ROCK
and
POP

Day by Day

ROCK
and
POP
Day by Day

Birthdays, Deaths
Hits and Facts

FRANK LAUFENBERG

Translated by Astrid Mick

Edited by Hugh Gregory

BLANDFORD

A BLANDFORD BOOK
First published in the UK 1992
by Blandford
(a Cassell imprint)
Villiers House
41/47 Strand
London
WC2N 5JE

Translation and English text copyright © 1992 Cassell plc

World copyright © 1990 Heel AG, Schindellegi, Switzerland

Distributed in the United States
by Sterling Publishing Co., Inc.
387 Park Avenue South, New York, NY 10016-8810

Distributed in Australia
by Capricorn Link (Australia) Pty Ltd
P. O. Box 665, Lane Cove, NSW 2066

A catalogue record for this book is available from the British Library

ISBN 0-7137-2319-X

Translated by Astrid Mick

Typeset by Puretech Corporation, India.
Printed in Great Britain by The Bath Press, Avon

Contents

Preface

There were many starting points possible for this book, most of which I considered at one time or another. In the end, I opted for the almanac or year-book approach – effectively a "book of days" – to present the information and based upon an artist's "known" date of birth.

Thus, let me state at the ourset, that should your favourite appear to be absent from the following pages, this is because I was unable to track down any record of a date of birth. In fact, many artists display a kind of vanity, often pushed by their management and record companies, which results in a reluctance to reveal a date of birth – or at least, to reveal the *true* date! The nature of the pop music business, with its perception of a young market, has always seemed to feel that the product sells better if the singer is presented as being that important few years younger. Let me quote an example from personal experience to illustrate just how these marketing myths are perpetuated long after it ceases to be of any importance to an artist and career. Just prior to the original German edition of the book going to the printer, I had the chance to talk with Spencer Davies. In the interview, he told me that during his success in the mid-60s with the Spencer Davies Group, their record company decided to make him younger by some two years. That "new birthday" became the accepted date, and which he never bothered to correct. But I can vouchsafe that he really was born on 17th July, 1937, as recorded herein!

I know all too well that a book of this nature can never hope to be complete. The music scene changes rapidly, new record artists come and go with remarkable speed, while others seem to be around for decades. I have tried to cover as much ground as is possible in the circumstances, from all the greats, to the one-hit wonders, from those who were household names for a fashonable period, to those who seem to appear in the charts seemingly from nowhere.

There are further notes following this Preface to assist use of the book. Nevertheless, I accepted the fact that in reading this book you are probably a fan of the music in some way or other – and the very nature of fandom guarantees that you will spot things you feel are incorrect, omitted, etc. Thus, whilst I update my data on almost a daily basis, new information is always welcome.

In looking throught the 366(*sic*) days of the year, I hope that you will find in the interconnection of names, songs, records and other miscellaneous facts the fascination and varied riches of the world of pop and rock.

Baden Baden, 1991   **Frank Laufenberg**

Using the book

The process outlined in the Preface whereby many artists seem to be younger than seems likely is still all too evident in the official biography or other information of many a star. Without the access to direct interview, we have had to accept the stated birthday in many cases, whilst suspecting that a "youth cure" has often taken place.

A further source of confusion over dates arises from the *secondary* recording in the UK of dates taken originally from US sources, often in the music press, record company press releases, music biographies, and so on. In the USA – and many places elsewhere – dates are recorded in the form month/day/year; in the UK the convention is day/month/year. Thus, unknowingly, many an American birthday has been incorrectly re-ascribed in the UK and thereon when that secondary source has been used elsewhere. It is always easy to spot for those born any day after the 12th of the month, but it represents an area of confusion if it is not obvious that a US source has been used at the very outset. we have tried wherever possible to double check the origins of such dates.

The style adopted throught this edition is based upon the British usage of day/month/year. This is also the case both birthdays – and for dates of death, sad and many as they are. Also, within each entry, listing of the success of an artist's records in the charts is based upon the following style:

  month/year/national chart/highest position reached of weeks in the chart

For example, taking the entry for Grandmaster Flash on the first page for Janauary 1st, we see the following:

  "White Lines (Don't Do It)" (11/83 UK 60; 2/84 RE-UK 7)

This indicates that in the UK charts, the record reached its highest position of No. 60 in November 1983; and that it also re-entered the chart in February of the following year and peaked at No.7. (Interestingly, re-enteries into the charts also occur several years apart, when a record is re-released, often in a new association with a movie or television commercial.)

The "Hits of the Day" are listed on the basis that the particular day on which the week's new chart appears coincides with the particular calendar date. It may seem confusing, but remember that the new record chart has been published on a number of different weekdays over the years in both the USA (see page 202) and UK. Thus, the "Hits" are the No. 1 records and are followed by the number of weeks for which they retained their top position.

Finally, the "Miscellany" entries are a series of facts and trivia that struck us as interesting and intriguing in their varying association with the history popular music.

F.L./H.G.

January

1st

Birthdays

Country Joe McDonald 1942 US singer and song-writer. Real name Joseph McDonald. In the late 60s he protested against the Vietnam War, mainly with his band, The Fish. When the war ended he turned to writing songs with an environmental flavour. Best known numbers: "Fixin' To Die Rag" from the first period; "Save the Whales" from the second period.

Grandmaster Flash 1958 US rapper and songwriter, considered by many to be the originator of rap, scratch and mix. Real name Joseph Sadler. Born in Barbados, he came to the New York's Bronx at an early age with his parents. In 1977 he began to work with a mobile discotheque in New York. Amongst others in the team were Kurtis Blow and Melle Mel, calling themselves Grandmaster Flash & The Furious Five. This set-up lasted until 1984, after which there were consider-able fluctuations in the group. Grandmaster hits were mainly in the UK, rather than in the USA: "The Mess-age" (8/82 UK 8), "White Lines (Don't Don't Do It)" (11/83 UK 60; 2/84 RE-UK 7) and "Step Off (Part 1)" (12/84 UK 8).

Xavier Cugat 1900 Band leader, singer, and song-writer, born in Spain. As a child he emigrated from his native Barcelona to Cuba, and from there to New York. In the late twenties specialized in Latin-American music, and became successful at the Waldorf-Astoria during the thirties. Greatest hits: "The Lady in Red" (5/35 US 3), "Perfidia (Tonight)" (1/41 US 3) and "Brazil" (1/43 US 2). He died on 27th October 1990.

Frank Pourcel 1928 French orchestra leader, who had his greatest international hit with his instrumental version of the Platters' hit "Only You" (4/59 US 9).

Morgan Fisher 1950 UK keyboard player with Love Affair, British Lions, Mott the Hoople and others. Also several solo LPs.

Johnny Young 1917 US blues musician, played guitar, harmonica, and mandolin, and sang. He died after a heart attack in Chicago on 18th April, 1974.

F. R. David 1954 Tunisian born singer and songwriter, who moved to France in 1964. Greatest international hit: "Words" (4/83 UK 2; 7/83 US 62).

Michael Hanson 1963 Canadian drummer with Glass Tiger.

Tony Dunmore 1952 UK bass player with Supercharge.

Deaths

Hank Williams 1953 US country musician. Died on the back seat of his Cadillac on his way to a performance in Canton, Ohio. Cause of death was quoted as being heart failure, an overdose of tablets, or simply alcoholism. Said to have influenced not only an entire generation of country singers and musicians, but also Bob Dylan. Born 17th Sept., 1923.

Maurice Chevalier 1972 French chansonnier and film actor – Trade mark: straw hat and cane. Born 12th Sept., 1888.

Moon Mullican 1967 US "King of Hillbilly Piano". Born 29th March, 1909.

Alexis Korner 1984 For many British musicians almost a father figure. Born 19th April, 1928.

Buck Ram 1991 US Manager and Writer

Hits of the Day

1955 "Let Me Go Lover" Joan Weber US 4 weeks.
1966 "Sounds of Silence" Simon & Garfunkel US 1 week.
1969 "Ob-La-Di Ob-La-Da" Marmalade UK 1 week.

Miscellany

1962 The Beatles made a trial recording in the Decca record studio. Dick Rowe, producer, rejected the band – he didn't like their sound, and in any case, 'the trend was away from guitar groups'. Human error. . . . ! However, listening to those recordings today, one could ask oneself if Dick Rowe didn't have a point back then. Of course, time has shown that they did improve as musicians – which in turn leads one to wonder about the point of such trial recordings, which can only demonstrate the standard at that moment, and not the possibilities for further development.

1964 British kids saw the programme *Top of the Pops* for the first time on television. Host Jimmy Saville introduced: Dusty Springfield with "I Wanna Be With You", the Rolling Stones with "I Wanna Be Your Man", Dave Clark 5 performed "Glad All Over", the Swinging Blue Jeans "Hippy Hippy Shake" and the Hollies "Stay".

studio during a live TV programme. However, his recording career lasted until 1958.

Kerry Minnear 1948 UK keyboard player with Gentle Giant.

Deaths

Erroll Garner 1977 US jazz pianist. Along with Dave Brubeck one of the most successful jazz musicians. His style based on Swing was unmistakeable. Born on 15th June, 1923.

Tex Ritter 1974 US country star. Died of a heart attack. Born on 12th Jan., 1907.

Eddie Heywood 1989 US pianist and songwriter. Born on 4th Dec., 1915.

Hits of the Day

1954 "Oh! My Pa-Pa" Eddie Fisher US 8 weeks.

2nd

Birthdays

Roger Miller 1936 US singer, guitarist and songwriter, successful both in pop and country charts. In the mid-fifties he went to Nashville as a songwriter, then became a drummer with the Faron Young Band, and finally a soloist. From 1960 to 1986, he was a regular in the country charts. Amongst his greatest hits are: "Dang Me" (6/64 US 7), "Chug-A-Lug" (9/64 US 9), "King of the Road" (1/65 US 4; 3/65 UK 1), "Engine Engine No. 9" (5/65 US 7, UK 33), and "England Swings" (11/65 US 8, UK 13). In 1985 he received the Tony Award for writing the Broadway musical *Big River*.

Chick Churchill 1942 UK keyboard player with Ten Years After, greatest hit "Love Like A Man" (6/70 UK 10). This group recorded outstanding LPs, until they split up in 1974 – Chick produced the solo LP, YOU AND ME which was a flop. Fifteen years later, and after Chick had earned his living as a studio musician, the four original members, Alvin Lee, Ric Lee, Leo Lyons, and Chick reformed in 1989 and produced the LP, ABOUT TIME.

Julius LaRosa 1930 US singer whose lucky *and* unlucky year was 1953. His greatest hit was "Eh Cumpari" (9/53 US 2), but on the 19th October 1953 he was fired from the

3rd

Birthdays

George Martin 1926 UK producer, permanently employed by EMI from 1950 to 1965. In the early days, he was concerned mainly with producing comedy recordings – by people like the Goons, Peter Sellers, Peter Ustinov and Bernard Cribbins but also artists such as Matt Monroe, Shirley Bassey or Temperance Seven. George became known worldwide by the fact that he signed the Beatles in 1962, and produced all their records until 1969. Other artists from the Brian Epstein stable also were recorded by him, e.g. Cilla Black, Billy J. Kramer, and Gerry & The Pacemakers. In 1965 he founded his own production company "Air". After 1970 he worked successfully with Jeff Beck, America, Neil Sedaka, UFO, Kenny Rogers, Ella Fitzgerald, Little River band and also with Paul McCartney in the post-Beatles period.

Stephen Stills 1945 US singer, guitarist, bass player, keyboard player and song writer. At the beginning of his career he had applied to a newspaper and looking for 'four crazy types' – he was rejected because of his bad teeth. Instead of Stephen, Michael Nesmith was chosen as one of the 'crazy types', who made their career as the Monkees. Another Monkee was Pete Tork – with whom Stills and Ritchie Furay had previously played in the New York folk group Au Go Go Singers. In March 1966, Stills, Furay and Neil Young became the founder members of Buffalo Springfield, to this day often reckoned to be the most under-rated group of the sixties. On May 5th, 1968 Buffalo Springfield appeared for the last time. Stephen Stills collaborated with Al Kooper and Mike Bloomfield on the LP SUPER SESSION. Afterwards with David Crosby and Graham Nash he formed Crosby, Stills & Nash. Neil Young joined the group at the Woodstock Festival on August 16, 1969 – and Crosby, Stills, Nash & Young were born. Their LP, DEJAVU, is one of the classics of the period. Main hit single "Woodstock" (3/70 US 11). Further hits as Crosby, Stills & Nash: "Just A Song Before I Go" (5/75 US 7) and "Wasted On The Way" (6/82 US 9). In addition to combined productions each member produced solo records, in which they helped each other. In September, 1988, after a gap of 14 years, they recorded together the LP AMERICAN DREAM.

Phillip Goodhand-Tait 1945 UK singer, keyboards, producer and singer. Originally a member of the British underground-band Circuit, he launched his solo career and cut a number of fine LPs. His songs are Lyrical and melodious – maybe too beautiful for the charts.

Van Dyke Parks 1941 US song writer, actor, producer and singer. Even as a child he appeared in Hollywood films, like. *The Swan* in 1956 with Grace Kelly. Later he studied piano and composition. As a producer he was connected with Judy Collins, Randy Newman, Ry Cooder, Phil Ochs, Arlo Guthrie and – most notably – the Beach Boys; their titles "Heroes and Villains" and "Surf's Up" show him at his best. He is supposed to have worked on his first solo-LP, SONG CYCLE, for four years (1968), earning him the nick-name 'The First Art Rocker'. His keyboard work on the Byrds release "Eight Miles High" was also impressive.

John Paul Jones 1946 UK bass player, keyboard player and song writer. Real name John Baldwin. He joined up with Jimmy Page in July 1968, in the death throes of the Yardbirds and they established themselves as Led Zeppelin in October 1968. Though never releasing any in the UK their first successful single was also their greatest hit, "Whole Lotta Love" (11/69 US 4). The band then went on to develop into an album group exclusively. However, the record company repeatedly lifted singles from their LPs. Led Zeppelin broke up after the death of drummer John Bonham, on 25th October 1980. Although numours of a reunion still abound.

Michael Zager 1943 US keyboard player and songwriter. Michael played with Ten Wheel Drive from 1968

to 1973, then got on to the disco bandwagon. As the Michael Zager Band he had a disco hit with "Let's All Chant" (3/78 US 36, UK 8).

Maxine Andrews 1918 US singer, one of the three Andrews Sisters. After a heart attack in 1982, she made her first solo LP in 1985! See Patti Andrews (16th Feb) for the Andrews Sisters hits.

Victoria Principal 1950 US actress in *Dallas*, Pam, who also once sang with Andy Gibb. Other sources quote her birth year as being 1945!

Deaths

Amos Milburn 1980 US blues pianist and singer. Died after a heart attack. Born 1st April, 1927.

Hits of the Day

1963	"The Next Time/Batchelor Boy" Cliff Richard UK 3 weeks
1970	"Raindrops Keep Falling On My Head" B. J. Thomas US 4 weeks
1976	"Saturday Night" Bay City Rollers US 1 week
1981	"Starting Over" John Lennon US 4 weeks

4th

Birthdays

Arthur Conley 1946 US soul singer and songwriter. Otis Redding discovered Arthur in 1965 and he signed him to his record label, Jotis. His first numbers were as Arthur and the Corvets. In 1967, when the soul-wave was at its height, he scored with the self-penned "Sweet Soul Music," produced by Otis Redding, (3/67 US 2, UK 7). However, the song closely resembled a number once written by Sam Cooke "Yeah Man". "Funky Street" (5/68 US 14, UK 46) was Arthur's and last hit.

John McLaughlin 1942 UK jazz/rock guitarist, pianist, and songwriter. John played a Gibson guitar designed to his own specifications, consisting of two necks with a total of 18 strings. His style was a synthesis of blues, jazz, flamenco, rock and Indian influences. Before founding the Mahavishnu Orchestra, he played together with such diverse musicians as the Four Tops, Wilson Pickett, Georgie Fame and Brian Auger. Together with poet and musian Pete Brown, (who was also Jack Bruce's co-writer for Cream) he set up his own group, then joined the Graham Bond Organisation alongside Ginger Baker and Jack Bruce. Finally he joined drummer Tony Williams' Lifetime. Then: 'John McLaughlin, a musician from England, has converted to hinduism and has become the world's best jazz and rock guitarist' (*Spiegel*, 1972). Later, he played together with such musical greats as Carlos Santana, Billy Cobham, Jerry Goodman and Jan Hammer. His BIRDS OF FIRE album was a seminal influence on the jazz-rock fusion trend of the early 1970s.

John Gorman 1937 UK singer and percufssionist with the Liverpool band Scaffold, who had their greatest hit with "Lily the Pink" (11/68 UK 1). Along with all three members of the group he was later with the comedy band Grimms.

Marcel King 1958 UK singer with the group Sweet Sensation, which had a few hits in the mid-70s, the greatest being "Sad Sweet Dreamer" (9/74 UK 1).

Bernard Sumner 1956 UK guitarist and singer, real name Bernard Dicken, who started as Bernard Albrecht with Joy Division in 1977, who in the same year had already tried their luck as Stiff Kittens and Warsaw. Singer Ian Curtis committed suicide on May 18, 1980. In 1981 the remaining members agreed to carry on as New Order with Berney taking over vocals. Hits: "Blue Monday" (3/83 UK 12; 8/83 RE-UK 9). "True Faith" (8/87 UK 4; 10/87 US 32) and "Blue Monday 1988" (5/88 UK 3), a re-mix of the first hit. In 1991, with Johnny Marr, he formed Electronic.

David Glasper 1965 UK singer and song writer for Breathe, who produced their first LP in 1988. Hits: "Hands To Heaven" (4/88 US 2; 7/88 UK 4), "How Can I Fall?" (9/88 US 3) and "Don't Tell Me Lies" (1/89 US 10).

Martin McAloon 1962 UK bass player with Prefab Sprout, formed in 1978.

Deaths

Phil Lynott 1986 Irish singer and bass player. He died of heart failure and pneumonia after taking a drugs overdose and lying in a coma for a week, Born 20th August, 1951.

Hits of the Day

1947 "White Christmas" Bing Crosby US 1 week
1957 "Singing the Blues" Guy Mitchell UK 1 week
1960 "El Paso" Marty Robbins US 2 weeks
1964 "There, I've Said It Again" Bobby Vinton US 4 weeks

1975 "Lucy In The Sky With Diamonds" Elton John US 2 weeks

5th

Birthdays

Sam Phillips 1923 US record producer and songwriter. He is considered to have discovered such rock greats as Elvis Presley, Jerry Lee Lewis, Johnny Cash, Carl Perkins, Charlie Rich and Roy Orbison. At least he was the one who gave young musicians a platform with his 1951 record company Sun Records. It is also true that Elvis Presley came to his studio in 1953 in order to sing on a record for his mother for $ 4. It was the beginning of an extraordinary career. Sam had worked previously as a disc jockey and show promoter in Memphis. Somewhere along the line he had noticed that black musicians in particular had hardly any opportunities for making recordings. He helped alleviate the situation by creating Sun Studios, where artists such as Howlin' Wolf, B. B. King, Jackie Brenston and Ike Turner made their first recordings. Sam also recorded Rufus Thomas, Junior Parker, Little Milton Campbell and James Cotton on his Sun label. Before that, he had tended to licence the masters to other record company like Chess in Chicago or RPM in Los Angeles. Among the most successful Sun singles released were "Blue Suede Shoes" by Carl Perkins, "I Walk The Line" by Johnny Cash, and "Whole Lotta Shakin' Goin' On" by Jerry Lee Lewis. He had sold Elvis Presley, after a few record releases, to RCA, for the enormous sum, in his eyes, of 35,000 dollars.

Phil Trim 1940 West Indian singer and songwriter, leader of Spanish group the Pop Tops, who had their greatest hit with "Mammy Blue" (10/71 UK 34; US 57).

Athol Guy 1940 Australian bass player with the Seekers, who immigrated to Britain in 1964. Their folk/pop combination went down well these; for three years the group produced one hit after another – "I'll Never Find Another You" (1/65 UK 1; 3/65 US 4) and "The Carnival Is Over" (10/65 UK 1) being their biggest two. The Seekers broke up in 1968. The later New Seekers contained neither Athol nor any other member of the original group!

Don Hartman 1946 US guitarist and singer with the underground band Frost, who produced three LPs but never had a hit.

Chris Stein 1950 US guitarist and songwriter in the group Blondie – beside Deborah Harry the most important musician in the band. (See 1st July under Debbie Harry.) After Blondie broke up in 1982, Chris set up his own record company before contracting a serious skin disease, from which Deborah nursed him back to health.

Biff Byford 1951 UK singer and songwriter of the heavy metal band Saxon, formed in 1977. Hits: "747 (Strangers In The Night)" (6/80 UK 13) and "And the Bands Played On" (4/81 UK 12).

George Brown 1949 US drummer with Kool & The Gang.

Deaths

Charles Mingus 1979 US jazz bass player, composer and orchestra leader. After suffering from muscular dystrophy for many years he finally died of a heart attack. In accordance with his last wishes, his widow scattered his ashes in the River Ganges. Born 22nd April, 1922.

Mal Evans 1976 Ex-road manager of the Beatles and 'Honorary Sheriff Of Los Angeles' – which, however, did not prevent his colleagues of the L.A. Police Dept. from shooting him. Mal threatened his girlfriend with a gun in their apartment; when the police ordered him to give himself up, he pointed his gun at them – and they shot him dead.

Hits of the Day

1946 "Symphony" Freddy Martin US 2 weeks
1952 "Slow Poke" Pee Wee King US 3 weeks
1980 "Please Don't Go" K.C. & the Sunshine Band US 1 week

6th

Birthdays

Sandy Denny 1941 UK singer and songwriter, several times voted best British folk singer. Full name Alexandra Elene MacLean Denny. After singing briefly with the Strawbs, in July 1968 she became the replacement for July Dyble as singer with Fairport Convention. With Sandy, the group had their only hit single, "Si Tu Dois Partir"

(7/69 UK 21) – a French version of Bob Dylan's "If You Gotta Go, Go Now". Sandy stayed with them until November 1969, then in March 1970 founded Fotheringay together with her husband, Trevor Lucas, and Jerry Donahue. They produced one LP and broke up in January, 1971. Then she started a solo career cutting a couple of solo albums before rejoining Fairport Convention in March 1974 where she stayed until January 1976, when she resumed her solo career. In addition, she sometimes appeared as vocalist for other artists like the Strawbs, Led Zeppelin, as well as in the rock opera "Tommy". Sandy died from injuries received from a fall down stairs on the 21st February, 1978.

Wilbert Harrison 1929 US singer and songwriter who also played several different instruments, and appeared as a 'one man band'. He made his first recording in 1952 – his greatest hit being "Kansas City" (4/59 US 1). "Let's Work Together" (12/69 US 32), one of his compositions, was a hit for Canned Heat in 1970, and for Brian Ferry in 1988 as a re-worked "Let's Stick Together '88".

Nino Tempo 1935 US saxophonist, singer and songwriter. He is said to have first performed as a three-year old; then aged seven he sang in the orchestra of Benny Goodman; later he played with Glenn Miller. Then, after working as a session saxophonist for several years, he formed a duo with his sister April Stevens in the early 60s. Their greatest hit was "Deep Purple" (9/63 US 1; 11/63 UK 17). April had already made solo recordings as a singer previously – after 1967 no further hits appeared and they both continued separately as soloists.

Doris Troy 1937 US singer and songwriter whose real surname is Payne. Doris started out with the Halos and Jay & Dee, and was also a backing singer for soul artists Chuck Jackson and Solomon Burke. As a soloist she had a hit with "Just One Look" (6/63 US 10). A cover-version of this number was a success for the British group the Hollies in 1964.

Adriano Celentano 1938 Italian singer, actor and songwriter. Adriano began his career at the Milan Rock Festival on 18th May, 1957. His first record was an Italian version of "Tutti Frutti". Greatest hits, "Una Festa Sui Prati" (6/67 G 10) and "Azzuro" (10/68 G 6). He set up his own record company, which he called Clan and probably derived from the fact that he was always surrounded by the family clan when he travelled. He is married to the singer Claudia Mori; he sang with her on her hit record "Non Succedera Pi" (6/82 Germany 12). He has been very successful in the Italian film industry.

Malcolm Young 1953 Australian guitarist, born in Glasgow but emigrated from Scotland with his family in

1963. Together with his younger brother Angus, he founded the hard rock band AC/DC in Sydney in 1973. The pair's oldest brother is George Young, once a member of the Easybeats.

Earl Scruggs 1924 US banjo player. After Earl had played in various groups, he met Lester Flatt in Bill Monroe's Band in 1945. The pair left Monroe in 1948 and founded the Foggy Mountain Boys. From 1952 onwards they were to be found as a duo in the C & W charts. 1949 they recorded "Foggy Mountain Breakdown", which became the title music for the film *Bonnie & Clyde* in 1968. In 1969 Earl received a Grammy (which corresponds to the film industry Oscar) award for this number. That year he separated from Lester Flatt and formed the Earl Scruggs Review.

Van McCoy 1944 US singer, songwriter and producer. Van began as a singer with the Marylanders, then founded the Starliters, who made their first recordings in 1959. Securing no hits, however, he set up his own record label in 1960. In 1961 until 1964 he was a producer at Scepter/Wand working with the Shirelles, among others, and then joined Leiter and Stoller as an arranger where he worked with the Drifters. After producing Gladys Knight he set up his own record company. His most succesful recordings under his own name were with "The Hustle" (4/75 US 1; UK 3) and "The Shuffle" (4/77 UK 4) for the Avco label. He died on 6th July, 1979.

Syd Barrett 1946 UK guitarist, singer and songwriter, whose real first name is Roger. In 1965 he founded Pink Floyd, whom he named after bluesmen Pink Anderson and Floyd Council. Without a doubt, Syd was responsible for the Floyd's musical direction in their early days. He wrote the hits "Arnold Layne" (3/67 UK 20) and "See Emily Play" (6/67 UK 6). In 1968 he left the group, and David Gilmour replaced him. Syd tried as a soloist – with the album THE MADCAP LAUGHS – but without success. The Floyd's "Shine On You Crazy Diamond" was their tribute to this founding member.

Kim Wilson 1951 US singer, harmonica player and song writer with the blues-rock band the Fabulous Thunderbirds, founded 1975. Greatest hit: "Tuff Enuff" (4/86 US 10).

Kathy Sledge 1959 US singer. She is the youngest sister in Sister Sledge.

Mark O'Toole 1964 UK bass player with Frankie Goes to Hollywood.

Hits of the Day

1956 "Rock Around the Clock" Bill Haley UK 2 weeks (2nd time)

1958	"At The Hop" Danny & The Juniors US 7 weeks	
1973	"You're So Vain" Carly Simon US 3 weeks	
1979	"YMCA" Village People UK 3 weeks	
1979	"Too Much Heaven" Bee Gees US 2 weeks	
1990	"Hangin' Tough" New Kids on the Block UK 2 weeks	

7th

Birthdays

Kenny Loggins 1948 US pop and rock singer, songwriter, and guitarist. In 1968 Kenny made his first recordings with the unsuccessful groups Gator Creek and Second Helping. After touring with the Electric Prunes in 1969, he became permanently employed as a songwriter – at $ 100 a week. In 1971 he wrote the number "The House At Pooh Corner" which became a big hit for the Nitty Gritty Dirt Band. After this success he received a solo recording contract, with former Buffalo Springfield and Poco member Jim Messina being hired as a producer. However, they decided to form the duo Loggins and Messina which stayed together for the next four years; their biggest hit was the million-seller, "Your Mama Don't Dance" (11/72 US 4). After separating they embarked on solo careers and Kenny notched up a string of hits with records like "Whenever I Call You Friend" (7/78 US 5), "I'm Alright" (7/80 US 7), "Footloose" (1/84 US 1; 4/84 UK 6), "Danger Zone" (5/86 US 2; 11/86 UK 45) and "Nobody's Fool" (7/88 US 8). Kenny remains in the charts especially through his film music. His brother Dave, songwriter and guitarist, made the excellent and underrated 1974 LP APPRENTICE (IN A MUSICAL WORKSHOP).

James West 1941 US singer who made his first record with the Echoes in 1959. From 1960 the trio called themselves the Innocents, two small successes followed with "Honest I Do" (8/60 US 28) and "Gee Whiz" (11/60 US 28). The group then had a hit with Kathy Young, "A Thousand Stars" (10/60 US 3). (Even after 1961 they turned up in the hit parades with Kathy).

Mike McGear 1944 UK singer and songwriter. Real name Michael McCartney, he is a step-brother of Ex-Beatle Paul McCartney. Mike was a member of Scaffold, which had Top Ten hits in the UK.

Dave Cousins 1945 UK singer, musician and songwriter. In 1967 Dave founded the Strawberry Hill Boys, who then made their first LP as the Strawbs in 1968. Greatest hit: "Part of the Union" (1/73 UK 2). Later Dave worked as a soloist, reforming the Strawbs for occasional gigs and working in local radio.

Paul Revere 1942 US keyboard instrumentalist. In 1959 he founded the duo Downbeats, together with singer and saxophonist Mark Lindsey they made some instrumental recordings. After the first minor hit, they formed the group Paul Revere & The Raiders. Between 1969 and 1971, they had 15 US Top 40 hits. (See 9th March, under Mark Lindsey.)

Danny Williams 1942 South African born singer who was successful in the UK between 1961 and 1964. His hits included "Moon River" (11/61 UK 1), from the film *Breakfast at Tiffany's* and "Wonderful World Of the Young" (4/62 UK 8). After a thirteen- year absence from the charts he had another hit with "Dancin' Easy" (7/77 UK 30).

Eldee Young 1936 US bass player, who in the early 50s played in the Clefs with Ramsey Lewis and Isaac Holt. These three founded Gentlemen of the Swing in 1956 and cut their first records that year re-naming themselves the Ramsey Lewis Trio. Greatest hit: "The In-Crowd" (7/65 US 5). In 1965 Ramsey Lewis carried on the group with other musicians; Eldee and Isaac, together with pianist Don Walker, founded the Young Holt Trio. After Walker left the trio in 1968, they called themselves Young- Holt Unlimited. Hit and million bestseller "Soulful Strut" (11/68 US 3); Barbara Acklin took this number, replaced the piano with her voice and called the song "Am I The Same Girl". In 1983 the Ramsey Lewis Trio re-grouped with the previous members.

Kathy Valentine 1959 US bass player, who joined the Go-Gos in 1980 for Margot Olavera.

Jack Greene 1930 US Country singer and drummer. Between 1965 and 1984 he was in the Country hit parades regularly. His greatest success was "There Goes My Everything" (10/66 C & W 1; US 65).

Deaths

Cyril Davies 1964 UK blues musician. In the 50s he played together with Alexis Korner, first banjo, later harmonica. In 1961 Korner and Davies founded the pioneering Blues Incorporated, who proceeded to revive and renew British blues. The next step was the Cyril Davies All-Stars, which included the pre-Stones Charlie Watts and Brian Jones. Occasionally, a young guy called Mick Jagger sang with the group. When Keith Richards joined, the Rolling Stones were born. Sadly, it was shortly after

the founding of this superband that Cyril died of leukaemia. Born 1932.

Larry Williams 1980 US rock'n'roller, who died of a gunshot wound. Born 10th May, 1935.

Hits of the Day

1950 "Rudolph, The Red-Nosed Reindeer" Gene Autreyo US 1 week

1955 "Finger Of Suspicion" Dickie Valentine UK 1 week

1956 "Memories Are Made Of This" Dean Martin US 6 weeks

1985 "Do They Know It's Christmas" Band Aid UK 4 weeks

1989 "Especially For You" Kylie Minogue & Jason Donovan UK 3 weeks

---

8th

Birthdays

David Bowie 1947 UK singer, saxophonist, and songwriter. Real name David Robert Hayward-Jones. "Space Oddity" (9/69 UK 5; 1/73 US 15; 10/75 Re-UK 1) was his first big hit; it has been re-released several times, maintaining a long-term success. Further No. 1 hits include "Fame" (6/75 US), "Ashes to Ashes" (8/80 UK), "Let's Dance" (3/83 UK & US). Together with Queen he recorded "Under Pressure" (11/81 UK 1; US 29); and with Mick Jagger a cover version of the old Martha Reeves hit Dancing In the Streets" (8/85 US 7; UK 1), which in the UK went straight to No. 1. In the meantime, Bowie has also made a name as an actor. Forgotten are the days when he appeared with George & The Dragon, The Konrads, Davie Jones with the King Bees (his first record, "Liza Jane/Louie Louie Go Home", appeared under this name on 5th June, 1964), The Manish Boys, Davy Jones, and Davy Jones & The Lower Third. In addition to his solo activities he has appeared since mid-1989 as singer of the band Tin Machine.

Lee Jackson 1943 UK bass guitarist, singer, and songwriter. He played with Blues Incorporated, and was a founder member of Nice – formed in September 1967 –

whose biggest hit single was "America" (7/68 UK 21). In 1970, he fronted his own group Jackson Heights for about one year. In August 1973 he joined Refugee. After that he played on records by blues man J. B. Hutto and by Tim Rose, made a solo album and became a record producer.

Terry Sylvester 1945 UK guitarist, singer, and songwriter. His career started as front man of the Escorts in Liverpool in 1962. He went on to the Swinging Blue Jeans as a replacement for Ralph Ellis in 1966, and then replaced Graham Nash in the Hollies in 1968 (when Nash went to the USA to found Crosby, Stills & Nash). Terry's first appearance with the Hollies is enshrined on their single "Sorry Suzanne". In May 1981, he left the band and founded Griffin & Sylvester, without chart success.

Little Anthony 1941 US singer and songwriter. Real name Anthony Gourdine, he was the lead singer with Little Anthony & the Imperials. In 1955 he sang with the DuPonts, and founded the Chesters vocal group in 1957, who were renamed the Imperials in 1958. Greatest hits: "Tears On My Pillow" (8/58 US 4) and "Goin' Out Of My Head" (11/64 US 6). (The former became a hit some 32 years later when covered by Kylie Minogue)

Shirley Bassey 1937 UK singer who was regularly in the UK charts from 1957 until 1973, and scored 12 Top Ten hits. The greatest included "As I Love You" (1/59 UK 1), and "Reach For The Stars/Climb Ev'ry Mountain" (7/61 UK). She is also known as the singer of title songs from the James Bond films like *Goldfinger* (10/64 UK 21; 1/65 US 8) and *Diamonds are Forever*. In 1987 she made the record "Rhythm Divine" with the Swiss band Yello.

Robert Krieger 1946 US guitarist and songwriter with the Doors, founded 1965. Before that he had played with fellow group member John Densmore in the Psychadelic Rangers. After the death of Jim Morrison on 3rd July, 1971, the remaining three Doors members recorded the LP NEW VOICES. He then founded the Butts Band with former Alan Bown vocalist Jess Roden and John Densmore. They made adequate but unsuccessful albums and 1977 saw the release of his first solo LP.

John Peterson 1942 US drummer with the Beau Brummels and from 1966 onwards with Harpers Bizarre, a band typifying the San Francisco garage and psychadelic sound.

Christy Lane 1940 US country singer, born Eleanor Johnston. From 1977 onwards successful in country charts. Her greatest success was "One Day At A Time" (3/80 C&W 1).

Mike Reno 1955 Canadian singer who began with Streetheart, and become co-founder of Loverboy in 1979,

who were successful in the US from 1980 onwards. Hits: "Lovin' Every Minute Of It" (8/85 US 9) and "This Could Be The Night" (1/86 US 10). Together with Ann Wilson, from the Canadian group Heart, he cut the hit "Almost Paradise . . . Love Theme from Footloose" (5/84 US 7).

Marcus Hutson 1943 US singer with the Whispers.

Mel Pritchard 1948 UK drummer with Barclay James Harvest.

Elvis Presley 1935 The first real star of rock'n'roll, for whom one would have to reserve a whole page for listing his hits alone. As with the case of the Beatles, we would like to refer to other literature on this artist. Kings merit their own books! Elvis died 16th August, 1977.

Deaths

Steve Clark 1991 UK guitarist with Def Leppard born 23rd April. 1960.

Hits of the Day

1954 "Oh, Mein Papa" Eddie Calvert UK 9 weeks
1966 "We Can Work It Out" Beatles US 2 weeks
1969 "Lily The Pink" Scaffold UK 1 week (2nd time)
1972 "I'd Like To Teach The World To Sing" New Seekers UK 4 weeks
1977 "You Don't Have To Be A Star" Marilyn McCoo & Billyo Davis US 1 week

---

9th

Birthdays

Jimmy Page 1944 UK guitarist and songwriter with Led Zeppelin, which evolved from the remains of the Yardbirds in October 1968. Although never a single, "Stairway to Heaven" is probably their best known title. (For Led Zeppelin defacts, see under band member Robert Plant, 20th August.)

Joan Baez 1941 US folk singer and songwriter, daughter of a Mexican doctor and an Irish teacher. Her career began at the end of the 50s. For years she was seen as the 'Queen of Protest'. It was she who during one of her concerts, introduced the newcomer Bob Dylan. Her greatest hit – and million bestseller – was the Bond's Opus "The Night They Drove Old Dixie Down" (8/71 US 3; UK 6).

Crystal Gayle 1951 US country singer, real name Brenda Gail Webb. She is the youngest sister of Loretta Lynn, with whom and another sister (Peggy Sue) she appeared as the Loretta Lynn Sisters. From 1970, she has featured regularly in the country charts. In 1979 she was the first country artist to tour China. Her greatest hits: "Don't It Make My Brown Eyes Blue" (8/77 US 2; 11/77 UK 5), "Talking In Your Sleep" (7/78 US 18; UK 11), and together with Eddie Rabbit, "You and I" (10/82 US 7).

Tim Hart 1948 UK folk singer, guitarist and songwriter. With Maddy Prior, he recorded some fine traditional English folk albums in the 1960s. Maddy and Tim then become the fellow founder members of the electric folk group Steeleye Span. Greatest hits: "Gaudete" (12/73 UK 14) and "All Around My Hat" (11/75 UK 5). A solo LP by Tim appeared in 1979 but he now lives in retirement on the Canary Islands.

Jimmy Boyd 1940 US children's singing star. Hits: "I Saw Mommy Kissing Santa Claus" (12/52 US 1) and, together with Frankie Laine, "Tell Me A Story" (3/53 US 4).

Scott Engel 1944 US singer and bass player with the Walker Brothers trio, founded 1964 in Los Angeles. They were more successful, and resident, in the UK than in their home country. Hits: "Make It Easy On Yourself" (8/65 UK 1; 10/65 US 16), and "The Sun Ain't Gonna Shine Anymore" (3/66 UK 1; US 13). Mid-1967 the Walker Brothers split up and tried their luck as solo artists. Scott, as Scott Walker, was successful with "Joanna" (5/68 UK7). In the mid-70s the three reformed briefly as the Walker Brothers. Hit: "No Regrets" (1/76 UK7). 1984 saw another solo LP appearing under the name of Scott Walker. By 1987 he was making TV ads for soft drinks in the UK, but his reputation continues to flourish among a small, but loyal, coterie of followers.

William Cowsill 1948 US guitarist and singer with the sibling group Cowsills. Greatest hits: "The Rain, The Park, & Other Things" (9/67 US 2) and "Hair" (3/69 US 2).

Roy Head 1943 US singer who started out in the mid-60s with his own band. After obtaining a record contract in 1965, they called themselves Roy Head & The Traits, which they used for their first and biggest hit "Treat Her Right" (9/65 US 2; 11/65 UK 30). After 1966 Roy left the group and tried his luck as a soloist. When he found he

was having no success in pop and rock music, he did as many rockers before him and became a country singer. Thus he had his greatest success with "Come To Me" (10/77 C&W 16).

David Johansen 1950 US singer and songwriter with the New York Dolls, formed 1971. After this pre-punk band was unable to make any real breakthrough, David continued in this direction first as the Dolls, then under his own name until 1979. After that he became more commercially orientated, releasing solo LPs; and in 1987 appeared as Buster Poindexter.

Domenico Modugno 1928 Italian singer and songwriter. In 1958 he won the San Remo Festival with the title "Nel Blu, Dipinto Di Blu (Volare)" (8/58 US 1; UK 10), which became his greatest international success.

Kenneth Kelly US singer with the group Manhattans, founded 1964.

Hits of the Day

1943	"Praise The Lord And Pass The Ammunition" Kay Kyser US 3 weeks
1961	"Wonderland By Night" Bert Kaempfert US 3 weeks
1971	"Grandad" Clive Dunn UK 3 weeks
1981	"Imagine" John Lennon UK 4 weeks
1988	"So Emotional" Whitney Houston US 1 week

10th

Birthdays

Johnny Ray 1927 US singer and songwriter, whose stage trademark was his choking sobs. Between 1951 and 1960 he was considered to be a superstar in the US and UK. Greatest hits: "Cry" (11/51 US 1), "Such A Night" (4/54 US 19; UK 1), "Just Walking In The Rain" (9/56 US 2; UK 1), and "Yes Tonight Josephine" (4/57 US 12; UK 1). In addition to his solo hits, he had some success in a duet with Doris Day, "Let's Walk Thata-Way" (7/53 UK 4), and with Frankie Laine. Johnny participated in three films, remained active into the 80s, and finally settled in Hollywood, where he died on Feb., 24th 1990 of liver failure.

Donald Fagen 1948 US keyboard player, singer and songwriter. In 1972 he founded Steely Dan with Walter

Becker. Greatest Hits: "Do It Again" (11/72 US 6; 8/75 UK 39), "Rikki Don't Lose That Number" (5/74 US 4; 3/79 UK 58), and "Hey Nineteen" (11/80 US 10). In 1981 the group split up. In 1982 soloist Donald released the album THE NIGHTFLY, with the hit "I.G.Y." (10/82 US 26), the abbreviation for "International Geo- Physical Year" (7/57 – 12/58). The song discussed critically what was being predicted at that time.

Rod Stewart 1945 UK singer and songwriter who joined the Faces in 1969 via the Five Dimensions (1963), the Hoochie Coochie Men (1964), Steampacket (1965), Shotgun Express, and the Jeff Beck Group (1966). On the side, he had attempted a solo career as early as October 1964, with "Good Morning Little Schoolgirl" on Decca, and in November 1965 with "The Day Will Come" under EMI, however, this was not to take off until November 1969. Greatest hits with the Faces: "Stay With me" (12/71 UK 6; US 17), and "Cindy Incidentally" (2/73 UK 2). Solo hits: "Maggie May" (7/71 US 1; 9/79 UK 1), "You Wear It Well" (8/72 UK 1; US 13), "Sailing" (8/75 UK 1; 9/76 RE-UK 3; 3/87 2nd RE-UK41), "Tonight's The Night (Gonna Be Alright)" (6/76 UK 5; 10/76 US 1), "I Don't Want To Talk About It/First Cut Is The Deepest" (2/77 is the B-side US 21; 4/77 as double A-side UK 1), "You're In My Heart (The Final Acclaim)" (10/77 UK 3; US 4), "Do Ya Think I'm Sexy" (11/78 UK & US 1), "Baby Jane" (6/83 UK 1; US 14), "Every Beat Of My Heart" (7/86 UK 2), and "My Heart Can't Tell You No" (12/88 US 4), and "Downtown Train" (11/89 US 3).

Jim Croce 1943 US singer, guitarist and songwriter. He made his first recordings in 1968, together with his wife Ingrid, for Capitol. He had his first success with the title "You Don't Mess Around With Jim" (7/72 US 8). Greatest hits: "Bad Bad Leroy Brown" (4/73 US 1), "Time In A Bottle" (11/73 US 1), and "I'll Have To Say I Love You In A Song" (3/74 US 9). His career was abruptly terminated by an air crash in which he and Maury Muehleisen, lead guitarist on all his records, were killed on 20th Sept, 1973.

Ronnie Hawkins 1935 US rock'n roll singer and pianist, who first accompanied on record the likes of Carl Perkins and Conway Twitty. From 1958 onwards he lived in Canada for 4 years where he founded the Hawks, which later became The Band. Greatest hit under his own name: "Mary Lou" (8/59 US 26).

Pat Benatar 1952 US singer; real name Patricia Andrzewski and singing professionally since 1980. Greatest hits: "Hit Me With Your Best Shot" (10/80 US 9), "Love Is A Battlefield" (9/83 US 5; 1/84 UK 49; 3/85 RE-UK 17), and "We Belong" (10/84 US 5; 1/85 UK 22).

Buddy Johnson 1912 US bandleader and songwriter successful since the 1930s. Greatest single hit: "That's The Stuff You Gotta Watch" (9/45 US 14). He died 20th Oct., 1984.

Sal Mineo 1939 US actor and singer. Starred alongside James Dean in *Rebel Without A Cause*. Greatest hit: "Start Movin' (In My Direction)" (5/57 US 9; UK 16). Sal was stabbed to death on 12th Feb., 1976.

Aynsley Dunbar 1946 UK drummer who played with the most a very wide variety of musicians – from John Mayall to Frank Zappa. From 1968 to 1970 he lead his own blues band the Aynsley Dunbar Retaliation, which featured Victor Brox on vocals and keyboards, and John Morsehead on lead guitar.

Michael Schenker 1955 First a member of the German hard rock band Scorpions, then joined the UK band UFO in 1973. In 1979 came the Michael Schenker Group; then together with Robin McAuley he appeared in the McAuley Schenker Group in 1987. Michael Schenker is probably the best known of German hard rock guitarists.

Nathan Moore 1965 UK singer with Brother Beyond who produced their first records in 1986. Hits: "The Harder I Try" (7/88 UK2), "He Ain't No Competition" (11/88 UK 6), and "Be My Twin" (1/89 UK 14).

Cyril Neville 1948 US singer and percussionist, who performs together with his brothers – the Neville Brothers.

Deaths

Howlin' Wolf 1976 US blues musician; real name Chester Burnett; of tremendous influence on white blues and rock. Unlike many Chicago bluesmen, he actually had minor pop chart success in the UK in 1964 with "Smoke-Stack Lightning". Died of cancer 20th Jan. 1976 in Hines, Illinois. Born 10th June, 1910 in Mississipi.

Zeb Turner 1978 US country rock player. Born 23rd June, 1915.

Hits of the Day

1953	"Don't Let The Stars Get In Your Eyes" Perry Como US 5 weeks
1958	"Great Balls Of Fire" Jerry Lee Lewis UK 2 weeks
1976	"Convoy" C. W. McCall US 1 week

11th

Birthdays

Slim Harpo 1924 US bluesman whose real name was James Moore. Greatest pop hits: "Rainin' In My heart" (5/61 US 34) – featuring the excellent blues guitarist Lightnin' Slim accompanied – and "Baby Scratch My Back" (1/66 US 16). His number "I'm A King Bee" is one of the strongest titles on the first Rolling Stones album. Slim died 31st Jan. 1970.

Frederick Dennis Green 1949 US singer and one of the many members of the US rock 'n' roll revival outfit Sha Na Na. Their early success was at the Woodstock Festival in 1969; the event's album features them on the oldie, "At The Hop". They produced the albums ROCK N' ROLL'S HERE TO STAY and THE GOLDEN AGE OF ROCK N' ROLL, had a weekly show on the American TV programme NBC, and because of the large number of members, the band were also known as 'The Dirty Dozen'. A number of individual talents emerged from the group, one of the best-known being Henry Gross, who was successful as a soloist with "Shannon" (4/76 US 6; UK 32).

Lee Ritenour 1952 US guitarist and songwriter. Lee is among the top session artists in the USA and can be heard on more than 200 successful albums. His greatest success as a soloist was "Is It You" (4/81 US 15).

Vicky Peterson 1960 US guitarist, singer and songwriter with the Bangles. (See 17th Jan. under Susanna Hoffs.)

Julie Roberts 1962 UK singer and songwriter for the group Working Week formed in 1984.

Hits of the Day

1957 "Singing The Blues" Tommy Steele UK 1 week
1962 "The Young Ones" Cliff Richard UK 6 weeks
1986 "West End Girls" Pet Shop Boys UK 2 weeks

Miscellany

1963 'Whisky-A-Go-Go', the first real American discotheque opened on Sunset Boulevard in Los Angeles. The proprietor was Elmer Valentine, a former policeman from Chicago. Over many years, several live albums were produced there and the venue was proved a great talent-spotting ground.

12th

Birthdays

Tex Ritter 1907 US country star whose real first names were Woodward Maurice. By the late 1930s he had become totally immersed in the mythology of the 'Wild West'. On the Houston radio station KPRC he sang cowboy songs and read cowboy fiction before going to Hollywood in 1936, where he played in about 85 films up until 1945, his horse "Whiteflash" appearing with him. Tex was always the shining hero; and along with Gene Autry and Roy Rogers he was the most well-known of the singing cowboys, although the films were always low-budget affairs. From 1944, until his death on 2nd Jan., 1974, he was successful mainly in the C & W charts. Greatest pop hits: "I'm Wastin' My Tears On You" (11/44 C&W 1; US 11), "High Noon" (9/52 US 12), and "I Dreamed Of A Hill-Billy Heaven" (6/61 C&W 5; US 20). In 1970, he stood – unsuccessfully – for US senator for Tennessee. Ironically, it was a few years later that the time was right for an actor in politics!

Long John Baldry 1941 UK singer with blues origins. He began with Cyril Davies in Blues Inc., founded the Hoochie Coochie Men, from which developed Steampacket. As a pop singer he had a hit with "Let The Heartache Begin" (11/67 UK 1) and the theme song from the Mexico Olympics. Subsequently, he has produced fine but unsuccessful LPs and now resides in Vancover, Canada.

Ray Price 1926 US country singer who appeared in the C&W charts regularly from 1952. Over the years he occupied the No. 1 slot eight times. His number "Crazy Arms" (5/56 C&W 1) was No. 1 for 20 weeks in succession and his greatest cross-over pop hit was "For The Good Times" (6/70 C&W 1; 8/70 US 11).

Abraham Tilmon 1949 US singer, songwriter and leader of the Detroit Emeralds, who produced their first record in 1968. Greatest hits: "Baby Let Me Take You (In My Arms)" (5/72 US 24), and "Feel The Need In Me" (2/73 UK 4). Abraham died in 1982 after a heart attack.

Glenn Yarborough 1930 US singer who began in 1959 with folk trio the Limeliters. After the group had broken up in 1963, he tried as a soloist. Greatest Hit: "Baby The Rain Must Fall" (3/65 US 12).

Maggie Bell 1945 UK singer whose career began in her native Scotland with Alex Harvey. When her boyfriend

Les, Alex's younger brother, founded Power, she joined them and Power became Stone the Crows. The band broke up after Les was fatally electrocuted during a performance in 1972. Maggie worked as a session singer; she can be heard with Rod Stewart on the title song of his LP EVERY PICTURE TELLS A STORY. Her solo career never took off, despite her great voice, and she became the singer with Midnight Flyers in the early 80s. Even this project was not successful, and finally Maggie continued as a session singer. As a soloist, her greatest success was "Hazell" (4/78 UK 37).

Charlie Gracie 1936 US singer and guitarist who made his first records in 1951. His best year was 1957, during which he achieved two hits in the USA and five in the UK. Greatest hits: "Butterfly" (2/57 US 1; 4/57 UK 12), and "Fabulous" (5/57 US 16; UK 8).

Fred McDowell 1904 US blues musician who played around the Mississippi in the area of his home town, besides working on the land from 1940 onwards. 'Rediscovery' ensured that he made his first recordings in 1959. Singer Bonnie Raitt referred to him as her ideal blues stylist and inspiration. He died 3rd July, 1972.

Mark Moore 1967 UK keyboard player and mastermind of 'S Express. Hits: "Theme From 'S Express" (4/88 UK 1), "Superfly Guy" (7/88 UK 5), and "Hey Music Lover" (2/89 UK 6).

Per Gessle 1959 Swedish guitarist, keyboard player, singer, and songwriter with the duo Roxette, which released their first LP in 1986. Before that, Per played with Gyllene Tider, who were successful only in Sweden. (For Roxette, see 30th May under Marie Fredricksson.)

Michael Barker 1953 UK drummer with the group Magnum.

Michael Blakey 1947 UK drummer with Christie.

Cynthia Robinson 1946 US trumpeter with Sly & The Family Stone.

Hits of the Day

1961 "Poetry In Motion" Johnny Tillotson UK 2 weeks
1963 "Go Away Little Girl" Steve Lawrence US 2 weeks
1974 "The Joker" Steve Miller US 1 week
1980 "Escape" Rupert Holmes US 1 week (2nd time)

13th

Birthdays

John Lees 1948 UK guitarist and songwriter with Barclay James Harvest. The band was formed in Oldham in 1966 out of two locally well-known groups; John had played with the Blues Keepers previously. From 1967 onwards, the members turned professional, and in 1968 they gained their first recording contract. Over the years the group made solid, successful LPs, but produced no single hits. The group's largest following is probably in Germany, where they had a hit with "Life Is For Livin' ". In 1977 John released a solo LP, "A Major Fancy," on the Harvest label.

Bobby Lester 1930 US singer, and first tenor with the Moonglows, who got their name from disc jockey and supporter Alan Freed. Freed had a popular radio show in the 50s called 'Moon Dog's Rock n' Roll Party'. On the side, he worked as a manager, contracted musicians and supported them – especially on his shows. For the Moonglows, this resulted in a total of seven hits in the R & B charts between 1954 and 1958. Their two greatest hits: "Sincerely" (12/54 R&B 1; 3/55 US 20), and "Ten Commandments of Love" (9/58 US 22; R&B 9). Bobby died on 15th October, 1980.

Fred White 1955 US drummer with the group Earth, Wind & Fire headed by his brother Maurice White.

Richard Anthony 1938 French singer and songwriter. Real name Ricardo Btesch. He had his first great hit in 1960 with "Nouvelle Vague". In France alone, over one million copies were sold of "J'entends Siffler Le Train" (original "500 Miles Away From Home" written/ adapted by US Folk/country singer Hedy West) in 1962. A further hit that year was "C'est Ma Faute" His fourth great hit in France was in 1969 with "Le Sirop – Typhon", a French version of "Lily The Pink". Along with Johnny Halliday and Eddie Mitchell, Richard was one of the first French artists to record rock 'n' roll, releasing a version of "Peggy Sue" in 1959; indeed he could be considered to be the only serious rival of Johnny Halliday. He was successful internationally with "Cin Cin", and "If I Loved You" (4/64 UK 18).

Graham McPherson 1961 UK singer and songwriter. In 1978 Graham joined the bluebeat/ska band the Invaders, which had formed in 1976. From January 1979 they became Madness, and September of the same year saw the release of their first single. After that, they had 15 Top 10 hits until 1983. Greatest hits: "It Must Be Love" (12/81 UK 4; 8/83 US 33), "House Of Fun" (5/82 UK 1), "Our House" (11/82 UK 5; 5/83 US 7), and "Wings Of A Dove" (8/83

UK 2). In 1985, Graham and another member of the group made a record as the Fink Brothers.

Trevor Rabin 1955 South African born guitarist, singer, bassist, and keyboard instrumentalist in the UK for Rabbitt, Streetband, Manfred Mann's Earth Band, Yes, and with solo LPs such as WOLF.

Deaths

Donny Hathaway 1979 US singer. He fell from the 15th floor of the New York Essex House Hotel, the police were unable to determine whether it was intentional or an accident. Previously and on the same day he had been working with Roberta Flack on a new LP. Born on 1st October, 1945.

Hits of the Day

1962 "The Twist" Chubby Checker US 2 weeks (then again 8/60)

14th

Birthdays

Allen Toussaint 1938 US singer, songwriter, pianist, producer and arranger from New Orleans, who made his first LP in 1958 as Al Tousan. This record contained the original version of Toussaint's "Java", which became a super-hit for Al Hirt in 1964. Since then this multi-talented artist has issued a deal of product, none of it too successful commercially. Instead, others made hits out of his songs – "The Band, Glen Campbell, Oak Ridge Boys, Devo, Boz Scaggs, Bonnie Raitt, Little Feat and many many more. Allen Toussaint remains a seminal and important figure in New Orleans R'n'B music.

Jack Jones 1938 US singer who inherited talent: his father Allen produced the early pop song "Donkey Serenade", and mother Irene Hervey was an actress. It was she who helped Jack enter the pop scene. He achieved 20 hits in the Hot 100 between 1962 and 1968, the most successful being "Wives & Lovers" (11/63 US 14) and "The Race Is On" (2/65 US 15).

Caterina Valente 1931 Italian singer from a well-known artistic family, Kurt Edelhagen took her into his orchestra as a singer in 1953. In 1954 she cut her first records with him. Especially successful in the Germany but also 12 other languages. She has had hits like. "The Breeze And I" (4/55 US 8; 8/55 UK 5) in many different countries.

Bob Bradbury 1956 UK singer and songwriter with Hello. Hits: "Tell Him" (11/74 UK 6), and "New York Groove" (10/75 UK 9).

Mike Tramp 1961 US singer and songwriter with the hard rock band White Lion founded in New York in 1984. They call their style 'rock 'n roar'. Hits "Wait" (2/88 US 8), and "When the Children Cry" (11/88 US 3).

Billie Jo Spears 1937 US singer who first appeared professionally aged 13. Between 1968 and 1984 she was very successful in Country hit parades. Hits: "Mr Walker, It's All over" (4/69 C&W 4), "Blanket On The Ground" (2/75 C&W 1, 7/75 UK 6), and "What I've Got In Mind" (2/76 C&W 5; 7/76 UK 4). In the UK she replaced Tammy Wynette as the best selling country artist.

L. L. Cool J. 1968 US rapper and rap writer. Real name James Todd Smith. He had his first successful numbers at the end of 1985 in the US R & B charts. "I Need Love" (7/87 US 14; 9/87 UK 8) brought him to a wider audience.

Geoff Tate 1959 US singer, keyboard player and songwriter with the hard rock band Queensryche.

Hits of the Day

1950	"I Can Dream, Can't I?" Andrews Sisters US 5 weeks
1955	"Mambo Italiano" Rosemary Clooney UK 1 week
1965	"Yeh Yeh" Georgie Fame UK 2 weeks
1978	"Baby Come Back" Player US 3 weeks
1984	"Pipes Of Peace" Paul McCartney UK 2 weeks
1989	"My Prerogative" Bobby Brown US 1 week

15th

Birthdays

Ronald Wayne Van Zandt 1948 US lead singer and songwriter for Lynyrd Skynyrd, which had formed while the members of the group were still at school in 1965 (the name of the group was a corruption of the name Leonard Skinner, one of their teachers). The group's first hit was also their greatest hit: "Sweet Home Alabama" (7/74 US

8), even though Ronnie originated from Jacksonville, Florida. Just as the group was about to peak as the most successful southern rock group, Van Zandt, Steve & Cassie Gaines were killed when their private plane crashed (20th October, 1977).

Gene Krupa 1909 US jazz drummer of the Big Band era who was second only to Buddy Rich. He played with the Benny Goodman Band from 1934 to 1938, appearing at the famous 'Live at Carnegie Hall' concert on 16th Jan., 1938. As a soloist, his biggest solo hits were "High On A Windy Hill" (2/41 US 2) and the B-side of the record "It All Comes Back To Me Now" (2/41 US 2). Gene died 16th October, 1973.

Captain Beefheart 1941 US singer and songwriter, real name Don Van Vliet. He went to school with Frank Zappa, who gave him the nickname Captain, and later produced his records. While his records have not been commercial successes, he has consistently appealed to the cognoscenti.

Earl Hooker 1930 US blues guitarist who also played banjo, drums, harmonica, and various keyboard instruments. Died 21st Feb., 1970.

Boris Blank 1953 Swiss sound technician, songwriter and singer with Yello.

Edward Bivins 1942 US singer with the Manhattans.

Pete Trewavas 1959 UK bass player with the group Marillion founded 1979.

Deaths

Jack Teagarden 1964 US jazz trombone player and orchestra leader. At the Monterey Festival in 1963 Jack had health problems due to lung disease and alcoholism. These were presumably the reasons for his death. Born on 20th August, 1905.

Hits of the Day

1944	"Shoo-Shoo Baby" Andrews Sisters US 9 weeks
1949	"A Little Bird Told Me" Evelyn Knight US 7 weeks
1949	"My Darling, My darling" Jo Stafford & Gordon MacRae US 1 week
1969	"Ob-La-Di-Ob-La-Da" Marmalade UK 2 weeks (2nd time)
1972	"American Pie" Don MacLean US 4 weeks
1977	"Don't Give Up On Us" David Soul UK 4 weeks

1977	"You Make Me Feel Like Dancing" Leo Sayer US 1 week
1983	"You Can't Hurry Love" Phil Collins UK 2 weeks
1983	"Down Under" Men At Work US 3 weeks

16th

Birthdays

Sade 1959 Singer and songwriter. Born in Nigeria, daughter of a British mother and Nigerian father, raised in England. Full name, Helen Folasade Adu. Sade studied fashion design in London at St. Martins School of Art, worked as a model and sang with Arriva in 1980. In 1981 she became a member of the radio band Pride. In 1983 she set up her own backing band. Greatest hits: "Your Love Is King" (3/84 UK 6), "Smooth Operator" (9/84 UK 19; 3/85 US 5), "Sweetest Taboo" (10/85 US 5; UK 31), "Never As Good As The First Time" (3/86 US 20), and "Paradise" (5/88 US 16; UK 29).

Bob Bogle 1937 US bass player, guitarist and songwriter with the Ventures, who made their first recordings in 1959. In the 60s a top instrumental band in the USA and Japan. Hits: "Walk Don't Run" (7/60 US 2; 9/60 UK 8), "Perfidia" (10/60 US 15; 12/60 UK 4), and "Hawaii Five-O" (3/69 US 4), the theme-tune of the TV programme of the same name.

Barbara Lynn 1942 US R & B singer, songwriter and guitarist. Full name, Barbara Lynn Ozen. Only hit: "You'll Lose A Good Thing" (6/62 US 8).

Ronnie Milsap 1946 US country singer, pianist and guitarist. Blind from birth, he became an excellent multi-instrumentalist by the time he was 12. First he played with the band of J. J. Cale, and then set up his own group in 1965. From 1973 onwards he could be found regularly in the country charts. By the end of 1988 he had been at No. 1 34 times. His greatest pop-hits: "It Was Almost Like A Song" (6/77 US 16), "(There's) No Gettin' Over Me" (6/81 US 5), and "Any Day Now" (5/82 US 14).

Jim Stafford 1944 US country/pop singer, songwriter, and guitarist. After moving from Florida to Nashville, he appeared as a one man band and made his first recording, which was produced by Lobo. From 1973 onwards he was successful in the pop charts. Hits: "Spiders & Snakes"

(11/73 US 3; 4/74 UK 14), "My Girl Bill" (4/74 US 12; 7/74 UK 20), and "Wildwood West" (7/74 US 7).

Phil Harris 1904 US band-leader, radio, TV, and film star, drummer, singer and songwriter. He began as a drummer in the 20s, in Francis Craig's Band. Between 1933 and 1952 he appeared in the US charts with several comedy singles. His greatest hits: "One-Zy, Two-Zy, (I Love You-Zy)" (3/46 US 2), and the million bestseller "The Thing" (11/50 US 1).

William Francis 1942 US keyboards player with Dr. Hook.

Paul Webb 1962 US bass player with Talk Talk.

Deaths

Clara Ward 1973 US gospel singer, who died aged 48 after a heart attack. She was in a coma for a week.

David Seville 1972 US songwriter. Born 27th Jan., 1919

David Whitfield 1980 UK singer. He died while working on a ship travelling around Australia. Born 2nd Feb., 1925.

Hits of the Day

1943	"There Are Such Things" Tommy Dorsey US 6 weeks
1953	"You Belong To Me" Jo Stafford UK 1 week
1964	"Glad All Over" Dave Clark Five UK 2 weeks
1965	"Come See About Me" Supremes US 1 week
1982	"Land Of Make Believe" Bucks Fizz UK 2 weeks
1988	"Heaven Is A Place On Earth" Belinda Carisle UK 2 weeks
1988	"Got My Mind Set On You" George Harrison US 1 week

Miscellany

1938 In Carnegie Hall in New York Benny Goodman recorded a concert, which was talked about for many years after, and which gave Swing the final breakthrough in the USA.

1957 The 'Cavern Club' opened its portals. Over the course of the next few years this Liverpool music cellar changed the face of British beat music. At first 'trad. jazz' was played there, then the Beatles started their legendary residency.

1967 A Festival took place in Monterey which, in retrospect was the first great rock spectacle. 50,000 saw among others Janis Joplin, Otis Redding, Jumi Hendrix The Who, The Mamas & The Papas, The Byrds, and Jefferson Airplane. It was filmed as *Monterey Pop* and has become a rock movie 'classic'.

17th

Birthdays

Chris Montez 1943 US singer who copied the style of his idol and protege Ritchie Valens. Real name Christopher Montanez. Chris was a school friend of the Beach Boys. He made his first record in 1960. Greatest hits: "Let's Dance" (8/62 US 4; 10/62 UK 2; 10/72 RE-UK 9; 4/79 RE-UK 47), "Some Kinda Fun" (12/62 US 43; UK 10), and "The More I See You" (4/66 US 16; 6/66 UK 3).

Mick Taylor 1948 UK guitarist. Mick's career started in 1965 with Ken Hensley in the Gods, which later became Uriah Heep. Mick left the Gods in June 1967 and joined John Mayall's Bluesbreakers as a replacement for Peter Green, who went on to found Fleetwood Mac. On 13th June, 1969 it was announced that Mick would be the replacement for Brian Jones, as a member of the Rolling Stones. In December 1974 he left the Stones and played briefly for Jack Bruce, then set up his own band in 1975 and worked as a session guitarist for Ron Wood, Gong and Bob Dylan.

Francoise Hardy 1944 French singer, guitarist and songwriter who had her first hit in her home country with the song "Tous Les Garcons Et Les Filles" in 1962. In 1963 she was successful with "Le Temps De L'Amour", in 1965 with "Mon Amie La Rose" and in 1973 with "Message Personnel".

William Hart 1945 US singer with the Delfonics, whose greatest hits "La-La Means I Love You" (2/68 US 4; 7/71 UK 19), and "Didn't I (Blow Your Mind This Time)" (1/70 US 10; 4/71 UK 22). The group was founded in 1965 by William and his brother Wilbert, and was originally called Four Gents.

Harold Miller 1931 US lead singer with the Rays, formed in New York in 1955. In the same year they made their first recordings. Greatest hit: "Silhouettes" (10/57 US 3). The B-side of this record was the number "Daddy Cool" which charted in the UK.

18th

Paul Young 1956 UK singer and songwriter. In 1977 he founded his first group, the Streetband, which secured a recording contract immediately. Their only hit was "Toast/Hold On" (11/78 UK 18). After that Paul lost his voice. The group broke up and several of the members left and formed the Q-Tips in September, and Paul joined them again as a singer when he recovered his voice. The Q-Tips rapidly developed into a group renowned for their live performances – however, their records remained on the shelf. Having performed over 700 live gigs in only 2 and a half years, Paul signed a solo-contract with CBS in September 1982. He broke through immediately with the Marvin Gaye composition "Wherever I Lay My Hat (That's My Home)" (6/83 UK 1). Further hits: "Come Back And Stay" (9/83 UK 4; 2/84 US 22), "Love Of The Common People" (11/83 UK 2), "I'm Gonna Tear Your Playhouse Down" (10/84 UK 9; 9/85 US 13), "Everything Must Change" (12/84 UK 9), and "Every Time You Go Away" (3/85 UK 4; 5/85 US 1).

Susanna Hoffs 1961 US singer and songwriter with the Bangles who, after playing as the Colours, first called themselves Bangs in 1981. At the beginning of 1982 a group from New Jersey appeared, also called Bangs, and told the girls from L. A. to change their name. In mid-1982 they made their first record as the Bangles. After several attempts, they had their first international hit with "Manic Monday" (1/86 US & UK 2), written by Prince under the pseudonym Christopher. Further hits were: "Walk Like An Egyptian" (9/86 US 1; UK 3), "Hazy Shade Of Winter" (11/87 US 2; 2/88 UK 11), and "Eternal Flame" (2/89 US & UK 1).

John Crawford 1960 US bass player, songwriter and singer with Berlin.

Deaths

Billy Stewart 1970 US singer. He was on the way to a performance when his car started to cross Highway 95 over the Neuse River in North Carolina, the car crashed through the guiderail and plunged into the river. He and two other passengers were killed. Born on 24th March, 1937.

Tommy Tucker 1982 US R&B artist and composer. Born on 5th March, 1933.

Hits of the Day

1976 "I Write The Songs" Barry Manilow US 1 week
1987 "Shake You Down" Gregory Abbott US 1 week

Birthdays

Bobby Goldsboro 1941 US singer, songwriter and guitarist, who had more than 20 hits between "See The Funny Little Clown" (1/64 US 9), and "Summer (The First Time)" (8/73 US 21; UK 9). His greatest hit: "Honey" (3/68 US 1; UK 2; 3/75 RE-UK 2). Bobby played lead guitar with the Candy Men, Roy Orbison's back-up group from 1962 to 1964.

David Ruffin 1941 US gospel and soul singer who was lead singer with the Temptations between 1964 and 1968. His greatest hit during his time with this band was "My Girl" (1/65 US 1; UK 43), after which he started a solo career. His first hit was "My Whole World Ended (The Moment You left Me)" (2/69 US 9). There followed a short, not particularly successful period of collaberation with his older brother Jimmy, then David continued to make solo records. Hit "Walk Away from Love" (11/75 US 9; UK 10). He teamed up with Former Temptation, Eddie Kendricks, which resulted in a tour with Hall & Oates in 1988. He died on June 1st, 1991.

Dave Greenslade 1943 UK keyboard instrumentalist with the legendary Chris Farlowe band, The Thunderbirds. A member of Colosseum from 1968 until 1971, then had his own group under his own name.

Tom Bailey 1956 UK singer, keyboard instrumentalist and songwriter of the Thompson Twins band, founded in 1977. Hits, "Hold Me Now" (11/83 UK 4; 1/84 US 3), "Doctor! Doctor!" (2/84 UK 3; 5/84 US 11), "You Take Me Up" (4/84 UK 2), "Lay Your Hands On Me" (12/84 UK 13; 9/85 US 6), and "King For A Day" (10/85 UK 22; 1/86 US 8).

Bob Rosenberg 1959 US singer, songwriter, and keyboard instrumentalist, drummer and mastermind of the group Will To Power, founded in 1987, who had their first success with a medley of hits by Peter Frampton and Lynyrd Skynyrd: "Baby, I Love Your Way/Freebird (Freebaby)" (9/88 US 1; 1/89 UK 6).

Deaths

Mel Appleby UK Vocalist. Died tragically young of cancer 1990. Born 11th July 1966.

Hits of the Day

1941	"We Three (My Echo, My Shadow & Me)" Ink Spots US 3 weeks
1957	"Singing The Blues" Guy Mitchell UK 1 week (2nd time)
1960	"Running Bear" Johnny Preston US 3 weeks
1975	"Down Down" Status Quo UK 1 week
1975	"Mandy" Barry Manilow US 1 week
1986	"That's What Friends Are For" Dionne & Friends US 4 weeks

19th

Birthdays

Janis Joplin 1943 US singer and songwriter, nicknamed 'Pearl', who sang the blues like no other white woman before or since. Janis came from Port Arthur, Texas and moved to San Francisco in 1966. In the same year she became a member of Big Brother & The Holding Company, and was a sensation at the Monterey Pop Festival in 1967. From 1968 onwards she played with her own band called Full Tilt Boogie. She did not live to experience her greatest single hit: "Me And Bobby McGee" (1/71 US 1); she was found dead of a heroin overdose in her motel room on the 4th of October, 1970. A line from "Me And Bobby McGee" went, 'Freedom's just another word for nothing left to do' Janis' motto was, 'Live to the hilt, love [violently] and die young.' She was the incarnation of the beatnik' philosophy. The film *The Rose* with Bette Midler was inspired by the life and death of Janis Joplin.

Phil Everly 1939 US singer, guitarist and songwriter. Phil is the younger of the two Everly Brothers (Donald & Philip). Ike and Margaret Everly, their parents, had made a name for themselves as folk and country musicians in the USA, especially in the Mid-West and the Deep South. Their sons appeared in the parents' radio show in 1945. When the parents retired, the sons made their first recordings from 1955 onwards first as C & W artists, then as a pop-duo. Their first hit was "Bye Bye Love" (5/57 US 2; UK 6), but their biggest hit was "All I Have To Do Is Dream" (4/58 US & UK 1). The brothers were regularly in the charts until till 1965, when their success began to wane. Finally they split up in 1973, but came together again in September of 1983. Both had unsuccessful attempts at solo careers. Don's birthday: 1st Feb., 1937, see there for further hits.

Shelley Fabares 1944 US singer and actress, real name Michele. She acted in three of Elvis Presley's films, and played the part of Mary Stone in the *Donna Reed Show*. In 1964 she married the successful record producer Lou Adler. Her only big hit was "Johnny Angel" (3/62 US 1; UK 41).

Dolly Parton 1946 US singer, songwriter and actor. She is the tenth most successful C & W artist of all time, and the most successful female Country artist ever. At the tender age of 11 she made her first record and went to Nashville in 1964. She became a member of the *Porter Wagoner TV Show* in 1967 and stayed until 1973. However, she also made solo recordings on the side. Her first appearance in the C & W charts was in January of 1967. From 1974 onwards, she scored regularly in the pop charts. Hits: "Jolene" (1/74 US 60; 5/76 UK 7), "Here You Come Again" (10/77 US 3; 4/84 UK 75), "9 To 5" (11/80 US 1; 2/81 UK 47), which was the title song in the film of the same name in which Dolly played one of the main parts, and in a duet with Kenny Rogers "Island In The Stream" (8/83 US 1; 10/83 UK 7).

Robert Palmer 1949 UK singer and songwriter, who was a member of Alan Bown Set, Dada, and Vinegar Joe, before beginning a very successful US solo career in 1974. Greatest hits: "Johnny and Mary" and "Looking For Clues" (11/80 UK 33). In 1985 he sang in a project with Duran-Duran musicians Andy and John Taylor, and Chic drummer Tony Thomson. They called themselves Power Station. Hits: "Some Like It Hot" (3/85 US 6; UK 14) and "Get It On" (5/85 UK 22; US 9). From 1986 onwards again a soloist – Hits: "Addicted to Love" (2/86 US 1; 5/86 UK 5), "I Didn't Mean To Turn You On" (7/86 UK 9; US 2), " . . . Simply Irresistible" (7/88 US 2) and "She Makes My Day" (10/88 UK 6).

Rod Evans 1945 UK singer, songwriter and founder member of Deep Purple, who was then replaced in 1970, after 3 LPs, by Ian Gillan. Appeared once more with Captain Beyond.

Dewey Bunnell 1951 US singer, guitarist and songwriter with America, who had their first and biggest hit: "Horse With No Name" (12/71 UK 3; 2/72 US 1). In the USA they were very successful scoring again with "Sister Golden Hair" (4/75 US 1).

Martha Davis 1951 US singer and songwriter, founder member of Motels in July 1978. Their first LP appeared in September 1979. Hits: "Only The Lonely" (4/82 US 9) and "Suddenly Last Summer" (9/83 US 9). From 1987 Martha had a solo career.

Laurie London 1944 UK child star, who at the age of 13 had a hit with "He's Got The Whole World In His Hand" (11/57 UK 12; 3/58 US 1).

Johnny O'Keefe 1935 Australian rock'n roll singer, biggest star in Australasia. He died on 6th Oct., 1978.

Michael Virtue 1957 UK keyboard player with UB40.

Deaths

Don Costa 1983 US songwriter and orchestra leader. Born 10th June, 1925.

Hits of the Day

1959	"O Billy Boy" Platters US 3 weeks	
1967	"I'm A Believer" Monkees UK 4 weeks	
1974	"Show and Tell" Al Wilson US 1 week	
1974	"You Won't Find Another Fool Like Me" New Seekers UK 1 week	
1980	"Brass In Pocket" Pretenders UK 2 weeks	
1980	"Rock With You" Michael Jackson US 4 weeks	
1985	"I Want to Know What Love Is" Foreigner UK 3 weeks	

20th

Birthdays

Eric Stewart 1945 UK singer, guitarist and songwriter. In 1963 he was a session musician in a Manchester studio when Glyn Ellis, alias Wayne Fontana, was looking for a back-up group for a recording session – thus was born Wayne Fontana and the Mindbenders. When Wayne left the group in the spring of 1966, the remaining members retained the name the Mindbenders, and promptly scored a hit with "A Groovy Kind Of Love" (1/66 UK 2, 4/66 US 2). Eric was the singer. In 1968 the band split up, Eric returned to session work and then reappeared in the charts in 1970 with Hot Legs and "Neanderthal Man" (7/70 UK 2, US 22). This band finally metamorphosed into 10 CC, who had any amount of hits in the seventies. The biggest were "Rubber Bullets" (5/73 UK 1, 9/73 US 73), "I'm Not In Love" (5/75 UK 1, US 2) and "Dreadlock Holiday" (8/78 UK 1, US 44). Finally Eric turned up again in the 80s in the company of Paul McCartney.

Ray Anthony 1922 US trumpeter and orchestra leader, who formed his own band in 1946 and produced hits regularly between 1950 and 1962. Real name: Raymond

Antonini. Also played with Glenn Miller and Jimmy Dorsey. Successful hit with Frank Sinatra "Melody Of Love" (1/55 US 19). Hits in his own right: "At Last" (2/52 US 2), "Dragnet" (8/53 US 2, 12/53 UK 7) and "Peter Gunn" (1/59 US 8). As an actor Ray appeared with Fred Astaire in *Daddy Long Legs* in 1955, and was married for some time to actress Mamie van Doren, nick-named 'Poor Man's Marilyn Monroe' in the USA – or 'Platinum Blonde Sexpot Of Hollywood B-Features'.

Billy Powell 1942 US singer with the O'Jays until 1976. Replaced by Sam Strain. Powell died of cancer on 26th May, 1977.

Ronald Townson 1941 US singer with the Fifth Dimension, whose biggest hit was "Aquarius/Let the Sunshine In" (3/69 US 1, UK 11).

Earl Grant 1931 US keyboard instrumentalist and singer, who had a hit with the tear-jerker "The End" (9/58 US 7). He died on 11th June, 1970.

Rick Evans 1943 US guitarist and singer, who played with the Eccentrics in 1962, along with Denny Zager. After the band had split up, these two met again in 1968 and recorded a piece which Evans had written in 1964. After a longish interval it became the biggest hit for Zager & Evans: "In the Year 2525 (Exordium & Terminus)" (6/69 US 1, 8/69 UK 1).

Paul Stanley 1950 US guitarist and songwriter with Kiss. Full name Paul Stanley Eisen. In 1978 all four members of the group made their own solo LPs – the one by Paul, entitled PAUL STANLEY, sold over a million copies.

Slim Whitman 1924 US country singer and yodeller. Real name Otis Dewey Whitman Jr. In 1950 Slim produced his first records and in 1952 first appeared in the UK charts; his success there continued into the 1970s. – Hits: "Indian Love Call" (7/52 US 9, 7/55 UK 7), "Rose Marie" (5/54 US 22, 7/55 UK 1). "Serenade" (6/56 UK 8), "I'll Take You Home Kathleen" (4/57 UK 7) and "Happy Anniversary" (10/74 UK 14). He appeared regularly in US country charts until the end of 1981.

George Grantham 1947 US drummer, one of the founder members of Poco.

Paul King 1960 UK singer and songwriter. In 1984 he formed the group King, which split up in 1986. Their biggest hits were: "Love & Pride" (1/85 UK 2, 7/85 US 55). and "Alone Without You" (8/85 UK 8). From 1987 Paul continued as a soloist.

Robin McAuley 1953 UK singer and songwriter, who played with the German guitarist Michael Schenker, brother of Rudolf Schenker of the Scorpions. From 1987, they were known as the McAuley Schenker Group (or MSG for short).

Melvyn Pritchard 1948 UK drummer with Barclay James Harvest.

Deaths

Alan Freed 1965 For many Americans he was the archetypical 'rock n' roll disc jockey'. He was the first to play R & B music by black artists in his programmes. Born 15th Dec., 1921.

Hits of the Day

1956 "16 Tons" Tennessee Ernie Ford UK 4 weeks
1966 "Keep On Running" Spencer Davis Group UK 1 week
1968 "Judy In Disguise" John Fred US 2 weeks
1979 "Le Freak" Chic US 3 weeks (3rd time)
1990 "Tears on my Pillow" Kylie Minogue UK 1 week
1990 "Nothing Compares 2U" Sinead O'Connor UK 4 weeks

21st

Birthdays

Mac Davis 1941 US singer, guitarist and songwriter. Although he was a musician from the early 60s, success came only after singers like Lou Rawls ("You're Good For Me"), Glen Campbell ("Within My Memory"), and particularly Elvis Presley ("In the Ghetto" and "Don't Cry Daddy") recorded his compositions. In 1969 Mac launched his own solo career. Greatest hits: "Baby Don't Get Hooked On Me" (7/72 US 1; 11/72 UK 29), and "Stop And Smell The Roses" (8/74 US 9). Mac had his own TV show in the USA from 1974 till 1976, and starred in several films as an actor.

Billy Ocean 1950 Singer and songwriter, who was born in Trinidad and grew up in London. Real name Leslie Sebastian Charles. In the early 70s he sang as an amateur with various bands in London and cut his first single in 1974 with Scorched Earth, which was unsuccessful. At the end of 1975 he obtained a contract with the record label

GTO, a number of hits followed: "Love Really Hurts Without You" (2/76 UK 2; 4/76 US 22), and "Red Light Spells Danger" (3/77 UK 2). In 1982 GTO Records was sold to CBS and he stopped recording for two years. And then when he resumed his career he was more successful than ever, notching up one hit after another: "Caribbean (European) Queen" (8/84 US 1; UK 6), "Loverboy" (12/84 UK 2; US 15), "Suddenly" (3/85 US 4; 5/85 UK 4), "When The Going Gets Tough, The Tough Get Going" (12/85 US 2; UK 1), "There'll Be Sad Songs (To Make Me Cry)" (4/86 US 1; UK 12), and "Get Outta My Dreams, Get Into My Car" (2/88 US 1; UK 3).

Telly Savalas 1924 US baldheaded film and TV star, real first name Aristotle. He had a single hit in the charts with a spoken version of the Bread hit "If" (2/75 UK 1). His career as an actor did not begin until he was 40. In the film *Birdman of Alcatraz* (1962) he was so convincing that he was nominated for an Oscar for the best supporting actor. This and many other roles show that he was underrated as merely Theo Kojak, a part he played from 1973 to 1978 on TV.

Edwin Starr 1942 US soul singer and songwriter, real name Charles Hatcher. He started with the group Future Tones and made his first recordings in 1957. He sang with Bill Doggett from 1963 to 1965. He has made records since 1965 under the name of Edwin Starr. From then until the late 70s he was an occasional visitor to the charts with hits like "Twenty-five Miles" (2/69 US 6; 9/69 UK 36), "War" (7/70 US 1, 10/70 UK 3), "Contact" (1/79 UK 6) and "H.A.P.P.Y. Radio" (5/79 UK 9).

Ritchie Havens 1941 US singer and guitarist whose soulful voice added an extra dimension to the folksongs in his repertoire. His first memorable appearance was at the Newport Folk Festival in 1966, but he reached the zenith of his career at the Woodstock Festival in 1969. His most commercial success was with the George Harrison composition "Here Comes The Sun" (3/71 US 16).

Snooks Eaglin 1936 US blues guitarist, singer and songwriter who was blind since childhood. Real first name Fird. In the early 1950s he played with Allen Toussaint and the Flamingoes. In the 1970s he worked primarily with Professor Longhair in his home town of New Orleans. Although Albert Collins and Little Richard Penniman appear as the authors of the song "Lucille", this number was allegedly written by Snooks.

Kristian Schultze 1945 Keyboard instrumentalist with Passport, Snowball and on sessions.

Pye Hastings 1947 UK guitarist and singer with Caravan.

Deaths

Jackie Wilson 1984 US singer and songwriter. He never awoke from a coma after collapsing on stage in 1975. He was the inspiration of many soul singers. Even white singers like Rod Stewart modelled there style on his performances. Born on 9th June, 1934.

Champion Jack Dupree 1992 US blues pianist and singer and long-time European resident. Born 4th July 1910.

Hits of the Day

1955 "Finger Of Suspicion" Dickie Valentine UK 2 weeks (2nd time)

1984 "Owner Of A Lonely Heart" Yes US 2 weeks

1989 "Two Hearts" Phil Collins US 2 weeks

Miscellany

1950 George Orwell (Eric Arthur Blair) died, and therefore, did not live to see how his novel *1984* written in 1949 would become more and more of a reality. A film of the book was made, which featured title song Sex Crime 1984 (11/84 UK 4) by the Eurythmics. Born 25th June, 1903 in India.

22nd

Birthdays

Sam Cooke 1935 US soul singers and songwriter. Sam started with the Highway Q.C.s and joined the Soul Stirrers in 1950, with whom he was lead singer until 1956. From 1956 he was more interested in pop music and made his first secular recordings under the name of Dale Cook although he reverted to Sam Cooke after one record. He had his first hit in 1957 with "You Send Me" (10/57 US 1, 1/58 UK 29). He was regularly in the charts until 1965, usually with his own compositions. On 11th December, 1964, he was shot dead in a motel in Los Angeles by a woman who alleged self defence; the circumstances were never clarified. Many singers subsequently covered his material. One of his records "Wonderful World" (7/60 US 12; UK 27; 3/86 RE-UK 2) became a hit all over again when it was used in a commercial for a jeans manufacturer. In

addition the Cooke family was represented in the charts by Cooke's daughter Linda, formerly a successful songwriter, she achieved even greater success after her marriage to Cecil Womack as Womack & Womack, and finally, a nephew of Sam Cooke, R. B. Greaves.

Adie Harris 1940 US singer, who was a member of the Shirelles – her nickname being Micki. The group formed while the girls were still at school. In 1958 they made their first recording, their last hit was in 1967. The most impressive hits were "Will You Love Me Tomorrow" (11/60 US 1; 2/61 UK 4), and "Soldier Boy" (3/62 US 1; 5/62 UK 23). Addie died on 10th June, 1982.

James P. Pennington 1949 US lead singer, guitarist and songwriter with the Exiles formed in 1963. The name was shortened to Exile in 1973. In its early days the group played rock, but with the help of the two British producers Mike Chapman and Nicky Chinn they were suddenly thrust into the limelight with hits like "Kiss You All Over" (7/78 US 1; UK 6). Since 1983 the group became more successful in the country charts, they managed to hit the No. 1 spot 10 times. Pennington left the group in 1989.

Malcolm MacLaren 1947 UK manager, songwriter and producer, who is considered by some to be a charlatan, and by others exceptionally talented. He managed or masterminded such artists as the Sex Pistols, Adam Ant and Bow Wow Wow. According to statements by his record company Malcolm can't really play a single instrument, and sees himself as 'musical painter, who shamelessly uses the sounds of any period'. He figured prominently in the punk movement which showed him that it is quite possible to enter the charts without a voice or musical talent. He started making records in his own name in 1982. His biggest hits: "Buffalo Gals" (12/82 Uk 9), and "Double Dutch" (7/83 UK 3).

Steve Perry 1949 US singer and songwriter. In 1977 joined the band Journey, founded in 1973. He also made records on the side as a soloist. Hits with the band: "Who's Crying Now" (7/81 US 4; 9/82 UK 46) and "Open Arms" (1/82 US 2); and as a soloist, "Oh Sherrie" (4/84 US 3). In February 1987 Journey announced they would no longer play together. Steve continued his solo career.

Michael Hutchence 1960 Australian singer and songwriter with the group INXS. The origins of this band go back to the year 1977. The Farriss Brothers formed in Sydney, and Michael was a founder member. From 1979 onwards the band called themselves INXS, their first record was released in May 1980. At first they were only successful in Australia, but soon became known worldwide. Hits: "What You Need" (1/86 US 5), "Need You Tonight" (10/87 US 1; UK 58; 11/88 RE-UK 2), "Devil

Inside" (2/88 US 2), "New Sensation" (1/88 UK 25; 5/88 US 3), and "Never Tear Us Apart" (6/88 UK 24; 8/88 US 7).

Graeme John Douglas 1950 UK guitarist, keyboard instrumentalist and songwriter with the Kursaal Flyers from their formation in 1974 until February 1977. Then he played with Eddie & The Hot Rods.

Nigel Pegrum 1949 UK drummer with Gnidrolog and Steeleye Span. Nigel also played on records by Michael Chapman, Richard Digance, John Otway & Wild Willy Barrett, Tim Hart, the Stender Band and Bernie's Autobahn Band.

Hits of the Day

1966 "The Sound Of Silence" Simon & Garfunkel US 1 week (2nd time)

1977 "I Wish" Stevie Wonder US 1 week

23rd

Birthdays

Robin Zander 1952 US singer, guitarist and songwriter with the band Cheap Trick from Chicago, founded in 1974. In 1977 their debut LP appeared. Hits: "I Want You To Want Me" (4/79 US 7; UK 29), "The Flame" (4/88 US 1), and "Don't Be Cruel" (8/88 US 4).

Django Reinhardt 1910 French jazz guitarist and composer who is considered to be one of the few Europeans to have influenced American jazz music. Born in Belgium his real first name was Jean Baptiste. Django became internationally known through his work with the violinist Stephan Grappelly, when he co-founded the quintet The Hot Club of France in 1934. In 1946 he played with Duke Ellington in the USA. There he did a lot towards the development of all guitar styles. Django who was a Romany, used clearly discernible influences of gypsy music in his melodies. He died on 16th May, 1953.

Herbert Hildebrandt 1943 German bass player, singer, and songwriter. He was a member of the Rattles between 1961 and 1968, and after that wrote and produced, for Pegasus and Soulful Dynamics. In the early 70s he was considered to be the most successful German composer – then he started to run clubs and discos. In 1988, when the Rattles re-grouped, he rejoined.

Pat Simmons 1950 US guitarist, singer, and songwriter with the Doobie Brothers, formed in September 1970 (doobie is a Californian slang term for a marijuana joint). The band's first record appeared in April, 1971. In March, 1982 the group declared they were splitting up, and in spring of 1983 Simmons' solo record appeared. His greatest success was "So Wrong" (3/83 US 30). After the lack of success of their various solo ventures, the Doobie Brothers reformed cutting the LP CYCLES in May, 1989; it featured almost the original line up. Greatest hits of the Doobie Brothers were "Long Train Runnin' " (4/74 US 8), "Black Water" (12/74 US 1), "What A Fool Believes" (1/79 US 1; UK 31), "Real Love" (9/80 US 5), and "The Doctor" (5/89 US 9),

Anita Pointer 1948 US singer with the group of sisters, Pointer Sisters. They made their first records in 1971. In 1976 they appeared in the film *Car Wash*. Hits, "Fire" (11/78 US 2; 3/79 UK 34), "He's So Shy" (7/80 US 3), "Slow Hand" (5/81 US 2; 8/81 UK 10), "Automatic" (1/84 US 5; 4/84 UK 2), "Jump For My Love" (4/84 US 3; 6/84 UK 6), "I'm So Excited" (8/84 US 9; 10/84 UK 11), and "Neutron Dance" (11/84 US 6; 1/85 UK 31).

Billy Cunningham 1950 US bass player with the Box Tops, formed in 1967. Billy left them in 1969.

Earl Falconer 1959 UK bass player with the group UB 40.

Deaths

Terry Kath 1978 US guitarist and songwriter with Chicago. He was playing about with a pistol, jokingly held it to his head and pressed the trigger – not realizing it was loaded. His replacement was Danny Dacus. Terry was born on 31st Jan., 1946.

Big Maybelle 1972 US singer, who also appeared as Mamie Webster. Her real name was Mabel Louise Smith. Cause of death was diabetes. Born on 1st May, 1924.

Edward "Kid" Ory 1973 US trombonist and band leader. Died of pneumonia and heart failure in Honolulu, Hawaii. Ory was born on 25th Dec., 1889.

Vic Ames 1978 US singer with the Ames Brothers. Born on 20th May, 1926.

Paul Robeson 1976 US singer. Born on 9th April, 1898.

Allen Collins 1990 US guitarist. Died of pneumonia. Born 23rd January 1952.

Hits of the Day

1953 "Comes Along A Love" Kay Starr UK 1 week
1959 "The Day The Rains Came" Jane Morgan UK 1 week
1965 "Downtown" Petula Clark US 2 weeks
1971 "Knock Three Times" Dawn US 3 weeks
1988 "The Way You Make Me Feel" Michael Jackson US 1 week

24th

Birthdays

Neil Diamond 1941 US singer, songwriter, and guitarist, who wrote so many numbers, he was unable to record them all himself. So other artists like the Monkees recorded his material including "I'm A Believer", which sold about 10 million copies. Neil made his debut as a performer with the folk group, Roadrunners between 1954 and 1956. In 1961 he signed his first record contract as a soloist. From 1966 onwards he appeared in the charts regularly. His million sellers were "Sweet Caroline (Good Times Never Seemed So Good)" (6/69 US 4; 2/71 UK 8), "Cracklin' Rosie" (8/70 US 1; 11/70 UK 3), "Song Sung Blue" (5/72 US 1; UK 14), and together with Barbra Streisand "You Don't Bring Me Flowers" (10/78 US 1; UK 5). He was quite competent as an actor in a new version of the Al Jolson film *The Jazz Singer*. He is still as popular as he ever was.

Aaron Neville 1941 US singer and songwriter with his brothers as the Neville Brothers and as a soloist. Solo hit, "Tell It Like It Is" (12/66 US 2) and in a duet with Linda Ronstadt, "Don't Know Much" (9/89 US 2; 11/89 UK 2). For the story of the Neville Brothers, see under 17th December, brother Art.

Jack Scott 1936 Canadian singer, songwriter, and guitarist, whose real name is Jack Scafone Jr. In 1946 he moved with his parents from his place of birth, Windsor, to Hazel Park, Michigan. From 1958 to 1960 he was successful in the USA mainly with self-composed songs. Hits: "My True Love" (6/58 US 3; 10/58 UK 9). and "Burning Bridges" (4/60 US 3; UK 23). He was still on the road in and around Detroit during the 80s.

Ray Stevens 1941 US singer, pianist, actor, comedian, songwriter and producer. Real name Ray Ragsdale. He was in the charts from 1961 onwards with – more often than not – novelty records his first Top Ten hit was "Ahab, the Arab" (6/62 US 5). His million bestseller was "Gitarzan" (4/69 US 8), "Everything Is Beautiful" (4/70 US 1; UK 6) and "The Streak" (4/74 US & UK 1). Although Ray continued to record in the 80s, he only managed to get into C&W charts.

Warren Zevon 1947 Canadian singer, son of Russian immigrants, songwriter and pianist. A US resident, he was successful with the title, "Werewolves of London" (3/78 US 21). In 1987 the record appeared again in Martin Scorsese's film *The Color Of Money*, starring Paul Newman and Tom Cruise. Warren wrote the number "Poor Poor Pitiful Me" (1/78 US 31) for Linda Ronstadt. Hindu Love Gods ref. In 1990, he collaborated with most of R.E.M for the album HINDU LOVE GODS.

Doug Kershaw 1936 US country/cajun violinist and songwriter, who made his first recordings together with his brother, Rusty, as the duo Rusty & Doug in 1953. Doug had already appeared on stage with his mother when he was 12. He formed the group Continental Playboys together with his brothers, Russell Lee alias Rusty, and Nelson alias Pee Wee. His autobiographical song, "Louisiana Man" was re-recorded by more than 600 different artists over the years. To many he is best known for his work with Bob Dylan. He made a comeback in 1970 after a bout of alcoholism.

John Belushi 1949 US singer, comedian and film actor who appeared with Dan Aykroyd as The Blues Brothers in the film of the same name. John was 'Jake Blues' and Dan 'Elwood Blues'. The whole thing was intended as a bit of fun for the TV programme 'Saturday Night Live', but it became a real hit. A hit for the duo was "Soul Man" (12/78 US 14). The film *Blues Brothers* made 32 million dollars in a space of only 2 months. Belushi died on 5th March, 1982 in Hollywood after a drugs overdose.

Jim Rutledge 1947 US singer and songwriter with the group Bloodrock, in which he replaced their lead singer, Warren Ham, in 1970. The group's only hit was "D.O.A." (1/71 US 36), and it featured Jim as lead vocalist.

Michael Chapman 1941 UK folk musician. Very much the iconoclast with a small but dedicated band of followers. Arguably, his best work is probably still his early LP FULLY QUALIFIED SURVIVOR which first appeard in 1969.

Deaths

Gene Austin 1972 US singer and songwriter. Born on 24th June, 1900.

James 'Shep' Sheppard 1970 US singer and founder of the band Shep & The Limelites formed in 1961. From 1956 to 1960 he was the lead singer with the Heartbeats, who had their biggest success with the number "A Thousand Miles Away" (12/56 US 53). An answer to this song became the biggest hit for Shep & The Limelites, "Daddy's Home" (3/61 US 2). Some years later, Cliff Richard covered it and it became a hit all over again (11/81 UK 2). James Sheppard was found dead in his car on the Long Island Expressway; he had been attacked, robbed, and beaten to death.

Gordon MacRea 1986 US film actor and singer. Born on 12th March, 1921.

Hits of the Day

1958	"Jailhouse Rock" Elvis Presley UK 3 weeks
1963	"Dance On" Shadows UK 1 week
1968	"The Ballad Of Bonnie And Clyde" Georgie Fame UK 1 week
1976	"Theme From Mahogany" Diana Ross US 1 week
1987	"Jack Your Body" Steve 'Silk' Hurly UK 2 weeks
1987	"At This Moment" Billy Vera & The Beaters US 2 weeks

ball when he was 6 years old. He became completely blind in 1950. He belonged to a long tradition of country-blues, singers like Big Bill Broonzy, which was the inspiration for artists like Arthur Big Boy Crudup. He died on 5th June, 1977.

Andy Cox 1956 UK guitarist and songwriter. Andy was a founder-member of the group The Beat in 1978. In 1983 he left and formed the band Fine Young Cannibals, with David Steele, another member of The Beat.

Ronnie Brandon 1946 US keyboard player with the McCoys.

Deaths

Chris Kenner 1976 US singer and songwriter. He died after a heart attack. Born on 25th Dec., 1929.

Hits of the Day

1957	"Garden Of Eden" Frankie Vaughan UK 4 weeks
1969	"Eloise" Barry Ryan
1975	"Ms. Grace" Tymes UK 1 week
1975	"Please Mr. Postman" Carpenters US 1 week
1986	"The Sun Always Shines On TV" A-Ha UK 2 weeks

Miscellany

1956 RCA released their first Elvis Presley record, with "Heartbreak Hotel" on the A-side, and "I Was The One" on the B-side. It was this record which became Elvis' first No. 1 hit on 3rd May, 1956. It stayed at No. 1 for 7 weeks.

25th

Birthdays

Etta James 1938 US singer and songwriter, real name Etta James Hawkins, nickname 'Miss Peaches' after the vocal group, Peaches. She was discovered by Johnny Otis in the early 50s, made her first records in 1954 and charted frequently up until 1970. Her biggest hit was "Tell Mama" (11/67 US 23). In recent years she has cut some fine albums with Allen Toussaint and Barry Beckett producing.

Richard Finch 1954 US bass player and songwriter. After meeting Harry Casey (K.C.) he formed K. C. & The Sunshine Band, who managed to hit a nerve with the disco-fad of the mid-1970s. For hits, see 31st Jan., under Casey (K.C).

Sleepy John Estes 1899 US blues guitarist, singer and songwriter. He lost the sight of his right eye playing base-

26th

Birthdays

Eartha Kitt 1928 US singer, dancer and actor. She began her career in Paris, before hitting Broadway in '*New Faces of 1952*'. Among her hits were "C'est Si Bon" (7/53 US 8) "Santa Baby" (11/53 US 4) and "Under The Bridges Of Paris" (4/55 UK 7), the latter being her first hit in the UK. After a long break during which she enhanced her reputation as a performer and an actress, she returned to the charts in 1983 with "Where Is My Man" (12/83 UK 36) and "I Love Men" (7/84 UK 50).

Huey 'Piano' Smith 1934 US R & B pianist and songwriter. Huey played with Earl King in the early 50s. From 1951 to 1954 he was a member of Eddie 'Guitar Slim' Jones' band. In between he played on many records by New Orleans-based musicians like Lloyd Price, Smiley Lewis, and Little Richard. In 1957 he formed his own band, Huey 'Piano' Smith and the Clowns, and charted with "Rocking Pneumonia & The Boogie Woogie Flu" (7/57 R&B 5) and "Don't You Just Know It" (3/58 R&B 4; US 9). The lead singer of The Clowns was Bobby Marchan, who left to pursue a solo career. Huey and his group were the lead backing musicians on the Frankie Ford hit, "Sea Cruise" (4/59 US 11). In the early 1970s Smith went into retirement.

Marshall Lieb 1939 US singer who sang with Phil Spector and Annette Kleinbard, alias Carol Connors, in the trio Teddy Bears. She had a big hit with "To Know Him Is To Love Him" (9/58 US 1; 12/58 UK 2).

Michel Delpech 1946 French singer and songwriter who was helped on his way by Jacques Brel, the latter helped Delpech get his first appearance at the Olympia Theatre in Paris. In 1965 he had his first big hit in his home country with "Chez Laurette"; it was followed by "L'Inventaire 66", (1966), "Wight Is Wight" (1969), "Pour Une Flirt" (1971), "Divorce" (1973) and "Le Chasseur" (1975).

Eddie Van Halen 1957 Dutch guitarist keyboard instrumentalist and songwriter of US band Van Halen, formed with his older brother Alex. See latter under 8th May, for hits and the history of the band.

Alice Babs 1924 Swedish jazz singer, film and TV star. Real surname Nilson. From the early 60s she was a member of the Swe-Danes-Trio, in which Svend Asmussen played as well. She even appeared in the UK charts as a soloist with "After You've Gone" (8/63 UK 43). In 1963, she recorded the LP SERENADE FOR SWEDEN with Duke Ellington. In 1975 she appeared at the Newport Festival.

David Briggs 1951 Australian Lead guitarist with the Little River Band, whose first LP was released in 1976. Briggs was replaced by Wayne Nelson in 1980.

Andrew Ridgeley 1963 UK guitarist, songwriter and 50% of Wham!, who had one hit after another between 1982 and 1986. The duo split up at the end of 1986. For a list of hits, see 25th June, under George Michael. Since the split Andrew has made various attempts at launching a new career in various walks of life.

Anna LaCazzio 1962 US singer and keyboard instrumentalist with Cock Robin. Hits: "When Your Heart Is Weak" (6/85 US 35) and "The Promise You Made" (5/86 UK 28).

Bert Heerink 1953 Dutch singer with Vandenberg. The group had a hit in the US with "Burning Heart" (1/83 US 39).

Norman Lamont Hassan 1958 UK keyboard instrumentalist, percussionist, trombonist and singer with UB40.

Derek Holt 1949 UK bassist and keyboard instrumentalist with the Climax Blues Band.

Deaths

John A. Lomax 1948 Important personality in US folk music, who was one of the first people to recognise the intrinsic significance of black music. Without his assiduous attention to the folk songs of the US much of its musical heritage would have disappeared. His son, Alan, has followed in his footsteps and became a vital force in rediscovery and documents many of the country blues artists. Born on the 23rd September, 1875.

Hits of the Day

1946	"Let It Snow! Let It Snow! Let It Snow!" Vaughan Monroe US 5 weeks
1961	"Are You Lonesome Tonight?" Elvis Presley UK 4 weeks
1963	"Walk Right In" Rooftop Singers US 2 weeks
1974	"You're 16" Ringo Starr US 1 week
1974	"Tiger Feet" Mud UK 4 weeks

27th

Birthdays

David Seville 1919 US songwriter, actor, and sound experimenter. Real name Ross Bagdasarian. In 1939 he wrote the song "Come On-A-My-House" which became a massive hit for Rosemary Clooney in 1951. In the early 50s he appeared in films like *Viva Zapata* (1952) and Hitchcock's *Rear Window* (1954). In order to work in recording studios and continue acting, he changed his name to David Seville. After several tries, he scored a hit with "Witch Doctor" (4/58 US 1), which encouraged him to invent the Chipmunks: he sang all the different voices, then mixed them at different tape speeds. Under this guise he had hits with, "The Chipmunk Song" (12/58 US 1) and "Alvin's Harmonica" (2/59 US 3). After his death on 16th Jan., 1972, further records by the Chipmunks appeared, which his son issued employing his Father's technique.

Bobby Bland 1930 US blues singer and songwriter. Real Christian names Robert Calvin, nickname 'Blue'. He started out in the late 40s with the gospel group Miniatures. In 1949 he was a member of the Beale Streeters, and played alongside musicians like B. B. King, Roscoe Gordon and Johnny Ace. From 1952 he started to cut solo records, and by 1957, he had become a fixture in the R&B charts. His most successful cross-over hits were, "Turn On Your Love Light" (12/61 R&B 2; US 28), and "Call On Me" (1/63 US 22; R&B 6). He has continued to tour regularly with B. B. King right up to the present day.

Nick Mason 1945 UK drummer, songwriter and in 1965, founder-member of Pink Floyd. In 1981 Nick released his solo LP, FICTITIOUS SPORT. Although it seemed as if Pink Floyd would finally split up in the mid-1980s when Roger Waters left, it was Nick and David Gilmour who kept the band together.

Kim Gardner 1948 UK bass player with Ashton, Gardner & Dyke, formed in 1968. The group had one hit single, "Resurrection Shuffle" (1/71 UK 3; 6/71 US 40). Previously, Kim was in Creation, who charted with "Painter Man" (11/66 UK 36). Kim also played on records by Mike Hugg, Badger, and Billy Burnette.

Seth Justman 1951 US keyboard player, singer and songwriter with the group J. Geils, formed in 1967. They cut their first album in 1970. After Peter Wolf left the group in 1983, Seth took over as lead singer. Hitherto, no hits have been forthcoming.

Elmore James 1918 US blues singer, guitarist and songwriter. Real surname Brooks. He is considered to be a model for many British blues and R&B musicians like. Eric Clapton who were quick to latch on to his bottleneck slide guitar technique. Elmore didn't start cutting records until the 1950s, when his hits included "Dust My Broom" (4/52 R&B 9) and "I Believe" (2/53 R&B 9). He appeared regularly in Chicago until shortly before his death on 24th May, 1963.

Kevin Coyne 1944 UK singer, guitarist, and songwriter, who made his first records in the late 60s with Siren, and released several solo LPs from 1972. His record

company always referred to him as an anti-star – which he has remained to this day. Now a German resident.

Helmut Zacharias 1920 German violinist and Orchestra leader. He had two international hits: "When The White Lilacs Bloom Again" (9/56 US 12) and "Tokyo Melody" (10/64 UK 9).

Miguel Drummond 1964 UK drummer with the band Curiosity Killed The Cat, formed in 1983.

Brian Downey 1951 UK drummer with Thin Lizzy, of which he was a founder-member in 1969.

Nedra Telley 1946 US singer with the Ronettes.

Deaths

Mahalia Jackson 1972 US 'Queen of Gospel'. She died after a long period of heart disease. Born on 26th October, 1911.

Hits of the Day

1940	"All The Things You Are" Tommy Dorsey US 2 weeks
1962	"Peppermint Twist" Joey Dee & The Starliters US 3 weeks
1966	"Michelle" Overlanders UK 3 weeks
1973	"Superstition" Stevie Wonder US 1 week
1973	"Blockbuster" Sweet UK 5 weeks
1979	"Hit Me With Your Rythm Stick" Ian Drury UK 1 week

28th

Birthdays

Mr Acker Bilk 1929 UK pop/jazz clarinetist and composer. Real first names, Bernard Stanley. 'Acker' is a British slang word for pal. After learning to play the clarinet during army service in Egypt in 1947, he formed his own group in 1958, this coincided with a boom in traditional and dixieland jazz. Between 1960 and 1963, he was at the peak of his popularity with hits like "Summer Set" (1/60 UK 5), "Buona Sera" (12/60 UK 7), "That's My Home" (7/61 UK 7) and "Stranger On The Shore" (11/61 UK 2; US 1). He returned to the UK charts with "Aria" (8/76 UK 5) after a protracted absence.

Achim Reichel 1944 German singer and songwriter who formed the Rattles in 1960. They developed a strong following at the Star Club in Hamburg in 1963, which led to 4 tours of the UK. The group's first hit was "La La La" in Germany, and their biggest was "Come On And Sing".

Brian Keenan 1944 UK drummer, who was a member of the US group, Chambers Brothers, from 1965 to 1973.

Corky Laing 1948 UK drummer of Mountain and West, Bruce & Laing. He has also issued solo records.

Dave Sharp 1959 UK guitarist and songwriter with the group Alarm, formed in 1981.

Robert Wyatt 1945 UK singer, drummer, keyboard player and songwriter who formed Soft Machine in 1966 and Matching Mole in 1971. After 1972, he recorded several solo LPs and he played as a studio musician with Kevin Coyne, Nick Mason and Phil Manzanera. Although he had a serious accident which left him paralysed from the waist down he is still one of the most inventive musicians currently working in the UK.

Arnold Muhren 1944 Dutch bass player and songwriter. He wrote the Cats' greatest hits.

Rick Allen 1946 US keyboard instrument player for the Box Tops.

Martin Leslie Fried 1944 US drummer with Cyrkle.

Deaths

Billy Fury 1983 UK singer. He had just launched a 'comeback' when he suffered a heart attack. Born 17th April, 1941.

Al Dexter 1984 US singer, songwriter, and guitarist. Born on 4th May, 1902.

Hits of the Day

1965 "Go Now" Moody Blues UK 1 week
1984 "Relax" Frankie Goes To Hollywood UK 5 weeks
1989 "Something's Gotten Hold Of My Heart" Mark Almond & Gene Pitney UK 4 weeks

---

Miscellany

1967 The first stage appearance of the Jimi Hendrix Experience takes place at London's Saville Theatre. "Hey Joe" had been released shortly before.

29th

Birthdays

Sacha Distel 1933 French guitarist, singer and songwriter. He learned to play the piano when he was 5 and the guitar at 15. While he was a student of philosophy he played dixieland jazz, then after hearing Dizzy Gillespie he became more interested in modern jazz. In 1950 he won a talent competition and, in the same year, he played with Stan Getz, the Modern Jazz Quartet, Lionel Hampton and Gillespie. At the time Sacha was considered to be an excellent jazz guitarist. In France he had his biggest success with "Scoubidou" (1959) and "Mon Bon Chapeau" (1960). On the international scene he arrived in the charts with "Raindrops Keep Falling On My Head" (1/70 UK 10), and "Adios Amigo". Sacha, who has recorded in 5 different languages, won a Grammy for the best song of the year in 1963 with the theme song for the film *The Seven Capital Sins*; as "The Good Life" it became a hit for Tony Bennett.

David Byron 1947 UK singer and songwriter of the band Uriah Heep, formed in 1969. From 1971 to 1978 they charted 17 times in Germany, however, they had no hits in their home country. Their most successful numbers were "Lady In Black", "Easy Livin' ", "Spider Woman" and "Free Me". At the end of the 70s David was fired from the band, as he could not get on with Ken Hensley, head of the band. He launched a solo career, formed Rough Diamond and the Byron band. David died on 28th Feb., 1985.

Mark Wynter 1943 UK singer, real name Terry Lewis. Mark was considered to be a British version of Frankie Avalon and Tommy Sands. From 1960 to 1964, he had nine so-called 'teen dream records' in the British charts. The most successful were "Venus In Blue Jeans" (10/62 UK 4), and "Go Away Little Girl" (12/62 UK 6). When success began to flag, he emigrated to Australia, but returned later on. In the meantime he has appeared in cabaret, musicals and pantomime.

Bobby Scott 1937 US singer, pianist, and songwriter, both in the pop and jazz sector. Hit: "Chain Gang" (1/56 US 13). Most successful composition "A Taste Of Honey" which became a hit for the Beatles and for Herb Alpert.

Frank Virtue 1933 US lead guitarist and head of the trio Virtues. His real name is Virtuoso. The group had formed in 1947, but did not have a hit until "Guitar Boogie Shuffle" (3/59 US 5). In 1962 Frank became the owner of a successful recording studio in his home town of Philadelphia.

Roddy Frame 1963 UK guitarist, songwriter and founder member of Aztec Camera. Hits: "Oblivious" (2/83 UK 47; 11/83 RE-UK 18), and "Somewhere In My Heart" (4/88 UK 3).

Bill Kirchen 1948 US singer, guitarist and songwriter with the country/rock band Commander Cody & His Lost Planet Airmen, formed in 1967. Biggest hit: "Hot Rod Lincoln" (3/72 US 9).

Tommy Ramone 1952 US drummer of the group Ramones, formed in 1974. Tommy was born Tom Erdelyi in Budapest.

Eddie Jackson 1961 US bassist and singer with Queensryche.

Deaths

"Cozy" Cole 1981 US drummer with Jelly Morton, Cab Calloway and Louis Armstrong. Died of cancer. Born 17th October, 1909.

Jesse Fuller 1976 US folk blues musician. Born 12th March, 1896.

Jimmy Durante 1980 US comedian, pianist, singer, and songwriter. After a heart attack in 1972 he was wheelchair bound. Goodnight Mr. Durante – wherever you are! Born on 10th Feb., 1893.

Willie Dixon 1992 US blues 'godfather'; singer, composer, bass player. Born 1st July, 1915

Hits of the Day

1944 "Me Heart Tells Me" Glen Gray US 5 weeks
1960 "Starry Eyed" Michael Holliday UK 1 week
1966 "We Can Work It Out" Beatles US 1 week (2nd time)
1969 "Albatross" Fleetwood Mac UK 1 week
1977 "Car Wash" Rose Royce US 1 week
1983 "Down Under" Men At Work UK 3 weeks

30th

Birthdays

Phil Collins 1951 UK drummer, singer, songwriter, and producer. In 1970 the group Genesis inserted a small ad for a drummer in the 'Melody Maker'. The group had formed in January 1967 from two amateur groups, Anon and Garden Wall, while at Charterhouse School. The founder members were Anthony Phillips, Michael Rutherford, Tony Banks, Peter Gabriel, and drummer Chris Stewart; the latter was replaced by John Silver and, he, in turn, by John Mayhew. The four original members continued, but they never found the right drummer until Phil Collins answered the ad. At this time he had already had a long career. As a child, he had been on TV, radio, film, and on stage (Like Steve Marriott, he had played the Artful Dodger in *Oliver Twist*.) After that he played with several groups including Flaming Youth. By the early 1970s Genesis were selling albums in vast quantities, but from 1978, they began to have hit singles with songs like "That's All" (12/83 UK 16; US 6), "Invisible Touch" (5/86 US 1; UK 15), "Land Of Confusion" (11/86 US 4; UK 14), and "Tonight, Tonight, Tonight" (2/87 US 3; UK 18). In addition to playing with Genesis, the 'hyper-active' Phil Collins also played with his own band, Brand X and in 1981, he embarked on a solo career, which has landed him a string of hits: "In The Air Tonight" (1/81 UK 2; 5/81 US 19), "You Can't Hurry Love" (11/82 US 10; UK 1), "Against All Odds" (2/84 US 1; UK 2), "Sussudio" (1/85 UK 12; 5/85 US 1), "One More Night" (2/85 US 1; 4/85 UK 4), "In the Air Tonight ('88 Remix)" (6/88 UK 4), "A Groovy Kind Of Love" (9/88 UK & US 1), "Two Hearts" (11/88 US 1; UK 6), and "Another Day In Paradise" (11/89 US 1; UK 2). (Even with all that he seems unfulfilled; he appears on so many records as a studio musician that he must manage on about two hours sleep a night). As an actor he appeared in the film *Buster* (1988) in the title role.

Steve Marriott 1947 UK singer, guitarist and songwriter. He came to prominence with the group Small Faces, formed in 1965, who managed twelve hits in the UK from 1965 to 1969, the biggest being "All Or Nothing" (8/66 UK 1), "Itchycoo Park" (8/67 UK 3; US 16; 12/75 RE-UK 9), and "Lazy Sunday" (4/68 UK 2; 3/76 RE-UK 39). In 1968 Steve formed Humble Pie, but their only hit was "Natural Born Bugie" (8/69 UK 4). From 1974, Steve Marriott played with a variety of people but was unable to regain his former status. He died in a fire at his home in Essex on April 20, 1991.

Ruth Brown 1928 US singer who had hits from 1949 to 1962. Real surname Weston. Ruth was discovered by Duke Ellington, who recommended her to the newly founded record company Atlantic. After cracking the upper echelons of the R&B charts with: "So Long" (9/49 R&B 4), "Teardrops from My Eyes" (10/50 R&B 1) and "5-10-15 Hours" (4/52 R&B 1), she had the million seller "(Mama) He Treats Your Daughter Mean" (3/53 US 23). Further pop hits included "Lucky Lips" (2/57 US 25), which became a hit for Cliff Richard later on, and "This Little Girl's Gone Rockin'" (9/58 US 24). In recent years, Ruth has appeared in TV shows, played on Broadway and in Las Vegas and can be seen in the films *Under The Rainbow* (1981) and *Hairspray* (1988).

Marty Balin 1943 US singer and songwriter. Real name Martin Buchwald. He formed Jefferson Airplane with Paul Kantner in 1965, and charted with "Somebody to Love" (4/67 US 5). In 1971 he left the band, but three years later returned to Jefferson Starship, a mutation of the former group. In this form they had one major hit with "Miracles" (8/75 US 3). In September 1978, Balin left the band and presented the rock opera *Rock Justice* which played for 4 days in the Old Waldorf Club in San Francisco the following year. In the spring of 1981 he released the solo single "Hearts" (5/81 US 8); it was extracted from his first solo LP, BALIN. In March 1985 Paul Kantner, Marty, and Jack Casady – 3 of the original members of Jefferson Airplane – formed the group KBC. By 1989 they had come full circle, with five original members from the early days of Jefferson Airplane reuniting and releasing records under their old name.

Jody Watley 1959 US singer and song writer. Started out as a dancer on the US TV series *Soul Train*. In 1977, with Jeffrey Daniels and Howard Hewett, she formed the trio, Shalamar. Biggest hit: "The Second Time Around" (11/79 UK 45; US 8). Jeffrey Daniels and Jody left the band in 1984 and were replaced by Micki Free and Delisa Davis. Jody carried on as a soloist and scored hits with "Looking For A New Love" (3/87 US 2; 5/87 UK 13), "Don't You Want Me" (10/87 US 6), "Real Love" (3/89 US 2; UK 31), and "Everything" (10/89 US 4).

Horst Jankowski 1936 German pianist, who won the annual prize for the best jazz pianist in the German Federal Republic between 1955 and 1965. Hit: "A Walk In The Black Forest" (5/65 UK 3; US 12).

Melvin Endsley 1934 US country singer and songwriter, whose biggest contribution was as writer of "Singing The Blues".

Marv Ross 1951 Guitarist, singer and songwriter. He formed Seafood Mama with his wife, Rindy, and had a hit in his hometown, Portland, with "Harden My Heart". Such was its success that he expanded the line up, renaming themselves Quarterflash. They re-recorded "Harden My Heart" (10/81 US 3), which was the first of a series of hits until 1985.

Deaths

Professor Longhair 1980 King of New Orleans piano. Born on 19th Dec., 1918.

Lightnin' Hopkins 1982 US blues musician. First name Sam. For the experts he was considered to be the 'most creative folk poet, and the King of Blues'. Born on 15th March, 1912.

Warren Smith 1980 One of the first US rock musicians. Died after a heart attack. Born 7th Feb., 1933.

Hits of the Day

1943	"Mister Five By Five" Harry James US 2 weeks
1953	"Outside Of Heaven" Eddie Fisher UK 1 week
1959	"One Night/I Got Stung" Elvis Presley UK 3 weeks
1961	"Will You Love Me Tomorrow" Shirelles US 2 weeks
1964	"Needles And Pins" Searchers UK 3 weeks
1982	"Oh Julie" Shakin' Stevens UK 1 week
1982	"I Can't Go For That" Hall & Oates US 1 week
1988	"I Think We're Alone Now" Tiffany UK 3 weeks
1988	"Need You Tonight" INXS US 1 week

31st

Birthdays

Harry Wayne Casey 1951 US songwriter, keyboard instrumentalist, and lead singer of the group for whom he abbreviated his surname to K.C., giving K.C. & The Sunshine Band its name. Together with Richard Finch he was the nucleus of the group, and between them they wrote most of the hits: "Get Down Tonight" (7/75 US 1; 3/75 UK 21), "That's The Way (I Like It)" (8/75 UK 4; 10/75 US 1), "(Shake, Shake, Shake) Shake Your Booty" (7/76 US 1; UK 22), "I'm Your Boogie Man" (2/77 US 1), "Please Don't Go" (8/79 US 1; 12/79 UK 3), and "Give It Up" (7/83 UK

1). On the 15th Jan., 1982 Harry Casey was badly injured in a car accident, however, by 1983 he had recovered sufficiently to set up his own record company, Meca.

Chuck Willis 1928 US R & B singer and songwriter, who was one of the trailblazers of the genre. In 1951 Chuck started out as an R & B artist with the Okeh label. His greatest success was his own composition "C. C. Rider" (4/57 US 12), because it was covered by so many other artists. His other influential record was "The Stroll" which was one of the many dance crazes of the period. Chuck didn't live long enough to savour his biggest hit as a singer, which, ironically enough, was called "What Am I Living For" (4/58 US 9), with the B-side "Hang Up My R n' R Shoes" (4/58 US 24). He inspired a wide diversity of artists like Elvis, Buddy Holly and the Drifters. In the spring of 1958 he became ill with peritonitis and died on 10th April.

Johnny Rotten 1956 UK singer and songwriter. Real name John Lydon, stage name derived from 'jolly rotten'. In 1975 he was a co-founder of the Sex Pistols. Hit: "God Save The Queen" (6/77 UK 2). In May 1978, after officially changing back to John Lydon, he left the Sex Pistols and announced the formation of his own group Public Image Ltd. Hits, "Public Image" (10/78 UK 9), and "This Is Not A Love Song" (9/83 UK 5). After their first hit they abbreviated the group name to P.I.L.

Phil Manzanera 1951 UK guitarist, and songwriter. In 1970 he was a founder-member of Quiet Sun, and from February 1972 was with Roxy Music. He worked on the solo projects of Bryan Ferry, Andy Mackay, Eno, John Cale, and Nico. After 1975 he released solo LPs, produced a single under the name of his old group Quiet Sun, founded 801, continued to play with Roxy Music, with Stomu Yamashta, The Explorers and in 1987 with John Wetton as Wetton/Manzanera.

Roosevelt Sykes 1906 US blues pianist, with the nickname 'The Honeydripper', who also appeared under the pseudonyms of The Blues Man, Dobby Bragg, Easy Papa Johnson, and Willie Kelly. Roosevelt wrote many well-known blues songs which were recorded from the late 1920s onwards. He died on 17th July, 1983.

Lloyd Cole 1961 UK singer and songwriter, who formed his group Commotions in 1982. From 1984 onwards Lloyd Cole & The Commotions were in the UK charts. Their biggest hits were "Brand New Friend" (9/85 UK 19) and "Lost Weekend" (11/85 UK 17). The band said

goodbye to their fans and split up with the release of LP *1984 – 1989*, which included all their hits. At the same time Cole announced that he was working on his first solo album with an American crew of musicians. His second solo album, DON'T GET WEIRD ON ME, was issued in 1991.

Bobby Hackett 1915 US cornetist, trumpeter and guitarist. Real Christian names Robert Leo. Bobby was considered to be the legitimate successor to the late Bix Beiderbecke. He played with the bands of Glenn Miller, Glen Gray, Jackie Gleason and his own orchestra among others. He died on the 7th June, 1976.

Adrian Vandenberg 1954 Dutch guitarist, keyboard instrumentalist, singer and songwriter. After playing on 25 LPs as a session guitarist in Holland, then becoming a member of the group Teaser, he formed his own band Vandenberg at the beginning of the 80s.

Terry Kath 1946 US guitarist, singer and songwriter with Chicago, of which he was a founder member in 1967. Terry died after a shooting accident on the 23rd Jan., 1978.

Cyril Stapleton 1914 UK orchestra leader who was one of the greats of British radio. His greatest record success was "Blue Star" (9/55 UK 2).

Allan Lomax 1915 US folk musician, son of John Lomax, who was popular as a singer and composer.

Deaths

Slim Harpo 1970 US R & B artist. Died after a heart attack. Born 11th January, 1924.

Buster Brown 1976 US singer and songwriter. Born 15th August, 1911.

Hits of the Day

1959	"Tom Dooley" Nilsen Brothers?
1963	"Diamonds" Jet Harris & Tony Meehan UK 3 weeks
1968	"Everlasting Love" Love Affair UK 2 weeks
1970	"I Want You Back" Jackson 5 US 1 week
1970	"Love Grows" Edison Lighthouse UK 5 weeks
1971	"My Sweet Lord" George Harrison UK 5 weeks
1976	"Mamma Mia" Abba UK 2 weeks
1976	"Love Roller Coaster" Ohio Players US 1 week
1981	"The Tide Is High" Blondie US 1 week

February

1st

Birthdays

Ray Sawyer 1937 US singer with the group Dr. Hook, formed in 1968. Later a soloist. The group had its first million bestseller with "Sylvia's Mother" (4/72 US 5; 6/72 UK 2). Ray usually sang parodic songs liberally laced with irony, written by Shel Silverstein. Further million sellers were, "The Cover Of 'Rolling Stone'" (12/72 US 6), "Only Sixteen" (1/76 US 6), "Sharing The Night Together" (9/78 US 6), "When You're In Love With A Beautiful Woman" (4/79 US 6; UK 1), and "Sexy Eyes" (2/80 US 5; 3/80 UK 4). Ray's trademark is an eye patch which he doesn't just wear for fun, as he lost an eye in a car accident.

Don Everly 1937 US singer and songwriter, the older of the two Everly Brothers. The brothers' parents were well-known country musicians in the US, and it was they who made sure that Don & Phil were heard on radio at ages 8 and 6 respectively. Later, Chet Atkins contracted them, which launched the career of the 'No. 1 duo of the rock era'. Their greatest hits: "Wake Up Little Susie" (9/57 US 1; 11/57 UK 2), "All I Have To Do Is Dream" (4/58 US & UK 1), "Bird Dog" (8/58 US 1; UK 2), "Cathy's Clown" (4/60 US & UK 1), "Walk Right Back" (2/61 US 7; UK 1), and "Temptation" (5/61 US 27; UK 1). Their last Top Ten hit was "The Price Of Love" (5/65 UK 2).

Rick James 1952 US singer, keyboard player, guitarist, and songwriter. Real name James Johnson. He formed his first group, Mynah Birds, in Toronto in 1967. Neil Young and Bruce Palmer (later of Buffalo Springfield), and Goldy McJohn (later of Steppenwolf) played with this group. The band even got a record contract with the Detroit record company, Motown, however, no records were ever released. In 1970 Rick went to London and formed the group Main Line. Over the next 7 years he was to spend time in London, Canada, and the USA. Rumour has it that he spent a longish period serving a prison sentence in the USA during that time, as he had deserted from the navy. In 1977 he formed the Stone City Band, and a little later on, secured solo recording contract with Motown. At last, records began to be released. Hits: "You And I" (7/78 US 13), and "Super Freak (Part 1)" (8/81 US 16). In 1991, he was in trouble with the law again, this time for forcibly imprisoning a woman and, allegedly, torturing her.

Joe Sample 1939 US keyboard player and songwriter with the Modern Jazz Sextet, formed in the 50s, which then became the Nitehawks, the Jazz Crusaders, and finally, in 1972, the Crusaders. In addition to his work with this band, he also produced solo records, played with the L.A. Express and became one of the most sought after session musicians in Los Angeles.

Bob Shane 1934 US singer and guitarist with the Kingston Trio, formed in 1957 in San Francisco. Greatest hits: "Tom Dooley" (9/58 US 1; 11/58 UK 5), "The Tijuana Jail" (3/59 US 12), "M.T.A." (6/59 US 15), and "Reverend Mr. Black" (4/63 US 8). After the group had split up in 1968, Shane formed the New Kingston trio in 1973.

Richard Williams 1950 US guitarist with the group Kansas, formed in 1970.

Walter Seyffer 1950 German rock singer with The Gravers, 9 Days Wonder, and Wintergarden.

Tommy Duffy 1944 US singer with the Brooklyn trio, Echoes. Hit: "Baby Blue" (3/61 US 12).

Deaths

Dick James 1986 UK singer, songwriter, music publisher and head of the record company, DJM (Dick James Music). He died of a heart attack. Born 1921.

Miscellany

1949 A new era for records: the US record company RCA released the first single record ever, which spun at 45 revolutions per minute (r.p.m).

1957 Frankie Vaughan was still at No. 1 in the UK charts, when Guy Mitchell returned for a third time with "Singing The Blues" to the No. 1 position, and had to share the position with Frankie Vaughan for a week.

2nd

Birthdays

Graham Nash 1942 UK guitarist, singer and songwriter. Together with his friend from schooldays, Allan Clarke, he formed the duo, Two Teens, in 1961, which changed to the Fourtones, the Deltas, and finally, in late 1962, to the Hollies. From 1963 to 1968, this group had 13 Top Ten hits in the UK (*see* under 5th April, Allan Clarke). During 1968 it became increasingly apparent that Graham no longer agreed with the musical direction of the Hollies. However, it was rumoured that the group was to produce a whole album of Bob Dylan songs, but it didn't stop Nash from leaving the band on 8th December, 1968. Shortly after that, Graham began rehearsing in London with David Crosby and Stephen Stills for their new trio project. In early 1969, in California, they signed a recording contract with the US company Atlantic Records, as Crosby, Stills & Nash. Perhaps, sunny California, was more attractive to Graham than rainy Blackpool. A little later, with the addition of Neil Young, the trio became a quartet. During the 1970s and 1980s the various members of the group played in different combinations together, or made solo records. In 1982, Graham decided to re-join the Hollies, but the project foundered and he carried on as before. At the end of the 1980s, after a long gap another album

appeared by Crosby, Stills, Nash & Young. Hits as Crosby Stills & Nash: "Marrakesh Express" (7/69 US 28; UK 17), "Just A Song Before I Go" (5/77 US 7), and "Wasted On The Way" (6/82 US 9). Greatest hits as Crosby, Stills, Nash & Young, "Woodstock" (3/70 US 11). Greatest solo hit "Chicago" (6/71 US 35).

David Whitfield 1925 UK singer. He was the first Briton to have a million-bestseller in the USA, "Cara Mia" (6/54 UK 1; 8/54 US 10). He was accompanied by the Mantovani Orchestra, Mantovani being the co-author of the song under the pseudonym Tulio Trapino. From 1953 to 1957 David was in the UK Top Ten 12 times. Further hits: "Answer Me" (10/53 UK 1), "Rags To Riches" (12/53 UK 3), "Santa Natale" (11/54 UK 2; US 19), "Ev'rywhere" (7/55 UK 3), and "My September Love" (3/56 UK 3). After his career as a pop star, David made an abortive attempt at light opera. He died on 16th Jan., 1980.

Stan Getz 1927 US tenor-saxophonist. Real name Stanley Gayetzsky. He began his career with Jack Teagarden (1943), Stan Kenton (1944/45), Benny Goodman and Jimmy Dorsey. Goodman once called him the 'best tenor-saxophonist of all time'. In 1947 Stan performed with his own trio, and in the same year joined Woody Herman, with whom he played until 1949. Together with guitarist Charlie Byrd he had a worldwide hit with "Desafinado" (9/62 US 15; 11/62 UK 11), and with singer Astrud Gilberto, "The Girl From Ipanema" (6/64 US 5; UK 29). He died on June 6, 1991.

Howard Bellamy 1946 US country singer, guitarist and songwriter, who appeared with his brother David as the Bellamy Brothers in 1958. From 1968 to 1971 the brothers were in a band called Jericho, and finally they scored an international hit with "Let Your Love Flow" (1/76 US 1; 4/76 UK 7), followed by a further pop hit, "If I Said You Have A Beautiful Body, Would You Hold It Against Me?" (5/79 US 39; 8/79 UK 3). After that, they appeared almost exclusively in the US country charts; from 1979 to 1988 they reached No. 1 ten times.

Skip Battin 1934 US bass player, real first name, Clyde. Together with Gary 'Flip' Paxton, he started the duo Skip & Flip at the end of the 1950s. Hits: "It Was I" (6/59 US 11), and "Cherry Pie" (4/60 US 11). After Skip had played with various groups during the 60s, he joined the Byrds in October 1969. He stayed with them until February 1973, when he cut a solo album. In February 1974, he joined the New Riders Of The Purple Sage, and then joined the newly re-formed Flying Burrito Brothers.

Derek Victor Schulman 1947 UK singer, saxophonist and bass player. Together with his brothers Phil and Ray, he formed Howlin' Wolves, who changed their name to Simon Dupree And The Big Sound. Greatest hits: "Kites"

(11/67 UK 9). In 1970 the three brothers became members of Gentle Giant, who produced a number of good albums.

John Patrick Weathers 1947 UK drummer with Eyes Of Blue, Graham Bond's Magick, Grease Band, Piblokto, and Gentle Giant.

Alan McKay 1948 US guitarist with Earth, Wind & Fire. Alan also played on recordings by Deodato, Ramsey Lewis, Deniece Williams, Emotions and Herbie Hancock among others.

Alan Caddy 1940 UK lead guitarist with the Tornados. Hits: "Telstar" (8/62 UK 1; 11/62 US 1) and "Globetrotter" (1/63 UK 5).

Whistling Jack Smith 1946 UK whistler, real name Billy Moeller. Only hit, "I Was Kaiser Bill's Batman" (3/67 UK 5; US 20).

Peter Macbeth 1943 UK bass player with the Foundations.

Deaths

Sid Vicious 1979 UK bass player with the Sex Pistols. He died of a drug overdose. Born 10th May, 1957.

Hits of the Day

1974 "The Way We Were" Barbra Streisand US 1 week
1980 "Too Much Too Young" Specials UK 2 weeks
1985 "I Want To Know What Love Is" Foreigner US 2 weeks

3rd

Birthdays

Melanie 1947 US singer and songwriter, surname Safka. In 1967 Columbia released "Beautiful People", which was a flop. Not until she had changed to the Buddah record company, did she have any success: "Lay Down (Candles In The Rain)" (4/70 US 6), together with the Edwin Hawkins 'Singers, "Ruby Tuesday" (9/70 UK 9) and "Brand New Key" (10/71 US 1; 1/72 UK 4). The last named record appeared on the Neighbourhood label, which she had started with her husband, Peter Schekeryk, in 1972. Melanie continued making records right into the 80s, although her voice still sounded as if she had just started taking singing lessons and needed a bit of help.

Frankie Vaughan 1928 UK singer, real name Frank Abelson. From 1954 to 1968 he achieved 11 Top ten hits in the UK, two of them with the Kaye Sisters, his most successful being "Green Door" (11/56 UK 2), "Garden Of Eden" (1/57 UK 1) and "Tower Of Strength" (11/61 UK 1). Frankie was one of many Britons who had specialised in covering American hits for the UK market. In 1960 he acted beside Marilyn Monroe and Yves Montand in the film *Let's Make Love*.

Val Doonican 1928 Irish singer and guitarist. First names Michael Valentine. By the mid-1940s Val could be heard on Irish radio, then he played drums with a touring band, and came to London in 1952 with the vocal group, The Four Ramblers. In 1959 Anthony Newley advised him to try his luck as a solo artist and got him his own radio show, 'A Date With Val'. From 1964 to 1967 Val was in the UK charts with 5 Top Ten hits, "Walk Tall" (10/64 UK 3), "The Special Years" (1/65 UK 7), "Elusive Butterfly" (3/66 UK 5), "What Would I Be" (11/66 UK 2), "If The Whole World Stopped Loving" (10/67 UK 3). His relaxed style, strongly reminiscent of Perry Como's, allowed him to continue in television long after his charting days were over.

Johnny Guitar Watson 1935 US guitarist, singer, pianist and songwriter, who changed his style from blues to disco. He cut his first record in 1952 as Young John Watson. He appeared in the R&B charts for the first with "Those Lonely, Lonely Nights" (10/55 R&B 10). He had his biggest hit with "A Real Mother For Ya" (4/77 UK 44; 7/77 US 41).

Stan Webb 1946 UK guitarist, singer and songwriter with the blues band Chicken Shack, formed in 1965. Hit: "I'd Rather Go Blind" (5/69 UK 14). In 1973 the band split up. Stan played for a short while with Savoy Brown, then formed Broken Glass in 1975, which was unsuccessful and so he formed Stan Webb's Chicken Shack.

Johnny Cymbal 1945 UK singer, songwriter and producer, who has lived in Canada since he was 7. Biggest hit, "Mr. Bass Man" (2/63 US 16; UK 24). After no more hits materialized as Johnny Cymbal, he recorded as Derek and scored with "Cinnamon" (10/68 US 11).

John Handy 1947 US jazz musician. Played alto sax, with Charles Mingus, among others, and as a soloist. He appeared in the pop charts with "Hard Work" (6/76 US 46).

4th

Birthdays

Dave Davies 1947 UK guitarist and songwriter with the Kinks. In order to escape being in the shadow of his brother Ray, he tried for a while to carve a solo career. His hits were "Death Of A Clown" (7/67 UK 3) and "Susannah's Still Alive" (12/67 UK 20).

Russell Arms 1929 US singer who was the star of the TV show 'Your Hit Parade', in which he sang the current hits of others. His only success was "Cinco Robles" (1/57 US 22).

Angelo D'Aleo 1940 US singer, first tenor with the Belmonts, who, after being abandoned by their lead singer Dion in 1960, had hits with "Tell Me Why" (5/61 US 18) and "Come On Little Angel" (7/62 US 28).

Alf Klimek 1956 Australian singer and songwriter who became known in our latitudes through the Spliff Radio Show in 1980. Before that, he had been a singer and clown with the Busby Berkley Roadshow. Together with 2 siblings and 2 musicians from Berlin he formed the group Other Ones. Their Hit was "Holiday" (7/87 G 4; US 29).

Laurence Tolhurst 1959 UK drummer, keyboard player and songwriter, with the group The Cure, formed in 1976.

Angie Buchzyk 1965 Keyboard player and singer with Dominoe.

Jim Lockhart 1949 Irish keyboard player with Horslips.

Deaths

Buddy Holly, Big Bopper, and Ritchie Valens 1959 US musicians who were killed on their way from Clear Lake to their next performance. They died in the wreckage of their aeroplane when it crashed a few minutes after takeoff, near Manson City, Iowa.

Joe Meek 1967 UK producer of the Tornados, Mike Berry, the Honeycombs and many other English artists. He shot himself on the anniversary of the death of his idol, Buddy Holly. Born 5th April, 1929.

Hits of the Day

1940	"Careless" Glenn Miller US 5 weeks
1968	"Hello Goodbye" Beatles UK 6 weeks/US 3 weeks
1968	"Green Tambourine" Lemon Pipers US 1 week
1973	"Crocodile Rock" Elton John US 3 weeks
1979	"Heart Of Glass" Blondie UK 4 weeks

Alice Cooper 1948 US singer, songwriter and performance artiste. Real name Vincent Furnier. After forming a band in 1965, which predominantly rehashed hits by the Rolling Stones under various different names, finally settled on calling itself Alice Cooper in 1966. In 1969 the first album by the band was released. At that time Vincent took snakes on stage and heavily disguised himself with kohl. In the early days this was intended to cover their lack of musical ability. By 1978 the public lost interest in Alice's shenanigans, but not before they had notched up a notable sequence of hits like "School's Out" (6/72 US 7; UK 1), "Elected" (10/72 US 28; UK 4), "Hello Hurray" (2/73 US 35; UK 6), "No More Mr. Nice Guy" (4/73 US 25; UK 10), "I Never Cry" (7/76 US 12), and "You And Me" (4/77 US 9). Although further records were released, Alice Cooper seemed to slip out of the limelight. However, in 1989 he turned up again with a new backing band; this time, though, without makeup and all the other paraphernalia and was able to relaunch his career with "Poison" (7/89 UK 2; 9/89 US 7).

John Steel 1941 UK drummer with the Animals. After the band split up, he worked in management with a former band colleague, Chas Chandler, who discovered people like Jimi Hendrix. John rejoined when the Animals made a comeback in 1983.

Florence LaRue 1944 US singer with the group Fifth Dimension, formed in 1966, and who had some success from 1967 to 1973. Biggest hits were "Aquarius/Let The Sunshine In" (3/69 US 1; UK 11) and "Wedding Bell Blues" (9/69 US 1; 1/70 UK 16).

Jerry Shirley 1952 UK drummer with Humble Pie. Previously he had played with groups like Apostolic Intervention, The Wages Of Sin, and Little Women. Later he formed the group Natural Gas, and from June 1982, he played with Fast Way.

Johnny Gambale 1942 US singer with the Classics whose only hit was "Till Then" (6/63 US 20).

Philip Ehart 1950 US drummer with Kansas.

Deaths

Louis Jordan 1975 US singer and saxophonist, who was considered to be the 'Jerry Lewis of R & B'. Died after developing pneumonia. Born 8th July, 1908.

Alex Harvey 1982 UK singer and songwriter. His band was known as the Sensational Alex Harvey Band. On tour in Belgium, when he died of a heart attack. Born 5th Feb., 1935.

Karen Carpenter 1983 US singer who had hits with her brother, Richard, as The Carpenters. Died of anorexia. Born 2nd March, 1950.

Liberace 1987 US pianist. Died of AIDS. Born 16th May, 1919.

Jethro 1989 US singer. Appeared with Henry Haynes as Homer & Jethro. Died of cancer. Born 10th March, 1923.

Trevor Lucas 1989 Australian guitarist, singer, songwriter and producer. He died after having a heart attack. Born 25th Dec., 1943.

Hits of the Day

1955 "Mambo Italiano" Rosemary Clooney UK 2 weeks (2nd time)

1965 "You've Lost That Lovin' Feelin'" Righteous Brothers UK 2 weeks

1978 "Uptown Top Ranking" Althia & Donna UK 1 week

1978 "Stayin' Alive" Bee Gees US 4 weeks

1984 "Karma Chameleon" Culture Club US 3 weeks

1989 "When I'm With You" Sheriff US 1 week

5th

Birthdays

Al Kooper 1944 US keyboard player, guitarist and songwriter. He was only 15 when he became a member of the Royal Teens who had just landed a hit with "Short Shorts". After that, he became a session musician, and tried his hand at songwriting. In 1965 he was one of the co-authors of "This Diamond Ring" by Gary Lewis & The Playboys. In the same year he provoked interest with his keyboard accompaniment on the Bob Dylan album, HIGHWAY 61 REVISTED, especially with the number, "Like A Rolling Stone". In 1966 he formed Blues Project, and a year later, Blood, Sweat & Tears. With both these groups he helped to establish jazz-rock music. He left Blood, Sweat & Tears again after their first album to make solo records, and could be heard on many records like ELECTRIC LADYLAND by Jimi Hendrix and LET IT BLEED by the Rolling Stones as a guest artist. He was also an excellent producer; particularly when working with new, young bands like Lynyrd Skynyrd. Occasionally he appears as a session musician under the pseudonym of Roosevelt Gook.

Bobby Brown 1969 US singer and songwriter. Began with the child group New Edition which was formed in 1982. Their first successful record was "Candy Girl" (4/83 R&B 1; US 46; UK 1). Further hits were "Cool It Now" (9/84 R&B 1; US 4), and "Mr. Telephone Man" (12/84 US 12; 2/85 UK 19). In 1986 Bobby left the group and began to cut solo records. Hits: "Don't Be Cruel" (8/88 US 8; UK 42; 3/89 RE-UK 13), "My Prerogative" (10/88 US 1; 12/88 UK 6), "Roni" (1/89 US 3; 11/89 UK 21), and "Rock Wit'cha" (8/89 US 7; UK 33).

James R. Cobb 1944 US lead guitarist and songwriter. In 1965 he was co-founder of the group Classics IV, and from the early 1970s onwards he played with Atlanta Rhythm Section. Hits by the Classics IV: "Spooky" (12/67 US 3), "Stormy" (10/68 US 5), and "Traces" (2/69 US 2); hits with Atlanta Rhythm Section: "So In To You" (1/77 US 7), and "Imaginary Lover" (3/78 US 7).

Alex Harvey 1935 UK singer and songwriter who made music from the mid-50s with varying degrees of success and various musicians. He scored a hit with a cover- version of "Delilah" (7/75 UK 7) backed by his group, Sensational Alex Harvey Band. He was successful also with "The Boston Tea Party" (6/76 UK 13). From 1954 he had played first in skiffle groups, then in R & B bands. After 1978 he dissolved his band and continued as a solo performer. The day before his birthday he died of a heart attack while touring in Belgium (4th Feb., 1982).

Claude King 1933 US country singer, guitarist and songwriter, who had got just one hit with "Wolverton Mountain" (5/62 US 6). Died in 1983.

Barret Strong 1941 US singer and songwriter. At the end of the 50s he met Berry Gordy Jr., founder of Tamla-Motown. He recorded the title "Moeny (That's What I Want)" (2/60 US 23) for Gordy, and it became his only hit. As a songwriter Barret became one of the most successful songwriters, teaming up with Norman Whitfield, they wrote lots of hits for the Temptations.

Henson Cargill 1941 US country singer, who had only one hit in the pop charts, "Skip A Rope" (12/67 US 25).

Cory Wells 1942 US singer with Three Dog Night, founded in 1968, and who had one hit after the other until 1975. The greatest were "Mama Told Me Not To Come" (5/70 US 1; 8/70 UK 3), "Joy To The World" (3/71 US 1; 5/71 UK 24), and "Black And White" (8/72 US 1). An attempted comeback by the group in the 80s failed.

Nigel Olsson 1949 UK drummer with the Spencer Davis Group which was already dissolving, then in the Elton John Band, with various sessions, and as a soloist on his own albums. Biggest hit single was "Dancin' Shoes" (12/78 US 18).

Chuck Winfield 1943 US saxophonist with the original line-up of Blood, Sweat & Tears.

Hits of the Day

1955	"Hearts Of Stone" Fontane Sisters US 3 weeks
1960	"Why" Anthony Newley UK 4 weeks
1966	"My Love" Petual Clark US 2 weeks
1966	"Yesterday Man" Chris Andrews
1969	"Blackberry Way" Move UK 1 week
1972	"Telegram Sam" T. Rex UK 2 weeks
1977	"Torn Between Two Lovers" Mary MacGregor US 2 weeks
1983	"Africa" Toto US 1 week

6th

Birthdays

Dave Berry 1941 UK singer, real name David Grundy, who was an ardent fan of Chuck Berry. For this reason he formed the group Cruisers in 1961, which performed almost exclusively hits by Chuck. As a soloist Dave had hits with "The Crying Game" (8/64 UK 5), "Little Things" (3/65 UK 5), and "Mama" (6/66 UK 5).

Fabian 1943 US singer and actor, real name Fabiano Forte. He was discovered by the owner of the Chancellor Records record company when he was only 14 years old who thought Fabian looked like a cross between Elvis Presley and Ricky Nelson. Without a doubt, Presley's military service period was Fabian's gain. Most of his 10 hits are from that period: "Turn me Loose" (3/59 US 9), "Tiger" (6/59 US 3), and "Hound Dog Man" (11/59 US 9).

The last song came from his first film which he made in 1959, and which started off his career as an actor.

Bob Marley 1945 Jamaican reggae-musician, real name Robert Nesta Marley. In 1961 he made his first recordings, but was not successful until he was put under contract by white Jamaican born Chris Blackwell, the owner of Island Records. Bob was the cult figure of the reggae movement. Hits: "No Woman No Cry" (9/75 UK 22; 6/81 RE-UK 8), "Jamming/Punky Reggae Party" (12/77 UK 9), "Is This Love" (2/78 UK 9), "Could You Be Loved" (6/80 UK 5), "Buffalo Soldier" (5/83 UK 4) and "One Love/People Get Ready" (4/84 UK 5). He was never able to achieve any success in the USA. However, Eric Clapton was successful there with Bob's composition, "I Shot The Sheriff".

Mike Batt 1950 UK musician, singer songwriter and producer, who was successful under several pseudonyms. As Mike Batt, "Summertime City" (8/75 UK 4), as Wombles, with "Remember You're A Womble" (4/74 UK 3), and "Wombling Merry Christmas" (12/74 UK 2). On the side, he produced Steeleye Span and the Kursaal Flyers. "Bright Eyes" (3/79 UK 1) was the most successful single of the year in the UK, written by Mike Batt, sung by Art Garfunkel. The music for the film *Caravans* is also by Mike.

Natalie Cole 1950 US singer, daughter of Nat 'King' Cole. Her first album appeared in 1975; in 1978 she was named best singer of the year in the USA. Hits: "I've Got Love On My Mind" (1/77 US 5), "Pink Cadillac" (2/88 US & UK 5), and "Miss You Like Crazy" (4/89 US 7; UK 2).

Punky Meadows 1950 US guitarist with Angel.

Rick Astley 1966 UK singer and songwriter. He began as a drummer with Give Way in 1983, became lead singer of FBI in 1984, and released solo records from 1987 onwards. Hits: "Never Gonna Give You Up" (8/87 UK 1; 12/87 US 1), "Whenever You Need Somebody" (10/87 UK 3), "When I Fall In Love" (12/87 UK 2), "Together Forever" (2/88 UK 2; 4/88 US 1), "She Wants To Dance With Me" (9/88 UK 6; 12/88 US 6), and "Take Me To Your Heart" (11/88 UK 8).

Deaths

Jesse Belvin 1960 US songwriter and singer. He died after a car accident. Born 15th Dec., 1933.

Hugo Montenegro 1981 Us orchestra leader who had his biggest hit with "The Good The Bad And The Ugly" (4/68 US 2; 9/68 UK 1). Born in 1925.

Hits of the Day

1953 "Don't Let the Stars Get In Your Eyes" Perry Como UK 5 weeks
1965 "You've Lost That Lovin' Feelin'" Righteous Brothers US 2 weeks
1982 "The Model" Kraftwerk UK 1 week
1982 "Centerfold" J. Geils Band US 6 weeks
1988 "Could've Been" Tiffany US 2 weeks

7th

Birthdays

King Curtis 1934 US saxophonist and songwriter he played with the Lionel Hampton band until 1954, and then with Nat Adderly and Oliver Nelson. He cut his first solo record in 1953 and then formed his own band, The Kingpins; they charted with "Soul Twist" (2/62 US 17). Curtis Ousley, his real name, played as a studio musician with Aretha Franklin, Brook Benton, Sam Cooke, Bobby Darin, the McGuire Sisters, the Coasters, the Shirelles, Nat 'King' Cole, Andy Williams, and hundreds of others. On 13th August, 1971, he was stabbed to death while trying to intervene in a fight between two men.

Warren Smith 1933 US rockabilly singer and songwriter, who began with the small but innovative record company Sun, like other artists, including Roy Orbison and Elvis Presley. He only got into the pop charts with "So Long I'm Gone" (6/57 US 72), but "Uranium Rock" and "Red Cadillac And A Black Moustache" were excellent examples of rockabilly. Such was the attention that label-mate, Elvis commanded that Warren was quickly relegated to a supporting role from which he never recovered. He died of a heart attack on 30th Jan., 1980.

Alan Lancaster 1949 UK bass player with The Spectres, The Highlights, The Traffic Jam, and Status Quo. After the band had announced their plans to break up, Lancaster moved to Australia for a spell. When he returned he attempted to claim ownership of the group's name: he failed. Instead he appeared sporadically with the Australian group Party Boys.

Earl King 1934 US R & B singer, guitarist, and songwriter, real name Earl Silas Johnson. In 1953 he made his first records and played typical New Orleans R & B with musicians like Huey 'Piano' Smith. His biggest hit was "Those Lonely, Lonely Nights" (8/55 R & B 7).

Juliette Greco 1927 French chansoneuse and actress. Juliette sang lyrics by Sartre and Camus, among others, brought the voice of post-war Parisian existentialists to a wider audience. Her hits were "Si Tu T'Imagines" (1950), "Les Feuilles Mortes" (1951), "Je Hais Les Dimanches" (1952), "Il n'y a Plus D'Apres" (1959) and "Paname" (1961).

Stoney Browder 1949 US guitarist and pianist with Dr. Buzzard's Original Savannah Band which later developed into Kid Creole & The Coconuts.

Steve Bronski 1960 UK keyboard player and songwriter, with the group named after him, Bronski Beat, formed in 1984.

Laurence Scott 1946 UK keyboard player with Isotope, Mike D'Abo, Brian Knight, and Long John Baldry. He also has a degree in dentistry.

David Bryan 1962 US keyboard player with Bon Jovi. Real name David Rashbaum.

Brian Travers 1959 UK saxophonist and songwriter with UB40; he also directs most of their videos.

Harvey Herskowitz 1943 US singer with Quotations.

Deaths

Matt Monroe 1985 UK singer. Died of cancer. Born 1st Dec., 1930.

Guitar Slim 1959 US blues musician. Died after developing pneumonia. Born on 10th Dec., 1926.

Hits of the Day

1942 "A String Of Pearls" Glenn Miller US 2 weeks
1970 "Venus" Shocking Blue US 1 week
1976 "50 Ways To Leave Your Lover" Paul Simon US 3 weeks
1981 "Woman" John Lennon UK 2 weeks
1981 "Celebration" Kool & The Gang US 2 weeks
1987 "Open Your Heart" Madonna US 1 week
1987 "I Knew You Were Waiting For Me" George Michael & Aretha Franklin UK 2 weeks

Miscellany

1964 1:35 pm. Kennedy Airport, New York. The Beatles are landing, and the police are confronted with 10,000 fans. They are powerless and the airport is paralysed for hours. Later it was said that this first US-Beatlemania was instigated and paid for by the group's record company. While the group is landing in the USA, a new EP by the Fab Four was being released in the UK, "All My Loving", "Ask Me Why", "Money", and "P.S. I Love You".

1980 From August to November 1979 Pink Floyd had been mixing the recordings for their album, THE WALL, in Los Angeles. On the 23rd November, 1979 the double album was released and within two weeks had sold 6 million copies. Now the whole thing had to be recorded live. The venue for this first performance was the sports arena in L.A.. From the 7th Feb. to the 13th Feb. 140,000 people watched the spectacle. After that THE WALL went on tour. Due to the formidable costs in mounting such an undertaking, THE WALL was performed only 29 times.

8th

Birthdays

England Dan 1950 US singer and songwriter whose real name is Danny Seals. His brother Jim is a member of Seals & Crofts. Together with John Ford Coley and Shane Keister, Danny formed the group Southwest F.O.B. in 1967 which had their biggest success with "Smell Of Incense" (10/68 US 56). When this project didn't seem to develop any further, Dan & John Ford formed a duo as England Dan & John Ford Coley. Their biggest hits were "I'd Really Love To See You Tonight" (6/76 US 2; 9/76 UK 26), "Nights Are Forever Without You" (10/76 US 10), "We'll Never Have To Say Goodbye Again" (2/78 US 9) and "Love Is The Answer" (3/79 US 10). After that, the duo split up, and Dan made several solo records as England Dan. Since 1983 Dan Seals has tended more towards country songs; and since 1985 he has had nine consecutive No. 1 hits in the country charts.

Tom Rush 1941 US folksinger and guitarist. Released his first album in 1963. Although he made several superb records, they were too good for commercial success.

John Williams 1932 US orchestra leader wrote scores for many films, e.g. *Jaws*, *Star Wars* and *E.T.*. Many of the themes charted individually.

Lonnie Johnson 1889 US blues and jazz guitarist, and singer. Real first name Alonzo. Lonnie played together with nearly all the greats in jazz history, and made records as Jimmy Jordan and Tom Jordan. He died 16th June, 1970.

Terry Melcher 1942 US producer, songwriter and singer. Terry is Doris Day's son. He began as Terry Day with very little success, finally he cut record with Bruce Johnson, who later joined the Beach Boys. First they called themselves Terry & Bruce, and then the Ripcords. As he didn't manage to get on as a singer, he tried his luck as a producer. He took care of the 1964 album LOVE HIM! by his mother, and then worked on the Byrds' first albums. He produced records until the mid-80s with varying degrees of success and cut a brace of albums under his own name.

Vince Neil 1961 US singer. Complete name Vince Neil Wharton. He has been a member of Motley Crue since their formation in 1981. Their first album appeared the same year. Since 1984, they have appeared regularly in the singles charts with hits like "Smokin' In The Boys' Room" (7/85 US 16), "Girls, Girls, Girls" (5/87 US 12; 8/87 UK 26) and "Doctor Feelgood" (9/89 US 6).

Ray Sharpe 1938 US singer, discovered by Lee Hazlewood in Las Vegas in 1959. Only hit was "Linda Lu" (7/59 US 46), on which he was accompanied by guitarists, Duane Eddy and Al Casey.

Creed Bratton 1943 US guitarist with Grass Roots, who were successful from 1966 to 1972. Creed left the group in 1969 and was replaced by Dennis Provisor.

Adolpho 'Fito' de la Parra 1946 US drummer with Canned Heat.

Deaths

Kurt Edelhagen 1982 Jazz musician and orchestra leader. Born 5th June, 1920.

Del Shannon 1990 US singer and guitarist. Suicide. Born 30th December, 1939.

Hits of the Day	
1941	"There I Go" Vaughn Monroe US 3 weeks
1947	"Huggin' And Chalkin'" Hoagy Carmichael US 2 weeks
1960	"Teen Angel" Mark Dinning US 2 weeks
1975	"January" Pilot UK 3 weeks

1975	"Fire" Ohio Players US 1 week
1986	"When The Going Gets Tough The Tough get Going" Billy Ocean UK 4 weeks

Miscellany

1931 James Dean born. He managed to become a legend with only three films: *East Of Eden*, *Rebel Without A Cause*, and *Giant*. These three films made him the idol of a disaffected young generation. He died on 30th September, 1955, when his Porsche crashed. He had just finished his third film.

9th

Birthdays

Carole King 1942 US songwriter and singer. Real name Klein. She formed one of the most successful songwriting teams of the 1960s with her erstwhile husband Gerry Goffin. They wrote more than 100 hits: "Up On The Roof", "Will You Love Me Tomorrow?", "The Locomotion", and many others. Carole was the composer of the team, and Gerry wrote the lyrics. In the early 60s she set up her own record company, which was not particularly successful. As a singer, Carole had her first hit with "It Might As Well Rain Until September" (8/62 US 22; UK 3; 10/72 RE-UK 43). In 1971 the album TAPESTRY was released which sold over 13 million copies worldwide; it included her biggest hit single, "It's Too Late" (5/71 US 1; 8/71 UK 6). Further hits like "Sweet Seasons" (1/72 US 9), "Jazzman" (8/74 US 2) and "Nightingale" (1/75 US 9) followed.

Barry Mann 1939 US songwriter and singer. In addition to collaborating with Goffin/King, Barry Mann was equally successful with his wife, Cynthia Weil. Among the songs the pair wrote were "Blame It On The Bossa Nova", "On Broadway", "We've Gotta Get Out Of This Place", "I'm Gonna Be Strong", and, with Phil Spector, "You've Lost That Lovin' Feelin'". Barry had only one hit by himself, "Who Put The Bomp?" (8/61 US 7), written by him, with Gerry Goffin.

Ernest Tubb 1914 US country singer and songwriter, nicknamed 'Texas Troubador'. In the mid 1930s he worked for various radio stations, and sang songs by his favourite artist, Jimmie Rogers. He made his first record in 1936. After writing his own million-seller, "Walkin' The Floor Over You" (8/41 US 23), he moved to Hollywood in 1943, and appeared in several films. From 1947, radio programmes were transmitted regularly from his record shop in Nashville. By the end of the 70s he had scored 80 hits in the country charts as a soloist, and several more, 95 duets with Red Foley and Loretta Lynn. He also made records with the Andrews Sisters, Wilburn Brothers and Willie Nelson. He died 6th September, 1984.

Holly Johnson 1960 UK singer and songwriter, real first name William. In 1978 he became a member of Big In Japan, and after making a few commercially unsuccessful records, he carried on as a solo artist. In August 1980 he was involved in the formation of Frankie Goes To Hollywood, whose first hit was "Relax" (1/84 UK 1; 4/84 US 67; 5/84 RE-UK 2; 1/85 RE-US 10); further hits included "Two Tribes" (6/84 UK 1) and "The Power Of Love" (12/84 UK 1). 1985 was a meagre year for the band hitwise, but then came "Rage Hard" (9/86 UK 4) the following year. After the group officially split-up in April 1987, Holly tried again as a solo artist. Hits included "Love Train" (1/89 UK 4), "Americanos" (4/89 UK 4) and "Atomic City" (6/89 UK 18).

Major Harris 1947 US singer. Began his career with the Jarmels. From 1971 to 1974, he was with the Delfonics, and then made solo records. His biggest hit and million-seller was "Love Won't Let Me Wait" (3/75 US 5; 8/75 UK 37).

Barbara Lewis 1943 US singer, songwriter and multi-instrumentalist. Barbara is alleged to have been writing songs since she was 9; she cut her first record in 1961. Her biggest hit was "Hello Stranger" (5/63 US 3).

Brian Bennett 1940 UK drummer and songwriter, who left the Krewcats in 1961 and replaced Tony Meehan in the Shadows.

Mark Mathis 1942 US singer with the Newbeats. Hit, "Bread And Butter" (8/64 US 2; UK 15).

Percy Nathan Rodgers 1970 US singer and songwriter with B.V.S.M.P. Hits were "I Need You" (7/88 UK 3) and "Be Gentle".

Dennis 'Dee Tee' Thomas 1951 US saxophonist with Kool & The Gang.

Deaths

Rev. James Cleveland 1991 US singer and songwriter. Born 23rd December 1932.

Percy Faith 1976 Canadian orchestra leader. Born 7th April, 1908.

Bill Haley 1981 US musician who paved the way for rock 'n' roll with "Rock Around The Clock". Born 6th July, 1925.

Sophie Tucker 1966 US singer. Born 13th Jan., 1884.

Hits of the Day

1946 "Doctor, Lawyer, Indian Chief" Betty Hutton US 2 weeks
1957 "Don't Forbid Me" Pat Boone US 1 week
1957 "Too Much" Elvis Presley US 3 weeks
1957 "Young Love" Sonny James US 1 week
1959 "Stagger Lee" Lloyd Price US 4 weeks
1963 "Hey Paula" Paul & Paula US 3 weeks
1974 "Love's Theme" Love Unlimited Orchestra US 1 week
1985 "I Know Him So Well" Elaine Paige & Barbara Dickson UK 4 weeks

---

10th

Birthdays

Roberta Flack 1939 US singer and pianist, who was successful both as a soloist, and in duets with Donny Hathaway and Peabo Bryson. She was discovered in the late 60s by Les McCann, and got a recording contract in 1969. Solo hits, "The First Time I Ever Saw Your Face" (3/72 US 1; 5/72 UK 14), "Killing Me Softly With His Song" (1/73 US 1; UK 6), and "Feel Like Makin' Love" (6/74 US 1; 8/74 UK 34). Hits with Donny Hathaway: "Where Is The Love" (6/72 US 5; 8/72 UK 29), "The Closer I Get To You" (2/78 US 2; 5/78 UK 42), and "Back Together Again" (5/80 UK 3); with Peabo Bryson, "Tonight I Celebrate My Love" (7/83 US 16; UK 2).

Chick Webb 1902 US drummer and band leader. Real first names William Henry. Chick, who was only about 5 ft. 2 and hump-backed, was considered to be one of the first to lead a big band from the drums, and (almost) drive it before him. Ella Fitzgerald had a million seller as a singer with Chick Webb, "A-Tisket, A-Tasket" (6/38 US 1). After Chick's death on 16th June, 1939, Ella continued to lead the band until 1942 when she embarked on a solo career.

Ral Donner 1943 US singer, who was also called 'Chicago-Elvis'. His greatest hit was "You Don't Know What You Got (Until You Lose It)" (7/61 US 4; 9/61 UK 25). Ral was the voice of Elvis in the film *This Is Elvis* He died on 6th April, 1984.

Peter Allen 1944 Australian singer, songwriter, and pianist, also known as the sometime husband of Liza Minelli (1964 – 1967). He wrote hits for Olivia Newton-John, "I Honestly Love You" and for Christopher Cross, "The Best That You Can Do". He made some good records in his own name like "I Go To Rio", but none of them impressed the record-buying public.

Robbie Nevil 1961 US singer, songwriter and guitarist. Robbie had his first hit with "C'Est La Vie" (10/86 US 2; 12/86 UK 3); further hits were "Dominoes" (2/87 US 14; 5/87 UK 26) and "Wot's It To Ya" (6/87 US 10). Robbie also wrote for El DeBarge, the Pointer Sisters and Vanity.

Rockin' Dopsie 1932 US singer and accordionist who record mainly zydeco material. Real name Alton Jay Rubin. By 1955 he was playing with Lafayette and in 1969 he made his first records. Along with Clifton Chenier and Queen Ida he is one of the most celebrated exponents of Zydeco music. He guested on Paul Simon's album GRACELAND.

Clifford T. Ward 1946 US singer and songwriter, whose greatest hit was "Gaye" (6/73 UK 8). Before that, he was an English teacher.

Don Wilson 1937 US guitarist and founder member of the Ventures.

Cory Lerios 1951 US keyboard/pianist and singer with the band Pablo Cruise, formed in 1973.

Hits of the Day

1940 "In The Mood" Glenn Miller US 12 weeks
1945 "Rum And Coca Cola" Andrews Sisters US 10 weeks
1958 "Don't" Elvis Presley US 5 weeks
1968 "Love Is Blue" Paul Mauriat US 5 weeks
1979 "Do Ya Think I'm Sexy" Rod Stewart US 4 weeks
1990 "Dub Be Good To Me" Beats International, featuring Lindy Layton UK 4 weeks

---

11th

Birthdays

Gene Vincent 1935 US singer and songwriter. Real name Eugene Vincent Craddock. In May 1955 Gene was commissioned out of the US navy, after breaking his leg in a motor bike accident while on a service trip. This injury was to handicap him for the rest of his life. In early 1956, when he was back home in Norfolk, 'Sheriff Tex Davis' the disk jockey at the local radio station WCMS, became interested in the up and coming young rock musician and helped Gene to edit his songs. Davis financed a demo tape which was sent to Capitol Records in April 1956, as they were looking out for their own 'Elvis Presley'. They contracted Gene, and shortly afterwards his first hit "Be-Bop-A-Lula" (6/56 US 7; 8/56 UK 16) appeared. After 1960, Gene moved to the UK, as he had more fans there than in the USA. Hits: "My Heart" (3/60 UK 16), and "Pistol Packin' Momma" (6/60 UK 15). On 17th April, 1960, he and his friend Eddie Cochran were involved in a serious car accident – Eddie died. Years later, while Gene was paying his father a visit, he was taken ill. After being taken to hospital, he died of internal haemorrhages on 12th October, 1971.

Bobby 'Boris' Pickett 1940 US novelty singer and songwriter. While attempting a career as a film actor, he remembered how he had wiled away the time, in his father's cinema watching Boris Karloff films: he promptly composed "Monster Mash". It was the perfect song for Hallowe'en 1962. It was his only hit (9/62 US 1; 5/73 RE-US 10; 9/73 UK 3) and did not chart in the UK until 1973, because the BBC refused to play it in 1962. When the record was re-released and charted in 1973, everyone started looking for Bobby: rumour has it, he was found driving a taxi in New York.

Gerry Goffin 1939 US songwriter who wrote more than 30 US Top Twenty Hits in the 60s with his erstwhile wife, Carole King (born 9th Feb., 1941). He is considered to be one of the most successful songwriters who never actually sang themselves. After their divorce success eluded him, in direct contrast to Carole King.

John Mills 1889 US guitarist, singer and oldest of the Mills Brothers. He was still with them when they had their first hit: "Tiger Rag" (11/31 US 1), and "Dinah" (1/32 US 1). John died in 1935, and the brothers' father, John senior, joined them, and stayed with them until 1956.

Ray Lake 1946 UK singer with Real Thing. Hits: "You To Me are Everything" (7/76 UK 1; 3/86 RE-UK 5) and "Can't Get By Without You" (9/76 UK 2; 5/86 RE-UK 5). (In the case of the RE-UK titles, these are so-called 'decade remixes', the old songs having been re-worked.)

Sergio Mendes 1941 Brazilian musician, one of the pioneers of the Bossa Nova. He became internationally known with Sergio Mendes & Brazil '66. Hits: "The Look Of Love" (5/68 US 4) and "The Fool On The Hill" (8/68 US 6). Without Brazil '66, he was successful with "Never Gonna Let You Go" (4/83 US 4; 7/83 UK 45).

Josh White 1908 US blues/folk singer, guitarist, and songwriter. Complete first names, Joshua Daniel. He was known for his unusual guitar tuning. In the late 1920s he worked as a guide for blind blues singer, Blind Lemon Jefferson. In 1932 Josh made his first recordings as Pinewood Tom and Tippy Barton. In the 1940s he made records as the Josh White Trio, with clarinetist Sidney Bechet. Josh died on 5th September, 1969 after a heart operation.

Johnny G. 1949 UK singer, multi-instrumentalist, and songwriter. Real name John Gotting. John started out in London pub-rock circles as a one man band. At the end of the 1970s he was in the group Lotus, with John Spencer, whom he worked with occasionally in the 1980s. In 1979 he recorded his first solo album.

Rochelle Fleming 1950 US lead singer with the trio, First Choice, which was formed as the Debronettes. Hits were "Armed And Extremely Dangerous" (3/73 US 28; 5/73 UK 16) and "Smarty Pants" (8/73 UK 9).

Earl Lewis 1941 US lead singer with the Channels. Their best known record was "The Closer You Are" (1956).

Neil Henderson 1953 UK guitarist and singer with Middle Of The Road. He joined the band, however, when the hits had dried up.

Hits of the Day

1950	"Chattanoogie Shoe Shine Boy" Red Foley US 8 weeks
1950	"Rag Mop" Ames Brothers US 2 weeks
1978	"Figaro" Brotherhood Of Man UK 1 week
1989	"Straight Up" Paula Abdul US 3 weeks

Miscellany

1963 10:30 to 23:00 hours: the Beatles are recording their first album – in its entirety.

12th

Birthdays

Ray Manzarek 1935 US keyboard player and pianist, and after Jim Morrison's death (3rd July, 1971) became vocalist of the Doors. Their number "Riders On The Storm" (7/71 US 14; UK 22, 3/76 RE-UK 33; 2/79 RE-UK 71) became a true rock classic, partly because of Ray's keyboard virtuosity. The remaining three members of the group made another two albums and finally, split up in 1973. Their only hit without Morrison was "The Mosquito" (9/72 US 85). After that, Ray released two solo albums, THE GOLDEN SCARAB (1974) and THE WHOLE THING STARTED WITH ROCK N'ROLL (1975); two more albums with his new group Nite City, NITE CITY (1977), and GOLDEN DAYS DIAMOND NIGHTS (1978) followed. In 1983 he produced a rock version of Carl Orff's *Carmina Burana*, with Philip Glass.

Lorne Greene 1915 Canadian actor and TV star. From 1940 to 1943 he was chief announcer on CBS radio. His international career took off in 1959, when he took the part of Ben Cartwright in *Bonanza*; it continued until 1973. From 1978 to 1980, he played Commander Adama in the TV series *Battlestar Galactica*, thus changing his field of action to outer space. Lorne had one hit with the spoken number "Ringo" (11/64 US 1; UK 22). He died 11th Sept., 1987.

Steve Hackett 1950 UK guitarist and songwriter. In August 1970 Steve joined Genesis as a replacement for Anthony Phillips. He played on the albums, NURSERY CRYME, FOXTROTT, SELLING ENGLAND BY THE POUND, THE LAMB LIES DOWN ON BROADWAY, and A TRICK OF THE TALE. In June 1977, he left the band, in order to devote himself to solo plans. In 1986 he appeared again with the band GTR. Hit: "When The Heart Rules The Mind" (5/86 US 14).

Will Glahe 1902 Accordionist and songwriter, who was celebrated as the Polka King in the 1930s in the USA. He had his greatest hit with the million-seller "Beer Barrel Polka" (5/39 US 1). For many years Glahe was one of the most successful German musicians in the USA and Japan. He died on 22nd November, 1989.

Moe Bandy 1944 US country singer and guitarist. He started as a musician with his father's band. On the side he appeared as a rodeo rider. He had his own TV show in the early 1970s with his group Mavericks. From 1973, he made fifty appearances in the country charts. His biggest success was "I Cheated Me Right Out Of You" (10/79

C&W 1). He was also in a duo with Joe Stampley, their biggest hit was "Just Good Ol' Boys" (7/79 C&W 1).

Kenny Dino 1942 US singer with one hit single, "Your Ma Said You Cried In Your Sleep Last Night" (11/61 US 24).

Gene McDaniels 1935 US singer, who was at the height of his powers between 1961 and 1963. His major hits were "A 100 Pounds Of Clay" (3/61 US 3) and "Tower Of Strength" (10/61 US 5; UK 49).

Vincent James 1951 UK singer with Sweet Sensation, whose biggest hit was "Sad Sweet Dreamer" (9/74 UK 1; 2/75 US 14).

Gil Moore 1951 Canadian drummer and singer with Triumph, formed in 1975.

Stanley Knight 1949 US guitarist with Black Oak Arkansas.

Deaths

Sal Mineo 1976 US singer and actor. He was stabbed to death in the road in Los Angeles while walking home. Born 10th Jan., 1939.

Hits of the Day

1955 "Sincerely" McGuire Sisters US 10 weeks
1969 "(If Paradise Is) Half As Nice" Amen Corner UK 2 weeks
1972 "Let's Stay Together" Al Green US 1 week
1977 "Don't Cry For Me Argentina" Julie Covington UK 1 week
1983 "Down Under" Men At Work US 1 week (2nd time)

13th

Birthdays

Peter Gabriel 1950 UK singer, flautist, and songwriter. At the end of 1966 he played with school group Garden Wall, and in January 1967, he became a founder member of Genesis. Peter left the group in May, 1975. The gradual growth in popularity of the group was directly due to his influence of combining rock music with theatre;

it was this element that gave Genesis its image. His role of vocalist was taken over by drummer Phil Collins. Peter produced a number of excellent solo albums after leaving Genesis, which were surprisingly commercial and yielded some highly successful singles: "Solsbury Hill" (4/77 UK 13), "Games Without Frontiers" (2/80 UK 4), "Sledgehammer" (5/86 US 1), and "Big Time" (11/86 US 8; 3/87 UK 13). "Don't Give Up" (11/86 UK 9) teamed him up with Kate Bush to remarkably good effect.

Peter Tork 1944 US singer and guitarist. He played with the Phoenix Singers before becoming a member of the Monkees in 1965. He was the first to leave the group on 30th Dec., 1968. In order to buy himself out of his contract he had to pay 160,000 dollars. Several of his projects thereafter failed completely. In the middle of 1970 the Monkees split up finally. In 1981 Peter toured Japan with his new band, New Monks. In an interview with the National Inquirer he said that he had worked as a waiter for the last few years, and for the rest he was a 'professional former success'. In 1986, 52 old Monkee episodes could be seen on the American TV station MTV – they were a great success. After that, Peter, Micky Dolenz, and David Jones regrouped as the Monkees, "That Was Then, This Is Now" (7/86 US 20).

Tennessee Ernie Ford 1919 US disc jockey, who become a singer and songwriter. Real name Ernest Jennings Ford. In 1948 he made his first country records. From 1955 to 1965 he had his own TV show. Later in his career, he concentrated more on gospel. Hits: "Mule Train" (11/49 US 9), "Give Me Your Word" (1/55 UK 1), "Ballad Of Davey Crockett" (3/55 US 5; 1/56 UK 3), and "16 Tons" (11/55 US 1; 1/56 UK 1). He died on October 17th 1991.

Gene Adams 1925 US singer and member of the Ames Brothers, who actually were brothers, but whose real surname was Urick. From 1948 to 1960 they had some success. Hits, see under brother Joe, on 3rd May. In 1960 the brothers split up.

Roy Dyke 1945 UK drummer, who played with the Remo Four in the mid-60s, then became a member of Ashton, Gardner & Dyke. When they split up, he played with Badger, Cafe Society, Pat Travers; and from the late 70s, in the German group, Bauer, Garn & Dyke, as he lived in Germany. He also played on records by Achim Reichel and Axel Zwingenberger.

Boudleaux Bryant 1920 US songwriter. He wrote eight million-sellers with his wife Felice, among them were hits for the Everly Brothers, Buddy Holly and Bob Luman. He died on 25th June, 1987.

King Floyd 1945 US singer and songwriter. He cut his first records in 1965, and had his first big success with the million selling "Groove Me" (12/70 US 6).

Edward John Gagliardi 1952 US bass player with Foreigner from their inception in 1976 until 1979. In 1982 he appeared again with the group Spys.

Roger Christian 1950 UK singer and songwriter with the Christians. However, he had left the group before they had finished work on their first album to start a solo career. In 1989 his album CHECKMATE was released.

Tony Butler 1957 UK bass player with the group Big Country, formed in 1982.

Peter Hook 1956 UK bass player with Joy Division, which turned into New Order in May, 1980, after lead singer Ian Curtis' suicide.

Dotty McGuire 1930 US singer with the McGuire Sisters. Hits by the sisters, see under Phyllis McGuire, 14th February.

Rod Dees 1951 UK bass player with Showaddywaddy.

Judy Cheeks 1954 US singer and songwriter.

Hits of the Day

1943	"When The Lights Go On Again (All Over The World)" Vaughn Monroe US 3 weeks
1943	"I Had The Craziest Dream" Harry James US 2 weeks
1961	"Calcutta" Lawrence Welk US 2 weeks
1971	"One Bad Apple" Osmonds US 5 weeks
1982	"A Town Called Malice" Jam UK 3 weeks

14th

Birthdays

Phyllis McGuire 1931 US singer with the McGuire Sisters. These were three real sisters, Christine, Dorothy (see above, yesterday), and the youngest, Phyllis. In the 1950s they were the most successful female vocal group in the USA, with hits like "Sincerely" (1/55 US 1; 7/55 UK 14), "Something's Gotta Give" (6/55 US 5), "He" (10/55 US 10) and "Sugartime" (12/57 US 1; 2/58 UK 14). The girls' manager was Alan Freed. Phyllis continued to appear as a solo artist in Las Vegas in the 1980s.

Eric Andersen 1943 US songwriter, singer, guitarist and harmonica player, who was discovered by Tom Paxton in San Francisco in 1963, when he appeared on stage with Janis Joplin. Eric wrote songs for Judy Collins, Johnny Cash, Joan Baez, Blues Project and Peter, Paul & Mary. He also worked with Tom Paxton and Phil Ochs. As an artist, he recorded regularly for a variety of record companies, but none of them ever sold well. He was even dubbed 'the new Bob Dylan', which was more a millstone than an asset. Brian Epstein was about to sign him up, but Brian died before the deal was finalised.

Lillie Bryant 1940 US singer, who had hits with Billy Ford, as Billy and Lillie: "La Dee Dah" (1/58 US 9) and "Lucky Ladybug" (12/58 US 14).

Roger Fisher 1950 US guitarist, who was co-founder of The Army in 1963; it later became White Heart in 1972, and finally Heart in 1974. In 1980 Roger left Heart to form his own band.

Tim Buckley 1947 US singer, songwriter, actor and film script writer, who was one of the most innovative musicians to emerge in the latter half of the 1960s. He died on 29th June, 1975.

Vic Briggs 1945 UK guitarist, with Brian Auger & Julie Driscoll, Steampacket, and from 1967, with Eric Burdon. Vic's stint with Burdon coincided with the contemporaneous psychedelic movement.

Magic Sam 1937 US blues singer, guitarist and songwriter. Real name Samuel Maghett. He also appeared as 'Good Rocking Sam'. Sam died on 1st Dec., 1969.

Doug Simril 1946 US guitarist and pianist, with the Steve Miller Band and Boz Scaggs.

Hits of the Day

1942	"Blues In The Night" Woody Herman US 4 weeks
1953	"Till I Waltz Again With You" Teresa Brewer US 7 weeks
1958	"The Story Of My Life" Michael Holliday UK 2 weeks
1968	"Mighty Quinn" Manfred Mann UK 2 weeks
1970	"Thank You" Sly & The Family Stone US 2 weeks
1987	"Livin' On A Prayer" Bon Jovi US 4 weeks

15th

Birthdays

Ali Campbell 1959 UK singer and rhythm guitarist with UB 40, formed in 1978, and named after the form for applying for unemployment benefit in the UK. Son of Ian Campbell, a leading figure of the UK folk music revival of the 1950s and 1960s. Hits have included "Red Red Wine" (8/83 UK 1; 1/84 US 34; 8/88 RE-US 1). Singer Chrissie Hynde of the Pretenders joined them for their re-working of "I Got You Babe" (7/85 US 28; UK 1).

Hank Locklin 1918 US country singer, guitarist and songwriter. After working on radio during the 1940s, he cut his first recordings in 1949. He appeared regularly in the country charts right into the 70s. His biggest cross-over hit was "Please Help Me, I'm Falling" (3/60 C&W 1; 5/60 US 8; 8/60 UK 9), but perhaps, his best known composition is "Send Me The Pillow You Dream On" (3/58 C&W 5).

Brian Holland 1941 US songwriter, who was a member of the team, Holland-Dozier-Holland (these were his brother Eddie and Lamont Dozier.) Between them they churned out hit after hit for the Tamla-Motown stable. Brian alone wrote "Please Mr. Postman", which became a hit for the Marvelettes, the Beatles and the Carpenters.

Mike & Dave Milliner 1962 UK singers and songwriters, with the Pasadenas. The five members of the group started out as a dance company called Finesse, which was in great demand in the 80s. They appeared in videos of many top stars and were featured in the film *Absolute Beginners*. In 1988 their debut album appeared, on which they collaborated with Pete Wingfield. Hit singles: "Tribute (Ride On)" (5/88 UK 5), and "Riding On A Train" (9/88 UK 13).

Denny Zager 1944 US singer and songwriter, who had an international hit with "In The Year 2525" (6/69 US 1; 8/69 UK 1). With Rick Evans, as Zager & Evans it is the only record by them to have appeared in the charts - real one hit wonders.

Melissa Manchester 1951 US singer, pianist and songwriter. Initially she was a backing singer, first in a background chorus with her friend Bette Midler, in the Harletts, and then she started a solo career. Hits: "Midnight Blue" (5/75 US 6), "Don't Cry Out Loud" (11/78 US 10) and "You Should Hear How She Talks About You" (5/82 US 5).

John Helliwell 1945 UK saxophonist and songwriter, with the Alan Bown Set, and from August, 1973, with the group Supertramp, formed in 1969.

Harold Arlen 1905 Singer and songwriter, real name Hyman Arluck. He wrote and sang "Stormy Weather" (3/33 US 1). From 1930 to 1960, he had more than 20 Top Ten compositions in the US charts, including "Over The Rainbow" and "Blues In The Night". He died on 23rd April, 1986.

Mick Avory 1944 UK drummer with the Kinks from 1964 to 1977. He was with them during their heyday.

David Brown 1947 US bassist, with Santana from 1969 to 1976, but was replaced by Douglas Rauch.

Michael Craig 1960 UK bassist, with Culture Club.

Deaths

Nat 'King' Cole 1965 US singer and pianist. Nat died of lung cancer. Born 17th March, 1919.

Little Walter 1968 US blues singer, guitarist and supremely harmonica player. He died of a head injury inflicted during a fight. Born 1st May, 1930.

Mike Bloomfield 1981 US blues guitarist, harmonica player, pianist and songwriter. He was found dead of a drug overdose in his car. Born 28th July, 1943.

Frederick Lowe 1988 US composer. Born 10th June, 1904.

Hits of the Day

1969   "Everyday People" Sly & The Family Stone US 4 weeks
1975   "You're No Good" Linda Ronstadt US 1 week
1986   "How Will I Know" Whitney Houston US 2 weeks

16th

Birthdays

Patti Andrews 1920 US lead singer and youngest of the Andrews Sisters. The sisters started appearing as a trio from the early 30s. In 1937 they made their first records, and they managed to close the gap left by 'the Boswell Sisters. The Andrews Sisters are probably one of the most successful all-female groups ever with sales of over 60 million records and 90 entries in the charts. Among their biggest hits were "Bei Mir Bist Du Schon" (1/38 US 1), "Ferryboat Serenade" (10/40 US 1), "Shoo Shoo Baby" (12/43 US 1), "Rum and Coca Cola" (1/45 US 1), "Christmas Island" (12/46 US 7; 12/47 RE-US 20; 1/49 RE-US 26), "I Can Dream, Can't I" (9/49 US 1) and "I Wanna Be Loved" (5/50 US 1). They sang and played with many other stars of the era like Les Paul, Danny Kaye, Dick Haymes, Burl Ives, Carmen Miranda, Ernest Tubb, Russ Morgan and Bing Crosby. They had 23 entries in the charts with Bing, the most successful being "Pistol Packin' Mama" (11/43 US 1), "A Hot Time In The Town Of Berlin" (9/44 US 1) and "Don't Fence Me In" (11/44 US 1). In between Patti tried her hand as a soloist. Her greatest success was "The Pussy Cat Song (Nyow! Nyow! Nyow!)" (1/49 US 12). In 1974 Patti and Maxene (Laverne had died in 1967) appeared in the nostalgic Broadway musical, *Over There.*

Sonny Bono 1935 US songwriter, singer and producer. Real first name Salvatore. In 1957 he started out as a songwriter for the record company Specialty. Then he became a session musician for Phil Spector. In 1963 he made his first records with Cher (as Caesar & Cleo); they married in 1964. From 1965 they were known as Sonny & Cher and were very successful (for their hits, see Cher, 20th May). Sonny had a solo hit with "Laugh At Me" (8/65 US 10; UK 9), and the couple divorced in 1974.

Bill Doggett 1916 US pianist and songwriter, who formed his first band in 1938. He made his first records with the Jimmy Munday Band in 1939. During the 40s he played and wrote arrangements for Lionel Hampton, Louis Jordan, Count Basie and Louis Armstrong. He played piano briefly with the Inkspots. Bill had his biggest hit under his own name with "Honky Tonk (Parts 1 & 2)" (8/56 US 2). He is considered to be the "Father of the Swing Organ".

Lyn Paul 1949 UK singer, real name Lynda Susan Belcher. She was a member of the New Seekers formed in 1969, who had their biggest hit with "I'd Like To Teach The World To Sing (In Perfect Harmony)" (12/71 UK 1; US 7). Later Lyn tried her luck as a solo artist, singing "It Oughta Sell A Million" (6/75 UK 37). It didn't, though . . .

Leon Ware 1940 US pianist, singer and songwriter. He made his first record in 1972. His greatest success was What's Your Name" (12/79 R&B 42). He wrote hits for Ike & Tina Turner, Marvin Gaye, Isley Brothers, Bobby Womack, Merry Clayton, Johnny Nash and Michael Jackson. He never managed to write a pop hit for himself.

Jimmy Wakely 1914 US country singer, guitarist, and pianist. He formed his first trio in 1937. In the early 40s he played on radio shows, which earned him the nickname 'Melody Kid'. From 1952 until 1957, Jimmy had his own radio show, and in 1961, a TV series with Tex Ritter. He had his first hit record in 1943, but his most successful solo record was "One Has My Name (The Other Has My Heart)" (10/48 US 10). However, with Margaret Whiting, he scored with "Slippin' Around" (9/49 US 1). He played in over 70 western films. He died 25th September, 1982.

Herbie & Harold Kalin 1939 US singer and songwriter who had their biggest hits as the Kalin Twins with "When" (6/58 US 5; UK 1) and "Forget Me Not" (9/58 US 12).

Otis Blackwell 1932 US songwriter, pianist and singer. Otis was considered to be one of the most influential R n' R composers but he also wrote for other artists like Tex Ritter. Over the years he wrote more than 900 songs, tailoring hits for Elvis, Jerry Lee Lewis and Jimmy Jones – but none for himself.

Andy Taylor 1961 UK lead guitarist and songwriter, who, in 1979, joined the group Duran Duran which had been formed the year before. In the mid-1980s he played with Power Station. In June, 1986 Andy left Duran Duran to pursue a solo career. Hit: "Take It Easy" (5/86 US 24).

Wayne King 1901 US saxophonist, orchestra leader and songwriter, who was nicknamed 'The King of the Waltz' in the USA. From 1930 to 1941 he was in the US charts with about 40 titles. His biggest hits were "Dream A Little Dream Of Me" (4/31 US 1) and "Goodnight Sweetheart" (10/31 US 1). He died 16th July, 1985.

Hits of the Day

1957 "Young Love" Tab Hunter US 6 weeks
1967 "This Is My Song" Petula Clark UK 2 weeks
1974 "The Way We Were" Barbra Streisand US 2 weeks (2nd time)
1980 "Coward Of The Country" Kenny Rogers UK 2 weeks
1980 "Do That To Me One More Time" Captain & Tennille US 1 week
1985 "Careless Whisper" Wham! US 3 weeks

17th

Birthdays

Gene Pitney 1941 US singer and songwriter, who wrote "He's A Rebel" for the Crystals and "Hello Mary Lou" for Ricky Nelson. He made his first records in 1959, with Ginny Arnell, as Jamie & Jane. From 1960, he recorded as a solo artist, and was very successful until 1968. His biggest hits were "(The Man Who Shot) Liberty Valance" (4/62 US 4), "Only Love Can Break A Heart" (9/62 US 2), "It Hurts To Be In Love" (7/64 US 7; 10/64 UK 36) and "I'm Gonna Be Strong" (10/64 US 9, UK 2). After a long absence from the charts, he suddenly re-appeared in 1989, with Marc Almond, on a remake of "Something's Gotten Hold Of My Heart" (1/89 UK 1); first time around, it reached No. 5 in the UK in November, 1967.

Tommy Edwards 1922 US singer and songwriter who wrote "That Chick's Too Young To Fry" for Louis Jordan. He was moderately successful as a singer from 1951 until 1960. His biggest hit was "It's All In The Game" (8/58 US 1; 10/58 UK 1), written by Charles Gates Dawes in 1912: Dawes was vice-President of the USA from 1925 to 1929 and received the Nobel Peace Prize in 1925 with G. A. Chamberlain for the Dawes Plan, which he developed himself.

John Leyton 1939 UK actor and singer who became known through his TV roles in the UK. He played the pop singer Johnny St. Cyr in the series *Harper's West One*. His manager at the time, Robert Stigwood (an Australian who was later to become a key figure in the business affairs of Cream and the Bee Gees, forming his own record company, later the Robert Stigwood Organisation RSO, in the early 1970s) had realized quite rightly that popularity on TV could be a useful springboard for a career as a singer. As with Tab Hunter and Anthony Newley, John Leyton became a pop star by accident rather than by design and consequently, had hits from 1961 until 1964 with "Johnny Remember Me" (8/61 UK 1) and "Wild Wind" (10/61 UK 2). His biggest success as an actor was in the film *The Great Escape* (1962), playing alongside Steve McQueen, Charles Bronson, James Coburn, James Garner, David McCallum and Richard Attenborough (before the 'Sir' tag).

Dodie Stevens 1947 US child singing star. Real name Geraldine Ann Pasquale. Her biggest hit (she was just 11 when it was recorded) was "Pink Shoe Laces" (2/59 US 3). No further hits since then.

Bobby Lewis 1933 US singer who grew up in an orphanage and was adopted by a family in Detroit at age 12. In 1956 he cut his first records and had his biggest hits with "Tossin' And Turnin'" (4/61 US 1) and "One Track Mind" (8/61 US 9).

Johnny Bush 1935 US singer, voted by magazine *Record World* to be the most promising singer of 1968 – a foolhardy prediction in the music business!

Orwill Hoppy Jones 1905 US singer with the Inkspots. Died 18th October, 1944.

Deaths

Thelonius Monk 1982 US jazz pianist and composer. Born 10th October, 1917.

Hits of the Day

1956	"Memories Are Made Of This" Dean Martin UK 4 weeks
1958	"Sugartime" McGuire Sisters US 4 weeks
1962	"Duke Of Earl" Gene Chandler US 3 weeks
1966	"These Boots Are Made For Walkin'" Nancy Sinatra UK 4 weeks

---

18th

Birthdays

Pee Wee King 1914 US accordionist, violinist, songwriter and bandleader. Real name Julius Frank Kuczynski. In 1936 he formed his own first band called Golden West Cowboys. From 1947 until 1957, he had his own radio show, and then, a TV show. In 1948, he started to chart with his own compositions like "Tennessee Waltz" (4/48 US 30) and "Slow Poke" (11/51 US 1); Redd Stewart was the leadsinger on all of Pee Wee King's records and the Lloyd T. 'Cowboy' Copas version of "Tennessee Waltz" became a million seller in 1948.

Juice Newton 1952 US country/pop singer. Real first names Judy Kay. At thirteen she was singing folk music and, in 1974, she went to Los Angeles with her band Silver Spur. From 1975, she cut records, but when the group split up in 1978, she started a solo career. After that she was a regular fixture in the country charts. Her versions of "Angel Of The Morning" (2/81 US 4) and "Queen Of Hearts" (5/81 US 2) were both million sellers.

Randy Crawford 1952 US singer who was originally more successful in the UK than at home; between 1979 and 1986 she had 10 hits there. The biggest were "One Day I'll Fly Away" (8/80 UK 2) and "Almaz" (11/86 UK 4). She was featured vocalist – but uncredited – on "Street Life" (8/79 UK 5; US 36) by the Crusaders.

John Travolta 1954 US singer and actor. His first success as an actor came with his part as Vinnie Barbarino in the TV series, *Welcome Back Kotter*, broadcast in 1975. The highpoint of his career was his part in the disco-film *Saturday Night Fever* (1977). Further films featuring John were *Grease*, *Blow Out*, and *Urban Cowboy*. Hits as a solo artist included "Let Her In" (5/76 US 10) and "Sandy" (10/78 UK 2); and duets with Olivia Newton-John "You're The One That I Want" (4/78 US & UK 1) and "Summer Nights" (8/78 US 5; UK 1).

Marty Simon 1948 UK drummer with Holy Smoke, Life, Sharks and April Wine. He also cropped up as a session musician on records by Eno, Leslie West, Patsy Gallant and Wilson Pickett.

Jimmy Jewell 1945 UK saxophonist and clarinetist with Ronnie Lane's Slim Chance, Keef Hartley, McGuinness-Flint, Gallagher & Lyle and many others.

Dennis de Young 1947 US singer, pianist and songwriter. In 1963 he met the brothers, John and Chuck Panozzo, in Chicago. This was where the foundations of the group Styx was laid. In 1968 they were still called the Tradewinds; finally, in 1970, they changed their name to Styx. 1974 was their watershed with the single "Lady" (12/74 US 6); it was followed by "Come Sail Away" (9/77 US 8), "Babe" (10/79 US 1; 1/80 UK 6), "The Best Of Times" (1/81 US 3), "Too Much Time On My Hands" (3/81 US 9), "Mr. Roboto" (2/83 US 3), and "Don't Let It End" (4/83 US 6). From 1984, Dennis cut solo records, scoring with "Desert Moon" (9/84 US 10).

Robin Bachman 1953 Canadian drummer. Played with Brave Belt from 1971 onwards, which later developed into Bachman-Turner Overdrive.

Irma Thomas 1941 US soul singer. Real name Irma Lee. Between 1960 and 1968 she was an occasional visitor to the R & B charts but her biggest pop hit was "Wish Someone Would Care" (3/64 US 17).

Austin Howard 1962 UK lead singer and songwriter with Ellis, Beggs & Howard, whose first hit was "Big Bubbles, No Troubles" (7/88 UK 59; 3/89 RE-UK 41). Previously, Austin had released some solo records, which were unsuccessful.

David Blue 1941 US singer and songwriter who recorded from 1963, but without any notable success. He died 2nd Dec., 1982.

Derek Pellici 1953 Australian drummer in the original line-up of Little River Band.

Yoko Ono 1933 Japanese, married to John Lennon in 1969, which supposedly led to the split up of the Beatles. She made some recordings with John Lennon which were too esoteric for mass approval. Even after the death of her husband she continued issuing records periodically. A tour in 1986 fell well short of her expectations.

Hits of the Day

1955 "Softly Softly" Ruby Murray UK 3 weeks
1956 "Great Pretender" Platters US 2 weeks
1956 "Rock And Roll Waltz" Kay Starr US 6 weeks
1965 "Tired Of Waiting For You" Kinks UK 1 week
1967 "Kind Of A Drag" Buckinghams US 2 weeks
1978 "Take A Chance On Me" Abba UK 3 weeks

19th

Birthdays

Smokey Robinson 1940 US singer and songwriter. Real first name, William, who wroter countless hits for himself, his group, the Miracles and for others, as well. He formed his first group called Matadors in 1955, when he was still at school, it would evolve into the Miracles later on. In 1958 "Got A Job" was released, the first single by the Miracles, it was the answer to "Get A Job" by the Silhouettes. In 1960 the Miracles had their first million seller for Motown Records with "Shop Around" (12/60 US 2). Further hits included "You've Really Got A Hold On Me" (12/62 US 8) and "Mickey's Monkey" (8/63 US 8). From 1967 the records were released under the name of Smokey Robinson & The Miracles, among the hits were "I Second That Emotion" (11/67 US 4; UK 27), "Baby, Baby Don't Cry" (1/69 US 8) and "The Tears Of A Clown" (8/70 UK 1; 10/70 US 1). On the 29th Jan., 1972, Smokey left the Miracles, became Vice-President of Tamla-Motown, and released solo albums on a regular basis, which included

hits like "Cruisin' " (10/79 US 4), and "Being With You" (2/81 US 2; 5/81 UK 1).

Lou Christie 1943 US singer, real name Lugee Alfredo Giovanni Sacco. He started out as the singer in the Classics with whom he made his first record in 1960 – it failed, which was followed by Lugee and The Lions In 1961 – they, too, failed. Finally, as Lou Christie, he had 5 Top 40 hits from 1963 to 1969. The most successful were "Two Faces Have I" (3/63 US 6), "Lightnin' Strikes" (12/65 US 1; UK 11) and "I'm Gonna Make You Mine" (8/69 US 10; UK 2).

Falco 1957 Austrian singer and songwriter, real name Johann Holzel. He started as a bass player with Drahdiwaberl and has been making solo records since 1980. His hits were "Der Kommissar", which was internationally successful for the British group After The Fire (2/83 US 5; 4/83 UK 47), "Rock Me Amadeus" (2/86 US & UK 1), "Vienna Calling" (4/86 US 18; UK 10), "Jeanny, Part 1" (8/86 UK 86) and "Coming Home (Jeanny Part 2, A Year Later)".

Dave Wakeling 1956 UK singer, guitarist and songwriter for the band The Beat, formed in September, 1978. Hits, "Tears Of A Clown/Ranking Full Stop" (12/79 UK 6), "Hands Off – She's Mine" (2/80 UK 7), "Mirror In The Bathroom" (5/80 UK 4), "Too Nice To Talk To" (12/80 UK 7) and "Can't Get Used To Losing You" (4/83 UK 3). In July 1983, the band split up, and Dave, with another former member of The Beat, formed the group General Public.

Eddie Hardin 1949 UK keyboard player, singer and songwriter. Eddie joined the Spencer Davis Group in April 1967 as a replacement for Steve Winwood. As, seemingly, he was no real replacement, the group had had its day. In October 1968 he and drummer Pete York left to form Hardin & York. Eddie called the duo the 'smallest Big Band in the world'. They were unsuccessful commercially.

Stan Kenton 1912 US pianist, songwriter and bandleader. In 1941 he formed his first jazz band. From 1944 to 1962 he was regularly in the charts, sometimes with vocalists like June Christy and sometimes as a pianist with his orchestra. His major hits, all million sellers, were "Artistry in Rhythm" (11/44 US 16), "Tampico" (7/45 US 3), and "Shoo-Fly Pie and Apple Pan Dowdy" (3/46 US 6). He died 25th August, 1979.

Bob Engemann 1936 US singer, with the Lettermen from their formation in 1960 until 1968. For hits, see 6th Nov., under fellow band member Jim Pike. After Engemann left the group, Gary Pike, Jim's brother, replaced him.

Mark Andes 1948 US bass player and singer with the band Spirit formed in L. A. in 1967. In 1971 he was co-founder of Jo Jo Gunne, and from 1976 a member of

Fireball, who had their biggest hit with "You Are The Woman" (9/76 US 9). In 1982 he joined the group Heart.

Lee Marvin 1924 US film actor, who murmured a little song in the film *Paint Your Wagon* which became a hit, "Wandrin' Star" (2/70 UK 1). He was a successful actor from 1951 onwards. He died of heart failure on 30th August, 1987.

Alan Merrill 1951 UK singer and bass player with the Arrows, who charted with "A Touch Too Much" (5/74 UK 8).

Czeslaw Wydrzycki 1939 Polish jazz-rock-musician. Made quite impressive albums as Niemen.

Andy Powell 1950 UK guitarist with the group Wishbone Ash formed in 1969.

Francis Buchholz 1950 German bass player with the Scorpions.

Tony Iommi 1949 UK guitarist with Black Sabbath.

Deaths

Bon Scott 1980 Australian/UK singer with AC/DC. Scott died after a night of heavy drinking by choking on his own vomit. Born 9th July, 1946.

Hits of the Day

1966 "Lightenin' Strikes" Lou Christie US 1 week
1972 "Without You" Nilsson US 4 weeks
1972 "Son Of My Father" Chicory Tip UK 4 weeks
1977 "When I Need You" Leo Sayer UK 3 weeks
1977 "Blinded By The Light" Manfred Mann's Earthband US 1 week
1983 "Baby Come To Me" Patti Austin & James Ingram US 2 weeks
1983 "Too Shy" Kajagoogoo UK 2 weeks

20th

Birthdays

Walter Becker 1950 US bass player and songwriter. During his time at university he met Donald Fagen. In 1969 the pair wrote film music for *You Got To Walk It Like You Talk It*, an early Richard Pryor film. However, the record was not released until the late 70s. In 1970 Walter and Donald became members of Demian, but never went

further than a cutting demo- recording. In 1971, as a duo, the pair cut demos for other artists, and in 1972 signed a contract as Steely Dan. They split up in the 80s, after recording a series of literate, jazzy albums that were the antithesis of the superficiality of the rock mainstream. A comeback has been mooted.

Barbara Ellis 1940 US singer with the Fleetwoods, who had their biggest hits with "Come Softly To Me" (3/59 US 1; UK 6) and "Mr. Blue" (9/59 US 1). The group continued recording until 1963.

Nancy Wilson 1940 US jazz singer who first recorded in 1956. Her biggest hit was "(You Don't Know) How Glad I Am" (7/64 US 11).

Jerome Geils 1946 US guitarist and founder of the J. Geils Band, formed in 1967. They first recorded in 1970. Despite an impressive live act they only achieved international status after their two biggest hits: the millionseller, "Centerfold" (11/81 US 1; 2/82 UK 3) and "Freeze-Frame" (2/82 US 4; 4/82 UK 27).

Buffy Sainte-Marie 1941 Canadian singer, guitarist and songwriter, of American Indian descent. Compositions like "Universal Soldier", "Until It's Time For You To Go" and "Up Where We Belong" were all written by her. Her biggest hit was "Soldier Blue" (7/71 UK 7), from the film of that name.

Randy California 1946 US guitarist with Spirit, Jay Ferguson, Kaptain Kopter, New Spirit and on several solo albums.

Alan Hull 1945 UK singer, pianist, guitarist, and songwriter with Lindisfarne, formed in the late 60s. Hits: "Meet Me On The Corner" (2/72 UK 5), "Lady Eleanor" (5/72 UK 3) and "Run For Home" (6/78 UK 10; 9/78 US 33).

Mark Reilly 1960 UK singer and songwriter for Matt Bianco, successful from 1984. Hits: "Get Out Of Your Lazy Bed" (2/84 UK 15), "Yeh Yeh" (10/85 UK 13) and "Don't Blame It On That Girl/Wap-Wam-Boogie" (6/88 UK 11).

Jimmy Yancey 1898 US blue 'boogie-woogie' pianist, singer and songwriter. Real first names James Edward. He made his first records in 1939 and was active until his death on 17th Sept., 1951.

Murv Shiner 1921 US country singer, guitarist and songwriter. Real first name Mervin. He made his first appearance, as a 16 year old, with his mother. He only had one big hit with the millionseller "Peter Cottontail" (3/50 US 8).

Louis Soloff 1944 US trumpeter with Blood, Sweat & Tears and session musician.

Hits of the Day

1959 "As I Love You" Shirley Bassey UK 4 weeks
1964 "Diane" Bachelors UK 1 week
1965 "This Diamond Ring" Gary Lewis US 2 weeks
1988 "I Should Be So Lucky" Kylie Minogue UK 5 weeks
1988 "Seasons Change" Expose US 1 week

21st

Birthdays

Jerry Harrison 1949 US guitarist, keyboard player, songwriter and singer. From 1970 to 1974 he was a member of the band Modern Lovers, which accompanied Jonathan Richman. In April 1976 Jerry watched the band Talking Heads, formed in 1974, and tried to join them. In September 1976 it worked, and in the spring of 1988 the first solo album by Jerry was released called CASUAL GODS.

Nina Simone 1933 US singer and songwriter. Real name Eunice Waymon. She tended towards jazz and played piano well. Pop hits: "I Love You, Porgy" (8/59 US 18), "Ain't Got No – I Got Life/Do What You Gotta Do" (10/68 UK 2) and "To Love Somebody" (1/69 UK 5), a cover version of the Bee Gees composition. In the 1970s her musical career suffered through her political outspokenness. In 1987 the self penned "My Baby Just Cares For Me" (10/87 UK 5) was used for a Chanel perfume commercial; it pushed her back into the limelight although she had written it in 1959.

Paul Newton 1945 UK bass player, who played with Greg Lake, Ken Hensley and Lee Kerslake in the Gods from September 1967 to the summer of 1968. After that, he planed with Mick Box and David Byron in Spice until December 1969. These three became the founder members of Uriah Heep. Paul stayed with them until the end of 1971. During the long history of Uriah Heep, the lineup was constantly changing the bass players, especially, never seemed to stay for very long: After Paul, they had Mark Clarke, Gary Thain, John Wetton, and Trevor Bolder.

Bob Colin Day 1942-61 UK singer who was in the Allisons with John Alford. Only hit: "Are You Sure" (2/61 UK 2).

Ranking Rogers 1961 UK drummer and singer. He started out as the drummer for the punk band Dum Dum Boys. In May 1979 he became a member of The Beat. When the group split up in July, 1983, he formed the group General Public, with Dave Wakeling (also a former member of The Beat).

Deaths

Janet Vogel 1980 US singer with the Skyliners. She committed suicide. Born 10th June, 1942.

Hits of the Day

1948 "I'm Looking Over A Four-Leaf Clover" Art Mooney US 5 weeks
1963 "Wayward Wind" Frank Ifield UK 3 weeks
1972 "Sacramento" Middle Of The Road
1976 "December '63" Four Seasons UK 2 weeks
1981 "Shaddap You Face" Joe Dolce UK 3 weeks
1981 "9 To 5" Dolly Parton US 1 week
1987 "Stand By Me" Ben E. King UK 3 weeks

22nd

Birthdays

Bobby Hendricks 1938 US singer with the Drifters. Lead singer on "Moonlight Bay" (6/58 US 72), and on the B-side "Drip Drop" (8/58 US 58). Then he was lead singer with the Swallows before having his only solo hit: "Itchy Twitchy Feeling" (8/58 US 25), with the Coasters backing him.

Louise Lopez 1943 US singer who sang lead vocals with her sister Lilian in Odyssey. Hits: "Native New Yorker" (11/77 US 21; UK 5), "Use It Up And Wear It Out" (6/80 UK 1), "If You're Lookin' For A Way Out" (9/80 UK 6), "Going Back To My Roots" (5/81 UK 4) and "Inside Out" (6/82 UK 3).

Oliver 1945 US singer, real name William Oliver Swofford. He was a member of The Good Earth before pursuing a solo career. Hits: "Good Morning Starshine" (5/69 US 3; 8/69 UK 6) and "Jean" (8/69 US 2). Nowadays, he performs as Bill Swofford in the USA.

Ernie K-Doe 1936 US singer and songwriter. Real name Ernest Kador Jr. He played typical New Orleans R & B. In 1954 he recorded with the Blue Diamonds, with Huey 'Piano' Smith in the lineup. From 1955, he pursued a solo career, but "Mother-In-Law" (3/61 US 1; 5/61 UK 29) was his only hit.

Del Wood 1920 US ragtime-pianist and singer, born Adelaide Hazelwood. From 1951 she appeared in the Grand Ole Opry, and had her biggest hit with the million seller "Down Yonder" (9/51 US 4).

Michael Wilton 1962 US guitarist, singer and songwriter with Queensryche.

Deaths

Florence Ballard 1976 US singer, who was an original member of the Supremes. When she left, in 1967 the group had had 20 chart hits. She was replaced by Cindy Birdsong. She received none of the royalties and she lost a legal case (for over 8.7 million dollars) against her record company Tamla Motown. She died in poverty, abandoned by her husband in a Detroit hospital after suffering a heart attack. Born 30th June, 1943.

Hits of the Day

1947 "Managua, Nicaragua" Freddy Martin US 3 weeks

1947 "Open The Door, Richard" Count Basie US 1 week

1957 "Young Love" Tab Hunter UK 7 weeks

1960 "Theme From A Summer Place" Percy Faith US 9 weeks

1962 "Rock-A-Hula Baby/Can't Help Falling In Love" Elvis Presley UK 4 weeks

1975 "Make Me Smile" Steve Harley & Cockney rebel UK 2 weeks

Miscellany

1956 In Hollywood, Grace Kelly and Bing Crosby record the title "True Love". It came from the film *High Society*, in which they both appeared alongside Frank Sinatra and Louis Armstrong. The record became a million seller. On the same day, in the same year, Elvis Presley appeared in the US charts with his first record, "Heartbreak Hotel". This record was to remain in the charts for 27 weeks and reached No. 1 on 3rd May.

23rd

Birthdays

Johnny Winter 1944 US blues guitarist, singer and songwriter. Only 15 years old, he made his first record in 1959 as Johnny & The Jammers; in keeping with his age, it was called "Schoolday Blues". During the next few years he played occasionally with his brother Edgar (an albino like himself) in several different groups. Among them were Black Plague and Gene Terry & The Downbeats. In 1968 he finally formed his first group with his brother. In 1969 they signed with CBS. In the following years he carried on in the old way, sometimes with and sometimes without his brother. Johnny never had a single hit, but the album LIVE/JOHNNY WINTER AND, in 1971, became a million seller.

Rusty Young 1946 US guitarist, singer and songwriter. He started out in 1964 with a very popular Colorado group, called Bonzee Cryque. In 1968, when Buffalo Springfield was on its last legs, he helped to complete their last album. Buffalo Springfield members, Jim Messina and Richie Furay formed the country-rock group Poco with Rusty Young in August 1968. From their formation until the spilt-up in October 1984 the lineup of Poco was changing constantly, with only Rusty lasting the course. In 1989 the group Poco came together again for a new album, with the same lineup from August 1968: Jim Messina, Richie Fury, George Grantham, Randy Meissner, and Rusty Young.

Howard Jones 1955 UK keyboardist, singer and songwriter, who first appeared in the charts in 1983. Hits: "New Song" (9/83 UK 3; US 27), "What Is Love" (11/83 UK 2; 4/84 US 33), "Things Can Only Get Better" (2/85 UK 6; US 5) and "No One Is To Blame" (3/86 UK 16; US 4). His nickname is 'Synth Wizard' and his specialty is vegetarian cookery. In 1987 he opened a restaurant in New York, which burned down after several months. Howard is also known for his social conscience: he worked with an anti-heroin project, a rehabilitation centre for drug addicts and alcoholics and organized a benefit concert for the victims of hurricane Irene in 1987.

David Sylvian 1958 UK singer, guitarist, keyboard player and songwriter. Real surname Blatt. He formed the group Japan in mid-1970, with his brother Steve, who changed his surname to Jansen. The group won first prize in a competition for upcoming young artists sponsored by German record company Ariola Hansa which had just opened a branch in London. In 1978 the first record by Japan appeared on this label – it failed. "Life In Japan", produced by Giorgio Moroder and released in May 1979, was unsuccessful except in Japan. During 1980, the group signed with Virgin Records and began to be successful. During the next few years, old recordings by the band were re-issued by Hansa and became hits: "Ghosts" (3/82 UK 5) and "I Second That Emotion" (7/82 UK 9). The group split up at the end of 1982. David worked with Ryuichi Sakamoto on "Bamboo Houses/Bamboo Music" (8/82 UK 30) and "Forbidden Colours" (7/83 UK 16) under the name of Sylvian Sakamoto; the latter title was from the film *Merry Christmas, Mr. Lawrence*, in which Sakamoto acted. After that, David worked as a solo artist, his biggest hit being "Red Guitar" (6/84 UK 17).

Michael Maxfield 1944 UK lead guitarist, with the Dakotas who were successful with Billy J. Kramer between 1963 and 1965. The band was managed by Brian Epstein and produced by George Martin; with such an influential combination behind them it was unevitable that they would be successful. They only charted once without Billy; it was an instrumental, "The Cruel Sea" (7/63 UK 18).

Robin Gray 1957 UK singer with the Dead End Kids who were successful with "Have I The Right" (3/77 UK 6).

Brad Whitford 1952 US guitarist with Aerosmith, formed in 1970.

Steve Priest 1950 UK bass player of the group Sweet, who were successful from 1971 to 1978.

Terry 'Tex' Comer 1949 UK bass player, guitarist and percussionist, with Warm Dust, Ace, and as a session musician.

Gary Giles 1952 UK bass player with Stray.

Deaths

Stan Laurel 1965 US film actor, real name Arthur Stanley Jefferson, who was half of the comedy duo Laurel and Hardy, with Oliver Hardy. 'Trail of the Lonesome Pine', etc. Born 16th June, 1890.

Hits of the Day

1961 "Sailor" Petula Clark UK 1 week
1974 "Devil Gate Drive" Suzi Quatro UK 2 weeks
1980 "Crazy Little Thing Called Love" Queen US 4 weeks

24th

Birthdays

Rupert Holmes 1947 British-born singer, songwriter and producer. His father was an American GI, his mother British. When Rupert was 6, the family moved to the state of New York. During his time at school he formed his first group, the Nomads, his main instrument being clarinet. He wrote and aranged for the Drifters, the Platters, Barbra Sreisand, Dolly Parton, Mac Davies, Manhattan Transfer and Gene Pitney. His biggest hit was "Timothy" (1/71 US 17) for the group Buoys. As a producer he worked for Sailor, Strawbs, Sparks and John Miles. Success as an artist came with titles like "Escape (The Pina Colada Song)" (10/79 US 1; 1/80 UK 23) and "Him" (1/80 US 6; 3/80 UK 31).

Nicky Hopkins 1944 UK pianist and songwriter, who was a session musician and a member of a vast number of different groups. He can be heard on "My Generation" by the Who, played with Screaming Lord Sutch and Cyril Davies, accompanied Jeff Beck, Jefferson Airplane, the Steve Miller Band, Quicksilver Message Service, the Rolling Stones and Sweet Thursday. His first solo album THE TIN MAN WAS A DREAMER (1972) featured George Harrison, Mick Taylor, Klaus Voormann, Jim Price and Bobby Keys. However it was unsuccessful.

Paul Jones 1942 UK singer and songwriter. Real name Paul Pond. He was co-founder of the band Manfred Mann and was lead vocalist on hits like "Do Wah Diddy Diddy" (7/64 UK 1; 9/64 US 1) and "Pretty Flamingo" (4/66 UK 1; 7/66 US 29). In 1966, Paul was replaced by Mike D'Abo as he wanted to go solo. His major hits were "High Time" (10/66 UK 4), and "I've Been A Bad Bad Boy" (1/67 UK 5). By the 1970s he had disappeared from the charts, but re-appeared in the Blues Band. He is also a regular broadcaster on Jazz FM and BBC Radio.

Dennis Waterman 1948 UK actor and singer. In common with many TV stars, Dennis has carved out a subordinate career as a singer on the strength of his acting ability. His biggest hit "I Could Be So Good For You" (10/80 UK 3), was featured in TV's series *MINDER*. In the UK he had his first success in 1962/63 as Neville Finch in *Fair Exchange* and in 1976 he was Sergeant Carter in *The Sweeney*. His most recent success was with "What Are We Gonna Get 'er Indoors" (12/83 UK 21).

Michel Legrand 1932 French pianist and composer. His father was Raymond Legrand who wrote violin arrangements for Dizzie Gillespie in 1952. Michel went to the USA and made records with Frankie Laine. After that he wrote almost 50 scores of film like the theme "Windmills Of Your Mind" from *The Thomas Crown Affair* in 1968 and "Summer Of '42" in 1972. Both compositions won him Oscars.

David Newman 1933 US saxophonist. From 1954, he played with T-Bone Walker and then with Ray Charles for 10 years. Finally David formed his own jazz group, but continued as a session musician working with Joe Cocker, the Neville Brothers, Herbie Mann, B. B. King and Doldinger's Passport.

Lonnie Turner 1947 US bass player with the Steve Miller Band formed in 1973. He also played on records by Dave Mason, Eddie Money and Tommy Tutone.

Colin Farley 1959 UK bass player and singer with Cutting Crew.

Deaths

Memphis Slim 1988 US blues veteran pianist Peter Chapman, alias Memphis Slim lived more or less permanently in France from 1961. He died of kidney failure in Paris. Born 3rd September, 1915.

Johnny Ray 1990 Died of liver failure, born 10th January, 1927.

Webb Pierce 1991 US singer and songwriter, born August 8th 1921.

Hits of the Day

1940	"Indian Summer" Tommy Dorsey	US 1 week
1958	"Get A Job" Silhouettes	US 2 weeks
1968	"Judy In Disguise" John Fred	
1973	"Killing Me Softly" Roberta Flack	US 4 weeks

25th

Birthdays

George Harrison 1943 UK singer, guitarist and songwriter. In the mid-1950s he became a member of his brother Pete's group, the Rebels. In 1958 he joined the Quarrymen, which developed into Johnny & The Moondogs, Johnny & The Silver Beatles, the Silver Beatles, and finally, in 1960, The Beatles. They are considered to have created new standards in pop music between 1962 and 1970. George wrote two of their most beautiful titles, "Here Comes The Sun" and "Something" (10/69 US & UK 1). He wrote "Tax Man" and "While My Guitar Gently Weeps", but was usually over shadowed by Lennon/McCartney. After the group split up, George embarked on a solo career. He had an international hit with "My Sweet Lord" (11/70 US 1; 1/71 UK 1), which later turned out to have been very similar to "He's So Fine" by the Chiffons. Harrison had to share the royalties. Further hits by him were "What Is Life" (2/71 US 10), "Give Me Love (Give Me Peace On Earth)" (5/73 US 1; UK 8), "All Those Years Ago" (5/81 US 2; UK 13), and "Got My Mind Set On You" (10/87 US 1; UK 2). He worked with the Travelling Wilburys. His commitment to the Bangladesh Benefit Concert at Madison Square Gardens on 1st August, 1971 was most impressive. He was the first of the 'Fab Four' to realize, 'There is more in life to being a Beatle.' In recent years he has devoted a lot of energy to the production company, Handmade Films.

Elkie Brooks 1945 UK singer. Real name Elaine Bookbinder; some books say she is the sister of Billy J. Kramer. At age 15 she made her debut as 'Manchester's Brenda Lee'. In 1972, with husband Peter Gage she formed the band Vinegar Joe. They made good records but little success. Elkie was more successful as a solo artist, "Pearl's A Singer" (4/77 UK 8). With Maggie Bell, she is certainly among the best British female rock singers.

Faron Young 1932 US country singer. 'The Young Sheriff' recorded from 1951 and regularly hit the country charts from 1953. He notched up a total of 85 hits, including five No. 1s He also hit the pop charts with "Hello Walls" (5/61 US 12) and "It's Four In The Morning" (7/72 UK 3). In addition to that he appeared in several westerns and was the founder and publisher of the newspaper, Music City News, in Nashville.

Ralph Edmond Stanley 1927 US country singer and banjo player, who formed the Clinch Mountain Boys with his older brother Carter Glen in 1946. They became the Stanley Brothers. From 1947, until Carter Glen's death in 1966, they made some of the best bluegrass records of all time. Their biggest hit was "How Far To Little Rock?" (3/60 C&W 17).

Foster Sylver 1962 US singer with the family group Sylvers. Initially, there were nine of them, before increasing to ten members; they formed in the wake of the success of the Jackson 5 and the Osmonds. Little Foster, aged 11 had a solo hit with "Misdemeanor" (6/73 US 22). Hits as Sylvers: "Boogie Fever" (2/76 US 1) and "Hot Line" (10/76 US 5).

Mike Peters 1959 UK singer, guitarist and songwriter, with the group Alarm, formed in 1981. Before that they had tried their luck as the punk band Toilets and as Seventeen. In October 1982 they released their first record. Their first success was "Where Were You Hidden When The Storm Broke" (1/84 UK 22) and their biggest hit was "Rain In The Summertime" (10/87 UK 18).

Juanita Curiel 1953 US singer, with the ladies disco troupe, Sugar & Spice, who finally renamed themselves Hot. They had a million seller with their biggest hit, "Angel In Your Arms" (2/77 US 6).

Roy Michaels 1942 US bass player and co-founder of Cat Mother & The All Night Newsboys, who played a danceable, relaxed folk-rock.

Jim 'Daryl' Gilmour 1958 Scottish born keyboard player and singer with the Canadian group Saga.

Deaths

Slim Gaillard 1991 US singer, pianist and songwriter; long-time European resident and inventor of the 'a-rooney' scat style. Born 1st January 1916.

Hits of the Day

1956	"Lisbon Antigua" Nelson Riddle US 4 weeks
1965	"I'll Never Find Another You" Seekers UK 2 weeks
1984	"Jump" Van Halen US 5 weeks
1989	"Belfast Child" Simple Minds UK 2 weeks

26th

Birthdays

Fats Domino 1928 US singer, songwriter and pianist. Real first name Antoine. Fats was influenced by Fats Waller and Albert Ammons. In the mid-1940s he joined the band of trumpeter Dave Bartholomew who recognized his talent and helped him to get a solo recording contract with Imperial Records in 1949. His very first records were hits in the US R&B charts, and so his first release, "The Fat Man" (2/50 R & B 1) became a million seller. He had his first hits in the pop charts with the two million sellers "Goin' Home" (6/52 US 30) and "Goin' To the River" (6/53 US 24). The broader white American public was introduced to Fats after Pat Boone had a No. 1 chart hit with Fats' title "Ain't That A Shame" (7/55 US 10 for Fats). The biggest hits for Fats were "I'm In Love Again" (4/56 US 3; 7/56 UK 12), "Blueberry Hill" (10/56 US 2; 12/56 UK 6), "Blue Monday" (1/57 US 5; 3/57 UK 23), "I'm Walkin'" (3/57 US 4; UK 19), "Valley Of Tears" (5/57 US 6; 7/57 UK 25), "Whole Lotta Loving" (11/58 US 6), "I Want To Walk You Home" (8/59 US 8; 10/59 UK 14), "Be My Guest" (10/59 US 8; 12/59 UK 19) and "Walking To New Orleans" (6/60 US 6; UK 19). Fats wrote most of his hits with Dave Bartholomew and was the pianist on records by colleagues like Lloyd Price and Joe Turner. In addition, Fats appeared in the movies, *Shake, Rattle & Roll, Jamboree, The Big Heat*, and *The Girl Can't Help It*.

Johnny Cash 1932 US country singer, guitarist and songwriter, who is listed as the third best country artist of all time, with a total of more than 110 solo hits. From 1951 to 1954, he was in the US Air Force, three years of that in the Federal Republic of Germany in Landsberg am Lech. It was here that he learned songwriting, playing the guitar, as well as forming his first group, the Landsberg Barbarians. He began his recording career with Sun Records in 1955 shortly after Elvis Presley. The first hits were "I Walk The Line" (9/56 US 17) and "Guess Things Happen That Way" (6/58 US 11). Just like Presley, however, he wasn't to be really successful until leaving Sun. On 14th July, 1958 Cash cut his first records for CBS. Up to 1986, he was to record 1,450 tracks. His biggest pop hit was the million seller, recorded live at San Quentin Prison, "A Boy Named Sue" (7/69 US 2; 9/69 UK 4). From 1961 he worked a great deal with June Carter, whom he married in 1968. His daughter Rosanna and his step-daughter Carlene Carter are both successful country singers.

Mitch Ryder 1945 US singer and songwriter. Real name William Levise. In 1963, after a stint with the Preps, he formed Billy Lee & The Rivieras, who made their first record that year. In July 1965 they wanted a new name and so they picked Mitch Ryder at random from the telephone directory; in order to make the name sound a bit more funky, they added Detroit Wheels, thus making Mitch Ryder & The Detroit Wheels. Their first hit "Jenny Takes A Ride" (12/65 US 10; 2/66 UK 33) was a combination of two R&B classics, "C. C. Rider" and "Jenny Jenny". Further hits were "Devil With A Blue Dress On & Good Golly Miss Molly" (10/66 US 4), and "Sock It To Me Baby"

(2/67 US 6). From mid-1967, Mitch attempted a solo career; his biggest hit was "What Now My Love" (9/67 US 30). His band Detroit Wheels released three further singles without him and then split up. In 1971 he formed a new band, Detroit. Further records followed, but success did not.

Bob 'Bear' Hite 1945 US lead singer, harmonica player and co-founder of Canned Heat in 1966. After a public appearance at the Monterey Pop Festival on the 16th June, 1967, he got a recording contract with Liberty Records. In October of the same year, the group's first album appeared. Hits: "On The Road Again" (7/68 UK 8; US 16), "Going Up The Country" (12/68 US 11; UK 19) and "Let's Work Together" (1/70 UK 2; 10/70 US 26). After guitarist Al Wilson left the band (dying shortly afterwards), Canned Heat sank into oblivion. Bob Hite died 5th April, 1981.

Betty Hutton 1921 US singer, real name Betty June Thornberg. Hollywood musical star in the 40s and 50s, she was in *Annie Get Your Gun* (1950). In 1938 she was singing in Vincent Lopez' band. He changed her surname to Hutton and she had a hit with "Igloo" (7/39 US 15). After appearing in the Broadway musicals *Two For The Show* and *Panama Hattie* in 1940, she went to Hollywood. She had her first main part in *The Fleet's In* (1942). From 1944 she recorded as a soloist and had her biggest hit with "Doctor, Lawyer, Indian Chief" (12/45 US 1) and the million seller "I Wish I Didn't Love You So" (9/47 US 5). Her nickname was 'Blonde Bombshell'.

Michael Bolton 1954 US singer and songwriter who wrote for Kenny Rogers, Jefferson Starship and Jennifer Rush. He formed his first rockband at the age of 13. At 15 (his mother had to sign for him) he had his first recording contract. After two unsuccessful albums, he became a member of Blackjack with whom he made another two albums, neither sold particularly well. In 1983, he launched a solo career. His greatest hit was "How Am I Supposed To Live Without You" (10/89 US 1).

Jackie Gleason 1916 US singer, composer, and orchestra leader who played on countless albums. "Melancholy Serenade" became a million seller for him (3/53 US 22), as the theme music for the TV series *The Honeymooners*. In addition, Jackie was an actor in several films, had his own TV show and was considered to have a pithy wit. He died 24th June, 1987.

Sandie Shaw 1947 UK singer. Real name Sandra Goodrich. Between 1964 and 1969, she had 8 Top Ten hits in the UK. The best were "(There's) Always Something There To Remind Me" (10/64 UK 1), "Long Live Love" (5/65 UK 1) and "Puppet On A String" (3/67 UK 1), the

winner of the Eurovision Song Contest in 1967. In 1984 she made a comeback with "Hand In Glove" (4/84 UK 27) assisted by Morrissey & The Smiths.

Paul Cotton 1943 US guitarist and singer. He began with Illinois Speed Press and joined Poco in November, 1970. His influence gave the band a much harder edge to their sound. After the group split up in October 1984, he went to Nashville as a songwriter and session musician.

Chic Hetti 1930 US singer with the Playmates who were successful from 1958 to 1962. Biggest hit was "Beep Beep" (11/58 US 4). The Playmates were what is widely termed as a novelty act.

John Jon 1961 UK singer. Real name John Andrew Foster. First, John was a member of Bust, then joined Bronski Beat as a replacement for Jimmy Somerville. Hit: "Hit That Perfect Beat" (11/85 UK 3).

Jim Crichton 1953 Canadian bass player, keyboard player and songwriter with Saga.

Bernie Bremond 1963 Australian saxophonist and singer with Johnny Diesel & The Injectors.

Hits of the Day

1966 "These Boots Are Made For Walking" Nancy Sinatra US 1 week
1969 "Where Do You Go To My Lovely" Peter Sarstedt UK 4 weeks
1973 "Blockbuster" Sweet
1977 "New Kid In Town" Eagles US 1 week

27th

Birthdays

Guy Mitchell 1927 US singer and actor of Yugoslavian origin. Real name Al Cernik. Even as a child he had recorded – he sang live for radio stations. After the war he became a singer in the band of Carmen Cavallaro. In 1950 Mitch Miller discovered him, and took him to CBS. Guy was to use Miller's orchestra on all his later records. Hits: "My Heart Cries For You" (12/50 US 2), "My Truly Truly Fair" (6/51 US 2), "Pittsburgh, Pennsylvania" (3/52 US 4), "She Wears Red Feathers" (2/53 UK 1), "Look At That Girl" (8/53 UK 10), "Singing The Blues" (10/56 US 1;

12/56 UK 1), "Rock-A-Billy" (4/57 US 10; UK 1) and "Heartaches By The Number" (10/59 US 1, UK 5). Guy appeared as an actor in films like the western *Whispering Smith* and on television in *The Guy Mitchell Show* (1957/58).

Steve Harley 1951 UK singer and songwriter, real name Steven Nice. In 1973 he placed an ad in the newspaper looking for another member for his group called Cockney Rebel. The first two hits appeared under that group name, "Judy Teen" (5/74 UK 5) and "Mr. Soft" (8/74 UK 8). After that the group was re-named Steve Harley & Cockney Rebel. They had a hit with "Make Me Smile (Come Up And See Me)" (2/75 UK 1); eventually Steve Harley disbanded the group. He had one further hit with "Here Comes The Sun" (7/76 UK 10).

Neal Schon 1954 US guitarist who became a member of Santana in January 1971 and then became a founder member of Journey in February 1973. On the side he guested on records by Azteca, Sammy Hagar and Joe Cocker. In addition he worked on the 'Schon & Hammer' project, with pianist Jan Hammer, in 1981/82. In 1984 Neal released a live-album, which included Sammy Hagar, Kenny Aaronson and Mike Shrieve.

Ben Webster 1909 US jazz musician, tenor saxophonist, pianist, and composer. He started as a pianist and then changed to tenor sax on the advice of Lester Young. In 1933 he started with Fletcher Henderson, playing with Cab Calloway among others. He became a permanent member of the Duke Ellington Band from 1939 until 1943, and again in 1948/49. His lyrical solo in "Cotton Tail" has become a classic. He also played on countless records by Oscar Peterson, Coleman Hawkins, Charlie Parker, Dizzy Gillespie, Teddy Wilson, Woody Hermann and Ella Fitzgerald. He was one of the most important tenor saxophonists of the swing-era. Ben died in Copenhagen on 20th September, 1973.

Garry Christian 1955 UK lead singer and songwriter of the Christians. With his brothers Henry and Roger he tried to land a recording contract from 1974. In 1974 they appeared in the talent contest 'Opportunity Knocks' under the name of Natural High. Before they finally got a recording contract in March 1986 as Christians, they called themselves Equal Temperaments and Gems. Hits: "Forgotten Town" (1/87 UK 22), "Idle World" (12/87 UK 14), "Harvest For The World" (10/88 UK 8) and "Words" (12/89 UK 18).

Clarence Joseph Garlow 1911 US blues musician and songwriter. His style of playing accordion influenced Clifton Chenier, the 'King of Zydeco Music'. Further pseudonyms of Clarence, Parran and Bon Ton.

Dexter Gordon 1923 US jazz saxophorist and composer. He started with the Lionel Hampton Band, then joined the Louis Armstrong Band, and then, Billy Eckstine's. From the mid-1940s, he toured the USA and Europe as a soloist. In 1986, he appeared in Tavernier's film *Round Midnight*, for which he was nominated for an Oscar. He died in Philadelphia on April 26, 1990.

Paul Humphries 1960 UK pianist and singer, with Orchestral Manoeuvres In The Dark(OMD).

Kevin Raleigh 1952 US singer and keyboard player, who, in 1978, joined the Michael Stanley Band, formed in 1974.

Adrian Smith 1957 UK guitarist, with Iron Maiden.

Vic Faulkner 1956 UK bass player, with Hello.

Hits of the Day

1954 "Secret Love" Doris Day US 8 weeks
1961 "Pony Time" Chubby Checker US 3 weeks
1964 "Anyone Who Had A Heart" Cilla Black UK 3 weeks
1984 "Relax" Frankie Goes To Hollywood
1988 "Father Figure" George Michael US 2 weeks

28th

Birthdays

Joe South 1940 US singer, guitarist, and songwriter. At the age of 12, Joe appeared regularly as a guitarist on a country radio station in his hometown of Atlanta. In 1957 he played in Pete Drake's band, and in 1958 he released his first solo record, "The Purple People Eater Meets The Witchdoctor" (7/58 US 47). In the early 60s he became a session guitarist in Nashville and in Muscle Shoals. He accompanied such artists as Marty Robbins, Eddy Arnold, Bob Dylan, Aretha Franklin and Simon & Garfunkel. At the same time he was composing for the Tams, "Untie Me" (10/62 US 60), and for Billy Joe Royal, "Down In the Boondocks" (7/65 US 9; 10/65 UK 38). His biggest hits as an artist were "Games People Play" (2/69 US 12; UK 6) and "Walk A Mile In My Shoes" (1/70 US 12). In 1971 Joe left the music business. This was partly because of the constant pressure of deadlines, and also because of his brother Tommy's death, which affected him deeply. For a while, he retired to Maui, Hawaii. He did not record again until 1975. No more chart hits. At the end of 1970, Lynn Anderson reached No. 1 in the US country charts with his composition "Rose Garden".

Brian Jones 1942 UK lead guitarist with the Rolling Stones until June, 1969. Some time later, on 3rd July, 1969, he was found dead in his swimming pool. Full name Lewis Brian Hopkins-Jones. Although he did not write for the group, he was the one who contributed to the 'bad boys' image of the band. Brian had already had drug problems in the early days of the Rolling Stones he took his first overdose in 1964. In addition, he was an alcoholic and took tablets to combat alcoholism. By 1967 he had been in hospital twice with nervous breakdowns. All this and his asthma prevented the Stones from touring in 1968. Added to which, he was obsessed by the conviction that his success was only due to his appearance, and that he had no talent. He also believed that Keith, Mick and Andrew Oldham were conspiring against him. His replacement was Mick Taylor who had previously played with John Mayall's Bluesbreakers.

John Fahey 1939 US guitarist, banjo player, songwriter, who obtained his Ph.D. with a thesis on the blues musician Charley Patton, record company owner, designer of album covers, and talent scout. (He discovered and recorded guitarist Leo Kottke). Extremely versatile and a true innovator.

Cindy Wilson 1957 US singer, guitarist, with the B 52s, formed in October, 1976. The group's name is derived from a Southern nickname for the 'highly-coiffed' hairstyle also called 'beehive' which is kept in position with masses of hairspray. Their first album appeard in the mid-1970s. Biggest hits: "Rock Lobster" (8/79 UK 37; 10/87 RE-UK 12), "Love Shack" (9/89 US 3) and "Roam" (12/89 US 3).

Barbara Acklin 1944 US R & B singer who cut her first record as Barbara Allen. Her biggest hit was "Love Makes A Woman" (7/68 US 15). In the mid-1960s she could often be heard as a background singer for the Chess label.

Svend Asmussen 1916 Danish violinist who was on tour for many years with the group Swe-Danes and Alice Babs until 1961. Even after that he often worked with Alice Babs. He also made records with Toots Thielemans, Stephane Grappelli and Jean-Luc Ponty.

Randy Jackson 1955 US singer, guitarist and pianist, with the trio Zebra formed in 1975. Before that he was with

groups like Shepherd's Bush, an acoustic duo with Felix Hanemann and Maelstrom.

Eddie Manion 1952 US saxophonist with Southside Johnny & Asbury Dukes.

Marty Sanders 1941 US lead guitarist with Jay & The Americans.

Marcus Lillington 1967 UK guitarist and songwriter with Breathe.

Philip Gould 1957 UK drummer with Level 42 until December 1987.

Deaths

David Byron 1985 UK singer for Uriah Heep and soloist. Born 29th Jan., 1947.

Bobby Bloom 1974 US singer who shot himself in a motel in Hollywood. After his hit "Montego Bay" (8/70 UK 3; US 8), he couldn't manage another hit which is thought to be the reason for his suicide. Another version is that the shooting was an accident; at any rate, Bobby did not live to see his number become a hit for the British group Amazulu in 1986.

Frankie Lymon 1968 US singer with the group Frankie Lymon & The Teenagers. He was just 25 years old when he died of an overdose of heroin. Born 30th September, 1942.

Manfred Weissleder 1980 It was he who established the Hamburg 'Star Club' and recruited all sorts of groups from Britain, including the Beatles. Weissleder was only 50 when he died.

Joe Vann 1984 US singer with the Duprees. Born on 3rd April, 1943.

Hits of the Day

1942 "Moonlight Cocktail" Glenn Miller US 10 weeks
1958 "Magic Moments" Perry Como UK 8 weeks
1968 "Cinderella Rockafella" Esther & Abi Ofarim UK 3 weeks
1970 "Bridge Over Troubled Waters" Simon & Garfunkel US 6 weeks
1976 "Theme From S. W. A. T." Rhythm Heritage US 1 week
1981 "I Love A Rainy Night" Eddie Rabbitt US 2 weeks

Miscellany

1966 The Closure of the Cavern Club, in which the Beatles were introduced in January 1961 by disc jockey Bob Wooler: they appeared 282 times. Souvenir hunters make sure that the stage on which the Fab Four stood is ripped out and sold in tiny pieces. The City of Liverpool thought about it a long time before deciding to clear the site. After the site at 8 Matthew Street had been used as a parking lot for a long time, the Club was pulled down finally in 1973. 50 paces further along, at 18 Matthew Street, Liverpool L2 6 RE, Merseyside, was where the Original Beatles Museum 'Cavern Mecca' was situated. Today a shopping centre, Cavern Walks, is on the site, in which there is a New Cavern Club. Liverpool honoured the Beatles with Beatles City in Sell Street, a small side road off Hanover Street. This is where the John Lennon Worldwide Memorial Club has been since 1980.

16th Jan., 1957 Opening of the club by Alan Sytner. At the beginning a pure jazz club which allowed only a little skiffle music. From June 1960 onwards R 'n' R bands were allowed to play there occasionally. The Club became the birthplace of the emerging 'Merseybeat'.

21st March, 1961 The Beatles appeared in the Cavern Club for the first time. From August 1961, they played there regularly.

9th November, 1961 Brian Epstein visited the Cavern Club for the first time, in order to listen to the Beatles.

18th August, 1962 Ringo Starr played for the first time as an official member of the Beatles.

3rd August, 1963 The Beatles appeared in the Cavern Club for the last time. On 28th Feb., 1966 the Cavern Club closed because of financial difficulties, but opened again during the course of the year.

10th Feb., 1973 The long-closed Cavern Club received another three months grace by British Rail, which wanted to pull it down in order to build an underground. It was hoped to save at least the stage area.

27th May, 1973 The Cavern Club is pulled down. Mick Jagger about the Cavern Club and the Star Club, 'Went and had a look at the Cavern Club. It's a shithole. All sealed up now. Just like the Star Club in Hamburg. The Beatles hung out there, and here, before they became megalomaniacs. Now, all that's left is the Beat.'

29th

Birthdays

Jimmy Dorsey 1904 US alto saxophonist, clarinetist and bandleader. He started out with his brother Tommy in 1928 as the Dorsey Brothers Orchestra, they had a total of 25 hits up to 1935. The biggest were "Lullaby Of Broadway" (4/35 US 1), with singer Bob Crosby, and "Chasing Shadows" (6/35 US 1), with singer Bob Eberle. With the change in musical taste in the USA, the brothers went their separate ways. Jimmy Dorsey managed exactly 100 hits from 1935 to 1950. The biggest of those were "Is It True What They Say About Dixie?" (5/36 US 1), "Change Partners" (10/38 US 1), "The Breeze And I" (5/40 US 1), "I Hear A Rhapsody" (1/41 US 1), "High On A Windy Hill" (2/41 US 1), "Amapola" (3/41 US 1), "My Sister And I" (5/41 US 1), "Green Eyes" (5/41 US 1), "Maria Elena" (5/41 US 1), "Blue Champagne" (7/41 US 1), "Tangerine" (4/42 US 1) and "Besame Mucho" (1/44 US 1). In 1953 the brothers joined up again. In January 1957 Jimmy signed another recording contract without his brother, and in April the title "So Rare" (2/57 US 2) hit the charts. Jimmy died 12th June, 1957.

Gretchen Christopher 1940 US singer who appeared in a duo with her friend Barbara Ellis. Then, when third member Gary Troxel joined them they called themselves Two Girls And A Guy. After they recorded "Come Softly To Me" (3/59 US 1; UK 6), they thought their group name was too complicated and they called themselves Fleetwoods. They had further hits until 1963: "Mr. Blue" (9/59 US 1), and "Tragedy" (4/61 US 10).

March

1st

Birthdays

Glenn Miller 1904 US bandleader, who formed his own band in 1937. Before that he played trombone with Ben Pollack, Red Nichols, Benny Goodman and the Dorsey Brothers. In 1935 he became the 'de facto' leader of Ray Noble's American band. On the side he arranged music for Glenn Gray and other popular orchestras of the era. By late 1941, he had established himself as a national celebrity in the USA. Between 1938 and 1948 he had about 130 records in the American charts. His biggest hits – all million bestsellers – were "Moonlight Serenade" (7/39 US 3; 3/54 UK 12; 1/76 RE-UK 13), "In The Mood" (10/39 US 1), "Tuxedo Junction" (2/40 US 1), "Pennsylvania 6-5000" (7/40 US 5), "Chattanooga Choo Choo" (9/41 US 1), "A String Of Pearls" (1/42 US 1), "Moonlight Cocktail" (2/42 US 1), and "(I've Got A Girl In) Kalamazoo" (8/42 US 1). In September 1942 Glenn Miller joined the US. Air Force and formed the most famous military orchestra of World War II. During 1944 he entertained the American troops in Britain, and on the 15th December, 1944, Glenn flew from London to Paris in a light aircraft to make preparations for a Christmas concert. His plane was never seen again – it is assumed to have crashed in the Channel.

Dinah Shore 1917 US singer, real first names Francis Rose. Between 1940 and 1957 she had more than 80 hits in the US pop charts. She had her first million seller with "Blues In The Night" (2/42 US 4); among her other hits were "I'll Walk Alone" (7/44 US 1), "The Gypsy" (4/46 US 1), "Anniversary Song" (3/47 US 1) and "Buttons And Bows" (9/48 US 1). Between 1951 and 1962 she had her own TV show, and in the 1970s she hosted the popular talkshow, *Dinah's Place*.

Harry Belafonte 1927 US singer and songwriter, real first names Harold George. He made his first recordings in 1949. Shortly after that, he specialised in folk music. He had his first hit with "Jamaica Farewell" (10/56 US 14). A perennial Christmas favourite was "Mary's Boy Child" (12/56 US 12; 11/57 UK 1; 11/58 RE-UK 10; 12/59 RE-UK 30). When Calypso became popular in the latter half of the 1950s, he re-worked all the popular standards like "Banana Boat (Day-O)" (1/57 US 5; 3/57 UK 2), and "Island In The Sun" (6/57 US 25; UK 2). However the memorable "Try To Remember" never got into the charts. Between 1953 and 1974 Harry appeared in 8 films, most impressive part being in *Carmen Jones* (1955). In 1987 he took the late Danny Kaye's position in UNICEF.

Jerry Fisher 1942 US singer who joined Blood, Sweat & Tears briefly as a replacement for David Clayton-Thomas in November, 1972.

Tony Ashton 1944 UK pianist, singer, and songwriter, who started out in the early 60s with the Remo Four. In 1968 he was co-founder of Ashton, Gardner & Dyke. Biggest hit: "Resurrection Shuffle" (1/71 UK 3; 6/71 US 40). Between September 1972 and October 1973 he was a member of Family, and from August 1976 to September 1977 he was with the Deep Purple off-shoot, Paice, Ashton & Lord. He helped countless musicians with their records by playing for them, and is highly-rated as a producer. In the early 1980s he was presenter of a music programme on UK TV Channel 4.

Mike d'Abo 1944 UK singer, pianist, and songwriter. He was a member of the Band Of Angels, and then, when Paul Jones left Manfred Mann in July 1966, he joined the group. Their biggest hits in Mike's time were "Ha Ha Said The Clown" (3/67 UK 4)s and "Mighty Quinn" (1/68 UK 1; 3/68 US 10). In June 1969 he left Manfred Mann to play Herod in *Jesus Christ Superstar*. Then he formed the duo Smith & d'Abo with Mike Smith; it was unsuccessful, as were the following solo albums.

Roger Daltrey 1945 UK singer. While he was always referred to as the "Voice", Pete Townsend was the 'leader' of the Who, therefore, the hits and history of the group are under Pete's entry, 13th May. As a soloist, Roger was successful with "Giving It All Away" (4/73 UK 5), and with "Without Your Love" (9/80 US 20). Roger also had a successful acting career in the films, *Tommy, Lisztomania* and *McVicar*.

John Carroll 1957 US guitarist, pianist, and singer with Fat City, which became the Starland Vocal Band; they had their only hit and million seller with "Afternoon Delight" (5/76 US 1; 8/76 UK 18).

Nik Kershaw 1958 UK musician and songwriter. His first record appeared in 1983, "I Won't Let The Sun Go Down On Me" (11/83 UK 47; 6/84 RE-UK 2), which only became a hit after the second single was released, "Wouldn't It Be Good" (2/84 UK 4). Further hits were. "The Riddle" (11/84 UK 3), "Wide Boy" (3/85 UK 9) and "Don Quixote" (8/85 UK 10).

Deaths

Gabor Szabo 1982 Hungarian jazz guitarist. Born 8th March, 1936.

Hits of the Day

1941	"Dream Valley" Sammy Kaye US 1 week
1947	"Open The Door, Richard" Three Flames US 1 week
1969	"Ob-La-Di-Ob-La-Da" Beatles
1975	"Best Of My Love" Eagles US 1 week
1980	"Atomic" Blondie UK 2 weeks
1986	"Kyrie" Mr. Mister US 2 weeks

2nd

Birthdays

Kurt Weill 1900 German composer, son of a Jewish cantor. Pupil of Engelbert Humperdinck and Ferruccio Busoni. He composed his first symphony in 1921. From 1926 he was involved with radical musical theatre. He wrote operas such as *The Protagonist* (1926), After that came a period of collabration with Bertolt Brecht: *The Threepenny Opera* (1928), Happy End (1929), and *The Rise And Fall of Mahogany City* (1930). In 1933 Weill emigrated to Paris first, and, then to the USA. His wife Lotte Lenya became a sympatic inter-preter of many of his songs, and 'Mack the Knife' from *The Threepenny Opera* has been covered by almost everyone at some point. He died on 3rd April, 1950 in New York.

Doc Watson 1923 US blues guitarist and songwriter, real first name Arthel.

Paul Dino 1939 US singer who had one hit, "Ginnie Bell" (1/61 US 38).

Keith Potger 1941 Australian guitarist with the Seekers, who was also in the original lineup of the New Seekers. Gradually he became involved with their production and management.

Tony Meehan 1942 UK drummer and songwriter with the Shadows during their halcyon days. Then he formed a duo with guitarist Jet Harris, also a member of the Shadows. Hits by the pair: "Diamonds" (1/63 UK 1), "Scarlett O'Hara" (4/63 UK 2) and "Applejack" (9/63 UK 4). After that he charted with "Song Of Mexico" (1/64 UK 39) credited to the Tony Meehan Combo.

Lou Reed 1943 US singer, guitarist and songwriter of the band Velvet Underground. Real name Louis Firbank. After the group broke up in 1970 he began a solo career. Hit, "Walk On The Wild Side" (2/73 US 16; 5/73 UK 10). His influence far exceeds his record sales, and is reflected in the devotion of his admirers.

Larry Carlton 1948 US guitarist and songwriter of the Crusaders from 1972 to 1977. Then he started a solo career while continuing to work as a session musician. His guitar work is featured on "The Theme From Hill Street Blues" (8/81 US 10) by Mike Post.

Rory Gallagher 1949 UK guitarist, singer and songwriter. He formed Taste in 1965, and then, after 1970, the Rory Gallagher Band. Rory was less of a singles artist, but more successful with his albums. He is reputedly charming but former band members vehemently disagree. Excellent live, though.

Eddie Money 1949 US singer and songwriter, real name Edward Mahoney. Before beginning a career as a singer, he was a policeman. His debut album appeared in 1978, which included his hit single "Baby Hold On" (2/78 US 11). Further hits were "Take Me Home Tonight" (8/86 US 4), "Walk On Water" (10/88 US 9) and "Peace In Our Time" (12/89 US 11).

Karen Carpenter 1950 US singer, who was the vocalist in the sibling-duo The Carpenters. Together with brother Richard (piano and keyboard) and the bass player Wes Jacobs she formed a jazz instrumental trio in 1965;

she played drums. After that the brother and sister team formed the group, Spectrum. In 1969, Karen and Richard sent a demo tape of their duo to Herb Alpert, proprietor of the record company A & M Records. He contracted them. Between 1970 & 1981 they recorded 20 Top Forty hits. The three most successful were "(They Long To Be) Close To You" (6/70 US 1; 9/70 UK 6), "Top Of The World" (10/73 US 1; UK 5) and "Please Mr. Postman" (11/74 US 1; 1/75 UK 2). By the late 1970s success was on the wane. Karen died on 4th February, 1983 of heart failure, probably caused by anorexia.

Dale Bozzio 1955 US singer and songwriter. In 1976 Dale was a Playboy Bunny; she continued to use this type of costume on stage during her musical career. With husband Terry, she worked with the Frank Zappa band. In 1980 she formed her own band, Missing Persons, but they never managed a hit single.

Jay Osmond 1955 US drummer with the sibling band: the Osmonds. Since then, he has been successful in the country charts with brothers Alan, Wayne, and Merrill.

Mark Evans 1956 Australian bass player with AC/DC from March 1974 to June 1977. He was replaced by Cliff Williams.

John Bon Jovi 1962 US singer and songwriter for the group Bon Jovi, formed in March 1983. Real name John Bongiovi. Their debut album appeared in January, 1984, and in 1987 they became the most successful American rock-band. Hits, "Runaway" (4/84 US 39), "You Give Love A Bad Name" (9/86 US 1; UK 14), "Wanted, Dead Or Alive" (4/87 US 7; UK 13), "Bad Medicine" (9/88 US 1; UK 17), "Born To Be My Baby" (11/88 US 3, UK 22), "I'll Be There For You" (2/89 US 1; 4/89 UK 18), "Lay Your Hands On Me" (6/89 US 7; 8/89 UK 18), and "Living In Sin" (10/89 US 9; 12/89 UK 35).

Deaths

Serge Gainsbourg 1991 French singer, actor and producer, born April 2nd, 1928.

Hits of the Day

1946 "Personality" Johnny Mercer US 2 weeks
1961 "Walk Right Back" Everly Brothers UK 3 weeks
1963 "Walk Like A Man" Four Seasons US 3 weeks
1967 "Release Me" Engelbert Humperdinck UK 6 weeks
1974 "Seasons In The Sun" Terry Jacks US 3 weeks

3rd

Birthdays

Little Junior Parker 1927 US singer and harmonica player, who was one of the early R & B artists to have success on the Sun label. Real first name, Herman. In the late 1940s he played with Sonny Boy Williamson and Howlin' Wolf, and in 1951, with the Beale Streeters, before forming his own group, the Blue Flames who made their first recordings in 1952. In 1953, now with Sun Records, he recorded the famous "Mystery Train", which was later covered by his Sun colleague Elvis Presley. He scored with "Feelin' Good" (10/53 R&B 5). During the 1960s he made soul and blues records. Hits: "Driving Wheel" (5/61 R&B 5), "In The Dark" (11/61 R&B 7) and "Annie Get Your Yo-Yo" (3/62 R&B 6). He died 18th November 1971.

Willie Chambers 1938 US guitarist and singer, one of the four Chambers Brothers, who had a hit with "Time Has Come Today" (8/68 US 11).

Mike Pender 1942 UK lead guitarist and singer with the Searchers, formed in Liverpool in early 1960s. Complete surname, Pendergast. In common with the Beatles, the Searchers came to prominence in Hamburg. In 1963 when any Liverpudlian group had a good chance of success their recording career took off. Anthony Jackson was the lead singer of the band until August 1964, when he left the Searchers, Frank Allen of Cliff Bennett & The Rebel Rousers joined as replacement, but Mike took over as lead singer. In 1966, the hey-day of the 'Mersey Sound' was over. In the case of the Searchers, their main problem was that they only ever managed to get cover versions into the charts. The group was able to tour continuously due to their pedigree, but the lineup was constantly changing. Mike Pender stayed throughout and still tours as Mike Pender's Searchers.

Jance Garfat 1944 US bass player and singer with the Sir Douglas Quintet and Dr. Hook.

Dave Mount 1947 UK drummer with Mud.

Christopher Hughes 1954 UK drummer with Adam & The Ants

Deaths

Danny Kaye 1987 Died of heart failure. Born 18th January, 1913.

Hits of the Day

1951 "If", Perry Como US 8 weeks
1973 "Cum On Feel The Noize" Slade UK 4 weeks
1975 "I Can Help" Billy Swan
1979 "Heart Of Glass" Blondie
1984 "99 Red Balloons" Nena UK 3 weeks

4th

Birthdays

Miriam Makeba 1932 South African singer, who was married to Hugh Masekela. She is considered to be the 'Queen of African Chanson'. Hit: "Pata Pata" (10/67 US 12).

Eric Allandale 1936 UK trumpeter with Foundations.

Michael Wilson 1944 UK drummer with Dave Dee, Dozy, Beaky, Mick & Tich. He was Mick.

Bobby Womack 1944 US soul singer, guitarist and songwriter. Together with his four brothers he formed the gospel group Womack Brothers who were known as the Valentinos between 1962 and 1964. Hits: "Lookin' For A Love" (7/62 R&B 8) and "It's All Over Now" (6/64 R&B 94) the latter became a No. 1 hit for the Rolling Stones in the UK in 7/64. Then Bobby toured with Sam Cooke, and later married his widow Barbara. (Coincidentally his brother Cecil later married Sam Cooke's daughter Linda, and who became famous as Womack & Womack in the 1980s). In 1965 Bobby began a solo career, and worked as a session guitarist with Wilson Pickett, the Box Tops, Joe Tex, Aretha Franklin and Janis Joplin. Biggest hits: "Harry Hippie" (12/72 US 31) and "Lookin' For A Love" (2/74 US 10). Both titles were million sellers.

Dieter Meier 1945 Swiss film maker, script writer, and singer for Yello, who cut their debut album in 1980; they are one of the few groups from a German-speaking background to have lasting international success. Hits: "Vicious Games" (4/85), "Desire" (7/85), "Call It Love" (3/87) and "The Race" (8/88 UK 7).

Robert Raymond 1946 US bass player with Sugarloaf.

Chris Squire 1948 UK bass player, singer and songwriter with the band Yes, formed in 1968. They were one of the top album groups in the 1970s. In common with the other members of Yes, Chris made solo records too.

Shakin' Stevens 1948 UK singer, real name Michael Barratt. During the 1960s he was forming groups like The Denims and Shakin' Stevens & The Sunsets. In 1969 his group played alongside the Rolling Stones in London. In 1977 he played in *Elvis*. In 1980 he finally made an impression on the charts with "This Ole House" (2/81 UK 1), "You Drive Me Crazy" (5/81 UK 2), "Green Door" (7/81 UK 1), "Oh Julie" (1/82 UK 1), "The Shakin' Stevens EP" (12/82 UK 2), "A Love Worth Waiting For" (3/84 UK 2), "Merry Christmas Everyone" (12/85 UK 1) and, with Bonnie Tyler, "A Rockin' Good Way" (1/84 UK 5).

Chris Rea 1951 UK singer, guitarist and songwriter, who was voted 'Newcomer of the Year' in 1978 in the USA. His record "Fool (If You Think It's Over)" (7/78 US 12; 10/78 UK 30) was the clincher. However after a seven year lull, he returned in 1985 with "Stainsby Girls" (3/85 UK 26), "Let's Dance" (6/87 UK 12), "On The Beach Summer '88" (8/88 UK 12) and "Road To Hell, Part 2" (10/89 UK 10).

St. Clair L. Palmer 1954 UK singer with Sweet Sensation. Hit: "Sad Sweet Dreamer" (9/74 UK 1; 1/75 US 14).

Boon Gould 1955 UK guitarist with Level 42, who left the group in March 1987 to try his luck as a soloist.

Patsy Kensit 1968 UK singer, songwriter and actress with Eighth Wonder, who had their first hit in 1985. Hits: "I'm Not Scared" (2/88 UK 7) and "Cross My Heart" (6/88 UK 13).

Deaths

Mike Patto 1979 UK singer. Member of Timebox and Spooky Tooth among others. Born 22 September, 1942.

Richard Manuel 1986 US singer and pianist with The Band. After appearing on stage in Florida, he hanged himself in his hotel room. He was suffering from severe depression. Born 3rd April, 1943.

Lloyd 'Tiny' Grimes 1989 US guitarist whose career had started as a drummer, pianist and dancer. Born 7th July, 1916.

Hits of the Day

1944 "Besame Mucho" Jimmy Dorsey US 7 week
1967 "Ruby Tuesday" Rolling Stones US 1 week
1978 "Love Is Thicker Than Water" Andy Gibb US 2 weeks
1985 "You're My Heart, You're My Soul" Modern Talking
1989 "Lost In Your Eyes" Debbie Gibson US 3 weeks

5th

Birthdays

J. B. Lenoir 1929 US blues guitarist and singer. He recorded from the early 1950s onwards. Hit: "Mama, Talk To Your Daughter" (7/55 R&B 11). His best known records is "Eisenhower Blues" (1954). The British blues revivalist, John Mayall, always said that Lenoir was his idol. He died 29th April, 1967.

Tommy Tucker 1933 US singer and pianist, real name Robert Higgenbotham. Hit: "Hi-Heel Sneakers" (2/64 US 11; UK 23). Tommy died on 17th January, 1982, from inhaling toxic vapours while painting the floor in his New York house.

Paul Evans 1938 US singer and songwriter. He wrote "When" for the Kalin Twins and "Roses Are Red" for Bobby Vinton. Among his own hits were, "Seven Little Girls Sitting In The Back Seat" (9/59 US 9; 11/59 UK 25) and "Happy-Go-Lucky-Me" (5/60 US 10). After Paul's disappearance from the charts, he returned with "Hello, This Is Joanie" (12/78 UK 6).

Derek Skinner 1944 UK drummer who joined the Swedish group Spotnicks in 1963.

Murray Head 1946 UK singer, songwriter and actor, who was a member of the cast of *Jesus Christ Superstar* as Judas. Hit single: "Superstar" (1/70 US 74; 1/71 RE-US 14). He was the lead vocalist on "One Night In Bangkok" (11/84 UK 12; 2/85 US 3), from the musical Chess. His solo album SAY IT AIN'T SO (1975) was good, but unfortunately, not very successful.

Eddie Hodges 1947 US singer and actor. He played the part of Frank Sinatra's son in the film, *A Hole In The Head* (1959). Hits: "I'm Gonna Knock On Your Door" (6/61 US 12; 9/61 UK 37) and "(Girls, Girls, Girls) Made To Love" (6/62 US 14; 8/62 UK 37).

Clodagh Rodgers 1947 Irish singer. Her biggest hits were "Come Back And Shake Me" (3/69 UK 3), "Goodnight Midnight" (7/69 UK 4), and "Jack In The Box" (3/71 UK 4). The whole thing was over by 1971.

Eddy Grant 1948 UK singer, songwriter, guitarist, pianist and producer. Real first names, Edward Montague. He formed his first group with schoolfriends – rehearsals were a problem as Eddy was the only one who could play an instrument. In 1966 the group the Equals debuted, playing R&B, with Ska influences. They got a recording contract, but the first releases were flops.

Their first hit was "Baby Come Back" (5/68 UK 1; 9/68 US 32) originally a B-side. In 1972 Eddy left the Equals and set up his own production and record company, Ice. Solo hits: "Do You Feel My Love" (11/80 UK 8), "I Don't Wanna Dance" (10/82 UK 1), "Electric Avenue" (1/83 UK 2; 4/83 US 2), and "Gimme Hope Jo'Anna" (1/88 UK 7).

Gary Grainger 1952 UK guitarist and drummer with Strider. He toured with the Faces, and then with Rod Stewart's band, where he wrote several hits.

Andy Gibb 1958 UK singer and younger brother of the brothers Gibb of the Bee Gees. Real first names, Andrew Roy. Between 1977 & 1981 his solo career was very successful in the USA: "I Just Wanna Be Your Everything" (4/77 US 1; 6/77 UK 26), "(Love Is) Thicker Than Water" (11/77 US 1) and "Shadow Dancing" (4/78 US 1). In the 1980s, however, he failed to sustain his run of hits. In 1983 he played one of the main parts in *Joseph And The Amazing Technicolor Dreamcoat*. On 10th March, 1988, while in the UK and having just signed a new recording contract with Island, he died in an Oxford hospital; it was often alleged that he had dabbled with drugs: the official cause of death was given as heart failure.

Deaths

Cowboy Copas, Patsy Cline, Hawkshaw Hawkins 1963 US country stars, who were on their way to Nashville from Kansas City, after giving a benefit concert for the widow of DJ Cactus Jack Call who had recently died in a car crash. Their private plane crashed near Dyersburg, Tennessee, killing all passengers.

John Belushi 1982 US singer, film actor and comedian. Member of the Blues Brothers. Died after taking a drug overdose. Born 24th January, 1949.

Hits of the Day

1949	"I've Got My Love To Keep Me Warm" Les Brown US 1 week
1949	"I Powder Your Face With Sunshine" Evelyn Knight US 1 week
1966	"Ballad Of The Green Berets" Barry Sadler US 5 weeks
1977	"Love Theme From A Star Is Born" Barbra Streisand US 3 weeks
1983	"Billie Jean" Michael Jackson US 7 weeks & UK 1 week

Miscellany

1960 Not since General Douglas McArthur had returned to the USA in 1945 after the surrender of the Japanese troops had another soldier created such a furore in the press as did Elvis Presley's discharge from the Army. After two years of military service he was discharged with the rank of sergeant at Fort Dix, New Jersey. A little later the album ELVIS IS BACK was released and in 1960, the film and record *G. I. Blues* followed.

6th

Birthdays

Walter 'Furry' Lewis 1893 US blues guitarist and harmonica player. He made records from the 1920s. Died 14th September, 1981.

Bob Wills 1905 US country singer, fiddler and songwriter. 'King of Western Swing'. In 1929 he formed his first group, the Wills Fiddle Band, which later became the Light Crust Doughboys. In 1933 he formed the Texas Playboys, who came to prominence in 1939. Especially his composition "San Antonio Rose" (6/39 US 15) and the subsequent reworking "New San Antonio Rose" (11/40 US 11; 3/43 RE-US 19) made him known nationally. Further hits were "We Might As Well Forget It" (9/44 US 11) and "You're From Texas" (11/44 US 14). Between 1934 & 1958, he had his own radio show in Tulsa and appeared in several westerns, like many of his C&W colleagues. In 1962, 1964, 1969 and 1973 he suffered a series of heart attacks; the last one in December 1973 sent him into a coma. He never came round and died on 13th May, 1975.

Wes Montgomery 1925 US jazz guitarist. Real first names John Leslie. He quickly developed his unique technique, thereby influencing a whole generation of other musicians. He started out in 1948 with Lionel Hampton, cutting his first solo records in 1957. He died on 15th June, 1968.

Sylvia Robinson 1936 US singer, who, with Mickey Baker, as Mickey & Sylvia, charted with "Love Is Strange" (1/57 US 11). Her maiden name was Vanderpool. As early as 1950 she was recording as Little Sylvia. She worked with McHouston 'Mickey' Baker until 1962, when she married Joe Robinson, the owner of All Platinum/Vibration Records. She appeared as a soloist in the charts on the Vibration label with the million seller "Pillow Talk" (3/73 US 3). Since then, she has founded the Sugarhill label, which for many years produced some of the best rappers in Harlem and the Bronx. In specialist circles Sylvia is considered to be the most dynamic black woman in the music business.

Flora Purim 1942 Brazilian singer, guitarist and percussionist. Airto Moreira taught her drumming then they married, cutting several records together. She also recorded with Miles Davis and Return to Forever.

David Gilmour 1944 UK guitarist and songwriter. He started out in 1966 with the group Jokers Wild and joined Pink Floyd as replacement for Syd Barrett in 1968. His first solo album was released in June 1978, and the second one in March 1984. After that, it seemed that Pink Floyd had died for good, but in 1987, it was David, in particular, who, with Nick Mason, made sure that Pink Floyd carried on.

Mickey Jupp 1944 UK singer, guitarist and songwriter, who wrote many great songs for himself as a soloist and for his group Legend – unfortunately, he was never successful in either capacity.

Mary Wilson 1944 US singer. With Diana Ross and Florence Ballard she formed the Primettes in 1959, who became the Supremes in 1961. Whereas the other members of the group voluntarily left or were replaced, Mary stayed the longest. Even in 1978 she was touring with Karen Ragland and Karen Jackson in the UK as the Supremes. After the tour, she was prohibited from using the name any longer. In the autumn of 1979 she released a solo album, and in 1984 her autobiography, *Dreamgirl: My Life As A Supreme* was published.

Hugh Grundy 1945 UK drummer with the Zombies.

Tony Klatka 1946 US trumpeter for Woody Herman and Blood, Sweat & Tears.

Kiki Dee 1947 UK singer, real name Pauline Matthews. For years she recorded without success. Then came her first hit "Amoureuse" (11/73 UK 13), and then "I've Got The Music In Me" (9/74 UK 19; US 12). She had an international hit with Elton John, "Don't Go Breaking My Heart" (7/76 UK & US 1).

Hits of the Day

1943	"I've Heard That Song Before" Harry James US 13 weeks	
1965	"My Girl" Temptations US 1 week	
1971	"Baby Jump" Mungo Jerry UK 2 weeks	
1976	"I Love To Love" Tina Charles UK 3 weeks	
1976	"Love Machine Part 1" Miracles US 1 week	
1982	"The Lion Sleeps Tonight" Tight Fit UK 3 weeks	
1989	"Something's Gotten Hold Of My Heart" Mark Almond & Gene Pitney	

7th

Birthdays

Danyel Gérard 1941 Real name, Gérard Daniel Kherlakian, son of an Armenian father and an Italian mother, was raised in Rio de Janeiro. When he was 12, he went to Paris. In 1954 he joined The Dangers. He made a name for himself as a composer of many French hits. Even Udo Jurgens and Caterina Valente sang his compositions. He had his first hit in France in 1962 with "Petit Gonzales". His biggest hit was "Butterfly" (9/71 UK 11).

Hamilton Bohannon 1942 US singer, songwriter and drummer. After studying at university, Hamilton worked as a music teacher. Between 1965 & 1967 he was the drummer in Stevie Wonder's band, then he became band leader and arranger for touring Motown artists. In 1974 he started his own career. Biggest hit: "Disco Stomp" (5/75 UK 6).

Chris White 1943 UK bass player, songwriter and producer. Member of the Zombies. In the late 80s the Zombies decided on a reunion. Chris was one of them.

Matthew Fisher 1946 UK pianist and songwriter, with Procol Harum. In 1968/69 he played with Joe Cocker, then he made solo records and accompanied Screaming Lord Sutch, Jerry Lee Lewis and Gary Brooker.

Peter Wolf 1946 US singer and songwriter. Real surname Blankfield. Peter worked as a disc-jockey for a Boston radio station and was renowned for his extensive knowledge of R&B. The band which evolved into the J. Geils Band in 1969 was called Hallucinations first. Peter joined them as vocalist in 1967. The first album by the band appeared in 1971, and on the 27th June, 1971, they played with the Allman Brothers, Mountain and the Beach Boys at the last performance at *Fillmore East*, when it closed down. Hits: "Must've Got Lost" (11/74 US 12), "Centerfold" (11/81 US 1; 2/82 UK 3) and "Freeze Frame" (2/82 US 4; 4/82 UK 27). In January 1983, Peter left the band and started a solo career. Hits: "Lights Out" (7/84 US 12) and "Come As You Are" (2/87 US 15).

Taylor Dayne 1962 US singer. Real name Lesley Wonderman. She started out as a dancer and, then joined the heavy metal group Felony. After that, she started her solo career. Hits: "Tell It To My Heart" (9/87 US 7; 1/88 UK 3), "Prove Your Love" (2/88 US 7; UK 8), "I'll Always Love You" (6/88 US 3), "Don't Rush Me" (11/88 US 2) and "With Every Beat Of My Heart" (10/89 US 5).

Deaths

Jack Anglin 1963 US country star with the duo Johnny & Jack. Anglin was on the way to the funeral of Patsy Cline when he died in a car crash on the way out of Nashville. Born 13th May, 1916.

Hits of the Day

1970 "Whole Lotta Love" Led Zeppelin
1979 "Wandrin' Star" Lee Marvin UK 3 weeks
1988 "Tell It To My Heart" Taylor Dayne

8th

Birthdays

Dick Hyman 1927 US composer, pianist and arranger. Dick played with Teddy Wilson, Benny Goodman, Lester Young, Mitch Miller and Percy Faith. Biggest hit with his jazz trio was "Moritat – A Theme From The Three-Penny Opera" (1/56 US 8; 3/56 UK 9).

Gabor Szabo 1936 Hungarian jazz guitarist and songwriter, who went to the USA in 1956. He died 1st March, 1982.

Ralph Ellis 1942 UK guitarist in the early days of the Swinging Blue Jeans. In 1966 he was replaced by Terry Sylvester (later of the Hollies).

Keef Hartley 1944 UK drummer with Rory Storm & The Hurricanes, Artwoods & the John Mayall Band. He formed the Keef Hartley Band in 1968, which became Dog Soldier in 1973. Throughout, Keef always worked as a studio musician with Michael Chapman and Vinegar Joe.

Mickey Dolenz 1945 US drummer and singer with the Monkees. As a child, this son of actor George Dolenz, played in the US TV-series *Circus Boy*. Then he released an unsuccessful single, and finally became a founder-member of the Monkees in October 1965. When three of the four original Monkees tried a comeback with "That Was Then, This Is Now" (6/86 US 20), Mickey was one of them.

Michael Allsup 1947 US guitarist with Three Dog Night.

Carol Bayer-Sager 1947 US singer and songwriter. As a teenager she penned "A Groovy Kind Of Love", which was a hit for the Mindbenders. Her songs became hits for the Doobie Brothers, Carly Simon, Frank Sinatra, Michael Jackson, Aretha Franklin and many others. She wrote the lyrics for many film scores. In 1982 she married Burt Bacharach. Carol had some hits on her own account with "You're Moving Out Today" (5/77 UK 6) and "Stronger Than Before" (5/81 US 30).

Randy Meisner 1947 US bass player and songwriter. Between 1964 & 1968 he played with the group Poor. In August 1968 he became a founder-member of Poco. He stayed until April 1969; in May 1969 he joined Rick Nelson's Stone Canyon Band where he stayed until June 1971, when he was recruited for Linda Ronstadt's touring band. In August 1971 they left Linda to form the Eagles. In September 1977, Randy left the Eagles to start a solo career. In November 1980 his first album appeared, HEARTS ON FIRE (2/81 US 19). At the reunion of Poco, Randy joined all the other original members.

Peggy March 1948 US singer. Born Margaret Battavio. Little Peggy March, she is considered to be the youngest singer ever to have had a No. 1 hit in the USA with "I Will Follow Him" (3/63 US 1).

Dave Lambert 1949 UK guitarist, singer and songwriter with the Strawbs.

Cheryl Baker 1954 UK singer with Bucks Fizz, who were formed in March 1981 for the Eurovision Song Contest. At this time, Cheryl had already had some experience with a similar group. In 1978 she was with the group Co-Co which had been formed for the same purpose. Co-Co and "Bad Old Days" (4/78 UK 13) did not win the Contest, but Bucks Fizz did with "Making Your Mind Up" (3/81 UK 1). After that, the four members decided to carry on with this artificially formed group. Further hits followed like "The Land Of Make Believe" (11/81 UK 1), "My Camera Never Lies" (3/82 UK 1), "Now These Days Are Gone" (6/82 UK 8) and "New Beginnings (Mamba Seyra)" (6/86 UK 8).

Clive Burr 1957 Drummer and singer with Iron Maiden between April 1980 & January 1983. His successor was Nicko McBrian who came from the group Trust, which, in turn, was the band Clive made an album with.

Pauline Murray 1958 UK singer with Penetrations.

Gary Numan 1958 UK singer, songwriter and keyboards. His first hit was credited to Tubeway Army, "Are Friends Electric" (5/79 UK 1). His other hits were credited to Gary Numan: "Cars" (9/79 UK 1; 3/80 US 9), "Complex" (11/79 UK 6), "We Are Glass" (5/80 UK 5), "I Die: You Die" (8/80 UK 6), "She Got Claws" (8/81 UK 6) and "We Take Mystery (To Bed)" (6/82 UK 9).

Richard Darbyshire 1960 UK singer, guitarist and songwriter with Living In A Box. Hits: "Living In A Box" (4/87 UK 5; 6/87 US 17), "Blow The House Down" (2/89 UK 10) and "Room In Your Heart" (9/89 UK 5).

Steve Grantley 1962 UK drummer, with Eighth Wonder.

Peter Gill 1964 UK drummer with Frankie Goes To Hollywood.

Deaths

Ron 'Pig-Pen' McKernan 1973 US keyboard player, singer and founder member of Grateful Dead. He was found dead in his hotel room. He was said to be suffering from a liver complaint. Born 8th September, 1946.

Stuart Hamblen 1989 US singer and actor. Died after an operation on a brain tumour. Born 20th October, 1908.

Hits of the Day

1947	"Anniversary Song" Dinah Shore US 2 weeks
1975	"If" Telly Savalas UK 2 weeks
1975	"Have You Never Been Mellow" Olivia Newton-John US 1 week
1976	"Mississippi" Pussycat
1986	"Chain Reaction" Diana Ross UK 3 weeks

9th

Birthdays

Billy Ford 1925 US singer in duets, with Lillie Bryant as Billy & Lillie. Hit: "La Dee Dah" (1/58 US 9).

Keely Smith 1928 US singer in the Louis Prima Band whom she married in 1953 to 1962. She had her first hit as a member of Louis Prima & His Orchestra, "Oh Babe!" (11/50 US 12); then she scored with Louis on "That Old Black Magic" (11/58 US 18). Shortly before that, Keely duetted with Frank Sinatra on "How Are Ya' Fixed For Love?" (5/58 US 22). In 1959 Louis and Keely appeared in the successful movie, *Hey Boy, Hey Girl*. As a soloist she had a hit in the UK with "You're Breaking My Heart" (3/65 UK 14).

Lloyd Price 1933 US R&B singer, pianist and song-writer. He formed his first band in 1949. From 1952, he hit the R&B charts with "Lawdy Miss Clawdy" (5/52 R&B 1), which featured Fats Domino on piano, and "Ooh Ooh Ooh" (11/52 R&B 4). Just as R&B caught on with white audiences in 1953, Lloyd was called up for military service. After his discharge in 1956, he set up his own record company, but signed a distribution deal with ABC Paramount. In 1963 he tried again, and setting up the record label Double-L. Hits: "Stagger Lee" (12/58 US 1; 2/59 UK 7), "Personality" (4/59 US 2; 6/59 UK 9) and "I'm Gonna Get Married" (8/59 US 3; UK 23).

Mickey Gilley 1936 US country singer and pianist, who cut his first record in 1953. In 1964 he set up his own record company, and between 1961 & 1989 he was co-owner of 'Gilley's' nightclub in Houston, which was featured in the film *Urban Cowboy*. As a singer Mickey had the bad luck to be a cousin of Jerry Lee Lewis, and as his style was similar to Jerry's, was constantly being accused of copying him. In 1974 he signed a recording contract with the Hugh Hefner's Playboy-label; he had four consecutive No. 1 hits in the C&W charts. He is still regularly in the C&W charts today and has had over 16 No. 1 hits. His biggest cross-over success was featured in the film *Urban Cowboy*, "Stand By Me" (5/80 C&W 1; US 22).

John Lee 1944 Australian singer with New World, who had five hits in the early 70s, the biggest being "Tom Tom Turnaround" (7/71 UK 6) and "Sister Jane" (5/72 UK 9).

Mark Lindsay 1944 US singer, saxophonist and song writer, with Paul Revere & The Raiders. His career started in 1959, when Mark and Paul Revere formed an instrumental duo; their first hit was, "Like, Long Hair" (3/61 US 38). But real success didn't arrive until 1966. Hits: "Kicks" (3/66 US 4), "Hungry" (6/66 US 6), "Good Thing" (12/66 US 4), and "Him Or Me – What's It Gonna Be" (4/67 US 5). Mark tried his luck as a soloist in 1969, and his biggest hit was the million seller "Arizona" (12/69 US 10). However, Mark remained connected with the Raiders by continuing the production chores.

Robin Trower 1945 UK guitarist, with the Paramounts, Procol Harum, Jude, and, finally, with his own Robin Trower Band.

Jim Cregan 1946 UK guitarist, bass player, and singer in various bands: Blossom Toes, Stud, Rod Stewart Band, Cockney Rebel among others. He is highly sought-after as a session musician.

Jimmy Fadden 1948 US guitarist and bass player, with the Nitty Gritty Dirt Band, and also as a session musician.

Jeffrey Osborne 1948 US singer, songwriter, and drummer. In 1970 he became a member of the R&B band LTD (Love, Togetherness & Devotion). They had their biggest hit with the million seller, "(Everytime I Turn Around) Back In Love Again" (10/77 US 4). In January 1982 Jeffrey decided to launch a solo career. He was successful immediately and became a fixture in the R&B charts. Pop hits: "On The Wings Of Love" (9/82 US 29; 6/84 UK 11), "Don't You Get So Mad" (7/83 US 25) and "Stay With Me Tonight" (11/83 US 30; 4/84 UK 18).

Martin David Fry 1958 UK singer and songwriter, with the group ABC, formed in 1980. Hits: "Poison Arrow" (2/82 UK 6; 1/83 US 25), "The Look Of Love" (5/82 UK 4; 8/82 US 18), "All Of My Heart" (9/82 UK 5) and "Be Near Me" (4/85 UK 26; 8/85 US 9). Both beautiful and successful was the hymn to Smokey Robinson, "When Smokey Sings" (6/87 UK 11; US 5). By the end of 1984, ABC were effectively a duo, with Martin and guitarist Mark White forming the nucleus and adding session musicians where appropriate.

Chris Thompson 1948 New Zealand singer, guitarist, and songwriter. In 1974 Chris came to Britain and two years later joined Manfred Mann's Earthband. He was lead vocalist on hits like "Blinded By The Light" (8/76 UK 6; 11/76 US 1) and "Davy's On The Road Again" (5/78 UK 6). In 1979 Thompson formed his own group Night. Their biggest hits were "Hot Summer Nights" (6/79 US 18) and "If You Remember Me" (8/79 US 17; 10/79 UK 42). After two albums he started a solo career, while continuing to work with Manfred Mann as an occasional vocalist. Solo records by Chris appeared continuously throughout the 1980s. His most notable achievement was "The Challenge (Face It)" (1989), title theme for the Wimbledon Tennis Championships 1989.

Trevor Burton 1949 UK guitarist with Move, Balls and, from 1976, the Steve Gibbons Band. As a session musician he worked with Gary Wright, Luther Grosvenor, Jim Capaldi and Paul Kossoff.

Hits of the Day

1959	"Venus" Frankie Avalon US 5 weeks
1974	"Jealous Mind" Alvin Stardust UK 1 week
1981	"Fade To Grey" Visage
1985	"You Spin Me Round (Like A Record)" Dead Or Alive UK 2 weeks
1985	"Can't Fight This Feeling" REO Speedwagon US 3 weeks

10th

Birthdays

Bix Beiderbecke 1903 US jazz cornet player, pianist and composer from Germany. Real first names Leon Bismarck. As an exponent of the Chicago style he was instrumental in the evolution of Swing. Bix gained his reputation as an excellent musician with Frankie Trumbauer. After that, he played with Jean Goldkette and Paul Whiteman. He, himself, charted on two separate occasions: "In A Mist" (2/28 US 20), a piano composition, and "At The Jazz Band Ball" (2/28 US 15). In 1950 a film of his life story was released entitled *Young Man With A Horn*. Bix died 6th August, 1931.

Jethro 1923 US string instrumentalist. Real name Kenneth Burns. He was known as Homer & Jethro in the duo with Henry Haynes. For hits, see under Homer on 27th July. Jethro died 2nd April, 1989.

Johnnie Allan 1938 US Cajun-Country musician. He did a wonderful '100 mph' version of Chuck Berry's "Promised Land".

Norman Blake 1938 US country session guitarist and singer. He worked with Kris Kristofferson, Johnny Cash and Bob Dylan, and made several solo albums.

Dean Torrence 1940 US singer. While still at school he formed the Barons with Jan Berry. Jan and Dean and a further Barons-member, Arnie Ginsburg, recorded "Jenny Lee" (6/58 US 8) in 1958 in Jan's garage. As Dean had to join the army for a six-month reserve exercise, the record appeared under the name of Jan & Arnie. When Dean returned from military service, Arnie went into the Navy. Jan & Dean signed a new contract with the record label Dore, which was owned by Herb Alpert. Hit: "Baby Talk" (8/59 US 10). They had their biggest hits with Liberty: "Surf City" (6/63 US 1; 8/63 UK 26) and "The Little Old Lady (From Pasadena)" (6/64 US 3). Jan & Dean are considered to be the co-founders of surf-sound. After Jan was involved in a serious road accident on 19th April, 1966, their career was over. Dean made some records as The Legendary Masked Surfers and opened a design studio in Hollywood. In 1978 the film biography *Dead Man's Curve* appeared and the duo staged a comeback.

Pete Nelson 1945 UK singer, with Flowerpot Men. Hit: "Let's Go To San Francisco" (8/67 UK 4). With White Plains. Hit: "My Baby Loves Lovin'" (2/70 UK 9; 4/70 US 13).

Tom Scholz 1947 US guitarist, keyboard player and songwriter from the band Boston, formed in 1975. Hits: "More Than A Feeling" (10/76 US 5; 1/77 UK 22), "Don't Look Back" (8/78 US 4; UK 43) and, after an eight year hiatus, "Amanda" (9/86 US 1).

Ted McKennan 1950 UK drummer with Tear Gas and later with the Sensational Alex Harvey Band, Rory Gallagher, Greg Lake and the Michael Schenker Group.

Tina Charles 1955 UK singer, real name Tina Hoskins. She started out with 5000 Volts, before making records as a soloist in 1976. Hits: "I Love To Love" (2/76 UK 1), "Dance Little Lady Dance" (8/76 UK 6) and "Dr. Love" (12/76 UK 4).

Bunny DeBarge 1955 US singer with the family group DeBarge.

Neneh Cherry 1964 US singer and songwriter, born in Stockholm. She is the step-daughter of jazz trumpeter Don Cherry. Without a doubt, Neneh can be counted amongst the greatest rising stars of 1989. In the early 80s she sang with UK new-wave group Rip Rig & Panic, which became Float Up CP. Following that she was a backing vocalist for the Slits and the The. Hits as a solo artist: "Buffalo Stance" (12/88 UK 3; 4/89 US 3) and "Man Child" (5/89 UK 5).

Deaths

Andy Gibb 1988 UK singer and younger brother of the Bee Gees. Official cause of death: heart failure. Born 5th March, 1958.

Doc Green 1989 US singer with the Drifters. Died of cancer. Born 8th October, 1934.

Hits of the Day

1951	"Be My Love" Mario Lanza	US 1 week
1960	"Poor Me" Adam Faith	UK 1 week
1962	"Hey, Baby" Bruce Channel	US 3 weeks
1979	"I Will Survive" Gloria Gaynor	US 2 weeks
1986	"Brother Louie" Modern Talking	

11th

Birthdays

Lawrence Welk 1903 US leader of polka and dance bands since the mid 1920s. Lawrence played accordion. He first appeared in the US pop charts in 1938. Hits: "I Won't Tell A Soul (I Love You)" (11/38 US 8), "The Moon Is A Silver Dollar" (3/39 US 7), "Don't Sweetheart Me" (3/44 US 2), and "Oh Happy Day" (1/53 US 5). On June 2nd, 1955, he had his own TV show which ran into the 1970s; it led to the hit and million seller "Calcutta" (12/60 US 1).

Art Todd 1920 US singer, who was successful with his wife, as Art & Dotty Todd, with "Broken Wings" (2/53 UK 6) and "Chanson D'Amour (Song Of Love)" (4/58 US 6).

Bob Lander 1942 Swedish guitarist and songwriter, real name Bob Starander. He was a member of the group Spotnicks formed in 1957. Biggest hit was "If You Could Read My Mind" (10/72).

Harvey Mandel 1945 US guitarist and songwriter, who started out with the Charlie Musselwhite Band, and began releasing solo albums in 1968. He also recorded with Barry Goldberg, Canned Heat, John Mayall, Don Sugarcane Harris and Love. Harvey's style of guitar playing was rooted in his home-city of Chicago and the Blues. The Rolling Stones are said to have wanted him as a replacement when Mick Taylor left them.

Mark Stein 1947 US singer and keyboard player with Vanilla Fudge, formed in 1966 and considered to be one of the first heavy rock bands. Vanilla Fudge can also be seen as the pioneers of 'long versions'. In 1968 they released the album THE BEAT GOES ON. It included a piece which told the entire history of music in 12 minutes? Their singles charts were radically abbreviated – perhaps, too radically! – thereby, losing much of the impact. Hit: "You Keep Me Hanging On" (7/67 US 6; UK 18). After the band split up in 1970, Mark formed Boomerang, and later played with Tommy Bolin, Dave Mason and Les Dudek.

'Blue' Weaver 1947 UK keyboard player. Real first name Mick. He began his career with the group Amen Corner, formed in 1966. After the band split up, he tried his luck as Wynder K. Frog and played with Keef Hartley, Fairweather, the Strawbs and from the mid 1970s, with the Bee Gees. He has also been a regular session musician for a vast number of artists.

George Kooymans 1948 Dutch guitarist, songwriter and the leader of Golden Earring. Hits: "Radar Love" (9/73 UK 7; 5/74 US 13) and "Twilight Zone" (11/82 US 10).

Bobby McFerrin 1950 US jazz singer and songwriter, whose voice is enormously versatile. He came from a very musical family. His father's voice was used on the sound track of the film *Porgy and Bess* in the Sydney Portier role. In the early 1980s Bobby recorded as a solo artist. His ability to modulate his phrasing and timing enabled him to encompass a diversity of styles. While he was best-known as a jazz-vocalist, he had an international hit with "Don't Worry Be Happy" (7/88 US 1; 9/88 UK 2), from the film *Cocktail*. However, seeing him perform once is sufficient to know that he can get away with anything.

Katie Kissoon 1951 UK singer who appeared with her brother as Mac & Katie Kissoon. For hits, see 11th November.

Mike Percy 1961 UK bass player with Dead Or Alive.

Bruce Watson 1961 UK guitarist and songwriter with Big Country.

Lenny Wolf 1962 US singer and songwriter, born in Hamburg, with the heavy metal group Kingdom Come.

Deaths

Sonny Terry 1986 US blues musician. Born 24th October, 1911.

Ken Colyer 1988 UK traditional jazz trumpeter, guitarist, and bandleader. Born 18th April, 1928.

Hits of the Day

1950	"The Cry Of The Wild Goose" Frankie Lane US 2 weeks
1955	"Give Me Your Word" Tennessee Ernie Ford UK 7 weeks
1965	"It's Not Unusual" Tom Jones UK 1 week
1967	"Love Is Here And Now You're Gone" Supremes US 1 week
1978	"Wuthering Heights" Kate Bush UK 4 weeks
1989	"Too Many Broken Hearts" Jason Donovan UK 2 weeks

Miscellany

1967 Dick James, Beatles publisher, announced that 446 different versions of "Yesterday" had appeared so far.

12th

Birthdays

Jesse Fuller 1896 US blues singer and songwriter, nickname 'Lone Cat'. In the 1920s he appeared as a film actor in Hollywood films. From the 50s he recorded and his best known composition was "San Francisco Bay Blues." He died on 29th January, 1976 of heart failure.

Gordon MacRae 1921 US film actor, in musicals *Oklahoma!* and *Carousel*, and singer. He started out in the Horace Heidt's orchestra and recorded countless duets with Jo Stafford like. "My Darling, My Darling" (11/48 US 1), " 'A' – You're Adorable (The Alphabet Song)" (3/49 US 4) and "Whispering Hope" (8/49 US 4). Solo hits: "It's Magic" (7/48 US 9), "Hair Of Gold, Eyes Of Blue" (8/48 US 7), or "The Secret" (9/58 US 18). He died 24th January, 1986.

Al Jarreau 1940 US jazz vocalist. He won a 'Grammy' four times as best jazz vocalist. Hits: "We're In This Love Together" (8/81 US 15), "Mornin'" (3/83 US 21; 5/83 UK 28) and "Moonlightning Theme" (3/87 UK 8; 5/87 US 23).

Brian O'Hara 1941 UK guitarist with the Fourmost.

Paul Kantner 1942 US guitarist, singer and songwriter. In 1965 he was a founder-member of Jefferson Airplane. Hits: "Somebody To Love" (5/67 US 5) and "White Rabbit" (7/67 US 8). In November 1970, with Grace Slick, he cut the album as Jefferson STARSHIP BLOWS AGAINST THE EMPIRE; by March 19th, 1974, Airplane had been dropped in preference to Starship. Hits: "Miracles" (9/75 US 3), "Count On Me" (3/78 US 8), and "Jane" (11/79 US 14; 1/80 UK 21). Kantner left the group in 1984, which had shortened its name to Starship in 1985 for legal reasons. In March 1985, Paul formed the KBC Band (with Paul Kantner, Marty Balin, and Jack Casady, all founder-members of Jefferson Airplane). At the end of 1988 there was a reformation of Jefferson Airplane in which nearly all the original members of the first group played together. In addition to his commitments with the bands mentioned, Paul also released solo albums, and played on records by Grace Slick, David Crosby, Papa John Creach and Micky Hart.

Mark Valentino 1942 US singer, real name Anthony Busillo. Only hit, "The Push And Kick" (11/62 US 27).

Liza Minnelli 1946 US singer and actress, daughter of Judy Garland and film producer Vincente Minnelli. When a child, she danced onstage while her mother sang. In 1972 Liza played the part of Sally Bowles in the film, *Cabaret*; – among her other films were *New York, New York* (1977), [*Arthur*] (1981) and *Arthurz On the Rocks*. Her most suc-

cessful album was LIZA WITH A 'Z' (1972) and her biggest hit single was "Losing My Mind" (8/89 UK 6), produced by the Pet Shop Boys.

Les Holroyd 1948 UK bass player, keyboard player and songwriter with Barclay James Harvest formed in September 1966. Before that he played with the blues group Heart & Soul & The Wickeds.

James Taylor 1948 US singer, guitarist, and songwriter. With his older brother Alex he formed the Fabulous Corsairs in 1964, but in 1965 he had a nervous breakdown. In 1966 he formed the group Flying Machine with his friend Danny Kortchmar before moving to England in 1968 and starting a solo career on the Beatles' Apple Label. After returning to the USA he had his first hit with "Fire And Rain" (9/70 US 3; 11/70 UK 42) and then a monster hit with "You've Got A Friend" (6/71 US 1; 8/71 UK 4), written by Carole King. Further Top Ten titles were, "Mockingbird" (2/74 US 5; UK 34), a duet with Carly Simon to whom he was married between 1972 & 1982, "How Sweet It Is (To Be Loved By You)" (6/75 US 5) and "Handy Man" (6/77 US 4). Together with Art Garfunkel and Paul Simon he had a hit with "(What A) Wonderful World" (1/78 US 17). Together with Dennis Wilson he appeared in the film *Two Lane Blacktop*. (1973)

Mike Gibbins 1949 UK drummer with Badfinger.

Simon Booth 1956 UK guitarist and songwriter with Working Week. Before that he played with Weekend.

Steve Harris 1956 UK bass player, songwriter, and in May 1976 co-founder of Iron Maiden.

Marlon Jackson 1957 US singer, member of the Jackson 5.

Deaths

Charlie Parker 1955 US jazz saxophonist, composer, and bandleader. Cause of death: perforated stomach, pneumonia, cirrhosis of the liver, and heart attack. Born 29th August, 1920.

Hits of the Day

1949	"Cruising Down The River" Blue Barron US 7 weeks
1954	"I See The Moon" Stargazers UK 5 weeks
1977	"Chanson D'Amour" Manhattan Transfer UK 3 weeks
1983	"Total Eclipse Of The Heart" Bonnie Tyler UK 2 weeks
1988	"Never Gonna Give You Up" Rick Astley US 2 weeks

13th

Birthdays

Sammy Kaye 1910 US woodwind instrumentalist, composer and orchestra leader. Between 1937 & 1953 he had more than 100 hits. His most successful were "Rosalie" (10/37 US 1), "Love Walked In" (3/38 US 1), "Dream Valley" (12/40 US 1), "Daddy" (5/41 US 1), "Chickery Chick" (10/45 US 1), "I'm A Big Girl Now" (3/46 US 1), "The Old Lamp-Lighter" (11/46 US 1), the million seller, "It Isn't Fair" (2/50 US 2), and "Harbour Lights" (9/50 US 1). He died 2nd June, 1987.

Mike Stoller 1933 US songwriter. His partnership with Jerry Leiber produced some of the greatest and best known hits of the rock 'n' roll era. Their success began in 1951 with "Hard Times", sung by Charles Brown. Shortly after that, Little Willie Littlefield got into the charts with "K.C. Lovin'". Years later, that song, renamed "Kansas City" was a million seller for Wilbert Harrison. Big Mama Thornton recorded "Hound Dog", which later became a massive hit for Elvis Presley, and the pair were to write 23 hits alone for Elvis, including "(You're So Square) Baby I Don't Care", "Don't", "Jailhouse Rock", "Just Tell Her Jim Said Hello", King Creole", "She's Not You" and "Treat Me Nice". In 1954 Mike and Jerry set up their own record label. The Robins who later became the Coasters, recorded compositions by the pair, on which their reputation was consolidated. Compositions like "Charlie Brown", "Poison Ivy", "Yakety Yak" and many more firmly established them in the vanguard of rock 'n' roll Songwriting teams. They appeared again in the 1970s as producers of Stealers Wheel & Peggy Lee. Royalties for their songs are still rolling in and the pair need never work again, but they do!

Neil Sedaka 1939 US singer and songwriter. Neil began his career in 1955 as a member of the Linc-Tones, which became the Tokens a year later. The group recorded unsuccessfully. In 1958 Neil left the band and carried on working as a soloist. That was the end of the Tokens chapter for the time being. In 1960 the group was reformed with a new line-up. The only original member was Hank Medress. Neil Sedaka's first hit was "Oh Carol" (10/59 US 9; UK 3), which was dedicated to Carole King but his biggest hit during that period was "Breaking Up Is Hard To Do" (7/62 US 1; UK 7). After 1966 Neil disappeared from the charts for eight years. He had to wait until 1974, when he signed with Elton John's Rocket label for his next hits "Laughter In The Rain" (11/74 US 1; 6/74 UK 15) and

"Bad Blood" (9/75 US 1). A hit for father Neil and daughter Dara was "Should've Never Let You Go" (5/80 US 19).

Daniel Bennie 1940 US singer with the Reflections. Hit, "(Just Like) Romeo And Juliet" (4/64 US 6).

Donald York 1949 US singer with Sha Na Na.

Jürgen Fritz 1953 German keyboard player and songwriter with Triumvirate, formed in 1970. The group had 3 albums in the charts in the USA, the greatest success being SPARTACUS (6/75 LP-US 27). After 1980 Jürgen was involved with various projects, sometimes more commercial, sometimes less so. In 1986 he formed the group Motive. In the meantime he has become a songwriter and producer.

Ronnie Rogers 1959 UK guitarist and songwriter with T'Pau. In 1982 he met singer Carol Decker in the group Lazers, then formed T'Pau with her in 1986.

Adam Clayton 1960 Irish bass player with U2.

Hits of the Day

1948	"Manana (Is Soon Enough For Me)" Peggy Lee US 7 weeks
1953	"She Wears Red Feathers" Guy Mitchell UK 4 weeks
1954	"Make Love To Me!" Jo Stafford US 7 weeks
1965	"Eight Days A Week" Beatles US 2 weeks
1965	"Downtown" Petula Clark
1976	"December '63" Four Seasons US 3 weeks

14th

Birthdays

Les Brown 1912 US orchestra leader and clarinettist. Full first names Lester Raymond. He started out as an arranger for Jimmy Dorsey and Larry Clinton before forming his own band at the end of the 1930s, cutting his first records in 1939. His biggest hits were the million seller "Sentimental Journey" (3/45 US 1), "My Dreams Are Getting Better All The Time" (3/45 US 1), both featuring Doris Day, and the million seller "I've Got My Love To Keep Me Warm" (12/48 US 1), which was the final major instrumental hit of the big band era. Les also accompanied hits by the Ames Brothers and Teresa Brewer. From 1947 he began a long association with Bob Hope for radio, TV and on tour. He also appeared regularly with his orchestra in TV shows by Steve Allen and Dean Martin.

Les Baxter 1922 US orchestra leader, pianist and composer, who has been successful since the 50s. Before that, he was a member of Mel Torme's backing group. The Mel-Tones. Then he became a staff arranger at Capitol records working with artists like Nat 'King' Cole. Among his hits were "April in Portugal" (4/53 US 2), "Unchained Melody" (4/55 US 1; UK 10) and "The Poor People Of Paris" (2/56 US 1).

Phil Phillips 1931 US singer and guitarist, who started out with the gospel group Gateway Quartet. Real name John Phillip Baptiste. After his only real hit with "Sea Of Love" (7/59 US 2) as Phil Phillips With The Twilights, he became a disc jockey.

Quincy Jones 1933 US trumpeter, producer, arranger, record company owner and songwriter; whatever he did, he did well. He started out as a jazz trumpeter and played with Lionel Hampton from 1950 to 1953. In 1961 he became musical director for the company Mercury Records, and in 1964 became vice-president. In between, he found time for many films and TV series. Quincy received 19 Grammies. He has arranged and produced literally hundreds of successful records. Probably his biggest successes were the Michael Jackson albums "OFF THE WALL", & BAD THRILLER. Chart hits under his name were, "Stuff Like That" (6/78 US 21; UK 34) – Ashford & Simpson and Chaka Khan were the vocalists – and "Razzamatazz" (6/81 UK 11). In 1989, with BACK ON THE BLOCK, he released an album which proved inspirational for others, especially the title, "I'll Be Good To You" (11/89 US 18), with vocals Ray Charles and Chaka Khan.

Jasper Carrott 1945 UK singer, comedian and songwriter, who had his biggest hit with "Funky Moped/Magic Roundabout" (8/75 UK 5).

Walter Parazaider 1945 US saxophonists with Chicago and session musician with the Bee Gees and Leon Russell.

Jona Lewie 1947 UK singer and songwriter. First success as Terry Dactyl & The Dinosaurs with "Seaside Shuffle" (7/72 UK 2), then under his own name. Hit: "Stop The Cavalry" (11/80 UK 3).

Peter Skellern 1947 UK singer and songwriter. Hits: "You're A Lady" (9/72 UK 3) and "Hold On To Love" (3/75 UK 14).

Ollie Halsall 1949 UK guitarist with Patto, Neil Innes, Grimms, Scaffold, Tempest, Kevin Ayers and Boxer. His guitar work figured prominently in the film *Jesus Christ Superstar*.

Chris Redburn 1957 UK bass player with Kenny.

Steve Lambert 1963 UK singer, guitarist and songwriter with Roman Holliday. Hit: "Don't Try To Stop It" (7/83 UK 14).

Deaths

Doc Pomus 1991 US singer and composer, born May 27th 1925.

Hits of the Day

1942	"(There'll Be Bluebirds Over) The White Cliffs Of Dover" Kay Kyser US 1 week
1963	"Summer Holiday" Cliff Richard UK 2 weeks
1981	"Jealous Guy" Roxy Music UK 2 weeks
1981	"9 To 5" Dolly Parton US 1 week (2 times)
1987	"Everything I Own" Boy George UK 2 weeks
1987	"Jacob's Ladder" Huey Lewis & The News US 1 week

15th

Birthdays

Sam 'Lightnin' Hopkins 1912 US blues singer, guitarist, and songwriter. Sam was considered to be one of last great blues singers. He worked with Alger 'Texas' Alexander from the late 1920s till 1937, and then again from 1945 into the 50s. He made his first records in 1946. One of his biggest hits was "Shotgun Blues" (9/50 R&B 5). He died 30th January, 1982.

Harry James 1916 US trumpeter, composer, and orchestra leader. He started out with Ben Pollack 1935/36, and played with Benny Goodman for the next two years. From 1938 onwards Harry had his own band. Hits: "You Made Me Love You" (11/41 US 5), "I Don't Want To Walk Without You" (2/42 US 1), "Easter Parade" (4/42 US 11; 4/46 RE-US 23), "Sleepy Lagoon" (4/42 US 1), "Mister Five By Five" (11/42 US 1), "I Had The Craziest Dream" (11/42 US 1) & "I've Heard That Song Before" (1/43 US 1). The last two titles were recorded with singer Helen

Forrest, and with newcomer Frank Sinatra he did "All Or Nothing At All" (6/43 US 1), "I'll Get By (As Long As I Have You)" (4/44 US 1) with singer Dick Haymes, recorded in April 1941, "I'm Beginning To See The Light" (1/45 US 1) with singer Kitty Kallen, and "It's Been A Long Time" (10/45 US 1) also with Kitty Kallen. Harry remained active in the music business until his death on 5th July, 1983.

Eddie Calvert 1922 UK trumpeter. Hits: "Oh Mein Papa" (12/53 US 6; UK 1), "Cherry Pink And Apple Blossom White" (4/55 UK 1), "John & Juli" (7/55 UK 6), and "Mandy" (2/58 UK 9). He died 7th August, 1978.

Carl Smith 1927 US country singer and guitarist. His first wife was June Carter. He started out in the 1940s, had his first country hit with "Let's Live A Little" (6/51 C&W 2), and his first No. 1 with "Let Old Mother Nature Have Her Way" (10/51 C&W 1). After that a further 100 hits were to follow. In 1977 Carl withdrew from the music business to his farm in Tennessee.

Arif Mardin 1932 US producer in a class of his own. He worked with Aretha Franklin, Roberta Flack, Bette Midler, Laura Nyro, Wilson Pickett, Herbie Mann, Average White Band, The Rascals, the Bee Gees and many more.

Phil Lesh 1940 US bass player with Grateful Dead. Real name Philip Chapman.

Mike Love 1941 US singer, saxophonist, and songwriter – alongside Brian Wilson the most important member of the Beach Boys formed in 1961; the group has had more than thirty in the US Top Forty hits since then. The biggest were "Surfin' U.S.A." (3/63 US 3; 8/63 UK 34), "Surfer Girl" (8/63 US 7), "Be True To Your School" (11/63 US 6), "Fun, Fun, Fun" (2/64 US 5), "I Get Around" (5/64 US 1; 7/64 UK 7), "When I Grow Up (To Be A Man)" (9/64 US 9; UK 27), "Dance, Dance, Dance" (11/64 US 8; 1/65 UK 24), "Help Me, Rhonda" (4/65 US 1; 6/65 UK 27), "California Girls" (7/65 US 3; 9/65 UK 26), "Barbara Ann" (1/66 US 2; UK 3), "Sloop John B." (4/66 US 3; UK 2), "Wouldn't It Be Nice" (7/66 US 8), "Good Vibrations" (10/66 US 1; UK 1), "Do It Again" (7/68 UK 1; US 20), "I Can Hear Music" (2/69 UK 10; US 24), "Break Away" (6/69 UK 6), "Cotton Fields" (5/70 UK 5), "Rock n' Roll Music" (6/76 US 5; UK 36), "Lady Linda" (6/79 UK 6) and "Kokomo" (9/88 US 1; 11/88 UK 25). Additionally, they hit with, "Wipeout" (7/87 US 12; UK 2) with the Fat Boys.

Hughie Flint 1942 UK drummer with Manfred Mann, Alexis Korner, John Mayall, Alan Price, Savoy Brown, Chicken Shack, McGuiness-Flint and finally with the Blues Band.

Joachim Kühn 1944 Considered to be one of the best and most versatile jazz-rock pianists in Europe.

Sly Stone 1944 US singer, songwriter, guitarist and keyboard player with his band Sly & The Family Stone, who released their first albums in 1967. Their biggest hits were "Dance To The Music" (2/68 US 8; 7/68 UK 7), "Everyday People" (11/68 US 1; 3/69 UK 32), "Hot Fun In the Summertime" (8/69 US 2), "Thank You (Fallettinme Be Mice Elf Agin)" (1/70 US 1), "Family Affair" (11/71 US 1; 1/72 UK 15) and "If You Want Me To Stay" (6/73 US 12). Sly is considered to be one of the founders of psychedelic soul and has been a major influence upon artists like Prince.

Howard Scott 1946 US guitarist with War.

Ry Cooder 1947 US guitarist, singer, and songwriter with Rising Sons, Captain Beefheart's Magic Band, on the debut album by Little Feat, with the Rolling Stones, and as a soloist. In 1979, he released the first digitally recorded rock-album BOP TILL YOU DROP. Ry has scored several films including *The Long Riders* (1980) and *Paris, Texas* (1985).

Dee Snider 1955 US singer and songwriter with the heavy rock band Twisted Sister, formed in 1976. The group spent a long period of their career in the UK, as they were considered to be a cheap copy of Kiss in the USA. First hits for Twisted Sister were "I Am (I'm Me)" (3/83 UK 18), and "We're Not Gonna Take It" (7/84 US 21).

Steve Coy 1962 UK drummer with Dead Or Alive.

Terence Trent d'Arby 1962 US singer and songwriter. He tried journalism, boxing, and then the army, which resulted in his being posted to Germany. During his time in the army he joined the Frankfurt group Touch. In early 1987, Terence, now living in London, started a solo career. He was celebrated as the 'future of soul music'!. First hits: "If You let Me Stay" (2/87 UK 7), "Wishing Well" (6/87 UK 4; 1/88 US 1), and "Sign Your Name" (1/88 UK 2; 5/88 US 4). He has various epithets, 'Big Mouth', 'Pretty Face', 'New Prince of Pop', 'Event of the Decade', and 'Soul Wonder'. At the end of 1989 he released his second album, awaited impatiently by the record company – it flopped, much to the delight of the press!

Rockwell 1964 US singer and songwriter. Real name Kennedy Gordy. He is the son of Tamla-Motown founder Berry Gordy. His first single-release became a million seller, "Somebody's Watching Me" (1/84 US 2; UK 6). It is possible that the record was helped to success by the fact that Michael Jackson was singing in the background. Mr. Gordy Rockwell did not manage another such hit.

Sabrina 1968 Italian singer. Surname Salerno. She was successful throughout Europe with "Boys" (2/88 UK 60; 6/88 RE-UK 3) and "All Of Me" (10/88 UK 25).

Deaths

Lester Young 1959 US jazz saxophonist and composer. He died after suffering a heart attack. Born 27th August, 1909.

Hits of the Day

1941	"Song Of The Volga Boatmen" Glenn Miller US 1 week
1947	"Managua, Nicaragua" Guy Lombardo US 1 week
1947	"Heartache" Ted Weems US 13 weeks
1952	"Wheel Of Fortune" Kay Starr US 10 weeks
1969	"Dizzy" Tommy Roe US 4 weeks
1975	"Black Water" Doobie Brothers US 1 week
1980	"Together We Are Beautiful" Fern Kinney UK 1 week
1986	"Sara" Starship US 1 week

Miscellany

1956 The premiere of *My Fair Lady* took place in New York. This musical evolved into the most successful piece in the history of modern theatre.

16th

Birthdays

Jerry Lewis 1926 US comedian, film actor, and singer. Real name Joseph Levitch. In 1946 he began working with Dean Martin. From 1949 onwards they made films together, in which Lewis usually played the part of the charming twit, and Martin the Latin lover. This successful partnership lasted some 10 years and 17 films. Combined hit, "That Certain Party" (12/48 US 22). In 1956 it was supposedly Dean Martin who wanted to carry on as a soloist. Jerry made about 40 films altogether with and without Martin. He was not as successful a singer as Dean Martin, and his only hit worthy of mention was "Rock-A-Bye Your Baby With A Dixie Melody" (11/56 US 10; 2/57 UK 12), which however, was a million seller. That title had been a hit for Al Jolson 10 years before in his film, *Al Jolson Story*.

Betty Johnson 1932 US singer who had her first hit with the wistful "I Want Eddie Fisher For Christmas" (11/54 US 22), and her biggest hit with "I Dreamed" (11/56 US 9). Her last hit was as trenchant as her first, "You Can't Get To Heaven On Rollerskates" (1/59 US 99).

Jerry Jeff Walker 1942 US singer, guitarist and songwriter. Real name Paul Crosby. In 1966 he formed the group Circus Maximus which then released albums. From 1968, Jerry worked mainly as a solo artist. He composed "Mr. Bojangles" (7/68 US 77), which however, was a hit for the Nitty Gritty Dirt Band (1/71 US 9). As a songwriter, he has a peerless reputation. More recently he has been connected with new wave country artists like Garth Brooks & Guy Clark.

Jerry Goodman 1943 US violinist in the band Flock formed in 1965. Their music slotted into the rather too-pat category of jazz-rock or fusion and was notable more for technical virtuosity than emotional content. Later he played with the Mahavishnu Orchestra and as a session musician.

Michael Bruce 1948 US guitarist and keyboard player who was one of the founder-members of Alice Cooper, until the group was disbanded in 1975. Michael released a solo album and then could be heard with the Billion Dollar Babies.

Ray Benson 1951 US guitarist, singer, songwriter, and leader of the country-swing group Asleep At The Wheel, formed in 1970. They could be heard regularly in the country charts from 1974 onwards. They had their biggest hit with "The Letter That Johnny Walker Read" (8/75 C&W 10).

Nancy Wilson 1954 US guitarist, singer and songwriter. In tandem with her sister Ann she formed nucleus of the group Heart. Nancy is backing vocalist and rhythm guitarist. She started out as a folksinger while her sister became a member of the hard rock band White Heart. Nancy finally joined the group and the band renamed itself Heart. Hits: "Magic Man" (7/76 US 9), "Barracuda" (5/77 US 11), "Tell It Like It Is" (11/80 US 8), "Never" (9/85 US 4; 3/88 UK 8), "These Dreams" (1/86 US 1; which was the B-side of "Never" in the UK), "Alone" (5/87 US 1; UK 3) and "Who Will You Run To" (8/87 US 7; UK 30).

Deaths

Tammi Terrell 1970 US singer, real name Tammi Montgomery. In 1961 she made her first records, then worked in the James Brown Revue. She was best known for her duets with Marvin Gaye. Biggest hits: "Your Precious Love" (9/67 US 5) and "Onion Song" (11/69 UK 9). Tammi collapsed onstage during a concert with Marvin Gaye, and died shortly after from a brain tumour. She was just 23 years old.

Aaron Thibeaux 'T-Bone' Walker 1975 US blues musician. He died after contracting pneumonia. Born 28th May, 1910.

Arthur Godfrey 1983 US singer. Born 31st August, 1903.

Hits of the Day

1940	"Darn That Dream" Benny Goodman US 1 week
1946	"Oh! What It Seemed To Be" Frankie Carle US 11 weeks
1956	"It's Almost Tomorrow" Dream Weavers UK 2 weeks
1968	"(Sittin' On) The Dock Of The Bay" Otis Redding US 4 weeks
1974	"Billy, Don't Be A Hero" Paper Lace UK 3 weeks

17th

Birthdays

Nat 'King' Cole 1917 US singer, pianist, and songwriter, real name Nathaniel Adams Coles. By 1934 he had his own band. In 1939 he formed the King Cole Trio, in which Oscar Moore played electric guitar which was quite unusual at the time. The trio rapidly became popular throughout the USA as an instrumental combo. Then, when Nat began to sing, his future career emerged clearly. The first hit was "Straighten Up And Fly Right" (4/44 US 9), followed by "(I Love You) For Sentimental Reasons" (11/46 US 1), "The Christmas Song" (11/46 US 3; 12/47 RE-US 23; 1/49 RE-US 24; 1/53 RE-US 30), "Nature Boy" (4/48 US 1), "Mona Lisa" (6/50 US 1), "Too Young" (4/51 US 1), "Pretend" (2/53 US 2; 4/53 UK 2), "Answer Me (My Love)" (2/54 US 6), "A Blossom Fell" (2/55 UK 3; 5/55 US 2), "When I Fall In Love" (4/57 UK 2; 12/87 RE-UK 4) and "Ramblin' Rose" (8/62 US 2; UK 5). Nat died 15th February, 1965 from cancer.

Adam Wade 1937 US singer, TV announcer and actor with three Top Ten hits in 1961, then everything was over.

"Take Good Care Of Her" (3/61 US 7), "The Writing On The Wall" (5/61 US 5), and "As If I Didn't Know" (7/61 US 10). Adam was the first black man to have a show on daytime television, and to have a gameshow *Musical Chairs* on one of the large US networks in 1975.

Clarence Collins 1939 US singer with Little Anthony & The Imperials.

Lewis Mathis 1939 US singer who appeared together with his brother as Dean & Mark. Only hit: "Tell Him No" (3/59 US 42). After Larry Henley had joined them, they called themselves the Newbeats. In 1964/65 they had three Top Twenty hits. Their biggest hit was "Bread And Butter" (8/64 US 2).

Vito Picone 1940 US lead singer with the white doo-wop quintet Elegants which had only one hit, "Little Star" (7/58 US 1; 9/58 UK 25).

Bob Johnson 1944 UK guitarist, singer, and songwriter with Steeleye Span.

Paul Pilnick 1944 UK guitarist with Jackie Lomax, Stealers Wheel, Badger, Deaf School and Joe Egan.

John Sebastian 1944 US singer, guitarist, harmonica player and songwriter for Lovin' Spoonful, formed by him in 1965. John began with the Even Dozen Jug Band, worked as a session musician, and was then with Mama Cass Elliott and Denny Doherty (later of the Mamas & Papas) and Zal Yanovsky in the Mugwumps. Between 1965 & 1968 Lovin' Spoonful had nine Top Twenty hits in the USA. The biggest were "Daydream" (2/66 US 2; 4/66 UK 2), "Did You Ever Have To Make Up Your Mind?" (5/66 US 2), and "Summer In The City" (7/66 US 1; UK 8). In 1968 the group split up, and John carried on as a soloist. He had a further hit and million seller with the theme song for the TV series, *Welcome Back, Kotter*, "Welcome Back" (3/76 US 1).

Harold Brown 1946 US drummer with War.

Pat Lloyd 1948 UK guitarist, with the Equals.

Scott Gorham 1951 UK guitarist, with Thin Lizzy.

Rena Jones 1954 US singer, with Champaign.

Mike Lindup 1959 UK keyboard player and singer with Level 42.

Claire Grogan 1962 UK singer and songwriter with Altered Images, formed in 1979. It was on account of Claire that the group got a recording contract, as she was the star in the cult films *Gregory's Girl* and *Comfort & Joy*. In 1984 the group split up. Hits: "Happy Birthday" (9/81 UK 2), "I Could Be Happy" (12/81 UK 7) and "Don't Talk To Me About Love" (3/83 UK 7).

Deaths

Samuel George 1982 US lead singer and drummer with the Capitols who had previsouly appeared as the 3 Caps. They had a Top Ten hit as the Capitols with "Cool Jerk" (4/66 US 7). He was 40 years old when he was stabbed to death.

Ric Grech 1990 UK singer, bassist and guitarist, born on November 1st, 1946.

Hits of the Day

1945 "Ac-Cent-Tchu-Ate The Positive" Johnny Mercer US 2 weeks

1956 "The Poor People Of Paris" Les Baxter US 6 weeks

1958 "Tequila" The Champs US 5 weeks

1960 "Running Bear" Johnny Preston UK 2 weeks

1966 "The Sun Ain't Gonna Shine Anymore" Walker Brothers UK 4 weeks

1979 "I Will Survive" Gloria Gaynor UK 4 weeks

1990 "The Power" Snap UK 2 weeks.

18th

Birthdays

Robert Lee Smith 1936 US soul singer with the Tams, who cut their first record in 1960.

Charley Pride 1938 US country singer. He was the first black C&W artist to attain ˝superstar status. In the meantime he has had a total of about 30 No. 1 hits in the C&W charts. His biggest cross-over success was the million seller "Kiss An Angel Good Mornin' " (11/71 US 21).

Kenny Lynch 1939 UK singer and actor. Hits: "Up On The Roof" (12/62 UK 10) & "You Can Never Stop Me Loving You" (6/63 UK 10).

Travis Pritchett 1939 US singer who together with Bob Weaver formed the duo Travis & Bob. Their only hit was "Tell Him No" (3/59 US 8).

Wilson Pickett 1941 US soul singer and songwriter. During 1960s he ranked with Otis Redding & James Brown as one of the best-known soul singers of the period.

In 1959 he became a member of the legendary Falcons, an R & B quintet from Detroit, whose only hit with Wilson as lead singer was "I Found A Love" (3/62 US 75; R & B 6). From 1963 he launched a solo career. After a few not particularly successful singles Wilson was taken to Memphis by Jerry Wexler, who teamed him with guitarist and producer Steve Cropper. With Cropper, his star went into the ascendant with hits like "Land Of A 1000 Dances" (7/66 US 6; 9/66 UK 22) & "Funky Broadway" (8/67 US 8). However, his two million sellers were "Don't Let The Green Grass Fool You" (1/71 US 17) and "Don't Knock My Love Pt. 1" (4/71 US 13), both of which were produced by Gamble & Huff.

Barry Wilson 1947 UK drummer. In 1961 he joined the Paramounts with whom he stayed until October 1966. In July 1967 he joined Procol Harum who had already recorded their hit "Whiter Shade of Pale". Barry also works as a session musician.

John Hartman 1950 US drummer with the Doobie Brothers.

Irene Cara 1959 US singer and actress. As a child she featured on Spanish-speaking radio and TV in New York. At age 8 she had a part in the Broadway musical *Maggie Flynn*, and at age 10 she sang with Roberta Flack and Sammy Davis Jr, in honour of Duke Ellington at Madison Square Garden. By the time she was 16, she appeared in TV series, like *Roots*. In 1980 she auditioned for a part in Alan Parker's film *Fame*, and got it. Finally she was allowed to sing the title song "Fame" (6/80 US 4; 7/82 UK 1). Further films followed like *Cotton Club*, and further hits, like "Flashdance ... What A Feeling" (4/83 US 1; 6/83 UK 2) and "Breakdance" (3/84 US 8).

Taja Sevelle 1962 US singer and songwriter, born in Minneapolis, and who was discovered by Prince. First hit: "Love Is Contagious" (2/88 UK 7).

Hits of the Day

1944 "Mairzy Doats" Merry Macs US 5 weeks

1950 "Music! Music! Music!" Teresa Brewer US 4 weeks

1965 "The Last Time" Rolling Stones UK 3 weeks

1967 "Penny Lane" Beatles US 1 week

1967 "Dear Mrs. Applebee" David Garrick

1972 "Heart Of Gold" Neil Young US 1 week

1972 "Without You" Nilsson UK 4 weeks

1978 "Night Fever" Bee Gees US 8 weeks

19th

Birthdays

Moms Mabley 1897 US comedian; real name Loretta Mary Aiken. She released several comedy albums, and got into the charts with the serious piece "Abraham, Martin And John" (7/69 US 35). This song was a hit also for Dion and for Marvin Gaye. Moms died 23rd May, 1975.

Lennie Tristano 1919 US jazz pianist, composer and bandleader. Lenny became completely blind after catching Spanish flu as a child. Inspite of this, he learned to play clarinet, saxophone and cello, as well as the piano. He was one of the most innovative of the post-bop pianists. Lennie died 18th November, 1978.

Ornette Coleman 1930 US jazz saxophonist, arranger and composer.

Clarence 'Frogman' Henry 1937 US singer, pianist, trombonist and songwriter. He started out with the Bobby Mitchell R & B band from 1953 to 1955 and carried on as a soloist there after. His first hit was "Ain't Got No Home" (12/56 US 20); it earned him the nickname 'Frogman'. His biggest hits were "But I Do" (3/61 US 4; UK 3) and "You Always Hurt The One You Love" (5/61 US 12; UK 6).

Robin Luke 1942 US singer, TV series actor, and songwriter. His only chart hit "Susie Darlin' " (8/58 US 5; 10/58 UK 23). His younger sister Susie was the inspiration for this song.

Paul Atkinson 1946 UK lead guitarist with the Zombies.

Derek Longmuir 1952 UK drummer with the Bay City Rollers.

Ricky Wilson 1953 US guitarist with B52s formed in 1976. His sister Cindy is the lead vocalist of the band. He died on October 12th, 1985.

Terry Hall 1959 UK singer and songwriter. He joined the Coventry Specials in 1978, who shortened their name to Specials shortly after. From 1979 to his departure in November 1981 the group had seven Top Ten hits, the biggest being "Too Much Too Young" (1/80 UK 1), and "Ghost Town" (1/81 UK 1). After that, Terry formed Fun Boy Three, who split up in 1983 after five Top Twenty hits in the UK. Biggest hits: "Tunnel Of Love" (2/83 UK 10), "Our Lips Are Sealed" (4/83 UK 7) and, with Bananarama, "It Ain't What You Do, It's The Way That You Do It" (2/82 UK 4). At the end of 1983, he formed Colour Field. Hit: "Thinking Of You" (1/85 UK 12).

Deaths

Paul Kossoff 1976 UK guitarist and songwriter. He died in his sleep on a flight from Los Angeles to New York. Born 14th September, 1950.

Gary Thain 1976 UK bass player who played with the Keef Hartley band from 1969 to 1971, and from 1972 to 1975 with Uriah Heep. He died from an overdose of tablets.

Hits of the Day

| 1964 | "Little Children" Billy J. Kramer UK 2 weeks |
| 1973 | "Mama Loo" Les Humphries Singers D 3 weeks |

20th

Birthdays

Ozzy Nelson 1906 US bandleader, songwriter, singer, multi-instrumentalist, radio and TV star; father of Ricky Nelson. In 1930 he led his first professional dance band. From 1932 onwards singer Harriet Hilliard appeared with the band, real name Peggy Lou Snyder. Ozzy, real names Oswald George, married her in 1935, which of course, makes her the mother of Ricky Nelson. Ozzy had about 40 hits from 1930 to 1940. The two biggest were "And Then Some" (7/35 US 1) and "White Sails (Beneath A Yellow Moon)" (7/39 US 2); both were sung by Ozzy too. From 1944 onwards the couple had a regular radio show as Ozzy & Harriet. From 1952 to 1966 the family story was carried over to television, which started the career of son Ricky. Ozzy died 3rd June, 1975.

Vera Lynn 1919 UK singer, real name Margaret Welsh. She started out as a singer with the Ambrose Orchestra and became the most successful British singer of the war and post-war era with the 'White Cliffs of Dover' forming the soundtrack to the period. Biggest hits: the million seller "Auf Weidersehn (Sweetheart)" (6/52 US 1; 11/52 UK 10), "Forget Me Not" (11/52 UK 7), and "My Son, My Son" (10/54 UK 1; US 28). Vera Lynn appeared on British television for many years after that. Her title "We'll Meet Again" (1/54 US 29) became known again, at least to cinema goers: in 1964 in the film *Dr. Strangelove, or how I learned to love the Bomb*, Peter Sellers who had several roles in the film, ends up riding a bomb like a rodeo rider on his bronco, to the accompaniement of "We'll Meet Again".

Vaughn Meader 1936 US comedy artist. In 1962 he had a million seller hit with the album THE 1ST FAMILY (12/62 LP US 1), which was a spoof on the life of the Kennedy family; he received a Grammy for 'Album of the Year'. After John F. Kennedy was assassinated on 22nd November, 1963, the album had disappeared from record shops by the very next day.

Jerry Reed 1937 US singer, guitarist, and songwriter who combined rock and country music. Complete name Jerry Reed Hubbard. Pop hits: "Amos Moses" (10/70 US 8) and "When You're Hot, You're Hot" (5/71 US 9). He wrote hits for others like, "Crazy Legs" for Gene Vincent and "Guitar Man" for Elvis. As an actor he appeared in *Gator* and *Smokey & The Bandit*, among others.

Joe Rivers 1937 US singer, who formed the R&B duo Johnnie & Joe together with his partner Johnnie Richards. They were successful once with "Over The Mountain, Across The Sea" (5/57 US 8; 9/60 RE-US 89).

Mike Settle 1941 US singer with First Edition. Later he was replaced by Kin Vassy. After that Mike could be heard on two albums by John Stewart.

Carl Palmer 1950 UK drummer, songwriter and singer. Various groups he played with were, Chris Farlowe's Thunderbirds, Crazy World Of Arthur Brown, Atomic Rooster, Emerson, Lake & Palmer, P.M., and Asia.

Jimmie Vaughan 1951 US guitarist, and Stevie Ray's older brother. In 1975 Jimmie was co-founder of the Fabulous Thunderbirds.

Fonso Martin 1956 UK singer and percussionist with Steel Pulse.

Deaths

Archie Bleyer 1989 US pianist, orchestra leader and founder of the record company Cadence. Born 12th June, 1909.

Hits of the Day

1959 "Smoke Gets In Your Eyes" Platters UK 1 week
1961 "Surrender" Elvis Presley US 2 weeks
1968 "The Legend Of Xanadu" Dave Dee & Co. UK 1 week
1971 "Me And Bobby McGee" Janis Joplin US 2 weeks
1971 "Hot Love" T. Rex UK 6 weeks
1982 "I Love Rock 'n' Roll" Joan Jett & The Blackhearts US 7 weeks

---

Miscellany

1960 After a lengthy break due to his military service, Elvis walked back into a recording studio. Many had predicted that he would never again be what he had been before March 1958 – the King of rock 'n' roll. Elvis played at soldier instead of his guitar for 2 years. He was discharged on 5th March, 1960. At 20:00 hours on 20th March he was standing in front of a microphone, in RCA studio B in Nashville. During the next 11 hours he recorded six new titles, "Make Me Know It" and "Soldier Boy" on the 20th, "Stuck On You", "Fame And Fortune", "Mess Of Blues", and "It Feels So Right" on the 21st March. Amongst the musicians accompanying him were his old friends Scotty Moore, D. J. Fontana, Hank Garland, Bob Moore, and Floyd Cramer. Elvis was in top form, and the pessimists turned out to be wrong.

1969 John Lennon married Yoko Ono Cox, 8 years his senior, in Gibraltar. This, for many friends of and experts on the Beatles, set the seal on the end of the group.

21st

Birthdays

Son House 1902 US singer, guitarist and songwriter. Real first names Eddie James. He is called the Father of folk-blues, and even if that does sound a bit high-faluting, he deserved it. Well-known blues musicians such as Robert Johnson or Muddy Waters were promoted by him early on. In 1930 Son made his first recordings. In the 1940s he had a longish break and worked for the New York Central Railroad for many years. In 1964, when interest in the blues was being rekindled, Son House was rediscovered. After that he recorded again with a number of white blues musicians like Al Wilson, who had shaped the career of Canned Heat.

Otis Spann 1930 US pianist, singer, and harmonica player. From 1953, Otis played with Muddy Waters, Sunnyland Slim, Little Walter and Jimmy Rogers, helping in the process, to develop the Chicago style of Urban Blues. It is said erroneously that he was the half-brother of Muddy Waters. However, they did play together. Otis can also be heard on records by Chuck Berry, Bo Diddley, Howlin' Wolf, Sonny Boy Williamson and Little Walter. For many years he was the house pianist of Chess Records. In 1964 he made an album in London with Eric Clapton and Jimmy Page, after which followed a fruitful period with Fleetwood Mac BLUES JAM AT CHESS: "The Biggest Thing Since Colossus", recorded with Otis Spann, Peter Green, Danny Kirwan, John McVie and S. P. Leary, was the product of this association. Otis died 24th April, 1970.

Vivian Stanshall 1943 UK singer with the Bonzo Dog Doo-Dah Band formed in 1966. In their early days the group played a mixture of dance music and traditional jazz. Their first singles were flops. Then they played in the MAGICAL MYSTERY TOUR by the Beatles, after which Paul McCartney produced the only hit by the group under the pseudonym Apollo C. Vermouth, "I'm The Urban Spaceman" (11/68 UK 5). Even cutting the Doo-Dah out of their name later on, did the band no good. However, it should be emphasised that their music was satirical, despite each members' musical accomplishments.

Rose Stone 1945 US keyboard player with Sly & The Family Stone.

Ray Dorset 1946 UK singer and songwriter who introduced a skiffle revival with the group Mungo Jerry in 1969. Biggest hits: "In The Summertime" (6/70 UK 1; US 3), "Baby Jump" (2/71 UK 1), "Lady Rose" (5/71 UK 5), and "Alright Alright Alright" (7/73 UK 3). Later Dorset tried to be a soloist, but had no success.

Roger Hodgson 1950 UK singer, guitarist, bass player, and songwriter with Supertramp. For hits, see 22nd July. In November 1982 Roger left the band and carried on as a soloist.

Deaths

Dean Martin Jr. 1987 US singer. Died after being involved in an accident with a plane. Born 17th November, 1952.

Hits of the Day

1942 "Rose O'Day" (The Filla-Da-Gusha Song) Freddy Martin US 2 weeks
1953 "The Doggie In The Window" Patti Page US 8 weeks
1955 "Tom Dooley" Kingston Trio
1964 "She Loves You" Beatles US 2 weeks
1964 "I Want To Hold Your Hand" Beatles
1981 "Keep On Loving You" REO Speedwagon US 1 week
1987 "Lean On Me" Club Nouveau US 2 weeks

22nd

Birthdays

Blue Barron 1911 US orchestra leader and trombone player. Real name Harry Friedland. He was successful from 1938 to 1951. His biggest hit was million seller "Cruising Down the River" (1/49 US 1). The record was succeeded in the charts by cover version by Russ Morgan.

Roger Whittaker 1936 UK singer and songwriter, born in Nairobi, son of a colonial official. He was called the singer of the silent, coffee drinking majority. All his initial hits were whistled. Hits: "Durham Town (The Leavin')" (11/69 UK 12), "I Don't Believe In If Anymore" (4/70 UK 8), "The Last Farewell" (4/75 US 19; 7/75 UK 2), "River Lady (A Little Goodbye)" (1976) and "Albany" (1982). He had a hit with "The Skye Boat Song" (11/86 UK 10), with Des O'Connor.

Johnny Ferguson 1937 US singer who worked as a disc jockey in the late 50s. As so many before him, he believed he was better than those whose records he played. His only hit was "Angela Jones" (2/60 US 27).

George Benson 1943 US guitarist and singer. In his younger days he played R&B, and made a first record as early as 1954 for RCA. He played with Brother Jack McDuff when he was nineteen, and in the early 1970s became house musician for CTI Records. For a number of years George belonged more in the jazz category, then he began to appear in the pop charts in 1976. Hits: "This Masquerade" (6/76 US 10), "On Broadway" (3/78 US 8), "Give Me The Night" (7/80 US 4; UK 7), "Love X Love" (10/80 UK 10), "Turn Your Love Around" (10/81 US 5; UK 29) and "In Your Eyes" (9/83 UK 7). His style of guitar playing was strongly influenced by Wes Montgomery.

Keith Relf 1943 UK singer, harmonica player, and songwriter. In 1963 he was a founder member of the Yardbirds, who had the following hits, "For Your Love" (3/65 UK 3; 5/65 US 6) and "Heart Full Of Soul" (6/65 UK 2; US 9). The lineup of the Yardbirds fluctuated quite a lot over the years, but Keith remained throughout. In 1969 he formed Renaissance who made good, but rather fey albums. Commercial success eluded them, however. He died 14th May, 1976.

Jeremy Clyde 1944 UK singer, guitarist and songwriter. In partnership with Chad Stuart, another British actor, he became popular in the USA as Chad & Jeremy between 1964 & 1966. Hit: "Summer Song" (8/64 US 7). In 1967 the two split up, as competition from other British duos like David & Jonathan and Peter & Gordon was too strong. They returned to acting, with Jeremy playing the main part in the 1976 TV series *Sexton Blake*.

Tony McPhee 1944 UK guitarist, singer, and songwriter, who benefitted from the mid-1960s blues boom in the UK. Between 1964 & 1966s, he played with the Groundhogs. Then Tony guested on records by Champion Jack Dupree (1966) and Eddie Boyd (1967). In 1968 the Groundhogs were reformed with Tony and another original member, bassist Peter Cruickshank. In 1969 the group changed direction, moving more towards rock than blues, and managed to reach a larger audience. In 1973 Tony released a solo album, which resulted in the band splitting up. By 1975, Tony had formed another version of the Groundhogs, of which he was the only original member. Tony is also a session musician with Mike Batt or and the John Dummer Blues Band.

Chuck Jackson 1945 US lead singer with the Independents who had the million selling hit, "Leaving Me" (4/73 US 21). He is not related to the other solo singer Chuck Jackson.

Patrick Olive 1947 UK guitarist and percussionist for Hot Chocolate.

Harry Vanda 1947 Australian guitarist and songwriter with the Easybeats formed in 1964. Harry was born Johannes Vandenberg in the Netherlands. Biggest hit: "Friday On My Mind" (10/66 UK 6; 3/67 US 16). In 1969 the Easybeats split up. Harry formed quite a successful writing team with former Easybeat member George Young. Later on, they tried their luck as Band Of Hope, Marcus Hook, Paintbox, and Flash & The Pan. Hits as the latter: "Waiting For A Train" (5/83 UK 7) and "Midnight Man".

Randy Hobbs 1948 US bass player with the McCoys and Johnny & Edgar Winter.

Andrew Lloyd Webber 1948 UK prodigy and composer of numerous extremely successful musicals, *Joseph And His Amazing Technicolour Dreamcoat* (1968), *Jesus Christ Superstar* (1970), *Evita* (1976), *Cats* (1981), *Starlight Express* (1984), *Phantom Of The Opera* (1985), *Chess* (1986) and *Aspects Of Love* (1989). Tim Rice wrote the lyrics for most of the musicals.

Susanne Sulley 1963 UK singer who joined Human League in October 1980.

Deaths

Mark Dinning 1986 US singer who died of a heart attack. Born 17th August, 1933.

Dave Guard 1991 US singer and guitarist, born 19th October, 1934.

Hits of the Day

1962 "Wonderful Land" Shadows UK 8 weeks
1975 "Bye Bye Baby" Bay City Rollers UK 6 weeks
1975 "My Eyes Adored You" Frankie Valli US 1 week
1980 "Going Underground" Jam UK 3 weeks
1980 "Another Brick In The Wall" Pink Floyd US 4 weeks
1986 "These Dreams" Heart US 1 week

23rd

Birthdays

Joan Crawford 1908 US actress who occasionally made a record. Greatest hit: "It's All So New To Me" (4/39 US 19). She died 10th May, 1977. Her real name was Lucille Le Sueur.

Louisiana Red 1936 US blues musician and songwriter. Real name Iverson Minter. His mother died of pneumonia a week after he was born. His father was lynched by the Ku-Klux-Klan in 1941. Iverson grew up first with his grandmother and then in an orphanage. At age 16 he was a member of a streetgang, and took part in a burglary of a food store, in which all the cash was taken. He was the only one caught, and sent to a corrective institution for boys, then he joined the army, and was sent off to Korea. It's hardly surprising he sings the blues.

Alan Blaikley 1940 UK songwriter. He formed a songwriting team with Ken Howard which was second only to Lennon/McCartney during the 1960s. They wrote ten Top Ten hits for Dave Dee, Dozy, Beaky, Mick & Tich exclusively. Furthermore they wrote for the Honeycombs, Herd, Lulu, Bay City Rollers, Petula Clark, Engelbert Humperdinck and Elvis Presley.

Dave Bartram 1952 UK singer with the R n' R revival group Showaddywaddy, who had 10 Top Ten hits between 1974 & 1982. Their biggest hits were "Hey Rock n' Roll" (5/74 UK 3), "Three Steps To Heaven" (5/75 UK 2), "Under The Moon Of Love" (11/76 UK 1), "When" (3/77 UK 3), "You Got What It Takes" (7/77 UK 2) and "I Wonder Why" (3/78 UK 2). Most of these hits were revamped r'n'r classics.

Chaka Khan 1953 US singer, real name Yvette Marie Stevens. As a teenager she worked for the Black Panther Movement, during which time she adopted the name Chaka Khan (chaka means 'fire'). In 1969 she joined Shades Of Black, in 1970 Look & Chain, and Lyfe, and in 1972 became the replacement lead singer for Paulette McWilliams with Ask Rufus, which finally became just Rufus in August 1973. They had their debut hit with the million seller written by Stevie Wonder, "Tell Me Something Good" (6/74 US 3). After that they became Rufus featuring Chaka Khan. Hit: "Sweet Thing" (1/76 US 5), also a million seller. Between 1978 & August 1979 the group were called Rufus & Chaka Khan, when she left the group completely to concentrate on a solo career. Hits: "I'm Every Woman" (10/78 US 21; 12/78 UK 11) and (5/89 UK 8, a remix), "I Feel For You" (9/84 US 3; UK 1), with rapper Grandmaster Melle Mel and Stevie Wonder playing harmonica, "Eye To Eye" (4/85 UK 16) and "Ain't Nobody" (remix) (7/89 UK 6).

Marti Pellow 1966 UK lead singer and songwriter with the group Wet Wet Wet. Real name Mark McLoughlin. The band was formed in 1982 as Vortex Motion, but changed their name that year to Wet Wet Wet, which referred to a line in the Scritti Politti-song "Getting, Having, And Holding". Hits: "Wishing I Was Lucky" (4/87 UK 6), "Sweet Little Mystery" (8/87 UK 5), "Angel Eyes (Home And Away)" (12/87 UK 5), "Temptation" (3/88 UK 12) and "Sweet Surrender" (9/89 UK 6).

Deaths

Bill Kenny 1978 US guitarist and singer. He joined the Inkspots as the replacement for Gerry Daniels. Success followed swiftly with Hits like "Address Unknown" (10/39 US 1), "We Three (My Echo, My Shadow, And Me)" (10/40 US 1), "I'm Making Believe" (10/44 US 1), "Into Each Life Some Rain Must Fall" (11/44 US 1), "The Gypsy" (5/46 US 1) and "To Each His Own" (8/46 US 1). From 1951 their hits dried up and, in 1952, the group split up. From then on there were two rival groups called Inkspots. Bill was born in 1915.

Jacob Miller 1980 Head of the reggae band Inner Circle. He died after a car crash. Born 4th May, 1956.

Hits of the Day

1946	"Oh! What It Seemed To Be" Frank Sinatra US 8 weeks
1961	"Wooden Heart" Elvis Presley UK 6 weeks

1963	"Our Day Will Come" Ruby & The Romantics US 1 week
1974	"Dark Lady" Cher US 1 week
1985	"Easy Lover" Philip Bailey & Phil Collins UK 4 weeks

24th

Birthdays

Dave Appell 1922 US leader of the band Applejacks. Hit: "Mexican Hat" (9/58 US 16). Later, he became a producer for Tony Orlando & Dawn, among others.

Billy Stewart 1937 US singer, composer, and pianist. Nickname: 'Fat Boy'. He began his career as a singer with the Rainbows in his native Washington. This band was also the starting point for other stars-to-be such as Marvin Gaye and Don Covay. Later on, Billy played with Bo Diddley's backing group. Bo promoted Billy helping him get a recording contract with Chess Records, Billy cut records for them from 1956 to 1967. He had his biggest hit with a very idiosyncratic version of Gershwin's "Summertime" (7/66 US 10; 9/66 UK 39). He died together with other musicians from his band in a tragic car accident on 17th January, 1970.

Colin Peterson 1946 Australian drummer. When Robert Stigwood signed the Bee Gees to recording a contract in February 1967 (hither to they had only been successful in Australia), they were joined in March that year, by guitarist Vince Melouney and Colin. In March 1969 both Vince and Colin left the band following internal disagreements.

Nick Lowe 1949 UK bass player, singer and songwriter. He formed Kippington Lodge in 1965 with guitarist Brinsley Schwarz, who released five singles during the following years, none of which charted. In October 1969 Nick and Brinsley decided to rename the group Brinsley Schwarz. 4 albums appeared, none of which became a commercial hit. In March 1975, the group split up, Nick became the producer of Kursaal Flyers, Dr. Feelgood and Graham Parker. He released two singles under the pseudonyms Disco Brothers and Tartan Horde, without success. In August 1976, his first solo single appeared, without success. Then he produced the Damned, Elvis Costello, the Clovers (Huey Lewis was a member of the group at the time) and David Edmunds. In July 1977, Nick became a member of Edmunds' group, Rockpile. On the side he carried on trying to establish a solo career. In 1978 onwards, he had hits with "I Love The Sound Of Breaking Glass" (3/78 UK 7) and "Cruel To Be Kind" (7/79 US & UK 12). In common with Mickey Jupp (whom he produced), Graham Parker, Elvis Costello, Ian Drury and Dave Edmunds, Nick Lowe was an ardent admirer of Chuck Berry, whose influence permeates his own output.

Mike Kellie 1945 UK drummer with Art, Spooky Tooth and Three Man Army. He has also worked as a session musician for Joe Cocker, Gary Wright, Luther Grosvenor, Jim Capaldi, Peter Frampton, Paul Kossoff, Splinter and Only Ones, among others.

Hits of the Day

1958 "Catch A Falling Star" Perry Como US 1 week
1973 "Love Train" O'Jays US 1 week
1979 "Tragedy" Bee Gees US 2 weeks
1984 "Hello" Lionel Richie UK 6 weeks

25th

Birthdays

Frankie Carle 1903 US pianist, bandleader and songwriter. Real name Francis Nunzio Carlone. As a teenager he played in dance bands, formed his own band, and joined Horace Heidt from 1939 until 1943. He became co-leader of the band, and then started his own band in 1944. Hits: "Oh! What It Seemed To Be" (1/46 US 1) and "Rumours Are Flying" (9/46 US 1). In both cases the Vocalist was Frankie's daughter Marjorie Hughes. In 1949, success waned.

Bonnie Guitar 1924 US guitarist and singer. Real surname Buckingham. She had her own group in the early 50s. In the mid-1950s she worked as a session guitarist in Los Angeles. In 1958 she set up her own record company, after which she became musical director of country music for Dot and ABC-Paramount. She scored, as an artist, with the crossover-hit "Dark Moon" (4/57 US 6).

Johnny Burnette 1934 US singer and songwriter. He was one of the arch-exponents of rockabilly music in the mid-1950s. He formed the Johnny Burnette Trio, with his brother Dorsey and a friend called Paul Burlison. His solo hits, however, had little to do with rockabilly: "Dreamin' " (7/60 US 11; 9/60 UK 5), and "You're Sixteen" (10/60 US 8; 1/61 UK 3). On the 14th August 1964 he drowned while fishing. His son Rocky (born 12th June, 1953) also became a singer.

Hoyt Axton 1938 US singer and songwriter, though considerably more successful as a writer. He must have inherited his talent from his mother who wrote the number "Heartbreak Hotel" for Elvis. Hoyt wrote "Greenback Dollar" for the Kingston Trio, "Joy To The World" and "Never Been To Spain" for Three Dog Night, "The Pusher" for Steppenwolf and the "No No Song" for Ringo Starr.

Anita Bryant 1940 US singer who was Miss Oklahoma in 1958, and was 2nd in the Miss America contest. Between 1959 & 1964 she had 11 hit records. Her biggest hits were "Paper Roses" (4/60 US 5; UK 24), and "In My Little Corner Of The World" (7/60 US 10).

Aretha Franklin 1942 US soul singer whose career took off in 1961 and has continued apace ever since. She cut her first recordings aged 14. In 1960 she signed with Columbia Records who treated her as a gospel/jazz singer. In 1967, when she signed to Atlantic Records her style changed subtly. This change was catalytic to her success; her hits included "I Never Loved A Man (The Way I Love You)" (3/67 US 9), "Respect" (4/67 US 1; 6/67 UK 10), "Baby I Love You" (7/67 US 4; UK 39), "Chain Of Fools" (12/67 US 2), "(Sweet Sweet Baby) Since You've Been Gone" (3/68 US 5), "Think" (5/68 US 7; UK 26), "I Say A Little Prayer" (8/68 US 10; UK 4), "See Saw" (11/68 US 14), "Don't Play That Song" (8/70 US 11; UK 13), "Bridge Over Troubled Water" (4/71 US 6), "Spanish Harlem" (7/71 US 2; 10/71 UK 14), "Rock Steady" (10/71 US 9), "Day Dreamin'" (3/72 US 5) and "Until You Come Back To Me (That's What I'm Gonna Do)" (11/73 US 3; 2/74 UK 26). All these records were million sellers. After James Brown she is the most influential soul singer around. After 1976 she was considered passé by many, but then the 'Queen of Soul' returned with "Freeway Of Love" (6/85 US 3) and "Who's Zoomin' Who" (9/85 US 7; 1/86 UK 11). In the 80s she has cut a few interesting duets with Eurythmics, Keith Richards and, the most successful, with George Michael, "I Knew You Were Waiting (For Me)" (1/87 UK & US 1), among others.

Elton John 1947 UK singer, pianist, and songwriter. Real name Reginald Kenneth Dwight. His career started in 1961 with Bluesology, who turned professional in 1965. The first record by Bluesology was "Come Back Baby", written by Elton. In December 1966 Long John Baldry became the vocalist of the group, which was renamed John Baldry Show shortly after. In June 1967 Elton joined the lyricist Bernie Taupin. In October Baldry released a solo record which became a No. 1 hit; the B-side "Lord You Made The Night Too Long" was the first recorded composition of John and Taupin. In March 1968 Elton John released his first single and, in June 1969, his first solo album appeared. His first hit single was "Your Song" (11/70 US 8; 1/71 UK 7). His biggest hits were "Crocodile Rock" (11/72 UK 5; US 1), "Goodbye Yellow Brick Road" (9/73 UK 6; US 2), "Benny And The Jets" (2/74 US 1), "Don't Let The Sun Go Down On Me" (6/74 UK 16; US 2), "Lucy In The Sky With Diamonds" (11/74 UK 10; US 1), "Philadelphia Freedom" (3/75 UK 12; US 1), "Someone Saved My Life Tonight" (6/75 UK 22; US 4), "Island Girl" (10/75 UK 14; US 1), "Sorry Seems To Be The Hardest Word" (11/76 UK 11; US 6), "Mama Can't Buy You Love" (6/79 US 9) and "Little Jeannie" (5/80 US 3; UK 33). They were all million sellers. His first No. 1 hit in Britain was a duet with Kiki Dee, "Don't Go Breaking My Heart" (7/76 UK & US 1), another million seller. Elton was successful during the 80s too. Hits: "Nikita" (10/85 UK 3; 1/86 US 7), "I Don't Wanna Go On With You Like That" (6/88 US 2; UK 30) and "Sacrifice" (6/90 UK 1). On 14th February, 1984 Elton married German sound technician Renate Blauel, it proved to be a short-lived liaison. Among his other ventures was chairmanship of Watford Football Club.

Jack Hall 1947 US bass player with Wet Willie, Yellow Dog and the Charlie Daniels Band.

John Rowles 1947 New Zealand singer who charted in 1968 with "If I Only Had Time" (3/68 UK 3), and "Hush Not A Word To Mary" (6/68 UK 12).

Michael Stanley 1948 US singer, guitarist, and songwriter who released two folk albums in the early 1970s. He formed his own group in 1974. The biggest hit by this band was "He Can't Love You" (11/80 US 33).

Maizie Williams 1951 UK singer with Boney M, born on Montserrat.

Steve Norman 1960 UK percussionist and saxophonist with the band Spandau Ballet, formed in 1979.

Deaths

Duster Bennett 1976 UK blues musician. Unfortunately, he died after a car accident. Born 23rd September, 1946.

Hits of the Day

1950	"If I Knew You Were Coming, I'd 've Baked A Cake" Eileen Barton US 10 weeks
1967	"Happy Together" Turtles US 3 weeks
1972	"A Horse With No Name" America US 3 weeks
1989	"The Living Years" Mike & The Mechanics US 1 week
1989	"Like A Prayer" Madonna UK 3 weeks

26th

Birthdays

Al Jolson 1886 US actor and singer, real name Asa Yoelson, born in Russian St. Petersberg. He had his first million seller in 1912 with "Ragging The Baby To Sleep" (7/12 US 1). Further timeless treasures were "The Spaniard That Blighted My Life" (5/13 US 1), "Swanee" (5/20 US 1) & "Sonny Boy" (10/28 US 1) from the film, *The Singing Fool*; the latter had the distinction of being the first million seller promoted through a film. Other hits were "The Anniversary Song" (2/47 US 2), "My Mammy" (2/47 US 18) and "April Showers" (4/47 US 15). It was Al who appeared in the first sound film, *The Jazz Singer* (1927). Two films were made about Jolson, *The Jolson Story*, and *Jolson Sings Again*. He died 23rd October, 1950.

Rufus Thomas 1917 US R & B singer, songwriter, dance inventor and disc jockey. He started his career as a member of the Rabbit Foot Minstrels in 1935. He made his first records as a soloist in 1950, and had his first success on the Sun label with the number "Bear Cat" (4/53 R&B 3). This song was an answer to Big Mama Thornton's song "Hound Dog". Pop hits were "Walking The Dog" (10/63 US 10) and "Do The Funky Chicken" (2/70 US 28; 4/70 UK 18). Between 1953 & 1974 he worked as a disc jockey for the radio station WDIA in Memphis. His daughter is the well-known soul singer Carla Thomas.

Fred Parris 1936 US lead singer and songwriter with the Five Satins. Hit: "In The Still Of The Night" (9/56 US 24). After Fred had made the record, he was conscripted into the Army and went to Japan. The band split up. Then the number became a hit and the Five Satins reformed with another lead singer, Bill Baker. When Fred was discharged from the army in January 1958, he took on his old job with the band, and Baker had to leave. In 1961, "In The

Still Of The Night" charted once again, albeit briefly. In 1982 Fred released a medley of old 1950s hits as Fred Parris & The Five Satins under the title, "Memories of Days Gone By" (2/82 US 71).

Rod Lauren 1940 US singer, who was meant to close the gap for RCA left by Elvis' military service. Rod's career was launched with a fan fare of publicity: one hit resulted, "If I Had A Girl" (12/59 US 31). Then Elvis returned – and Rod disappeared.

Diana Ross 1944 US lead singer with the Supremes and, from 1970, as a solo singer. Hits: with the Supremes, "Where Did Our Love Go" (7/64 US 1; 9/64 UK 3), "Baby Love" (10/64 US & UK 1), "Come See About Me" (11/64 US 1; 1/65 UK 27), "Stop In The Name Of Love" (2/65 US 1; UK 7), "Back In My Arms Again" (5/65 US 1), "I Hear A Symphony" (10/65 US 1), "You Can't Hurry Love" (8/66 US 1; UK 3), "You Keep Me Hanging On" (10/66 US 1; 12/66 UK 8), "Love Is Here And Now You're Gone" (1/67 US 1; UK 17) and "Happening" (4/67 US 1; UK 6). After this, all records were credited to Diana Ross & The Supremes, and the hits just kept on coming, "Love Child" (10/68 US 1; UK 15) and, the last before splitting up, "Someday We'll Be Together Again" (11/69 US 1; UK 13). As a solo artist, she was seldom far from the top of the charts: "Ain't No Mountain High Enough" (8/70 US 1; UK 6), "Touch Me In The Morning" (6/73 US 1; UK 9), "Theme From Mahogany (Do You Know Where You're Going To)" (11/75 US 1; 4/76 UK 5), "Love Hangover" (4/76 US 1; UK 10), and "Upside Down" (7/80 UK 2; US 1). Diana Ross topped the charts twice within the UK "I'm Still Waiting" (4/71 UK 1) and "Chain Reaction" (1/86 UK 1). In addition to all the No. 1 hits mentioned, there were countless top ten hits, some of which were duets with other Motown artists like Michael Jackson, Marvin Gaye, Smokey Robinson, Stevie Wonder & the Temptations. One more hit should be mentioned, which stood at No. 1 for 9 consecutive weeks in the USA, "Endless Love" (7/81 US 1; 9/81 UK 7), another duet – this time with Lionel Richie.

Fran Sheehan 1946 US bass player with Boston.

Richard Tandy 1948 UK keyboard and guitar player with ELO. As a session musician, he played with Kiki Dee, Dave Edmunds and the Everly Brothers.

Steve Tyler 1948 US lead singer and songwriter with the band Aerosmith formed in 1970. Biggest hits were "Dream On" (10/73 US 59; 1/76 RE-US 6), and "Walk This Way" (11/76 US 10). In the early 1980s the band split up, but then reformed in April 1984. Hits: "Dude (Looks Like A Lady)" (10/87 US 14), "Angel" (1/88 US 3), "Love In

An Elevator" (9/89 US 5; UK 13), and "Janie's Got A Gun" (11/89 US 4).

Vicky Lawrence 1949 US singer, actress and, briefly, wife of Bob Russell, who wrote songs like "Honey" and "Little Green Apples". He wrote his wife's only hit, "The Night The Lights Went Out In Georgia" (2/73 US 1). Between 1967 & 1969 Vicky was featured regularly on the Carol Burnett Show and, from 1983, starred in the US TV-series *Mama's Family*.

Ronnie McDowell 1950 US singer and Elvis imitator. After his idol's death he sang, "The King Is Gone" (9/77 US 13); while it was his only hit, it was a million seller.

Teddy Pendergrass 1950 US singer and drummer. In 1969 he began his career as the drummer with Harold Melvin & The Blue Notes. In 1970 he replaced their lead singer John Atkins, which marked the turning point in their career. Hits: "If You Don't Know Me By Now" (9/72 US 3; 1/73 UK 9) and "The Love I Lost (Part 1)" (9/73 US 7; 1/74 UK 21), both records were million sellers. In 1976 Teddy started a solo career. Hit and million seller: "Close The Door" (7/78 US 25). On the 18th March, 1982 he had a serious car accident, which seriously incapacitated him for the best part of two years. In 1984 he resumed his career, recording the duet "Hold Me" (6/84 US 46; R&B 5; 1/86 UK 44) with the completely unknown Whitney Houston.

William Lyall 1953 UK pianist and flautist with Pilot, Alan Parsons Project, and as a session musician with Dollar, and Sheena Easton.

Deaths

Eddie Lang 1933 US guitarist. He died as the result of an operation for tonsilitis. Born 25th October, 1902.

Hits of the Day

1949	"Cruising Down The River" Russ Morgan US 7 weeks
1955	"The Ballad Of Davy Crockett" Bill Hayes US 5 weeks
1969	"I Heard It Through The Grapevine" Marvin Gaye UK 3 weeks
1977	"Rich Girl" Hall & Oates US 2 weeks
1983	"Is There Something I Should Know" Duran Duran UK 2 weeks
1988	"Man In The Mirror" Michael Jackson US 2 weeks
1988	"Don't Turn Around" Aswad UK 2 weeks

27th

Birthdays

Leroy Carr 1905 US blues pianist. In the 20s he accompanied various artists at dances and so-called house parties. From the late 1920s he cut his own records, usually accompanied by Scrapper Blackwell. The "Sloppy Drunk Blues" concerned one of Leroy's favourite pastimes, which is probably why he died of alcoholism on 29th April, 1935.

Richard Hayman 1920 US pianist, harmonica player and orchestra leader. He was successful from 1953 to 1961, hit "Ruby" (4/53 US 3).

Tom Edwards 1923 US radio disc jockey, who was one of the first to promote Elvis Presley on the radio. He himself was successful with two narrated records with orchestral backing; the themes of the numbers was the perennial conflict between generations. He told the adults "What Is A Teenage Girl?" (2/57 US 57), and the other side of the record was "What Is A Teenage Boy?". Tom died 24th July, 1981.

Sarah Vaughan 1924 US singer and pianist, who was successful from 1949 to 1966. She studied piano from 1930 to 1939. In 1942 she won an amateur competition at the Apollo Theatre in Harlem, which led to a contract with the Earl Hines band as a vocalist and second pianist. This, in turn, led to positions with the orchestras of Billy Eckstine and Dizzy Gillespie; she recorded the classic "Lover Man" with the latter. From 1945 she made records as a soloist, her nickname was 'The Divine One'. Hits: "Nature Boy" (7/48 US 9), "Make Yourself Comfortable" (11/54 US 6), "Whatever Lola Wants" (4/55 US 6) and "Broken Hearted Melody" (7/59 US 7; 9/59 UK 7). She was active right into the 1980s. She died on April 3rd, 1990.

John Marascalco 1931 US songwriter who wrote many of the great R n' R numbers of the 50s like "Rip It Up" and "Good Golly Miss Molly".

Bo Winberg 1939 Swedish guitarist, songwriter and leader of the Spotnicks. Bo remained with the group through thick and thin, and stayed true to the band over the years, giving the group its trademark sound. Hit: "Hava Nagila" (1/63 UK 13).

Janis Martin 1940 US singer who signed a recording contract with RCA shortly after Elvis Presley. RCA were of the opinion that Janis was the female Elvis. She had broadcast on radio as an eleven year old, and at thirteen she appeared at the Tobacco Festival with Ernest Tubb. At fifteen she had a recording contract, but her only success was "Will You, Willyum" (5/56 US 50). After that, RCA tried to emphasize the connection with Elvis, but "My Boy Elvis" was a flop. After 1958 and a baby her career was over, inspite of several comeback attempts.

Andy Bown 1947 UK guitarist, keyboard player and songwriter with the group Herd formed in September 1966, and which split up in October 1969. After this, Andy played with Mike Hugg, Leslie Duncan, Memphis Slim, Tim Hardin, Chris Jagger, Marmalade, Pink Floyd, and Peter Frampton. He released solo albums in 1972, 1973, and 1976 respectively, and has played bass with Status Quo since 1973.

Tony Banks 1950 UK pianist, singer and songwriter. In January 1967 he was one of the musicians whom Jonathan King christened Genesis. He has remained with the group throughout their career. As did the other members, Banks released solo albums, which however, were not as successful as those of his colleagues. In 1989 he started a new project called Bankstatement.

Felix Haug 1952 Swiss multi-talent musician and songwriter, who joined the group Double after stints with Yello and Ping Pong. Their biggest hit was "The Captain Of Her Heart" (1/86 UK 8; 6/86 US 16).

Walter Stocker 1953 US lead guitarist with the Babys and as a session musician with Air Supply and Rod Stewart.

Bill MacKenzie 1957 UK singer and songwriter, who formed the cabaret-combo Absorbic Ones together with Alan Rankine in 1976. In 1979 they renamed themselves Associates, set up their own label and released their first record. Their first one was "Party Fears Two" (2/82 UK 9). In February 1985 the group split up.

Clark Datchler 1961 UK singer and songwriter, who after releasing two successful solo records with Rak Records, became co-founder of the trio Johnny Hates Jazz in 1985. Hits: "Shattered Dreams" (4/87 UK 5; 3/88 US 2), "I Don't Want To Be A Hero" (8/87 UK 11; 7/88 US 31) and "Turn Back The Clock" (11/87 UK 12).

Hits of the Day

1959	"Side Saddle" Russ Conway UK 4 weeks
1965	"Stop! In The Name Of Love" Supremes US 2 weeks
1968	"Lady Madonna" Beatles UK 2 weeks
1976	"Save Your Kisses For Me" Brotherhood Of Man UK 6 weeks
1982	"Seven Tears" Goombay Dance Band UK 3 weeks

Miscellany

1952 The first record by the Sun label appeared at number 175 by Sam Phillips, "Drivin' Slow/Flat Tire" sung by Johnny London. Before that, Phillips had made his presence felt with "Blues In My Condition" by Walter Horton and Jack Kelly by sending test discs to the local radio stations. However, interest was so meagre that Phillips did not even release the record on the market. The instrumental by saxophonist, Johnny London, failed to make the crucial break through for Sun label as well. Sun 209 appeared on 19th July, 1954, "That's Alright Mama," by Elvis, and with that times changed for Sam Phillips.

28th

Birthdays

Paul Whiteman 1890 US violinist and orchestra leader, the "King of Jazz", who is considered to be the most popular bandleader of the swing era. Started out as a violinist with the Denver & San Francisco Symphony Orchestra. In 1919 he formed his own first band. From 1920 to 1954 he had 220 hits. He had 26 No. 1s in the US charts. His biggest hits were million sellers, "Whispering/Japanese Sandman" (10/20 US 1), "Wang Wang Blues" (12/20 US 2), "3 O'Clock In The Morning" (11/22 US 1), and "Linger Awhile" (2/24 US 1). It was Paul who, with his orchestra, accompanied George Gershwin at the premiere of 'Rhapsody In Blue' in the New York Aeolian Hall on 12th February, 1924. He also played with Bix Beiderbecke and other great jazz musicians in the late 20s and made the first recordings with Bing Crosby in 1927. Bing sang compositions like "My Blue Heaven" (10/27 US 1), in which Red Nichols played trumpet. Paul died 29th December, 1967.

Jay Livingston 1915 US songwriter; standards like "Tammy", "Golden Earrings", "Buttons & Bows", "Mona Lisa" and "Whatever Will Be Will Be" were composed by him. Jay usually wrote with Ray Evans. The Livingston/Evans team had their first hit in 1948. They also worked on many film and TV scores, like *Bonanza*.

Thad Jones 1923 US trumpeter, composer, and bandleader. Real first names, Thaddeus Joseph. He started out in the Count Basie orchestra, from which Thad, with Mel Lewis, began the Lewis-Jones Band. During the course of his career he played with many famous jazz musicians. In February 1985, he became the leader of the Count Basie Band. He died of cancer on 20th August, 1986 aged 62.

Charlie McCoy 1941 US harmonica player. He was a session musician on many records by great US stars. His metier was versatility: working with Bob Dylan, Quincy Jones, Waylon Jennings and B.J. Thomas.

Charles Portz 1945 US bass player with the Nightriders, who became the Crossfires and then, the Turtles.

Sally Carr 1948 UK singer with Middle Of The Road, who lived up to their name musically speaking. Formed in Scotland in 1970, after a successful debut, they found themselves stranded penniless in Genoa, Italy, and were unable to pay for their return fare back to Britain. Just as in a fairytale, an RCA director happened to hear the group at his Italian holiday resort, and sent them straight off to the studio. The first single which appeared in October 1970, became their first hit 6 months later, "Chirpy Chirpy Cheep Cheep" (6/71 UK 1). This was the first of a series of hits for Sally Carr, which included "Tweedle Dee Tweedle Dum" (9/71 UK 2), "Soley Soley" (12/71 UK 5), "Sacramento" (4/72 UK 23), "Samson And Delilah" (7/72 UK 26), "Bottom's Up" (9/72) and "Yellow Boomerang" (3/73).

John Evan 1948 UK keyboard player. Both Ian Anderson and Glenn Cornick were members of John Evan's Smash in 1966/67; later, they formed Jethro Tull in November 1967. Thereupon, John dissolved his band, studied chemistry, and in April 1970 joined his old colleagues in Jethro Tull. He stayed until June 1980 and then carried on as a session musician.

Milan Williams 1948 US pianist, singer, guitarist and songwriter with the Commodores.

Mark Spiro 1957 US keyboard player and singer who turned up in 1985/86 as a session musician with Anne Murray, Laura Brannigan and Richard T. Bear.

Deaths

W. C. Handy 1958 US blues songwriter and cornettist. Born 16th November, 1873.

Arthur 'Big Boy' Crudup 1974 US blues guitarist and singer. He died in poverty after a stroke. Born 24th August, 1905.

Hits of the Day

1963 "Foot Tapper" Shadows UK 1 week
1970 "Bridge Over Troubled Water" Simon & Garfunkel UK 3 weeks

1981	"This Ole House" Shakin' Stevens UK 3 weeks
1981	"Rapture" Blondie US 2 weeks
1987	"Respectable" Mel & Kim UK 1 week

29th

Birthdays

Moon Mullican 1909 US country pianist, singer and bandleader. Real first name Aubrey. He was called the 'King of Hillbilly Piano Players' and his style of piano playing influenced the development of rock n' roll. He had his first band in the mid-1930s. In the early 40s he played with the Blue Ridge Playboys and the Texas Wanderers and, finally, made records as a soloist from 1946. His most successful numbers were "New Pretty Blond (Jole Blon)" (2/47 C&W 2) and "I'll Sail My Ship Alone" (3/50 C&W 1). He died on 1st January, 1967.

Pearl Bailey 1918 US singer and actress. When 13 she won her first competition for youngsters, and won a second competition at the Apollo in New York. In 1946 she had her first success as an actress and in 1947, she made her first records. Among her most celebrated film roles were in *Carmen Jones* (1954), *St. Louis Blues* (1958) with Nat 'King' Cole, *Porgy And Bess* (1959) and *All The Fine Young Cannibals* (1960); The title of the latter was the inspiration for the name of the British group Fine Young Cannibals. Her biggest hit was "Takes Two To Tango" (9/52 US 7).

Donny Conn 1930 US singer with the trio Playmates, whose biggest hit was "Beep Beep" (11/58 US 4).

Eden Kane 1942 UK singer, real name Richard Sarstedt. He had five Top Ten hits from 1961 to 1964: "Well I Ask You" (6/61 UK 1), "Get Lost" (9/61 UK 10), "Forget Me Not" (1/62 UK 3), "I Don't Know Why" (5/62 UK 7) and "Boys Cry" (1/64 UK 8). With his solo career behind him, Eden made an abortive attempt at stardom as the Sarstedt Brothers with siblings Clive and Peter. Clive and Peter also tried their luck as soloists: Clive failed totally, while Peter scored with "Where Do You Go To, My Lovely?".

Vangelis 1943 Greek multi-instrumentalist and composer, real name Evangelos Papathanassiou. He started out as a member of the rock band Formynx. After the military junta took power in Greece, Vangelis fled to Paris in 1967. With other exiled Greeks, he formed the band Aphrodite's Child, who had an international million seller with "Rain And Tears" (10/68 UK 30), which was supposedly reminiscent of Johann Pachelbel's Canon in D. After the band split up, he worked as a session musician and on solo projects, scoring the sound track for the film "Chariots Of Fire" (9/81 UK 12; 2/82 US 1), for which he received an Oscar. From 1980, he worked with Jon Anderson, singer with the group Yes, as Jon & Vangelis. Hits: "I Hear You Now" (1/80 UK 8), and "I'll Find My Way Home" (12/81 UK 6).

Mike Shepstone 1944 US drummer and songwriter with the British band I Rokes, who were as popular as the Beatles in Italy in the mid-1960s. Their biggest hit was "Piangi Con Me (Cry With Me)" a million seller in Italy in 1967. An English version of this title composition was a hit for Grass Roots in the US that year, "Let's Live For Today" (6/67 US 8). In 1973 Mike formed the duo, Shepstone & Dibbins, with Peter Dibbins and they charted in Germany in 1974 with "Shady Lady".

Terry Jacks 1946 Canadian singer, guitarist, songwriter and producer. He began as a rhythm guitarist and lead singer with the Canadian group Chessmen. During a TV show for a Canadian television station he met Susan Pesklevits whom he married later on, and with whom he formed the quartet Poppy Family. Hit and million seller: "Which Way You Goin' Billy" (4/70 US 2; 8/70 UK 7). In 1973 both the group and the marriage broke up, and the two carried on as solo artists. Terry had his biggest hit with "Seasons In The Sun" (1/74 US 1; 3/74 UK 1) and "If You Go Away" (6/74 UK 8), both were Jacques Brel compositions, with English lyrics by Rod McKuen: the original versions being "Le Moribond" and "Ne Me Quittes Pas" respectively.

Bobby Kimball 1947 US leadsinger and songwriter with Toto. Real name Robert Toteaux. Before that he sang with S.S. Fools. When the group Toto was founded in 1978, all the members were already sought-after session musicians. Even after the formation of the group, each continued to work on sessions for other artists. Hits, with Toto: "Hold The Line" (10/78 US 5; 2/79 UK 14), "Rosanna" (4/82 US 5; 4/83 UK 12), and "Africa" (10/82 US 1; 2/83 UK 3). In 1984 Bobby left the group and was replaced by Dennis Frederiksen. In 1985 Bobby became a member of Far Corporation, formed by Frank Farian. Their most successful record was a version of the old Led Zeppelin composition, "Stairway To Heaven" (11/85 UK 8). In 1989 Bobby started a solo career.

Andy Parker 1953 UK drummer with UFO.

Hits of the Day

1941 "Amapola" Jimmy Dorsey US 10 weeks
1969 "Atlantis" Donovan
1975 "Lady Marmalade" La Belle US 1 week
1986 "Living Doll" Cliff Richard & The Young Ones UK 3 weeks
1986 "Rock Me Amadeus" Falco US 3 weeks

30th

Birthdays

Frankie Lane 1913 US singer, real name Frank LoVecchio. He began his career in 1937 with the Freddy Carlone Band, replacing Perry Como, who had started a successful solo career. Before that among other things he survived the Depression years by entering so-called 'Dance Marathon Contests' holding the world record for years of 3,501 hours, which was set in Atlantic City in 1932. Laine did not stay with Freddy Carlone for long. Shortly after, he became a singer on a radio station in New York. After the 2nd World War, with pianist Carl Fischer, he was a sensation in a Hollywood nightclub. Between 1947 & 1969 he had hits with the million sellers, "That's My Desire" (3/47 US 4), "That Lucky Old Sun" (8/49 US 1), "Mule Train" (11/49 US 1), "The Cry Of The Wild Goose" (2/50 US 1), "Jezebel" (5/51 US 2), "Jealousy" (11/51 US 3), "Sugar Bush" (with Doris Day) (6/52 US 7), "High Noon" (7/52 US 5; 11/52 UK 7) and "I Believe" (2/53 US 2; 4/53 UK 1). Other hits – not million sellers though were "Hey Joe" (8/53 US 6, 10/53 UK 1), "Answer Me" (10/53 US 24; UK 1) and "A Woman In Love" (11/55 US 19; 9/56 UK 1). Besides that, Frankie cut duets with Jimmy Boyd on "Tell Me A Story" (3/53 US 4; 5/53 UK 5), Johnnie Ray, Jo Stafford, and Doris Day.

Sonny Boy Williamson 1914 US blues singer and harmonica player. Real first names John Lee. This is the "original" Sonny Boy Williamson. He worked with small bands in Chicago until 1945, then as a soloist: his biggest hit was "Shake The Boogie" (2/47 R&B 4). He was murdered 1st June, 1948.

Rolf Harris 1930 Australian singer, pianist and songwriter. Hits: "Tie Me Kangaroo Down Sport" (7/60 UK 9; 6/63 US 3), "Sun Arise" (10/62 UK 3) and "Two Little Boys" (11/69 UK 1). From 1970 Rolf had regular TV shows on BBC and was especially popular on children's programmes.

Graeme Edge 1942 UK drummer and songwriter with the Moody Blues. He also made solo albums from 1975.

Eric Clapton 1945 UK guitarist, singer and songwriter. His career began in January 1963 with the Roosters. In September of the same year he became a member of Casey Jones & The Engineers, and finally in October of the same year he joined the Yardbirds. He stayed with them until March 1965, then went to John Mayall's Bluesbreakers, staying with them until July 1966, when he formed one of the first so-called super groups, Cream, with Ginger Baker and Jack Bruce. Hits: the million seller "Sunshine Of Your Love" (1/68 US 5; 10/68 UK 25) and "White Room" (10/68 US 6; 1/69 UK 28). By November 1968 it was all over, and from February 1969 to February 1970 he played with Blind Faith, another super group, which included Ric Grech and Steve Winwood in addition to Eric and Ginger. In spring 1970 he played with Delaney & Bonnie & Friends for three months, forming Derek & the Dominos in May 1970; this lasted until April 1971. Hit: "Layla" (3/71 US 51; 5/72 RE-US 10; 8/72 UK 7; 3/82 RE-UK 4). From April 1974 to the present day, he has worked as a solo artist with varying backing musicians. In the meantime, he has worked with a vast number of different artists as a session musician. He conceded later that he had suffered from drug related problems. Hits: "I Shot The Sheriff" (7/74 US 1; UK 9), "Lay Down Sally" (12/77 UK 39; US 3), "Promises" (10/78 US 9; UK 37). Clapton, who has the nickname 'Slowhand', has always sold albums by the truck load and his fans are as loyal as ever.

Jim Dandy 1948 US singer and songwriter, real name Jim Mangrum. In July 1971 an amateur group called Nobody Else renamed themselves Black Oak Arkansas. Jim was born in that town. In the same year, 1971, the first album by the group appeared in the charts. Their biggest hit single was "Jim Dandy" (12/73 US 25). In 1980 the band split up, the reasons given being difficulties with the record company and Jim's heart attack. In 1984 Jim released a solo record. He was going to be a member of Black Sabbath, but nothing came of it.

Dave Ball 1950 UK guitarist with Procol Harum and Bedlam.

Samuel McFadin 1952 US guitarist and leadsinger with Flash Cadillac & The Continental Kids, a group of six students who played music in the style of the 1950s. Hit,

"Did You Boogie (With Your Baby)" (8/76 US 29). The well known DJ Wolfman Jack can also be heard on this record.

Lene Lovich 1954 US singer and songwriter. She was born Marlene Premilovich in Detroit, of an English mother and Yugoslavian father. At age 13 she came to the UK with her mother. In 1979, she had her first UK hit with "Lucky Number" (2/79 UK 3). It is still her biggest to date. Among other names, she has been called 'England's answer to Nina Hagen', 'Horror Puss', 'a cross between Rapunzel and Snow-White' and, even, 'a refreshing eccentric'.

Randy Vanwarmer 1955 US singer, guitarist and songwriter who moved to Britain with his mother, when he was 12, after his father had died in a car accident. He tried his luck as a musician there, but then returned to the USA and had his first success with the million seller "Just When I Needed You Most" (3/79 US 4; 8/79 UK 8).

Tracy Chapman 1964 US singer, guitarist, and songwriter. In 1988 she was Newcomer of the Year. Her first big hit was "Fast Car" (6/88 UK 5; US 6).

Deaths

Dick Haymes 1980 Singer born in Argentina 13th September, 1916.

Mantovani 1980 Italian violinist, songwriter and composer. Born 15th November, 1905.

Soeur Sourire 1985 Belgian nun, who committed suicide. Her real name was Jeannie Deckers, and as a sister in an order she was called Soeur Luc-Gabrielle. She had her biggest hit with the self-penned "Dominique" (11/63 US 1; UK 7). She was known as the Singing Nun in the USA and in the UK. 'Sister Smile' was 52 years old.

Hits of the Day

1940	"When You Wish Upon A Star" Glenn Miller US 5 weeks
1956	"Rock n' Roll Waltz" Kay Starr UK 1 week
1957	"Butterfly" Andy Williams US 3 weeks
1957	"Party Doll" Buddy Knox US 1 week
1963	"He's So Fine" Chiffons US 4 weeks
1974	"Sunshine On My Shoulder" John Denver US 1 week
1985	"One More Night" Phil Collins US 2 weeks

31st

Birthdays

Lefty Frizzell 1928 US country singer, guitarist, and composer. Real name William Orville. From 1950 until his death he was in the country charts quite regularly. His biggest crossover hit was "I Want To Be With You Always" (8/51 US 29). He died on 19th July, 1975.

Shirley Jones 1934 US actress and singer. In the 50s she played in film musicals such as *Oklahoma* and *Carousel*. In 1960 she won an Oscar for best supporting role in the film, *Elmer Gantry*. In 1969 she was brilliant in the TV film *Silent Night, Lonely Night*. She formed the nucleus of the Partridge family with step-son David Cassidy, which was a successful TV series from 1970 to 1974. This was about an obviously very musical family who sang a little song in each episode; David Cassidy was the featured vocalist, whose hits are under 12th April.

John D. Loudermilk 1934 US songwriter, and singer. He gained his first musical experience as a drummer with the Salvation Army, where he learned to play guitar, ukulele, trumpets and saxophone. At age 12 he appeared beside Tex Ritter on TV and at 13, he had his own radio show as Johnny Dee. In one programme he sang the self-penned "A Rose And A Baby"; George Hamilton IV recorded it and it became a Top Ten hit. John went and made his first records as Ebe Sneezer and Johnny Dee. As Dee he had a hit with "Sittin' In The Balcony" (3/57 US 38) which Eddie Cochran heard and recorded (3/57 US 18). After that, Loudermilk wrote any number of titles for others: "Tobacco Road", "Indian Reservation", "Abilene", "Norman", "Sad Movies", "Waterloo" and "Ebony Eyes". John D. Loudermilk's hits: "Language Of Love" (11/61 US 32; 1/62 US 13) and "Blue Train" (12/63).

Richard Chamberlain 1935 US actor and part-time singer. He became popular in the early 1960s in his role as a doctor in the US TV series Dr. Kildare. Film company MGM capitalised on his popularity and signed him as a recording artist. In 1962 and 1963 five hits in the US and UK charts respectively. The biggest hit success was the "Theme From Dr. Kildare" (Three Stars Will Shine Tonight) (6/62 US 10; UK 12); the series *Dr Kildare* was based on the German series *Black Forest Clinic*. The other hits were "Love Me Tender" (10/62 US 21; UK 15), "All I Have To Do Is Dream" (2/63 US 14), and "Hi- Lili, Hi-Lo" (2/63 UK 20). Chamberlain also became popular through such TV series as *Shogun*, and *Thornbirds*.

Herb Alpert 1937 US trumpeter, songwriter, singer, producer and record company owner. He managed Jan & Dean with Lou Adler. The pair also produced 15 novelty-hits, including the title "Alley-Oop" by Dante & The Evergreens (5/60 US 15). He formed A&M Records with his friend Jerry Moss: the initials of their surnames providing the label name. A&M Records started out in a garage in 1962 and became an international company. They produced Herb's first hit "The Lonely Bull" for 200 dollars (10/62 US 6; 1/63 UK 22). Other hits were "Taste Of Honey" (9/65 US 7), "This Guy's In Love With You" (5/68 US 1; UK 3), "Rise" (7/79 US 1; 10/79 UK 13) and "Diamonds" (4/87 US 5; 6/87 UK 27) sung by Janet Jackson and Lisa Keith.

Mouth 1937 Dutch singer, real name Willem Duyn. He started as a drummer in the Holland-Quartet and then became a singer with the Jay-Jays. After a spell as a disc jockey, he finally formed the band Speedway in 1970. In 1971 he formed the duo Mouth & MacNeal. For hits see 5th May under Maggie MacNeal.

Rod Allen 1944 UK guitarist with the Fortunes.

Mick Ralphs 1944 UK guitarist, pianist and songwriter. In 1968 he was co-founder of Mott The Hoople and then of Bad Company in 1973.

Allan Nichol 1946 US lead guitarist with the Turtles.

Al Goodman 1947 US singer and songwriter with the Corvettes and the Vipers, who changed their name to Moments. The group was successful between 1968 & 1980 with million sellers like "Love On A Two Way Street" (4/70 US 3), "Sexy Mama" (1/74 US 17), "Dolly My Love" (7/75 UK 10) and "Jack In The Box" (1/77 UK 7). In the mid-1970s they recorded with the instrumental group Whatnuts; as Moments & Whatnuts, they scored with "Girls" (3/75 UK 3). At the end of the 1970s they changed their name again to Ray, Goodman & Brown and had a million seller with "Special Lady" (1/80 US 5).

Thijs Van Leer 1948 Dutch keyboard player, flautist and songwriter. He was a founder-member of Focus and made solo albums aswell.

Richard Hughes 1950 US drummer with the Winter brothers.

Pat McGlynn 1958 UK guitarist. In November 1977 he replaced Ian Mitchell in the Bay City Rollers, who were on their last legs at that time. The crucial factor was finding a face with teen appeal for the magazines. In 1978 McGlynn's first solo album appeared.

Angus Young 1959 Australian lead guitarist and songwriter, with AC/DC; his trademark is wearing schoolboy uniforms with shorts on stage.

Deaths

O'Kelly Isley 1986 US singer with the Isley Brothers. Born 25th December, 1937.

Hits of the Day

1945	"My Dreams Are getting Better All The Time" Les Brown US 7 weeks
1945	"Candy" Johnny Mercer, Jo Stafford, & Pied Pipers US 1 week
1960	"My Ole Man's A Dustman" Lonnie Donegan UK 4 weeks
1962	"Don't Break The Heart That Loves You" Connie Francis US 1 week
1973	"Killing me Softly" Roberta Flack US 1 week
1973	"Twelfth Of Never" Donny Osmond UK 1 week
1984	"Footloose" Kenny Loggins US 3 weeks

April

1st

Birthdays

Alberta Hunter 1895 US blues singer and songwriter who also sang under the names May Alix, Helen Roberts and Josephine Beatty. She made her first records in 1921 with the Fletcher Henderson Orchestra. In 1922 Alberta filled in for Bessie Smith in the musical comedy *How Come*. During the course of her long career, she made records with almost all the greats of jazz and blues. She had the one hit under her own name, "Beale Street Blues" (10/27 US 16). She died 17th October, 1984.

Bob Nolan 1908 US country singer and songwriter. Real name Robert Clarence Nobles. In 1934 he was a founder member of Sons Of The Pioneers, who started making records that year. The group also appeared in many films in the course of their career. Biggest hits included "Tumbling Tumbleweeds" (12/34 US 13) and "Cool Water" (8/41 US 25). The Sons Of The Pioneers charted once more with Vaughn Monroe, with "Cool Water" (7/48 US 9). Nolan also recorded as a soloist. He died 15th June, 1980.

Art Lund 1915 US singer and actor, who began his career as Art London with Jimmie Joy's band, before joining Benny Goodman. He had his first hit "Winter Weather" (1/42 US 24), while with that band; it was a duet with Peggy Lee. After an interruption for military service Art returned to Benny Goodman and had the hit, "Blue Skies" (8/46 US 9). From 1947 he made solo records. His first was also his most successful, the million seller "Mam'selle" (4/47 US 1). In 1956 Art was the star of the Broadway musical *The Most Happy Fella*. He died on May 30th, 1990.

Arthur Smith 1921 US country guitarist and songwriter. He had his biggest crossover success with the composition "Guitar Boogie" (7/48 US 25). In the 1950s he set up his own recording studio, in which, in the mid-1950s,

he and Don Remo recorded the instrumental "Feudin' Banjos" for MGM. This recording later became well-known through Eric Weissberg's version "Duelling Banjos" in the film, *Deliverance*. Arthur had to get lawyers to sort this out. He won the case after two years of legal wrangling, and is now officially considered to be its composer.

Amos Milburn 1927 US blues and R&B pianist, singer and songwriter. In 1945 he formed his own band and made his first records in 1946. His best known records were "Chicken Shack Boogie" (11/48), "Bewildered" (12/48), "Roomin' House Boogie" (9/49), and "Bad Bad Whiskey" (11/50) which all reached the No. 1 spot in the US R&B charts. After suffering his first stroke in 1970, Amos withdrew from the music business. He died after a second stroke on 3rd January, 1980.

Debbie Reynolds 1932 US actress and singer, real first names Mary Frances. She made her first film in 1948. In Hollywood she was the typical "girl next door" type. In 1950, she played the part of the "boop-boop-a-doo" singer Helen Kane in *3 Little Words*. Kane had been famous in the USA in the late 20s and sang the original version of "I Wanna Be Loved By You", later popularised by Marilyn Monroe in the film, *Some Like It Hot*. In 1952 Debbie acted alongside Gene Kelly in *Singing In The Rain*. Debbie had her two biggest hits as a singer with titles songs featured in films: from the film *Two Weeks With Love* came the million seller, "Aba Daba Honeymoon" (2/51 US 3), which was a duet with Carleton Carpenter, and "Tammy" (7/57 US 1; UK 2) from *Tammy & The Batchelor*. A few further records followed, then her singing career was over. From 26th September, 1955 until 1959 Debbie was married to singing star (at the time) Eddie Fisher. Eddie left Debbie to become the husband of Elizabeth Taylor. The offspring of the Reynolds/Fisher marriage was Carrie Fisher who played the part of Princess Leia in *Star Wars*.

Jim Brown 1934 US singer who formed a duo with his sister Maxine in the early 1950s until their youngest sister joined them in 1955 and they became The Browns. They charted with "The Three Bells" (8/59 US 1; UK 6) and "The

Old Lamplighter" (3/60 US 5). Up until then, they had often been in the country charts. Jim became a country star, who was successful into the 1980s. The sisters set up a recording studio.

Rudolf Isley 1939 US singer and songwriter with the Isley Brothers.

Alan Blakely 1942 UK guitarist, pianist, singer and songwriter with the Tremeloes.

Frank Gari 1942 US actor, and singer, who was in the US charts in 1960/61 with three titles and then was never heard of again. His biggest hit was "Lullaby Of Love" (4/61 US 23).

Philip Margo 1942 US drummer, guitarist, and singer with The Tokens. Hits: "Tonight I Fell In Love" (3/61 US 15) and "The Lion Sleeps Tonight" (11/61 US 1; UK 11). From 1973, three of The Tokens, the brothers Philip and Mitch, with Jay Siegel, recorded as Cross Country. Biggest hit was "In The Midnight Hour" (8/73 US 30).

John Barbata 1945 US drummer who started with the Sentinels, then joined the Turtles in June, 1966, appearing on their biggest hits. Then he replaced Dallas Taylor in Crosby, Stills, Nash & Young, and ended up with Jefferson Starship in 1974. He also played as a session musician on a number of records by artists like Dave Mason, Ry Cooder and John Sebastian.

Jimmy Cliff 1948 Jamaican singer and songwriter. Real name James Chambers. He made records from 1962 and was among the first to be successful with reggae. Hits: "Wonderful World, Beautiful People" (10/69 UK 6; 12/69 US 25), "Vietnam" (4/70) and "Wild World (8/70 UK 8). Among his outstanding compositions were "You Can Get It If You Really Want" and "Too Many Rivers To Cross". As an actor, he appeared in *The Harder They Come* (1972), in which a young musician leaves his rural home to find his fortune in the big city – Jimmy played himself.

Simon Cowe 1948 UK guitarist, mandolinist and singer with Lindisfarne and Jack The Lad.

Ronnie Lane 1948 US bass player, singer and songwriter with the group Small Faces formed in June 1965. Then after Steve Marriott had left, and Ron Wood and Rod Stewart had joined, they became the Faces in February 1969 continuing until May 1973. In September of that year he formed his own group Ronnie Lane & Slim Chance. During the course of the 70s he made records with Ron Wood and Pete Townsend, and could be heard as a session musician with Roy Harper and Wings. In the late 1970s a

solo album by Ronnie appeared. Since then, he has been suffering from multiple sclerosis.

Gil Scott-Heron 1949 US singer, pianist and songwriter, whose songs were critically outspoken on racial issues in the USA and South Africa. Atomic warfare, drugs and alcohol are also targets of criticism in his lyrics – not exactly chart material.

Billy Currie 1950 UK pianist and songwriter in Ultravox, formed in 1973, who were also called 'Kings of Electro- Pop'. He can be heard on records by Visage, Phillip Lynott and Gary Numan.

Jeff Porcaro 1954 US drummer with Toto and a much sought-after session musician.

Mark White 1961 UK guitarist and songwriter with ABC.

Deaths

Scott Joplin 1917 US ragtime composer. Born 24th November, 1868.

Marvin Gaye 1984 US soul singer and songwriter. He was shot dead by his father during an argument, the day before his birthday, 2nd April, 1939.

Hits of the Day

1967 "Let's Spend The Night Together" Rolling Stones
1974 "Dan The Banjo Man" Dan The Banjo Man
1989 "Eternal Flame" Bangles US 1 week

2nd

Birthdays

Herbert Mills 1912 US singer with the Mills Brothers, whose career began in the 1930s and lasted about 40 years. "Tiger Rag" (11/31 US 1) was their first million seller. Further hits were "Dinah" (1/32 US 1), "Paper Doll" (10/42 US 20; 7/43 RE-US 1), "You Always Hurt The One You Love" (6/44 US 1), "Glow Worm" (9/52 US 2; 1/53 UK 10) and "Cab Driver" (1/68 US 23), which was their last hit. "Paper Doll" alone sold 6 million copies.

Lou Monte 1917 US singer and guitarist, who had his first hit with "At The Darktown Strutters' Ball" (2/54 US 7) and his biggest hit with "Pepino The Italian Mouse" (12/62 US 5).

Serge Gainsbourg 1928 French actor, singer, pianist, guitarist and songwriter. Real name Lucien Ginzberg. He had his first hit in 1959 with "Le Poinconneur de Lilas". Other hits were "La Javanaise" (1962), "Bonnie & Clyde" (1968) with Briggitte Bardot, "Je Suis Venu Te Dire Que Je M'En Vais" (1974), "Aux Armes Et Caetera" (1978), and "Love On The Beat" (1984). His biggest international hit was with Jane Birkin on the controversial "Je T'Aime . . . Moi Non Plus" (7/69 UK 2; 10/69 RE-UK 1; US 58). He died on March 3rd, 1991.

Marvin Gaye 1939 US soul singer and songwriter. The stages of his career were Rainbows; his own first band Marquees (1957), and then as a member of Harvey & The Moonglows, who scored with "Ten Command-ments Of Love" (10/58 US 9). In 1960 Marvin Gaye went to Detroit and became a session drummer with Tamla-Motown. In 1961 he married Anna Gordy, sister of Tamla- Motown chief Berry Gordy Jr., thereby becoming one of the Motown clan. At first he played the drums for the early hits by Smokey Robinson & The Miracles, then he made solo records. His fourth single became his first success, "Stubborn Kind Of Fellow" (10/62 US 46). Biggest hits: "I Heard It Through The Grapevine" (11/68 US 1; 2/69 UK 1), "Let's Get It On" (7/73 US 1; 9/73 UK 31), "Got To Give It Up" (4/77 US 1; UK 7) and "Sexual Healing" (10/82 US 3; UK 4). In addi-tion there were any number of Top Ten hits – some were duets with Diana Ross, Tammi Terrell, Mary Wells and Kim Weston. On the 1st April, 1984 Marvin was shot dead by his father.

Leon Russell 1941 US multi-instrumentalist, song-writer and singer. He also cut C&W records under the name of Hank Wilson. As a session musician, Leon played with everyone from Jerry Lee Lewis, to Bob Lind, The Crystals, Frank Sinatra, Glen Campbell, Bob Dylan, Rolling Stones, Joe Cocker, to Phil Spector. He was con-sidered to be one of the first important session musicians in the USA. In 1970 he organized the band for the Mad Dogs & Englishmen-tour with Joe Cocker, which made Leon a star too. He cut several solo records, which were good but not very successful. Biggest hit: "Tight Rope" (8/72 US 11).

Phil Castrodale 1942 US singer with the Reflections.

Larry Coryell 1943 US jazz-rock guitarist and song-writer in a class of his own. As a soloist, and with Eleventh, House he made outstanding albums.

Glen Dale 1943 UK guitarist with the Fortunes.

Kurt Winter 1946 Guitarist. In 1969 he replaced Randy Bachman in the Canadian group Guess Who? for three years.

Emmylou Harris 1947 US singer, guitarist and song-writer, who started as a folk-singer in the late 1960s and made her first records in 1969. After that she played and sang a great deal with the Flying Burrito Brothers and Gram Parsons, whom she was friendly with until his death in 1973. In 1975 she formed her own band and had some success in the country charts. Both as a solo artist and duetting with Dolly Parton, Linda Ronstadt, Earl Thomas Conley, Charlie Louvin, Buck Owens and Don Williams she had around 50 C&W hits. She had seven No. 1s, but never quite managed to hit the top of the pop charts.

Leon Wilkeson 1952 US bass player with Lynyrd Sky-nyrd and the Rossington-Collins Band.

David Robinson 1953 US drummer with Jonathan Richman & Modern Lovers. In 1976 he was a founder member of Cars.

Gregory Abbott 1956 US singer and songwriter. First hit: "Shake You Down" (10/86 US 1; UK 6).

Keren Jane Woodward 1963 US singer with Banana-rama, whose first record appeared in 1981. Hits: "Really Saying Something" (4/82 UK 5), "Shy Boy" (7/82 UK 4), "Na Na Hey Kiss Him Goodbye" (2/83 UK 5), a cover version of the old hit by Steam, "Cruel Sum-mer" (7/83 UK 8; 7/84 US 9), "Robert de Niro's Wait-ing" (3/84 UK 3), "Venus" (5/86 UK 8; US 1) a new recording of the old hit by Shocking Blue, "I Heard A Rumour" (7/87 UK 14; US 4), "Love In The First Degree" (10/87 UK 3), "I Want You Back" (4/88 UK 5) and "Help" (2/89 UK 3).

Deaths

Buddy Rich 1987 US jazz drummer and orchestra leader. Born 30th June, 1917.

Hits of the Day

1964 "Can't Buy Me Love" Beatles UK 3 weeks
1966 "19th Nervous Breakdown" Rolling Stones
1977 "Knowing Me, Knowing You" Abba UK 5 weeks

3rd

Birthdays

Doris Day 1924 US actress and singer, real name Doris von Kappelhoff. Doris wanted to be a dancer, but injured her legs and decided on a singing career. She began her career in the late 1930s, with Barney Rapp's band, who in addition to leading his own band in Doris' hometown Cincinatti, also had his own nightclub. It was Barney who disliked the surname Kappelhoff, and advised Doris to call herself Day, after her favourite song at the time, "Day After Day". Then she joined Fred Waring's Band and, then, Bob Crosby's. Between 1943 & 1946 Doris was the singer with the Les Brown Band. Hits: "My Dreams Are Getting Better All The Time" (3/45 US 1) and "Sentimental Journey" (3/45 US 1). From the end of 1947 her records appeared under her own name. Hits: "Love Somebody" (5/48 US 1), "It's Magic" (7/48 US 2), "A Guy Is A Guy" (3/52 US 1), "Secret Love" (1/54 US 1; 4/54 UK 1) and "Whatever Will Be Will Be (Que Sera, Sera)" (6/56 US 2; UK 1). Doris also duetted with Frankie Laine on "Sugarbush" (6/52 US 7; 11/52 UK 8) and Johnny Ray on "A Full Time Job" (12/52 US 20; 4/53 UK 11). From 1949 Doris was one of the most popular actresses around, because she was so natural and unaffected. In addition, she was a talented comedienne. Among her most successful films were *Pillow Talk* (1959), *Midnight Lace* (1960) and *A Touch Of Mink* (1961). It can only have been a 'touch', as it was Doris Day who said it was 'a crime to kill an animal to make a fur coat.'

Don Gibson 1928 US country singer, guitarist, and songwriter. He wrote Faron Young's, hit "Sweet Dreams" (1956) and the Ray Charles hit "I Can't Stop Loving You"; his nickname was 'Mr. Country Soul'. His biggest pop-hits were "Oh Lonesome Me" (3/58 US 7), "Blue Blue Day" (6/58 US 20) and "Sea Of Heartbreak" (6/61 US 21; 8/61 UK 14). All his records were produced by Chet Atkins.

Jimmy McGriff 1936 US jazz and R&B keyboard player and songwriter of a special class. He was also in the pop-charts with "I've Got A Woman, Part 1" (10/62 US 20).

Jeff Barry 1938 US songwriter and singer. He wrote many hits with his wife Ellie Greenwich in the early 1960s including "Da Doo Ron Ron", "Be My Baby", "Then He Kissed Me", "Tell Laura I Love Her", "Hanky Panky", "River Deep, Mountain High" and "Leader Of The Pack". The couple also charted as artists as the Raindrops. Biggest hit: "The Kind Of Boy You Can't Forget" (8/63 US 17).

Philippe Wynne 1938 US leadsinger of the Detroit Spinners from January 1971. He joined the group, replacing G. C. Cameron, who wanted to start a solo career. Hits, with Wynne: "I'll Be Around" (8/72 US 8), "Could It Be I'm Falling In Love" (12/72 US 4; 4/73 UK 11), "One Of A Kind (Love Affair)" (4/73 US 11), together with Dionne Warwicke, "Then Came You" (7/74 US 1; 10/74 UK 29), "They Just Can't Stop It (The Games People Play)" (8/75 US 5), and "The Rubber Band Man" (9/76 US 2; UK 16), all the aforementioned records were million sellers. In early 1977, Wynne left the group and was replaced by John Edwards. Nothing came of Wynne's planned solo career. He died 14th July, 1984. In the USA the group was always known as the Spinners; while in the UK in December 1970, they had to change their name to Motown Spinners because a very popular folk group from Liverpool of that name already existed. When the group's contract with Motown was up in 1972 they became known as Detroit Spinners in the UK.

Jan Berry 1941 US singer. While still at high school in Los Angeles, Jan and his friend Dean Torrence, formed a group called Barons. Jan and Dean and another member of the Barons, Arnie Ginsburg, recorded "Jennie Lee" (6/58 US 8) in Jan's garage. Shortly afterwards Dean was drafted to the army and "Jennie Lee" was released on Doris Day's label, Arwin. Jan and Arnie were credited as writers. When Dean returned in 1959, Arnie joined the Navy. The duo Jan & Dean signed a recording contract with Herb Alpert's and Lou Adler's company Dore. Hits: "Baby Talk" (8/59 US 10), "Surf City" (6/63 US 1; 8/63 UK 26), "Drag City" (12/63 US 10), "Dead Man's Curve" (3/64 US 8) and "The Little Old Lady (From Pasadena)" (6/64 US 3). Beach Boy Brian Wilson helped out with the lyrics and vocals on "Surf City"; then Dean Torrence helped out the Beach Boys with the vocals on "Barbara Ann" – he sang the lead. On 19th April 1966 Jan was involved in a serious road accident. After making *Dead Man's Curve*, a biographical film about the duo, the pair tried a comeback in 1978.

Wayne Newton 1942 US singer, multi- instrumentalist, and top entertainer in Las Vegas. His success began after an appearance in the Jackie Gleason TV show in 1962. Bobby Darin saw him in the show, signed him up and produced his first record. His first hit was Bert Kaempfert's "Danke Schon" (7/63 US 13) and his biggest was "Daddy Don't You Walk So Fast" (4/72 US 4).

Richard Manuel 1943 US singer and pianist for the The Band, formed in 1967 in Woodstock. All members played in Ronnie Hawkins' backing group, Hawks, before that. The group gave their last concert at the end of November 1976 on Thanksgiving Day and, then split up; at the time it was filmed by Martin Scorsese as *The Last Waltz*. On 4th March, 1986, Manuel committed suicide.

Joe Vann 1943 US lead singer with the Duprees, real name Joseph Canzano. Biggest hit: "You Belong To Me" (8/62 US 7). In the late 60s the group renamed themselves The Italian Asphalt & Pavement Company, who almost had a hit with "Check Yourself" (5/70 US 97). Joe died 28th February, 1984.

Tony Orlando 1944 US singer, real name Michael Anthony Orlando Cassavitis. He had his first hits with "Half-way To Paradise" (5/61 US 39) and "Bless You" (8/61 US 15; UK 5) and then, for a while, nothing happened. He worked as a promoter in the record industry, then as a manager for a music publisher. At the end of the 1960s a new group called Wind was formed in a New York studio – the leadsinger was Tony Orlando. Hit: "Make Believe" (9/69 US 28). In 1970 Hank Medress, once a member of the Tokens, and now a producer for Bell-Records, received a demo tape from Thelma Hopkins and Joyce Vincent, who called themselves Dawn. He asked Tony to dub a lead vocal over the finished tape, and thus began the career of Tony Orlando & Dawn. Their biggest hits (all million sellers) were, "Candida" (7/70 US 3; 1/71 UK 9), "Knock Three Times" (11/70 US 1; 4/71 UK 1), "Tie A Yellow Ribbon Round The Old Oak Tree" (2/73 US & UK 1), "Say, Has Anybody Seen My Sweet Gypsy Rose?" (7/73 US 3; UK 12) and "He Don't Love You (Like I Love You)" (3/75 US 1). In 1977 Tony Orlando retired from the music business, only to return later as a soloist.

Barry Pritchard 1944 UK lead guitarist with the Fortunes, who were successful from 1965 to 1972.

Dee Murray 1946 UK bass player with the Spencer Davis Group from October 1968 to July 1969, then in Elton John's backing band and, then as a session musician.

Richard Thompson 1949 UK guitarist and songwriter, one of the best exponents of the folk-rock genre. In 1967 he was a founder member of Fairport Convention. He stayed with them until January 1971. After that, he made solo records, sang with his wife Linda, worked as a session musician and turned up as a member of the Albion Country Band in October 1972. After that he recorded as Richard & Linda Thompson and worked with J. J. Cale, T-Bone Burnett, Gerry Rafferty, Julie Covington & Sandy Denny, among others. Richard Thompson's work, now fronting his own band, is widely regarded as being one of the best-kept secrets in the British Isles.

Mel Schacher 1951 US bass player and singer who began his career as a member of the group ? & The Mysterians in their last days. In 1969 he joined the Fabulous Pack, which became Grand Funk Railroad in 1970. In 1976 when leadsinger Mark Farner wanted to try a solo career, the group split up and Mel continued with the others in the trio Flint.

David Nicholson 1952 UK bass player, keyboard player and songwriter with Blue.

Mick Mars 1955 US lead guitarist and songwriter with Mötley Crüe.

Nick Richards 1960 UK singer, songwriter and in 1985 founder of the band, Boys Don't Cry, who had a hit with their debut single "I Wanna Be A Cowboy" (4/86 US 12).

Eddie Murphy 1961 US actor and singer. First hit, "Party All The Time" (10/85 US 2), written and produced by Rick James. Eddie is considered to be a natural comedian. Best known films: *Beverly Hills Cop*, *48 Hours* and *The Golden Child*.

John Griffith 1962 US singer, guitarist, and keyboard player. In 1980 he played with the Ratfinks, who changed their name to Red Rockers.

Deaths

Kurt Weill 1950 US composer of German origin, who composed his most successful pieces with lyrics by Bertolt Brecht. Born 2nd March, 1900.

Sarah Vaughan 1990 US singer, born on March 27th, 1924.

Hits of the Day

1961	"Runaway" Del Shannon US 4 weeks
1971	"Just My Imagination" Temptations US 2 weeks
1976	"Disco Lady" Johnny Taylor US 4 weeks
1989	"Looking For Freedom" David Hasselhoff

4th

Birthdays

Muddy Waters 1915 US blues guitarist, singer, and songwriter in a class of his own. Real name McKinley Morganfield. In 1941 he cut his first records. His best known records are "Long Distance Call" (4/51 R&B 8), "I'm You Hoochie Coochie Man" (3/54 R&B 3), and "Manish Boy" (7/55 R&B 5). He died 30th April, 1983.

Margo J. Sylvia US lead singer with the Tune Weavers formed in 1956, who had their only hit with "Happy Birthday Baby" (9/57 US 5).

Hugh Masekela 1939 South African trumpeter, bandleader, singer and songwriter. His only hit is, "Grazing In The Grass" (6/68 US 1). He was married to the singer Miriam Makeba, and has been a valuable critic of apartheid throughout a long exile from his home-land.

Major Lance 1941 US soul singer who was successful between 1963 and 1965. After trying his hand at amateur boxing and as a dancer with Record Hop TV-Shows, he sang with Five Gospel Harmonaires and became a member with the Ideals. In 1959 he made his first solo records. Hits: "The Monkey Time" (7/63 US 8), and "Um, Um, Um, Um, Um, Um" (1/64 US 5; UK 40). In 1975 he set up his own record label with Al Jackson of the MGs. Between 1978 & 1981 he was in prison for drug offences.

Kris Jensen 1942 US singer and guitarist with one hit, "Torture" (9/62 US 20).

Doug Ferguson 1947 UK bass player. He began in 1968 with Strange Brew, who later shortened their name to Brew. Then he was with the Mike Scott band for about a year, back with Brew for a further 6 months, and finally with Andy Ward and Andy Latimer in Philip Goodhand-Tait's backing group. These three musicians, with Peter Bardens, formed the group Camel in the spring of 1972.

Berry Oakley 1948 US bass player and songwriter with the Allman Brothers Band, who were in the ascendant in the early 1970s. Success did not last long, as two key members of the band died in motorcycle crashes, Duane Allman on 29th October, 1971, and Berry Oakley on 11th November, 1972.

Dicken 1950 UK singer, lead guitarist, and songwriter, with Mr. Big, formed in 1973. Real name Jeff Robert Pain. Only hit: "Romeo" (2/77 UK 4). After the band split up, he carried on as a soloist.

Pip Pyle 1950 UK drummer with Hatfield & The North, National Health and as a session musician.

Peter Haycock 1952 UK singer, guitarist and songwriter with the Climax Chicago Blues Band formed in 1968, who somewhere along the line, dropped Chicago from their name. Along with crossing out part of the name most of the blues seemed to get lost as well. Hits: "Couldn't Get It Right" (10/76 UK 10; 2/77 US 3) and "I Love You" (2/81 US 12).

Dave Hill 1952 UK guitarist with Ambrose Slade, who shortened their name to Slade and were successful from 1971 onwards. In the mid 1970s Slade's success waned, but

in 1983 they returned to the higher echelon of the charts; curiously, it was the first time they had achieved any real success in the USA.

Gary Moore 1954 Irish songwriter, singer, and guitarist. In the first half of the 1970s he played with Dr. Strangely Strange, Skid Row, Thin Lizzy and Colosseum before starting a solo career. His biggest hits were "Parisienne Walkways" (4/79 UK 8), with vocals by Phil Lynott, "Empty Rooms" (8/84 UK 51; 7/85 RE-UK 23) and "Out In The Fields" (5/85 UK 5).

Julie Forsyth 1958 UK singer. She guested on Donovan's album COSMIC WHEELS, and then became a member of Guys n' Dolls, who were successful with "There's A Whole Lot Of Loving" (3/75 UK 2) and "You Don't Have To Say You Love Me" (2/76 UK 5).

Deaths

Red Sovine 1980 US country singer. Born 17th July, 1918.

Hits of the Day

1963	"Summer Holiday" Cliff Richard UK 1 week (2nd time)
1964	"Can't Buy Me Love" The Beatles US 5 weeks
1982	"Too Shy" Kajogoogoo
1987	"Let It Be" Ferry Aid UK 3 weeks
1987	"Nothing's Gonna Stop Us Now" Starship US 2 weeks

5th

Birthdays

Frank Warner 1903 US singer, banjo player, and songwriter. He was vice-president of the Country Song & Dance Society Of America. Frank remained committed to traditional American folk music throughout his life.

Gale Storm 1922 US singer and actress, real name Josephine Owaissa Cottle. She came to Hollywood at the end of the 1930s and was the lead in many films throughout the 1940s and the early 1950s. From 1952 to 1955 she had her own TV series, *My Little Margie*, and from 1956 to 1960 the *Gale Storm Show*. In the USA she had 6 records in the

Top Ten from 1955 to 1957. Biggest hits: "I Hear You Knocking" (10/55 US 2) and "Dark Moon" (4/57 US 4).

Tony Williams 1928 US singer and co-founder of the Platters in 1953. In 1954 he made his first records, including "Only You", which was then rejected by the record company Federal as not worth releasing. In 1955, the Platters signed to Mercury and re-recorded "Only You". Tony sang the lead on all of their major hits: "Only You (And You Alone)" (10/55 US 5), "The Great Pretender" (12/55 US 1) (both appeared in the UK as A and B sides of the same record) (9/56 UK 5), "My Prayer" (7/56 US 1; 11/56 UK 4), "Twilight Time" (4/58 US 1; UK 3), and "Smoke Gets In Your Eyes" (11/58 US 1; 1/59 UK 1). In June 1960 Tony left the Platters for a solo career; he was replaced by Sonny Turner. Tony had no hits without the Platters and they had none without him. A group called the Platters still haunt the Club circuit, but it is doubtful whether any original members remain.

Joe Meek 1929 UK record producer and sound-creator. Real first name, Robert. After serving in the army where he worked as a radar technician, he became an engineer in television, and then worked in a recording studio. He worked on the early hits by Lonnie Donegan, and began to write under his own name, like "Put A Ring On Her Finger", which was for a hit Tommy Steele. After that, he went free-lance and built his own studio in North London, setting up his own record label. His first big hit on his own label was "Angela Jones" (6/60 UK 7) for Michael Cox. Joe Meek was recruited by Robert Stigwood to produce actor John Leyton. On the strength of John Leyton's hits, Joe's career was properly launched and he was sought out by other British artists, like Mike Berry & The Outlaws, Tornados, Heinz, Honeycombs and Screaming Lord Sutch. After success began to wane, he committed suicide on the anniversary of the death of his idol Buddy Holly, 3rd February, 1967.

Billy Bland 1932 US singer, who made his first records in 1955. His biggest hit was "Let The Little Girl Dance" (2/60 US 7; 5/60 UK 15).

Allan Clarke 1941 UK singer and songwriter with the Hollies. Before that he had played with Graham Nash as the duo Guytones and Two Teens. After adding further members these became the Fourtones, the Deltas, and finally, in 1962, the Hollies. At the beginning of 1963, British recording companies were on the hunt for other Beatles-type groups. An EMI producer discovered the Hollies in Liverpool's Cavern Club and invited them to play in London. The Hollies passed the test and cut their first records on April 4, 1963. Biggest hits: "Just One Look" (2/64 UK 2), "I'm Alive" (5/65 UK 1), "I Can't Let Go" (2/66 UK 2), "Bus Stop" (6/66 UK & US 5), "Stop Stop Stop" (10/66 UK 2; US 7), "Carrie-Anne" (6/67 UK 3; US 9), "Sorry Suzanne" (3/69 UK 3); "He Ain't Heavy, He's My Brother" (10/69 UK 3; 12/69 US 7; 9/88 RE-UK 1), (the latter's renewed success could be explained by the fact that it was used by a US beer company 'Miller Lite' for a TV commercial), "Long Cool Woman (In A Black Dress)" (6/72 US 2; 9/72 UK 32), "The Air That I Breathe" (2/74 UK 2; 4/74 US 6). In the mid-1970s the group split up, and reformed in 1983. In between Allan tried his luck unsuccessfully as a solo artist several times. He sang on the Alan Parsons' album I ROBOT.

David LaFlamme 1941 US violinist, guitarist, singer, and songwriter for It's A Beautiful Day, who recorded "White Bird" in 1969, it failed to reach the charts. David LaFlamme recorded it again on a solo album, this time it reached the lowly No. 89 in the USA in December 1976.

David Swarbrick 1941 UK violinist, and singer, who made records with Martin Carthy, and played for Fairport Convention from September 1969. In between he was a session musician, playing with Sandy Denny, Al Stewart, Alain Stivell, Heads, Hands & Feet and the Seekers.

Nicholas Caldwell 1944 US singer with the Whispers.

Crispian St. Peters 1944 UK singer and guitarist. Real name Robin Peter Smith. Hits: "You Were On My Mind" (1/66 UK 2; 7/67 US 36) and "Pied Piper" (3/66 UK 5; 6/66 US 4).

Agnetha 1950 Swedish singer with Abba. Real Name Agnetha Ase Fältskog. She also made several solo records.

Everett Morton 1951 UK drummer with The Beat. Before that he played with Joan Armatrading's band.

Stan Ridgway 1954 US singer and songwriter with the band Wall Of Voodoo, formed in 1979. Biggest hit: "Mexican Radio" (3/83 US 58; UK 64). From 1983 he made solo records. Hit: "Camouflage" (7/86 UK 4).

Pia Zadora 1955 US singer. Real last name Schipani. As a solo artist she was fairly successful internationally, particularly on a duet with Jermaine Jackson, "When The Rain Begins To Fall" (10/84). Solo hits: "Let's Dance Tonight" (2/85), and "Little Bit Of Heaven" (6/85). Her millionaire husband bought her into films such as *Butterfly* (1982), *A Lonely Lady* (1983), and *Hairspray* (1988).

Deaths

Bob Hite 1981 US singer with Canned Heat. Born 26th February, 1945.

Danny 1983 US singer with Danny & The Juniors. Danny committed suicide. Born 10th May, 1941.

Hits of the Day

1941 "I Hear A Rhapsody" Jimmy Dorsey US 2 weeks
1975 "Lovin' You" Minnie Riperton US 1 week
1976 "Rocky" Frank Farian G 4 weeks

6th

Birthdays

Gerry Mulligan 1927 US jazz saxophonist, composer and bandleader. He played with the Gene Krupa band in 1946/47, with Miles Davis 1948-50, and made his first solo record in 1951.

Merle Haggard 1938 US country singer, guitarist, violinist and songwriter. During his youth it seemed that he would spend most of his time in and out of corrective institutions and prisons until a three year spell in the notorious San Quentin prison for armed robbery made him turn over a new leaf. After that, he worked in clubs, and made his first records in 1962. In 1965 he signed a recording contract with Capitol. His two biggest crossover hits were "Okie From Muskogee" (10/69 C&W 1; US 41), and "If We Make It Through December" (10/73 C&W 1; US 28). Merle is the fourth most successful country artists of all time. By the end of 1988 he had just about 90 hits, of which 34 had reached No. 1 in the C&W charts. In addition there were another four which were duets: Clint Eastwood, Janie Fricke, George Jones and Willie Nelson. It was only natural that the US film industry should make use of such a well-known artist. He has appeared in several TV series. Haggard is considered to be one of the most scintillating and honest country musicians.

Hedy West 1938 US singer, guitarist and songwriter, whose composition "500 Miles" became a world hit for several artists. In the early 1980s she left the music business after her daughter was born.

Julie Rogers 1943 UK singer, real name Julie Rolls. A cover-version of the Argentine song "La Novia" gave her the hit "The Wedding" (8/64 UK 3; 11/64 US 10). A second successful number was "Like A Child" (12/64 UK 21).

Michelle Gilliam Phillips 1944 US singer. Born Holly Michelle Gilliam. In 1962 she started out with the group Journeymen, who later became the Mamas & Papas; they had their biggest hits between 1966 and 1967: "California Dreaming" (1/66 US 4; 4/66 UK 23), "Monday, Monday" (4/66 US 1; UK 3) and "Dedicated To The One I Love" (2/67 US 2; UK 2). In 1970 Michelle separated from her husband John Phillips – also a member of Mamas & Papas – whom she had married in 1962 and tried her luck as an actress. She played one of the main roles beside Dennis Hopper in the film *The Last Movie*, later she was married to him for 8 years. Further films included *Dillinger* and Ken Russell's film-bio of Rudolph Valentino in 1976. In 1977 she made a solo record which flopped.

Tony Connor 1947 UK drummer with Audience, Jackson Heights and Hot Chocolate from 1974.

Patrick Hernandez 1952 Belgian singer and songwriter who had a Disco-hit with "Born To Be Alive" (6/79 US 16; UK 10).

Stan Cullimore 1962 UK guitarist, singer and songwriter with the Housemartins.

Michael Damian 1962 US singer, keyboard player, songwriter, and actor. In 1979 he made a debut single, nothing came of it. From 1981 onwards he acted in the daily soap opera *The Young & The Restless*, and from 1985 onwards recorded solo albums. Only hit so far, "Rock On" (3/89 US 1), from the film, *Dream A Little Dream*, which is a cover-version of the old David Essex hit.

Deaths

Ral Donner 1984 US singer, nickname 'Chicago-Elvis'; died of cancer. Born 10th February, 1943.

Hits of the Day

1956 "It's Almost Tomorrow" Dream Weavers UK 1 week (2nd time)
1957 "Butterfly" Charlie Gracie US 2 weeks
1957 "Round And Round" Perry Como US 2 weeks
1968 "Mighty Quinn" Manfred Mann
1974 "Hooked On A Feeling" Blue Swede US 1 week
1974 "Seasons In The Sun" Terry Jacks UK 4 weeks

Miscellany

1971 The Rolling Stones announce the formation of their own record company Rolling Stones Records in Cannes. Trade mark: a tongue sticking out!

7th

Birthdays

Percy Faith 1908 Canadian orchestra leader, pianist, and composer. In the 1920s he played the piano accompaniment to silent movies in cinemas. In 1950 he was employed by the record company CBS as an A & R man. In the same year he wrote the hit, "My Heart Cries For You", for Guy Mitchell. Percy Faith can be heard on many records by Tony Bennett, Rosemary Clooney, Sarah Vaughan, Doris Day and Johnny Mathis. He was one of the principal band-leaders and arrangers of the era. He recorded a total of 85 albums for CBS, and had hits with "Delicado" (4/52 US 1), "Song From Moulin Rouge" (4/53 US 1) and "Theme From A Summer Place" (1/60 US 1; 3/60 UK 2). Percy died 9th February, 1976.

Billie Holiday 1915 US blues singer considered to be the greatest of all time. She was born Eleanor Gough. She took on the name Holiday from guitarist Clarence Holiday whose illegitimate daughter she was. After difficult early years, Billie was discovered in 1933 by jazz critic John Hammond. She made a record with Benny Goodman, "Riffin' The Scotch" (1/34 US 6), and started a successful collaboration with Teddy Wilson which lasted until 1938. In the late 1930s she sang with Count Basie and Artie Shaw. She was also credited as co-writer of many compositions like "God Bless The Child", which was later recorded by Blood, Sweat & Tears and Diana Ross. Her most successful hits were "The Way You Look Tonight" (11/36 US 3), "Pennies From Heaven" (1/37 US 3), "Carelessly" (4/37 US 1) and "I'm Gonna Lock My Heart" (8/38 US 2). Billie died 17th July, 1959. In 1972 her life story was told in the film *Lady Sings The Blues*, her part was played by Diana Ross.

Mongo Santamaria 1922 Cuban percussionist, bandleader and songwriter. Real first name, Ramon. In 1950 he came to New York via Mexico City, and played with the Perez Prado band for three years, and then for seven years with Tito Puente. He was also on records by George Shearing, Dizzy Gillespie and Jack McDuff. From 1958, onwards Mongo made his own records. His music can be described as a fusion of Latin, R&B, jazz and soul. He had one hit-single with "Water Melon Man" (3/63 US 10).

Bobby Bare 1935 US country guitarist, singer and songwriter. In 1956 he made his first records and was successful with "The All American Boy" (12/58 US 2), which mistakenly credited Bill Parsons as the artist. When this record reached the charts, Bobby Bare was just completing his military service, so Bill Parsons toured the USA

and mimed to Bobby Bare's record. Further pop hits by Bobby were "Detroit City" (6/63 US 16), and "500 Miles Away From Home" (10/63 US 10). He appeared regularly in the country charts until 1986 and had a total 70 hits. His most successful was "Marie Laveaux" (5/74 C&W 1), his only No. 1 in the C&W charts. Bobby also sang in German and had a hit there.

Charley Thomas 1937 US lead singer with the Drifters from 1964 to 1966. He was the replacement for Rudy Lewis who died of a heart attack in 1964. Hits by the Drifters with Charley were "Under The Boardwalk" (6/64 US 4) and "Saturday Night At The Movies" (11/64 US 18; 4/72 UK 3).

Freddie Hubbard 1938 US jazz trumpeter, pianist, and composer.

Ravi Shankar 1919 Indian sitar player from whom George Harrison took lessons.

Mick Abrahams 1943 UK guitarist, with Jethro Tull, his own band Blodwyn Pig, as a solo artist and as a session musician with Gary Wright, among others.

Spencer Dryden 1943 US drummer with Jefferson Airplane and its splinter groups, then from 1971, he was with New Riders Of the Purple Sage.

Bill Kreutzmann 1946 US drummer with Grateful Dead and as a session musician with Crosby, Stills & Nash and David Bromberg.

Pat Bennett 1947 US singer with the Chiffons. Hits: "He's So Fine" (2/63 US 1; 4/63 UK 16), "One Fine Day" (6/63 US 5; UK 29) and "Sweet Talking Guy" (5/66 US 10, UK 31; 3/72 RE-UK 4). The four girl singers of the Chiffons also recorded for other companies as the Four Pennies, which however, were not particularly successful.

Florian Schneider 1947 German computer musician with Kraftwerk, one of the few German bands to be internationally successful. Hits: "Autobahn" (5/75 US 25; UK 11) and "Computer Love/The Model" (12/81 UK 1).

Carol Douglas 1948 US singer. She started in the early 1970s as a member of the Chantels after their hits had dried up and started a solo career in 1974. Only hit: "Doctor's Orders" (11/74 US 11).

John Oates 1949 US singer, guitarist, keyboard player and songwriter. In 1967 he was a member of the Masters and met Daryl Hall. They discovered shared interests, got together and played in various R&B groups, then went their separate ways, and met again in 1969 in the band Gulliver. After a further separation of several years, they signed a recording contract in 1972 as Hall & Oates. In 1974 the album ABANDONED LUNCHEONETTE appeared which was later referred to as the first real album by the pair. From 1976 they regularly hit the upper echelons of the charts. Biggest hits: "Sara Smile" (1/76 US 4), "Rich Girl" (1/77 US 1), "Kiss On My List" (11/80 UK 33; 1/81 US 1), "Private Eyes" (8/81 US 1), "I Can't Go For That (No Can Do)" (11/81 US 1; 1/82 UK 8) and "Maneater" (10/82 US 1; UK 6), all the above were million sellers. Other successful records were "She's Gone" (2/74 US 60; 7/76 RE-US 7), "Out Of Touch" (9/84 US 1) and "Everything Your Heart Desires" (4/88 US 3).

Steve Ellis 1950 UK singer, songwriter and leader of Love Affair. Hit: "Everlasting Love" (1/68 UK 1). At the end of 1969 after four further Top Twenty hits, the group split up, Steve formed the band Ellis, who made two albums, and then sang with the Widowmakers in 1976.

Janis Ian 1951 US singer, guitarist, pianist, and songwriter. Real name Janis Eddy Fink. She started having piano lessons when she was three; by the time she was 11 she was playing guitar, at 12 she wrote her own songs and appeared in public. At 16 she made her first record, it became a hit, "Society's Child (Baby I've Been Thinking)" (5/67 US 14), which no radio stations would play to begin with. Only after appearing on TV in a Leonard Bernstein special, did the record become a hit. After that she recorded various albums with different companies but at 19 her career seemed to be over. In 1974 her album STARS appeared on the market. In the titlesong she sings of the highs and lows and the fears and the hopes of so-called stars. This album also included her most successful single, "At Seventeen" (6/75 US 3).

Simon Climie 1960 UK singer, and songwriter. In 1981 Simon decided to become a songwriter, and signed a contract with Chrysalis Music. His compositions became hits for artists like Pat Benatar, Smokey Robinson, Leo Sayer, Roger Daltrey and Jeff Beck. In 1985 he met Rob Fisher at a recording session by the group Scritti Politti. In March 1986 the pair signed a contract as Climie Fisher with EMI. In August 1986 their debut single "This Is Me" (5/88 UK 22) appeared; which didn't get into the charts until it was re-released later on. The same thing happened to the second single, "Keeping The Mystery Alive" (4/88). From August 1987 success came right away with hits like "Love Changes (Everything)" (9/87 UK 67; 3/88 RE-UK 2; 5/88 US 23) and "Rise To The Occasion" (12/87 UK 10). Simon also was the writer of the Aretha Franklin/George Michael hit "I Knew You Were Waiting (For Me)".

Deaths

Kit Lambert 1981 Manager and producer of the Who into the 70s.

Hits of the Day

1962	"Johnny Angel" Shelley Fabares US 2 weeks
1973	"The Night The Lights Went Out In Georgia" Vicki Lawrence US 2 weeks
1973	"Get Down" Gilbert O'Sullivan UK 2 weeks
1979	"I Will Survive" Gloria Gaynor US 1 week (2nd time)
1990	"Vogue" Madonna UK 4 weeks
1990	"Killer" Adanski UK 4 weeks

Miscellany

1956 Columbia Records announce that from now on all pop records will only appear as 45s, and that 78s will be reserved for the 'hillbilly market' only.

8th

Birthdays

Jacques Brel 1929 French singer and songwriter of Belgian origins. The themes of his songs were mainly ordinary people, his home country of Flanders, criticism of social ills and of bourgeois society. Among his most successful songs were "Quand On N'A Que L'Amour" (1956), "Le Moribond" (1961), "Ne Me Quittes Pas", "Le Plat Pays" (both 1962), "Les Bonbons" (1967) and "Vesoul" (1968). "Ne Me Quittes Pas" became a hit in the English speaking world by other artists as "If You Go Away". His most commercial composition was "Le Moribond", which became a world hit for Terry Jacks in the English version "Seasons In The Sun". Brel died 9th October, 1978.

Connie Stevens 1938 US actress and singer. Real name Concetta Rosalie Ann Ingolia. She played the part of Cricket Blake in the TV series *Hawaiian Eye* from 1959 to 1963. In 1964/65 she was Wendy in *Wendy And Me*. Then together with Edward 'Kookie' Byrnes she had the hit "Kookie, Kookie (Lend Me Your Comb)" (4/59 US 4; UK 27). As a soloist Connie was successful with "16 Reasons" (2/60 US 3; 5/60 UK 9). Along with Debbie Reynolds and Liz Taylor she was one of the wives of Eddie Fisher.

Roger Chapman 1942 UK singer and songwriter with the nickname 'Chappo'. He was one of the founder-members of Family and Streetwalkers. Also he contributed to records by Ellis, Thin Lizzy, Mike Batt, the Riffburglars and Box Of Frogs. From 1979, Roger made solo records.

As a singer for Mike Oldfield he had the hit, "Shadow On The Wall" (10/83).

Steve Howe 1947 UK guitarist and songwriter who joined the group Yes replacing Peter Banks in March 1970 after stints with Syndicates, The In Crowd, Tomorrow, and Bodast. In 1981 he became a member of Asia, and in 1986 formed the group GTR with Steve Hackett among others. Steve also released two solo albums and collaborated with Lou Reed, the Dregs and Frankie Goes To Hollywood.

Reg Isidore 1949 UK drummer with Peter Bardens, Quiver, High Tensions, Skaterlines and the Robin Trower Band.

John Schneider 1954 US actor and country singer. He played the part of Bo Duke in the TV series *Dukes Of Hazzard* from 1979 to 1985. He has been successful in country charts since 1981. His biggest crossover hit was "It's Now Or Never" (5/81 US 14).

Julian Lennon 1963 UK guitarist, singer and songwriter. Unmistakably, both in looks and in sound, the son of John Lennon. In 1984 his first records appeared. Hits: "Too Late For Goodbyes" (10/84 UK 6; 1/85 US 5), and "Valotte" (10/84 US 9). His recording debut was "Ya Ya" on the album WALLS AND BRIDGES by his father – Julian, aged just 11, played drums.

Deaths

King Oliver 1938 US jazz musician. Born 11th May, 1885.

Hits of the Day

1965	"Concrete & Clay" Unit 4 Plus 2 UK 1 week
1978	"Matchstalk Men & Matchstalk Cats & Dogs" Brian & Michael UK 3 weeks
1989	"The Look" Roxette US 1 week

9th

Birthdays

Paul Robeson 1898 US singer and actor. In 1925 he played the lead part in Eugene O'Neill's *Emperor Jones*, and in 1933 the same part in the film version. In 1930 he played Othello in London, in 1932, in *Showboat*, and in 1936 in the film version of *Showboat*. His most successful records were "Steal Away" (12/25 US 13), "Deep River"

(10/27 US 19) and "Ol' Man River" (6/28 US 7). In the 1930s and 1940s he appeared in several other films. Paul died 23rd January, 1976.

Carl Perkins 1932 US singer, guitarist and songwriter. As were many young rock 'n roll artists of the mid-1950s, Carl Perkins was under contract to the small label Sun. At the end of 1955 he wrote the song "Blue Suede Shoes" and recorded it in January 1956. Just as he was starting to promote it, he was involved in a car accident on 21st March, 1956 on the way to a New York TV station. His brother was killed in the accident, and so was his manager. Carl was hospitalised for several months and couldn't promote his record. In the meantime, Elvis Presley recorded "Blue Suede Shoes", which may not have happened if Carl Perkins had not had his accident. This accident appeared to end his career, before it had got under way. "Blue Suede Shoes" (3/56 US 2; 5/56 UK 10) remained his only success. For many Perkins was the definitive rockabilly artist. The Beatles recorded his compositions "Matchbox", "Honey Don't", and "Everybody's Trying To Be My Baby". Later Carl played country music and in 1986 recorded the album CLASS OF '55 with old pals from the Sun-era, Roy Orbison, Jerry Lee Lewis and Johnny Cash. To this day, he remains active: one of the great originals of the rock 'n' roll era.

Gene Parsons 1944 US drummer, guitarist, bassist and singer. In 1963 he started with the Castaways, remaining for nearly three years, then with Cajun Gibb & Gene for almost two years. In the spring of 1968 he became a member of Nashville West, and in November 1968 he replaced Keven Kelley as drummer with the Byrds. In August 1972 Gene left the group for a solo career. After that, he toured in a duo with Gib Guilbeau alias 'Cajun Gib', played briefly with the reformed Flying Burrito Brothers and then worked as an A & R man for a record company.

Emil Stucchio 1944 US leadsinger with the Classics, only hit, "Till Then" (6/63 US 20). The group started out as the Perennials and made their first records in 1959.

Les Gray 1946 UK leadsinger with Mud, formed in 1966. Their hit-making period lasted from 1973 to 1976. Biggest hits: "Tiger Feet" (1/74 UK 1), "Lonely This Christmas" (11/74 UK 1) and "Oh Boy" (4/75 UK 1). After Mud, Les made solo records; his biggest hit was "A Groovy Kind Of Love" (2/77 UK 32).

Philip Wright 1948 UK leadsinger and drummer with the group Paper Lace formed in 1969. Hits: "Billy, Don't Be A Hero" (2/74 UK 1) and "The Night Chicago Died" (5/74 UK 3; US 1).

Blackie Lawless 1956 US leadsinger, songwriter and bassist with the group W.A.S.P. (We Are Sexual Perverts, or White Anglo Saxon Protestants), formed by him in 1982. Nickname of the band, 'the butcher boys of heavy rock'. Before that, Blackie had been a member of the New York Dolls during their last few months together, and with the duo Sister. First hits with W.A.S.P. were "Mean Man" (3/89 UK 21) and "The Real Me" (5/89 UK 23).

Mark Kelly 1961 UK keyboard player with Marillion.

Deaths

Phil Ochs 1976 US folk protest singer and songwriter. Hanged himself in his sister's apartment. Born 19th December, 1940.

Brook Benton 1988 US singer. Died after contracting an inflammatory disease of the spinal column. Born 19th September, 1931.

Hits of the Day

1966 "You're My Soul And Inspiration" Righteous Brothers US 3 weeks
1977 "Dancing Queen" Abba US 1 week
1983 "Let's Dance" David Bowie UK 3 weeks
1984 "Big In Japan" Alphaville
1988 "Get Outta My Dreams, Get Into My Car" Billy Ocean US 2 weeks
1988 "Heart" Pet Shop Boys UK 3 weeks

10th

Birthdays

Martin Denny 1921 US composer, arranger and pianist. Biggest hit, as The Exotic Sounds of Martin Denny, "Quiet Village" (4/59 US 4), and as Martin Denny & His Orchestra, "A Taste Of Honey" (7/62 US 50).

Sheb Wooley 1921 US country singer, songwriter, and actor. He played the part of killer Ben Miller in *High Noon* (1952) and the part of Peter Nolan in the TV series *Rawhide* from 1959 to 1965. He was also in *Rocky Mountain, Giant* and *Hoosiers*. From the mid-50s Sheb recorded and his biggest hit was "The Purple People Eater" (6/58 US 1; UK 12). In addition, Sheb was successful under the pseudonym Ben Colder. Usually, as Ben, he made parodies of pop- country

hits: "Don't Go Near The Indians" was turned into "Don't Go Near The Eskimos" (11/62 US 62) and "Harper Valley P.T.A." became "Harper Valley P.T.A. (Later That Same Day)" (10/68 US 67). In the 1960s he was successful in the country charts: "That's My Pa" (1/62 C&W 1).

Nate Nelson 1932 US lead singer. In 1954, he joined the Flamingos formed in Chicago in 1952. Hit: "I Only Have Eyes For You" (6/59 US 11). In 1966 Nate became a member of the Platters. He died 1st June, 1984.

Bobbie Smith 1936 US leadsinger with the Spinners, who were formed as the Domingoes and renamed themselves Spinners in 1961. The line up changed quite often over the course of the years. Bobby was one of the few to remain in the band for a long time. In 1970 the group was called Motown Spinners on the British market, and then renamed Detroit Spinners after they had left the Motown label, in order to avoid confusion with the Liverpudlian folk-group, the Spinners. Hits: "I'll Be Around" (8/72 US 3), "Could It Be I'm Falling In Love" (12/72 US 4; 4/73 UK 11), "One Of A Kind (Love Affair)" (4/73 US 11), "Then Came You" (7/74 US 1; 10/74 UK 29) with Dionne Warwicke, "They Just Can't Stop It (The Games People Play)" (8/75 US 5), "The Rubber Band Man" (9/76 US 2; UK 16) and "Working My Way Back To You" (12/79 US 2; 2/80 UK 1). All of these records were million sellers.

Ricky Valance 1940 UK singer who was successful with a cover-version of the Ray Peterson hit "Tell Laura I Love Her" (8/60 UK 1), although the BBC refused to play it. It was his only success.

Bunny Wailer 1947 Jamaican bassist, singer and conga player with the Wailers. Real name Neville O'Reilly Livingston. Peter Tosh and Bob Marley played with the Wailers. Bunny has been releasing solo albums since 1980.

Dave Peverett 1950 UK singer, guitarist, and songwriter with Savoy Brown, and from 1971 with Foghat. Biggest hit: "Slow Ride" (12/75 US 20). Dave has been given the nickname 'Lonesome'.

Katrina Leskanich 1959 Singer and guitarist with the English/American quartet Katrina & The Waves. Hits: "Walking On Sunshine" (3/85 US 9; 5/85 UK 8), and "That's The Way" (7/89 US 16).

Brian Setzer 1959 US leadsinger, guitarist and songwriter with the Stray Cats, who formed in New York in 1979, and then went to the UK, where classic 1950s rockabilly as played by the group became very popular. Hits: "Rock This Town" (2/81 UK 9; 9/82 US 9), "Stray Cat Strut" (4/81 UK 11; 12/82 US 3) and "(She's) Sexy And Seventeen" (8/83 US 5; UK 29). All three hits were produced by Dave Edmunds. After the Stray Cats split up in

1984, Brian made solo records. In the spring of 1989 the original lineup of Stray Cats came together again.

Deaths

Chuck Willis 1958 US rock 'n' roller. Developed peritonitis in the spring of 1958 and died after a serious operation. (Other sources say he was killed after a car accident). Born 31st January, 1928.

Stu Sutcliffe 1962 UK bass player in the early days of the Beatles. When the group returned to Liverpool after a guest appearance in the Starclub in Hamburg, Stu stayed on to study art. He died at the age of 21 of a brain tumour.

Hits of the Day

1953	"Broken Wings" Stargazers UK 1 week	
1954	"Wanted" Perry Como US 8 week	
1965	"I'm Telling You Now" Freddie & The Dreamers US 2 weeks	
1968	"Congratulations" Cliff Richard UK 2 weeks	

Miscellany

1956 In Birmingham, Alabama, 6 white racists climb onto the stage during a Not 'King' Cole concert and beat him up.

1970 Paul McCartney announces he will no longer play with the Beatles – a week later his first solo album appears on the market.

1970 Jim Morrison politely asked the audience during a concert by the Doors, "Would you like to see my cock?", Ray Manzarek bundled him off the stage.

Much Too Young" (1/80 UK 1), and "Ghost Town" (6/81 UK 1). After the release of "Ghost Town", Hall, Staples and a further member, Lynval Golding, left the band to start Fun Boys Three. Hits: "It Ain't What You Do, It's The Way That You Do It" (2/82 UK 4), which they did with Bananarama, and "Our Lips Are Sealed" (4/83 UK 7).

Stuart Adamson 1958 UK singer, songwriter and guitarist. From 1978 to 1982, with Richard Jobson, he was the nucleus of the Skids. Then Adamson formed his own group which he called Big Country, who were successful from 1983. Hits: "In A Big Country" (5/83 UK 17; 10/83 US 17), "Wonderland" (1/84 UK 8), "Look Away" (4/86 UK 7) and "King Of Emotion" (8/88 UK 16).

Lee Sheridan 1949 UK singer with Brotherhood Of Man, who won the Grand Prix Eurovision at The Hague in 1976 with the title "Save Your Kisses For Me" (3/76 UK 1; 5/76 US 27). Further hits, "United We Stand" (2/70 UK 10; 4/70 US 13), "Angelo" (7/77 UK 1), and "Figaro" (1/78 UK 1).

Delroy Pearson 1970 UK singer with Five Star, consisting of 5 siblings. First hit: "All Fall Down" (5/85 UK 15).

Deaths

Dave 1988 US soul singer. Surname Prater. Successful in a duet with Samuel Moore as Sam & Dave. He died in a car accident. Born 9th May, 1937.

Hits of the Day

1963	"How Do You Do It" Gerry & The Pacemakers UK 3 weeks	
1970	"Let It Be" Beatles US 2 weeks	
1981	"Kiss On My List" Hall & Oates US 3 weeks	

11th

Birthdays

Tony Victor 1943 US singer with the Classics. Biggest hit: "Till Then" (6/63 US 20).

Neville Staples 1956 Jamaican singer. In the middle of 1977, he appeared with Terry Hall as leadsinger of the Specials, who were considered to be the founders of the 'New Ska Blue Beat Movement'. The band had a total of seven Top Ten hits in the British charts. Biggest hits: "Too

12th

Birthdays

Lionel Hampton 1913 US vibraphonist, drummer, pianist, singer and bandleader. He made his first records in 1929 as a drummer and pianist with Paul Howard. A little later he played with Louis Armstrong, and over the next few decades Lionel was to play with just about every major jazz musician. He appeared in the pop charts with his orchestra between 1937 and 1950. His major hits were

"After I've Gone" (11/37 US 6), "Hey! Ba-Ba-Re- Bop" (3/46 US 9) and "Rag Mop" (2/50 US 7).

Hound Dog Taylor 1917 US blues guitarist, pianist, singer and songwriter. Real first names Theodore Roosevelt. He started working with artists like Elmore James and Sonny Boy Williamson (Alex Miller) in the latter half of the 1920s, but only started making records in the early 1960s. Taylor died 17th December, 1975.

Helen Forrest 1918 US singer. She sang with the bands of Artie Shaw, Benny Goodman, and Harry James, from 1938 to 1943 the biggest hits respectively being, "They Say" (12/38 US 1) and "Thanks For Ev'rything" (1/39 US 1) with Shaw, "I Can't Love You Anymore (Anymore Than I Do)" (5/40 US 5) and "Taking A Chance On Love" (4/43 US 1) with Goodman, and "I Don't Want To Walk Without You" (2/42 US 1) and "I've Heard That Song Before" (1/43 US 1) with James. In 1944 she was also very successful as a solo artist, with "Time Waits For No One" (7/44 US 2). She also sang very successfully in a duet with Dick Haymes, greatest hit, "I'll Buy That Dream" (9/45 US 2).

Billy Vaughn 1919 US orchestra leader and arranger who began his career with the Hilltoppers. Hits: "P.S. I Love You" (6/53 US 4) and "Only You" (1/56 UK 3). In 1955 Billy left the Hilltoppers and became A&R director of Dot-Records. It was he who arranged hits by Pat Boone, Gale Storm and the Fontane Sisters, with backing from his orchestra. Instrumental hits for Billy Vaughn were "Melody Of Love" (12/54 US 2), "The Shifting Whispering Sands (Parts 1 and 2)" (9/55 US 5; 1/56 UK 20), "Sail Along Silvery Moon" (12/57 US 5), "La Paloma" (8/58 US 20) and "Wheels" (2/61 US 28). A hit for the Fontane Sisters featuring Billy Vaughn's Orchestra was "Hearts Of Stone" (12/54 US 1). Billy was more successful than any other orchestra leader during the rock era. He died on 14th September, 1991.

Ned Miller 1925 US country singer and songwriter, who had his greatest success with crossover hit, "From A Jack To A King" (12/62 US 6; 2/63 UK 2). He still appeared in the country charts throughout the 1970s.

Tiny Tim 1930 US novelty singer and ukelele player. Real name Herbert Khaury. His biggest hit was "Tip Toe Thru The Tulips" (5/68 US 17).

Herbie Hancock 1940 US keyboard player, composer and bandleader. He worked with Donald Byrd in New York in 1961. After that, he played with Oliver Nelson, Eric Dolphy, Dexter Gordon, and from 1963 to 1968 with Miles Davis. Herbie has been successful both in jazz and pop. In 1974 he released the solo album HEADHUNTERS, which included hit single "Rockit" (7/83 UK 8).

John Kay 1944 Singer, guitarist, and songwriter of German origin, with the Canadian group Steppenwolf; real name Joachim Krauledat. In 1958 he emigrated to Canada after fleeing from the German Democratic Republic. In 1967 he formed the group Sparrow who released an unsuccessful single. The group moved from Canada to California and changed their name to Steppenwolf after the novel by Hermann Hesse. They were successful from 1968 onwards. Hits: "Born To Be Wild" (7/68 US 2; UK 30), "Magic Carpet Ride" (10/68 US 3) and "Rock Me" (3/69 US 10). In February 1972 John announced the group was splitting up, and shortly after that his first solo album appeared. Exactly two years later the group reformed. Throughout the 1980s, he alternated between his solo career and Steppenwolf.

David Cassidy 1950 US actor and singer. He had one of the leading roles in the TV series *Partridge Family*, which was shown between 1970 and 1974 on US television. The story concerned a very musical family who sang a song in each episode, some of which became hits: "I Think I Love You" (10/70 US 1; 2/71 UK 18), "Doesn't Somebody Want To Be Wanted" (2/71 US 6), "I'll Meet You Halfway" (5/71 US 9) and "Breaking Up Is Hard To Do" (7/72 US 28; UK 3). In addition to his membership of the Partridge Family, David was also making solo records from 1971 onwards. Hits: "Cherish" (11/71 US 9), "How Can I Be Sure" (5/72 US 25; 9/72 UK 1), "Daydreamer" (10/73 UK 1). In 1978 David announced, 'I've just got to stop working. I've worked 18 hours a day, seven days a week. It's enough.' At the time *Man Under Cover* was just running on TV in which he played the part of Officer Dan Shay. After some years of absence from the charts he returned with "The Last Kiss" (2/85 UK 6).

Alexander Briley 1956 US singer with Village People.

Will Sergeant 1958 UK guitarist and songwriter with the group Echo & The Bunnymen formed in 1978. Before joining the group Will had been a chef in a restaurant.

Deaths

Josephine Baker 1975 French singer and dancer of American origin. Born 3rd June, 1906.

Hits of the Day

1957	"Cumberland Gap" Lonnie Donegan UK 5 weeks
1969	"Aquarius/Let The Sunshine In" Fifth Dimension US 6 weeks
1975	"Philadelphia Freedom" Elton John US 2 weeks
1980	"Working My Way back To You" Spinners UK 2 weeks

13th

Birthdays

Horace Kay 1934 US singer with the Tams, who made their first records in 1960. Hit, "What Kind Of Fool (Do You Think I Am)" (12/63 US 9). A re-release of the title "Hey Girl Don't Bother Me" (7/64 US 41; 7/71 UK 1) pushed the band back into the limelight in the 1970s, at least in the UK.

Lester Chambers 1940 US percussionist, harmonica player, and singer with the Chambers Brothers. He also worked with Bonnie Raitt and Ry Cooder.

Jim Pons 1943 US bass player with the Leaves, then with the Turtles, Mothers Of Invention and Flo & Eddie.

John Casady 1944 US bass player with Jefferson Airplane from 1965 to 1973. In addition he was a founder-member of Hot Tuna in 1970, whose last album appeared 1977. In between John played with spin-off groups from Jefferson Airplane. In the mid-1980s he teamed up with Paul Kantner and Marty Balin as the KBC band.

Lowell George 1945 US singer, guitarist, and songwriter. After playing with Factory, the Standells, the Seeds, and briefly with Frank Zappa, he formed Little Feat in March 1970. While the live-album WAITING FOR COLUMBUS, was their most commercially successful – released in March 1978 and became a million seller – DIXIE CHICKEN was their most impressive. Lowell worked on many albums by other artists and recorded one solo album. In April 1979 he disbanded Little Feat. Two months later he died on 29th June, 1979.

Al Green 1946 US singer and songwriter who started to record in 1967. Hits and million sellers: "Tired Of Being Alone" (7/71 US 11; 10/71 UK 4), "Let's Stay Together" (12/71 US 1; UK 7), "Look What You Done For Me" (4/72 US 4), "I'm Still In Love With You" (7/72 US 3; UK 35), "You Ought To Be With Me" (10/72 US 3), "Call Me (Come Back Home)" (2/73 US 10), "Here I Am (Come And Take Me)" (7/73 US 10) and "Sha-La-La (Make Me Happy)" (9/74 US 7; 11/74 UK 20). After his career waned in the late 1970s, Al became a gospel singer and a minister with the Full Tabernacle Church in Memphis. In 1988 he appeared again in the charts in partnership with Annie Lennox on "Put A Little Love In Your Heart" (11/88 US 9; UK 28) from the film *Scrooge*. In 1989 Al recorded "The Message Is Love" (10/89 UK 38) with Arthur Baker & The Backbeat Disciples.

Roy Loney 1946 US singer and guitarist with the Flamin' Groovies, who had previously called themselves Chosen Few and Lost and Found. Roy also made solo records.

Pieter Sweval 1948 US bassist with Looking Glass formed in 1971. After that he played with Starz from 1975.

Peabo Bryson 1951 US soul singer and songwriter. He was called the 'King Of The Black Love Ballad'. He started out in 1965 with Al Freeman & The Upsetters. He sang with Moses Dillard & The Tex-Town Display from 1968 to 1973. In 1970 he made his first solo record, and from 1976 he became a fixture in the R&B charts. His biggest cross-over hit, "Tonight, I Celebrate My Love" (7/83 US 16; UK 2), was a duet with Roberta Flack; her former partner Donny Hathaway died in rather tragic circumstances. After that he had a solo hit with "If Ever You're In My Arms Again" (5/84 US 10). He also recorded duets with Natalie Cole.

Louis Johnson 1955 US bassist, guitarist, pianist, singer and songwriter. He was discovered with his brother George by Quincy Jones, who promoted them and produced them. In 1971 the brothers joined Billy Preston. In the mid-1970s they played with Quincy Jones again. Hits, as Brothers Johnson, "I'll Be Good To You" (5/76 US 3), "Strawberry Letter 23" (7/77 US 5; UK 35), and "Stomp" (2/80 UK 6; US 7). Just like his brother, Louis is a much sought-after session musician.

Wayne Lewis 1957 US keyboard player, singer, and songwriter with the group Atlantic Starr formed in 1976.

Hits of the Day

1956	"Poor People Of Paris" Winifred Atwell UK 3 weeks
1957	"All Shook Up" Elvis Presley US 9 weeks
1959	"Come Softly To Me" Fleetwoods US 4 weeks
1967	"Something Stupid" Nancy & Frank Sinatra UK 2 weeks
1968	"Honey" Bobby Goldsboro US 5 weeks
1974	"Bennie & The Jets" Elton John US 1 week
1985	"We Are The World" USA For Africa US 4 weeks

Miscellany

1962 In Hamburg and its environs posters appeared announcing, 'Your troubles are over! The time of village music is over! Friday April 13th is opening night at the Star Club!'

1971 The Rolling Stones severed their ties with Decca Records and have set up their own record company. As with many other things they were way behind the Beatles by several years. Their first single appeared on their Rolling Stones label (trade mark, a red tongue) on this date, "Brown Sugar/Bitch/Let It Rock". Exactly a week later came the album STICKY FINGERS which turned out to be a masterpiece and is probably one of their most consistent albums.

14th

Birthdays

Buddy Knox 1933 US singer and songwriter. Real first name Wayne. He was a member of Jimmy Bowen & The Rhythm Orchids. Hit: "I'm Stickin' With You" (2/57 US 14). He also had solo hits, "Party Doll" (2/57 US 1; 5/57 UK 29) and "Hula Love" (9/57 US 9). Later Buddy Knox set up his own record label.

Loretta Lynn 1935 US country singer. Maiden name Loretta Webb. At age 14 she married Oliver Lynn. She had about 80 hits in the country charts from 1960 to 1980 and hit No. 1 sixteen times. She sang duets with Conway Twitty. Her autobiography, 'Coalminer's Daughter', was turned into a film.

Tony Burrows 1942 UK singer, songwriter, and producer. He sang with Kestrels, Ivy League, Flowerpot Men, Edison Lighthouse, White Plains, and The Pipkins. He also worked as a backing vocalist for Elton John, John Barry, Matthew Fisher, Chris Spedding and Kiki Dee.

Ritchie Blackmore 1945 UK guitarist and songwriter. From spring 1962 he played Screaming Lord Sutch's band, the Savages, and in 1963 with the Outlaws, who were produced by Joe Meek. Meek tended to use the Outlaws as the house band, backing other artists like Heinz, Tom Jones, John Leyton and Mike Berry. In 1964/65 Ritchie joined the Wild Boys, who became the backing group for Heinz. At the end of 1965 three of the Wild Boys got stuck in Hamburg, played for artists on the Polydor record label, and then formed the Three Musketeers. In 1966 Ritchie played in Neil Christian's backing band, the Crusaders. In 1967, in Hamburg again, he formed Mandrake Root. At the end of the same year Jon Lord, who was playing with the Flowerpot Men, was looking for a guitarist for his own group. In February 1968 they formed Roundabout, and in

April changed the group's name to Deep Purple: they modelled the group on Vanilla Fudge. Their first hit was "Hush" (8/68 US 4). From 1970 they became successful in the UK, having hits with "Black Night" (8/70 UK 2) and "Smoke On The Water" (5/73 US 4; 4/77 UK 21). At the end of 1974 the announcement came that Ritchie was leaving the group, and in the spring of 1975, his own band Rainbow was formed. Hits: "Since You've Been Gone" (9/79 UK 6), "All Night Long" (2/80 UK 5) and "I Surrender" (1/81 UK 3). In late 1984 Deep Purple was re-formed with the original line-up from the early 1970s – Blackmore, Glover, Gillan, Lord and Paice. It is said that each member received an offer of 2 million dollars to reform. The album PERFECT STRANGERS was later released.

Patrick Fairley 1946 UK bassist and guitarist with Marmalade.

Larry Ferguson 1948 UK keyboard player with Hot Chocolate.

June Millington 1949 US singer, guitarist and songwriter with the all-female group Fanny formed in 1970. Before that she had played with Svelts and Wild Honey. The idea for the group name Fanny came from George Harrison. Hit: "Butter Boy" (2/75 US 29). Shortly after that the band split up. June released a duet album with her sister Jean, and then carried on as a solo artist.

Sonja Kristina 1949 UK singer, guitarist, pianist and songwriter with Curved Air. Hit: "Back Street Luv" (8/71 UK 4).

Jerry Knight 1952 US bassist, singer, and keyboard player with Raydio, Bill Withers and various other groups.

Deaths

Pete Farndon 1983 UK bassist with the Pretenders. He died in his bath after a drug overdose. Born 12th June, 1952.

Thurston Harris 1990 US singer, born July 11th 1931.

Hits of the Day

1945 "I'm Beginning To See The Light" Harry James US 2 weeks

1958 "He's Got The Whole World (In His Hands)" Laurie London US 4 weeks

1966 "Somebody Help Me" Spencer Davis Group UK 2 weeks

1979 "Bright Eyes" Art Garfunkel UK 6 weeks

1979 "What A Fool Believes" Doobie Brothers US 1 week

15th

Birthdays

Bessie Smith 1894 US blues singer and songwriter who was one of the best in the business. At the beginning of her singing career she toured with Ma Rainey's band. Her recording career began with the million seller "Downhearted Blues" (6/23 US 1). She also appeared with Louis Armstrong and other top jazz musicians. By 1932 her recording career was over. She died on 26th September, 1937 after a car accident.

Roy Clark 1933 US country singer and banjo player. In the late 1940s he won the National Country Music Banjo Competition twice. From 1963 he had over 50 country hits. His biggest crossover hit was "Yesterday When I Was Young" (6/69 US 19). Roy also played in several TV series.

Bob Luman 1938 US rockabilly singer, songwriter and guitarist. Hit: "Let's Think About Living" (9/60 US 7; UK 6). He was regularly in the C&W charts until 1978. He died 27th December, 1978.

Marty Wilde 1939 UK singer and songwriter who was successful from 1958 to 1962. Major hits: "Endless Sleep" (7/58 UK 4), "Donna" (3/59 UK 3), "A Teenager In Love" (6/59 UK 2) and "Sea Of Love" (9/59 UK 3) – all cover versions of US hits. Then Marty, real name Reginald Smith, married Joyce Baker of the Vernon Girls, who had several hits in the UK in the early 1960s. The couple's children Ricky and Kim, are following in their parents' footsteps.

Dave Edmunds 1944 UK guitarist, singer, songwriter and producer. After playing in groups like 99ers, Raiders, and Image, he made his first record with Human Beinz. In spring 1968 after the first record had flopped, they changed their name to Love Sculpture and had their first hit with "Sabre Dance" (11/68 UK 5). In the spring of 1969 the group split up. In 1970 Dave recorded an old Smiley Lewis song, "I Hear You Knocking" (11/70 UK 1; US 4). His record company EMI were not interested in it, but his manager Gordon Mills had set up his own label, MAM; it was released on this label and sold over 3 million copies. Over the next few years Dave was successful in partnership with Nick Lowe and with Rockpile. Other solo hits included "Baby I Love You" (1/73 UK 8), "Born To Be With You" (6/73 UK 5) and "Girls Talk" (6/79 UK 4). He produced Shakin' Stevens, Stray Cats, Fabulous Thunderbirds, Flamin' Groovies, Everly Brothers, Mason Ruffner, Nick Lowe, Elvis Costello, Dion and many others.

Michael Chapman 1947 Australian songwriter who worked in the UK with Nicky Chinn from the early 1970s. Among the artists they worked with were Sweet, Mud, Suzi Quatro. Their success as Chinni-Chap was comparable to that of the Stock, Aitken & Waterman.

Wooley Wolstenhome 1947 UK keyboard player and singer with the group Barclay James Harvest formed in 1966 from the group Blues Keepers. Real first name Stuart. In June 1979 he left the band to work on a solo career.

Marsha Hunt 1949 UK singer, who played one of the main parts in the London version of the musical *Hair*. After that, she became a focus of attention for the gossip columns of the tabloid press. She tried several times unsuccessfully in various groups or as a solo artist, but she only had the one hit, "Keep The Customer Satisfied" (5/70 UK 41). Her greatest success was a court decision. In 1975, an English court named Mick Jagger as the father of Marsha Hunt's daughter Karis.

Phil Mogg 1952 UK singer and songwriter with UFO formed by him in 1969. Best known number "Boogie" (7/71); greatest success "Prince Kajuku" (10/71).

Nick Kamen 1962 UK singer. He became famous for a TV commercial for jeans in which he undressed in a laundrette. Madonna must have seen the commercial as she wrote and produced Nick's first hit, "Each Time You Break My Heart" (11/86 UK 5). Another hit was "Loving You Is Sweeter Than Ever" (3/87 UK 16).

Graeme Clark 1966 UK bassist, songwriter and singer with Wet Wet Wet.

Samantha Fox 1966 UK singer, who came to prominence as a 'topless model'. Hits: "Touch Me (I Want Your Body)" (3/86 UK 3; 10/86 US 4), "Do Ya Do Ya (Wanna Please Me)" (6/86 UK 10), "Nothing's Gonna Stop Me Now" (5/87 UK 8), "Naughty Girls (Need Love Too)" (3/88 US 3; 5/88 UK 31), and "I Only Wanna Be With You" (1/89 UK 16; US 31).

Hits of the Day

1965 "The Minute You're Gone" Cliff Richard UK 1 week

1967 "Somethin' Stupid" Frank & Nancy Sinatra US 4 weeks

1972 "First Time I Ever Saw Your Face" Roberta Flack US 6 weeks

1972 "Amazing Grace" Royal Scots Dragoon Guards Band UK 5 weeks

1989 "She Drives Me Crazy" Fine Young Cannibals US 1 week

1989 "Eternal Flame" Bangles UK 4 weeks

16th

Birthdays

Charlie Chaplin 1889 Born in London; started as a film comedian in Hollywood in 1914. Charlie was not only an actor, but also a film director, script writer, producer, and composer, who wrote for example the international hit, "Limelight". In May 1953 it went to No. 5 in the US charts with Frank Chacksfield and his orchestra. Chaplin died 25th December, 1977.

Roy Hamilton 1929 US R&B ballad singer. He boxed for the Golden Gloves in the Heavy-weight class. In 1947 he won first prize at an amateur contest in the Apollo Theatre. In 1948 Roy started out with the Searchlight Gospel Singers. He was successful as a solo artist from 1954 to 1961. His first hit was "You Never Walk Alone" (2/54 R&B 1; US 21) and his biggest was "Unchained Melody" (4/55 US 6). He died 20th July, 1969.

Ed Townsend 1929 US R&B singer. Hit: "For Your Love" (4/58 US 13).

Herbie Mann 1930 US flautist, saxophonist and songwriter. Real name Herbert Jay Solomon. He was one of the first to adopt Bossa Nova in jazz and helped to breakdown the musical barriers by incorporating R&B, hard rock, calypso, reggae and disco in his arrangements. He first recorded with the Mat Mathews Quintet in 1953, cutting his first solo album in 1954. Probably his best known composition is "Memphis Underground" (5/69 US 44), while his biggest hit was "Hijack" (2/75 US 14).

Perry Botkin Jr. 1933 US producer, composer and arranger. Together with Barry De Vorzon he wrote "Cotton's Dream" for the film *Bless The Beasts And Children*; then, it became the theme song for the TV series *The Young And The Restless*. Finally Nadia Comaneci, the Rumanian gymnast, used it at the Olympic Games in Montreal in 1976 – where it became a hit as "Nadia's Theme" (8/76 US 8).

Bobby Vinton 1935 US singer, real first names Stanley Robert. His father was a bandleader. The son formed his first own band while still at school; this lineup was used as a backing-up band for the artists appearing in Dick Clark's 'Caravan Of Stars' in 1960. From 1962 to 1975 Bobby was successful as a soloist. Hits: "Roses Are Red (My Love)" (6/62 US 1; 8/62 UK 15), "Blue Velvet" (8/63 US 1), "There! I've Said It Again" (11/63 US 1; UK 34), "Mr. Lonely" (10/64 US 1), "I Love How You Love Me" (11/68 US 9) and "My Melody Of Love" (9/74 US 3).

Dusty Springfield 1939 UK singer, real name Mary Catherine Isabel Bernadette O'Brien. She began with The Lana Sisters, and then formed the folk-trio The Springfields with brother Tom, and Tim Field in the early 60s. Hits: "Island Of Dreams" (12/62 UK 5), and "Say I Won't Be There" (3/63 UK 5). From autumn 1963 Dusty worked as a solo artist. From 1968 onwards she had ten Top Ten hits in the UK alone, with the most successful being "You Don't Have To Say You Love Me" (3/66 UK 1; 5/66 US 4). Cliff Richard said of her that she had the 'blackest' voice he had ever heard in a white woman. And Martha Reeves, a black American singer, was under the impression that Dusty was black. From 1973 to 1978 she made no records, with one exception, she was a backing vocalist on a record by Anne Murray (1975). In 1978 she tried a comeback but in the end it was the Pet Shop Boys who helped Dusty back into the charts, when they joined forces for "What Have I Done To Deserve This" (8/87 UK 2; 12/87 US 2). Then again as a solo artist, "Nothing Has Been Proved" (2/89 UK 16) from the film *Scandal* concerning the Profumo affair, and "In Private" (12/89 UK 14).

Stefan Grossman 1945 US guitarist with the Fugs and as a soloist.

Gerry Rafferty 1947 UK singer, guitarist and songwriter. In 1968 he was a member of the folk group Humblebums, who split up in 1970 after releasing two albums. In 1971 Gerry released his first solo album which was unsuccessful. In 1972 he formed Stealers Wheel, which 'was to be a Scottish version of Crosby, Stills, Nash & Young'. Hit: "Stuck In The Middle With You" (3/73 US 6; 5/73 UK 8). In March 1975 the group split up. Gerry had difficulties with his management and record company during the following years. In 1978 he got a new recording contract and released the album CITY TO CITY, which included the hits "Baker Street" (2/78 UK 3; 4/78 US 2) and "Night Owl" (5/79 UK 5). In the 1980s he released other records which failed to create an impression. In November 1987 he produced the Scottish twins Proclaimers.

Kurt Maloo 1953 Swiss multi-musician with Troppo, Ping Pong, both solo and with Felix Haug as a duo. Hit: "The Captain Of Her Heart" (1/86 UK 8; 6/86 US 16).

Jimmy Osmond 1963 US singer and youngest of the Osmond Brothers. Hits, as 'Little Jimmy Osmond': "Long-Haired Lover From Liverpool" (4/72 US 38; 11/72 UK 1) and "Tweedle Dee" (1/73 US 59; 3/73 UK 4).

Deaths

Morris Stoloff 1980 US orchestra leader and pianist. Born 1st August, 1898.

Hits of the Day

1954 "Secret Love" Doris Day UK 1 week
1969 "The Israelites" Desmond Dekker UK 1 week
1977 "Don't Give Up On Us" David Soul US 1 week

17th

Birthdays

James Last 1929 German orchestra leader, composer, and bassist. In 1950, as a young bassist, he won the Jazz-poll in Germany. From 1955 he wrote arrangements for Freddy, Caterina Valente and Helmut Zacharias. In 1964 he signed a recording contract for his orchestra with Polydor. Ever since, he has been successful worldwide with the James Last Band. In the UK alone he appeared in the LP-charts with 52 records between 1967 and 1987, and thus is the second most successful after Elvis Presley. The most successful were "THIS IS JAMES LAST" (4/67 UK 6), TEN YEARS NON-STOP JUBILEE (7/75 UK 5), MAKE THE PARTY LAST (11/75 UK 3), LAST THE WHOLE NIGHT LONG (4/79 UK 2) and LEAVE THE BEST TO LAST (9/85 UK 10). In the German LP-charts James Last had 100 entries between 1965 and 1985.

Chris Barber 1930 UK trombonist. In 1949 he formed his own first band. In 1950 he played with Lonnie Donegan in Ken Colyer's band which became the Chris Barber Jazzband in 1954. This band was joined by clarinettist Monty Sunshine who was responsible for Chris Barber's hit, "Petite Fleur" (1/59 US 5; UK 3); ironically Chris himself was not even featured. The best known number by Barber is "Ice Cream". In 1967 Paul McCartney wrote "Cat Call" for Chris Barber.

Alexander Graves 1930 US singer with the Moonglows. Hits: "Sincerely" (3/55 US 20), and "Ten Commandments Of Love" (9/58 US 22).

Billy Fury 1941 UK singer, real name Ronald Wycherly. He had eleven hits in the Top Ten between 1959 and 1966, which included "Halfway To Paradise" (5/61 UK 3), "Jealousy" (9/61 UK 2), "Like I've Never Been Gone" (2/63 UK 3) and "When Will You Say I Love You" (5/63 UK 3). In addition he appeared as a film actor in *That'll Be The Day*, playing the part of Stormy Tempest; among other actors featured were Ringo Starr and David Essex. In Sep-

tember 1982 Billy attempted a comeback. He died 28th January, 1983.

Jan Hammer 1948 Czech keyboard player and composer who went to the USA in 1968. He started out as a bar pianist in Boston, then he accompanied Sarah Vaughan for a year on tour in the USA, Canada and Japan. After that he played with Jeremy Steig, the Mahavishnu Orchestra between 1970 and 1974, and Jeremy Goodman. This was followed by further records with David Earle, and Neil Schon. His biggest success came when he scored the popular TV series *Miami Vice*. Hits: "Miami Vice Theme" (9/85 US 1; UK 5) and "Crockett's Theme" (9/87 UK 2).

Michael Sembello 1954 US guitarist, producer, composer and singer. From 1974 to 1979 he played guitar on Stevie Wonder's albums. Michael's major hit was "Maniac" (6/83 US 1; 8/83 UK 43), from the film *Flashdance*. He is a highly sought-after session musician.

Pete Shelley 1955 UK guitarist and songwriter, real name Peter McNeish. He formed the New Wave punk group Buzzcocks with Howard DeVito in 1975. Hits: "Ever Fallen In Love (With Someone You Shouldn't've)" (9/78 UK 12) and "Promises" (11/78 UK 20). In 1981 the band split up. Pete carried on as a soloist. The group re-formed in 1990.

Deaths

Eddie Cochran 1960 US singer, guitarist and songwriter. Eddie had been playing for a week at the Hippodrome in Bristol. In the early hours of the morning he was driving towards London when one of his tyres burst near Chippenham. Cochran suffered multiple head injuries, and died several hours later in a Bath hospital. Songwriter Sharon Sheeley and fellow rockstar Gene Vincent were also in the car, but survived the accident. However, Gene was badly injured and had to spend several months in hospital. Eddie was born 3rd October, 1938.

Felix Pappalardi 1983 US bassist, songwriter, and producer with Mountain. He was 44 years old when he was shot dead by his wife.

Hits of the Day

1943 "Moonlight Becomes You" Bing Crosby US 2 weeks
1953 "(How Much Is) That Doggie In The Window" Lita Roza UK 1 week
1971 "Joy To The World" Three Dog Night US 6 weeks
1982 "My Camera Never Lies" Bucks Fizz UK 1 week

Miscellany

1964 The first album by the Rolling Stones was released in the UK, called ROLLING STONES.

1970 The first solo album by Paul McCartney appeared, entitled, McCARTNEY. He played all the instruments himself.

18th

Birthdays

Little Brother Montgomery 1906 US blues pianist and singer. Eureal Wilford are his real first names. From 1930 he made solo records and backed other blues singers.

Clarence 'Gatemouth' Brown 1924 US blues & country singer, guitarist, violinist, drummer and songwriter. He played country/bluegrass music in the early 1940s, then made his first blues records in 1947. Hits: "Mary Is Fine" (11/49 R&B 8) and "My Time Is Expensive" (11/49 R&B 9). Clarence was the best-known 'Texas Blues Guitarist' in the early 1950s. Finally, he went back to country music and made successful records with Roy Clark.

Ken Colyer 1928 UK traditional jazz trumpeter, guitarist and bandleader. In 1949 he formed his own first band, he also formed the Crane River Jazzband in 1951 he played with the Christie Bros Stompers, and from 1953 with Ken Colyer's Jazzmen. For a while Lonnie Donegan and Chris Barber were in his band, with Chris taking it over in 1954, the band being renamed the Chris Barber band. Then Ken formed his own group, which he ran until 1985. Ken died 11th March, 1988.

Glen Hardin 1939 US pianist for the Crickets after Buddy Holly's death.

Mike Vickers 1941 UK guitarist, saxophonist, flautist and clarinetist in the early days of Manfred Mann.

Tony Reeves 1943 UK bassist and flautist, with John Mayall, Colosseum, and Greenslade.

John Kane 1946 Australian singer with New World, who had five hits in the UK-charts from 1971 to 1973. Hits included "Tom Tom Turnaround" (7/71 UK 6) and "Sister Jane" (5/72 UK 9).

Hayley Mills 1946 UK child actress. In 1959 she had her first part in the film *Tiger Bay*. She received an award for it at the Berlin Film Festival, and then received a five-year contract with Walt Disney. In 1960 she received an hon-oury children's Oscar for her part in the film *Pollyanna*. She also had two records in the US charts with "Let's Get Together" (9/61 US 8; UK 17), from the film, *The Parent Trap* and "Johnny Jingo" (3/62 US 21).

Skip Spence 1946 Canadian drummer and guitarist. Real first name Alexander. He played with Jefferson Airplane as a drummer, and as a guitarist with Moby Grape.

Andy Kyriacou 1958 UK drummer with the band Modern Romance formed in 1980.

Les Pattison 1958 UK bassist with Echo & The Bunnymen.

Shirlie 1962 UK singer and composer. Last name, Holliman. With her colleague Pepsi De Macque she was a member of the group Wham! From 1987, she was successful as Pepsi & Shirlie. Hits: "Heartache" (1/87 UK 2) and "Goodbye Stranger" (5/87 UK 9).

Deaths

Johnny Young 1974 US blues guitarist and singer. He died after a heart attack. Born 1st January, 1917.

Hits of the Day

1970 "All Kinds Of Everything" Dana UK 2 weeks
1981 "Making Your Mind Up" Bucks Fizz UK 3 weeks
1987 "I Knew You Were Waiting (For Me)" Aretha Franklin & George Michael US 2 weeks

19th

Birthdays

Alexis Korner 1928 Guitarist, singer, and songwriter, born in Paris, who said of himself he was a European. In 1961 he formed Blues Incorporated a group in which many young English musicians learned their trades. Among the early members were Cyril Davies, Charlie Watts and Dick Heckstall-Smith. Over the years until the band split up in 1967, Mick Jagger, Jack Bruce, Ginger Baker, Hughie Flint, Graham Bond, Long John Baldry, and Terry Cox had all been members. Alexis helped to form Led Zeppelin and Free. His other projects included New Church and, from 1970, CCS (Collective Consciousness Society). Hits:

"Whole Lotta Love" (10/70 UK 13), "Walkin'" (2/71 UK 7) and "Tap Turns On The Water" (9/71 UK 5). He died 1st January, 1984.

Dickie Goodman 1934 US comedian. Real first name, Richard. He was successful with partner Bill Buchanan as Buchanan & Goodman on "The Flying Saucer (Part 1 & 2)" (8/56 US 3). In the 1970s Dickie carried on as a solo artist. Hit: "Mister Jaws" (9/75 US 4). He died 6th November, 1989.

Bobby Russell 1941 US songwriter and singer. He wrote international hits for others, like "Honey", "Little Green Apples" and "The Night The Lights Went Out In Georgia". He only had one Top Thirty hit, "Saturday Morning Confusion" (7/71 US 28).

Alan Price 1942 UK pianist, singer, songwriter, arranger and producer. He played keyboards on the first hits by the Animals: "The House Of The Rising Sun" (6/64 UK 1; 8/64 US 1; 10/72 RE-UK 25; 9/82 RE-UK 11) and "We've Gotta Get Out Of This Place" (7/65 UK 2; US 13). In 1965 he left the Animals and formed the Alan Price Set. Hits: "Simon Smith & His Amazing Dancing Bear" (3/67 UK 4) and "The House That Jack Built" (8/67 UK 4). In the early 1970s he recorded with Georgie Fame, as Fame & Price Together. Hit: "Rosetta" (4/71 UK 11). In 1974 Price released the album, BETWEEN YESTERDAY AND TODAY, which yielded the single "Jarrow Song" (5/74 UK 6). In 1976, and again in 1983, the original Animals came together again briefly. In 1989 Alan had a hit in Germany with "Changes", which was used for a VW commercial.

Eva Graham 1943 UK singer, real name Evelyn May Beatson. She was the lead vocalist with the New Seekers, who were formed in 1969. Hits: "Never Ending Song Of Love" (7/71 UK 2), "I'd Like To Teach The World To Sing" (In Perfect Harmony) (12/71 UK 7), "Beg, Steal Or Borrow" (3/72 UK 2) and "You Won't Find Another Fool Like Me" (11/73 UK 1).

Tim Curry 1946 UK actor and singer. In 1968 he appeared in the London production of *Hair* for 15 months. In the film *The Rocky Horror Picture Show*, produced in 1975, he played the part of Dr. Frank N. Furter, the transvestite from outer space. Tim was also a rocksinger from 1980 onwards, producing good but unsuccessful records. His only hit was "I Do The Rock" (2/80).

Mark Volman 1947 US singer, guitarist and songwriter, who formed his first group in 1961 with his friend Howard Kaylan, whom he has always worked with. First, they formed the Nightriders which became the Crossfires, who made their first record in 1963. In 1965 they became the Turtles. Hits: "Happy Together" (2/67 US 1; UK 12),

"She'd Rather Be With Me" (5/67 US 3; UK 4), and "Elenore" (10/68 US 6; UK 7). After the band split up in 1970, the pair became members of Frank Zappa's Mothers Of Invention. In 1972 they made records as a duo, and called themselves Phlorescent Leech & Eddie, then later, Flo & Eddie. In 1985 they carried on touring as the Turtles.

Deaths

Willie Mabon 1985 US blues pianist, singer, and harmonica player. He died in Paris after a long illness. Born 24th October, 1925.

Steve Conway 1952 UK singer. He died after a heart operation. Born 24th October, 1920.

Hits of the Day

1941	"There'll Be Some Changes" Benny Goodman US 4 weeks
1941	"High On A Windy Hill" Jimmy Dorsey US 2 weeks
1980	"Call Me" Blondie US 5 weeks
1986	"A Different Corner" George Michael UK 3 weeks
1986	"Kiss" Prince US 2 weeks

Miscellany

1980 This had never happened in the history of the Billboard country chart: female singers in all first five positions, 1. Crystal Gayle, 2. Dottie West, 3. Debbie Boone, 4. Emmylou Harris, 5. Tammy Wynette (with George Jones)!

20th

Birthdays

Bob Braun 1929 US artist, real name Robert Earl Brown. Only hit, "Till Death Us Do Part" (7/62 US 26), a spoken record. He presented a TV show in Cincinnati.

Johnny Tillotson 1939 US singer, who was successful between 1960 and 1965. Hits: "Poetry In Motion" (10/60 US 2; 12/60 UK 1), "Without You" (8/61 US 7), "It Keeps Right On A-Hurtin'" (5/62 US 3), "You Can Never Stop Me Loving You" (8/63 US 18) and "Talk Back Trembling Lips" (11/63 US 7).

Craig Frost 1948 US keyboard player, who joined the hardrock band Grand Funk Railroad as the fourth member in 1972. With his arrival and the dropping of 'Railroad' was the beginning of Grand Funk's most successful period. After 1976 the band fell apart, Craig became a member of Flint, and later played in Bob Seger's Silver Bullet Band.

Luther Vandross 1951 US singer, producer, and songwriter. He began as a singer of advertising jingles, and then became a session singer. He had his first hits in the R&B charts as Luther in 1976. From 1981 he was in the pop charts under his full name. Hit, "Stop To Love" (11/86 US 15; 9/87 UK 24). He worked on countless albums by other artists, and was also a member of the session group Round Tree.

Deaths

Steve Marriott 1990 UK singer, songwriter & guitarist. Born 30th January 1947.

Johnny Shines 1992 US blues guitarist, singer and contemporary of Robert Johnson. Born 26 April 1915.

Hits of the Day

1974 "TSOP" MFSB US 2 weeks
1985 "We Are The World" USA For Africa UK 2 weeks

21st

Birthdays

Ira Louvin 1924 US country singer. Real name Lonnie Ira Loudermilk. He was in the Mountain Boys, with his brother Charlie, and after that in his own radio show. In the mid-1940s he played with Charlie Monroe's Kentucky Partners, and from 1947 with his brother as the Louvin Brothers. They cut their first records in 1949; they had a total of 12 hits in the C&W charts, the biggest being "I Don't Believe You've Met My Baby" (1/56 C&W 1). In 1963 they split up, and Ira died 20th June, 1965.

Ernie Maresca 1939 US songwriter and singer, who managed again and again to adapt hits in such a way that they turned into new hits without anyone feeling plagiarised. He wrote "Runaround Sue" and "The Wanderer", which became hits for Dion. For himself he wrote "Shout! Shout! (Knock Yourself Out)" (3/62 US 6).

Iggy Pop 1947 US singer, songwriter, and drummer. Real name James Jewel Osterberg. In 1964 Iggy became drummer and singer with the Iguanas from which his name Iggy was derived, and later he played drums for Junior Wells, Buddy Guy, and the Shangri-Las. In 1965 he joined the Prime Movers, and in 1966 he joined the Butterfield Blues Band as a drummer. In 1967 he formed the Psychedelic Stooges, who became the Stooges in 1969. In 1971 the band split up, and Iggy began to earn his living mowing lawns at the golf clubs in Florida. Then in 1972, Iggy and David Bowie wrote "China Girl" together, and a new version of the Stooges was formed, which however split up again in 1974. In 1975 Iggy disappeared completely from the scene. It emerged later on that he spent some time in a psychiatric clinic in order to get rid of his drug problem. The only person to visit him during this period was David Bowie. In April 1977 Iggy's first solo album appeared, THE IDIOT. From then on he released further records at regular intervals.

Alan Wagner 1947 UK guitarist with Foundations.

John Weider 1947 UK violinist and guitarist. He started out with John Mayall in 1963, played with the Animals from 1967 to 1968, and then with Family, and Stud. He worked as a session musician and also made solo records.

Paul Davis 1948 US singer and songwriter who made records from 1970 onwards. Hits: "I Go Crazy" (8/77 US 7), which was in the charts for 40 weeks, and " '65 Love Affair" (2/82 US 6).

Nicole Barclay 1951 US keyboard player with Fanny.

Robert Smith 1959 UK singer, guitarist, and songwriter with the group Easycure formed in 1976, and which became The Cure later. From 1980 they were successful with hits, like "The Love Cats" (10/83 UK 7), "Lullaby" (4/89 UK 5) and "Love Song" (8/89 US 2; UK 18).

Deaths

Earl Hooker 1970 US blues musician, died of tuberculosis. Born 15th January, 1930.

Sandy Denny 1978 UK folk singer. Died as the result of falling down stairs. Born 6th January, 1941. (Other versions say 16th January)

Hits of the Day

1951 "How High The Moon" Les Paul & Mary Ford US 9 weeks

1956 "Heartbreak Hotel" Elvis Presley US 8 weeks
1958 "Twilight Time" Platters US 1 week
1962 "Good Luck Charm" Elvis Presley US 2 weeks
1973 "Tie A Yellow Ribbon Round The Old Oak Tree"
Dawn UK & US 4 weeks
1979 "Knock On Wood" Amii Stewart US 1 week
1984 "Against All Odds" Phil Collins US 3 weeks

22nd

Birthdays

Charles Mingus 1922 US jazz bassist, composer and orchestra leader. From 1941 to 1943 he played with Louis Armstrong, from 1946 to 1948 with Lionel Hampton, and later on with Charlie Parker, and Duke Ellington. About the mid-1950s he went solo. Mingus was popular also with non jazz players: Joni Mitchell dedicated an album to him 1979 on which she recorded four of his compositions. Mingus is considered to be one of the most important pioneers of free jazz. He died 5th January 1979.

Glen Campbell 1936 US guitarist, singer, and songwriter, to be found both in pop and country charts. He started to tour with his band, Glen Campbell and the Western Wranglers between 1954 and 1958. In 1960 he became a member of the Champs. He became an outstanding session musician backing the Beach Boys in 1965 when Brian Wilson was ill. From 1968 to 1972 he had his own TV show *The Glen Campbell Goodtime Hour*. He co-starred in the films, *True Grit, Norwood* and *Strange Homecoming*. Hits: "Wichita Lineman" (11/68 US 3; 1/69 UK 7), "Galveston" (3/69 US 4; 5/69 U 14), "Rinestone Cowboy" (5/75 US 1; 10/75 UK 4) and "Southern Nights" (2/77 US 1; 5/77 UK 28) all million sellers.

Mel Carter 1943 US singer and actor. Mel was already singing on radio in his hometown when he was only four years old. At age 9 he was onstage with Lionel Hampton. In the early 1950s he became a member of various gospel groups. In 1957 he was voted top gospel tenor. Mel made his first solo record in 1959. Hit: "Hold Me, Thrill Me, Kiss Me" (6/65 US 8). He appeared as an actor in the TV series *Quincy* and *Magnum P.I.*

Joshua Rifkin 1944 US pianist and songwriter. He studied composition with Karl-Heinz Stockhausen in Germany. He had an early interest in folk music and became a member of the Even Dozen Jug Band. In 1978 he arranged the album WILD FLOWERS for Judy Collins which included "Both Sides Now". In 1970 he released three albums of piano rags by Scott Joplin. He led the Baroque Ensemble Of The Merseyside Chamber Music Society as a sideline.

Larry Groce 1948 US pop folk singer and songwriter. He started out as a compiler of children's songs for record productions by Walt Disney. He had his only hit with a novelty song recorded live in Santa Monica, "Junk Food Junkie" (1/76 US 9).

Pete Carr 1950 US guitarist and singer with partner Lenny LeBlanc (both were session musicians in the studio, Muscle Shoals, Alabama) as the duo LeBlanc & Carr. Hit: "Falling" (10/77 US 13).

Peter Frampton 1950 UK guitarist, singer, and songwriter. He formed Herd when he was 16. Hits: "From The Underworld" (9/67 UK 6) and "Paradise Lost" (12/67 UK 15). Then he formed Humble Pie in 1969, whose only hit was "Natural Born Bugie" (8/69 UK 4). In July 1972, Peter Frampton formed Camel, and in 1974 he became a solo artist. At the end of 1975, he was supposedly going to retire from the record business and gave a farewell concert, which became a bestseller as double-album FRAMPTON COMES ALIVE. From this album, the hits "Show Me The Way" (2/76 US 6; 5/76 UK 10) and "I'm In You" (5/77 US 2; 7/77 UK 41) were extracted. After that came further record releases. In June 1978 he broke several bones in a car accident, but was soon up and about again. However, hits became less frequent.

Paul Carrack 1951 UK keyboard player and singer with Ace, who had a hit with "How Long" (11/74 UK 20; 3/75 US 3). After leaving Ace he joined Roxy Music as a replacement for Brian Eno, and then became a member of Squeeze and Nick Lowe's band. Paul formed Mike & The Mechanics with Mike Rutherford in 1985, singing their hits, "Silent Running" (11/85 US 6; 2/86 UK 21), "All I Need Is A Miracle" (3/86 US 5) and "The Living Years" (1/89 US 1; UK 2). On the side he worked on solo projects by Roger Waters, RADIO K.A.O.S and continued to make solo records every now and then. Hit: "Don't Shed A Tear" (11/87 US 9).

Arthur Baker 1955 US disc jockey, mixer, and producer. In the mid-1980s he made a name for himself remixing material by Cyndi Lauper, Hall & Oates, Bruce Springsteen, Diana Ross, New Edition and Freeze. In 1989 he released the first record in his own name as Arthur Baker & The Backbeat Disciples. Hit: "The Message Is Love" (10/89 UK 38), sung by Al Green.

Craig Logan 1969 UK bass player with Bros. In 1989 he left the twins.

Deaths

Earl Hines 1983 US jazz and blues pianist. Nickname, 'Fatha'. Born 28th December, 1903.

Hits of the Day

1944 "It's Love Love Love" Guy Lombardo US 2 weeks
1965 "Ticket To Ride" Beatles UK 3 weeks
1989 "Like A Prayer" Madonna US 3 weeks

Miscellany

1968 Herb Alpert wanted to offer something special to his audiences during a TV special on the occasion of his tenth album – the trumpeter thought he'd sing a song. It was "This Guy's In Love With You" which was not intended for release as a record. But shortly after the programme, demand was so great that Alpert released it first on an album and later as a single – it became a million seller.

23rd

Birthdays

Roy Orbison 1936 US singer and songwriter. In 1952 he formed his own group the Wink Westeners; in the mid-1950s he formed the Teen Kings, with whom he recorded "Ooby Dooby" in Norman Petty's studio in late 1955; it was released as a single in West Texas and New Mexico. A few weeks later, it was re-recorded, this time in the Sun studios in Memphis. This time "Ooby Dooby" (6/56 US 59) entered the chart. He caused a commotion in 1958 when the Everly Brothers recorded his composition "Claudette". From 1960 to 1965 Roy had international hits with "Only The Lonely" (6/60 US 2; 8/60 UK 1), "Running Scared" (4/61 US 1; UK 9), "Crying" (8/61 US 2; UK 9), "It's Over" (4/64 US 9; UK 1) and "Oh, Pretty Woman" (8/64 US & UK 1). Several private tragedies hit him after 1965: his wife Claudette died after a motor bike accident,

and two of his sons died in 1968 when his house burned down. Nothing was heard of Roy Orbison for quite a while until he produced a record with Emmylou Harris in 1980. Then, with his old Sun colleagues Jerry Lee Lewis, Carl Perkins, and Johnny Cash, he released the album CLASS OF '55 in 1986. On 30th September, 1987 a number of very high-class artists collaborated in the production of a video 'A Black And White Night' – starring Roy Orbison. Among them were Bruce Springsteen, Jackson Brown and Elvis Costello. At the same time Orbison started recording a new solo album. Shortly afterwards, he became a member of the band Travelling Wilburys, which comprised Bob Dylan, Jeff Lynne, Tom Petty and George Harrison; in the autumn of 1988 the album TRAVELLING WILBURYS VOL. 1 appeared. Just when the release of his solo album MYSTERY GIRL was announced, Roy died on 6th December, 1988. The first single from the album was "You Got It" (1/89 US 9; UK 3).

Ray Peterson 1939 US singer, with records on the market from 1958. Hits: "Tell Laura I Love Her" (6/60 US 7) and "Corinna, Corinna" (11/60 US 9; 1/61 UK 41).

John Miles 1949 UK singer, keyboard player, guitarist and songwriter. Alan Parsons produced the hit "Music" (3/76 UK 3) for him in the Abbey Road Studios. In 1977 his "Slow Down" (3/77 US 34; 6/77 UK 10) marked the beginning of the end of his solo career. He is on various albums by Alan Parsons as a singer and guitarist. John also plays in Tina Turner's band.

Michael Narada Walden 1952 US singer, songwriter, drummer, and producer. As a teenager he played with such groups as Ted Nugent & The Amboy Dukes, MC 5, Bob Seger System, and Deacon Williams & The Soul Revival. In 1972 he became a member of John McLaughlin's Mahavishnu Orchestra. After the band split up in 1976, Walden made solo records and worked as a session musician with Jeff Beck, Carlos Santana, Weather Report, Rick James, Roy Buchanan, Tommy Bolin, and others. He also made a name for himself as a producer of Stacy Lattislaw, Whitney Houston and Sister Sledge.

Steve Clarke 1960 UK lead guitarist with Def Leppard, died on 8th January, 1991.

Deaths

Peter Ham 1975 UK guitarist, and leader of the Iveys, who developed into Badfinger. When success began to wane, he hanged himself. Born 27th April, 1947.

Johnny Thunders 1991 US singer and guitarist with New York Dolls and Heartbreakers.

Harold Arlen 1986 US composer and singer. Born 15th February, 1905.

Hits of the Day

1954 "I See The Moon" Stargazers UK 1 week (2nd time)

1964 "World Without Love" Peter & Gordon UK 2 weeks

1969 "Get Back" Beatles UK 6 weeks

1977 "Don't Leave Me This Way" Thelma Houston US 1 week

1983 "Come On Eileen" Dexy's Midnight Runners US 1 week

1988 "Where Do Broken Hearts Go" Whitney Houston US 2 weeks

24th

Birthdays

Freddy Scott 1933 US singer and songwriter with hits from 1963 to 1967. Greatest success, "Hey Girl" (7/63 US 10).

Barbra Streisand 1942 US actress, singer and songwriter. Real names Barbara Joan. In 1962 she made her debut on Broadway in *I Can Get it From You Wholesale*, and played the lead part in *Funny Girl* in 1964. Her film debut was *Funny Girl* in 1968, and with Katherine Hepburn she immediately won the Oscar for 'Best Actress Of The Year'. Then her career as a singer began with a song from *Funny Girl*: "People" (4/64 US 5). Other hits like "The Way We Were" (11/73 US 1; 3/74 UK 31), "Evergreen" (12/76 US 1; 4/77 UK 3) and "Woman In Love" (9/80 US & UK 1). Hits in duet with various partners: "You Don't Bring Me Flowers" (10/78 US 1; UK 5) with Neil Diamond; "Guilty" (11/80 US 3; UK 34) with Barry Gibb; "No More Tears (Enough Is Enough)" (10/79 US 1; UK 3) with Donna Summer, and "Till I Loved You" (10/88 US 25; UK 16) with Don Johnson. Her career as a movie star continued apace with *A Star Is Born, Hello Dolly, Funny Lady, The Way We Were* among others. In the film *Yentl* (1983) she was the producer, director, and played the main part.

Bernard St. Clair Lee Calhoun Henderson 1944 US singer, also with Hues Corporation.

Tony Visconti 1944 US producer. He started as a guitarist in schoolbands, then became a bassist, backing Tony Bennett and Milton Berle. Together He made a demo tape with his wife as Tony & Sigrid, which was released by RCA but never reached the charts. After that he went to Britain and worked with Move, Procol Harum, Joe Cocker, Georgie Fame and Denny Cordell. His first major successes as a producer came with T. Rex, and David Bowie. Among his other clients were the Strawbs, Mary Hopkin (whom he married later), Tom Paxton, Ralph McTell, Thin Lizzy, Osibisa, Gentle Giant, Boomtown Rats and the Stranglers.

Doug Clifford 1945 US drummer, who was in the original lineup of Creedence Clearwater Revival, released a solo record in 1972, and could be heard on records by Tom Fogerty, the Don Harrison Band, and others during the 1970s.

Robert Knight 1945 US singer who made records from 1960. He had his first hit with "Everlasting Love" (9/67 US 13; 1/68 UK 40); 3/74 RE-UK 19). A further success was "Love On A Mountain Top" (11/73 UK 10).

Glen Cornick 1947 UK bass player with Jethro Tull from 1968 to 1971, then with Wild Turkey, Karthago, and finally with Bob Welch in Paris.

Hubert Ann Kelly 1947 US singer with Hues Corporation. Hit and million seller: "Rock The Boat" (5/74 US 1; 7/74 UK 6).

Steve York 1948 UK bassist with Graham Bond, East Of Eden, Manfred Mann Chapter 3, Dada, Vinegar Joe, and as a session musician.

Jack Blades 1954 US bassist and singer with Night Ranger, who released their debut album in 1982. Hits: "Sister Christian" (3/84 US 5), and "Sentimental Street" (5/85 US 8).

Captain Sensible 1954 UK bass player, guitarist, and singer. Real name Ray Burnes. After playing in various bands from 1970, he became a founder-member of The Damned in May 1976. In February 1978 the band split up. Sensible who was bassist with the band, became a guitarist and member of the Softies. After that he formed a band called King. In 1979 The Damned reformed and since 1982 he has been a solo artist too. "Happy Talk (6/82 UK 1) and "Wot" (8/82 UK 26). In August 1984 he left The Damned.

Boris Williams 1958 UK drummer with The Cure.

Deaths

Otis Spann 1970 US blues musician. Even after a heart attack Otis did not restrict his alcohol intake. In early 1970

the doctors diagnosed cancer of the liver. He probably died of acute heart failure. Born 21st March, 1930.

Hits of the Day

1948 "Now Is The Hour" Bing Crosby US 3 weeks
1953 "I Believe" Frankie Lane UK 9 weeks
1959 "It Doesn't Matter Anymore" Buddy Holly UK 3 weeks
1965 "Game Of Love" Wayne Fontana & The Mindbenders US 1 week
1968 "What A Wonderful World/Cabaret" Louis Armstrong UK 4 weeks
1982 "Ebony & Ivory" Stevie Wonder & Paul McCartney UK 3 weeks

---

25th

Birthdays

Earl Bostic 1913 US alto saxophonist, clarinettist, flautist, songwriter and orchestra leader. He played with Cab Calloway, Lionel Hampton, and Paul Whiteman's band. In 1944 he formed his own group. The number "Flamingo" (11/51 R&B 1), though not in the pop charts, was nevertheless a million seller. Earl died 28th October, 1965.

Ella Fitzgerald 1918 US First Lady of Jazz! In 1934 she won an amateur contest at The Harlem Operahouse and at the Apollo Theatre. In 1935 she became a member of Chick Webb & His Orchestra. Hit: "A-Tisket, A-Tasket" (6/38 US 1). After Chick's death in 1939, Ella led the band until 1942. Solo records by her appeared from 1936. Hits, with the Inkspots: "I'm Making Believe" (11/44 US 1), and "Into Each Life Some Rain Must Fall" (11/44 US 1). Her last notable hit was "Mack The Knife" (5/60 US 27) which was recorded live on 13th February, 1960 in the Deutchlandhalle in Berlin.

Albert King 1923 US blues singer, guitarist, and drummer. Real name Albert Nelson. In the late 1940s/early 1950s he was in the gospel group Harmony Kings. He made his first records in 1953, and in 1956 he formed his own group. From 1961 to 1979 Albert was regularly in the R & B charts. Hits: "Don't Throw Your Love On Me So Strong" (12/61 R&B 14), and "Cold Feet" (1/68 R&B 20; US 67).

Jerry Leiber 1933 US songwriter, who wrote many of the early R 'n' R hits with Mike Stoller (see birthday of Mike, 13th March).

Tony Christie 1943 UK singer, real name Anthony Fitzgerald. Hits: "I Did What I Did For Maria" (5/71 UK 2) and "Is This The Way To Amarillo" (11/71 UK 18).

Stu Cook 1945 US bassist in the original lineup of Creedence Clearwater Revival. After that, he played on records by his former band colleagues Doug Clifford, and Tom Fogerty, with the Don Harrison Band, and Roky Erickson & The Aliens.

Dave Lawson 1945 UK pianist with Episode Six, Alan Bown and Greenslade. After that as a session musician with Sally Oldfield, Shadows, John Martyn, Bill Wyman and Jimmy Page.

Björn Ulvaeus 1945 Swedish guitarist and composer for Abba. He had his hits in the early 1960s with the Hootenanny Singers, who mixed pop hits with a folk repertoire. Then he started working together with Benny Andersson, who was as a pianist in the Hep Stars. Benny was engaged to singer Anni-Frid Lyngstad, and Bjorn married Agnetha Faltskog (also a pop singer in Sweden) in 1971. In 1972 the four released their first record under the group name Bjorn, Benny, Agnetha & Anni-Frid, "People Need Love", which reached No. 2 in the Swedish charts. In 1973 they abbreviated the group name to their initials, ABBA, and participated in the Swedish finals for the Grand Prix Eurovision with "Ring Ring". The title was not chosen. Instead they won the European contest a year later with the number "Waterloo" (4/74 UK 1; 6/74 US 6). Their career turned them into the most successful group since the Beatles generating a number of hits up to 1983. In the UK they had 9 No. 1 hits and one in the USA including "Fernando" (3/76 UK 1; 9/76 US 13), "Dancing Queen" (8/76 UK 1; 12/76 US 1) and "Take A Chance On Me" (2/78 UK 1; 4/78 US 3). In 1978 Bjorn and Agnetha were divorced. From 1983 onwards the Abba members went their separate ways. In 1984 Bjorn wrote the musical *Chess* with Benny Andersson and Tim Rice.

Mike Kennedy 1946 Singer and guitarist. Real name Michael Kogel. In the early 1960s he played with Michael & The Firebirds. The German producer Nils Nobach introduced Michael to the Spanish group Los Bravos, with whom he recorded "Black Is Black" (6/66 UK 2; 8/66 US 4; 8/66 US 4). However, it later became known that apart from Michael no one from the group Los Bravos had been present in the studio during production. A further hit followed, "I Don't Care" (9/66 UK 16). In 1969 Michael left the band and turned up as a solo artist in Spain under the name Mike Kennedy, where he hit the No. 1 spot with "La Lluvia". After various attempts to launch his career in Britain and Germany he remained in Spain.

Michael Brown 1949 US keyboard player, and songwriter for the group Left Banke formed in 1966, also Montage, Stories and Beckies. Real name Lukowsky.

Steven Ferrone 1950 UK drummer and session musician with Brian Auger's Oblivion Express, Bloodstone, and as a replacement for the late Robbie McIntosh in the Average White Band. Steven is also a highly sought-after session musician.

Cory Daye 1953 US lead singer with Dr. Buzzard's Original Savannah Band. Biggest success, "Whispering/Cherchez La Femme/C'est Si Bon (11/76 US 27). The band tried to transalate the style of the 1930s to the discotheque era. After the founder of the band, August Darnell, left the band in 1980 to form Kid Creole & The Coconuts, the group disappeared from the scene.

Fish 1958 UK singer and songwriter. Real name Derek William Dick. In 1980 he joined the group Silmarillion formed in December 1978 which was shortened to Marillion. From 1982 they appeared in the charts with "Kayleigh" (5/85 UK 2), "Lavender" (9/85 UK 5) and "Incommunicado" (5/87 UK 6). In September 1988 Fish left because of 'musical differences' within the group, and started a solo career. First hit: "State Of Mind" (10/89 UK 32).

Billy Rankin 1959 UK guitarist, singer, keyboard player and songwriter, who played with Zal in 1976 and then, after several changes of direction, became a member of Nazareth in 1981. From 1983 he was a solo artist.

Andy Bell 1964 UK singer with Erasure, formed in 1985 as a new project by Vince Clark, who had already helped form Depeche Mode, Yazoo and Assembly. Andy had previously sung with the group Void, and then replied to an ad in the Melody Maker, placed by Vince. Hits for Erasure: "Sometimes" (10/86 UK 2), "Victim Of Love" (5/87 UK 7), "The Circus" (10/87 UK 6), "Ship Of Fools" (2/88 UK 6), "Chains Of Love" (6/88 UK 11; US 12), "A Little Respect" (10/88 UK 4; US 14), "Crackers International" (12/88 UK 2) and "Drama!" (9/89 UK 4).

Hits of the Day

1958	"Whole Lotta Love" Marvin Rainwater UK 3 weeks
1960	"Stuck On You" Elvis Presley US 4 weeks
1970	"ABC" Jackson 5 US 2 weeks
1970	"Mademoiselle Ninette" Soulful Dynamics

1977	"Lay Back In The Arms Of Someone" Smokie
1987	"La Isla Bonita" Madonna UK 2 weeks
1988	"Heart" Pet Shop Boys

26th

Birthdays

Ma Rainey 1886 US blues singer. Born Gertrude Malissa Pridgett. She was said to be the 'Pioneer of Female Blues Singers', and was the idol of Bessie Smith. In 1923 she made her first records. Hit: "See Rider Blues" (1/25 US 14), Louis Armstrong and Fletcher Henderson among others played on this record. Ma was also known under the pseudonyms Mama Can Can, Lila Patterson and Anne Smith. In 1933 she retired from the music business. After suffering a heart attack she died 22nd December, 1939. In 1985 her life was the subject of the Broadway musical *Ma Rainey's Black Bottom*.

Jörgen Ingmann 1925 Danish guitarist and songwriter. His version of "Apache" (1/61 US 2) was unsuccessful in Britain only because it was a Shadows hit there. Together with Grethe Ingmann he won the Grand Prix Eurovision for Denmark in London with the title "Dansevise".

Duane Eddy 1938 US guitarist and songwriter who was discovered by Lee Hazlewood in 1957 and promoted by him. Hits: "Rebel Rouser" (6/58 US 6; 9/58 UK 19), "Forty Miles Of Bad Road" (6/59 US 9; 9/59 UK 11), "Because They're Young" (5/60 US 4; 8/60 UK 2), "Pepe" (12/60 US 18; UK 2) and "(Dance With The) Guitar Man" (10/62 US 12; UK 4). Eddy with his twangy guitar is considered to be the No. 1 R 'n R instrumentalist. After disappearing from the charts for about 20 years in the mid 1960s, he returned with the group Art Of Noise, scoring with "Peter Gunn" (3/86 UK 8; 8/86 US 50). In 1987 a new album appeared which had been recorded with such musicians as Jeff Lynne, Paul McCartney, George Harrison, John Fogerty and Ry Cooder.

Maurice Williams 1938 US singer and songwriter. In 1955 he formed the Royal Charms which a little later on became the Gladiolas. Hit: "Little Darlin'" (4/57 US 41). In 1959 they changed their name again to Maurice Williams & The Zodiacs. Hit: "Stay" (10/60 US 1; UK 14), this title written by Williams was later a Top Twenty hit for the Four Seasons, Jackson Browne and the Hollies too.

Bobby Rydell 1940 US singer, real name Robert Louis Ridarelli. Among his school friends were Fabian and Frankie Avalon, all from Philadelphia, and all of them had one goal in mind, to become stars. With Frankie as a trumpeter, and Bobby on drums they played with Rocco & The Saints in 1956, and in 1957 he made his first records. As did many high school teen-idols of those days Bobby played in several mediocre films. Bobby's hits included "We Got Love" (10/59 US 6), "Wild One" (2/60 US 2; UK 7), "Swinging School" (5/60 US 5), "Volare" (7/60 US 4; 9/60 UK 22) and "Forget Him" (3/63 UK 13; 11/63 US 4). He had no more hits after 1963: the Beatles came and the teen-idols were replaced.

Claudine Clark 1941 US singer and songwriter. In 1958 she cut her first records. Hit: "Party Lights" (6/62 US 5). In addition she made records under the pseudonym Joy Dawn.

Gary Wright 1943 US pianist, singer, and songwriter who helped to form the group Spooky Tooth in the UK in 1967. When the group split up in 1970, he carried on as a soloist without success. Between 1973 and 1974 he rejoined Spooky Tooth, but left for another stab at a solo career. Hits: "Dream Weaver" (1/76 US 2) and "Love Is Alive" (4/76 US 2). Gary played in the TV series *Captain Video* as a 7 year old in 1950.

Giorgio Moroder 1944 South Tyrolean singer, songwriter and producer who plays several instruments and speaks five languages. As Giorgio he had the hits, "Looky, Looky" (6/69) and "Underdog" (2/71) in Germany. From the beginning of the 1980s he was a successful composer in the USA, writing a number of successful film scores. He received an Oscar for *Midnight Express*, *Flashdance* and for the title song of *Top Gun*. Hits with Paul Engemann: "Reach Out" (8/84) (this title was the official theme of the Olympic Games in L.A.), and with Phil Oakey "Together In Electric Dreams" (9/84 UK 3). For the Olympic Games in Korea in 1988 Giorgio wrote the number "Hand In Hand" (9/88), which was successful worldwide. The rumour that Moroder has won a total of 150 golden discs is absolutely correct! The variety of musicians produced by him range from Michael Holm, Ricky Shayne, and Mary Roos via Donna Summer right to Sigue Sigue Sputnik.

Tony Murray 1945 UK bass player with the Troggs.

Ronny Dayton 1946 US 'Hot Rod' musician. Real name Bucky Wilkin. Hit for Ronny & The Daytonas, "G.T.O." (8/64 US 4).

Jimmy Hall 1949 US singer, saxophonist, and songwriter for Wet Willie who play typical 'Southern Boogie

Rock'. Hit: "Keep On Smilin'" (5/74 US 10). The band lasted from 1970 to 1980. After 1980 Jimmy played on records by Jeff Beck and Charlie Daniels.

Roger Taylor 1960 UK drummer who came from the punk group Scent Organs in 1979 to join the group Duran Duran formed a year before. He also played with Arcadia. In April 1986 Roger announced he wanted to take a break for a year and recover. He did not return to Duran Duran.

Deaths

Count Basie 1984 US jazz pianist and orchestra leader. Born on 21st August, 1904.

Dexter Gordon 1990 US saxophonist and actor, born on 27th February, 1923.

Hits of the Day

1971	"Rose Garden" Lynn Anderson
1975	"Another Somebody Done Somebody Wrong Song" B.J. Thomas US 1 week
1980	"Call Me" Blondie UK 1 week

27th

Birthdays

Maxine Brown 1932 US singer with the Browns, a trio comprised three sisters. Hit: "The Three Bells" (7/59 US 1; 9/57 UK 6). After that the three only had one more hit, "The Old Lamplighter" (3/60 US 5).

Cuba Gooding 1944 US leadsinger with Main Ingredient. When he replaced Donald McPherson who died on 4th July, 1971, the band started to be successful. Hits and million sellers, "Everybody Plays The Fool" (7/72 US 3) and "Just Don't Want To Be Lonely" (2/74 US 10; 6/74 UK 27).

Peter Ham 1947 UK guitarist and songwriter. In July 1968, after playing in David Garrick's backing group, he signed a recording contract with Apple Records. Paul McCartney had heard a demo tape by him and was interested. Peter's group called itself Iveys. After several unsuccessful record releases the band changed their name to Badfinger in December, 1969. Now the hits came pouring in: "Come And Get It" (1/70 UK 4; US 7), "No Matter What" (10/70 US 8; 1/71 UK 5) and "Day After Day" (12/71 US 4; UK 10). Peter also wrote some hits for other artists, like the No. 1 for Harry Nilsson, "Without You". When success waned, Ham hanged himself on 23rd April, 1975.

Ann Peebles 1947 US singer and songwriter. She had her first successes in the R&B charts in 1969. Her composition "I Can't Stand The Rain" (9/73 US 38) became a hit again in 1978 for Eruption.

Kate Pierson 1948 US organist and singer with the B 52s who were formed in October 1976.

Ace Frehley 1950 US guitarist, singer and songwriter with Kiss, and solo. Real first name Paul. As a soloist he had the hit, "New York Groove" (10/78 US 13). The trademark of the group Kiss formed in 1972 was full make-up, which the members were never seen without. Not until 1982 did they discard this image when it was unnecessary for their continued success. In the same year, Ace left the group and formed his own band Frehley's Comet a little later.

Sheena Easton 1959 UK singer and actress, real name Sheena Orr. In 1980 she began her career in the BBC TV documentary 'The Big Time' in which she played a singer. Hits: "Morning Train (Nine To Five)" (7/80 UK 3; 2/81 US 4), "For Your Eyes Only" (6/81 UK 8; US 4) from the James Bond film of the same name, and "The Lover In Me" (11/88 US 2; 1/89 UK 15). Also in a duet with Kenny Rogers, "We've Got Tonight" (1/83 US 6; UK 28).

Deaths

Mike Brant 1975 French pop star. He took his life inexplicably at the height of his career. Born 2nd February, 1947.

Z. Z. Hill 1984 US R&B artist. He died after a heart attack. Born 30th September, 1935.

28th

Birthdays

Peter Anders 1941 US singer, songwriter, and producer; real name Peter Andreoli. He recorded under several different group names in the mid-1960s with Vincent Poncia and other US session musician. As Videls (1960), Trade Winds, "New York's A Lonely Town" (2/65 US 32) and as Innocence "There's Got To Be A Word!" (12/66 US 34). In the late 1960s Anders and Poncia released an album as a duo and from 1972, Peter made solo records.

John Wolters 1945 US drummer and singer with Dr. Hook.

Vito Balsamo 1946 US leadsinger with Vito & The Salutations, who had two smallish hits in 1962/63.

Brian Miller 1947 UK keyboard player with Isotope, Turning Point and Sally Oldfield.

Bob Robertson 1951 UK saxophonist and pianist with Supercharge and Rumour.

Edwin Jobson 1955 UK multi-instrumentalist. He played with Fat Grapple, Curved Air, Bryan Ferry, Roxy Music, Jethro Tull and U.K. He recorded as a solo artist and is much a sought-after session musician in the UK.

Andy LeGear 1960 UK lead guitarist with Rosetta Stone, who were to follow in the footsteps of the Bay City Rollers.

Enid Williams 1960 UK bass player and singer with Girlschool, who had a hit "St. Valentine's Day Massacre" (2/81 UK 5) with the group Motorhead, as Headgirl.

Deaths

Tom Donahue 1975 US disc jockey and producer. Born 21st May, 1928.

B.W. Stephenson 1988 US singer and songwriter, born 5th October 1949.

Hits of the Day

1946	"I'm A Big Girl Now" Sammy Kaye US 1 week
1963	"I Will Follow Him" Little Peggy March US 3 weeks
1967	"Puppet On A String" Sandie Shaw UK 3 weeks
1968	"Words" Bee Gees
1987	"You're The Voice" John Farnham

Hits of the Day

1958	"Witch Doctor" David Seville US 3 weeks
1960	"Do You Mind" Anthony Newley UK 1 week
1966	"You Don't Have To Say You Love Me" Dusty Springfield UK 1 week
1979	"Heart Of Glass" Blondie US 1 week
1980	"Weekend" Earth & Fire

29th

Birthdays

Duke Ellington 1899 US pianist, songwriter, leader of his own orchestra and one of the most popular personalities in the history of jazz. Real first names Edward Kennedy. He was active as a bandleader from 1918. He came to New York and, in 1923 from 1927, played in the New York 'Cotton Club' for five years. As a composer he influenced countless musicians including those of modern free-jazz. Hits: "Three Little Words" (10/30 US 1), "Cocktail For Two" (5/34 US 1), "Moon Glow" (10/34 US 2), "Solitude" (10/34 US 2) and "I Let A Song Go Out Of My Heart" (3/38 US 1). Another unforgettable number was Duke Ellington's theme, "Take The 'A' Train" (7/41 US 11; 7/43 RE-US 19), written by Billy Strayhorn. He recorded frequently with Ella Fitzgerald. Duke died 24th May, 1974.

Russ Morgan 1904 US pianist, songwriter, trombonist and orchestra leader. Russ was successful with his orchestra in the USA from 1935. Biggest hits: "The Merry-Go-Round Broke Down" (6/37 US 1), "I've Got A Pocketful Of Dreams" (8/38 US 1), in which Morgan was vocalist, the million seller "Cruising Down The River" (2/49 US 1) and "Forever And Ever" (3/49 US 1). As a composer he had, among others, the successful hit, "You're Nobody Till Somebody Loves You". Russ died 8th August, 1969.

Donald Mills 1915 US singer with the Mills Brothers formed in the late 1920s. From 1956 until 1982 the Mills Brothers were only a trio, and later still they consisted only of Donald and his son John.

Carl Gardner 1928 US singer. In 1954 he joined the Robins, formed in 1947, and was featured on the hit "Smokey Joe's Cafe" (12/55 R&B 10). In 1955 Carl formed the group the Coasters and became their lead singer. Hits: "Yakety Yak" (6/58 US 1; 8/58 UK 12), "Charlie Brown" (2/59 US 2; UK 6), "Along Come Jones" (5/59 US 9), and "Poison Ivy" (8/59 US 7; 10/59 UK 15).

Ray Baretto 1929 US percussionist, songwriter, arranger and bandleader. He became known when he replaced Mongo Santamaria with Tito Puente in the 50s. After four years with the band Ray set up his own group, Charanga, made solo records and worked as a session musician with the Rolling Stones, George Benson, Herbie Mann, Bee Gees, Average White Band, and many others. He had the hit, "El Watusi" (4/63 US 17) under his own name.

Lonnie Donegan 1931 UK singer, songwriter and string instrumentalist. Real first name, Anthony. He was one of the first superstars in the UK in the 1950s. He helped to start the skiffle craze when he was in Ken Colyer's band, and in 1953, he played with Chris Barber. In 1954 he recorded "Rock Island Line" (1/56 UK 8; 3/56 US 8), which became a hit 2 years later. By the end of 1962 he had had seventeen Top Ten hits in the UK; the biggest were "Cumberland Gap" (4/57 UK 1), "Gamblin' Man/Putting On The Style" (6/57 UK 1), "Does Your Chewing Gum Lose Its Flavour (On The Bedpost Overnight)" (2/59 UK 3; 8/61 US 5) and "My Old Man's A Dustman" (3/60 UK 1).

Otis Rush 1934 US blues singer, guitarist, and harmonica player. He had his own group called Little Otis. Biggest hit under his own name was "I Can't Quit You Baby" (10/56 R&B 6).

April Stevens 1936 US singer who, with brother Nino Tempo, had the hits, "Deep Purple" (9/63 US 1; 11/63 UK 17) and "Whispering" (12/63 US 11; UK 20). April made solo records too, with title, "Teach Me Tiger" (11/59 US 86) being the best known.

Klaus Voormann 1938 German musician born in Berlin. 1966 was his year: he designed the cover for the Beatles album REVOLVER and replaced Jack Bruce as bass player in Manfred Mann. After that Klaus became a highly sought-after session musician in the UK and USA and played in the Plastic Ono Band from 1969 to 1974. He participated in the 'Concert For Bangladesh' and is on records by Carly Simon, Howlin' Wolf, Gary Wright, B. B. King, Jerry Lee Lewis, Peter Frampton, Art Garfunkel, Donovan, Keith Moon, Nilsson; he also guested on the various solo albums by each individual member of the Beatles. In the early 1980s Klaus returned to Germany to work as a producer; his first successful production was Trio.

Vincent Poncia 1942 US singer, songwriter, and producer. He was in several bands like Videls, Trade Winds and Innocence. From the early 1970s he worked more as a producer with Melissa Manchester, Ringo Starr, Kiss, Fanny and Ellen Foley, among others.

Hugh Hopper 1945 UK bassist with Soft Machine, as a soloist, and as a songwriter for Isotope.

Tommy James 1947 US singer, songwriter and leader of the band Tommy James & The Shondells formed by him in 1959. Real name Thomas Jackson. In 1963 they recorded "Hanky Panky" (6/66 US 1; UK 38), which was not successful until about 3 years later. Further hits: "I Think We're Alone Now" (2/67 US 4), "Mony Mony" (4/68 US 3; 6/68 UK 1), "Crimson And Clover" (12/68 US 1) and "Crystal Blue Persuasion" (6/69 US 2). In 1970, Tommy launched a solo career, scoring with "Draggin' The Line" (6/71 US 4). After a break of nine years, he released "Three Times In Love" (1/80 US 19).

Michael Karoli 1948 German guitarist with Can.

Bob 'Willard' Henke 1951 US bass player with Dr. Hook.

Deborah Iyall 1954 US singer with the San Francisco 'new wave' quintet Romeo Void, formed in 1979. Only hit: "A Girl In Trouble (Is A Temporary Thing)" (9/84 US 35).

Mark Kendall 1957 US lead guitarist and songwriter with Great White.

Deaths

Leroy Carr 1935 US blues-pianist and singer, who literally drank himself to death. Born 27th March, 1905.

Cisco Houston 1961 US folk singer and guitarist. Born 18th August, 1918.

J. B. Lenoir 1967 US blues musician. Died as a result of a car accident. Born 5th March, 1929.

Hits of the Day

1950 "The Third Man Theme" Anton Karas US 11 weeks

1955 "Cherry Pink And Apple Blossom White" Perez Prado UK 2 weeks

1978 "Night Fever" Bee Gees UK 2 weeks

Miscellany

1968 The musical *Hair* had its Broadway premiere. As with most other musicals it had already been tried out beforehand. It appeared at the Public Theatre, Off-Broadway, on 17th October, 1967, and created quite a stir. *Hair* was performed 1,750 times on Broadway and is, perhaps, one of the most successful musicals ever.

30th

Birthdays

'Reverend' Gary Davis 1896 US guitarist, harmonica player, pianist, blues singer, and songwriter. At a young age he was partially blind and in 1926 he lost his sight completely. He was considered to be one of the best gospel, blues and ragtime guitarists and singers. He died 5th May, 1972.

Johnny Horton 1927 US country and pop singer. In 1951 he made his first records. Hits: "The Battle Of New Orleans" (4/59 US 1; 6/59 UK 16), "Sink The Bismarck" (3/60 US 3) and "North To Alaska" (9/60 US 4; 1/61 UK 23). Johnny died after a car accident on 5th November, 1960. His birthdate is also given as the 3rd April.

Bobby Marchan 1930 US singer. In 1955 he started out as an R&B singer, then became a member of Huey 'Piano' Smith & The Clowns. In 1959 he relaunched his solo career. Hit: "There's Something On Your Mind, Part 2" (6/60 US 31).

Willie Nelson 1933 US 'King Of The Outlaw Country Movement' and songwriter, composing "Crazy" for Patsy Cline and "Hello Walls", a million seller in 1960 for Faron Young. He had his first records in the C&W charts in 1962. Since then he has had over 100 entries and is the eighth most successful country artist. His biggest pop hit was "Always On My Mind" (3/82 US 5). He also duetted with Waylon Jennings and Julio Iglesias. Hit for Julio/Willie: "To All The Girls I've Loved Before" (3/84 US 5; UK 17). Willie also appeared in several films like *The Electric Horseman*, and *Honeysuckle Rose*.

Jerry Lordan 1934 UK guitarist, singer, and songwriter. In the mid-50s he formed the duo Lee & Jerry Elvin. In 1960 Jerry became a singer, charting with "Who Could Be Bluer" (2/60 UK 17). But he made a name for himself as the composer of instrumentals. He wrote "Apache" for Jorgen Ingmann and the Shadows, and for the latter, "Atlantis" and "Wonderful Land", which became a hit years later for Mike Oldfield.

Johnny Farina 1941 US guitarist, and songwriter. With his brother Santo, as Santo & Johnny, they had the instrumental hit "Sleep Walk" (7/59 US 1; 10/59 UK 22).

Bobby Vee 1943 US singer, real name Robert Thomas Velline. He formed the Shadows in 1959 with his brother and a few friends. Buddy Holly was to have appeared in Bobby Vee's hometown Fargo in North Dakota on 3rd February, 1959. As is well-known, Buddy Holly died in a plane crash before that. The Shadows knew Holly's entire repertoire, and appeared that evening instead of their idol; therefore, they profited from his death. Unfortunate really. A little later they landed a record contract, with the first record credited to Bobby Vee & The Shadows; thereafter, all were attributed to Bobby Vee. Hits: "Take Good Care Of My Baby" (8/61 US 1; 10/61 UK 3), "Run To Him" (11/61 US 2; UK 6), "The Night Has A Thousand Eyes" (12/62 US 3; 2/63 UK 3) and "Come Back When You Grow Up" (7/67 US 3). Bobby appeared in several rather witless film musicals in the early 1960s.

Richard Shoff 1944 US singer with the Sandpipers who started out as the Grads.

Mike Deacon 1945 UK keyboard player with Greatest Show On Earth, Juicy Lucy, Vinegar Joe, Suzi Quatro and John Entwhistle's Ox. Sought-after studio musician in the UK.

Merrill Osmond 1953 US singer with the Osmonds.

Deaths

Richard Farina 1966 US singer, songwriter, and multi-instrumentalist. The son of Irish-Cuban parents, he supplied the IRA with weapons in the mid-1950s, when they still carried for him the aura of a romantic rebel movement. In the late 1950s he met Mimi, the younger sister of Joan Baez, whom he married. After that he travelled through Europe, recorded in London in 1963, appeared at folk festivals and at Newport in 1965. His songs were later recorded by Fairport Convention, Sandy Denny and Ian Matthews. Richard died after a motorbike accident. Born in 1936.

Muddy Waters 1983 US blues musician who died of a heart attack. Born 4th April, 1915.

Hits of the Day

1949 "Careless Hands" Mel Torme US 1 week
1954 "Such A Night" Johnnie Ray UK 1 week
1955 "Cherry Pink And Apple Blossom White" Perez Prado US 10 weeks
1966 "Good Lovin'" Young Rascals US 1 week
1977 "Southern Nights" Glen Campbell US 1 week
1983 "Beat It" Michael Jackson US 3 weeks (2nd time)
1983 "True" Spandau Ballet UK 4 weeks
1984 "People Are People" Depeche Mode
1988 "Theme From S-Express" S-Express UK 2 weeks

May

1st

Birthdays

Kate Smith 1907 US singer whose career of hits stretched from 1927 to 1948. Hits included "When The Moon Comes Over The Mountain" (9/31 US 1), which was the theme to her long-running radio programme and "River, Stay 'Way From My Door" (1/32 US 1). She then became a host of a TV show. It was Kate Smith who popularised the Irving Berlin composition "God Bless America" (4/39 US 10; 7/40 RE-US 5; 1/42 RE-US 23), written in 1918 for the patriotic show *Yip, Yip, Haphank*. Irving himself had decided not to use the piece in 1918 as it seemed a bit over the top. After Kate recorded the title it very quickly became the unofficial national anthem. Kate died 17th June, 1986.

Big Maybelle 1924 US blues singer, whose real name was Mabel Louise Smith. She also appeared as Mamie Webster. From 1944 she recorded with the Christine Chatman Orchestra, Quincy Jones and King Curtis. Solo hits were "Gabbin' Blues" (1/53 R&B 3) and "My Country Man" (11/53 R&B 5). In the 1960s she starred at the Apollo Theatre and at Carnegie Hall in New York. From 1967, she suffered from ill-health, and she died on 23rd January, 1972.

Sonny James 1929 US country and pop singer, guitarist and songwriter. Nickname, 'The Southern Gentleman'. Real name James Loden. He began to be successful in 1953. By 1983 he had more than 70 C&W hits, with 23 hitting the No. 1 spot. His biggest crossover hits were "Young Love" (12/56 US 1; 2/57 UK 11) and "First Date, First Kiss, First Love" (3/57 US 25).

Little Walter 1930 US singer, guitarist, harmonica player and songwriter. Real name Marion Walter Jacobs. He developed his own style of playing the blues' harmonica. From 1947, he cut solo records. Biggest hits were "Juke" (9/52 R&B 1) and "My Babe" (3/55 R&B 1). The Rolling Stones said he was the musician to have influenced them most and they paid tribute by recording "Confessin' The Blues". Walter died 15th February, 1968 as the result of head injuries sustained during a fight.

Judy Collins 1939 US singer, guitarist, pianist and songwriter. Her first records were released in 1961. For a long time, Judy was second only to Joan Baez as the most popular female folk singer in the US. From 1968, her audience increased, as she recorded better known material like "Both Sides Now" (11/68 US 8; 1/70 UK 14), "Amazing Grace" (12/70 UK 5; US 15) and "Send In The Clowns" (5/75 UK 6; US 36; 9/77 RE-US 19). During the 1960s, she was politically active travelling the southern states with Pete Seeger and Phil Ochs encouraging blacks to make use of their vote. Later, Judy who was a pacifist, sang protest songs against the Vietnam War.

Rita Coolidge 1945 US singer, daughter of a Baptist father and a Cherokee Indian mother. She started to sing in the 1960s with a band called R. C. & The Moonpies. In the late 1960s her sister Priscilla married songwriter and producer Booker T. Jones, who was successful with the band Booker T. & The MGs. This helped Rita's career. She took part in Joe Cocker's tour 'Mad Dogs & Englishmen' and became a member of Delaney & Bonnie's group. In 1969 she had her first solo hit in the US. Biggest solo hits: "(Your Love Has Lifted Me) Higher And Higher" (5/77 US 2) and "We're All Alone" (7/77 UK 6; 9/77 US 7). She sang "All Time High" (7/83 US 36) for the James Bond film *Octopussy*. She was married to Kris Kristofferson between 1973 & 1979.

Mimi Farina 1945 US singer who made three albums with her husband Richard Farina, which however, were not commercially successful. She is Joan Baez' sister.

Ray Parker Jr. 1954 US guitarist, singer and songwriter. He started his career as a studio musician with Boz Scaggs, LaBelle, Barry White, Marvin Gaye and Stevie Wonder. From 1977, he was successful with his group Raydio. Hits: "Jack & Jill" (1/78 US 8; 4/78 UK 11), and

"You Can't Change That" (4/79 US 9). From 1980, the band was called Ray Parker Jr. & Raydio. Hit: "A Woman Needs Love (Just Like You Do)" (3/81 US 4). From 1982, Ray worked as a soloist. Hits: "The Other Woman" (3/82 US 4) and "Ghostbusters" (6/84 US 1; 8/84 UK 2).

Rick Driscoll 1957 UK guitarist with Kenny.

Steve Farris 1957 US guitarist with Mr. Mister, who recorded from 1984.

Phil Smith 1959 UK saxophonist with Haircut 100, and session musician with Toyah and Chi Coltrane.

Owen Paul 1962 UK singer and songwriter, who made solo records from 1983. Before that he was a member of a band called The Venigmas. Only hit: "My Favourite Waste Of Time" (5/86 UK 3).

Deaths

Spike Jones 1965 US songwriter and leader of the comedy band, The City Slickers. Born 14th December, 1911.

Hits of the Day

1965 "Mrs. Brown You've Got A Lovely Daughter" Herman's Hermits US 3 weeks
1971 "Double Barrell" Dave & Ansil Collins UK 2 weeks
1976 "Let Your Love Flow" Bellamy Brothers US 1 week

2nd

Birthdays

Teddy Stauffer 1902 Swiss bandleader who went to Berlin in 1929 with his Original Teddies bringing swing music to the Germans. He remained there until 1933. Real first names Ernest Henri. In 1941 he emigrated to America and was partly responsible for turning the Mexican fishing village Acapulco into a 'Jet Set Resort'. He died in August, 1991.

Bing Crosby 1904 US singer, real first names Harry Lillis. He was considered to be the most popular entertainer of the first half of the 20th century. He was discovered in 1929 by orchestra leader Paul Whiteman, who engaged him and his partner at the time, Al Rinker. After a third singer, Harry Barris, joined them they called themselves the Rhythm Boys. In 1930 the trio left Whiteman, and in 1931 Bing recieved a solo contract with CBS radio. The next 30 years saw Bing Crosby accumulating a total of 340 hits in the US pop charts, 23 of them with the Andrews Sisters. He had a total of 16 singles that were million sellers, and hit No. 1 40 times in the USA. He has cut innumerable records, but "White Christmas" (10/42 US 1; 12/43 RE-US 6; 12/44 RE-US 5; 12/45 RE-US 1; 12/46 RE-US 1; 12/47 RE-US 3; 12/48 RE-US 6; 12/49 RE-US 5; 12/50 RE-US 13; 12/51 RE-US 13; 12/53 RE-US 21; 12/54 RE-US 21; 12/55 RE-US 7; 12/56 RE-US 65; 12/57 RE-US 34; 12/58 RE-US 66; 12/59 RE-US 59; 12/60 RE-US 26; 12/61 RE-US 12; 12/62 RE-US 38; 12/77 UK 5) is one of the biggest selling records of all time. Estimates vary from 30 to over 130 million copies of this record alone of being sold. Bing starred in more than 50 films, and played the part of a priest in *Going My Way*, which got an Oscar for best film of the year in 1945. Bing died in Madrid on 14th October, 1977.

Link Wray 1929 US rock guitarist, singer and songwriter of American Indian extraction. In the early 1950s he became a member of family group Palomino Ranch Gang, cutting his first records as Lucky Wray in 1956. As Link Wray & His Ray Men he had a hit with "Rumble" (4/58 US 16). In 1977 a rockabilly album appeared, which he recorded with Robert Gordon.

Engelbert Humperdinck 1936 UK singer, born in Madras, India, who came to England in 1947. Real name Arnold George Dorsey. In 1958 he made his first records under his real name, but when Tom Jones' manager renamed him Englebert Humperdinck in 1965 (after the German composer), he started to be successful. Hits: "Release Me" (1/67 UK 1; 4/67 US 4), "The Last Waltz" (8/67 UK 1; US 25) and the million seller "After The Lovin' " (10/76 US 8). By the end of the 1960s he had had eight Top Ten hits in the UK, he moved to the US. In Las Vegas he has still a considerable following to this day. German producers Jack White and Dieter Bohlen produced records right into the 80s.

Hilton Valentine 1943 UK guitarist in the early days of the Animals. His birthday is given also as 21st May.

John Verity 1944 UK guitarist and singer with Argent since their formation in 1969, as a studio musician and a solo artist.

Randy Cain 1945 US singer with the Four Gents, formed in 1965. They cut their first records in 1967, changing their name to Delfonics. In 1971 Randy was replaced by Major Harris.

Goldy McJohn 1945 Canadian keyboard player with Steppenwolf.

Lesley Gore 1946 US singer and actress. She was discovered by Quincy Jones while she was singing in a hotel in Manhattan. She was successful between 1963 & 1967. Biggest hits: "It's My Party" (5/63 US 1; UK 9) and "You Don't Own Me" (12/63 US 2).

Lou Gramm 1950 US singer and songwriter, first with Black Sheep, then from 1976 with Foreigner, whose first album in 1977 sold more than 3 million copies. Hits: "Feels Like The First Time" (3/77 US 4; 5/78 UK 39), "Cold As Ice" (7/77 US 6; 7/78 UK 24), "Hot Blooded" (7/78 US 3; 10/78 UK 42), "Double Vision" (9/78 US 2), "Urgent" (7/81 US 4), "Waiting For A Girl Like You" (10/81 US 2; 12/81 UK 8), "I Want To Know What Love Is" (12/84 US & UK 1), "Say You Will" (12/87 US 6) and "I Don't Want To Live Without You" (3/88 US 5). From 1987, Lou also had a solo career. Hits: "Midnight Blue" (1/87 US 5) and "Just Between You And Me" (10/89 US 6).

John Callis 1951 UK guitarist with the Rezillos and, from 1980, played synthesizer for Human League.

Prescott Niles 1954 US bass player with The Knack.

Dr. Robert 1961 UK singer, guitarist and songwriter for the Blow Monkeys, who were successful from 1985. Real name, Robert Howard. First hits: "Digging Your Scene" (3/86 UK 12; 5/86 US 14) and "It Doesn't Have To Be This Way" (1/87 UK 5). He duetted with Kym Mazelle, having the hit, "Wait" (1/89 UK 7).

Deaths

June Hutton 1973 US singer. Born 11th August, 1921.

Larry Clinton 1985 US bandleader and composer. Born 17th August, 1909.

Hits of the Day

1942	"Deep In The Heart Of Texas" Alvino Ray US 1 week	
1963	"From me To You" Beatles UK 7 weeks	
1970	"Spirit In The Sky" Norman Greenbaum UK 2 weeks	
1981	"Morning Train (Nine To Five)" Sheena Easton US 2 weeks	
1987	"(I Just) Died In Your Arms" Cutting Crew US 2 weeks	

3rd

Birthdays

Pete Seeger 1919 US folksinger, guitarist, and songwriter. Mentor to the entire folk-scene of the 50s and 60s in the USA. Although he had no hits, compositions such as "We Shall Overcome", "Where Have All The Flowers Gone" and his version of "Guantanamera" continue to be widely influential.

Joe Ames 1924 US singer and oldest of the Ames Brothers, who were successful in the USA from 1949 to 1960. Real surname of the brothers, Urick. Biggest hits: "Rag Mop" (1/50 US 1), "Sentimental Me" (1/50 US 1), "Undecided" (9/51 US 2), "You, You, You" (6/53 US 1) and "The Naughty Lady Of Shady Lane" (11/54 US 3; 2/55 UK 6).

James Brown 1928 US R&B and soul singer and songwriter, with one of the most dynamic live acts in the world. In the R&B charts, he is ahead of Aretha Franklin as most successful artist of all time. In the mid-1950s he formed his own group, the Famous Flames, and cut a demo tape of his own composition "Please Please Please" (4/56 R&B 5; US 105) in November 1955, which got him a recording contract with the King label in 1956. He had his first big hit with "Try Me" (11/58 R&B 1; US 48). Among his other most famous records are "Papa's Got A Brand New Bag" (7/65 US 8; 9/65 UK 25), "I Got You (I Feel Good)" (11/65 US 3; 2/66 UK 29), "It's A Man's Man's Man's World" (4/66 US 8; 6/66 UK 13), "Cold Sweat" (7/67 US 7), "I Got The Feelin' " (3/68 US 6) and "Get Up I Feel Like Being A Sexmachine" (7/70 US 15; 10/70 UK 32). In 1974, the hits dried up in the USA; the James Brown-era seemed to be over. But then he sang "Living In America" (12/85 US 4; UK 5) for *Rocky IV*, which re-established him. At the end of the 1980s, and after several 'run-ins' with the law, he was sent to jail for a series of offences.

Dave Dudley 1928 US country singer, guitarist and songwriter. Real name David Pedruska. After playing as a semi-professional in several baseball teams, where his arms were injured, he worked as a D. J. from 1955. First he formed a trio and then carried on as a solo artist. Greatest hits: "Six Days On The Road" (6/63 C&W 2; US 32) and "The Pool Shark" (3/70 C&W 1). Dave is very popular with truckers.

Georges Moustaki 1934 Born of Greek emigrants in Alexandria. Real name Joseph Moustacci. When he was 17, he went to Paris, worked as a journalist and on his first compositions. In 1958 he wrote the lyrics for the song "Milord" which became a hit for Edith Piaf. As an artist George was a star throughout the 60s in France. Among his biggest successes was "Le Métèque" in 1969.

Frankie Valli 1934 US singer. Real name Francis Castelluccio. In 1949 he was a founder member of the Variety Trio, which split up at the end of 1952. In 1953 he recorded "My Mother's Eyes" under the name of Frank Valley, which sold so few copies that it is worth 200 dollars among collectors today. After a further attempt as a member of the Variatones, he became a member of the group The Four Lovers in 1956, who had a hit with "You're The Apple Of My Eye" (5/56 US 62). After several changes of lineup, this group became the Four Seasons in 1961. From 1962 they had one hit after another: "Sherry" (8/62 US 1; 10/62 UK 8), "Big Girls Don't Cry" (10/62 US 1; 1/63 UK 13), "Walk Like A Man" (1/63 US 1; 3/63 UK 12) & "Rag Doll" (6/64 US 1; 8/64 UK 2). From 1966, Frankie Valli started his own career, while still working with the Four Seasons. Hits: "Can't Take My Eyes Off You" (5/67 US 2), "My Eyes Adored You" (11/74 US 1; 2/75 UK 5), and "Grease" (5/78 US 1; 8/78 UK 3). In addition, usually with different musicians, the odd record as the Four Seasons. Hits: "Who Loves You" (8/75 US 3; UK 6), and "December, 1963 (Oh What A Night)" (12/75 US & UK 1). Even during the 1980s new records by Frankie Valli with the Four Seasons continued to appear.

Pete Staples 1944 UK bass player, with Ten Foot Five, and from 1965 with the Troggs. Peter was present at a reunion of the Troggs in 1972.

John Richardson 1947 UK drummer with the Rubettes and as a session musician.

Mary Hopkin 1950 UK singer, who had her biggest hits on the Beatles' record label Apple: "Those Were The Days" (9/68 UK 1; US 2), "Goodbye" (4/69 UK 2; US 13), "Temma Harbour" (1/70 UK 6; US 39), and "Knock Knock Who's There" (3/70 UK 2). Shortly after that she married the well-known British producer Toni Visconti and only sang occasionally as backing vocalist on records by Ralph McTell, David Bowie and Thin Lizzy. In 1981 she became lead vocalist of the group Sundance who were unsuccessful.

Christopher Cross 1951 US singer, guitarist, and songwriter. Real surname Geppert. In 1971 he became a member of the hardrock band Flash, who supported Zeppelin and Deep Purple on US tours. In 1973 he left the group to concentrate on his writing. In 1975 he formed his own band, and in 1978 he got a recording contract. Hits, "Ride Like The Wind" (2/80 US 2), "Sailing" (6/80 UK 1), "Arthur's Theme (Best That You Can Do)" (8/81 US 1; 1/82 UK 7) and "Think Of Laura" (12/83 US 9).

Steve Jones 1955 UK guitarist, and singer with the Sex Pistols, Professionals, Generation X and Iggy Pop.

David Ball 1959 UK pianist, and songwriter. In 1979, he was the co-founder of the techno-pop duo Soft Cell with Marc Almond. Hits, see under Marc 9th July. In 1984 Soft Cell split up.

Philip Cilia 1960 UK guitarist and songwriter in the duo Waterfront.

Deaths

Les Harvey 1972 UK guitarist with Stone The Crows. He was electrocuted by his microphone during a concert in Swansea.

Helmut Koellen 1977 String instrumentalist with Triumvirat. He had just completed his first album. He was listening to tapes in his car in a closed garage with the engine running. Born 2nd March, 1950.

Hits of the Day

1969	"Crimson And Clover" Tommy James & Shondells
1975	"Oh Boy" Mud UK 2 weeks
1975	"He Don't Love You" Tony Orlando & Dawn US 3 weeks
1976	"Fernando" Abba
1980	"Geno" Dexy's Midnight Runners UK 2 weeks
1986	"Addicted To Love" Robert Palmer US 1 week

4th

Birthdays

Al Dexter 1902 US country singer, songwriter, violinist, and guitarist. Born Clarence Albert Poindexter. He cut his first records in 1936. Hits, "Pistol Packin' Mama" (6/43 US 1), and "Guitar Polka" (3/46 US 16). He died 28th January, 1984.

Maynard Ferguson 1928 Canadian jazz trumpeter and orchestra leader. He played in the Jimmy Dorsey and Stan Kenton big bands in the USA. In 1957 he formed his own orchestra. He had his biggest pop hit with "Gonna Fly Now (Theme From 'Rocky')" (4/77 US 28).

Ed Cassidy 1930 US drummer, who was a member of Spirit from 1967 to 1970. After the band split up, it reformed in the mid-70s.

Ron Carter 1934 US jazz bass player, singer and songwriter, who also played other instruments. He played on over 500 records, some of them of historical importance, and regularly released solo records.

Richard Burns 1941 US leadsinger with the Hondells who had their only hit with "Little Honda" (9/64 US 9).

Nickolas Ashford 1942 US singer, songwriter, and producer. In 1964 he met Valerie Simpson in a Harlem church. In the same year they recorded unsuccessfully as Valerie & Nick. In 1966 they had their first hit as writers with their composition "Let's Go Get Stoned" sung by Ray Charles. In 1967 their composition "Ain't No Mountain High Enough" with Marvin Gaye and Tammi Terrell was their first Top Twenty hit in the USA; and it became a No. 1 later on for Diana Ross. In 1973 they signed a recording contract and released records as Ashford & Simpson. Own hit: "Solid" (11/84 US 12; 1/85 UK 3). They wrote and produced for other artists like Gladys Knight and Chaka Khan.

Ronnie Bond 1943 UK drummer, and in 1964 founder member of the Troggs. After the band split up in 1969, Ronnie released a solo record, but rejoined in 1972 when the band reformed.

Peggy Santiglia 1944 US leadsinger with the Angels, who replaced Linda Jansen in 1962. Hit: "My Boyfriend's Back" (8/63 US 1).

George Wadenius 1945 Swedish guitarist and bass player with Blood, Sweat & Tears, and as a session musician.

Zal Cleminson 1949 UK guitarist with the Sensational Alex Harvey Band, Nazareth, and as a session musician.

Bruce Day 1951 US bass player and singer from 1977 with the group Pablo Cruise, formed in 1973. Before that he played with Santana.

Colin Bass 1951 UK bass player with Foundations, Clancy, Steve Hillage and Camel.

Jackie Jackson 1951 US singer, real first names Sigmund Esco. Jackie is the oldest of the many Jackson Brothers and was a founder member of the trio in 1963. During the course of the next few years, the younger brothers successively joined the band, and they called themselves the Jackson 5. In 1968 they made their first records,

the leadsinger being Michael Jackson. From 1976, after changing record companies from Motown to Epic/CBS, they called themselves just Jacksons.

Jacob Miller 1956 Jamaican singer, songwriter and leader of the reggae group Inner Circle, whose biggest hit was "Everything Is Great" (2/79 UK 37). Jacob died in a car accident on 23rd March, 1980.

Jay Aston 1961 UK singer with Bucks Fizz. For hits, see under colleague Cheryl Baker on 8th March.

Deaths

Paul Butterfield 1987 US singer, harmonica player, and songwriter. Born 17th December, 1942.

Hits of the Day	
1940	"The Woodpecker Song" Glenn Miller US 7 weeks
1946	"Prisoner Of Love" Perry Como US 3 weeks
1956	"No Other Love" Ronnie Hilton UK 6 weeks
1961	"Blue Moon" Marcels UK 2 weeks
1974	"Waterloo" Abba UK 2 weeks
1974	"The Loco-Motion" Grand Funk US 2 weeks
1985	"Move Closer" Phyllis Nelson UK 1 week

5th

Birthdays

Blind Willie McTell 1901 US blues guitarist, singer and songwriter. Real first names Willie Samuel. Recorded from the 1920s. Died on 19th August, 1959.

Monica Lewis 1925 US singer. Successful in the 1940s and 1950s. Biggest hit, "Midnight Masquerade" (4/47 US 16). Later she became a TV and film actress.

Ace Cannon 1934 US alto saxophonist. He played in Bill Black's combo. As a soloist he had an instrumental hit with "Tuff" (12/61 US 17).

Johnnie Taylor 1937 US singer. He started in the early 50s with the gospel group Highway QCs, and then became a member of the Five Echoes, with whom he first recorded in 1954. After that he joined the Soul Stirrers as the replacement for Sam Cooke, cutting his first solo records in 1961. Hits: "Who's Making Love" (10/68 US 5), "I Believe In You (You Believe In Me)" (6/73 US 11) and "Disco Lady" (2/76 US 1; 4/76 UK 25).

Tammy Wynette 1942 US country singer. Real name Virginia Wynette Pugh. In 1966 she had her first success in the US country charts, her last hit was in 1980. She managed a total of twenty No. 1 hits. Her biggest crossover hits were "D-I-V-O-R-C-E" (6/68 US 63; 6/75 UK 12) and "Stand By Your Man" (11/68 US 19; 4/75 UK 1). She was married to country singing star George Jones from 1968 to 1975.

Bill Ward 1948 UK drummer and songwriter with Black Sabbath.

Eddy Amoo 1950 UK guitarist, singer, keyboard player and songwriter with Real Thing. In 1976 he joined the band which was formed in 1970, and they were immediately successful: "You To Me Are Everything" (6/76 UK 1; 3/86 RE-UK 5), "Can't Get By Without You" (9/76 UK 2; 5/86 RE-UK 6) and "Can You Feel The Force" (2/79 UK 5; 8/86 RE-UK 24). The RE-UKs were remix versions.

Maggie MacNeal 1950 Dutch singer in the duo Mouth & MacNeal. Real name Sjoukje van Spijker. Hits: "How Do You Do" (4/72 US 8), "Hello-A" (6/72) and "I See A Star" (5/74 UK 8). Maggie was also featured on records by Jan Akkerman, Cuby & The Blizzards and Livin' Blues. Her attempts as a soloist were unsuccessful.

Ian McCulloch 1959 UK guitarist, singer, songwriter and leader of Echo & The Bunnymen. Ian formed the Crucial Three in May 1977. Demos by the band led nowhere. In July 1978 they tried under the name A Shallow Madness – nothing doing. In November 1978 they cut their debut as Echo & The Bunnymen, signing a recording contract shortly afterwards. Hits: "The Cutter" (1/83 UK 8) and "The Killing Moon" (1/84 UK 9).

Kevin Paul Mooney 1962 UK bass player in the early days of Adam & The Ants.

Kevin Saunderson 1964 US songwriter, and producer with Inner City. His mother is supposed to have sung in the original Supremes line-up. Kevin is considered to be one of the most sought after 'dance' producers, he has remixed versions of records by Wee Papa Girl Rappers, Neneh Cherry and Paula Abdul.

Deaths

'Reverend' Gary Davis US blues musician. Born 30th April 1896.

Hits of the Day

1945	"Dream" Pied Pipers	US 1 week
1956	"Hot Diggity" Perry Como	US 1 week
1960	"Cathy's Clown" Everly Brothers	UK 7 weeks
1962	"Soldier Boy" Shirelles	US 3 weeks
1966	"Pretty Flamingo" Manfred Mann	UK 3 weeks
1979	"Reunited" Peaches & Herb	US 4 weeks
1984	"The Reflex" Duran Duran	UK 4 weeks
1986	"Midnight Lady" Chris Norman	

6th

Birthdays

Rudolph Valentino 1895 US actor and idol of the silent movie era. Real name Rodolpho Guglielmi di Valentino. Died 23rd August, 1926.

Carmen Cavallaro 1913 US pianist and orchestra leader. Greatest hit, based on a theme by Chopin was the million seller "Polonaise in A" (6/45 US 3). A version of this composition with lyrics gave Perry Como his first No. 1 in the same year.

Herbie Cox 1939 US leadsinger with the Cleftones, a doo-wop group formed in 1955, originally called Silvertones. Between 1956 & 1962 they were regularly in the charts, with their biggest hit being "Heart And Soul" (5/61 US 18). In the 1970s they appeared regularly on the 'rock'n'roll' oldies circuit.

Colin Earl 1942 UK keyboard player with Mungo Jerry and Foghat.

Bob Seger 1945 US singer, songwriter and guitarist, who first recorded 1966. In 1964 he formed his own first rock trio, Decibels. After that he played with Town Criers and Doug Brown & The Omens. The Omens musicians recorded a parody of the "Ballad Of The Green Berets" in March 1966 under the pseudonym Beach Bums; in their version it was 'yellow berets'. Barry Sadler threatened to sue them, and the record was withdrawn. In May 1966, Bob cut his first record under his own name. From January 1968 he had a contract with Capitol Records as Bob Seger System. Hit: "Ramblin' Gamblin' Man" (12/68 US 17). From 1971, Bob became a solo artist, backed by the Silver Bullet Band. Hits: "Night Moves" (12/76 US 4), "Still The Same" (5/78 US 4), "Fire Lake" (2/80 US 6), "Against The

Wind" (5/80 US 5), "Tryin' To Live My Life Without You" (9/81 US 5), "Shame On The Moon" (12/82 US 2) and "Shake Down" (5/87 US 1), etc.

Mary MacGregor 1948 US singer. Her first hit was a million seller, "Torn Between Two Lovers" (11/76 US 1; 2/77 UK 4).

Davey Johnstone 1951 UK guitarist in Elton John's band and session musician. Also made solo records originally, a folk banjoist dubbed 'Shaggis'.

Larry Steinbachek 1960 UK keyboard player with Bronski Beat.

Deaths

Dickie Valentine 1971 UK singer who died in a car accident. Born 4th November, 1929.

Kai Winding 1983 Danish trombone player and composer. He died of a brain tumour. Born 18th May, 1922.

Hits of the Day

1944 "I Love You" Bing Crosby US 5 weeks
1950 "The Third Man Theme" Guy Lombardo US 11 weeks

7th

Birthdays

Jim Lowe 1927 US singer and songwriter. His career started as a DJ. He composed "Gambler's Guitar" for Dusty Draper. Then he became successful himself with "The Green Door" (9/56 US 1; UK 8). This title became a No. 1 for Shakin' Stevens in 1981.

Teresa Brewer 1931 US singer. Real name Teresa Breuer. She broadcasted in a local radio show at the age of 5. From 1949 onwards she recorded and became a star in the 1950s. Hits: "Music! Music! Music!" (2/50 US 1), "Till I Waltz Again With You" (12/52 US 1), "Ricochet (Rick-O-Shay)" (10/53 US 2), "Let Me Go Lover!" (12/54 US 6; 2/55 UK 9), "A Tear Fell" (2/56 US 5; 4/56 UK 2), "A Sweet Old Fashioned Girl" (6/56 US 7; UK 3) and "You Send Me" (11/57 US 8).

Johnny Maestro 1939 US singer. Real surname Mastrangelo. He was the lead vocalist in the group Crests, formed in 1955, and who recorded from 1957 onwards. Biggest hit: "16 Candles" (11/58 US 2). He was successful as a soloist from 1961 with the hit, "Model Girl" (2/61 US 20), and in the late 1960s as a leadsinger with Brooklyn Bridge, who scored with "Worst That Could Happen" (12/68 US 3).

Jimmy Ruffin 1939 US singer and brother of David Ruffin who was leadsinger of the Temptations from 1964 to 1968. Jimmy began in 1961 as a backing vocalist with Motown Productions. Hits: "What Becomes Of The Broken Hearted" (8/66 US 7; 10/66 UK 10; 7/74 RE-UK 4), "Farewell Is A Lonely Sound" (2/70 UK 8), "I'll Say Forever My Love" (7/70 UK 7), "It's Wonderful" (10/70 UK 6), and "Hold On To My Love" (3/80 US 10; 5/80 UK 7). He also duetted with his brother, which however, were unsuccessful.

Rick West 1943 UK guitarist with the Tremeloes. Real name Richard Westwood.

Bill Danoff 1946 US singer and songwriter. He wrote the hit, "Take Me Home, Country Roads", with John Denver, and, with his wife Taffy, sang in the folk quintet Fat City. They both became members of the Starland Vocal Band. Hit: "Afternoon Delight" (5/76 US 1; 8/76 UK 18), on John Denver's record label.

Ray Monette 1946 US guitarist who replaced Paul Warren in Rare Earth.

Pete Wingfield 1948 UK pianist, songwriter, producer and singer. He started out with the group Jellybread. In 1975 he released a solo album which included the hit single, "18 With A Bullet" (6/75 UK 7; 8/75 US 15). Pete is a sought-after British session musician and producer.

Keith 1949 US singer. Real name James Barry Keefer. Only Top Ten success, "98.6" (12/66 US 7; UK 24), the backing vocalists were the Tokens.

Hits of the Day

1949 "A – You're Adorable" Perry Como US 2 weeks
1954 "Secret Love" Doris Day UK 1 week (2nd time)
1964 "Don't Throw Your Love Away" Searchers UK 2 weeks
1966 "Monday Monday" Mamas & Papas US 3 weeks
1977 "Free" Deniece Williams UK 2 weeks
1977 "Hotel California" Eagles US 1 week
1988 "Wishing Well" Terence Trent D'Arby US 1 week

8th

Birthdays

Red Nichols 1905 US trumpeter and bandleader. Real firstnames Ernest Loring, nicknamed 'Red' because of his red hair. In the early days, musicians such as Glenn Miller, the Dorsey brothers, Benny Goodman and Gene Krupa all played in his band. Red was also leader of the Charleston Chasers, who were successful from 1927 to 1931. A hit and million seller for Red Nichols & His 5 Pennies was "Ida, Sweet As Apple Cider" (11/27 US 1). He died 28th June, 1965.

Robert Johnson 1911 US blues singer, guitarist and songwriter. About 1930 he worked with Son House, later with Howlin' Wolf, Sonny Boy Williamson, and Elmore James. He made his only records in a hotel room in San Antonio in 1936, and in a backroom of an office block in Dallas in 1937. Only "Terraplane Blues" could be loosely termed a hit among black audiences. For many, Robert remains an inspirational figure in the development of rock music, even though he died 16th August, 1938. In fact loosely, his composition "Cross Roads Blues" has been re-worked by many musicians like Cream, Jimi Hendrix, Johnny Winter, Muddy Waters and Bonnie Raitt; all of whom have cited Johnson as their model. The film *Cross-roads* (1986), with music by Ry Cooder and Sonny Terry, was allegedly inspired by Johnson's short life. A musical giant!

Gary Glitter 1940 UK singer and songwriter, real name Paul Gadd. His career in the music business started in the late 1950s as Paul Russell & His Rebels. In January 1960 he first recorded as Paul Raven, and in November 1961 he formed the group Paul Raven & Boston International. In June 1968 he recorded as Paul Monday, in October 1969 as Rubber Buckett, and in October 1970 (now again as Paul Raven) he was featured on the album JESUS CHRIST SUPERSTAR as a priest. From 1972, he became known as Gary Glitter. Hits: "Rock & Roll" (6/72 UK 2; US 7), "I'm The Leader Of The Gang (I Am)" (7/73 UK 1), "I Love You Love Me Love" (11/73 UK 1), "Always Yours" (6/74 UK 1) and "Another Rock & Roll Christmas" (12/84 UK 7). In 1988 the British band Time-lords immortalised him in their song "Doctorin" The Tardis" (6/88 UK 1) with the line, 'Everybody Loves Gary Glitter.'

Rick Nelson 1940 US singer, TV star and actor. Real first names Eric Hilliard. Son of well-known bandleader Ozzie and the singer Harriet Nelson. From March 1949 Ricky appeared with his brother, David, in their parents' radio show, *The Adventures Of Ozzie & Harriet*; it was transferred to television in 1952, and ran until 1966. Ricky recorded from 1957 and became one of the first 'teen idols' of the rock era. After three hits for the record company Verve, he changed over to Imperial, where he was backed by Bob Luman's Band. James Burton played lead guitar with them. Hits: "A Teenager's Romance" (5/57 US 2), "Poor Little Fool" (7/58 US 1; UK 4), "Travellin' Man" (4/61 US 1) with the B-side, "Hello Mary Lou" (5/61 US 9). In the UK "Hello Mary Lou/Travellin' Man" (6/61 UK 2) was counted as a double A-side. Up until then, the records appeared under the name Ricky Nelson, after that the 'y' was done away with, as he said he was too old for that now. Further hits: "Teenage Idol" (8/62 US 5; UK 39), "It's Up To You" (12/62 US 6; UK 22), and "For You" (12/63 US 6; UK 14). From 1969 he played as Rick Nelson & The Stone Canyon Band. Hit: "Garden Party" (9/72 US 6). On the film acting side he was particularly memorable in the part of a young sharpshooter in the film *Rio Bravo* (1959). He died 31st December, 1985.

John Fred 1941 US singer with John Fred & His Play-boy Band. Real name John Fred Gourrier. In 1956 he founded the Playboys as a white group who were going to play rhythm & blues, who recorded From 1958. Hit and million seller, "Judy In Disguise (With Glasses)" (11/67 US 1; 1/68 UK 3). The composition was intended to be a parody of the Beatles song "Lucy In The Sky (With Diamonds)".

Paul Samwell-Smith 1943 UK bass player and songwriter with the Yardbirds. In June 1966 he left the band and was replaced by Jimmy Page who shortly after advanced to lead guitarist. Paul became a producer of various UK artists, returning in the late 1970s as a session musician on records by Chris de Burgh, Illusion, Cat Stevens and Carly Simon. Then he formed Box Of Frogs. In 1990, he produced Beverly Craven's album.

Toni Tennille 1943 US singer, who was successful with her husband Daryl Dragon as Captain & Tennille from 1975 to 1979. Hits, all million sellers: "Love Will Keep Us Together" (4/75 US 1), "The Way I Wanna Touch You" (9/75 US 4; 1/76 UK 28), "Lonely Night (Angel Face)" (1/76 US 3), "Shop Around" (5/76 US 4), "Muskrat Love" (9/76 US 4) and "Do That To Me One More Time" (10/79 US 1; 2/80 UK 7). In 1984 a solo album by Toni appeared, and a second in 1987, neither created much interest.

Keith Jarrett 1945 US jazz pianist and world class composer.

Philip Bailey 1951 US singer, percussionist and songwriter. In 1971, after leaving the Stoval Sisters' Band, he joined Earth, Wind & Fire as second lead singer, beside Maurice White. In addition to his work with the band he released solo records, usually gospel. In 1984 he made the album CHINESE WALL. In it he sang a duet with Phil Collins, "Easy Lover" (11/84 US 2; 3/85 UK 1). After that Phil Collins' solo career escalated. In addition to all that, Philip occasionally sang on records by Deniece Williams, Kenny Loggins and Stevie Wonder.

Chris Frantz 1951 US drummer and songwriter with Talking Heads and Tom Tom Club.

Billy Burnette 1953 US guitarist, singer, and songwriter who was trying to follow in the footsteps of his father Dorsey Burnette. He made his first records when he was 11, and in the early 1980s his first albums appeared. In August 1988 he and another American called Rick Vito, replaced Lindsey Buckingham in Fleetwood Mac.

Alex Van Halen 1955 US drummer and songwriter. Like his brother Edward he was born in Nijmegen, Netherlands. The family emigrated to the USA in 1968. Early on, the brothers formed Mammoth, then Rat Salade, and finally, in 1974, Van Halen. In 1978 they started to chart regularly.

Deaths

Graham Bond 1974 UK keyboard player and leader of the Graham Bond Organisation. He jumped in front of a train arriving at Finsbury Park Tube Station; nobody knew why. Born 28th October, 1937.

Hits of the Day

1948	"Nature Boy" Nat 'King' Cole US 8 weeks
1976	"Fernando" Abba UK 4 weeks
1976	"Welcome Back Kotter" John Sebastian US 1 week
1982	"Chariots Of Fire" Vangelis US 1 week

Miscellany

1970 The last album by the Beatles LET IT BE is released. It was less of a co-production by the band, but rather a collection of hitherto unpublished songs remixed by Phil Spector. He had added a string section to most of the tracks, much to the chagrin of the Beatles, especially Paul McCartney.

9th

Birthdays

Frank Chacksfield 1914 UK pianist and orchestra leader. He started out in the 1930s as a bandleader, and recorded from 1948. His biggest hits were "Limelight (Terry's Theme)" (5/53 US 5; UK 2), and the million seller "Ebb Tide" (8/53 US 2; 2/54 UK 9).

Hank Snow 1914 The best-known Canadian-born country artist and songwriter since the end of the 1940s. Real first names Clarence Eugene; nickname 'The Singing Ranger'. He made his first records in 1936 and then moved to the USA in the mid-1940s. Biggest crossover hits: "I'm Movin' On" (7/50 US 27), and the million seller "I Don't Hurt Anymore" (7/54 US 22). He had over forty Top Ten country hits between 1949 and 1974.

Sonny Curtis 1937 US guitarist and songwriter with the Crickets, formed in the mid-1950s. He also played on records by Waylon Jennings, Eric Clapton, Crystal Gayle, Charlie Door, Bobby Bear and Ricky Skaggs.

Dave 1937 US soul singer. Surname Prater. He recorded with Sam Moore as Sam & Dave. On 11th April, 1988 died in a car crash. See under 12th October, Sam Moore.

Nokie Edwards 1939 US lead guitarist and songwriter with the Ventures until 1968. In that year he was replaced by Jerry McGee, and then rejoined in 1972. Hits: "Walk – Don't Run" (7/60 US 2; 9/60 UK 8), "Perfidia" (11/60 US 15; UK 4), "Walk, Don't Run '64" (7/64 US 8) and "Hawaii Five-O" (3/69 US 4).

Mike Milward 1942 UK guitarist with the Fourmost.

Tommy Roe 1942 US singer, guitarist and songwriter. While still at school he formed the group Satins in 1958, and they recorded Tommy's composition "Sheila", which he had written when he was 14. However, that version sunk without trace. From 1962, he was a soloist. He re-recorded "Sheila" (7/62 US 1; 9/62 UK 3), and this time it worked. Further hits: "Everybody" (10/63 US 3; UK 9), "Sweet Pea" (6/66 US 8), "Hooray For Hazel" (9/66 US 6), "Dizzy" (2/69 US 1; 4/69 UK 1), and "Jam Up Jelly Tight" (11/69 US 8). In the mid-1960s Tommy emigrated to the UK, but returned to the USA in 1969. As did many of his colleagues, who had been successful in the USA in the 1960s, Tommy turned to country music. His biggest hit was "Let's Be Fools Like That Again" (12/86 C&W 38).

Don Dannemann 1944 US lead guitarist and song-writer with Cyrkle. Hit: "Red Rubber Ball" (5/66 US 2). In the 1970s he worked as a producer.

Richie Furay 1944 US guitarist, singer, and songwriter. In 1966 he was a founder member of Buffalo Springfield, and of Poco in 1968. In 1974 he was co-founder of the Souther-Hillman-Furay Band, before starting a solo career. In the late 1980s Richie was back at the reunion of Poco.

Steve Katz 1945 US singer, guitarist and songwriter. He started out with the Ragtime Jug Stompers, then with Jim Kweskin's Even Dozen Jug Band. In 1965 he was a co-founder of the Blues Project. Al Kooper also played with that band. Katz and Kooper formed Blood, Sweat & Tears in 1968. In 1972 Steve became a member of American Flyer and then worked as an A & R manager for Mercury Records.

Clint Holmes 1946 US singer, born in England and emigrated to the USA with his parents. He had his biggest hit there with the million seller "Playground In My Mind" (3/73 US 2).

Richard Hudson 1948 UK instrumentalist, singer, and songwriter with the Strawbs, for whom he wrote their biggest hit "Part Of The Union" (1/73 UK 2), with another band member, John Ford. With Ford, he formed the duo Hudson Ford, Hit: "Pick Up The Pieces" (8/73 UK 8). The pair recorded in 1979 under the name The Monks. Hit: "Nice Legs Shame About The Face" (4/79 UK 19).

Billy Joel 1949 US singer, pianist, and songwriter. Real first names William Martin. In 1964 he formed his first group, the Echoes, which later became the Lost Souls. In the late 1960s he played with the Hassles, and after that with drummer Jon Small in the hard rock duo Attila, starting a solo career in 1972. Hits: "Just The Way You Are" (11/77 US 3; 2/78 UK 19), "My Life" (11/78 US 3; UK 12), "It's Still Rock & Roll To Me" (5/80 US 1; 8/80 UK 14), "Tell Her About It" (7/83 US 1; 12/83 UK 4), "Uptown Girl" (9/83 US 3; UK 1), "An Innocent Man" (12/83 US 10; 2/84 UK 8), "You're Only Human (Second Win)" (7/85 US 9) and "We Didn't Start The Fire" (9/89 UK 8; US 1).

Pete Birrell 1941 UK bass player with Freddie & The Dreamers.

John Edwards 1953 UK bass player with Status Quo in their later phase from May 1986.

David Gahan 1962 UK leadsinger, and co-founder of Depeche Mode, who have charted regularly since 1981: "See You" (2/82 UK 6), "Everything Counts" (7/83 UK 6), "People Are People" (4/84 UK 4; 5/85 US 13), "Master And Servant" (8/84 UK 9), "Stripped" (2/86 UK 15), "Strangelove" (5/87 UK 16; 7/87 US 76; 9/88 RE-US 50), "Never Let Me Down Again" (9/87 UK 22) and "Behind The Wheel/Route 66" (1/88 UK 21).

Paul David Heaton 1962 UK singer, songwriter, and founder of the group Housemartins in 1984. Biggest hits: "Happy Hour" (6/86 UK 3), and "Caravan Of Love" (12/86 UK 1). In February Heaton announced the band had only been projected to last three years, and it was time to split up. In May 1988 the last single by the band appeared. At the middle of 1989 came Heaton's new project: together with David Hemmingway, also a former member of Housemartins, he formed Beautiful South. First hits: "Song For Whoever" (6/89 UK 2) and "You Keep It All In" (9/89 UK 8).

Hits of the Day

1942 "Tangerine" Jimmy Dorsey US 6 weeks
1942 "I Don't Want To Walk Without You" Harry James US 2 weeks
1964 "Hello Dolly" Louis Armstrong US 1 week
1970 "American Woman/No Sugar Tonight" Guess Who US 3 weeks
1970 "Let It Be" Beatles
1981 "Stand And Deliver" Adam & The Ants UK 5 weeks
1987 "Nothing's Gonna Stop Us Now" Starship UK 4 weeks

10th

Birthdays

Fred Astaire 1899 US dancer, choreographer, actor, and singer. Real name Frederick Austerlitz. He formed a team with his sister in 1917 and they appeared in the most important Broadway musicals of the era; it was a team that would last until 1931. After that Fred appeared as a soloist in about 40 films, ten of them with Ginger Rogers. As a singer he had 36 hits in the US pop charts between 1929 and 1951, 8 of them reaching No. 1. Biggest hits: "Night And Day" (12/32 US 1) and "Cheek To Cheek" (8/35 US 1). He was the dancing idol for countless artists, not least. Michael Jackson, who always worshiped Fred Astaire, and dedicated his autobiography *Moonwalk* to him. Fred died 22nd June, 1987 of a lung disease.

Dimitri Tiomkin 1899 US pianist and composer of Russian origins, who emigrated to the USA in 1925. He has written the most varied types of music for countless Hollywood films since the early 1930s. He won two Oscars for the music of the film *High Noon* (1952) alone; won an Oscar for *The High And The Mighty* (1954) and *The Old Man And The Sea* (1958). His scores for *Gunfight At The OK Coral* (1957), *Rio Bravo* (1959), *The Alamo* (1960), *The Guns Of Navarone* (1961) and *Tchaikovsky* (1970) were equally memorable. Tiomkin died 11th November, 1979.

Bert Weedon 1920 UK guitarist and songwriter. In the early 1950s he played with Stephane Grappelli and Django Reinhardt, and Ted Heath in the late 1960s with Cliff Richard and Dickie Valentine. As a solo artist Bert was successful with "Guitar Boogie Shuffle" (5/59 UK 10). His books on guitar playing, 'Play In A Day', and 'Play Every Day', greatly influenced young British musicians. The books sold over a million copies.

Larry Williams 1935 US pianist, singer, and songwriter. He started out in the backing band of Lloyd Price wanting to follow in his footsteps. Hits as a soloist: "Short Fat Fannie" (6/57 US 5; 9/57 UK 21), and "Bony Moronie" (11/57 US 14; 1/58 UK 11). After that, he disappeared from sight for a while. In 1960 he was sentenced for drug offences. Later, it was rumoured that he earned more by pimping than from his records. Finally, he was found shot, slumped behind the wheel of his car. The official verdict was suicide, rumours of murder continued for years.

Henry Fambrough 1938 US singer with the Detroit Spinners.

Arthur Alexander 1940 US R&B singer, and songwriter. In 1960 he cut his first records. Biggest hits: "You Better Move On" (3/62 US 24), later a success for the Rolling Stones – and "Anna (Go To Him)" (11/62 R&B 10; US 68), which the Beatles covered on their first album. Both compositions were by Alexander.

Danny 1941 US leadsinger. Surname Rapp. In 1955 he was a co-founder of the Juvenairs, who became Danny & The Juniors. Hits: "At The Hop" (12/57 US 1; UK 3; 7/76 RE-UK 39), and "Rock 'n Roll Is Here To Stay" (3/58 US 19). Danny died by committing suicide on 5th April, 1983.

Jackie Lomax 1944 UK singer with Dee & The Dynamites, and the Undertakers who played in Hamburg at the same time as the Beatles. Brian Epstein put him under contract and formed the group Lomax Alliance around him. After Epstein's death he was the first artist on the Apple label. The single, "Sour Milk Sea" was written in 1968 and produced by George Harrison. On the album, IS THIS WHAT YOU WANT?, (1969) George Harrison, Eric Clapton, Ringo Starr and Paul McCartney all guested, but

to no avail. After that Jackie went to the States disillusioned, then came back to the UK in 1974, and became a member of Badger – still nothing.

Donovan 1946 UK singer, songwriter and guitarist. Surname Leitch. He is considered to be one of the better known UK folk singers. Hits: "Catch The Wind" (3/65 UK 4; 5/65 US 23), "Colours" (6/65 UK 4), "Sunshine Superman" (7/66 US 1; 12/66 UK 3), "Mellow Yellow" (11/66 US 2; UK 8), "Hurdy Gurdy Man" (5/68 UK 4; US 5) and "Atlantis" (12/68 UK 23; 4/69 US 7). Then from 1974 to 1981 he sank out of sight like the legendary island he sang about. Attempts to revive his career in the 1980s failed, despite groups like Happy Mondays extolling his virtues.

Graham Gouldman 1946 UK guitarist, singer and songwriter. He formed his own first band Whirlwinds in 1963 in his hometown of Manchester, then in 1965 the Mockingbirds. The group released a few unsuccessful singles, and regularly played as a warm-up band before the BBC TV programme Top Of The Pops. In the meantime, however, he had been building a reputation as a songwriter for the Yardbirds, Herman's Hermits, Hollies, Jeff Beck and Wayne Fontana. In 1966 and 1967 Graham released several solo singles, which were unsuccessful. In March 1968 he replaced Bob Lang as a member of the Mindbenders, but in November of the same year, the group finally split up. Gouldman and Eric Stewart bought the Inner City Recording Studio in Manchester and renamed it Strawberry Studios. In October 1969 Graham moved to the USA and wrote for the Bubblegum-Enterprise Kasenatz/Katz, the management company behind groups like Ohio Express, Crazy Elephant and 1910 Fruitgum Company; all were session musicians. At any rate, "Sausalito (Is The Place To Go)" (9/69 US 86) was sung by Graham Gouldman. In November 1969 Kasenatz/Katz booked the Strawberry Studios for three months. Gouldman and Stewart called up Lol Creme and Kevin Godley whom they had worked with before, and recorded there for the American firm. At the time Graham was writing and was vocalist on "Susan's Tuba", a million seller in France for Freddie & The Dreamers, In August 1970, the studio fees from Kasenatz/Katz enabled them to re-equip the Strawberry Studios. While Graham, Eric, Lol, and Kevin were rehearsing they wrote "Neanderthal Man" (7/70 UK 2; US 22), recorded it as Hotlegs, and sold it to Philips Records for an advance of 500 pounds sterling. The record sold 2 million copies worldwide. In 1971, the four of them formed 10 CC. Hits: "Rubber Bullets" (5/73 UK 1), "I'm Not In Love" (5/75 UK 1; US 2), "The Things We Do For Love" (11/76 UK 6; 1/77 US 5), and "Dreadlock Holiday" (8/78 UK 1). In the early 1980s, Graham released solo records as 10 CC fell apart: the official date of disbanding was given as October 1983. Shortly after, Graham started a new project with US artist Andrew Gold, called 'Wax'. Hit: "Building A Bridge To Your Heart" (8/87 UK 12).

Dave Mason 1946 UK guitarist, singer and songwriter. In April 1967, after working as a roadie for Spencer Davis and the Hellions, he became a founder member of Traffic and was lead vocalist on "Hole In My Shoe" (9/67 UK 2). In December 1967, he left the band after 'musical differences' with Steve Winwood. He played briefly with Delaney and Bonnie Bramlett, then began a solo career. Hit: "We Just Disagree" (9/77 US 12). As a session musician he worked with the Rolling Stones, George Harrison, Cass Elliott, Graham Nash, Wings, Steven Stills, Ron Wood and Donovan.

Vic Elmes 1947 UK guitarist with Christie.

Jay Ferguson 1947 US singer, and keyboard player with the band Spirit formed in 1967. When it fell apart again in 1970, he formed Jo Jo Gunne, whose biggest hit was "Run Run Run" (3/72 UK 6; US 27). Jay started a solo career and had a hit with "Thunder Island" (1/78 US 9).

Ron Banks 1951 US leadsinger with the Dramatics, who made their first records in 1966. Hits: "Whatcha See Is Whatcha Get" (7/71 US 9) and "In The Rain" (2/72 US 5). In 1978 Banks joined the George Clinton project, Brides of Funkenstein, who scored with "Disco To Go" (9/78 R&B 7). From 1983, Ron Banks was a solo artist, charting with "Make It Easy On Yourself" (12/83 R&B 31).

Sly 1952 Jamaican drummer and songwriter. Complete name Noel Charles Dunbar. In 1969 he played on the hit "Double Barrel" by Dave & Ansil Collins. In the mid-1970s Sly and bassist Robbie Shakespeare were considered to be *the* ace rhythm section of reggae. They played with almost every Jamaican artists of significance: Peter Tosh, Jimmy Cliff, Gregory Isaacs, Bunny Wailer and Burning Spear. In 1977 Sly released two solo albums, and in 1978, with Robbie, he set up his own record company, Taxi. In the same year they appeared as Sly & Robbie. In 1987 they recorded the excellent album RHYTHM KILLERS, which included "Boops (Here To Go)" (3/87 UK 12).

Sid Vicious 1957 UK bass player, singer, and songwriter he joined the Sex Pistols in February 1977 after leaving The Flowers Of Romance. Sid, real name John Simon Beverly, released one solo album. He died 2nd February, 1979.

Bono 1960 Irish singer and songwriter. Real name Paul Hewson. In 1976 he formed Feedback with friends. The band played at smaller events mainly covering hits and renamed themselves The Hype. When Dick Evans left in order to form Virgin Prunes, the bandname was changed once more, to U2. Paul got the name Bono Vox – 'good voice' – from an advertisement for a hearing aid retailer. Hits: "New Years Day" (1/83 UK 10), "Pride (In The Name Of Love)" (9/84 UK 3; US 33), "With Or Without You" (3/87 US 1; UK 4), "I Still Haven't Found What I'm Looking For" (6/87 US 1; UK 6), "Desire" (10/88 UK 1; US 3), "Angel Of Harlem" (12/88 UK 9; US 14), "When Love Comes To Town" (4/89 UK 6), with B. B. King, and "All I Want Is You" (6/89 UK 4). In 1991, they released the long awaited ACHTUNG BABY!, which sold by the Trabant load.

Hits of the Day

1947 "Linda" Ray Noble US 2 weeks
1986 "Rock Me Amadeus" Falco UK 1 week
1986 "West End Girls" Pet Shop Boys US 1 week

11th

Birthdays

Alma Gluck 1884 US singer born in Bucharest, Rumania. At the age of 5 she emigrated to the USA with her parents. Real name Reba Fiersohn. Her career began on 16th November, 1909: she played the part of Sophie in Jules Massanet's opera *Werther* (written in 1892) at the New York Metropolitan Opera House. Next morning the critics were full of enthusiasm, and Alma Gluck was a star. Her record "Carry Me Back To Old Virginny" (2/15 US 1), was a million seller in the USA in 1915, and is thought to be the first record with a recording on both sides. Up until then there was only one side of music. This means that the first B-side of all time was "Old Black Joe". Alma had a total of 19 hits in the USA from 1911 to 1919. The daughter of her first marriage was successful author and critic Marcia Davenport. During her second marriage to violinist Efrem Zimbalist who accompanied her on most of her records, she had a son. Efrem Zimbalist Jr. became a well-known film and TV actor, as the private detective Stuart Bailey in *77 Sunset Strip* and in *The F.B.I.*, his daughter Stephanie is featured in *Remington Steele*. Alma Gluck died 27th October, 1938.

King Oliver 1885 US cornet player, bandleader, and songwriter. Real first name Joseph. Right after the first world war he became one of the jazz greats; his band was the launching pad for the young unknown Louis Armstrong. He was one of the first black Jazz musicians to make commercially successful records. Among Oliver his biggest hits were "Dipper Mouth Blues" (1/24 US 9) and "St. James Infirmary" (2/30 US 9). He died 8th April, 1938.

Irving Berlin 1888 US composer, born in Temun, Russia. In 1892, with his father, a cantor, he fled from the Cossack pogroms to the USA. Israel Baline, his real name, grew up in the Lower East Side of New York. At age 14 he left home, played piano in saloons and appeared as a singing waiter. In 1907 his first song was published, "Marie From Sunny Italy". In 1910 he had his only entry in the US charts as an artist with the novelty-song, "Oh, How That German Could Love!" (6/10 US 10). With the rise of ragtime came Irving's first monster success as a songwriter, "Alexander's Ragtime Band"; it was published in 1911 and was soon included in every band's repertoire: by 1947, eight different versions had hit the top 6 of the US charts, two of them at No. 1: Arthur Collins & Byron Harlan (1911) and Bing Crosby & Connee Boswell (1938). Irving also wrote several musicals, among them *Annie Get Your Gun* (1946). His most famous song though must be "White Christmas": Bing Crosby's version is reputedly, the biggest selling record, worldwide, of all time. Irving Berlin died 22nd September, 1989 at the age of 101.

Don Howard 1935 US singer who had his only hit at age 17, the million seller "Oh Happy Day" (12/52 US 4).

Carla Bley 1938 US pianist, singer, songwriter and band-leader, a multi-talented jazz musician. Born Carla Borg.

Eric Burdon 1941 UK singer and songwriter. He started as a singer with the Animals. Hits: "The House Of The Rising Sun" (6/64 UK 1; 8/64 US 1; 10/72 RE-UK 25; 9/82 RE-UK 11), "Don't Let Me Be Misunderstood" (2/65 UK 3; US 15) and "We've Gotta Get Out Of This Place" (7/65 UK 2; US 13). When Alan Price left the band in 1966, Eric formed Eric Burdon & The Animals. Hits: "See Rider" (9/66 US 10) "When I Was Young" (4/67 US 15) and "San Franciscan Nights" (8/67 US 9; 10/67 UK 7). In 1970 he formed Eric Burdon & War. Hit: "Spill The Wine" (5/70 US 3). After that he disappeared until Udo Lindenberg re-discovered him in the late 1970s and took him on tour. New records by Eric appeared occasionally and, in 1977 and 1983, there were reunions of the Animals for recording purposes. He appeared in the odd film, but long term success remained elusive. In 1986 his autobiography was published, called 'I Used To Be An Animal But I'm All

Right Now'. In 1988 a solo album of the same name appeared.

Les Chadwick 1943 UK bass player with Gerry & The Pacemakers.

Deaths

Lester Flatt 1979 US country musician. Born 28th June, 1914.

Bob Marley 1981 Cult figure of the reggae movement. Died of cancer. Born 6th February, 1945.

Hits of the Day

1959	"Happy Organ" Dave Cortez US 1 week
1968	"Delilah" Tom Jones
1985	"19" Paul Hardcastle UK 5 weeks
1985	"Crazy For You" Madonna US 1 week
1987	"La Isla Bonita" Madonna

12th

Birthdays

Burt Bacharach 1928 US songwriter and pianist. He wrote nearly all the early hits for Dionne Warwick and several for Gene Pitney with Hal David. He was married to actress Angela Dickinson, then to Carole Bayer-Sager, with whom he formed a songwriting partnership. Burt tried as a recording artist, but without success.

Ian Drury 1942 UK singer and songwriter. In 1970 Ian formed Kilburn & The High Roads, who recorded their first album in 1974. The band fell apart in June 1976, and Ian launched a solo career backed by the Blockheads. His first successful singles, "Sex & Drugs & Rock 'n' Roll" and "Sweet Gene Vincent," illustrated the quality of the groups that had had to resort to playing in pubs in the latter half of the 1970s. Ian's public performances were also reminiscent of his idol Gene Vincent, as he had contracted polio when he was seven and was partially paralysed. His first hits were "What A Waste" (4/78 UK 9), "Hit Me With Your Rhythm Stick" (12/78 UK 1), and "Reasons To Be Cheerful" (8/79 UK 3).

Billy Swan 1942 US singer, songwriter, keyboard player, guitarist and producer. Billy Swan stood at the door of Elvis Presley's house, 'Graceland', in the 1960s and checked the visitors. He had formed the group Mert Mitley & The Rhythm Steppers in the late 1950s and composed "Lover Please," which was covered by Clyde McPhatter in 1962. Billy then went to Nashville, produced the first three albums by Tony Joe White and toured with Kris Kristofferson, until he had his own hit "I Can Help" (9/74 US 1; 12/74 UK 6). In 1986 he formed Black Tie with Randy Meisner.

James Purify 1944 US singer, who had a hit "I'm Your Puppet" (9/66 US 6; 4/76 UK 12), with his cousin Bobby Dickey, as James & Bobby Purify. In the late 1960s Dickey left James, who continued as a soloist until 1974, after which Ben Moore became 'Bobby Purify'.

Robert MacVitte 1946 US drummer with Sugarloaf.

Ian McLagan 1946 UK pianist with the Small Faces, later the Faces, as a session musician and soloist.

Steve Winwood 1948 UK singer, keyboard player, composer and producer. He began his career in 1963 with the Spencer Davis Group. Hits: "Keep On Running" (12/65 UK 1), "Somebody Help Me" (3/66 UK 1), "Gimme Some Loving" (11/66 UK 2; US 7) and "I'm A Man" (1/67 UK 9; 3/67 US 10). In April 1967 he was a co-founder of Traffic. Hit: "Hole In My Shoe" (9/67 UK 2). In 1969 he was a co-founder of Blind Faith for the only album. After that Traffic reformed and carried on until 1974. During the next year or so Steve worked with Stomu Yamashta and Klaus Schulze. From 1977 he went solo. Hits: "While You See A Chance" (2/81 US 7), "Higher Love" (6/86 US 1; UK 13), "Valerie" (9/87 UK 19; US 9), "Roll With It" (6/88 US 1), "Don't Know What The Night Can Do" (8/88 US 6) and "Holding On" (11/88 US 11).

Billy Squier 1950 US singer, guitarist and songwriter. He started out with the Sidewinders and Piper, then as a soloist. Hits: "The Stroke" (5/81 US 17), and "Rock Me Tonite" (7/84 US 15).

Shannon 1957 US singer. Complete name Brenda Shannon Greene. Hits, million seller, "Let The Music Play" (11/83 US 8; 1/84 UK 14) and "Give Me Tonight" (4/84 UK 24).

Terry McKee 1960 UK drummer with Rosetta Stone.

Billy Duffy 1961 UK lead guitarist and songwriter, who joined Death Cult in April 1983 after leaving Theatre Of Hate. From January 1984, they called themselves Cult.

Hits of the Day

1945 "There! I've Said It Again" Vaughn Monroe US 6 weeks

1958 "All I Have To Do Is Dream" Everly Brothers US 5 weeks

1979 "Born To Be Alive" Patrick Hernandez

1984 "Hello" Lionel Richie US 2 weeks

13th

Birthdays

Johnny Wright 1914 US country singer. He formed the duo Johnny & Jack, with Jack Anglin, who made their first records in 1947. The two had already formed the Tennessee Mountain Boys in 1938. Johnny & Jack had their biggest success with "Oh Baby Mine (I Get So Lonely)" (4/54 C&W 1). They stayed together until Jack Anglin's death. Johnny was married to singer Kitty Wells.

Jack Anglin 1916 US country singer and guitarist in the duo Johnny & Jack. He died 7th March, 1963.

Eberhard Schoener 1938 German pianist and innovative composer. He worked with Sting and Deep Purple, among others.

Joe Brown 1941 UK singer and guitarist. He started with the skiffle group The Spacemen. From 1959, the same musicians appeared as Joe Brown & The Bruvvers, having three Top Ten hits: "A Picture Of You" (6/62 UK 2), "It Only Took A Minute" (11/62 UK 6) and "That's What Love Will Do" (2/63 UK 3). In the early 1970s, together with his wife Vicky (in the British charts in the 1960s as one of the Vernon Girls), he formed the country-style group Brown's Home Brew. In addition, he worked as an actor. His daughter Sam Brown became successful in the late 1980s as a singer.

Ritchie Valens 1941 US singer, guitarist, and songwriter. Hit: "Donna" (11/58 US 2; 3/59 UK 29). Real name Richard Valenzuela. He was bound for stardom when he died in the plane crash that killed Buddy Holly and Big Bopper on 3rd February, 1959. The film *La Bamba* dramatised his life-story in 1987.

Mary Wells 1943 US singer and songwriter. She recorded from 1961. Major hits: "The One Who Really Loves

You" (3/62 US 8), "You Beat Me To The Punch" (8/62 US 9), "Two Lovers" (12/62 US 7) and "My Guy" (4/64 US 1; UK 5; 7/72 RE-UK 14). All the above named were written and produced by Smokey Robinson. Mary also recorded duets with Marvin Gaye.

Magic Dick 1945 US harmonica player for the J. Geils Band. Real name Richard Salwitz.

Marlon Hargis 1949 US keyboard player and singer with Exile.

Overend Watts 1949 UK bass player, singer and song-writer with Mott The Hoople and British Lions.

Danny Kirwan 1950 UK guitarist, singer and song-writer. He started with Boiler House, then with Fleetwood Mac from 1968 to 1972, then with Chris Youlden and then as a solo artist.

Stevie Wonder 1950 US multi-instrumentalist, singer, songwriter and producer. Real name Steveland Morris Hardaway/Judkins. In August 1962 he released his first record as Little Stevie Wonder. Since 1963, he has hit the No. 1 spot eight times in the US charts: "Fingertips, Part 2" (6/63 US 1), "Superstition" (11/72 US 1; 2/73 UK 11), "You Are The Sunshine Of My Life" (3/73 US 1; 5/73 UK 7), "You Haven't Done Nothin'" (8/74 US 1; 10/74 UK 30), "I Wish" (12/76 US 1; UK 12), "Sir Duke" (4/77 US 1; UK 2), "I Just Called To Say I Love You" (8/84 US & UK 1) and "Part-Time Lover" (9/85 US 1; UK 3). He also recorded with other Motown artists and duetted with Paul McCartney on "Ebony And Ivory" (4/82 US; UK 1); fur-thermore, he has played harmonica on countless records by other artists.

Paul Thompson 1951 UK drummer. Best known for his work in Roxy Music and its 'spin-off' groups.

Johnny Logan 1955 Australian singer and songwriter. Real name Sean Patrick O'Hara. In 1980 he won the Grand Prix Eurovision for Ireland with the title "What's Another Year" (5/80 UK 1). In 1987 he won another Grand Prix with the self-composed "Hold me Now" (5/87 UK 2), again for Ireland.

Kim McAuliffe 1959 UK guitarist, singer and song-writer with Girlschool.

Deaths

James Gideon Tanner 1960 US country musician. Born on 6th June, 1885.

Bob Wills 1975 US country musician. Born 6th March, 1905.

Joan Weber 1981 US singer with one hit, "Let Me Go, Lover" (12/54 US 1; 2/55 UK 16). Born 1936.

Chet Baker 1988 US jazz trumpeter and singer. Died after a fall from the window of his hotel room in Amster-dam. Born 23rd December, 1929.

Hits of the Day

1955	"Stranger In Paradise" Tony Bennett UK 2 weeks
1965	"King Of The Road" Roger Miller UK 1 week
1967	"Penny Lane" Beatles
1967	"The Happening" Supremes US 1 week
1978	"If I Can't Have You" Yvonne Elliman US 1 week
1989	"I'll Be There For You" Bon Jovi US 1 week
1989	"Hand On Your Heart" Kylie Minogue UK 1 week

14th

Birthdays

Sidney Bechet 1897 US clarinetist, saxophonist and composer. Strongly influenced by New Orleans jazz, he played with King Oliver, Mamie Smith and Duke Elling-ton. Million seller in France "Les Oignons" (1949). His composition "Petite Fleur" was a hit for Chris Barber in 1959. Bechet died in 1959 near Paris on his birthday.

Mike Preston 1934 UK singer. Hits: "Mr. Blue" (10/59 UK 12), and "Marry Me" (3/61 UK 14).

Bobby Darin 1936 US singer, pianist, guitarist, drum-mer, songwriter and film actor. Real name Walden Robert Cassotto. He was nominated for an Oscar for his part in the film *Captain Newman, M.D.*. He cut his first records in March 1956 as a member of the Jaybirds. He had his first hit with "Splish Splash" (6/58 US 3; 8/58 UK 18), and his second with "Early In The Morning" (7/58 US 24); he had recorded the latter as Ding Dongs for another record com-pany before "Splish Splash", but his new record company bought the rights and re-released it as Rinky Dinks. Fur-ther hits: "Dream Lover" (4/59 US 2; UK 1), "Mack The Knife" (8/59 US & UK 1), "You Must Have Been A Beau-tiful Baby" (9/61 US 5; UK 10), "Things" (7/62 US 3; UK 2), "You're The Reason I'm Living" (1/63 US 3) and "If I

Were A Carpenter" (9/66 US 8; UK 9). He was married to actress Sandra Dee from 1960 to 1967. In 1968 he set up his own record company. He died 20th December, 1973.

Troy Shondell 1940 US singer and songwriter. Hit: "This Time" (9/61 US 6; 11/61 UK 22). Later he tried as a country artist.

Jack Bruce 1943 UK bassist, keyboard and harmonica player, singer and songwriter, with Graham Bond, John Mayall and Manfred Mann (he played on the record "Pretty Flamingo"). In the middle of 1966 he formed Cream with Eric Clapton and Ginger Baker, whose hits included "I Feel Free" (12/66 UK 11), "Sunshine Of Your Love" (1/68 US 5; 10/68 UK 25) and "White Room" (10/68 US 6; 1/69 UK 28). At the end of 1969 the band fell apart, Jack carried on as a soloist, formed West, Bruce & Laing and, later still, his own band. He has occasionally done session works subsequently for old friends.

Derek Leckenby 1943 UK guitarist with Herman's Hermits.

Gene Cornish 1944 Canadian guitarist, singer, and bassist with the Young Rascals, Rascals, Bulldog and Fotomaker.

Al Ciner 1947 US guitarist, singer, and songwriter with American Breed, Rufus, Three Dog Night, Tina Turner and Daddy Dewdrops.

Art Grant 1950 UK bassist with the Edgar Broughton Band.

Jay Beckenstein 1951 US saxophonist, songwriter and leader of Spyro Gyra, who had their biggest hit single with "Morning Dance" (6/79 US 24; UK 17).

David Byrne 1952 US singer, guitarist, songwriter and film-maker. In the early 1970s he began his musical career in the duo Wizadi, then with Artistics, and from May 1977 as Talking Heads, who have been recording since 1978. Hits: "Once In A Lifetime" (2/81 UK 14), "Burning Down The House" (7/83 US 9) and "Road To Nowhere" (11/85 UK 6). David also released solo records. Impressive also was his film *True Stories* and the corresponding score.

Tom Cochrane 1953 Canadian singer, guitarist, and songwriter. Cousin of Eddie Cochran (who dropped the 'e' from his name). In November 1977 he joined the group Red Rider, formed in 1976. Before that he had already released several singles and written the soundtrack for a film. In 1980 the group's debut album appeared; from the mid-1980s their records were credited to Tom Cochrane & Red Rider.

Ian Astbury 1962 UK singer, songwriter and leader of the group Southern Death Cult formed in 1982, who called themselves Death Cult from July 1983, and Cult from January 1984. Hits: "She Sells Sanctuary" (5/85 UK 15), "Rain" (10/85 UK 17), "Love Removal Machine" (2/87 UK 18), and "Lil' Devil" (5/87 UK 11).

Fab Morvan 1966 US singer. Born in Haiti, emigrating with his family to Miami in 1970. In 1985 he met Rob Platus, with whom he formed Milli Vanilli. In 1989 they were hailed as Newcomers of the Year in the USA, with one hit after another: "Girl You Know It's True" (10/88 UK 3; 1/89 US 2), "Baby Don't Forget My Number" (12/88 UK 16; 4/89 US 1), "Blame It On The Rain" (10/89 US 1), and "Girl I'm Gonna Miss You" (8/89 US 1; UK 2).

Deaths

Sidney Bechet 1959 see above.

Keith Relf 1976 UK singer with the Yardbirds. Electrocuted, found dead, holding an electric guitar in his hand by his 8-year old son. Born 22nd March, 1943.

Hits of the Day

1949	"Riders In The Sky (A Cowboy Legend)" Vaughn Monroe US 12 weeks
1949	"Forever And Ever" Russ Morgan US 3 weeks
1955	"Unchained Melody" Les Baxter US 2 weeks
1955	"Dance With Me Henry" Georgia Gibbs US 3 weeks
1973	"Get Down" Gilbert O'Sullivan
1977	"When I Need You" Leo Sayer US 1 week
1988	"Anything For You" Gloria Estefan & Miami Sound Machine US 2 weeks
1988	"Perfect" Fairground Attraction UK 1 week

15th

Birthdays

Eddy Arnold 1918 US country singer and songwriter. Complete first name Richard Edward, nickname, 'The Tennessee Ploughboy'. He became popular at Nashville's Grand Ole Opry as a singer with Pee Wee King & His Golden West Cowboys, with whom he appeared from 1940 to 1943. In 1945 Colonel Tom Parker took over managing him for 8 years and turned him into a star. Eddy was thought to be the most successful country artist of all time, as he was equally successful in the country and pop charts, making him the first artist to 'crossover'. He was at the peak of his popularity in the late 1940s. Million sellers: "I'll Hold You In My Heart (Till I Can Hold You In My Arms)" (11/47 US 22), "Anytime" (5/48 US 17), "Bouquet Of Roses" (6/48 US 13), and "Just A Little Lovin (Will Go A Long, Long Way) (9/48 US 13). After a lengthy absence from the upper echelons of the charts he had another monster hit with "Make The World Go Away" (10/65 US 6; 2/66 UK 8).

Trini Lopez 1937 US singer, guitarist songwriter and actor who was immensely successful between 1963 and 1967. His records were especially popular in the emerging discos. The two biggest hits were "If I Had A Hammer" (7/63 US 3; 9/63 UK 4), and "America" (12/63). His appearance in *The Dirty Dozen* failed to widen his appeal.

Tich 1944 UK lead guitarist with Dave Dee, Dozy, Beaky, Mick & Tich. Real name Ian Amey.

Rod Coombes 1946 UK drummer with Lulu, Cat Stevens, Jeff Beck, Juicy Lucy, Stealers Wheel and the Strawbs.

Graham Goble 1947 Australian guitarist, singer and songwriter. In 1972 he formed the band Mississippi, which became the Little River Band in 1975. However, Graham Goble is now the only original member of the group.

Brian Eno 1948 UK synthesizer player producer and experimental composer. Complete name Brian Peter George St. John Le Baptiste de la Salle Eno. In 1971 he was a founder member of Roxy Music. In July 1973 he left the group for a solo career and worked as a session musician with David Bowie and Talking Heads, among others.

Dennis Fredericksen 1951 US singer, who took over from Bobby Kimball as leadsinger with Toto. Dennis was later replaced by Joseph Williams in 1986.

Mike Oldfield 1953 UK multi-instrumentalist and songwriter who formed and recorded with the group Sallyangie, when aged 14, with his sister Sally. The next step was the band Barefeet, then in 1971 he was first bassist, and then guitarist, in Kevin Ayers' group The Whole World. In 1972 he cut a solo album TUBULAR BELLS, which made him world-famous at a stroke; it took him eight months to record the album, as he played nearly all the instruments himself. When passages of it were used in the film *The Exorcist*, "Tubular Bells" (2/74 US 7; 6/74 UK 31) became a hit. After that, Mike was especially successful in Europe. Hits: "In Dulce Jubilo/On Horseback" (12/75 UK 4), "Portsmouth" (11/76 UK 3), "Moonlight Shadow"

(5/83 UK 4) sung by Maggie Reilly, "Shadow On The Wall" (10/83) sung by Roger Chapman, "Pictures In The Dark" (12/85) and "Innocent" (7/89). Anita Hegerland sang on the last two records. She is now Mrs. Oldfield.

Julian Brookhouse 1963 UK guitarist with the group Curiosity Killed The Cat formed in 1983.

Hits of the Day

1959	"A Fool Such As I/I Need Your Love Tonight" Elvis Presley UK 5 weeks
1971	"Knock Three Times" Dawn UK 5 weeks
1976	"Boogie Fever" Sylvers US 1 week
1982	"A Little Peace" Nicole UK 2 weeks
1982	"Ebony And Ivory" Paul McCartney & Stevie Wonder US 7 weeks

---

16th

Birthdays

Woody Herman 1913 US jazz musician, who was a clarinetist and saxophonist in various bands, before becoming leader of his own orchestra in 1936. Real first names Woodrow Charles. First he played blues, and then in the 1940s Swing/Bepop. The 'Four Brothers' sound played on four saxophones became famous. Stravinsky dedicated his Ebony Concerto to Woody. Hits, on which he was sometimes a singer, "Blue Flame" (3/41 US 5), "Blues In The Night" (12/41 US 1), "Amen" (6/42 US 5), "Laura" (4/45 US 4) and "Caldonia" (5/45 US 2). Woody died 29th October, 1987.

Liberace 1919 US pianist. Best-known title, "September Song" (5/52 US 27). For many years he was a star in Las Vegas. Died 4th February, 1987.

Isaak Holt 1932 US drummer and songwriter in the Ramsey Lewis Trio and later with Eldee Young who also played with Lewis, as Young-Holt Unlimited. Hit and million seller, "Soulful Strut" (11/68 US 3).

Billy Cobham 1944 US drummer and songwriter, at home both with jazz and rock. He put out a number of good solo records especially impressive was his session work with Carlos Santana and John McLaughlin on LOVE, DEVOTION AND SURRENDER (1973).

Nicky Chinn 1945 UK songwriter in partnership with Michael Chapman. For the duo's hits see under 15th April.

Roger Earl 1946 UK drummer. He played with Savoy Brown from 1968 to 1971 and was then a co-founder of Foghat.

Robert Fripp 1946 UK guitarist, keyboard player, producer and songwriter. In 1967 he formed Giles, Giles, & Fripp, who renamed themselves King Crimson in 1969. He worked often and well with Brian Eno. In addition, he did session work for David Bowie, Hall & Oates, Peter Gabriel and Talking Heads.

Barbara Lee 1947 US singer with the Chiffons. For hits see 7th April under Pat Bennett.

Darrell Sweet 1947 UK drummer with the Shadettes, which developed into Nazareth.

William Spooner 1949 US guitarist and singer with the Tubes since 1975.

Jonathan Richman 1951 US guitarist and songwriter. Hits: "Roadrunner" (7/77 UK 11) and "Egyptian Reggae" (10/77 UK 5).

Allen Wentz 1951 US bassist, pianist and singer with Wild Cherry, Garcons, and Lizzy Mercier Descloux.

Richard Page 1953 US leadsinger, bassist and songwriter. In the late 1970s he formed the group Pages, which became Mr. Mister in 1982. He started as a session musician for Quincy Jones, James Ingram, Molly Hatchet and as a songwriter for Donna Summer, Michael Jackson, Kenny Loggins and Al Jarreau. In 1984 the first record by Mr. Mister appeared. Hits: "Broken Wings" (9/85 US 1; UK 4), "Kyrie" (12/85 US 1; UK 11), and "Is It Love" (3/86 US 8).

Hazel O'Connor 1955 UK singer, songwriter, and actress who made records from 1978. She played the main part in the film *Breaking Glass* in 1980. Hits: "Eighth Day" (8/80 UK 5), from *Breaking Glass*, and "Will You" (5/81 UK 8).

Glenn Gregory 1958 UK singer and songwriter with the group Heaven 17 formed in 1980. Hits: "Temptation" (4/83 UK 2) and "Come Live With Me" (6/83 UK 5).

Jock Bartley 1959 Canadian guitarist and singer with the US band Firefall, formed in 1974. Before that he had played with the Fallen Angels, Gram Parsons' band, and as a replacement for Tommy Bolin in Zephyr.

Janet Jackson 1966 US singer, and the youngest of 9 children of the Jackson Clan. In 1973 she appeared publicly for the first time during a show by her brothers in the MGM Grand Hotel in Las Vegas. In 1977 she appeared in various TV programmes, and a little later she was in *Fame*. In 1982 she made her first, not particularly successful, album. In 1986 she became a superstar overnight. Hits: "What Have You Done For Me Lately" (2/86 US 4; UK 3), "Nasty" (5/86 US 3; UK 19), "When I Think Of You" (8/86 US 1; UK 10), "Let's Wait Awhile" (1/87 US 2; 3/87 UK 3), "Miss You Much" (9/89 US 1; UK 22) and "Rhythm Nation" (11/89 US 2).

Deaths

Django Reinhardt 1953 Gypsy jazz guitarist of immense fame. He died as the result of a brain haemorrhage. Born in Belgium 23rd January, 1910.

Ernie Freeman 1981 US producer and arranger. Died of a heart attack. Born 16th August, 1922.

Sammy Davis, Jr 1990 US singer, actor and entertainer, born 8th December 1925.

Hits of the Day

1953	"Song From Moulin Rouge (Where Is Your Heart)" Percy Faith US 10 weeks
1958	"Who's Sorry Now?" Conny Francis UK 6 weeks
1964	"My Guy" Mary Wells US 2 weeks
1970	"Back Home" England World Cup Squad UK 3 weeks
1981	"Bette Davis Eyes" Kim Carnes US 5 weeks
1987	"With Or Without You" U2 US 3 weeks

17th

Birthdays

Pervis Jackson 1938 US singer with the Spinners.

Taj Mahal 1940 US singer, songwriter and multi-instrumentalist. Real name Henry Saint Clair Fredericks. He formed the blues-rock band Rising Sons with Ry Cooder in 1965, then played with Canned Heat and made his first solo album in 1968. He is also a session musician, and played on early records by the Pointer Sisters.

Jesse Winchester 1944 US singer, guitarist and song-writer who began to make albums from 1971 onwards, which were produced by either Robbie Robertson, The Band, or Todd Rundgren. In 1973 Jesse took Canadian citizenship in order to avoid being called up for the Vietnam War. After an amnesty for conscientious objectors had been announced in 1977 he returned to the USA. Biggest hit: "Say What" (4/81 US 32).

Andy Latimer 1949 UK guitarist, bassist, singer, flautist, pianist and songwriter, with Brew, Philip Goodhand-Tait's backing band and, finally, Camel in 1971. Even though the group's line-up changed quite a bit over the years, Andy was always with them!

Bill Bruford 1950 UK drummer, and songwriter with Yes (1970 to 1972), and with King Crimson (1973 to 1975 and again from 1981 to 1984). He also worked as a session musician for Genesis, as well as making solo albums. In 1989 he made a new album with Yes-colleagues Rick Wakemann, Jon Anderson, and Steve Howe.

George Johnson 1953 US guitarist, with his younger brother, Louis, as the Brothers Johnson. For hits see under his brother, 13th April.

Paul Di'Anno 1959 UK singer who was an original member of the group Iron Maiden formed in 1977. In 1981, when they were on the way to success, Paul left the band and was replaced by Bruce Dickinson formerly of Samson.

Enya 1961 Irish singer, pianist, and songwriter. Real name Enya Ni Bhraonàin. In 1980 she became part of the family group Clannad formed in 1976 (*clannad* = Gaelic for family). She was on two of their albums and then left the group in 1982. After writing several film scores for the BBC, she had her first solo hit as Enya in 1988, "Orinoco Flow (Sail Away)" (10/88 UK 1; 1/89 US 24).

Hits of the Day

1952 "Kiss Of Fire" Georgia Gibbs US 7 weeks
1952 "Blue Tango" Leroy Anderson US 5 weeks
1957 "Rock-A-Billy" Guy Mitchell UK 1 week
1962 "Nut Rocker" B. Bumble & The Stingers UK 1 week
1975 "Stand By Your Man" Tammy Wynette UK 3 weeks
1980 "What's Another Year" Johnny Logan UK 2 weeks
1986 "The Chicken Song" Spitting Image UK 3 weeks
1986 "Greatest Love Of All" Whitney Houston US 3 weeks

18th

Birthdays

Joe Turner 1911 US R&B singer and songwriter. He started out in his early days in partnership with boogie-woogie pianist Pete Johnson. His first real success came with the 'Spirituals To Swing' Concert in 1938 at Carnegie Hall. In the same year Joe made his first solo records, while continuing as vocalist in Pete Johnson's All-Star Orchestra. Hits: "S. K. Blues, Parts 1 & 2" (5/45 R&B 3). As a solo artist Joe had a million seller with "Chains Of Love" (9/51 US 30), "Honey Hush" (12/53 US 23), "Flip Flop And Fly" (3/55 R&B 2) and "Corinna, Corinna" (4/56 R&B 2). He recorded "Shake Rattle And Roll" (5/54 R&B 1; 8/54 US 22) before Bill Haley, and was still appearing in public in 1982. He died 23rd November, 1985.

Perry Como 1912 US singer, real name Pierino Como. In 1933 he left his successful hairdressing business to become a singer in the Freddy Carlone Band. He sang in Ted Weems Band from 1937 to 1942, before starting a solo career in 1943. Throughout his career, he notched up an extraordinary 147 hits between 1943 & 1975. Among the biggest were "Till The End Of Time" (8/45 US 1), "Prisoner Of Love" (3/46 US 1), "Surrender" (6/46 US 1), "Chi-Baba, Chi-Baba (My Bambino Go To Sleep)" (5/47 US 1), " 'A' – You're Adorable" (4/49 US 1), "Some Enchanted Evening" (4/49 US 1), "Hoop-Dee-Do" (4/50 US 1), "If" (1/51 US 1), "Don't Let The Stars Get In Your Eyes" (12/52 US 1; UK 1), "No Other Love" (6/53 US 1), "Wanted" (3/54 US 1; 6/54 UK 4), "Hot Diggity (Dog Ziggity Boom)" (3/56 US 1; 5/56 UK 4), "Round And Round" (2/57 US 1), and "Catch A Falling Star/Magic Moments" (1/58 US & UK 1). Between 1948 & 1963 he had his own TV show.

Kai Winding 1922 Danish trombonist and composer. His family emigrated to the USA in 1934, where Kai played with Shorty Allen in 1940, Alvino Rey in 1941 and in army bands from 1942. After military service, he went to Benny Goodman (1945/46), Stan Kenton (1947), and Charlie Ventura (1948). After that, he worked with his own groups and as a session musician. In the 1950s Kay played together with the J.J. Johnson quintet, and in the 1960s he composed film scores among other things. His only chart success was from this period, "More" (7/63 US 8), the theme from the film *Mondo Cane*. He also worked as a producer, agent, entrepeneur and teacher, as well as appearing regularly at jazz festivals. Kai died 6th May, 1983.

Alma Cogan 1932 UK singer, who started her career beside Audrey Hepburn in the chorus of *High Button Shoes*, a West End musical in London. In 1952 she made her first records. Hits: "Bell Bottom Blues" (3/54 UK 4), "I Can't Tell A Waltz From A Tango" (12/54 UK 6), "Dreamboat" (5/55 UK 1) and "Never Do A Tango With An Eskimo" (12/55 UK 6). Another well-known record was "Tennessee Waltz" (11/64). Between 1959 and 1961, she was the first singer in Great Britain to have a regular 'prime-time' TV show. She died 26th October, 1966.

Albert Hammond 1942 UK songwriter, guitarist and singer. He wrote many hits with his colleague Mike Hazlewood. They also sang together in many groups under various pseudonyms like Family Dogg and Magic Lanterns. Albert was successful in the early 1970s as a solo artist with "It Never Rains In Southern California" (10/72 US 5) and "Free Electric Band" (5/73 UK 19). Since then, he has turned his attention to songwriting for others.

Feliciano Tavares 1948 US singer and one of the five Tavares Brothers.

Rick Wakeman 1949 UK pianist and songwriter with the Strawbs, Yes, and as a session musician; he was featured on several albums by David Bowie, like SPACE ODDITY and played with Elton John, Al Stewart, Lou Reed, Hudson & Ford and Philip Goodhand-Tait. From 1972, he also made a number of solo albums. In 1989 Jon Anderson, Bill Bruford, Steve Howe, and Rick all former members of Yes joined up to record a new album.

William Wallace 1949 Canadian bassist and singer from 1972 with Guess Who.

George Weyman 1949 UK drummer with Edison Lighthouse.

Wreckless Eric 1954 UK singer, guitarist, pianist, and songwriter. Recorded several good but unsuccessful albums and "Whole Wide World". Real name Eric Goulden.

Toyah 1958 UK singer, songwriter and actress. Surname Wilcox. Multi-coloured dyed hair and flamboyant concerts were her trademark. In 1976 she made her first television appearance, before turning to the cinema, where she starred in films like *Jubilee* (1977) and *Quadrophenia* (1979). She made her recording debut in 1976, reaching a peak in 1981 with 'Four From Toyah' (EP) (2/81 UK 4), and "Thunder In The Mountains" (10/81 UK 4). In 1987 she married Robert Fripp, leader of King Crimson.

Simon Ellis 1961 UK keyboard player and songwriter with Ellis, Beggs & Howard.

Deaths

Leroy Anderson 1975 US orchestra leader and composer. Born 29th June, 1908.

Ian Curtis 1980 UK leadsinger and songwriter for Joy Division, which became New Order after Ian's death. Ian committed suicide by hanging when suffering from depression.

Hits of the Day

1946 "The Gypsy" Dinah Shore US 8 weeks
1959 "Kansas City" Wilbert Harrison US 2 weeks
1961 "On The Rebound" Floyd Cramer UK 1 week
1963 "If You Wanna Be Happy" Jimmy Soul US 2 weeks
1967 "Silence Is Golden" Tremeloes UK 3 weeks
1968 "Tighten Up" Archie Bell & The Drells US 2 weeks
1974 "The Streak" Ray Stevens US 3 weeks
1974 "Sugar Baby Love" Rubettes UK 4 weeks
1981 "In The Air Tonight" Phil Collins
1985 "Don't You (Forget About Me)" Simple Minds US 1 week

19th

Birthdays

Mickey Newbury 1940 US singer and songwriter who wrote for Elvis Presley, Jerry Lee Lewis, Ray Charles, Johnny Cash, Kenny Rogers, and many others. Real first name Milton. For himself he had the one hit, "An American Trilogy" (11/71 US 26).

Pete Townshend 1945 UK guitarist, songwriter and leader of the Who formed in 1964. In the early 1960s three of the Who members were playing in the Detours. When drummer Keith Moon arrived as the fourth member, they called themselves High Numbers, and made their first record, "I'm The Face/Zoot Suit", which was unsuccessful. Shortly afterwards they changed their name to The

Who, and released their first single under that name, "I Can't Explain" (2/65 UK 8), which included Jimmy Page as a session guitarist. Further hits: "My Generation" (11/65 UK 2), "I'm A Boy" (9/66 UK 2), "Happy Jack" (12/66 UK 3; 4/67 US 24), "Pictures Of Lily" (4/67 UK 4), and "Pinball Wizard" (3/69 UK 4; US 19). The latter was extracted from the rock-opera 'Tommy', one of their most celebrated works; it was made into a full-length film. Throughout the 1970s The Who had further success, until Keith Moon died 7th September, 1978. The other members had already worked on solo projects, and the band began to crumble apart. Pete released his first solo album, WHO CAME FIRST, in 1972, then EMPTY GLASS in 1980, and then the excellent WHITE CITY in 1985, which included the single. "Face The Face" (11/85 US 26). In 1986 he wrote the book, Horse's Neck. In the late 1980s the Who joined up again for a tour, rumours abound that they will tour in 1992.

Philip Rudd 1946 Australian drummer with AC/DC. He was a founder member in 1974, remaining until August 1983, and being replaced by Simon Wright.

Paul Brady 1947 Irish singer, multi- instrumentalist and songwriter. He started with groups like Kult and Rockhouse, was a member of the Johnstons until 1972, and then played with Planxty. From the early 1980s he made solo records. He is highly thought of by his musical colleagues, having opened on tours for Dire Straits, and Eric Clapton, but he has never quite managed real success. Others have successfully covered his material, like Tina Turner's hit "Paradise Is Here" and "Steel Claw".

Jerry Hyman 1947 US trombonist with Blood, Sweat & Tears since their first album in 1968.

Dusty Hill 1949 US singer, bass player, and songwriter with the Texan group Z.Z. Top.

Romeo Challenger 1950 UK drummer with Black Widow and Showaddywaddy.

Mike Wedgwood 1950 UK bass player with Curved Air, and Caravan.

Grace Jones 1952 Jamaican model, singer, songwriter and film actress (in 1985 as May Day, the adversary of Roger Moore alias James Bond in *A View To Kill*). In 1976 she was a sought-after model who appeared on the covers of Vogue and Elle. In 1977 she released her first record, "Sorry". After signing with Island records, where she was produced by Chris Blackwell, she had hits with "I've Seen That Face before" (8/81), and "Slave To Rhythm" (10/85 UK 12).

Barbara Joyce Lomas 1952 US leadsinger with the group King David House Rockers formed in 1972, who changed their name to Madison Street Express, and finally became the New York disco-septet, B. T. Express, – B.T. for Brooklyn Trucking. Hits: "Do It (Til You're Satisfied)" (9/74 US 2), and "Express" (1/75 US 4; 3/75 UK 34), both titles being million sellers.

Joey Ramone 1952 US singer with the Ramones. Real name Jeffrey Hyman. The band was formed in 1974, and is considered to be America's most popular punk-rock band. First hit: "Sheena Is A Punk Rocker" (5/77 UK 22), biggest hit, "Baby I Love You" (1/80 UK 8).

Martyn Ware 1956 UK synthesizer player and songwriter who helped to form Human League in 1977. In October 1980, before they became successful, he left. One record, released unsuccessfully in 1978, later became a hit, "Being Boiled" (1/82 UK 6). In the meantime, Martyn had formed Heaven 17. Their first record appeared in March 1981. Hits: "Temptation" (4/83 UK 3) and "Come Live With Me" (6/83 UK 5). In 1987 Ware was co-producer of the extremely successful first album THE HARD LINE ACCORDING TO TERENCE TRENT D'ARBY.

Yazz 1960 UK singer. Real name Yasmin Evans. After a spell as a session vocalist for British mixers and disc jockeys like Coldcut with "Doctorin' The House" (2/88 UK 6), she embarked on a successful solo career. Hits: "The Only Way Is Up" (7/88 UK 1), "Stand Up For Your Love Rights" (10/88 UK 2), "Fine Time" (2/89 UK 9) and "Where Has All The Love Gone?" (4/89 UK 16).

Ben Volpeliere-Pierrot 1965 UK singer and songwriter with the group Curiosity Killed The Cat formed in 1983. The first record, "Misfit" appeared in August 1986, but did not become a hit until about a year later when it was re- released. Biggest hits: "Down To Earth" (12/86 UK 3), "Ordinary Day" (4/87 UK 11), "Misfit" (6/87 UK 7) and "Name And Number" (9/89 UK 14).

Deaths

Coleman Hawkins 1969 US jazz musician and tenor saxophonist. Born 21st November, 1904.

Hits of the Day

1973 "You Are The Sunshine Of My Life" Stevie Wonder US 1 week
1973 "See My Baby Jive" Wizard UK 4 weeks

20th

Birthdays

Vic Ames 1926 US singer with the Ames Brothers. Hits, see brother Joe under 3rd May. Vic died 23rd January, 1978.

Teddy Randazzo 1937 US singer and songwriter. He started as an accordion player and singer with the Three Chuckles, who appeared in the films, *Rock, Rock, Rock*, and *The Girl Can't Help It*. Hit: "Runaround" (11/54 US 20). From 1958, he went solo, having a minor hit with "The Way Of A Clown" (4/60 US 44). He made a name for himself as a songwriter, composing. "Goin' Out Of My Head", among others.

Shorty Long 1940 US singer, pianist, and songwriter. Real first names Frederick Earl. In 1962 he made his first records. Biggest hit: "Here Comes The Judge" (6/68 US 8; UK 30). He drowned on 29th June, 1969.

Paula 1942 US singer, real name Jill Jackson. Together with Ray Hildebrand she formed the duo Paul & Paula. Hits: "Hey Paula" (12/62 US 1; 2/63 UK 8), and "Young Lovers" (3/63 US 6; UK 9).

Terry Smith 1943 UK guitarist with J. J. Jackson, If, Zzebra, and as a session musician with Georgie Fame and Tony Ashton.

Joe Cocker 1944 UK singer and songwriter. He started in 1959 with the Cavaliers, who later called themselves Vance Arnold & The Avengers and then the Grease Band. In 1964 Joe received his first solo contract. His version of the Beatles number "I'll Cry Instead" was a flop. However, he was more successful with another Beatles' cover, "With A Little Help From My Friends" (10/68 UK 1). Further hits: "Delta Lady" (9/69 UK 10), "The Letter" (4/70 US 7; 7/70 UK 39) and "You Are So Beautiful" (1/75 US 5). Joe only emerged again in 1982 after alcohol and drugs problems. He sang "Up Where We Belong" (8/82 US 1; 1/83 UK 7) with Jennifer Warnes. His biggest hit single in recent years was "When The Night Comes" (10/89 US 11).

Cher 1946 US singer. Real name Cherilynn Sarkasian La Pierre (other spellings are possible). She started out as a session singer with Phil Spector. In 1963 she married her colleague Salvatore Bono, and in the same year a record by the pair appeared as Caesar & Cleo. She tried a solo career in 1964, calling herself Bonnie Jo Mason and Cherilyn. In 1965, as Sonny And Cher, the duo had a run of hits: "I Got You Babe" (7/65 US & UK 1), "Baby Don't Go" (8/65 US 8; UK 11), "The Beat Goes On" (1/67 US 6; UK 29), "All I Ever Need Is You" (10/71 US 7; 1/72 UK 8) and "A Cowboy's Work Is Never Done" (2/72 US 8). From 1965 onwards her solo career took off too. Hits: "Bang Bang (My Baby Shot Me Down)" (3/66 US 2; UK 3), "Gypsys, Tramps And Thieves" (9/71 US 1; 11/71 UK 4), "Half-Breed" (8/73 US 1) and "Dark Lady" (1/74 US 1; UK 36). She was divorced from Sonny Bono on 26th June, 1974, 4 days later she married Gregg Allman of the Allman Brothers band. And after 9 days she announced that she would seek another divorce. After 5 years without a hit, she returned with "Take Me Home" (2/79 US 8). Since 1982 her acting career has created interest; in 1984 she was nominated for an Oscar for the best supporting role in the film *Silkwood*. In 1988 she won an Oscar as best actress for her part in *Moonstruck*. In the meantime, her records have continued to sell well: "I Found Someone" (11/87 US 10; UK 5), "We All Sleep Alone" (4/88 US 14), "After All" (3/89 US 6) with Peter Cetera, "If I Could Turn Back Time" (7/89 US 3; 9/89 UK 6) and "Just Like Jesse James" (10/89 US 8).

Steve Broughton 1950 UK drummer with the Edgar Broughton Band and as a session musician with Roy Harper, Mike Oldfield and Sean Taylor.

Warren Cann 1951 Canadian drummer and songwriter with the group Tiger Lily formed in 1973, which turned into Ultravox in 1976.

Jimmy Henderson 1954 US lead guitarist with Black Oak Arkansas.

Steve George 1955 UK keyboard player, singer, songwriter and saxophonist with Mr. Mister.

Jane Wiedlin 1958 US guitarist, singer, songwriter and actress. In 1978 she was a co-founder of the female rock group Go-Gos. Hits: "We Got The Beat" (1/82 US 2) and "Vacation" (7/82 US 8). In 1983 she released a solo album and then with Russell Mael of the Sparks sang "Cool Places" (4/83 US 49). In 1984 Jane left the Go-Gos and was replaced by Paula Jean Brown. She carried on working on her solo career. Hit: "Rush Hour" (5/88 US 9; 8/88 UK 12).

John and Susan Cowsill 1960 US twins who sang in the family group Cowsills.

Nick Heyward 1961 UK singer, guitarist and songwriter who formed Haircut 100 in 1980. Hits: "Favourite Shirts (boy Meets Girl)" (10/81 UK 4), "Love Plus One" (1/82 UK 3), "Fantastic Day" (4/82 UK 9), and "Nobody's Fool" (8/82 UK 9). In 1983 he began a solo career. Hits: "Whistle Down The Wind" (3/83 UK 13), "Take That Situation" (6/83 UK 11) and "Blue Head For A Blue Day" (9/83 UK 14).

Brian Nash 1963 UK guitarist with Frankie Goes To Hollywood.

Hits of the Day

1965 "Where Are You Now (My Love) Jackie Trent UK 1 week
1967 "Groovin'" Young Rascals US 2 weeks
1972 "Metal Guru" T. Rex UK 4 weeks
1978 "With A Little Luck" Wings US 2 weeks
1989 "Forever Your Girl" Paula Abdul US 2 weeks
1989 "Ferry Cross The Mersey" The Christians, Holly Johnson, Paul McCartney, Gerry Marsden, & Stocko Aitken Waterman UK 3 weeks

Miscellany

1851 Emile Berliner born in Hanover. At age 19 he emigrated to the USA, where he invented the contact microphone in 1877. With this and other inventions he made considerable contributions towards the invention of the telephone. Ten years later, in 1887 he invented the gramophone and the record. He also invented a process for manufacturing records.

21st

Birthdays

Fats Waller 1904 US jazz pianist, singer and songwriter, real first name Thomas. From 1929 he was a soloist and leader of his own group. He is considered to be one of the arch-exponents of swing, writing such famous songs as "Ain't Misbehavin'" (11/29 US 17), his first hit, "Honeysuckle Rose" (2/35 US 17), and "I'm Gonna Sit Right Down And Write Myself A Letter" (6/35 US 5). Biggest hits – all in the USA – "Truckin'" (8/35), "A Little Bit Independent" (12/35), "All My Life" (5/36), "It's A Sin To Tell A Lie" (6/36), "Smarty" (7/37) and "Two Sleepy People" (11/38). He died 15th December, 1943.

Dennis Day 1917 US singer. Real name Eugene Patrick McNulty. From 1930 until 1960s he played and sang in the Jack Benny Show. He had his biggest hit in his own right with "Mam'selle" (5/47 US 8). He died 22nd May, 1988.

Tom Donahue 1928 US disc jockey, who encouraged and produced many a San Francisco group like Grateful Dead. It was he who helped Jefferson Airplane obtain a record contract. He died 28th April, 1975.

Tony Sheridan 1940 UK singer, guitarist, and songwriter. Real name Anthony Esmond Sheridan McGinnity. He began as a skiffle musician and backed Marty Wilde, Conway Twitty, Gene Vincent and many other musicians, who travelled to Britain. In 1961 he recorded in Hamburg with the Beat Brothers, also known as the Beatles. With the global interest in Beatlemania, his records "My Bonnie" 2/64 US 26) and "Skinny Minny" (7/64) became popular especially in Germany. Following that he tried to make his way as a rock musician in Germany, and now lives there permanently.

Ronald Isley 1941 US leadsinger and songwriter of the Isley Brothers. The three brothers O'Kelly, Rudolph and Ronald formed a gospel group in the early 1950s in their hometown Cincinnati. In 1957 they moved to New York and made their first records. They had their first notable success with "Shout" (9/59 US 47), which Joey Dee made into hit in 1962, and Lulu in 1964. Biggest hits for the Isley Brothers, "It's Your Thing" (3/69 US 2), "That Lady" (7/73 US 6; 9/73 UK 14) and "Fight That Power" (6/75 US 4). In the UK, "This Old Heart Of Mine" (4/66 UK 47; 10/68 RE-UK 3) and "Behind A Painted Smile" (4/69 UK 5) became big hits when re-released by Motown. In 1973 the trio expanded: the two younger brothers Ernie and Marvin and Cousin Jasper also joined. It was these three who left the band in 1984 and carried on as Isley, Jasper, Isley.

Vince Crane 1943 UK keyboard player, singer and songwriter. Real name Vincent Rodney Chessman. He wrote the hit "Fire" (6/68 UK 1; 9/68 US 2) with Arthur Brown for the Crazy World Of Arthur Brown, of which he was a member. In 1969 he formed the group Atomic Rooster with drummer Carl Palmer. Hit: "The Devil's Answer" (7/71 UK 4). Later on he played with Dexy's Midnight Runners. In February 1989 Vince committed suicide with an overdose of sleeping tablets.

Marcie Bane 1944 US singer with one hit, "Bobby's Girl" (10/62 US 3).

Leo Sayer 1948 UK singer and songwriter, who was promoted and made into a star by Adam Faith, a rockstar of the 1960s. Real first names Gerard Hugh. In 1972 he started his career as a member of the Patches. Their manager was Dave Courtney, ex-drummer with Adam Faith. Courtney and Sayer wrote a few songs, which they played to Adam Faith and he put Leo under contract. Hits: "The Show Must Go On" (12/73 UK 2), "Long Tall Glasses" (9/74 UK 4; 2/75 US 9), "You Make Me Feel Like Dancing" (10/76 UK 2; US 1), "When I Need You" (1/77 UK & US 1) and "More Than I Can Say" (7/80 UK 2; 9/80 US 2). In the 1980s nothing much was heard of Leo, due to contractual difficulties with management and record company.

Tim Lever 1961 UK pianist and saxophonist from August 1983 with the group Dead Or Alive, formed in 1980.

Deaths

Juan Llossas 1957 Tango king. Born 27th July, 1900.

Vaughn Monroe 1973 US singer and bandleader. Born 7th October, 1911.

Hits of the Day

1964	"Juliet" Four Pennies UK 1 week
1977	"I Don't Want To Talk About It/The First Cut Is The Deepest" Rod Stewart UK 4 weeks
1977	"Sir Duke" Stevie Wonder US 3 weeks
1983	"Let's Dance" David Bowie US 1 week
1984	"Send Me An Angel" Real Life
1988	"With A Little Help From My Friends/She's Leaving Home" Wet Wet Wet/Billy Braggs UK 4 weeks

---

22nd

Birthdays

Charles Aznavour 1924 French actor, singer and songwriter of Armenian descent. Real name Shahnour Varenagh Aznavourian. He is one of those artists whose career was promoted by Edith Piaf. Among his greatest hits in France were "Viens Au Creux De Mon Epauls" (1954), "Sur Ma Vie" (1955), "On Ne Sait Jamais" (1956), "Sa Jeunesse (Hier Encore)" (1957), "Je Ne Peux Pas Rentrer Chez Moi" (1959), "Tu Te Laisse Aller" (1960), "Je M'Voyais Déjà" (1961), "La Mama" (1963), "La Bohème" (1966), "Désormais" (1969), "Mourir D'Amier" (1971) and "Comme Ils Disent" (1973). Hit outside France "She" (6/74 UK 1). One of his most impressive contributions as an actor was his role in *Shoot The Pianist* (1959), directed by Francois Truffaut.

Kenny Ball 1931 UK trumpeter, singer and songwriter for his band Kenny Ball & His Jazzmen, formed in 1958. Hits: "Midnight In Moscow" (11/61 UK 2; 1/62 US 2), "March Of the Siamese Children" (2/62 UK 4), "The Green Leaves Of Summer" (5/62 UK 7) and "Sukiyaki" (1/63 UK 10). With the beat era, the hits stopped coming.

Al Brown 1934 US bandleader with Al Brown's Tunetoppers formed in 1953. Only hit: "The Madison" (4/60 US 23).

Bruce Rowlands 1941 UK drummer with Joe Cocker, Grease Band, Gallagher & Lyle, Fairport Convention, Bryan Ferry, Ralph McTell, Bill Wyman, Slim Chance and others.

Bernie Taupin 1950 UK lyricist for Elton John. He also made solo records, which, however, were not successful.

Jerry Dammers 1954 UK pianist and songwriter for the Specials. Some sources give his birthday as 22nd April.

Al Corley 1955 US actor, singer, and songwriter. From Denver-clan to rock 'n roll. He was especially popular in West Germany where he had a hit with "Square Rooms" (9/84).

Iva Davis 1955 Australian singer, guitarist, and songwriter. He formed the group Flowers in January 1980, and in the same year the band had their first Top Ten hit in Australia. In February 1981 they changed their name to Icehouse. From 1983, they were internationally successful with "Hey Little Girl" (2/83 UK 17), "Crazy" (10/87 US 14; 2/88 UK 38) and "Electric Blue" (2/88 US 7).

Dalbello 1959 Canadian singer, actress, presenter and songwriter. First name Lisa. At age 12 she wrote her first songs, and when she was 13 she was a sought-after young presenter. She composed for Heart, Queensryche, and the English lyrics for Nena. Biggest hit for herself, "Tango" (11/87).

Morrissey 1959 UK singer and songwriter. First name Stephen Patrick. In November 1982 he formed The Smiths, the first single appeared in May 1983, the first hit was "This Charming Man" (11/83 UK 25). After that the group quickly developed into a cult band, which split up in the Autumn of 1987. Biggest hits: "Heaven Knows I'm Miserable Now" (6/84 UK 10), and "Sheila Take A Bow" (4/87 UK 10). From 1988, Morrissey worked as a solo artist with hits like "Suedehead" (2/88 UK 5), "Every Day Is Like Sunday" (6/88 UK 9), "The Last Of The Famous International Playboys" (2/89 UK 6) and "Interesting Drug" (4/89 UK 9).

Deaths

Dennis Day 1988 US singer. Born 21st May, 1917.

Hits of the Day

1948 "You Can't Be True, Dear" Ken Griffin US 7 weeks
1961 "Mother-In-Law" Ernie K. Doe US 1 week
1965 "Ticket To Ride" Beatles US 1 week
1965 "The Last Time" Rolling Stones
1968 "Young Girl" Union Gap featuring Gary Puckett UK 4 weeks
1976 "Silly Love Songs" Wings US 1 week

23rd

Birthdays

Artie Shaw 1910 US clarinettist, composer and orchestra leader. Real name Arthur Arshawsky. He played with different bands like Red Nichols and Vincent Lopez, before forming one of the most successful orchestras of the swing-era in 1936. Alongside Benny Goodman he is considered to be the greatest clarinettist of that time. Hits: "Begin The Beguine" (9/38 US 1), "They Say" (12/38 US 1), "Thanks For Ev'rything" (1/39 US 1) and "Frenesi" (7/40 US 1). Shaw was married eight times, among his wives were Lana Turner and Ava Gardner. Later he became a theatre producer and in the 1980s he started a new orchestra.

Robert Blackwell 1918 US composer and producer of many early rock 'n' roll hits such as "Long Tall Sally" and "Rip It Up". His nickname was 'Bumps'. He died on March 9, 1985.

Helen O'Connell 1920 US singer, who sang in Jimmy Dorsey's orchestra from 1939 to 1943, usually in a duo with Bob Eberly. Hits: "Amapola" (3/41 US 1), "Green Eyes" (5/41 US 1) and "Tangerine" (4/42 US 1). She had several hits in the early 1950s as a solo artist. Biggest hit: "Slow Poke" (12/51 US 8). In 1953 she started a TV show with Bob and Ray Anthony.

Rosemary Clooney 1928 US singer who was among the most popular artists in the 1950s. She started out in Tony Pastor's band in the late 1940s. From the early 1950s she was a soloist, but her first hit was a duet with Guy Mitchell, "You're Just In Love" (2/51 US 24). Further hits for Rosemary, "Come On- A-My House" (7/51 US 1), "Tenderly" (3/52 US 17), "Half As Much" (5/52 US 1; 11/52 UK 3), "Botch-A-Me" (Ba-Ba-Baciami Piccina)" (6/52 US 2), "Hey There" (7/54 US 1; 9/55 UK 4), "This Ole House" (8/54 US 1; 10/54 UK 1), "Mambo Italiano" (11/54 US 10; UK 1) and "Mangos" (3/57 US 10; UK 17). As an actress she took part in more than 50 films, among them *White Christmas*. After a lengthy period of personal problems she turned up again in the late 1970s as a successful jazz and ballad singer.

Robert Moog 1934 The inventor of the electronic synthesizer instrument named after him.

Norman Johnson 1944 US leadsinger with the Showmen, who sang a tribute to rock 'n'roll in the early 1960s, "It Will Stand" (11/61 US 61; 7/64 RE-US 80). In 1968 Norman signed a recording contract with Invictus, a record company set up by the Tamla-Motown songwriting team Holland/Dozier/Holland. Norman, who has the nickname 'General', formed the Gentlemen, who a little later were renamed Chairmen Of The Board. Hits: "Give Me Just A Little More Time" (1/70 US 3; 8/70 UK 3), "(You've Got Me) Danging On A String" (5/70 US 38; 11/70 UK 5) and "Pay To The Piper" (11/70 US 13; 5/71 UK 34). In 1976 the group split up, Norman cut six unsuccessful singles flops. In 1981 the group had a reunion, this time as the Chairmen. Kevin Rowland of Dexy's Midnight Runners was much influenced by Johnson's style of singing.

Daniel Klein 1946 US bass player with the J. Geils Band.

Bill Hunt 1947 UK pianist and trumpeter with Hannibal, ELO and Wizzard.

Rick Fenn 1953 UK guitarist with Hamilton Gray and 10CC. He also worked with Mike Oldfield and Nick Mason.

Deaths

Eddy Howard 1963 US orchestra leader, singer and songwriter. Born 12th September, 1914.

Moms Mabley 1975 US singer. Born 19th March, 1897.

Hits of the Day

1960 "Cathy's Clown" Everly Brothers US 5 weeks
1988 "Ella elle l'a" France Gall

24th

Birthdays

Archie Shepp 1937 US jazz saxophonist, pianist, songwriter and bandleader.

Chong 1940 Canadian, full name Thomas Chong. Together with Californian Richard Marin, alias Cheech, he was considered to be one of the leading rock parodists. Hits as Cheech & Chong, "Basketball Jones featuring Tyrone Shoelaces" (9/73 US 15), and "Earache My Eye featuring Alice Bowie" (8/74 US 9). From 1980, the team appeared in films.

Bob Dylan 1941 US songwriter, singer, guitarist, and occasionally a film actor. Real name Robert Allen Zimmermann, his name was inspired by poet Dylan Thomas. In December 1960 he went to New York and began to play in the folk clubs of Greenwich Village. In October 1961 he obtained a recording contract with CBS. There is hardly a musician who set as many trends as he did during his career: first, he, alongside Joan Baez, was a speaker for the folk-protest-movement and then started folk-rock in 1965. Hits: "Times They Are A-Changin' " (3/65 UK 9), "Subterranean Homesick Blues" (4/65 US 39; UK 9), "Like A Rolling Stone" (7/65 US 2; UK 4), "Positively 4th Street" (10/65 US 7; UK 8), "Rainy Day Women 12 & 35" (4/66 US 2; UK 7) and "Lay Lady Lay" (7/69 US 7; 9/69 UK 5). Many of his compositions were successfully covered by other artists.

Derek Quinn 1942 UK lead guitarist with Freddy & The Dreamers.

Patti LaBelle 1944 US singer. Real name Patricia Holt. In 1961 Patti and Cindy Birdsong were members of the group Ordettes, while schoolfriends Sarah Dash and Nona Hendryx were singing with the band Bell Capris. When the two groups split up in 1962, the four girls carried on as Patti LaBelle & The Blue Belles. In 1967 Cindy Birdsong joined the Supremes; in 1971 the long name was changed to LaBelle. Hit and million seller: "Lady Marmalade" (1/75 US 1; 3/75 UK 17). After 1976 the girls embarked on solo careers. Hits for Patti, "New Attitude" (2/85 US 17), and with Michael McDonald, "On My Own" (3/86 US 1; 5/86 UK 2).

Dave 1945 UK singer, guitarist, and songwriter. Surname, Peacock. In 1970 he played briefly with Charles Hodges in the band Black Claw, in 1975 they were both in the Albert Lee Band and, with drummer Mick Burt, they finally formed the trio Chas & Dave, who charted from 1978. Hits: "Rabbit" (11/80 UK 8), and "Ain't No Pleasing You" (3/82

UK 2). Their music was a mixture of rock 'n' roll and Cockney rhyming slang. Their record company, Rockney, was also Mick's nickname. They had a hit "Ossie's Dream (Spurs Are On Their Way To Wembley)" (5/81 UK 5) with the football team Tottenham Hotspurs and "Snooker Loopy" (5/86 UK 6) with Match Room Mob. Dave was also on records by Magna Carta and Dave Edmunds.

Steve Upton 1946 UK drummer with Wishbone Ash.

Rosanne Cash 1955 US country singer and songwriter. Daughter of Johnny Cash. From the late 1970s she was successful in the country charts and, to date, has had ten No. 1 hits. Only crossover success, "Seven Year Ache" (2/81 C&W 1; 4/81 US 22). She is married to songwriter Rodney Crowell.

Deaths

Elmore James 1963 US blues musician. Died of a heart attack. Born 27th January, 1918.

Duke Ellington 1974 US jazz musician and composer. He died of lung cancer. Born 29th April, 1899.

Gene Clark 1991 US singer, guitarist and songwriter. Born November 11th, 1941.

Hits of the Day

1952 "A Guy Is A Guy" Doris Day US 1 week
1957 "Butterfly" Andy Williams UK 2 weeks
1962 "Good Luck Charm" Elvis Presley UK 5 weeks
1969 "Get Back" Beatles US 5 weeks
1975 "Shining Star" Earth, Wind & Fire US 1 week

25th

Birthdays

Hal David 1921 US lyrics writer, who wrote countless hits with Burt Bacharach.

Miles Davis 1926 US jazz trumpeter, songwriter, and bandleader. He is considered to be one of the most influential but also most controversial jazz musicians of all time. German jazz critic Werner Burkhard wrote about him,

"Once again, our dear Lord, in a fit of absentmindedness, has lent a great gift, (as with Richard Wagner and Herbert von Karajan) to a great arsehole." In the 1940s Miles played in the bands of Charlie Parker, Benny Carter and Billy Eckstine. From his memoirs, which appeared in the late 1980s, one can see that Miles was well aware of his importance, saying "I have revolutionized music five or six times." He died after years of ill-health on 25th September, 1991.

Kitty Kallen 1926 US singer, who recorded from the early 1940s. She started out in the orchestra of Jack Teagarden and then changed over to Jimmy Dorsey. Hits: "They're Either Too Young Or Too Old" (12/43 US 2) and "Besame Mucho" (1/44 US 1). From 1945, she sang in Harry James' band. Hits: "I'm Beginning To See The Light" (1/45 US 1) and "It's Been A Long Long Time" (10/45 US 1). From 1949 Kitty was successful as a solo artist: "Little Things Mean A Lot" (4/54 US 1; 6/54 UK 1), "In The Chapel In The Moonlight" (7/54 US 4) and "My Colouring Book" (12/62 US 18).

Norman Petty 1927 US pianist, songwriter and producer. In the early 1950s he led his own trio and built his own studio in Clovis, Texas in 1954. He recorded his two biggest hits there: the Duke Ellington Composition "Mood Indigo" (9/54 US 14) and "On The Alamo" (12/54 US 29). With the earnings from these two titles he carried on extending his studio and recorded the Buddy Knox million seller "Party Doll". After that he invited artists from further afield to use his studio, among them were Buddy Holly & The Crickets. Norman became their manager and also co-wrote several of their hits. In 1958 Holly left Petty; after Buddy's death he bought up the rights of unreleased recordings and demo tapes, reworked them in his studio, and inspite of all criticism, turned them into hits. Further hits from his studio were "Sugar Shack" with Jimmy Gilmour & The Fireballs and "Wheels" with the String-A-Longs. In the early 1970s he sold his rights to the Buddy Holly catalogue to Paul McCartney. Norman died 15th August, 1984.

Tom T. Hall 1936 US country singer, guitarist and songwriter. He had his own band, the Kentucky Travellers, when he was 16. After that he became a disc jockey and broadcasted on AFN radio in the German Federal Republic from 1957 to 1961. In 1964 he went to Nashville. From 1967 he appeared regularly in the country charts and managed a total of seven No. 1 hits and over 50 entries. His biggest crossover hit was "I Love" (12/73 US 12). Tom became known for the narrative content of his songs, exemplified by the Jeannie C. Riley hit, "Harper Valley P.T.A.", in 1968.

Brian Davison 1942 UK drummer with Nice, Refugee and Every Which Way.

Poli Palmer 1943 UK pianist and drummer with Matthews Southern Comfort, Family, Streetwalkers, Peter Frampton, Roger Chapman, Pete Townshend, Deep Feelings, Bakerloo and Blossom Toes. Real first name John.

Jessi Colter 1947 US singer, keyboard player and songwriter. Real name Miriam Johnson Jennings. At age 16 she married rock-guitarist Duane Eddy, whom she divorced in 1968. In 1969 she married country artist Waylon Jennings. Pop hit: "I'm Not Lisa" (4/75 US 4).

Mitchell Margo 1947 US pianist, drummer and singer with The Tokens, who became Cross Country in 1973.

Klaus Meine 1948 Singer and songwriter with the German group Copernicus, who changed their name to the Scorpions in 1971. This group is one of the few German groups to have huge record sales in the USA, France, and Japan. Biggest hits: "Rock You Like A Hurricane" (3/84 US 25) and "Still Loving You" (11/84).

Jean Millington 1950 US bass player and songwriter with Fanny. As a session musician she has worked with David Bowie, Keith Moon and Barbra Streisand.

Robert Steinhardt 1950 US violinist, singer and songwriter with the band Kansas until 1982.

John Grimaldi 1955 UK guitarist with Argent from 1974.

Paul Weller 1958 UK leadsinger, guitarist and songwriter for The Jam, one of the pioneering 'new wave' bands, formed in 1975; they released their first records in 1977. Among their hits were "Going Underground" (3/80 UK 1; 1/83 RE-UK 21), "Start" (8/80 UK 1), "Town Called Malice" (2/82 UK 1) and "Beat Surrender" (12/82 UK 1). At the beginning of 1983 The Jam split up and, in March 1983, the first single by Weller's new project Style Council, appeared, "Speak Like A Child" (3/83 UK 4). Other Hits: "Long Hot Summer" (8/83 UK 3), "My Ever Changing Moods" (2/84 UK 5; US 29), "Groovin' (You're The Best Thing)" (5/84 UK 5), "Shout To The Top" (10/84 UK 7), "Walls Come Tumbling Down" (5/85 UK 6) and "It Didn't Matter" (1/87 UK 9).

Deaths

Sonny Boy Williamson 1965 US singer and acchetypal harmonica player, also known as Aleck Rice Miller. Born on 5th December, 1899.

Roy Brown 1981 US R&B singer and songwriter. Born on 10th September, 1925.

26th

Birthdays

Peggy Lee 1920 US singer, songwriter and actress. Real name Norma Delores Egstrom. She started as a nightclub singer in Hollywood with the bands of Jack Wardlaw and Will Osborne. In 1941 Benny Goodman saw Peggy and signed her up for his band until 1943. Hits: "Somebody Else Is Taking My Place" (3/42 US 1) and her first million seller "Why Don't You Do Right?" (1/43 US 4). She was successful as a solo artist from 1945. Hits: "Golden Earrings" (11/47 US 2), "Manana" (1/48 US 1), "Lover" (6/52 US 3), "Mr. Wonderful" (3/56 US 14; 5/57 UK 5) and "Fever" (7/58 US 8; UK 5). From 1950 onwards Peggy appeared in several films. She was even nominated for an Oscar for her role in *Pete Kelly's Blues* (1955). Even after her great success as a soloist she carried on working for Quincy Jones, Duke Ellington and others. Her last hit was written by Leiber/Stoller, "Is That All There Is" (9/69 US 11). Yes, that's all – but maybe it hasn't been so bad.

Jaki Liebezeit 1939 German drummer with Can and later a sought-after session musician.

Ray Ennis 1942 UK lead guitarist, singer, and songwriter with the Swinging Blue Jeans, who formed in May 1958 as The Bluegenes. Up until then, Ray had played skiffle. In 1963 they changed their name to Swinging Blue Jeans. The success of The Beatles had a knock-on effect for other Mersey sound groups like Swinging Blue Jeans. Hits: "Hippy Hippy Shake" (12/63 UK 2; 3/64 US 24) and "You're No Good" (6/64 UK 3). In 1968 the group split up after several changes of lineup, but in 1973 Ray reformed the group with a new lineup to tour Europe. In 1976 he turned up with Racing Cars and the hit "They Shoot Horses, Don't They" (2/77 UK 14).

Levon Helm 1943 US drummer in the Canadian group Levon & The Hawks, who backed Ronnie Hawkins in the first half of the 1960s. In 1965 Bob Dylan invited them to become his backing band and they accepted. After Dylan crashed his motorbike and had to take a lengthy break, they called themselves The Band and released the highly praised MUSIC FROM THE BIG PINK album in 1968. Levon later became a sought-after session musician and released solo records too.

Verden Allen 1944 UK pianist with Mott The Hoople.

Garry Peterson 1945 Canadian drummer and founder member of Guess Who until 1976, then with Burton Cummings, and in 1984 on an album by BTO.

Stevie Nicks 1948 US singer and songwriter. She became a member of the group Fritz with Lindsey Buckingham. After the band split up in 1971, they carried on working as a duo. In 1973 they recorded their debut album. When it turned out to be a flop, Buckingham continued working as a session musician and toured with Don Everly, while Stevie jobbed as a waitress in a bar in Hollywood. When the British band Fleetwood Mac was looking for an injection of new life at the beginning of 1975, as Bob Welch had left, they came upon this duo. With Buckingham-Nicks on board Fleetwood Mac were revitalised. In 1977 the album RUMOURS appeared which sold over 25 million copies. From 1981 solo records by Stevie appeared. Hits: "Stop Draggin' My Heart Around" (8/81 US 3), "Stand Back" (6/83 US 5), "Talk To Me" (11/85 US 4) and "Rooms On Fire" (5/89 US & UK 16).

Mick Ronson 1949 UK guitarist, pianist, bass player and singer. Member of Mott The Hoople, sessions with David Bowie, Bob Dylan, David Cassidy, Meatloaf, Dalbello, and Lou Reed, and also as a solo artist.

Philip-Michael Thomas 1949 US actor and singer. He has been successful as 'Detective Ricardo Tubbs' in *Miami Vice* since 1984, but less so as a singer.

Hank Williams Jr. 1949 US country singer, songwriter and multi-instrumentalist. Real first name Randall. For a long time he was over shadowed by his father's career, but established his own identity. From 1964 'Bocephus' has had over 80 hits in the country charts, with more than 10 hitting the No. 1 spot. Hank is considered to be an excellent showman, and was voted Entertainer of the Year by the Country Music Association in 1987 and 1988.

Colin Vearncombe 1951 UK singer, guitarist, pianist and songwriter. In January 1981, he formed the trio Black. From 1981 to 1985 some singles appeared, which were all unsuccessful. From 1986, when Colin was working alone under the name Black, he was successful. Hits: "Wonderful Life" (9/86 UK 72; 8/87 RE-UK 8), "Sweetest Smile" (6/87 UK 8) and "Everything's Coming Up Roses" (1/88).

Bernie Flint 1952 UK singer, whose biggest hit was "I Don't Want To Put A Hold On You" (3/77 UK 3).

Marian Gold 1958 Singer and songwriter with Alphaville, a band from Munster, Germany, who had their first hit in 1984, "Big In Japan" (8/84 UK 8; 11/84 US 66), followed by "Sounds Like A Melody" (6/84), "Forever Young" (3/85 US 93; 10/88 RE-US 67) and "Dance With Me" (4/86).

Wayne Hussey 1959 UK guitarist, singer and songwriter. He played with Pauline Murray, Dead Or Alive, and the ska-punk group Walkie Talkies, before becoming a member of Sisters Of Mercy in June, 1983. In December 1985 he was a founder-member of Sisterhood, who changed their name to Mission. Biggest hits: "Waste Land" (1/87 UK 11), and "Tower Of Strength" (2/88 UK 12).

Chris Duffy 1960 UK singer and songwriter with Waterfront, who released "Cry" (4/89 US 10; UK 17) in October 1988; it did not become a hit until about 6 months later.

Deaths

Jimmie Rodgers 1933 US country star and 'Father Of Country Music'. He died of TB. Born 8th September, 1897.

Billy Powell 1977 US singer and founder member of the O'Jays. Died of cancer. Born 20th January, 1942.

Hits of the Day

1945 "Sentimental Journey" Les Brown US 9 weeks
1962 "Stranger On The Shore" Mr. Acker Bilk US 1 week
1966 "Paint It Black" Rolling Stones UK 1 week
1973 "Frankenstein" Edgar Winter Group US 1 week
1979 "Sunday Girl" Blondie UK 3 weeks
1984 "Let's Hear It For The Boys" Deniece Williams US 2 weeks

---

27th

Birthdays

Ramsey Lewis 1935 US keyboard player and songwriter. First he played with the Clefs, and when they split up in 1955, Lewis, together with bass player Eldee Young and drummer Isaac 'Red' Holt formed the Ramsey Lewis Trio. Hit: "The In Crowd" (7/65 US 5). In 1965 the trio fell apart. Holt and Young carried on as the Young-Holt Trio.

Lewis got hold of Cleveland Eaton as his new bass player and Maurice White as drummer (later of Earth, Wind & Fire). Hit: "Wade In the Water" (7/66 US 19; 4/72 UK 31). In 1982 the original trio reformed.

Don Williams 1939 US country singer, guitarist, songwriter and film actor. Real first names Donald Ray. He managed more than 15 No. 1 country hits, but was also successful in the pop charts. Don started out in the pop-folk group Pozo-Seco Singers, worked as a songwriter in Nashville from the early 1970s, and made solo records. From 1972 he was in the country charts. Pop-hits, "I Recall A Gypsy Woman" (6/76 UK 13) and "I Believe In You" (9/80 US 24).

Cilla Black 1943 UK singer, real name Priscilla White. She was the cloakroom attendant in the Cavern Club, when she was signed up by Brian Epstein. He had heard how she occasionally appeared in public as 'Swinging Cilla' with bands like Kingsize Taylor & The Dominoes and the Beatles. His intuition was right. Between 1963 and 1974 she had a total of 11 Top Ten hits. Biggest hits: "Anyone Who Had A Heart" (2/64 UK 1), "You're My World" (5/64 UK 1; 7/64 US 26), "You've Lost That Lovin' Feeling" (1/65 UK 2), "Surround Yourself With Sorrow" (2/69 UK 3) and "Something Tells Me (Something Is Gonna Happen Tonight)" (11/71 UK 3).

Bruce Cockburn 1945 Canadian singer, guitarist and songwriter. From 1971 he released solo records which at first were successful only in Canada, then later in the USA. Biggest hit: "Wondering Where The Lions Are" (3/80 US 21). His commitment to political and social issues is obvious in his music and is probably not suitable for the charts – a shame, as lyrically, he is more inventive than most.

Marty Kristian 1947 UK guitarist and singer of German origin with the New Seekers. Born in Leipzig, East Germany, real name Martin Vanags.

Peter Sears 1948 US bass player and pianist. He played with Steamhammer, Rod Stewart, Ron Wood and Kim Foley, before becoming a member of Jefferson Starship in 1975.

James Mitchell 1949 US singer with the Detroit Emeralds.

Siouxsie Sioux 1957 UK singer, guitarist, pianist and songwriter. Real name Susan Dallion. The group Banshees was formed in 1976; among the original line up was Sid Vicious who played drums, later he joined the Sex Pistols. Hits for Siouxsie & The Banshees: "Hongkong Garden"

(8/78 UK 7), "Dear Prudence" (10/83 UK 3), "This Wheel's On Fire" (1/87 UK 14) and "Peek-A- Boo" (7/88 UK 16). In the early 1980s she formed an additional band with another member of the Banshees, and called them Creatures. Hit: "Right Now" (7/83 UK 14).

Neil Finn 1958 New Zealand singer, and guitarist. In May 1977 he replaced Phil Judd in Split Enz (Phil had been a founder member in October 1972). Another founder member of the band was Neil's older brother Tim, but it was Neil's influence that gave the group its first hit, "I Got You" (8/80 UK 12). In 1985 Tim left the group for a solo career and Neil formed the new band Crowded House. Hits: "Don't Dream It's Over" (1/87 US 2; UK 27) and "Something So Strong" (5/87 US 7).

Deaths

Little Willie John 1968 US R&B musician. Died after a heart attack in Washington State Prison, in which he was serving a sentence for manslaughter. Born 15th November, 1937.

Onie Wheeler 1984 US country singer, composer and harmonica player. Born on 10th November, 1921.

Hits of the Day

1955 "Cherry Pink & Apple Blossom White" Eddie Calvert UK 4 weeks
1961 "Wheels" Billy Vaughn
1965 "Long Live Love" Sandie Shaw UK 3 weeks
1967 "Puppet On A String" Sandie Shaw
1972 "Oh Girl" Chi-Lites US 1 week

28th

Birthdays

Andy Kirk 1898 US trumpeter and bandleader. He was already playing with various bands in the 1920s, before becoming successful in the mid-1930s as Andy Kirk & His Twelve Clouds Of Joy with "Until The Real Thing Comes Along" (7/36 US 1) and "I Won't Tell A Soul (I Love You)" (10/38 US 1).

Aaron 'T-Bone' Walker 1910 US singer, guitarist, pianist and songwriter. 'T-Bone' is derived from his real second name Thibeaux. He was one of the first blues guitarists to amplify his guitar with electricity in 1935. He toured with 'Medicine Shows' in the 1920s. In 1929 he made his first records, and from 1930 to 1934 he played with Cab Calloway, Milt Larkins and Ma Rainey, among others. In 1940 'T-Bone' formed his own band, but also played as a session musician on Freddie Slack's "Rifette" (5/43 US 19). Hits under his own name were "Bobby Sox Blues" (1/47 R&B 3), "Call It Stormy Monday (But Tuesday Is Just As Bad)" (1/48 R&B 5) and "T-Bone Shuffle" (3/49 R&B 7). Walker was considered to be one of the first rock musicians before the term had been invented. B. B. King always referred to himself as a pupil of Walker's. Aaron died on 16th March, 1975.

Papa John Creach 1917 US violinist with bands like Jefferson Airplane and Hot Tuna. He also made solo albums.

Cathy Carr 1936 US singer. Biggest hit: "Ivory Tower" (3/56 US 2).

Prince Buster 1938 Jamaican musician and songwriter, who is considered to be a co-founder of the ska and reggae movement. Real surname Campbell. In 1962 he was recording a combination of ska and blue beat, which later became known as reggae. Only hit: "Al Capone" (2/67 UK 18).

Tony Mansfield 1943 UK drummer with Billy J. Kramer & The Dakotas.

Gladys Knight 1944 US singer, who formed the family-based group Gladys Knight & The Pips in 1952 with two cousins, her older brother Merald, and her sister Brenda. They first recorded in 1958. Hits: "Every Beat Of My Heart" (5/61 US 6), "I Heard It Through The Grapevine" (10/67 US 2), "Neither One Of Us (Wants To Be The First To Say Goodbye)" (1/73 US 2; 5/73 UK 31), "Midnight Train To Georgia" (9/73 US 1; 5/76 UK 10), "I've Got To Use My Imagination" (11/73 US 4), "Best Thing That Ever Happened To Me" (2/74 US 3; 8/75 UK 7), "On And On" (5/74 US 5), "The Way We Were/Try To Remember" (4/75 UK 4; US 11), "Baby Don't Change Your Mind" (5/77 UK 4), "Come Back And Finish What You Started" (6/78 UK 15), "Love Overboard" (1/88 US 13) and "Licence To Kill" (6/89 UK 6), from the James Bond film of the same name.

Billy Vera 1944 US singer and songwriter. Real name William McCord Jr. In 1967/68 he recorded with Judy Clay Patten. In 1968 he could still be heard as Billy & The Beaters. In 1979 he revived the Beaters and, in January

1981, he made a live recording of "At This Moment" (9/81 US 79; 11/86 RE-US 1) at the Roxy in L.A. The song "At This Moment" had been revived in the American TV series, *Family Ties*, which generated fresh interest.

John Fogerty 1945 US guitarist, singer, and songwriter, leader of Creedence Clearwater Revival, who made their first records in 1959 as Blue Velvets. In 1964 they called themselves Golliwogs and, in 1967, success arrived as CCR. Hits: "Proud Mary" (1/69 US 2; UK 8), "Bad Moon Rising" (5/69 US 2; 7/69 UK 1), "Green River" (8/69 US 2; 10/69 UK 19), "Travellin' Band/Who'll Stop The Rain" (1/70 US 2; 4/70 UK 8), "Up Around The Bend" (4/70 US 4; 6/70 UK 3), "Lookin' Out My Back Door" (8/70 US 2), "Have You Ever Seen The Rain" (1/71 US 8; 3/71 UK 36), "Hey Tonight" (2/71), and "Sweet Hitch Hiker" (7/71 US 6; UK 36). In October 1972 the group split up. John Fogerty started a one man band, Blue Ridge Rangers. Hit: "Jambalaya (On The Bayou)" (12/72 US 16). He then recorded under his own name. Hit, "Rockin' All Over The World" (9/75 US 27). After that it seemed to be over, but contractual difficulties with his record company were to blame for his long absence from the charts. He returned with "Old Man Down The Road" (12/84 US 10).

Ray Laidlaw 1948 UK drummer with Lindisfarne and Jack The Lad.

Steve Strange 1959 UK singer and songwriter. Real name Harrington, He was a roadie for Generation X, then with Chrissie Hynde he was co-founder of the Moors Murderers at the end of 1977, then with Photon, and finally he opened the club, Blitz, with drummer Rusty Egan who had previously been in Rich Kids. For many, Steve was the instigator of the 'New Romantic Trend' which began about 1978. Hits: "Fade To Grey" (12/80 UK 8) and "Mind Of A Toy" (3/81 UK 13) with Visage. In the mid-1980s he opened the London disco Camden Palace, a counterpart to New York's Studio '54, after which he tried as a singer with Strange Cruise. But the public wouldn't fall for a singing clothes-horse twice.

Roland Gift 1962 UK singer and songwriter for the group Fine Young Cannibals. Since 1985 they have been successful. Hits: "Johnny Come Home" (6/85 UK 8), "Suspicious Minds" (1/86 UK 8), "She Drives Me Crazy" (1/89 UK 5; US 1) and "Good Thing" (4/89 UK 7; US 1). In between Roland was also active as an actor. He played the lead male role in the film *Sammy & Rosie Get Laid*, and took part in *Scandal*.

Brad Hopkins 1963 Bassist and songwriter with the Canadian group Chalk Circle.

Kylie Minogue 1968 Australian singer. She started as an actress in the TV series *Neighbours*. When it was shown in the UK, within weeks she had become sought-after as a singer. She had her first hit in Australia with a version of Little Eva's "Locomotion" (8/88 UK 2; US 3). Her further hits were master-minded by the British production team Stock/Aitken/Waterman which guaranteed immediate success: "I Should Be So Lucky" (1/88 UK 1; 5/88 US 28), "Got To Be Certain" (5/88 UK 2), with Jason Donovan "Especially For You" (12/88 UK 1), "Hand On Your Heart" (5/89 UK 1), and "Never Too Late" (11/89 UK 4).

Hits of the Day

1964	"You're My World" Cilla Black UK 4 weeks
1966	"When A Man Loves A Woman" Percy Sledge US 2 weeks
1983	"Flashdance" What A Feeling Irene Cara US 6 weeks
1983	"Candy Girl" New Edition UK 1 week
1988	"One More Try" George Michael US 3 weeks

29th

Birthdays

Roy Crewsden 1941 UK guitarist with Freddie & The Dreamers.

Sir Monti Rock III 1942 US singer, with Disco Tex & The Sex-O-Lettes, which was a bunch of session musicians under the leadership of producer Bob Crewe. His real name is Joseph Moses Aponte Montanez Jr., born in The Bronx, and owner of a chain of hairdressing shops called 'Mr. Monti's Salons'. Hits: "Get Dancing" (11/74 US 10; UK 8), and "I Wanna Dance Wit' Choo" (4/75 UK 6; US 23). Sir Monti played the part of a disc jockey in the film *Saturday Night Fever*.

Gary Brooker 1945 UK keyboard player, songwriter and singer. From 1962 he played with the Paramounts, who secured a recording contract with Parlophone in 1963, recording six singles and one EP, of which only "Poison Ivy" (1/64 UK 35) charted. Other members of the group included Robin Trower and Barrie 'B.J.' Wilson, and all worked as the backing band for Sandie Shaw and Chris Andrews. At the end of 1966 Gary wrote several songs with Keith Reid, these he recorded together with session musicians. They didn't plan to form a permanent group until they became successful. Their first release was "Whiter Shade Of Pale" (5/67 UK 1; US 5; 4/72 RE-UK 13). Then the band was formed under the name Procol Harum and it included Robin Trower and B. J. Wilson. Further hits: "Homburg" (10/67 UK 6; US 34) and "Conquistador" (5/72 US 16; 8/72 UK 22). In 1977 the band split up. Gary played as a session musician for Eric Clapton on the album ANOTHER TICKET; he has released solo records since 1979.

Francis 'Mike' Rossi 1949 UK lead guitarist, singer, songwriter and leader of Status Quo. His birthdate is also given as 29th April, and 25th May. For hits, see 12th October, under fellow band member Rick Parfitt.

Rebbie Jackson 1950 US singer and oldest member of the Jackson siblings. Real first name Maureen. In 1974 when the Jackson 5 and her various brothers had established themselves as stars, Rebbie started to make regular appearances, first with the Jacksons and then as a solo artist from 1977. Michael helped his sister on the hit, "Centipede" (10/84 US 24).

Mel Gaynor 1959 UK drummer with Simple Minds from 1982.

Deaths

Fanny Brice 1951 US comedienne, dancer, and singer. Born 29th October, 1891.

John Cipollina 1989 US guitarist with Quicksilver Messanger Service. Born 24th August, 1943.

Hits of the Day

1943	"That Old Black Magic"	Glenn Miller US 1 week
1961	"Travellin' Man"	Ricky Nelson US 1 week
1965	"Help Me Ronda"	Beach Boys US 2 weeks
1972	"Beautiful Sunday"	Daniel Boone
1976	"Love Hangover"	Diana Ross US 2 weeks
1982	"House Of Fun"	Madness UK 2 weeks
1989	"The Look"	Roxette

Miscellany

1942 In the middle of a lovely Californian spring in a Los Angeles studio Bing Crosby is recording "White Christmas" which over the years is to prove the biggest selling single of all time.

30th

Birthdays

Benny Goodman 1909 US clarinetist, songwriter, and orchestra leader. He was playing with Art Kassel when he was 16. From 1925 to 1929 he made a name for himself with Ben Pollack, then played with Arnold Johnson, and Red Nichols, and became a sought-after session musician in New York. In 1934 he formed his own first band. Until 1953 Goodman had more than 160 hits in the American charts, 16 of which were No. 1. His most successful records (those which were at No. 1 for four weeks or more), were "Goody Goody" (2/36 US 1) and "The Glory Of Love" (2/36 US 1) – both were sung by Helen Ward – then "Goodnight My Love" (1/37 US 1), sung by Ella Fitzgerald, "Don't Be That Way" (3/38 US 1), "And The Angels Sing" (4/39 US 1), sung by Martha Tilton, "There'll be Some Changes Made" (3/41 US 1), sung by Louise Tobin and "Jersey Bounce" (3/42 US 1). In 1956 a film was made about the 'King of Swing', called *The Benny Goodman Story*. He died 13th June, 1986.

Lenny Davidson 1944 UK guitarist and bass player with Dave Clark Five.

Pete Way 1952 UK bass player with UFO.

Nicky 'Topper' Headon 1957 UK drummer with Clash, and from 1986 as a solo artist.

Marie Frederickson 1958 Swedish leadsinger and guitarist with the duo Roxette, who released their first album, PEARLS OF PASSION, in 1986. Marie was already a solo star in Sweden. In 1988 the album LOOK SHARP was released, four singles were extracted and all charted in the US: "The Look" (2/89 US 1; 4/89 UK 7), "Dressed For Success" (4/89 US 14), "Listen To Your Heart" (8/89 US 1), and "Dangerous" (12/89 US 2).

Robert Tepper 1958 US singer, keyboard player, guitarist and bassist. First hit was "No Easy Way Out" (1/86 US 22) from the film *Rocky IV*.

Deaths

Paul Desmond 1977 US jazz saxophonist and composer. Died of cancer. Born 25th November, 1924.

Carl Radle 1980 UK bassist. Died of a chronic kidney disease. Born 18th June, 1945.

Art Lund 1990 US singer and actor, born 1st April 1915.

31st

Birthdays

Clint Eastwood 1930 US actor, and director. He had his first major success as Rowdy Yates in the TV series *Rawhide*; he was featured from the beginning of the series in 1959 right through to the end in 1966. He became a world star in three spaghetti-westerns, produced in Italy in 1966. Clint turned singer in the film *Paint Your Wagon* (1969); he even hit the country charts with "Bar Room Buddies" (5/80 C&W 1), a duet with Merle Haggard, and "Beer's To You" (11/80 C&W 55), with Ray Charles, from the film *Any Which Way You Can*. He became Mayor of Carmel in California.

Peter Yarrow 1938 US singer, and songwriter with Peter, Paul & Mary, who were formed in 1961 and were successful from 1962 to 1970. Before that, Peter had been a folk singer. Hits for the trio: "Puff The Magic Dragon" (3/63 US 2), "Blowin' In The Wind" (6/63 US 2; 10/63 UK 13) and "Leaving On A Jetplane" (10/69 US 1; 1/70 UK 2). In 1971 the trio split up, and all three tried as solo artists. Peter even made recordings in German. In 1978 they joined up again, but the folk trend had petered out. Peter scored as a songwriter, composing "Torn Between Two Lovers" (11/76 US 1), a hit for Mary McGregor.

Augie Meyer 1940 US pianist with the Sir Douglas Quintet.

Junior Campbell 1947 UK guitarist, keyboard player, singer and songwriter. Real first name William. The group Dean Ford & The Gaylords became Marmalade in 1966. Hits: "Ob-La- Di, Ob-La-Da" (12/68 UK 1), "Reflections Of My Life" (12/69 UK 3; 3/70 US 10) and "Rainbow" (7/70 UK 3). From 1972, Campbell worked as a solo artist, charting with "Hallelujah Freedom" (10/72 UK 10).

John Bonham 1948 UK drummer and songwriter with Band Of Joy, and from July 1968, with the New Yardbirds, which shortly after became Led Zeppelin. John also played with Joe Cocker, Chris Farlowe, Wings, Roy Wood and Tim Rose. He died 25th September, 1980.

David Sterry 1954 Australian singer, guitarist and songwriter with Real Life. First hit, "Send Me An Angel" (1/84 US 29; 5/89 RE-US 26).

Corey Hart 1962 Canadian singer, keyboard player and songwriter. Hits: "Sunglasses At Night" (5/84 US 7), and "Never Surrender" (6/85 US 3).

Wendy Smith 1963 UK singer with the band Prefab Sprout formed in 1978.

Johnny Diesel 1966 US guitarist and songwriter. When Johnny was 11, he emigrated to Australia with his parents. In the summer of 1986 he formed the band Johnny Diesel & The Injectors in Perth. Their first single appeared in the spring of 1989.

Deaths

Billy Strayhorn 1967 US composer and pianist. Died of cancer. Born 29th November, 1915.

June

1st

Birthdays

Johnny Bond 1915 US country singer, songwriter and actor. Real name Cyrus Whitfield Bond. He managed to get into films with the help of Gene Autry and appeared in many B-westerns as a singing cowboy. He wrote books, like the 'Tex Ritter Story' and his autobiography 'Reflections'. Johnny really enjoyed singing about drunks and had his greatest hit with "10 Little Bottles" (2/65 C&W 2). Johnny died 12th June, 1978.

Nelson Riddle 1921 US trombonist, composer and orchestra leader. He played with Charlie Spivak and Tommy Dorsey in the 1940s. It was Nelson who brought Frank Sinatra back into circulation in the early 1950s when he was having problems. Nelson and his orchestra accompanied Nat King Cole, Ella Mae Morse and, in the 1980s, Linda Ronstadt among others. Riddle himself had a hit with his orchestra, "Lisbon Antigua" (12/55 US 1), which had been written in Portugal in 1937, and which he had polished up. In 1975 he received an Oscar for his musical score of the film *The Great Gatsby*. He died 6th October, 1985.

Marilyn Monroe 1926 US actress and singer. Real name Norma Jean Baker. She got her first film role in 1948. Her roles in *Asphalt Jungle*, and *All About Eve* (1950) launched her career; with *Niagara, Gentlemen Prefer Blondes*, and *How To Marry A Millionaire*, she became a superstar. She could play the naive sex-bomb type like nobody else could, and became the archetypal sex symbol. She often sang very affecting songs in her films, but only charted once with "River Of No Return" (7/54 US 30), surprising, because she sang very professionally. Further film highpoints were *River Of No Return*, and *There's No Business Like Showbusiness* (1954), *Seven Year Itch* (1955), *Bus Stop* (1956), *The Princess And The Showgirl* (1957), *Some Like It Hot* (1959), *Let's Make Love* (1960), and *The Misfits* (1961). Marilyn died 5th August, 1962.

Pat Boone 1934 US singer and film actor, great- great grandson of the legendary pioneer Daniel Boone. Real first names, Charles Eugene. Pat made his first records in 1953. From 1955 until 1962 he was the 'All-American Superstar'. Hits: "Ain't That A Shame" (7/55 US 1; 11/55 UK 7), "I'll Be Home" (2/56 US 4; 4/56 UK 1), "I Almost Lost My Mind" (6/56 US 1; 8/56 UK 14), "Don't Forbid Me" (12/56 US 1; 2/57 UK 2), "Love Letters In The Sand" (5/57 US 1; UK 2), "April Love" (10/57 US 1; 12/57 UK 7), "Moody River" (5/61 US 1; 7/61 UK 18), and "Speedy Gonzales" (6/62 US 6; UK 2). In 1954, before his career started, he married Shirley Foley, daughter of the well-known US country star, Red Foley. Debby, one of the four Boone daughters had a hit with "You Light Up My Life" (9/77 US 1 for 10 weeks!). The whole family tends to be present at recordings as the Boone Family. Pat, unlike Elvis Presley, always projected a clean and wholesome image: a complete antithesis to the spirit of rock n' roll as represented by such upcoming stars as Fats Domino, Chuck Berry or Little Richard. In 15 films Pat showed his countrymen how a decent American is supposed to live.

Linda Scott 1945 US singer, real name Linda Joy Sampson. 1961 was her year, "I've Told Every Little Star" (3/61 US 3; 5/61 UK 7) and "Don't Bet Money Honey" (7/61 US 9). After 1964 she disappeared from the charts.

Ron Wood 1947 UK guitarist, bassist, singer and songwriter with the Faces and Rolling Stones. He is in the vanguard of the very best British guitarists and is a much sought-after session musician, recording with Eric Clapton, The Band, and Bob Dylan, among others. He has also recorded his own solo albums.

Mike Levine 1949 Canadian keyboard player and songwriter with Triumph. The members of this trio started playing together for the first time in 1975. In 1978 they went on their first tour of the USA.

Charlene 1950 US singer. Born Charlene D'Angelo, later surname Duncan. In 1977 she cut a record which was to become her biggest hit five years later, "I've Never Been To Me" (9/77 US 97; 3/82 RE-US 3; 5/82 UK 1).

Graham Russell 1950 Australian singer and songwriter for the group Air Supply formed in 1976, who were internationally successful from 1980. The biggest of their eight Top Ten hits in the USA were "All Out Of Love" (6/80 US 2; 9/80 UK 11), "The One That You Love" (5/81 US 1) and "Making Love Out Of Nothing At All" (7/83 US 2).

Alan Wilder 1959 UK pianist, singer and songwriter. He started with the Hitmen and then joined Depeche Mode in January 1982 as a replacement for Vince Clarke.

Simon Gallup 1960 UK bass player, who replaced Michael Dempsey with Cure in January 1980.

Mike Joyce 1963 UK drummer with the group Smiths formed in 1982, and with Adult Net from 1985.

Jason Donovan 1968 Australian TV actor and singer. He was in a TV series at age 11. His international career began when he played the partner of Kylie Minogue in *Neighbours*. When this series was shown on British TV, Stock Aitken Waterman made the two main actors into 'teen idols'. Hits: "Nothing Can Divide Us" (9/88 UK 5) in a duet with Kylie, "Especially For You" (12/88 UK 1), and "Too Many Broken Hearts" (3/89 UK 1), "Sealed With A Kiss" (6/89 UK 1), "Everyday (Love You More)" (9/89 UK 2) and "When You Come Back To Me" (12/89 UK 2).

Deaths

Sonny Boy Williamson 1948 US harmonica player. Was murdered in Chicago. Born 30th March, 1914.

David Ruffin US vocalist. Born 18th January, 1991.

Nate Nelson 1984 US singer with the Flamingos. Born 10th April, 1932.

Hits of the Day

1959 "Battle Of New Orleans" Johnny Horton US 6 weeks
1961 "Surrender" Elvis Presley UK 4 weeks
1963 "It's My Party" Lesley Gore US 2 weeks
1968 "Mrs. Robinson" Simon & Garfunkel US 3 weeks

Miscellany

1967 The album SGT. PEPPER'S LONELY HEARTS CLUB BAND is released, which is regarded as a milestone in pop history. The record went gold on the same day. John Lennon said of this album, "It was a highpoint."

2nd

Birthdays

Sammy Turner 1932 US singer. Real name Samuel Black. He started as leadsinger with the Twisters, and then was successful as a soloist with an old English folk-song from 1750, "Lavender Blue" (6/59 US 3). That was followed by "Always" (11/59 US 19; UK 26). Then he made records for different record companies, like Motown, 20th Century Fox, and Verve, which however, were unsuccessful.

Otis Williams 1936 US leadsinger with Charms, who made their first records in 1953. Hits: "Hearts Of Stone" (11/54 US 15) and "Ivory Tower" (3/56 US 11). Later Otis became a country singer.

Jimmy Jones 1937 US singer. He started as a tap-dancer in the 1950s, became a member of the R&B group Spark Of Rhythm in 1955, and in 1956 formed his own band, Savoys, whom he later renamed Pretenders. Not until he became a soloist, did success arrive, with "Handy Man" (12/59 US 2; 3/60 UK 3), and "Good Timin'" (4/60 US 3; 6/60 UK 1).

Charles Miller 1939 US saxophonist, flautist, and singer with War, and as a session musician.

William Guest 1941 US singer with Gladys Knight & The Pips.

Charlie Watts 1941 UK drummer who began his career in 1961 with Blues Incorporated, before becoming a founder member of the Rolling Stones in 1962.

Marvin Hamlisch 1944 US pianist, and composer of numerous soundtracks. Hit: "The Entertainer" (3/74 UK 25; US 3) from the film *The Sting*. Marvin got an Oscar and a Grammy in 1973 for "The Way We Were" from the film of the same name.

Antone 'Chubby' Tavares 1947 US leadsinger with the group Tavares, consisting of five brothers, and who appeared as Chubby & The Tavares from 1964 to 1969. Hits: "It Only Takes A Minute" (7/75 US 10; 5/86 UK 46), "Heaven Must Be Missing An Angel" (6/76 US 15; UK 4), "Don't Take Away The Music" (10/76 UK 4; 12/76 US 34) and "Whodunit" (3/77 US 22; UK 4).

Michael Steele 1959 US bass player, singer and songwriter for the Bangles.

Tony Hadley 1960 UK singer. In 1976 he was a founder-member of the Makers, which became Spandau Ballet in 1979. The band has been successful since 1980.

Hits: "To Cut A Long Story Short" (11/80 UK 5), "Chant No. 1 (I Don't Need This Pressure On)" (7/81 UK 3), "True" (4/83 UK 1; 8/83 US 4), "Gold" (8/83 UK 2; 12/83 US 29), "Only When You Leave" (6/84 UK 3; US 34), "Fight For Ourselves" (7/86 UK 15) and "Through The Barricades" (11/86 UK 6).

David White 1965 UK guitarist and songwriter with Brother Beyond.

Deaths

Sammy Kaye 1987 US trumpeter, songwriter, and bandleader. Born 13th March, 1910.

Hits of the Day

1956	"Moonglow And Theme From Picnic" Morris Stoloff US 3 weeks
1962	"I Can't Stop Loving You" Ray Charles US 5 weeks
1966	"Strangers In The Night" Frank Sinatra UK 3 weeks
1973	"My Love" Paul McCartney & Wings US 4 weeks
1979	"Hot Stuff" Donna Summer US 1 week
1984	"Wake Me Up Before You Go Go" Wham! UK 2 weeks
1990	"World In Motion" England Fc/New Order UK 2 weeks

3rd

Birthdays

Josephine Baker 1906 French dancer, singer, and film actress of American origin. In 1925 she had a breakthrough in Paris with the dance troupe Black Birds. She was dressed in a banana leaf skirt! She celebrated one success after the other in the Folies Bergeres. Josephine was committed to equality among races and adopted numerous children of different nationalities. She died 12th April, 1975.

Curtis Mayfield 1942 US singer and songwriter. He started in 1957 as a singer with the Roosters, who changed their name to Impressions in 1958. In those early days, Jerry Butler was the leadsinger with the band. He started a solo career in 1958, when Curtis took over as lead singer. Hits: "It's All Right" (9/63 US 4) and "Amen" (11/64 US 7). Curtis left the Impressions in 1970 and carried on as a solo artist. Hits: "Freddie's Dead" (8/72 US 4) and "Superfly" (11/72 US 8). He is an excellent songwriter and has written for and produced many other artists.

Michael Clarke 1943 US drummer with the Byrds, the Flying Burrito Brothers, Firefall, and as a session musician on records by Sean Phillips, Chris Hillman, Barry McGuire and Roger McGuinn.

Anita Harris 1944 UK singer. Greatest hit: "Just Lovin' You" (6/67 UK 6).

Ian Hunter 1946 UK singer, guitarist, and songwriter. The *Melody Maker* carried an ad for a singer for the group Silence. Ian answered it. Shortly afterwards, the band's name was changed to Mott The Hoople, – that was 1969. But success did not arrive until David Bowie helped them. Hits: "All The Young Dudes" (8/72 UK 3; US 37) and "Roll Away The Stone" (11/73 UK 8). The group split up at the end of 1974. In the next few years, Ian sometimes went solo, scoring with "Once Bitten Twice Shy" (5/75 UK 14), and sometimes worked with Mick Ronson as the Hunter-Ronson Band. Ian is also on records by Ellen Foley and Mountain.

Mickey Finn 1947 UK guitarist and percussionist. In October 1969 he joined T. Rex, replacing Steve Peregrine Took, and formed the nucleus of the band with Marc Bolan. When T. Rex broke through, Bolan dominated the band.

Florian Pilkington-Miksa 1950 UK drummer with Curved Air.

Suzi Quatro 1950 US singer, bass player and songwriter who found her fortune in the UK. Hits, "Can The Can" (5/73 UK 1), "48 Crash" (7/73 UK 3), "Devil Gate Drive" (2/74 UK 1), and "If You Can't Give Me Love" (3/78 UK 4). In her home country she had only one hit in a duet with Smokie leadsinger Chris Norman, "Stumblin' In" (11/78 UK 41; 1/79 US 4).

Deniece Williams 1951 US singer and songwriter. She was a member of Wonderlove, Stevie Wonder's back-up group from 1972 to 1975. After that she started a solo career. Hits: "Free" (12/76 US 25; 4/77 UK 1) and "Let's Hear It For The Boy" (4/84 US 1; UK 2). She was also successful, with Johnny Mathis, on "Too Much, Too Little, Too Late" (4/78 US 1; UK 3).

Billy Powell 1952 US pianist with Lynyrd Skynyrd, 38 Special, Rossington-Collins Band and Allen Collins.

Dan Hill 1954 Canadian singer and songwriter. Hits: "Sometimes When We Touch" (11/77 US 3; 2/78 UK 13) and "Can't We Try" (5/87 US 6).

Deaths

Mississippi Fred McDowell 1972 US blues musician. Born 12th January, 1904.

Ozzie Nelson 1975 US singer, multi- instrumentalist, bandleader, songwriter and TV star. Born 20th March, 1906.

Hits of the Day

1950 "Hoop Dee-Doo" Perry Como with Fontane Sisters US 2 weeks

1957 "Love Letters In The Sand" Pat Boone US 7 weeks

1967 "Respect" Aretha Franklin US 2 weeks

1972 "I'll Take You There" Staple Singers US 1 week

1978 "Too Much, Too Little, Too Late" Johnny Mathis & Deniece Williams US 1 week

1985 "You Can Win If You Want" Modern Talking

1989 "Rock On" Michael Damian US 1 week

4th

Birthdays

Oliver Nelson 1932 US saxophonist, flautist, composer and bandleader. He made records with Louis Jordan, Count Basie, Quincy Jones and Wes Montgomery. Oliver died 27th October, 1975.

Freddy Fender 1937 US singer and songwriter of Mexican origin. Real name Baldemar Huerta. He recorded songs in Spanish with a rockabilly flavour for small record labels from 1956 to 1959. He spent time from 1960 to 1963 in the State Prison of Louisiana for a drug offence. From 1963 to 1968 he released records on a small label in New Orleans. Success came when Freddy sang a song partly in English and partly in Spanish, "Before The Next Teardrop Falls" (2/75 US 1). The following record was a million seller, "Wasted Days And Wasted Nights" (6/75 US 8). After 1976 he disappeared into obscurity.

Cliff Bennett 1940 UK singer with Cliff Bennett & The Rebel Rousers formed in 1959. For the next nine years he was constantly on tour in Britain and West Germany. Frank Allen was a member of his group part of the time, who was later with the Searchers, Roy Young, Nicky Hopkins and Chas Hodges. In 1961 he took on two horn players in his band and was produced by Joe Meek. With his help, Cliff released four records, but all of them flopped. However, groups with brass sections did not become established until the Mersey sound was on the wane. Hits: "One Way Love" (10/64 UK 9) and "Got To Get You Into My Life" (8/66 UK 6). After the band had split up, he formed Toe Fat in 1969, which included Ken Hensley and Lee Kerslake, who would shortly form Uriah Heep. In 1971 Cliff formed Cliff Bennett's Rebellion, and Shanghai in 1974.

Roger Ball 1944 UK saxophonist, pianist and songwriter for Mogul Trash, Vinegar Joe, Mike McGear and Kiki Dee, before becoming a founder member of the Average White Band in 1972.

Gordon Waller 1945 UK singer, and guitarist with the duo Peter & Gordon formed in 1964. Peter Asher's sister Jane was Paul McCartney's girlfriend, and Paul gave Peter & Gordon "A World Without Love" (3/64 UK 1; 5/64 US 1). Other hits included "I Go To Pieces" (1/65 US 9), "True Love Ways" (4/65 UK 2; US 14) and "Lady Godiva" (9/66 UK 16; US 6). One of their best songs was "Woman" (2/66 UK 28; US 14); however it is possible, that it might have become their biggest hit, if it had been known that Paul McCartney wrote it under the pseudonym Webb. In 1968 the duo split up. Solo attempts by Waller were unsuccessful.

Peter Van Hooke 1950 UK drummer, who was a session musician on records by Van Morrison, Marshall Hain, Chas Jankel, Sheena Easton, Sally Oldfield, and many others, before becoming a member of Mike & The Mechanics in 1985.

Jimmy McCulloch 1952 UK guitarist. He started with the Scottish group One In A Million in the mid-1960s. He came to popularity as a member of Thunderclap Newman, which was followed by spells with John Mayall, Stone The Crows, Blue and, finally, Wings in 1974. He stayed with them until November 1977, joined the Small Faces briefly, played on records by Nick Gilder, Roy Harper, and Roger Daltrey, and had just formed his own band Dukes, when he died in mysterious circumstances on 27th September, 1979.

Colin McKee 1961 UK bass player with Rosetta Stone.

El DeBarge 1962 US leadsinger, and keyboard player with the family group DeBarge, consisting of five members, and who have been successful since 1983. Records appeared under his name as El DeBarge with DeBarge, or as DeBarge only. Hits: "Rhythm Of The Night" (2/85 US 3; 4/85 UK 4), "Who's Holding Donna Now" (6/85 US 6) and "Who's Johnny" (4/86 US 3) from the film *Short Circuit*.

Deaths

Stiv Bators 1991 US singer and guitarist

Hits of the Day

1969 "Dizzy" Tommy Roe UK 1 week
1983 "Every Breath You Take" Police UK 4 weeks

5th

Birthdays

Bill Hayes 1926 US actor, and singer. He was the star of several TV series, including *Your Shows Of Shows*, and *Days Of Our Lives*. Hit: "The Ballad Of Davy Crockett" (2/55 US 1; 1/56 UK 2). The title came from a Walt Disney series and was sung by Fess Parker in the original. However, as the latter had not released it on a record, Bill recorded it and had a hit. The original version by Fess was released later.

Floyd Butler 1941 US singer with the Friends Of Distinction. Hits see 4th November under Harry Elston.

Don Reid 1945 US country leadsinger. In 1960 he joined the gospel trio Kingsmen formed in 1955. In order to avoid being confused with the pop group of the same name, they renamed themselves Statler Brothers in 1963. They took the name from a box of tissues which happened to be lying on the table, so they just might have called themselves Kleenex Brothers! They had their first big hit with the title "Flowers On The Wall" (9/65 C&W 2; 11/65 US 4; 2/66 UK 38). In the meantime they are still in the country charts, having amassed over 60 hits.

Freddy Stone 1946 US guitarist. Real name Fred Stewart. He formed the nucleus of Sly & The Family Stone with brother Sly.

Tom Evans 1947 UK bass player and songwriter with Badfinger. In the mid-1960s three of the four musicians, who first called themselves Iveys in 1968, then became Badfinger in December 1969, had played in David Garrick's backing-up group. Tom Evans and Peter Ham had sent a demo tape to the newly formed Beatles company 'Apple'. Paul McCartney liked the tape so much that he offered them a contract. For hits, see 27th April, under Peter Ham. After Ham's suicide in April 1975, the group split up, but reformed again in 1978 for a few years. Tom committed suicide on 18th November, 1983.

Laurie Anderson 1950 US violinist, singer, songwriter and performance artist. Among Laurie's large creative output, music takes up only a small percentage. She must have been rather surprised herself when her record "O Superman" (10/81 UK 2) became a hit. The record was 8 minutes long, and was voted by British disco-kids as the record you have to play if you want to clear the dancefloor.

Ronnie Dyson 1950 US singer belonging to the group of many young musicians who came into show business via the musical *Hair*. Hit: "(If You Let Me Make Love To You Then) Why Can't I Touch You" (6/70 US 8). Ronnie was successful in the R&B charts until 1983. He died on November 11th, 1990.

Richard Butler 1956 UK singer and songwriter with the group Psychodelic Furs formed in 1977. Hits: "Pretty In Pink" (8/86 UK 18) and "Heartbreak Beat" (3/87 US 26).

Keith Marshall 1956 UK singer, lead guitarist and songwriter with Hello. Hits: "Tell Him" (11/74 UK 6) and "New York Groove" (10/75 UK 9). Keith was a solo artist in the 1980s. His biggest hit was "Only Crying" (4/81 UK 12).

Deaths

Sleepy John Estes 1977 US blues guitarist and singer. Born 25th January, 1899.

Hits of the Day

1954 "Little Things Mean A Lot" Kitty Allen US 9 weeks
1961 "Runnin' Scared" Roy Orbison US 1 week
1976 "No Charge" J. J. Barrie UK 1 week

6th

Birthdays

James Gideon Tanner 1885 US country fiddler, bandleader, and comedian with Gid Tanner & His Skillet Lickers. Million seller: "Down Yonder" (8/34 US 10). He died 13th May, 1960.

Gary U. S. Bonds 1939 US singer and songwriter. Real surname Anderson. Hits: "New Orleans" (10/60 US 6; 1/61 UK 16), "Quarter To Three" (5/61 US 1; 7/61 UK 7) and "School Is Out" (7/61 US 5). After 1962, obscurity seemed to beckon, but in the early 1980s Bruce Springsteen collaborated with him on an album. Hit: "This Little Girl" (4/81 US 11).

Joe Stampley 1943 US country singer and songwriter. He made his first records in 1957 and became leadsinger with the Uniques in the mid-1960s. From 1971 he was a solo artist, who appeared mainly in the country charts, where he hit the No. 1 spot four times. His biggest pop hit was "Soul Song" (11/72 C&W 1; 1/73 US 37).

Peter Albin 1944 US bass player, singer and songwriter with Big Brother & The Holding Company.

Edgar Froese 1944 German synthesizer player, guitarist and songwriter with Tangerine Dream from Berlin. He also made solo records.

Terry Williams 1947 US singer with the New Christy Minstrels, First Edition and Kenny Rogers.

Shorty Beck 1948 Dutch drummer with Shocking Blue. Real name Cornelies van der Beek.

Richard Sinclair 1948 UK bass player with Caravan, Hatfield & The North and Camel.

Dee C. Lee 1961 UK singer and songwriter. She started as a backing vocalist with Wham! and Style Council. From 1985 she was a solo artist. First hit: "See The Day" (11/85 UK 3).

Deaths

Stan Getz 1991 US saxophonist best known with the Dave Brubeck Quartet. Born 2nd February 1927.

Hits of the Day

1942 "Somebody Else Is Taking My Place" Benny Goodman US 3 weeks

---

1964 "Chapel Of Love" Dixie Cups US 3 weeks
1970 "Yellow River" Christie UK 1 week
1983 "Juliet" Robin Gibb
1987 "You Keep Me Hanging On" Kim Wilde US 1 week
1987 "I Wanna Dance With Somebody (Who Loves Me)" Whitney Houston UK 2 weeks

7th

Birthdays

Dolores Gray 1924 US singer, dancer, and actress, who began her career in Rudy Vallee's radio shows. In 1945 she sang with Wayne King's band. She started making records in the early 1950s. Her biggest hit was "Shrimp Boats" (11/51 US 16).

Tom Jones 1940 UK singer. Real name Thomas Jones Woodward. Just like Dean Martin, Tom Jones too was a coalminer. In his spare time he performed as Tommy Scott, and formed a trio called Senators in 1963. After moving from Wales to London, he started a solo career in 1964. Hits: "It's Not Unusual" (2/65 UK 1; 4/65 US 10; 5/87 RE-UK 17), "Green Green Grass Of Home" (11/66 UK 1; US 11), "I'll Never Fall In Love Again" (7/67 UK 2; 9/67 US 49; 7/69 RE-US 6), "Im Coming Home" (11/67 UK 2), "Delilah" (2/68 UK 2; US 15), "Help Yourself" (7/68 UK 5; US 35), and "She's A Lady" (1/71 UK 13; US 2). Having worked the cabaret circuit for several years in Las Vegas, he suddenly returned to the charts with "A Boy From Nowhere" (4/87 UK 2) and, with Art Of Noise, "Kiss" (10/88 UK 5; 12/88 US 31), a composition by Prince.

Miguel Rios 1944 Spanish singer who recorded the hit, "A Song Of Joy" (6/70 US 14; UK 16) with his uncle Waldo de los Rios' orchestra.

Clarence White 1944 US guitarist and singer with the Byrds, Everly Brothers, Flying Burritos, Rick Nelson, Gene Clark, Randy Newman, Maria Muldaur, Joe Cocker, Rita Coolidge and Arlo Guthrie. He died 14th June, 1973.

Mickey Jones 1946 UK lead guitarist and singer with Man, and also as a session musician for Peter Frampton.

Joey Scarbury 1955 US singer and pianist, who made his first record aged 13. After that, he was on productions by hitmaker Mike Post, and as a background singer with Loretta Lynn. When Mike Post was looking for a singer for the theme of the TV series *Greatest American Hero*, he remembered Joey and made the record with him. It became, whether you believe it or not, his only hit, "Theme From Greatest American Hero (Believe It Or Not)" (5/81 US 2).

Paddy McAloon 1957 UK singer, and guitarist with the group Prefab Sprout formed in 1978. The name is derived from Pepper Sprout from the Nancy Sinatra hit "Jackson", which Paddy had misunderstood. In 1984 they got their first recording contract having had one success on an Independent-label the previous year. Hits: "When Love Breaks Down" (11/85 UK 25) and "The King Of Rock n' Roll" (4/88 UK 7).

Prince 1958 US singer, songwriter, film actor, multi-instrumentalist and producer. Real name Prince Rogers Nelson. In 1977 he secured his first recording contract and has been successful since 1979. Hits: "I Wanna Be Your Lover" (11/79 US 11; 1/80 UK 41), "1999" (10/82 US 44; 1/83 UK 25; 6/83 RE-US 12; 1/85 RE-UK 2), "Little Red Corvette" (2/83 US 6; 4/83 UK 54; 11/83 RE-UK 66; and in 1/85 as the B-side of "1999" RE-UK 2), "When Doves Cry" (6/84 US 1; UK 4), "Let's Go Crazy" (8/84 US 1; 2/85 UK 7), "Purple Rain" (9/84 UK 8; US 2), "Raspberry Beret" (5/85 US 2; 7/85 UK 25), "Kiss" (2/86 US 1; UK 6), "Sign Of The Times" (3/87 US 3; UK 10), "U Got The Look" (8/87 US 2; UK 11), "Alphabet St." (4/88 US 8; UK 9), and "Batman" (6/89 US 1; UK 2).

Deaths

Meade Lux Lewis 1964 US blues and boogie pianist and songwriter. He died after a car accident. Born 4th September, 1905.

Bobby Hackett 1976 US trumpeter. Born 31st January, 1915.

Hits of the Day

1941	"My Sister And I" Jimmy Dorsey US 2 weeks
1947	"Mam'selle" Art Lund US 2 weeks
1952	"Here In My Heart" Al Martino US 3 weeks
1957	"Yes Tonight, Josephine" Johnnie Ray UK 3 weeks

1975	"Whispering Grass" Windsor Davies & Don Estelle UK 3 weeks
1975	"Thank God I'm A Country Boy" John Denver US 1 week
1982	"Ebony & Ivory" Paul McCartney & Stevie Wonder
1986	"Spirit In The Sky" Doctor & The Medics UK 3 weeks
1986	"Live To Tell" Madonna US 1 week

8th

Birthdays

Nancy Sinatra 1940 US singer and actress, daughter of 'Ol' Blues Eyes'. She was successful between 1965 and 1971, sometimes with her father, sometimes with Lee Hazlewood and sometimes solo. Hits: solo, "These Boots Are Made For Walking" (1/66 US & UK 1), "How Does That Grab You Darlin'?" (4/66 US 7; UK 19) and "Sugar Town" (11/66 US 5; 1/67 UK 8); with Frank, "Somethin' Stupid" (3/67 US & UK 1); and with Lee Hazlewood "Jackson" (6/67 US 14), and "Did You Ever" (8/71 UK 2). She was married to colleague Tommy Sands from 1960 until 1965. She made her first TV appearance in 1959 with her father and Elvis Presley, with whom she also appeared in the film *Speedway*.

Chuck Negron 1942 US singer with Three Dog Night.

Boz Scaggs 1944 US singer, guitarist, and songwriter. Real first names William Royce. He started out, with and without Steve Miller, in bands like Markmen (1959), Ardells (1961), Fabulous Knighttrains (1961), and Wigs (1963). In 1964 Boz went to Europe and recorded his first solo album in Sweden, which only appeared there. He travelled until 1967, then returned to the States and at the end of September 1967 he became a member of the Steve Miller Band. At the end of 1968, after two albums, he left Steve, on account of "musical differences of opinion", and made a superb solo album with excellent studio musicians, like Duane Allman, which however, was unsuccessful. But he did have one success in the early 1970s. Hit and million seller "Lowdown" (7/76 US 3).

Mick Box 1947 UK lead guitarist with Uriah Heep.

Julie Driscoll 1947 UK singer. She was still working for the Yardbirds' fan club when she joined Steampacket, which included musicians like Rod Stewart, Long John Baldry and Brian Auger. When Brian formed his own band she joined it. Hit for Julie Driscoll, Brian Auger & The Trinity, "This Wheel's On Fire" (4/68 UK 5). After Julie left the band in 1969, she married the jazz-rock pianist Keith Tippett, and sang with his group Centipede.

Jeff Rich 1953 UK drummer. He worked as a session musician from 1974 on 2 albums by Stretch, Jackie Lynton, Charles Musclewhite and Judie Tzuke. He has been a member of Status Quo since mid-1986.

Bonnie Tyler 1953 UK singer and songwriter. Real name Gaynor Hopkins. She won a youth contest at age 17. After that she became popular on the pub and club scene in her native Wales. In 1976 she had to have an operation on her larynx, after which she had the voice which became her trademark: the female Rod Stewart. Hits: "Lost In France" (10/76 UK 9), "It's A Heartache" (12/77 UK 4; 3/78 US 3), "Total Eclipse Of The Heart" (2/83 UK 1; 7/83 US 1), "Holding Out For A Hero" (2/84 US 34; 8/85 UK 2) and "A Rockin' Good Way" (1/84 UK 5), with Shakin' Stevens.

Russel Christian 1956 UK saxophonist and singer with the Christians.

Mick Hucknall 1960 UK singer and songwriter. Between 1979 and 1983 he released several unsuccessful albums in the UK with his group Frantic Elevators, and then formed Simply Red in 1984. With them came success. Hits: "Money's Too Tight (To Mention)" (6/85 UK 13; 7/86 US 28), "Holding Back The Years" (11/85 UK 51; 4/86 US 1; RE-UK 2), "The Right Thing" (2/87 UK 11; US 27), "Ev'ry Time We Say Goodbye" (11/87 UK 11), "It's Only Love" (1/89 UK 13), and "If You Don't Know Me By Now" (4/89 UK 2; US 1).

Nick Rhodes 1962 UK keyboard player, guitarist and songwriter with Duran Duran and Arcadia.

Robert Pilatus 1965 Singer, son of a US soldier and German mother, born in New York, grew up in Munich. After working as a model, dancer, and backing singer, he appeared together with colleague Fab Morvan as Empire Bizarre in 1987, and as Milli Vanilli in 1988. Hits, see under Fab, 14th April.

Doris May Pearson 1966 UK singer with the sibling group 5 Star.

Neil Mitchell 1968 UK pianist with Wet Wet Wet.

Deaths

Laverne Andrews 1967 US singer with the Andrews Sisters. Died of cancer. Born 6th July, 1915.

Jimmy Rushing 1972 US singer. Died after a short illness. Born 16th August, 1903.

Hits of the Day

1967 "A Whiter Shade Of Pale" – Procol Harum UK 6 weeks

1974 "Band On The Run" – Paul McCartney & Wings – US 1 week

1985 "Everybody Wants To Rule The World" – Tears For Fears US 2 weeks

---

Miscellany

1969 After meeting with Mick Jagger and Keith Richard, Brian Jones announces he is leaving the Rolling Stones. "I want to play my kind of music, and the Stones' music is no longer my kind of music."

9th

Birthdays

Cole Porter 1891 US composer and lyricist. He was one of the most important US musical and song writers. His songs became evergreens. Beside Irving Berlin he was the only one who wrote both music and lyrics. At first, though, things didn't seem to be going right for young Cole. His first compositions for Broadway musicals in 1915 and 1916 were unsuccessful. He went to Paris, joined the Foreign Legion, and later became a French artillery officer. After the war, he married and remained in Europe during the 1920s. He composed periodically, until finally returning to the USA in 1928, he wrote the hit "Let's Do It" for the Broadway show, *Paris*. With that his career took off. Among his best known musicals are *Around The World In 80 Days* (1946), *Kiss Me Kate* (1948), *Can Can* (1953), *Silk Stockings* (1955). He also wrote music for films like *High Society* (1956). Among his best known compositions are "Begin The Beguine", "Don't Fence Me In", "Night And Day", "I've Got You Under My Skin", and "True Love". Once he charted himself with "You're The Top" (1/35 US 10) from the musical, *Anything Goes*; for this, he sang and accompanied himself on the piano. In 1937 Cole had a serious riding accident: his horse fell on top of him and smashed both his legs. He had to undergo countless operations, still finally lost his right leg in 1958. The film *Night & Day* (1946) was about the life of Cole Porter, with Cole portrayed by Cary Grant. Cole died 15th October, 1964.

Les Paul 1916 US guitarist, real name Lester William Pollfuss. He began his career in the 1930s as a country musician and comedian, under the names Hot Rod Red and Rhubarb Red. Between 1939 and 1940 he played with Fred Waring. After that, he worked as a session musician for several years and with his own trio, recording with Bing Crosby and his own hit "It's Been A Long Long Time" (10/45 US 1). From 1948 he was a solo artist and used double-tracking for the first time. His biggest success though was with his wife Mary Ford between 1950 and 1961. Biggest hits: "Mockin' Bird Hill" (2/51 US 2), "How High The Moon" (3/51 US 1), "The World Is Waiting For The Sunrise" (8/51 US 2) and "Vaya Con Dios" (6/53 US 1; 11/53 UK 7), all million sellers. He designed the legendary Les Paul guitar for the Gibson company.

Johnny Ace 1929 US singer, pianist, and songwriter. Real name John Marshall Alexander Jr. He played with B. B. King's band, and then, with Earl Forrest and Bobby Bland he formed the Beale Streeters. After that he appeared as a solo artist. Hits: "My Song" (8/52 R&B 1), "The Clock" (7/53 R&B 1), and "Pledging My Love" (1/55 R&B 1; US 17). On Christmas Eve of 1954 he appeared in Houston. Backstage he played Russian Roulette for a laugh to impress his entourage, the gun went off and he died a day later. He did not live to see his only pop hit.

Jackie Wilson 1934 US singer and songwriter. He began his career with a gospel group, became an amateur boxer and appeared as a solo singer. In 1953 he joined Billy Ward & His Dominoes as a replacement for Clyde McPhatter. Hit with Jackie as a leadsinger, "You Can't Keep A Good Man Down" (9/53 R&B 8). In 1957 he went solo again. Hits: "Reet Petite" (11/57 UK 6; 11/86 RE-UK 1), "Lonely Teardrops" (11/58 US 7), "Night" (3/60 US 4), "Baby, Work Out" (3/63 US 5), "(Your Love Keeps Lifting Me) Higher And Higher" (8/67 US 6; 5/69 UK 11; 7/87 RE-UK 15) and "I Get The Sweetest Feeling" (7/68 US 34; 7/72 UK 9; 5/75 RE-UK 25; 2/87 RE-UK 3). After a heart attack on 29th September, 1975, he fell into a coma from which he never awoke. He died, after lying in hospital for years, on 21st January, 1984. Many great soul and pop stars see him as their idol. His god-daughter is Jody Watley.

Billy Hatton 1941 UK bass player with Fourmost.

Jon Lord 1941 UK pianist and songwriter. When he was 9 he started piano lessons. His first attempts as a professional musician were with the Bill Ashton combo, the National Youth Orchestra, Red Bludd's Bluesmusicians, which became first the Art Woods Combo and, finally, the Artwoods in 1963. They released several unsuccessful singles and albums up to 1967. For their last attempt they changed their name to St. Valentine's Day Massacre. After that Jon worked as a session musician with Nick Simper for the Flowerpot Men. Together, they formed the group Roundabout in February 1968 with several other musicians. This was to be the nucleus of Deep Purple, formed a month later. He stayed with Deep Purple until Spring of 1976, then he formed the trio Paice, Ashton, & Lord, until September 1977. In 1978 he joined Whitesnake and reformed Deep Purple for a reunion. In between, Jon kept on releasing solo records.

Stuart Edwards 1946 UK lead guitarist with Edison Lighthouse.

Mitch Mitchell 1947 UK drummer. Real first name John. He played with the session band on the TV programme *Ready, Steady, Go!*, and with Georgie Fame's Blue Flames, before joining the Jimi Hendrix Experience in September 1966. After the trio split up, he played with Ramatam, Free Creek, Randy California, Roger Chapman and Dave Morrison.

Francis Monkman 1949 UK synthesizer player with Curved Air, Camel, Sky, Phil Manzanera, and as a session musician. Also made solo albums.

Trevor Bolder 1950 UK bass player with the Spiders From Mars, David Bowie's backing-up band, then with Uriah Heep. He can be heard on records by Dana Gillespie and Wishbone Ash.

Terry Uttley 1951 UK bass player with Smokie. In 1983/84 he played on records by Agnetha and Verity.

Peter Byrne 1954 UK singer, who joined up with Rob Fisher in the early 1980s and formed Nakes Eyes. Hits: "Always Something There To Remind Me" (3/83 US 8) and "Promises Promises" (7/83 US 11). After further hits failed to materialise, the pair split up and Rob Fisher formed Climie Fisher with Simon Climie.

Hits of the Day

1958	"Purple People Eater" Sheb Wooley US 6 weeks
1979	"Love You Inside Out" Bee Gees US 1 week
1984	"Time After Time" Cyndi Lauper US 2 weeks
1990	"Sacrifice/Healing Hands" Elton John UK 5 weeks

10th

Birthdays

Frederic Loewe 1904 US musicals composer, born in Vienna as Friedrich Lowe, and lived in the US from 1924. He started to work with lyricist Alan Jay Lerner in the early 1940s. Among his best-known achievements were *Paint Your Wagon* (1951), *My Fair Lady* (1956), *Camelot* (1960) and the film *Gigi* (1958). Lowe died 15th February, 1988.

Howlin' Wolf 1910 US blues musician, real name Chester Burnett. He was considered to be one of the most original blues musicians. In the 1930s he played with Robert Johnson and Sonny Boy Williamson, while working as a share cropper. In 1947 he formed his own trio with Junior Parker and the 13-year old James Cotton; he had another sideline: he worked as a disc jockey at a radio station in Memphis. From 1948 he recorded for the Sun label, which was still run by Chess at that time. Hits: "How Many More Years" (12/51 R&B 4), "Smokestack Lightning" (3/56 R&B 8) and "I Ask For Water" (11/56 R&B 8). Many of his compositions were later reworked by rock artists. Chester died of cancer on 10th January, 1976.

Judy Garland 1922 US film actress and singer. Real name Frances Gumm. She started out as a child star and played her first part in *Broadway Melody Of 1938* (1937), singing a birthday greeting for Clark Gable. In the film *Wizard Of Oz* (1939), which made her world famous, she sang "Somewhere Over The Rainbow" (9/39 US 5). After that, Judy was regularly in the charts until the mid 1950s. Hits: "I'm Nobody's Baby" (7/40 US 3), "For Me And My Gal" (1/42 US 3) with Gene Kelly, "The Trolley Song" (11/44 US 5), and "Yah-Ta-Ta Yah-Ta-Ta (Talk, Talk, Talk)" (5/45 US 5) with Bing Crosby. In the early 1950s she was an international star onstage in London and New York. After suffering personal difficulties for some years, she returned to the film business in 1954 with the film, *A Star Is Born*, and stayed until 1963. Liza Minelli is her daughter. Judy died in London on 22nd June, 1969.

Don Costa 1925 US composer, conductor, arranger and producer. In the 1940s/50s he wrote arrangements for Vic Damone, Sarah Vaughan, Vaughn Monroe, Eydie Gorme, Steve Lawrence, and made a star out of 16-year old Paul Anka. Don had the hit "Never On Sunday" (8/60 US 19; 10/60 UK 27) with his orchestra. After that, he formed his own production company which looked after Little Anthony & The Imperials and Trini Lopez. Frank Sinatra was also accompanied for several years by Don Costa and his orchestra. Don has worked with Barbra Streisand, Perry Como, Dean Martin and the Osmonds. He died 19th January, 1983.

Shirley Alston 1941 US leadsinger and songwriter for the Shirelles. Real surname Owens. During her schooldays she formed the group Poquellos, which developed into the Shirelles, who made their first records in 1958. Hits: "Will You Love Me Tomorrow" (11/60 US 1; 2/61 UK 4), "Dedicated To The One I Love" (1/61 US 3), "Soldier Boy" (3/62 US 1; 5/62 UK 23) and "Foolish Little Girl" (3/63 US 4; UK 38). In 1975 Shirley left the group to start a solo career. Nothing came of it.

Janet Vogel 1942 US singer with the Skyliners. Biggest hit: "Since I Don't Have You" (2/59 US 12). She committed suicide 21st February, 1980.

Rick Price 1944 UK bass player with Move, Wizzard, Roy Wood and Brains.

Perry Kibble 1949 US pianist, singer, and songwriter with Taste Of Honey formed in 1971, who had two big hits: "Boogie Oogie Oogie" (6/78 US 1; UK 3) and "Sukiyaki" (3/81 US 3).

Mark Shaw 1961 UK singer and songwriter for the group Then Jericho formed in 1983. Hits: "The Motive" (7/87 UK 18) and "Big Area" (1/89 UK 13).

Deaths

Adie Harris 1982 US singer, one of the four Shirelles. Born 22nd January, 1940.

Hits of the Day

1944 "I'll Get By (As Long As I Have You)" Harry James US 6 weeks

1950 "Sentimental Me" Ames Brothers US 1 week

1972 "Candy Man" Sammy Davis Jr. US 2 weeks

1972 "Vincent" Don McLean UK 2 weeks

1974 "Waterloo" Abba

1978 "You're The One I Want" John Travolta & Olivia Newton-John US 1 week

1985 "19" Paul Hardcastle

1989 "Wind Beneath My Wings" Bette Midler US 1 week

1989 "Sealed With A Kiss" Jason Donovan UK 2 weeks

11th

Birthdays

James 'Pookie' Hudson 1934 US lead singer with Spaniels, who were formed in 1952. In 1955 there were personnel changes within the group, Hudson too left the band briefly, but then came back again in 1956. Biggest hit: "Goodnite Sweetheart, Goodnite" (6/54 US 24). In 1961 he left the band and formed the New Spaniels in 1975.

Jud Strunk 1936 US singer and TV comedian. Complete name Justin Strunk Jr. Biggest hit: "Daisy A Day" (2/73 US 14). He died 15th October, 1981.

Joey Dee 1940 US singer and songwriter. Real name Joseph DiNicola. In 1958 he formed Joey Dee & The Starlighters in New Jersey, who were discovered in the New York bar, Peppermint Lounge, and peaked with the emerging twist craze. Hits: "The Peppermint Twist – Part 1" (11/61 US 1; 2/62 UK 33), "Shout – Part 1" (3/62 US 6), "Ya Ya" (8/62), and "What Kind Of Fool Is This" (9/62 US 18). After 1963 success waned in the USA but continued in Europe. Other later members of the Starlighters included Felix Cavaliere, Gene Cornish, and Eddie Brigati, who later became the Young Rascals. Jimi Hendrix too was a member of Joey Dee's backing band in 1965/6.

John Lawton 1946 UK singer with Lucifer's Friend, the Les Humphries Singers, and from 1976 with Uriah Heep for two years. After that, he made a solo album, and returned to Lucifer's Friend, then to Rebel.

Glenn Leonard 1947 US singer. In 1975 he replaced Damon Harris in the Temptations, who had left. By 1988, he had left the group.

Lynsey De Paul 1950 UK singer and songwriter, real surname Rubin. Hits: "Sugar Me" (8/72 UK 5), "No Honestly" (11/74 UK 7), and "Rock Bottom" (3/77 UK 19) with Mike Moran.

Donnie Van Zant 1952 US singer and songwriter. After being a member of with Sweet Rooster, various other groups, and working as a brakeman on the railroad, he formed 38 Special in 1975. It is possible that the fact that Donnie's older brother Ronnie was a member of Lynyrd Skynyrd, helped him to get a recording contract. In 1977, 38 Special's debut album appeared. Hits: "Caught Up In You" (5/82 US 10), "Like No Other Night" (5/86 US 14) and "Second Chance" (2/89 US 6).

Frank Beard 1949 US drummer and songwriter of ZZ Top formed in 1969.

Hits of the Day

1966 "Paint It Black" Rolling Stones US 2 weeks
1966 "Sloop John B." Beach Boys
1969 "The Ballad Of John And Yoko" Beatles UK 3 weeks
1977 "I'm Your Boogie Man" K. C. & The Sunshine Band US 1 week

---

Miscellany

1969 The record "Space Oddity" by David Bowie is released, which proves to be a foundation stone for a worldwide career. However, things dragged at the beginning: the record reached the British charts on 6th September, 1969, and got to No. 48, for one week, then dropped out again. On the 20th September, 1969 it was in the charts again, this time at No. 5 for 13 weeks. In January 1973 it was in the US charts, at No. 15. In October 1975 it was in the charts in Britain again, this time, at last, at No. 1!

12th

Birthdays

Archie Bleyer 1909 US pianist and orchestra leader. He was already appearing with his own band in 1934. In 1952 he set up the record company Cadence, with whom such artists as Julius La Rosa, the Chordettes, and the Everly Brothers had hits. Successful records for Archie on his own label were "Hernando's Hideaway" (5/54 US 2), with a castanet solo by Maria Alba, and "The Naughty Lady Of Shady Lane" (12/54 US 17). In 1964 Bleyer withdrew from the record business. He died 20th March, 1989.

Vic Damone 1928 US singer and actor. Real name Vito Farinola. He is one of the most successful ballad singers of the post-war period. He had more than 40 hits between 1947 and 1965. Biggest hits: "Again" (4/49 US 6), "You're Breaking My Heart" (6/49 US 1), "Tzena, Tzena, Tzena" (7/50 US 6), "My Heart Cries For You" (12/50 US 4), "My Truly, Truly Fair" (6/51 US 4) and "On The Street Where You Live" (4/56 US 4; 5/58 UK 1). Vic appeared in several films and hosted his own TV show in 1956/7.

Chick Corea 1941 US jazz pianist, composer, and bandleader, who is considered to be one of the most important pianists of jazz-rock. Real first names Armando Anthony.

He played with Herbie Mann and Miles Davis, among others, and formed Return To Forever in 1971.

Roy Harper 1941 UK underground folk-rock singer. He released several albums which generated little interest. However, British musicians loved him. Pink Floyd enlisted Roy as singer on "Have A Cigar", Led Zeppelin dedicated "Hats Off To Harper" to him. His albums featured members of Pink Floyd, Led Zeppelin, Who, Yes, and in 1970, the entire lineup of The Nice as guest musicians, but all to no avail.

Len Barry 1942 US singer, real name Leonard Borisoff. He began as a leadsinger of the band Dovells formed in 1957. Hits: "Bristol Stomp" (9/61 US 2) and "You Can't Sit Down" (4/63 US 3). After that, Len left the group for a solo career. Hits: "1-2-3" (9/65 US 2; 11/65 UK 3), and "Like A Baby" (1/66 US 27; UK 10). After his career was over, he was reputedly a waiter in a bar in Philadelphia.

Reg Presley 1943 UK singer, songwriter, and leader of the Troggs. Real name Reg Maurice Ball. The group was formed as the Troglodytes in 1964 and was discovered by Kinks manager, Larry Page, in 1965. In 1966 they shortened there name to Troggs and released their first record. Their records were very often not played on radios around the world, (or at least in English speaking countries) because of so-called 'suggestive lyrics'. Nevertheless, they had plenty of hits: "Wild Thing" (5/66 UK 2; US 1), "With A Girl Like You" (7/66 UK 1; US 29), "I Can't Control Myself" (9/66 UK 2; US 43), "Anyway That You Want Me" (12/66 UK 8) "Give It To Me" (2/67 UK 12) and "Love Is All Around" (10/67 UK 5; US 7). The latter was a bit of a departure and very tongue-in-cheek as it seemed to embrace 'Flower-Power', which highly amused Reg. By the early 1970s the Troggs were finished, although they still released the odd record.

Barry Bailey 1948 US lead guitarist with Badger (1974), and Atlanta Rhythm Section. He also played on records by Al Kooper, Paul Davis – "Ride 'Em Cowboy" (1975) – Mylon Lefevre and Frankie Miller.

Lyn Collins 1948 US singer. She started in the mid-1960s with Charles Pikes & The Scholars and from 1969 was a member of in the James Brown Revue. Now and again she was allowed to make a solo recording under Brown's eagle-eye. Hit: "Think (About It)" (7/72 R&B 9).

Bun E. Carlos 1951 US drummer with Cheap Trick. Real name Brad Carlson.

Brad Delp 1951 US leadsinger, and founder of Boston with Tom Scholz in the mid-1970s. For hits, see 10th March under Scholz. When the band appeared in the charts again with a new record after 8 years, only Tom and Brad remained of the original line-up.

Pete Farndon 1952 UK bass player for two years with the Australian band Bushwackers, and then in 1978 founder member of the Pretenders. In June 1982 he was replaced by Malcolm Foster – Pete had drug problems, which led to his death on 14th April, 1983.

Dale Krantz 1952 US singer with the Rossington-Collins Band, which was formed in 1979 out of the five surviving members of Lynyrd Skynyrd. Dale had previously been a backing vocalist for 38 Special.

Rocky Burnette 1953 US singer, son of Johnny Burnette. He is trying to follow in his father's footsteps. First hit: "Tired Of Toein' The Line" (6/80 US 8).

Deaths

Jimmy Dorsey 1957 US orchestra leader, brother of Tommy Dorsey. Born on 29th February, 1904.

Johnny Bond 1978 US country singer and actor. Born on 1st June, 1915.

Hits of the Day

1943	"Taking A Chance On Love" Benny Goodman US 3 weeks
1961	"Travellin' Man" Ricky Nelson US 1 week (2nd time)
1965	"Back In My Arms" Supremes US 1 week
1971	"Want Ads" Honey Cone US 1 week
1976	"Combine Harvester" Wurzels UK 2 weeks
1976	"Silly Love Songs" Wings US 4 weeks (2nd time)
1982	"Goody Two Shoes" Adam & The Ants UK 2 weeks

13th

Birthdays

Slim Dusty 1927 Australian singer, who is the most popular country artist in his homeland. Real name David Gordon Kirkpatrick. He had a hit with "Pub With No Beer" (1/59 UK 3).

Attila Zoller 1927 Hungarian jazz guitarist and composer who played with Albert Mangelsdorff, Oscar Pettiford and Kenny Clarke. In 1959 he went to the USA and played with Stan Getz, and from 1962 until 1965 with Herbie Mann. In addition, he also made solo albums.

Bobby Freeman 1940 US singer and songwriter. At the age of 14 he formed the group Romancers, later the Vocaleers. But he was more successful as a solo artist. Hits: "Do You Want To Dance" (5/58 US 5) and "C'mon And Swim" (7/64 US 5).

Esther Ofarim 1941 Israeli singer, who was successful with her husband Abi, as Esther & Abi Ofarim. Real name Esther Zaied. Hits: "Morning Of My Life" (7/67), and "Cindarella Rockefella" (2/68 UK 1). From the early 1970s she carried on without her husband or hits.

Dennis Locorriere 1949 US guitarist, singer, and songwriter. He and Ray Sawyer (*viz*) formed the group Dr. Hook in 1968.

Howard Leese 1951 Canadian pianist with Heart, and as a session musician with Dixon House, Randy Meisner and Spirit.

Robert Donaldson 1954 US keyboard player and trumpeter with his band Bo Donaldson & The Heywoods, who had their only hit with the Paper Lace song "Billy Don't Be A Hero" (4/74 US 1).

Jorge Santana 1954 Mexican guitarist, younger brother of Carlos. In 1971 he formed the band Malo, which stayed together until 1974. Biggest Hit, "Suavecito" (3/72 US 18). Jorge also played with the Fania All-Stars as a soloist.

Rolf Brendel 1957 German drummer with Nena.

Deniece Lisa Maria Pearson 1968 UK leadsinger with the sibling group Five Star. In 1983 the three sisters Lorraine, Doris, and Deniece, asked their father, a former professional guitarist and songwriter, to let them record one of their compositions. Father Buster had backed artists like Wilson Pickett. Lee Dorsey, Desmond Dekker and Jimmy Cliff, as a member of a touring band in Britain in the 1960s. He had also worked as a songwriter and producer for an independent reggae-label; he was so enthusiastic about his daughters, demo, which Lorraine had written, that he used his connections. They made their first television appearance in September 1983. In the meantime their two brothers Stedman and Delroy had joined the sisters and they became Five Star. From 1985 they were in the British charts regularly with hits like "System Addict" (1/86 UK 3), "Rain Or Shine" (9/86 UK 2), and "The Slightest Touch" (4/87 UK 4).

Deaths

Clyde McPhatter 1972 US singer who died of a heart attack. Born 5th November, 1933.

Benny Goodman 1986 US King of Swing. Born 30th May, 1909.

Hits of the Day

1942	"Jersey Bounce" Benny Goodman US 4 weeks
1970	"Long And Winding Road" Beatles US 2 weeks
1970	"In The Summertime" Mungo Jerry UK 8 weeks
1981	"Being With You" Smokey Robinson UK 2 weeks
1987	"Always" Atlantic Starr US 1 week

14th

Birthdays

Burl Ives 1909 US film actor, singer, author, storyteller, and banjo player. Complete name Burle Icle Ivanhoe Ives. He played countless character parts on Broadway, on television and in films; he played beside James Dean in the film *East Of Eden* in 1955, received an Oscar for best supporting role in the film *The Big Country*. In the same year he played the part of Big Daddy in *Cat On A Hot Tin Roof*. In 1959 he played beside Alec Guiness in the British film *Our Man In Havanna*. If anyone was needed to play the part of a large landowner of the Southern USA, Ives was the man. He received several awards from his work in country and folk music, and from the 1940s until the 1960s he was considered to be one of the most popular folksingers. His interest in American folk music started in the early 30s. He earned his living in a variety of jobs, appearing as a singer and banjo player and collecting folksongs, which later, when he had amassed more than 500, were published in books. He charted with "Lavender Blue (Dilly Dilly)" (2/49 US 16), "Riders In The Sky (Cowboy Legend)" (4/49 US 21), "On Top Of Old Smoky" (5/51 US 10), "A Little Bitty Tear" (12/61 US & UK 9), and "Funny Way Of Laughin' " 4/62 US 10; UK 29).

Julie Felix 1941 US singer who sought success as Britain's answer to Joan Baez. Only hit: "If I Could (El Condor Pasa)" (4/70 UK 19).

Muff Winwood 1943 UK bass player and record producer who played with the Spencer Davis Group in their early days, and was always over-shadowed by his younger brother Stevie.

Rod Argent 1945 UK keyboard player, singer, and songwriter, who formed the Zombies in 1963. Hits: "She's Not There" (8/64 UK 12; 10/64 US 2), "Tell Her No" (1/65 US 6) and "Time Of The Season" (2/69 US 3). When the last hit got into the charts the group had already split up. Rod started his own group Argent. Greatest hit: "Hold Your Head Up" (3/72 UK 5; 6/72 US 5). In June 1976 this band split up too, and Rod tried as a solo artist credited as San Jose he had a hit just in time for the World Soccer Cup, with "Argentine Melody" (Cancion de Argentina) (6/78 UK 14), featuring Rodriguez Argentina. Rod was ubiquitous as a session musician.

Alan White 1949 UK drummer, with the Plastic Ono Band and with Yes from 1972. He also made solo records and is a much sought-after session musician.

Jimmy Lea 1952 UK bassist, pianist and songwriter for Slade. For hits see 4th April, under Dave Hill.

Nick van Eede 1959 UK singer and songwriter with the group Cutting Crew, who were the new band of 1986. Hits: "(I Just) Died In Your Arms" (8/86 UK 4; 3/87 US 1) and "I've Been In Love Before" (10/86 UK 31; 9/87 US 9; 11/87 RE-UK 24).

Boy George 1961 UK singer, and songwriter with Culture Club. Real name O'Dowd. He began his career as a short term member of Bow Wow Wow, and then formed Culture Club in 1981. Hits: "Do You Really Want To Hurt Me" (9/82 UK 1; 11/82 US 2), "Time (Clock Of The Heart)" (11/82 UK 3; 4/83 US 2), "Church Of The Poison Mind" (4/83 UK 2; 10/83 US 10), "Karma Chameleon" (9/83 UK 1; 12/83 US 1), "Victims" (12/83 UK 3), "It's A Miracle" (3/84 UK 4), "Miss Me Blind" (3/84 US 5), "War Song" (9/84 UK 2; US 17), and "Move Away" (3/86 UK 7; US 12). In early 1987, George started a solo career too. Hits: "Everything I Own" (3/87 UK 1) and "To Be Reborn" (11/87 UK 13).

DeGarmo Chris 1963 US guitarist and songwriter with Queensryche.

Deaths

Wynonie Harris 1969 US R&B singer. Born 24th August, 1915.

Clarence White 1973 US guitarist with the Byrds. He was run over by a drunk driver. Born 7th June, 1944.

Hits of the Day

1986 "On My Own" Pattie La Belle and Michael McDonald US 3 weeks

---

15th

Birthdays

David Rose 1910 UK composer, pianist and orchestra leader, born in London and moved to Chicago with his parents when he was four. He studied at Chicago Musical College, played as a pianist in various bands in the late 1920s and worked as an arranger. In 1936 he made a name for himself by arranging the title "It's Been So Long" (2/36 US 1) for Benny Goodman. In the late 1930s he became a free-lance arranger in Hollywood. There he married Martha Raye (1938 – 1941), and Judy Garland (1941 – 1943). In 1943 he made his first record, "Holiday For Strings" (6/43 US 2). Further hits were "Calypso Melody" (3/57 US 42 – but still a million seller!), and "The Stripper" (5/62 US 1). He wrote and arranged music for many TV series like *Bonanza*, and *Little House On The Prairie* and also for films. Tony Martin and the comedian Red Skelton worked with David on radio and television programmes; David and his orchestra also played on many records by Connie Francis. He died on August 23rd, 1990.

Erroll Garner 1921 US legendary jazz pianist. He only appeared in the charts once with "Misty" (10/54 US 30), which he wrote himself and five years later it became a hit for Johnny Mathis. Garner died 2nd January, 1977.

Waylon Jennings 1937 US country singer, bass player and songwriter. Waylon, with Willie Nelson, Tompall Glaser and Jessi Colter (his wife since 1969), was one of the 'outlaws' of US country music. In the second half of the 1950s he worked as a D.J. in Lubbock, Texas and became friends with Buddy Holly. Buddy produced Waylon's first record "Jole Blon" in 1958. Shortly after, Waylon became bassist in Buddy Holly's backing band; and escaped the plane crash on 3rd February, 1959, because he drew lots with Big Bopper for the seat on the plane and lost. In the early 1960s Waylon formed a strongly folk-oriented group, called the Waylors. In 1965 he signed with RCA, as a solo artist. However, the material he was expected to sing was rubbish and he, with Willie Nelson, began to protest in the early 1970s against the patronizing attitude towards artists by record companies and producers. After that, he was allowed to produce his own records. This branded him an 'outlaw'. Crossover hits in the pop charts were "Luckenbach, Texas (Back To The Basics Of Love)" (5/77 US 25) and "Theme From The Dukes Of Hazzard (Good Ol' Boys)" (9/80 US 21). He was also successful duetting with Willie Nelson: "Good Hearted

Woman" (2/76 US 25). Waylon is the eleventh most successful country musician. By the end of 1988 he had hit the top of the C&W charts sixteen times, either alone, or with other artists.

Harry Nilsson 1941 US singer and songwriter who started in the early 1960s as Johnny Niles. Real name Harry Edward Nelson III. His compositions were recorded by the Ronettes, the Monkees, and Three Dog Night: not only did he compose, but he also sang on the demo tapes as a result, it was noted that he had quite a good voice himself. Hits: "Everybody's Talking" (8/69 US 6; UK 23), "Without You" (12/71 US 1; 2/72 UK 1) and "Coconut" (6/72 US 8). Nilsson was known to be a close friend of John Lennon and Ringo Starr.

Johnny Hallyday 1943 French singer who managed to adapt to each trend over thirty years, which is probably why he was called the 'chameleon idol'. Real name Jean Philippe Smet. He had his first hit in 1960 with "Souvenirs, Souvenirs". In 1961, when the twist had just arrived, he recorded the French version of "Let's Twist Again": "Viens Dancer Le Twist". He liked to see himself (as in his hit of 1963), as "L'Idole De La Jeunesse". One of his last great successes was in 1986, "Quelque Chose De Tennessee". Johnny was married to his colleague Silvie Vartan, and is the father of David Hallyday.

Demis Roussos 1946 Greek singer with Aphrodite's Child, and as a solo artist. Hit for the band, "Rain And Tears" (11/68 UK 30). Solo hits, "Good-bye, My Love, Good-bye" (4/73), "Happy To Be On An Island In The Sun" (11/75 UK 5), and "The Roussos Phenomenon" (6/76 UK 1) – the last of which was an EP, with four tracks, including two which had been very successful in Germany: "Forever And Ever", "Sing An Ode To Love", "So Dreamy" and "My Friend The Wind".

Russel Hitchcock 1949 Australian singer with the duo Air Supply. See 1st June, under Graham Russell.

Michael Lutz 1949 US bass player with Brownsville Station.

Noddy Holder 1950 UK singer, guitarist and songwriter for Slade. Hits see 4th April, under Dave Hill.

Steve Walsh 1951 US singer, songwriter and pianist. In 1972 Steve became a member of the band White Clover, formed the year before, who shortly afterwards became Kansas. Hits: "Carry On Wayward Son" (12/76 US 11) and "Dust In The Wind" (1/78 US 6). In January 1981 Steve left the band, was replaced by John Elefante, and made solo records. In late 1983 Kansas split up. In 1986 they reformed with Steve. Hit: "All I Wanted" (11/86 US 19).

Richie Puente 1953 US percussionist and clarinetist with Foxy. He also played with Mink DeVille and Peter Frampton.

Terri Gibbs 1954 US country singer and pianist who was blind since birth. As a child she sang with a gospel group and had her own band from 1974, called Sound Dimension. She worked in a restaurant called 'Steak & Ale' in her hometown Augusta between 1975 and 1980, then she had the hit, "Somebody's Knockin' " (1/83 US 13). Since then, she has been in the country charts regularly.

Brett Gillis 1957 US singer and guitarist with Rubicon, who made two albums in the late 1970s. In 1979 they became the trio Stereo, and later still Night Ranger, who released their first album in 1982.

Neil Arthur 1958 UK synthesizer player, singer, songwriter, and half of Blancmange. In 1978 Neil was a member of Viewfinders. When he met Steven Luscombe, they formed L360 together. After this project failed to work, they parted, joined up again, and formed Blancmange (after the British pudding). Hits, "Living On The Ceiling" (10/82 UK 7) and "Don't Tell Me" (4/84 UK 8). In 1986 they split up again.

Deaths

Wes Montgomery 1968 US guitarist. Born 6th March, 1925

Bob Nolan 1980 US country singer and songwriter. Born 1st April, 1908.

Pete de Freitas 1989 West-Indian drummer with the British group Echo & The Bunnymen. Died after a traffic accident. Born 2nd August, 1961.

Hits of the Day

1956	"I'll Be Home" Pat Boone UK 5 weeks
1963	"Sukiyaki" Kyo Sakamoto US 3 weeks
1974	"Billy, Don't Be A Hero" Bo Donaldson & Theo Heywoods US 2 weeks
1974	"The Streak" Ray Stevens UK 1 week
1985	"You'll Never Walk Alone" The Crowd UK 2 weeks
1987	"I Wanna Dance With Somebody (Who Loves Me) Whitney Houston

---

16th

Birthdays

Stan Laurel 1890 UK actor, the thin one of Laurel & Hardy. Real surname Jefferson. In 1917 he made his first film *Lucky Dog* with Oliver Hardy in USA. The song "The Trail Of The Lonesome Pine" (11/75 UK 2) recorded in 1937, was a posthumous hit for Laurel & Hardy. He died 23rd February, 1965.

Billy 'Crash' Craddock 1939 US country singer with a touch of rock n' roll. He started out in the mid-1950s with his brother Ronald, in the rockband Four Rebels, who made their first record in 1957. In 1959 he tried as a soloist, failed and withdrew from the music business. He returned in the early 1970s, this time with more success: "Rub It In" (6/74 US 16). He carried on appearing in the country charts until 1983 and then it was all over.

Lamont Dozier 1940 US songwriter and singer. In partnership with the two brothers Brian and Eddie Holland he is one of Tamla-Motown's most successful songwriters. Attempts to sing his own material were not particularly successful. In 1961 he recorded as Lamont Anthony and, in the early 1970s, he duetted with Brian Holland. Then he gave up, reverting to a solo career under his real name. Biggest hit: "Trying To Hold On To My Woman" (12/73 US 15). The songwriting team of Holland/Dozier/Holland finished their liaison with Motown in 1968 – they formed their own company Invictus/Hot Wax.

Edward Levert 1942 US singer with the band Triumphs formed in 1958. As Mascots they made their first record in 1961, then they called themselves O'Jays after a disc-jockey in Cleveland called Eddie O'Jay. Hits: "Backstabbers" (7/72 US 3; 9/72 UK 14), "Love Train" (1/73 US 1; 3/73 UK 9), "For The Love Of Money" (4/74 US 9), "I Love Music" (11/75 US 5; 1/76 UK 13; 4/78 RE-UK 36), and "Use Ta Be My Girl" (4/78 US 4; 6/78 UK 12). Two of Edward's sons, Gerald and Sean, are members of the trio Levert.

John Rostill 1942 UK bassist and songwriter. He started with the group Interns. When Brian Locking of the Shadows became a Jehovah's Witness and wanted to leave the group in 1967, John joined and stayed until their official split-up in October, 1969. John died 26th November, 1973.

Peter Hoorelbeke 1945 US drummer who in 1971 joined the band Rare Earth formed in 1969, replaced Pete Rivera and took over as leadsinger.

Ian Matthews 1946 UK singer and songwriter. Complete name Ian Matthew McDonald. In 1966 he became a member of the group Pyramid which released one unsuccessful single. In the autumn of 1967 he joined Fairport Convention as leadsinger. After two albums with them, he formed Matthew's Southern Comfort in January, 1969. Greatest hit, "Woodstock" (9/70 UK 1; 3/71 US 23). From January 1971 Ian was a solo artist, whose biggest hit was "Shake It" (11/78 US 13).

Gino Vannelli 1952 Canadian singer and songwriter. From 1974 he was successful with hits like "I Just Wanna Stop" (9/78 US 4), and "Living Inside Myself" (3/81 US 6).

Malcolm Paul Mortimer 1953 UK drummer with Gentle Giant, G. T. Moore & The Reggae Guitars, and Jona Lewie.

Ian Mosley 1953 UK drummer with Curved Air, The Gordon Giltrap Band, Steve Hackett and, from November 1983, Marillion.

Deaths

Chick Webb 1939 US jazz drummer. Died of tuberculosis. Born 10th February, 1902.

Lonnie Johnson 1970 US blues and jazz guitarist and singer. Born 8th February, 1889.

James Honeyman-Scott 1982 UK guitarist with the Pretenders. Died of a drugs overdose. Born 4th November, 1957.

Hits of the Day

1956	"Wayward Wind" Gogi Grant US 8 weeks
1973	"Can The Can" Suzi Quatro UK 1 week
1975	"Paloma Blanca" George Baker Selection
1979	"Ring My Bell" Anita Ward UK 2 weeks
1979	"Hot Stuff" Donna Summer US 2 weeks (2nd time)
1984	"Two Tribes" Frankie Goes To Hollywood UK 9 weeks

Miscellany

1967 A three-day festival begins in Monterey, California. It was organised by producer Lou Adler and John Phillips of the Mamas & Papas. There had never before been such a coming together of 'crack' musicians within three days.

To name just a few: Otis Redding, Jefferson Airplane, The Who, Canned Heat, The Byrds, Blood, Sweat & Tears, Janis Joplin and Jimi Hendrix.

17th

Birthdays

Red Foley 1910 US country singer and songwriter who was also known as a gospel singer. Real first names Clyde Julian. He has regularly appeared in the country charts since the 1940s. Hits: "Smoke On The Water" (9/44 US 7), "Chattanoogie Shoe Shine Boy" (1/50 US 1) and "Cincinnatti Dancing Pig" (9/50 US 7). Red was a radio broadcaster in the 1930s. With TV catching on, he was soon in evidence there. Red Foley was Pat Boone's father-in-law. He died 19th September, 1968.

Dean Martin 1917 US singer and actor. Real name Dino Crocetti. After he had tried just about everything, miner, boxer, gas-station attendant, etc etc., he had the idea, when 27, to be a singer. In 1946 the owner of a club in Atlanta needed something special for his cabaret: he put Dean on stage together with the young comedian Jerry Lewis. Over the next few years Dean and Jerry made a number of successful film comedies. They also recorded together. Their greatest success was "That Certain Party" (12/48 US 22). In the late 1950s Dean proved in at least two films that he was very versatile. After that, he continued to diversify, appearing in westerns like *Rio Bravo* in 1959. In addition, from the early 1950s, his singing career was equally successful with forty hits between 1948 and 1969: "That's Amore" (11/53 US 2; 1/54 UK 2), "Memories Are Made Of This" (12/55 US & UK 1), "Return To Me" (4/58 US 4; 6/58 UK 2) and "Everybody Loves Somebody" (6/64 US 1; 8/64 UK 11). He was also one of the Frank Sinatra clan, known as 'The Rat Pack'. Dean had his own TV show in the USA from 1965 until 1974. His birthday is also quoted as being 7th of June.

Dickey Doo 1939 US singer and leader of Dickey Doo & The Don'ts. Real name Dave Allred. Dickey had been a drummer with the Rhythm Orchids previously. Greatest hit with his own group, "Click Clack" (2/58 US 28).

Norman Kuhlke 1942 UK drummer with the original lineup of the Swinging Blue Jeans.

Barry Manilow 1944 US singer, pianist, and songwriter. Real name Barry Allan Pinkus. His career started as a jingle writer, penning the McDonald slogan 'You Deserve A Break Today,' among others. While continuing his work on jingles, he had his first success as amusician in 1972: he met Bette Midler who made him her musical director. In 1974, Barry himself became a star with hits like "Mandy" (11/74 US 1; 2/75 UK 11), "I Write The Songs" (11/75 US 1), "Looks Like We Made It" (5/77 US 1), "Can't Smile Without You" (2/78 US 3), and "Copacabana (At The Copa)" (6/78 US 8; UK 42). All of them were million sellers.

Chris Spedding 1944 UK guitarist, singer and songwriter. He is probably one of the most active session guitarists in the UK, having played with Pete Brown's Battered Ornaments, formed in 1967, the Jack Bruce Band and Sharks formed by Andy Fraser in 1973. Additionally, he has worked with Elton John, Nina Hagen, Tom Waits, Gilbert O'Sullivan, Harry Nilsson, John Cale, David Essex, Roy Harper, Wombles, Jeff Wayne, Mike Batt and Lesley Duncan, just to name a few. As a solo artist he has released some pretty good rock 'n' roll records like "Motor Bikin' " (8/75 UK 14).

Eric Lewis UK bassist and pianist with Middle Of The Road.

Lenny LeBlanc 1951 US bass player, singer, and songwriter. He was successful as the duo LeBlanc & Carr with Pete Carr. Hit: "Falling" (10/77 US 13). Lenny and Pete were both studio musicians in the Muscle Shoals Studios in Alabama.

Deaths

Kate Smith 1986 US singer and TV presenter. Born 1st May, 1907.

Hits of the Day

1965	"Crying In The Chapel" Elvis Presley UK 1 week
1967	"Groovin' " Young Rascals US 2 weeks (2nd time)
1978	"You're The One That I Want" John Travolta & Olivia Newton-John UK 9 weeks
1978	"Shadow Dancing" Andy Gibb US 7 weeks
1989	"I'll Be Loving You Forever" New Kids On The Block US 2 weeks

18th

Birthdays

Kay Kyser 1906 US trumpeter and leader of his own orchestra, who were once the most popular of the so-called 'sweet dance bands'. From 1935 until 1948 he had 78 hits, with ten No. 1s including six million sellers: "The Umbrella Man" (12/38), "Three Little Fishes" (5/39), "(Lights Out) Until Reveille" (7/41), "(There'll Be Blue-birds Over) The White Cliffs Of Dover" (12/41), "Who Wouldn't Love You" (4/42), "Jingle, Jangle, Jingle" (7/42), "He Wears A Pair Of Silver Wings" (7/42), "Strip Polka" (10/42), "Praise The Lord And Pass The Ammunitions!" (10/42), "Ole Buttermilk Sky" (9/46) and "Woody Wood-pecker" (6/48 US 1). Kay died 23rd July, 1985.

Johnny Pearson 1925 UK pianist, bandleader and songwriter. He had the international hit "Cast Your Fate To The Wind" (12/64 UK 5; 3/65 US 10) with Sounds Orchestral. As a soloist he had a further hit with "Sleepy Shores" (12/71 UK 8). In addition, he collaborated with Cilla Black, Shirley Bassey, Lena Horne and Conny Fran-cis.

Don 'Sugarcane' Harris 1938 US jazz musician and songwriter. Don took violin lessons as a child, but earned his living as a pianist and singer to begin with in local groups, and then as a bassist and guitarist with his partner of many years Dewey Terry, as the duo Don & Dewey. It was not until after all that, that his international career as a violinist took off. In the mid-1960s he played with Johnny Otis, Little Richard, Frank Zappa and, finally, John Mayall. He is one of the leading jazz-rock violinists.

James Paul McCartney 1942 UK singer, bassist, pian-ist (but also plays other instruments), songwriter, and one of the most successful musicians of all time. He wrote countless million sellers for the Beatles with fellow group member John Lennon, and, between 1962 and 1978, either alone or with others a total of 43 million sellers. On 11th April, 1970 Paul announced he would never again record with John Lennon. On 17th April, his first solo record appeared, which he had recorded at home alone. In 1971 he formed Wings with his wife Linda, guitarist Denny Laine, drummer Denny Seiwell and, a little later, guitarist Henry McCullough. From the late 1970s Paul was a so-loist. Of all his compositions, "Yesterday" is perhaps the best known with almost 1,200 different versions by the end of 1972, in existence, making the most-often recorded song around. Until 1991, "Mull Of Kintyre" was biggest selling single in the UK, having sold 2.5 million copies. In

1990 Paul was awarded a Grammy by the American rec-ord industry for his life's work.

Carl Radle 1945 UK bass player with Eric Clapton, Leon Russell, Joe Cocker, George Harrison, Freddie King, Delaney & Bonnie, and J. J. Cale. Carl was a sought-after session musician. He died 30th May, 1980.

Alison Moyet 1961 UK singer and songwriter. Com-plete name, Genevieve Alison-Jane Moyet, and her French father gave her the nickname Alf. She sang with such groups as Vicars and Screaming Abdabs, before forming Yazoo with Vince Clark at the beginning of 1982, just after he had left Depeche Mode. Hits: "Only You" (4/82 UK 2), "Don't Go" (7/82 UK 3), and "Nobody's Diary" (5/83 UK 3). In mid-1983 they went their separate ways. Clark formed Assembly first, and then Erasure, and Moyet be-came a solo artist. Hits: "All Cried Out" (10/74 UK 8), "That Ole Devil Called Love" (3/85 UK 2), "Is This Love" (12/86 UK 3), "Weak In The Presence Of Beauty" (3/87 UK 6) and "Love Letters" (11/87 UK 4).

Hits of the Day

1977 "Lucille" Kenny Rogers UK 1 week
1977 "Dreams" Fleetwood Mac US 1 week
1984 "Self Control" Laura Branigan
1988 "Doctorin' The Tardis" Timelords UK 1 week
1988 "Together Forever" Rick Astley US 1 week

19th

Birthdays

Guy Lombardo 1902 Canadian orchestra leader who formed his own band in 1924, with his brothers Carmen and Lebert, which was called Guy Lombardo & His Royal Canadians. Later, fourth brother Victor joined the band too. Guy was the leader, Carmen saxophonist and vocalist. By 1955 the brothers had sold over 100 million records and had reached No. 1 26 times in the US charts. Their first hit was "Charmaine!" (9/27 US 1), which stayed at the top for 7 weeks and became a million seller again for Mantovani in 1951. Over the years, the band became an integral part of New Year's Eve celebrations all over North America: they played on radio. The New Year had virtually arrived when Guy Lombardo began to play "Auld Lang Syne", but he never charted with it. Among his greatest hits:

"You're Driving Me Crazy! (What Did I Do?)" (11/30), "We Just Can't Say Goodbye" (8/32), "Stars Fell On Alabama" (10/34), "Red Sails In The Sunset" (10/35), "Boo Hoo" (3/37), "September In The Rain" (4/37), "It Looks Like Rain In Cherry Blossom Lane" (5/37) and "The Third Man Theme" (3/50) – all these records stayed at No. 1 in the USA for at least a month. Guy died 5th November, 1977, and his brother Carmen on 17th April, 1971.

Charlie Drake 1925 UK singer and comedian. Hits: "Splish Splash" (8/58 UK 7) and "My Boomerang Won't Come Back" (10/61 UK 14; 2/62 US 21). Later, he became a TV star in Britain.

Tommy de Vito 1928 US guitarist and singer. He formed the group Variatones in 1955 with his brother Nick, Frankie Valli and Hank Majewski, which became the Four Lovers in 1956, and the Four Seasons in 1961. In 1971 he retired from the music business.

Shirley Goodman 1936 US singer. She made her first records as Shirley Pixley with Leonard Lee in 1952. Hit for Shirley & Lee, "Let The Good Times Roll" (8/56 US 20). In 1963 they split up and everything seemed to be over. However, Shirley carried on with Jesse Hill as Shirley & Jesse, and worked with Mac Rebennack alias Dr. John in New Orleans. In 1975 she re-appeared as Shirley & Company, releasing "Shame, Shame, Shame" (1/75 US 12; UK 6), one of the first disco-hits.

Al Wilson 1939 US singer and drummer who began his career with the Jewels, the Rollers, and with Johnny 'Legs' Harris & The Statesmen. His first hit as a solo singer was "The Snake" produced by Johnny Rivers in 1968, but he really came into his own with "Show And Tell" (10/73 US 1).

Elaine 'Spanky' McFarlane 1942 US lead singer and songwriter with Spanky & Our Gang formed in 1966. Biggest hit: "Sunday Will Never Be The Same" (5/67 US 9). In 1982 she joined the reunion of Mamas & Papas as a replacement for the late Mama Cass.

Robin Box 1944 UK guitarist. First he was a session musician with Peter & Gordon and Paul Jones, then lead guitarist with White Plains.

Peter Bardens 1945 UK pianist with the Cheynes (beside Mick Fleetwood), Them in 1964, then Shotgun Express (beside Rod Stewart and Peter Green), Village and Camel. In 1978 he left Camel as he had quarrelled with the other leader of the band, Andy Latimer. In 1987 his first solo album SEEN ON EARTH was released, featuring the single "In Dreams" (12/87).

Nick Drake 1948 UK singer, guitarist and songwriter, born in Burma, who spent the first two years of life in Bombay, before moving to Britain with his parents in 1950. He released three outstanding albums between 1970 and 1972, which were 'too good' for the general public. He was found dead on 25th November, 1974.

Ann Wilson 1950 US singer and songwriter with Heart. For hits and history of the band see 16th March under sister Nancy. Ann had the hit "Almost Paradise . . . Love Theme From Footloose" (5/84 US 7), with Mike Reno and then "Surrender To Me (From Tequila Sunrise)" (12/88 US 6), with Robin Zander.

Snips 1951 UK singer with Sharks and Baker Gurvitz Army. Then he became a solo artist – good singer, but little success.

Larry Dunn 1953 US keyboard player with Earth, Wind & Fire. Real name Lawrence Dunnhill. As a session musician he recorded with Ramsey Lewis, Deniece Williams, Lenny White and Herbert Laws.

Gwen Owens 1953 US singer, one of the Trio Hot. Hit and million seller: "Angel In Your Arms" (2/77 US 6).

Mark DeBarge 1959 US singer, trumpeter and saxophonist with the sibling group DeBarge.

Paula Abdul 1963 US singer, dancer, and choreographer. When videos became important marketing tools in the mid-1980s, many artists learned how to dance. Paula helped some of them like Janet Jackson, Z. Z. Top and George Michael with the choreography. There is no doubt that Paula's videos helped her to sell records by the truck load. Hits: "Straight Up" (12/88 US 1; 3/89 UK 3), "(It's Just) The Way That You Love Me" (12/88 US 88; 9/89 RE-US 3), "Forever Your Girl" (3/89 US 1; 6/89 UK 24), "Cold Hearted" (6/89 US 1) and "Opposites Attract" (12/89 US 1).

Hits of the Day

Year		
1959	"Roulette" Russ Conway	UK 2 weeks
1961	"Moody River" Pat Boone	US 1 week
1965	"I Can't Help Myself" Four Tops	US 1 week
1969	"Jumping Jack Flash" Rolling Stones	UK 2 weeks
1971	"It's Too Late/I Fell The Earth Move" Carole King	US 5 weeks
1971	"Chirpy Chirpy Cheep Cheep" Middle Of the Road	UK 5 weeks

Miscellany

1956 It was announced that the two actors Jerry Lewis and Dean Martin no longer wished to film together (after a total of 16 films). The last film had been *Hollywood Or Bust*. The initiative came from Lewis who was fed up with being the butt of Martin's jokes. It was rumoured then that at least Dean Martin's career was over; wrong, as we now know. Martin had looked ahead and been recording successfully since 1949.

20th

Birthdays

Chet Atkins 1924 US country guitarist, producer, and arranger, who discovered pianist Floyd Cramer. Real first names Chester Burton. After working in various radio shows like Red Foley's from 1942 he made his first solo record in 1946. From 1947 he recorded a number of successful albums for RCA. In 1950 he became a session musician and producer in Nashville, working with artists like Hank Snow, Waylon Jennings, Perry Como and Al Hirt. Between 1968 and 1982 he was vice-president of RCA records. He is considered to be the man who partly defined the 'Nashville sound'. His greatest solo success was "Yakety Axe" (6/65 C&W 4).

Eric Dolphy 1928 US jazz musician. Eric played alto saxophone, flute recorder and bass clarinet. His style was a synthesis of hard-bop and experimental. He died 29th June, 1964.

Billy Guy 1936 US singer, he became a founder member of the Coasters in 1955, and stayed with the group over the years.

Mickie Most 1936 UK songwriter, producer and singer. Real name Michael Hayes. In the late 1950s he appeared with Alex Murray alias Alex Wharton as the Most Brothers. They were accompanied by the later Shadows Hank Marvin, Bruce Welch, and Jet Harris. In 1959 Mickie married a South African and went to live in her home country for three years. He formed Mickie Most & The Playboys, and made cover versions of American hits for the South African market. In this way he had eleven No. 1 hits during that time. In 1962 he returned to Britain, and as he was unsuccessful as a singer, he started producing. His first successful productions were for the Animals; particularly "House Of The Rising Sun", which made him a rich man. He went on to produce the Nashville Teens, Herman's Hermits, Donovan, Lulu and the Jeff Beck group with singer Rod Stewart. In 1969 Mickie set up his own record company RAK: in 1973, 14 out of 18 releases got into the charts. Among these were records by Cozy Powell, Suzi Quatro, Mud, Hot Chocolate and Kenny. Further hits followed by Smokie, Chris Spedding, New World, CCS, Harpo and the Arrows.

Jerry Keller 1937 US singer and songwriter. Only hit: "Here Comes Summer" (6/59 US 14; 8/59 UK 1).

Brian Wilson 1942 US keyboard player, bassist, singer and songwriter for the Beach Boys, who were the only band to withstand the Beatles 'invasion' in the USA in 1964. The group formed in 1961 and first called themselves Kenny & The Cadets, then Carl & The Passions and then, Pendletones. They made their first record in 1961 as the Beach Boys. At this point, members of the group were the brothers Brian, Carl (guitar), and Dennis Wilson (drums), along with Mike Love as leadsinger, and Al Jardine (guitar). Their major hits were "I Get Around" (5/64 US 7; UK 1), "Help Me Rhonda" (4/65 US 1; 6/65 UK 27), "Barbara Ann" (1/66 US 2; UK 3), "Sloop John B." (4/66 US 3; UK 2), "Good Vibrations" (10/66 US & UK 1; 7/76 RE-UK 18), and "Do It Again" (7/68 UK 1; US 20). He tried to launch a solo career in 1966 and had a hit with "Caroline, No" (3/66 US 32), but his next solo album didn't appear until 1990.

Anne Murray 1945 Canadian singer, who cut her first records in 1969. She and Joni Mitchell were the first Canadian women to have million sellers in the USA. Hits: "Snowbird" (7/70 US 8; 10/70 UK 23) and "You Needed Me" (7/78 US 1; 12/78 UK 22). From 1983 she only reached the pop charts occasionally, but was regularly in the C&W charts.

Nigel Morris 1948 UK drummer with Stomu Yamashta and Isotope.

Alan Longmuir 1949 UK bassist and pianist with the Bay City Rollers.

Lionel Richie 1949 US singer, keyboard player and songwriter. He formed The Mighty Mystics in 1967, which became the Commodores in the same year, and from 1981 he made solo records. The first hits for the Commodores appeared in 1974, the biggest being "Three Times A Lady" (6/78 US 1; 8/78 UK 1) and "Still" (9/79 US 1; 11/79 UK 4). Hits as a soloist: "Truly" (10/82 US 1; UK 6), "All Night Long" (9/83 US 1; UK 2), "Hello" (2/84 US & UK 1), "Say You, Say Me" (11/85 US 1; UK 8) and "Dancing On The Ceiling" (7/86 US 2; UK 7). Additionally he had a hit with Diana Ross, "Endless Love" (7/81 US 1; 9/81 UK 7). Further successes as a songwriter were, "Lady" for Kenny Rogers and "We Are The World" for USA for Africa, the latter was co-written with Michael Jackson.

Cyndi Lauper 1953 US singer and songwriter. She took her first steps with Blue Angels, and has been successful as a solo artist since 1984. Hits: "Girls Just Want To Have Fun" (12/83 US & UK 2), "Time After Time" (4/84 US 1; UK 3), "She Bop" (7/84 US 3), "True Colors" (8/86 US 1; UK 12) and "I Drove All Night" (5/89 US 6; UK 7).

Michael Anthony 1955 US bassist with Van Halen.

Kelly Johnson 1958 UK guitarist and singer with Girlschool.

Nigel John Taylor 1960 UK bassist with Duran Duran and Power Station.

Deaths

Ira Louvin 1965 US country singer of Louvin Brothers. Died after a car accident. Born 21st April, 1924.

Hits of the Day

1942 "Sleepy Lagoon" Harry James US 4 weeks
1963 "I Like It" Gerry & The Pacemakers UK 4 weeks
1981 "Stars on 45" Stars On 45 US 1 week
1987 "Head To Toe" Lisa Lisa & Cult Jam US 1 week
1987 "Star Trekkin' " The Firm UK 2 weeks

21st

Birthdays

Lalo Schifrin 1932 Argentinian pianist, composer and conductor. Real first name Boris. He studied music, sociology and law at the University of Buenos Aires and then continued to study music in Paris from 1953 until 1955. Lalo is one of the most successful composers in Hollywood; his reputation as a jazz musician has grown through his partnership with Dizzy Gillespie. Best-known film scores are for *Cincinatti Kid* (1965) and *Bullit* (1968). His most successful scores for TV series are *Mannix* and "Mission Impossible" (1/68 US 41). He had a hit in the UK with his orchestra, playing the theme from "Jaws" (10/76 UK 14).

O. C. Smith 1932 US singer, real first names Ocie Lee. His career started in 1951 during his military service with the US Air Force. After his national service in 1955, he was with the Sy Oliver Band, made his first solo record in 1956, and was leadsinger with the Count Basie Band from 1961 until 1963. He had some success as a solo artist in 1968 with "Son Of Hickory Holler's Tramp" (2/68 US 40; 5/68 UK 2), "Little Green Apples" (8/68 US 2) and "Daddy's Little Man" (8/69 US 34).

Deodato 1942 Brazilian pianist, composer, arranger and producer. Complete name Eumire Deodato Almeida. His biggest personal hit was "Also Sprach Zarathustra" (2/73 US 2; 5/73 UK 7). As a producer he looked after Kool & The Gang from 1979 to 1982.

Ray Davies 1944 UK singer, guitarist and songwriter for the Kinks, formed in 1962. Real first names Raymond Douglas. He was the nucleus of the band with his brother Dave. Hits: "You Really Got Me" (8/64 UK 1; US 7), "All Day And All Of The Night" (10/64 UK 2; 12/64 US 7), "Tired Of Waiting For You" (1/65 UK 1; 3/65 US 6), "Sunny Afternoon" (6/66 UK 1; 8/66 US 14), "Waterloo Sunset" (5/67 UK 2), "Lola" (7/70 UK 2; US 9), "Apeman" (12/70 UK 5), and "Come Dancing" (8/83 UK 12; 5/83 US 6). Even if they no longer appear in the singles charts, they still make good albums.

Jon Hiseman 1944 UK drummer and songwriter with John Mayall, Jack Bruce and Colosseum among others.

Chris Britton 1945 UK guitarist with the Troggs from 1965 to 1969. He played lead guitar on their hits. In 1969 he released one unsuccessful solo album.

Brenda Holloway 1946 US singer, and songwriter. Hit: "Every Little Bit Hurts" (5/64 US 13). Later, she was a backing chorus vocalist for Joe Cocker.

Joey Molland 1947 UK guitarist with Badfinger and Natural Gas.

Joey Kramer 1950 US drummer with Aerosmith.

Alan Silson 1951 UK guitarist and harmonica player with Smokie.

Nils Lofgren 1953 US guitarist, singer, and songwriter. He played with Neil Young's backing band, then with Grin, and from 1976 as a solo artist with several good but unsuccessful albums. From 1984 he played with Bruce Springsteen's band. Recently, he has resumed his solo career.

Mark Brzezicki 1957 UK drummer with the group Big Country formed in 1982. As a session musician he recorded with Pete Townshend and Midge Ure.

Deaths

Bert Kaempfert 1980 Orchestra leader and songwriter. Born 16th October, 1923.

June Christy 1990 US singer and songwriter. Born November 20th, 1925.

Hits of the Day

1941 "Daddy" Sammy Kaye US 8 weeks
1947 "Peg O' My Heart" Harmonicats US 8 weeks
1975 "Love Will Keep Us Together" Captain & Tennille US 4 weeks
1980 "Crying" Don McLean UK 3 weeks

22nd

Birthdays

Kris Kristofferson 1936 US singer, guitarist, songwriter and actor. Many of his compositions were covered by other artists: "Me And Bobby McGee" was Janis Joplin's biggest hit. Kris himself had a million seller with "Why Me" (4/73 US 16). He was married to Rita Coolidge from 1973 until 1979 and they recorded a couple of albums together. As an actor he came to prominence in 1971, playing the main part in *Cisco Pike* (1972) and Billy in *Pat Garrett And Billy The Kid* (1973). Further well-known roles were in *A Star Is Born* (1976), *Convoy* (1978) and *Heaven's Gate* (1980).

Jimmy Castor 1943 US singer, saxophonist and songwriter. In 1957 he was in the Teenchords with Frankie Lymon's brother, Lewis. A year before that, he recorded "I Promise To Remember" with the group Juniors. Jimmy played saxophone on "Rinky Dink" by Dave 'Baby' Cortez in 1962. His first solo success was in 1966 with "Hey, Leroy, Your Mama's Calling You" (12/66 US 31). In 1972, he formed the Jimmy Castor Bunch and had his biggest hits with "Troglodyte (Cave Man)" (5/72 US 6) and "The Bertha Butt Boogie (Part 1)" (2/75 US 16). Later he turned to 'disco' trend.

Peter Asher 1944 UK singer, songwriter, and producer. He formed the duo Peter & Gordon, with Gordon Waller, who were successful between 1964 and 1967. Hits: "A World Without Love" (3/64 UK 1; 5/64 US 1), "Nobody I Know" (6/64 UK 10; US 12), "I Go To Pieces" (1/65 US 9), "True Love Ways" (4/65 UK 2; US 14), "To Know You Is To Love You" (6/65 UK 5; US 24), and "Lady Godiva" (9/66 UK 16; US 6). In 1968 Peter & Gordon split up, Peter became an A&R manager with the Beatles company Apple. Since the early 1970s he has worked as a very successful producer in the USA with James Taylor and Linda Ronstadt; and in the 1980s, with 10,000 Maniacs.

Howard Kaylan 1945 US leadsinger with the band Turtles, formed in 1963. Real surname Kaplan. His career was linked with that of his fellow band member Mark Volman (see 19th April).

Todd Rundgren 1948 US singer, guitarist, producer and songwriter. He started in bands like Money and Wood's Truckstop. In 1967 he formed Nazz. Hit: "We Gotta Get You A Woman" (11/70 US 20). In 1970, he released records under the pseudonym Runt, and, in 1972, he reverted to his own name. Hit: "Hello It's Me" (10/73 US 5). After that, he formed Utopia, who had a hit with "Set Me Free" (2/80 US 27). He produced groups and artists like Badfinger, Tubes, Grand Funk, Fanny, Sparks, New York Dolls, Meat Loaf and Patti Smith.

Alan Osmond 1949 US guitarist, singer and songwriter with the Osmonds, the oldest of the brothers. Alan also produced several hits for the group.

Green Gartside 1956 UK singer and songwriter with the group Scritti Politti formed in 1977. Complete surname Strohmeyer-Gartside. From 1981 he was in the British charts with hits "Wood Beez (Pray Like Aretha Franklin)" (3/84 UK 10), "The Word Girl" (5/85 UK 6), "Perfect Way" (9/85 US 11) and "Oh, Patti (Don't Feel Sorry For Lover Boy)" (5/88 UK 13).

Jimmy Somerville 1961 UK singer and songwriter. In 1984 he was a co-founder of the trio Bronski Beat. Hits with Jimmy as the singer, "Smalltown Boy" (6/84 UK 3), "Why?" (9/84 UK 6), and in a duet with Marc Almond, "I Feel Love (Medley)" (4/85 UK 3). In May 1985 he left the band and was replaced by John Jon. Jimmy formed the duo Communards with keyboard player Richard Coles. Hits: "Don't Leave Me This Way" (8/86 UK 1; 12/86 US 40), "So Cold The Night" (11/86 UK 8) and "Never Can Say Goodbye" (11/87 UK 4). Since 1989 he has made solo records. Hit: "Comment Te Dire Adieu" (11/89 UK 14).

Tommy Cunningham 1965 UK drummer with Wet Wet Wet.

Deaths

Judy Garland 1969 US actress and singer. She died of an overdose of sleeping tablets in London. Born 10th June, 1922.

Fred Astaire 1987 US dancer. Died of a lung disease. Born 10th May, 1899.

Hits of the Day

1940	"Imagination" Glenn Miller US 3 weeks
1968	"This Guy's In Love With You" Herb Alpert US 4 weeks
1974	"Always Yours" Gary Glitter UK 1 week

23rd

Birthdays

Zeb Turner 1915 US country boogie-woogie specialist and songwriter. Real name William Edward Grisham. He wrote the song "That's When The Heartache Begins". Zeb played a part in the film *My Darling Clementine*. His only hits were "Tennessee Boogie" (9/49 C&W 11) and "Chew Tobacco Rag" (4/51 C&W 8). He died 10th January, 1978.

Dotty Todd 1923 US singer. She was successful with husband Art. See 11th March.

June Carter 1929 US country singer and songwriter. She was a a member of the group Carter Family, but also worked as a soloist. She started out in 1943 with her sisters Helen and Anita, as the Carter Sisters. In the early 1960s she wrote "Ring Of Fire", which became a big hit for her husband to be, Johnny Cash (they married in 1968). She also recorded a number of duets with him.

Adam Faith 1940 UK singer and actor. Real name Terence Nelhams. In 1956 Adam was co-founder of a skiffle group called The Worried Men. In 1958 he made his first records which were all flops; at the time he was one of the many British singers copying Elvis. In 1959 he tried again, and succeeded. The biggest of 24 hits were "What Do You Want" (11/59 UK 1), "Poor Me" (1/60 UK 1), and "Someone Else's Baby" (4/60 UK 2). The hits continued until 1966, after which he produced Roger Daltrey and managed Leo Sayer. Adam is now an *'eminence gris'* of the UK record industry.

Rosetta Hightower 1944 US singer, who cut her first records as a member of the Orlons. Hits: "The Wah Watusi" (6/62 US 2), "Don't Hang Up" (10/62 US 4) and "South Street" (2/63 US 3). After 1968 she tried to launch a solo in the UK, not very successfully though.

Paul Goddard 1945 US bass player with Atlanta Rhythm Section and Al Kooper.

Betty Dragstra 1952 Dutch singer with Pussycat. The band had their greatest hit with "Mississippi" (8/76 UK 1).

Richard Coles 1962 UK keyboard player and song-writer with the Communards.

Deaths

Elton Britt 1972 US country singer and songwriter. Born 7th July, 1917.

Hits of the Day

1951	"Too Young" Nat 'King' Cole US 5 weeks
1960	"Three Steps To Heaven" Eddie Cochran UK 2 weeks
1966	"Paperback Writer" Beatles UK 2 weeks
1973	"Rubber Bullets" 10 CC UK 1 week
1984	"The Reflex" Duran Duran US 2 weeks

24th

Birthdays

Gene Austin 1900 US singer, pianist and songwriter. Real name Eugene Lucas. He was one of the most popular singers in the latter half of the 1920s: between 1925 and 1929 he reached No. 1 in the US charts 9 times. His biggest hits, which were also million sellers, were "My Blue Heaven" (12/27 US 1) and "Ramona" (5/28 US 1). He died 24th January, 1972.

Mick Fleetwood 1942 UK drummer. He played with the Cheynes, the Bo Street Runners, Peter B's Looners, and Shotgun Express before joining John Mayall's Bluesbreakers in July 1966. At that time, Peter Green and John McVie were with Mayall as well. All three of them were fired after one month, and formed their own blues band, Peter Green's Fleetwood Mac. Hits from this period: "Albatross" (12/68 UK 1; 5/73 RE-UK 2), "Man Of The World" (4/69 UK 2) and "Oh Well" (10/69 UK 2). In the meantime, 'Peter Green' had been dropped from the name, and finally he left the band. After a bout of 'musical chairs' in the line-up the only survivors were Mick and McVie. In the mid-1970s the changes of personnel and a lack of music direction militated against a cohesive unit. The band was transformed by the duo Lindsey/Buckingham which resulted in the outstanding album RUMOURS, from which several singles were extracted: "Dreams" (4/77 US 1; 7/77 UK 24), "Don't Stop" (7/77 US 3), and "You Making Loving Fun" (10/77 US 9). Further hits included "Tusk" (10/79 US 8; UK 6), "Hold On" (6/82 US 4), "Big Love" (3/87 US 5); UK 9), "Little Lies" (8/87 US 4; UK 5), and "Everywhere" (12/87 US 14; 4/88 UK 4). Mick also released solo albums, and as Mick Fleetwood's Zoo.

Jeff Beck 1944 UK guitarist and songwriter. In March 1965 he succeeded Eric Clapton in the Yardbirds, and from February 1967 until July 1972, he had his own band, then he played with the group Beck, Bogert, Appice until April 1974. Despite his musical ability, he always had a reputation for awakwardness. He made a number of solo records and is a highly sought-after session musician. As a solo artist, he had his biggest hit with "Hi-Ho Silver Lining" (3/67 UK 14; 11/72 RE-UK 17; 10/82 RE-UK 62); on which he was lead vocalist.

Arthur Brown 1944 UK singer and songwriter who had a hit with the group Crazy World Of Arthur Brown formed in 1966, "Fire" (6/68 UK 1; 9/68 US 2). After that he made good albums which however were not commercially successful. In the early 1980s he made another good attempt at a comeback with former band colleague Vince Crane, but again no hit materialised. He also sang on the first album by Alan Parsons.

Charlie Whitney 1944 UK guitarist with Family, Streetwalkers, Roger Chapman, Rhead Brothers, Eddie Money and Axis Point.

Chris Wood 1944 UK flautist, saxophonist, pianist and singer. He was a member of Traffic and Ginger Baker's Air Force. Chris was a much sought-after session musician who played on records by Fat Mattress, Sky, Jimi Hendrix, Free Creek and Crawler. He died 12th July, 1983.

Patrick Moraz 1948 Swiss keyboard player. He started with his own band, then played with Mainhorse, Refugee and finally in 1974 with Yes. In 1976 he became a solo artist and then, replacement for Mike Pinder with Moody Blues in 1981. He also worked with Bill Bruford.

Astro 1957 UK trumpeter and announcer for UB 40. Real name Terence Wilson. He is usually the central figure in their stage shows.

Andrew McClusky 1959 UK synthesizer player, singer, bassist, guitarist and songwriter for the band Orchestral Manoeuvres In The Dark, formed in 1978, who were successful from 1980. Hits: "Enola Gay" (10/80 UK 8), "Souvenir" (8/81 UK 3), "Joan Of Arc" (10/81 UK 5), "Maid Of Orleans (The Waltz Of Joan Of Arc)" (1/82 UK 4), "Locomotion" (4/84 UK 5), "So In Love" (5/85 UK 27; 7/85 US 26), "If You Leave" (3/86 US 4; 5/86 UK 48), "(Forever) Live And Die" (9/86 UK 11; US 19) and "Dreaming" (3/88 US 16).

Curt Smith 1961 UK singer, bassist and songwriter with the duo Tears For Fears formed in 1981. They had their first hit with "Mad World" (10/82 UK 3). Biggest hits: "Change" (2/83 UK 4), "Pale Shelter" (4/83 UK 5), "Shout" (12/84 UK 4; 6/85 US 1), "Everybody Wants To Rule The World" (3/85 UK 2; 5/86 RE-UK 5), "Head Over Heels" (6/85 UK 12; 9/85 US 3) and "Sowing The Seeds Of Love" (9/89 UK 5; US 2).

Glenn Allan Medeiros 1970 US singer, born in Hawaii. Hit: "Nothing's Gonna Change My Love For You" (2/87 US 12; 6/88 UK 1).

Deaths

Jackie Gleason 1987 US orchestra leader and film actor. Died of cancer. Born 26th February, 1916.

Hits of the Day

1950	"I Wanna Be Loved" Andrew Sisters US 2 weeks
1955	"Unchained Melody" Jimmy Young UK 3 weeks
1965	"I'm Alive" Hollies UK 1 week
1989	"Satisfied" Richard Marx US 1 week
1989	"Back To Life" Soul II Soul UK 4 weeks

25th

Birthdays

Clifton Chenier 1925 US singer and songwriter. He is considered to be the 'King Of Zydeco Music', the Cajun music of black people, the main instrument being the accordion. He made his first records in 1954 after being discovered in the street by a talent scout. He died 12th December, 1987.

Eddie Floyd 1935 US soul singer and songwriter. In 1955 he became a founder member and lead singer of the Falcons. Hit: "You're So Fine" (4/59 US 17). In 1961 Wilson Pickett joined them as an additional vocalist. In 1963 the band split up and Eddie carried on as a solo artist. Hits, "Knock On Wood" (9/66 US 28; 3/67 UK 19), and "Bring It On Home To Me" (10/68 US 17).

Carly Simon 1945 US singer and songwriter. She appeared as the Simon Sisters in April 1964 together with her sister Lucy. After making a few children's and folk records, Lucy got married in 1966. Carly carried on as a solo artist, with some success from 1971: "That's The Way I've Always Heard It Should Be" (4/71 US 10), "You're So Vain" (12/72 US 1; UK 3), "Nobody Does It Better" (7/77 US 2; UK 7), "You Belong To Me" (8/77 US 6), "Jesse" (8/80 US 11), and "Coming Around Again" (10/86 US 18; 1/87 UK 10). She was married to James Taylor from 3rd November, 1972 until 1982; they duetted on "Mockingbird" (2/74 US 5; UK 34).

Allen Lanier 1946 US keyboard player, guitarist and singer with Blue Öyster Cult.

Ian McDonald 1946 UK multi-instrumentalist. In 1968 he joined the group Giles, Giles, & Fripp formed the year before, which became King Crimson in January 1969. In December 1969 Ian left the band and, with another former member, formed McDonald & Giles. In 1971 he played with Centipede and on "Electric Warrior" by T. Rex. In 1974 he joined King Crimson again and then in 1976, played with Ian Lloyd in the USA. While working with Lloyd, Ian met Mick Jones and they formed Foreigner later that same year. In 1980 Ian left Foreigner.

Clint Warwick 1949 UK bass player with the original lineup of Moody Blues.

Tim Finn 1952 New Zealand singer, pianist and songwriter. In 1972 the seeds were sown in Auckland for the later group Split Enz; their first album appeared in 1976. The band was especially successful in the Antipodes. First international hit, "I Got You" (8/80 UK 12; US 53). In 1983 Tim released his debut solo album ESCAPE; it included "Fraction Too Much Friction" which never got into the charts.

David Paich 1954 US keyboard player, singer and songwriter for Toto. The group was formed in 1978. Before that, David played with Rural Still Life.

George Michael 1963 UK singer and songwriter. Real name Georgios Panayiotou. He formed a ska-band called Executives in 1979 with his friend Andrew Ridgeley and others. In 1981 the pair changed their style and name to Wham!. Hits: "Young Guns (Go For It)" (10/82 UK 3), "Bad Boys" (5/83 UK 2), "Club Tropicana" (7/83 UK 3), "Wake Me Up Before You Go-Go" (5/84 UK 1; 9/84 US 1), "Freedom" (10/84 UK 1; 7/85 US 3), "Everything She Wants/Last Christmas" (12/84 UK 2; US 1), "I'm Your Man" (11/85 UK 1; US 3) and "The Edge Of Heaven" (6/86 UK 1; US 10). At the end of 1986 the two members of Wham! announced they were going their separate ways. George had already released two solo singles before, "Careless Whisper" (8/84 UK 1; 12/84 US 1), and "A Different Corner" (4/86 UK 1; US 7). Further solo hits, "I Knew You Were Waiting (For Me)" (1/87 UK & US 1), a duet with Aretha Franklin, "I Want Your Sex" (6/87 UK 3; US 2), "Faith" (10/87 UK 2; US 1), "Father Figure" (1/88 UK 11; US 1), "One More Try" (4/88 UK 8; US 1), "Monkey" (7/88 UK 13; US 1) and "Kissing A Fool" (10/88 US 5; 12/88 UK 18).

Deaths

Johnny Mercer 1976 US songwriter and singer. Born 18th November, 1909.

Boudleaux Bryant 1987 US songwriter. Died of cancer. Born 13th February, 1920.

Hits of the Day

1964 "It's Over" Roy Orbison UK 2 weeks
1966 "Paperback Writer" Beatles US 1 week
1977 "Show You The Way To Go" The Jacksons UK 1 week
1977 "Got To Give It Up" Marvin Gaye US 1 week
1988 "Foolish Beat" Debbie Gibson US 1 week
1988 "I Owe You Nothing" Bros UK 2 weeks

Miscellany

1967 In the Abbey Road Studios the worldwide television programme Our World broadcast for the first time the title "All You Need Is Love" by the Beatles. Other participants were Marianne Faithfull, Keith Moon, Eric Clapton, Graham Nash, Gary Leeds, and Rolling Stones members Mick Jagger and Keith Richards. Estimates as to the number of viewers of this programme ranged from 150 to 400 million.

26th

Birthdays

Big Bill Broonzy 1893 US blues singer and guitarist. He was one of the first to come to the attention of white audiences. Hit: "Romance In The Dark" (11/40 US 23), with Lil Green. He had an enormous influence on other contemporary blues artists. Bill died 14th August, 1958.

Billy Davis Jr. 1940 US singer with the group Fifth Dimension formed in 1966. Hits: "Up-Up And Away" (6/67 US 7), "Stoned Soul Picnic" (6/68 US 3), "Aquarius/Let The Sunshine In" (3/69 US 1; UK 11), "Wedding Bell Blues" (9/69 US 1; 1/70 UK 26), "One Less Bell To Answer" (11/70 US 2) and "(Last Night) I Didn't Get To Sleep At All" (4/72 US 8). In November 1975 Billy and another member of Fifth Dimension, his wife Marilyn McCoo, left the group and carried on as a duo. Hit: "You Don't Have To Be A Star (To Be In My Show)" (9/76 US 1; 3/77 UK 7). In 1980 the two split up professionally.

Larry Taylor 1942 US bass player with Canned Heat, Harvey Mandel, John Mayall, and Tom Waits.

Georgie Fame 1943 UK singer and pianist. Real name Clive Powell. He is considered to be one of the best British R&B artists. Georgie made his recording debut as a pianist on "Pistol Packin' Mama" by Gene Vincent. In 1961 he became a member of Billy Fury's backing group The Blue Flames. In 1962, now no longer with Billy Fury, the Blue Flames expanded from four to seven musicians, adding a brass section. In 1963 Georgie got a recording contract as a solo artist. Hits: "Yeh Yeh" (12/64 UK 1; 2/65 US 21), "Get Away" (6/66 UK 1) and "Ballad Of Bonnie & Clyde" (12/67 UK 1; 2/68 US 7). Then he formed the duo Fame and Price with Alan Price. Hit: "Rosetta" (4/71 UK 1).

Jean Knight 1943 US soul singer with one hit, "Mr. Big Stuff" (5/71 US 2).

Richard McCracken 1948 UK bass player with Taste, Stud, Spencer Davis, Kevin Ayers, Axis Point and others.

Junior Daye 1950 UK singer with Sweet Sensation.

Rindy Ross 1951 US singer and saxophonist with Seafood Mama, who had her first regional hit in her hometown Portland in 1980 with "Harden My Heart" (10/81 US 3); it became a success nationally after the group renamed itself Quarterflash and re-released it.

Mick Jones 1955 UK guitarist and songwriter. He formed the group Clash in 1976 with Joe Strummer (see under 21st August). Mick stayed until 1983 and then formed Big Audio Dynamite. First hit, "E = MC2 (E equals MC squared)" (3/86 UK 11).

Chris Isaak 1956 US singer, guitarist, and songwriter. Real first names Christopher Joseph. In 1985 he made his first records.

Patti Smythe 1957 US singer who released her first records in 1982 with Scandal. She had her first success with "The Warrior" (6/84 US 7). From 1987 Patti made solo records.

Terri Nunn 1961 US singer and songwriter with Berlin. Biggest hit: "Take My Breath Away" (6/86 US 1; 9/86 UK 1), the love theme from the film *Top Gun*.

Hits of the Day

1943	"As Time Goes By" Rudy Vallee US 4 weeks
1953	"I'm Walking Behind You" Eddie Fisher UK 1 week
1961	"Quarter To Three" Gary U.S. Bonds US 2 weeks
1965	"Mr. Tambourine Man" Byrds US 1 week
1976	"You To Me Are Everything" Real Thing UK 3 weeks
1982	"I've Never Been To Me" Charlene UK 1 week

27th

Birthdays

Doc Pomus 1925 US songwriter. Real first name Jerome. He wrote many memorable hits of the 1950s and 1960s with Mort Shuman. Apart from Leiber and Stoller they were the most successful songwriting team rock 'n' roll era. They had their greatest hits in the 1960s. Although handicapped by polio, Doc started out as a blues musician. During that time he composed for Joe Turner and Ray Charles. He wrote the hit "Young Blood" for the Coasters with Leiber/Stoller. His first successful collaboration with Mort Shuman was "A Teenager In Love" for Dion & The Belmonts in 1959. This was followed by hits for Fabian, Andy Williams, Bobby Darin, Jimmy Clanton, Gary U. S. Bonds, Gene McDaniels, the Drifters, Jay & The Americans, Ben E. King, Elvis Presley and many others. He died on 14th March, 1991.

Björn Thelin 1942 Swedish bass player with the original line-up of the Spotnicks.

Bruce Johnston 1944 US singer. Together, he formed the Ripcords in the early 1960s with Terry Melcher, son of

Doris Day. Biggest hit: "Hey Little Cobra" (12/63 US 4). They also had two smallish hits as Bruce & Terry in 1964. When Brian Wilson of the Beach Boys said at the end of 1964 that he wished to concentrate on composing and producing, he was replaced by Glen Campbell in January 1965, and he in turn was replaced by Bruce in April 1965. Since the 1970s Bruce has alternated between the Beach Boys and his solo career.

Louis Risbrook 1953 US bass player with B. T. Express.

Miscellany

1971 Bill Graham, born in Berlin (real name Wolfgang Grajonca), closed Fillmore East in New York after a good-bye concert. In the autumn of the same year Fillmore West in San Francisco is closed too: the reason being the exorbitant fees of the bands.

Hits of the Day

1958 "ON The Street Where You Live" Vic Damone UK 2 weeks

1960 "Everybody's Somebody's Fool" Connie Francis US 2 weeks

1964 "World Without Love" Pater & Gordon US 1 week

1970 "The Love You Save/I Found That Girl" Jackson 5 US 2 weeks

1970 "El Condor Pasa" Simon & Garfunkel

1981 "One Day In Your Life" Michael Jackson UK 2 weeks

1981 "Bette Davis Eyes" Kim Carnes US 4 weeks (2nd time)

1987 "I Wanna Dance With Somebody (Who Loves Me)" Whitney Houston US 2 weeks

---

28th

Birthdays

Richard Rodgers 1902 US composer. He wrote hits like "My Funny Valentine" (1937) with lyricist Lorenz Hart from 1919 to 1943. After that he worked with Oscar Hammerstein, composing musicals like *Oklahoma!* (1943), *South Pacific* (1949), *The King And I* (1951) and *The Sound Of Music* (1959). He also wrote film scores. Richard died 30th December, 1979.

Lester Flatt 1914 US country guitarist and singer. He turned professional in 1939. He formed his own band, the Foggy Mountain Boys with Earl Scruggs in 1948, who were one of the best bluegrass groups of the day. Their best-known record was "Foggy Mountain Breakdown (Theme from Bonnie & Clyde)" (3/68 US 55), which was recorded in 1949. In 1969 Lester and Earl parted. Lester died 11th May, 1979.

George Morgan 1924 US country singer and songwriter. He had his biggest country hit with "Candy Kisses" (2/49 C&W 1). He crossed over into the pop charts once with "Room Full Of Roses" (10/49 US 25). George recorded until shortly before his death on 7th July, 1975.

Bobby Harrison 1943 UK drummer with the original lineup of Procol Harum. He stayed until July 1967 and then formed his own group Freedom. He played with Snafu in 1973/4 and with Matthew Fisher.

Dave Knights 1945 UK guitarist and bassist in the original lineup of Procol Harum. He left the group in March 1969, and went into management. Both he and the aforementioned Bobby Harrison played on the best known Procol Harum hit, "A Whiter Shade Of Pale".

Deaths

Red Nichols 1965 US orchestra leader. Born 8th May, 1905.

Harry Mills 1982 US singer with the Mills Brothers. Born on 19th August, 1913.

Hits of the Day

1941 "Dolores" Tommy Dorsey US 1 week

1947 "Chi-Baba, Chi-Baba (My Bambino Goes To Sleep)" Perry Como US 3 weeks

1947 "Temptation (Tim-Tayshun)" Red Ingle US 1 week

1957 "Gamblin' Man/Putting On The Style" Lonnie Donegan UK 2 weeks

1962 "Come Outside" Mike Sarne UK 2 weeks

1969 "Love Theme From 'Romeo And Juliet' " Henry Mancini US 2 weeks

1975 "I'm Not In Love" 10 CC UK 2 weeks

1980 "Coming Up" Paul McCartney US 3 weeks

1986 "The Edge Of Heaven" Wham! UK 2 weeks

29th

Birthdays

Leroy Anderson 1908 US composer, conductor and arranger. In 1935 he became the arranger for Arthur Fiedler & The Boston Pops Orchestra. It was Fielder who first popularised many of Anderson's compositions. Hits as Leroy Anderson & His 'Pops' Concert Orchestra, "The Syncopated Clock" (3/51 US 12), which became well-known as the theme of the TV programme Late Show, and "Blue Tango" (12/51 US 1). Both titles were million sellers. Many will know Anderson as the writer of "Sleigh Ride", a US Christmas standard, and also from "The Typewriter" (11/53 US 21), which was featured in a Jerry Lewis film. Leroy died 18th May, 1975.

Leonard Lee 1935 US singer and songwriter. He was successful in Shirley & Lee with Shirley Goodman (see 19th June). Then he tried as a soloist, but had no hits. Leonard died 23rd October, 1976.

Billy Storm 1938 US leadsinger with Valiants. After that he was a soloist with one hit, "I've Come Of Age" (4/59 US 28).

Little Eva 1945 US singer. Real name Eva Narcissus Boyd. She was a babysitter for Carole King and her husband-at- the-time Gerry Goffin, when the pair suggested that Eva sing a new composition, "The Locomotion" (6/62 US 1; 9/62 UK 2; 7/72 RE- UK 11). Further hits, "Let's Turkey Trot" (2/63 US 20; UK 13), and – with Big Dee Irvin – "Swinging On A Star" (5/63 US 38; 11/63 UK 7).

Johnnie Richardson 1945 US singer who recorded with Joe Rivers as Johnnie & Joe. Hit: "Over The Mountain, Across The Sea" (5/57 US 8). In 1963 she was a member of the Jaynettes whose only hit was "Sally, Go 'Round The Roses" (9/63 R&B 4).

Carlo Santanna 1947 UK guitarist and singer with Paperlace.

Dervin & Lincoln Gordon 1948 UK twins who joined the Equals in 1965 as leadsinger (Dervin), rhythm-guitar (Lincoln) and songwriters (both). At the end of 1966, the first record by the group was released; the A-side was "Hold Me Closer". It failed to chart, but the B-side "Baby Come Back" (5/68 UK 1; 9/68 US 32), was played by the disc jockeys and became a hit. Further hits were "Softly" (12/68), "Green Light" (3/69), "Michael And The Slipper Tree" (4/69 UK 24), "Viva Bobby Joe" (7/69 UK 6), "Rub A Dub Dub" (12/69 UK 34) and "Black Skin Blue Eyed Boys" (12/70 UK 9).

Ian Paice 1948 UK drummer, songwriter and producer. He was a founder member of Deep Purple with Rod Evans in March 1968, having left the group Maze. Before that, he had played in such groups as Georgie & The Rave Ons, Shindigs, and M 15. After Deep Purple split up in March 1976, Ian, with Jon Lord and Tony Ashton, formed the trio Paice, Ashton & Lord until September 1977. In July 1979 Ian joined Whitesnake as a drummer, replacing David Dowle. This group split up in autumn 1981. Ian played on several albums with Gary Moore, and then finally returned to Deep Purple in autumn 1984, which had reformed with the original lineup from the early 1970s.

Colin Hay 1953 Australian singer, guitarist and songwriter with Men At Work, formed in Melbourne in 1979 by Scottish born Colin. Hits: "Down Under" (11/82 US 1; 1/83 UK 1), "Who Can It be Now?" (7/82 US 1), "Overkill" (4/83 US 3; UK 21) and "It's A Mistake" (7/83 US 6; UK 33). In 1985 the band split up. In 1987 a solo record by Colin appeared which failed to impress.

Stedman Pearson 1964 UK singer with the sibling group Five Star formed in 1983.

Deaths

Eric Dolphy 1964 US jazz musician. Born 20th June, 1928

Shorty Long 1969 US singer. Capsized his boat and drowned. Born 20th May, 1940.

Tim Buckley 1975 US artist. Died of an overdose of heroin. Born 14th February, 1947

Lowell George 1979 US singer, guitarist and songwriter with Little Feat and as a soloist. Cause of death was given as a heart attack. Born 13th April, 1945.

Hits of the Day

1961	"Runaway" Del Shannon UK 3 weeks
1974	"Sundown" Gordon Lightfoot US 1 week
1974	"She" Charles Aznavour UK 4 weeks
1985	"Frankie" Sister Sledge UK 4 weeks
1985	"Heaven" Bryan Adams US 1 week

30th

Birthdays

Buddy Rich 1917 US jazz drummer and orchestra leader. Real first name Bernard. From 1938 Buddy played with Bunny Berigan, Artie Shaw (1939), Tommy Dorsey (1939-42, 44-46) and Harry James (1953/54). In between he also played with Nat 'King' Cole, Charlie Parker and, from 1946, his own orchestra. He is supposed to have a great technique by other drummers. Buddy died 2nd April, 1987.

June Valli 1930 US singer. She was successful from 1952 after winning in Arthur Godfrey's *Talent Scouts* TV programme. Hits: "Crying In The Chapel" (8/53 US 4), "Unchained Melody" (5/55 US 29), and "Apple Green" (3/60 US 29).

Dave Van Ronk 1936 US folk-blues singer, guitarist and songwriter. In the mid-1950s he played in traditional jazzbands, and after that got involved in the folk-scene in Greenwich Village and appeared with such musicians as Jack Elliott, Phil Ochs and Bob Dylan. In 1963 he played at the Newport Folk Festival and formed the Ragtime Jug Stompers. Many fans at the time thought Dave would became a great star – they were wrong.

Larry Hall 1941 US singer. Only hit: "Sandy" (11/59 US 15).

Larry Henley 1941 US leadsinger with the trio New-beats. Biggest hits: "Bread And Butter" (8/64 US 2; UK 15) and "Run Baby Run (Back Into My Arms)" (10/65 US 12; 10/71 UK 10).

Florence Ballard 1943 US singer in the original lineup of the Supremes. Florence left the group in 1967 and was replaced by Cindy Birdsong. She died 22nd February, 1976.

Eddie Rambeau 1943 US singer and songwriter. Real name Edward Flurie. Hit: "Concrete & Clay" (5/65 US 35).

Gene Cotton 1944 US singer and songwriter. In 1967 he made his first album. Hit: "Before My Heart Finds Out" (2/78 US 23).

Glenn Shorrock 1944 UK singer and songwriter in the Little River Band, formed in Australia in 1975. He emigrated to Australia with his parents as a teenager and became a member of the teeniebopper band Twilights who were very successful in the 1960s; he also played with Esperanto. From 1976 the Little River Band were successful internationally with "Reminiscing" (7/78 US 3), "Lonesome Loser" (7/79 US 6) and "The Night Owl" (8/81 US 6). Glenn left the group in June 1983 to start a solo career and was replaced by John Farnham. In 1987 Glenn returned to the band and Farnham started to make solo records.

Billy Brown 1946 US singer, whose career paralleled that of Al Goodman, see 31st March.

Theo Klouwer 1947 Dutch drummer with Cats.

Andy Scott UK guitarist with Sweet.

Stanley Clarke 1951 US jazz bassist and songwriter, who can also play piano and keyboards, guitar, flute and can sing. He became a member of Return To Forever and was a highly sought-after studio musician with Aretha Franklin, Santana, Deodato, Al DiMeola, Paul McCartney, La Toyah Jackson and George Duke. In addition, he released solo albums. In 1989 he turned up with the group Animal Logic.

Stefan Zauner 1952 German singer, pianist and songwriter who was successful mainly in Germany but had a hit in Britain, "Keeping The Dream Alive" (12/88 UK 14).

Hits of the Day

1973 "Give Me Love" George Harrison US 1 week
1973 "Skweeze Me, Pleeze Me" Slade UK 3 weeks
1979 "Are Friends Electric" Tubeway Army UK 4 weeks
1979 "Ring My Bell" Anita Ward US 2 weeks

July

1st

Birthday

Alvino Rey 1911 US guitarist and bandleader. Real name Alvin McBurney. After playing with Russ Morgan, Freddy Martin, and Horace Heidt, he formed his own band in 1939. It was successful between 1941 and 1948. His major hit was "Deep In The Heart Of Texas" (2/42 US 1). Alvino is considered to be one of the first musicians to play an amplified guitar.

Willie Dixon 1915 US singer, guitarist, bassist, composer and producer. As James Dixon he won the Heavyweight Boxing Championship for the Golden Gloves of Chicago in 1936. He formed his first group called the Five Breezes, then the Four Jumps Of Jive, and the Big Three Trio. Dixon wrote hundreds of blues songs and produced most blues artists, working in Chicago in the 1970s. He himself was only in the R&B charts once with "Walking The Blues" (9/55 R&B 6). He died 29th January 1992.

Bobby Day 1932 US singer and songwriter. Real name Robert Byrd. In 1950 he formed the Hollywood Flames. Hit: "Buzz-Buzz-Buzz" (11/57 US 11), who were also known as The Flames, 4 Flames, Hollywood 4 Flames, Jets, Tangiers, and finally as the Satellites. Greatest hit for Bobby Day "Rockin' Robin" (8/58 US 2). In 1960 he worked with Earl Nelson who had been leadsinger on their only hit as the Hollywood Flames and after that, in the duo Bob & Earl, but was then replaced by Bob Relf. He died on 15th July, 1990.

James Cotton 1935 US bluessinger, guitarist, harmonica player and songwriter. In 1954 he made his first record for Sun records and was in Muddy Waters' band from 1955 to 1966. After that, he formed his own blues band and made records as a solo artist or as an accompanying musician, but he never had a hit.

Delaney Bramlett 1939 US guitarist, singer, and songwriter. He made records from 1968 with Bonnie, his wife. In 1969 they went on tour with Blind Faith. Shortly after, Eric Clapton played with Delaney, Bonnie & Friends, but it didn't last. In 1982 they split up: band and marriage: both went solo, even though their greatest hit was "Never Ending Song Of Love" (5/71 US 13).

Deborah Harry 1945 US singer, songwriter and film actress. She started with the folk-rock band Wind In The Willows, who released an album in 1968. After that she worked as a Playboy Bunny and barmaid. In the early 1970s she joined the glitter-rock band Stilettoes as a singer. Later, guitarist Chris Stein became a member of the band. In 1974 Harry and Stein left the band and formed Angel & The Snakes, which became Blondie in 1975. Hits: "Denis" (2/78 UK 2), "Heart Of Glass" (1/79 UK 1; 3/79 US 1), "Sunday Girl" (5/79 UK 1), "Dreaming" (9/79 UK 2), "Atomic" (2/80 UK 1; 6/80 US 39), "Call Me" (3/80 US & UK 1), "The Tide Is High" (11/80 UK & US 1) and "Rapture" (1/81 UK 5; US 1). In autumn 1982 Blondie split up: Deborah carried on as a solo artist. Hit: "French Kissin' (In The USA)" (11/86 UK 8).

June Monteiro 1946 US singer with the Toys. Born on Jamaica. Hit: "A Lover's Concerto" (9/65 US 2; 11/65 UK 5).

Marc Benno 1947 US songwriter, guitarist, singer and keyboard player. In the late 1960s he formed the Asylum Choir with Leon Russell. He played on records by Rita Coolidge and Johnny Nash, and as a soloist in the 1970s.

John Ford 1948 UK bassist, singer and songwriter, whose career ran parallel to that of Richard Hudson (see 9th May).

John Farnham 1949 UK singer who emigrated to Australia with his parents when he was ten. When he was 18 he made his first single, "Sadie (The Cleaning Lady)" which reached No. 1 in the Australian charts. Up to 1981 he released any number of singles and albums as a soloist. In 1982 he replaced Glenn Shorrock as leadsinger with the Little River Band. In 1986 he returned to his solo career.

Hits: "You're The Voice" (3/87 UK 6) and "Age Of Reason" (9/88).

Fred Schneider 1951 US keyboard player and singer with the group B 52s, formed in 1976.

Dan Aykroyd 1952 Canadian film actor, singer, comedian and songwriter. He appeared together with John Belushi in the NBC TV show *Saturday Night Live* as the Blues Brothers and the Bees from 1975 to 1979. What they hadn't reckoned with, was that they would sell lots of records as the Blues Brothers. Hit: "Soul Man" (12/78 US 14). After Belushi's death 5th March, 1982, Dan carried on mainly as an actor, in films like *Ghostbusters*.

Leon Chancler 1952 US drummer. In 1971 he started with Herbie Hancock and became a sought-after studio musician, who made records with Santana, Flora Purim, the O'Jays, Crusaders and George Duke.

Evelyn 'Champagne' King 1960 US singer who was washed up on the disco wave. She was working as a cleaning lady at the Sigma Sound studios in Philadelphica when she was discovered. Major hits: "Shame" (6/78 US 9) and "Love Come Down" (8/82 US 17; UK 7).

Vito Bratta 1961 US guitarist and songwriter with White Lion.

Hits of the Day

1944	"I'll Be Seeing You" Bing Crosby US 4 weeks
1965	"Crying In The Chapel" Elvis Presley UK 1 week (2nd time)
1967	"Windy" Association US 4 weeks
1972	"Song Sung Blue" Neil Diamond US 1 week
1972	"Take Me Back 'Ome" Slade UK 1 week

2nd

Birthdays

Marvin Rainwater 1925 US singer and songwriter. The real surname of this Cherokee Indian is Percy. Rainwater was his mother's maiden name. After studying veterinary medicine, he became a member of Red Foley's group in 1946. Marvin began to write songs which were covered by Teresa Brewer, Justin Tubb and Connie Fran-

cis. Consequently, he got his own record contract: the hits like "Gonna Find Me A Bluebird" (5/57 US 18) and "Whole Lotta Woman" (3/58 UK 1) followed. In the early 1960s he underwent an operation on his vocal chords which, for a while, ended his singing career.

Lee Allen 1926 US tenor saxophonist on countless records which were recorded in New Orleans in the 1950s. He was also a regular member of Fats Domino's band. Hit: "Walkin' With Mr. Lee" (1/58 US 54).

Randy Starr 1930 US singer, guitarist and songwriter. Real name Warren Nadel. Hit: "After School" (4/57 US 32). He formed the instrumental duo Islanders with Frank Metis (born in Nurnberg, Germany) in the late 1950s. Hit: "The Enchanted Sea" (9/59 US 15). From 1970 he worked as a dentist.

Tom Springfield 1934 UK singer, and songwriter. Real name Dion O'Brien. He formed the Springfields in 1960 with his younger sister Dusty and Tim Field. Hits: "Silver Threads And Golden Needles" (9/62 US 20), "Island Of Dreams" (12/62 UK 5) and "Say I Won't Be There" (3/63 UK 5). In October 1963 Dusty left the group and began a solo career. Tom worked as a writer and producer, especially with the Seekers, composing "I'll Never Find Another You", "A World Of Our Own", "The Carnival Is Over" and "Georgie Girl".

Paul Williams 1939 US singer with the Temptations, and who was a founder member in 1960. In 1971 he was replaced by Richard Street. Paul died 17th August, 1973.

Leapy Lee 1942 UK singer and songwriter. Real name Lee Graham. Hit: "Little Arrows" (8/68 UK 2; 10/68 US 16).

Peter Cruickshank 1945 UK bass player with Groundhogs.

Hans Bathelt 1950 German drummer with one of the many lineups of Triumvirat from Cologne. He drummed on four albums by the band from 1972 to 1976.

Joe Puerta 1951 US leadsinger, bassist and songwriter with Ambrosia. Hits: "How Much I Feel" (9/78 US 3) and "Biggest Part Of Me" (4/80 US 3). He played on records by Chi Coltrane as a session musician, then with the Alan Parsons Project, Al Stewart and Chris Rea. In the latter half of the 1980s Joe turned up with Bruce Hornsby.

Peter Briquette 1954 UK bass player with Boomtown Rats.

Hits of the Day

1954	"Cara Mia" David Whitfield UK 10 weeks
1966	"Strangers In The Night" Frank Sinatra US 1 week
1969	"Something In The Air" Thunderclap Newman UK 3 weeks
1977	"So You Win Again" Hot Chocolate UK 3 weeks
1977	"Gonna Fly Now" Bill Conti US 1 week
1983	"Baby Jane" Rod Stewart UK 3 weeks
1988	"Dirty Diana" Michael Jackson US 1 week

3rd

Birthdays

Mississippi John Hurt 1893 US blues guitarist, singer and songwriter, who had recorded since the 1920s. He died 2nd November, 1966.

Fontella Bass 1940 US soul singer and pianist. Biggest hit: "Rescue Me" (10/65 US 4; 12/65 UK 11).

Judith Durham 1943 Australian leadsinger with the Seekers who were formed in Melbourne in 1964. They came to the UK in the same year. Hits: "I'll Never Find Another You" (1/65 UK 1; 3/65 US 4), "A World Of Our Own" (4/65 UK 3; US 19), "The Carnival Is Over" (10/65 UK 1), "Morningtown Ride" (11/66 UK 2) and "Georgy Girl" (12/66 US 2; 2/67 UK 3). In 1967 she started a solo career, her only hit was "Olive Tree" (6/67 UK 33).

Johnny Lee 1945 US country singer and songwriter. Real name John Lee Ham. In the early 1960s he played in rock bands, then he formed his own group Road Runners. After serving as a soldier in Vietnam, he played in Mickey Gilley's band in the latter's club in Pasadena, Texas. Later he opened his own club only a few miles away. On the side he worked on a solo career. It began with "Lookin' For Love" (7/80 US 5) from the film *Urban Cowboy*. Over the next few years he was often in the country charts, where he hit the No. 1 position 5 times, but these were inadequate credentials for the pop charts.

Paul Barrère 1948 US guitarist and singer with Little Feat. He made solo records too and played as a session musician with Nicolette Larson, Robert Palmer, Carly Simon, Johnny Nash and Bonnie Raitt.

Johnnie Wilder 1949 US leadsinger with Heatwave, formed in Kaiserslautern, Germany, in 1972, where Wilder was a G.I. Hits and million sellers: "Boogie Nights" (1/77 UK 2; 7/77 US 2), "The Groove Line" (1/78 UK 12; 5/78 US 7), and "Always And Forever" (1/78 US 18; 11/78 UK 9). In 1979 Johnnie had a serious car accident and was paralysed from the neck down.

Mike Corby 1955 UK guitarist, keyboard player and singer with the group Babys, formed in 1976.

Laura Brannigan 1957 US singer. Hits: "Gloria" (7/82 US 2; 12/82 UK 5), "Solitaire" (3/83 US 7) and "Self Control" (4/84 US 4; 7/84 UK 5).

Stephen Pearcy 1959 US singer and songwriter with Ratt, formed in the early 1980s. Their first hit was "Round And Round" (6/84 US 12).

Vince Clarke 1960 UK songwriter and pianist. Vince is one of the most scintillating personalities of British electro-pop. In 1976 he formed Depeche Mode. Hits: "New Life" (6/81 UK 11) and "Just Can't Get Enough" (9/81 UK 8). In December 1981 he left the band and formed Yazoo with Alison Moyet. Hits: "Only You" (4/82 UK 2), "Don't Go" (7/82 UK 3) and "Nobody's Diary" (5/83 UK 3). Alison left in autumn 1983, and became successful as a soloist. Then, Vince recorded "Never Never" (11/83 UK 4) with Fergal Sharkey as Assembly. In 1985 there followed a short unproductive spell with Paul Quinn; and in the same year, Vince started a new project with Andy Bell called Erasure. Major hits: "Sometimes" (10/86 UK 2), "Chains Of Love" (6/88 UK 11; US 12), "A Little Respect" (10/88 UK 4; 12/88 US 14), "Crackers International" (12/88 UK 2), "Drama" (9/89 UK 4) and "You Surround Me" (12/89 UK 15).

Stephen Morgan 1960 Australian bassist and singer with Icehouse.

Deaths

Brian Jones 1969 UK guitarist with the Rolling Stones. He was found drowned in his swimming pool. Born 28th February, 1942.

Jim Morrison 1971 US singer and songwriter with the Doors. He died in his bathtub in Paris – official cause of death, heart failure. Born 8th December, 1943.

Mississippi Fred McDowell 1972 US blues musician. Born 12th January, 1904.

Rudy Vallee 1986 US singer, actor, and songwriter. Born 28th July, 1901.

Hits of the Day

1943 "Comin' In On A Wing And A Prayer" Song Spinners US 3 weeks
1948 "Woody Woodpecker" Kay Kayser US 6 weeks
1953 "I Believe" Frankie Laine UK 6 weeks (2nd time)
1959 "Dream Lover" Bobby Darin UK 4 weeks
1965 "I Can't Help Myself" 4 Tops US 1 week (2nd time)
1968 "Baby Come Back" Equals UK 3 weeks
1982 "Happy Talk" Captain Sensible UK 2 weeks
1982 "Don't You Want Me" Human League US 3 weeks

4th

Birthdays

Louis Armstrong 1900 US jazz musician, trumpeter, singer, songwriter and 'incarnation of New Orleans jazz'. His inspiration was King Oliver in 1917, played in Kid Ory's band, and then with Fate Marable for 2 years on a Mississippi steamboat. In 1922 he was back with King Oliver, from 1924 with Fletcher Henderson and various other bands until forming his own band in 1926. At this time he was reckoned to be the world's best jazz trumpeter. He became really popular when, in addition to playing the trumpet, he began to sing as well: audiences really took to his gravelly voice. Among his hits in the pop charts were "All Of Me" (2/32 US 1), "Takes Two To Tango" (10/52 US 19; 12/52 UK 6), "Mack The Knife" (2/56 US 20; 4/56 UK 8), "Hello Dolly" (2/64 US 1; 6/64 UK 4) and "What A Wonderful World" (2/68 UK 1; 2/88 US 32). He is also featured on records by Fletcher Henderson, King Oliver, Bessie Smith, Carly Smith and Clarence Williams. Armstrong, whose nicknames were 'Pops' and 'Satchmo', also appeared in various films, like *High Society*. He died 6th July, 1971.

Charlie Monroe 1903 US country musician who appeared in Chicago together with his brothers Bill and Birch between 1929 & 1934. In 1936, having teamed up with Bill, formed the Monroe Brothers and made their first records: they played together for two years. In 1938 they split up, Charlie formed his own band, Kentucky Partners, with whom he made good but not particularly successful records. Charlie died 27th September, 1975.

Champion Jack Dupree 1910 US blues pianist, singer and songwriter who lived in Europe since 1958. Died Hanover Germany 21st January 1992.

Mitch Miller 1911 US orchestra leader and producer for such artists as Tony Bennett, Johnny Mathis, Frank Sinatra, Frankie Laine and Percy Faith's orchestra. He studied classical oboe, and played with the CBS Symphony Orchestra from 1936 to 1947. In the 1950s he first made a name for himself the SING ALONG WITH MITCH albums and TV programmes. Hits, with his own orchestra, "Tzena Tzena Tzena" (7/50 US 3), "Yellow Rose Of Texas" (8/55 US 1; 10/55 UK 2) and "River Kwai March" (1/58 US 20).

Gilbert Lopez 1934 US singer, with the Tune Weavers. Gilbert is the brother of Margo Sylvia.

Bill Withers 1938 US singer, guitarist and songwriter. In 1970 Bill cut his first records, produced by Booker T. Jones. Hits: "Ain't No Sunshine" (7/71 US 3), "Lean On Me" (4/72 US 1; 8/72 UK 18), "Use Me" (8/72 US 2) and "Lovely Day" (12/77 US 30; UK 7; 9/88 RE-UK 4). Furthermore, he had a hit with "Just The Two Of Us" (2/81 US 2; 5/81 UK 34) with saxophonist Grover Washington Jr.

Alan 'Blind Owl' Wilson 1943 US singer, guitarist, harmonica player and songwriter, with Canned Heat. John Lee Hooker once referred to him as the greatest harmonica player of all time. Hits, see 26th February under Bob Hite. Alan died 3rd September, 1970.

Jeremy Spencer 1948 UK guitarist, singer and songwriter. He was a founder member of Fleetwood Mac in July 1967, after playing with the Levi Set before that. In 1970 he released a solo album. In February 1971 he told the other band members in a hotel room in L.A. during a tour, that he was popping out for a minute. He wasn't seen for two years. Later it became known that Jeremy, like Peter Green before him, could no longer stand the pressure of success with Fleetwood Mac. He joined the Children Of God sect, and in 1973 released an album entitled JEREMY SPENCER & THE CHILDREN OF GOD. It wasn't until 1979 that another album by him appeared.

Ralph Johnson 1951 US drummer with Earth, Wind & Fire.

John Waite 1955 UK singer, bassist and songwriter. In 1976 John was a member of the Babys. Hits: "Isn't It Time" (10/77 US 13) and "Everytime I Think Of You" (1/79 US 13). In the spring of 1981 the band split up, and John carried on as a solo artist. First hit: "Missing You" (6/84 US 1; 9/84 UK 9). In 1988 he became a founder member of Bad English. Hits: "When I See You Smile" (9/89 US 1) and "Price Of Love" (12/89 US 5).

Deaths

Donald McPherson 1971 US leadsinger with Main Ingredient. He had leukaemia. Born 9th July, 1941.

Hits of the Day

1953	"I'm Walking Behind You" Eddie Fisher US 7 weeks	
1958	"All I Have To Do Is Dream/Claudette" Everly Brothers UK 7 weeks	
1964	"I Get Around" Beach Boys US 2 weeks	
1987	"It's A Sin" Pet Shop Boys UK 3 weeks	

Miscellany

1958 Vic Damone is still at No. 1 position in the UK with "On The Street Where You Live". The Everly Brothers join him and so two records are at No. 1 for one week.

5th

Birthdays

Smiley Lewis 1913 US R&B singer, guitarist and songwriter. Real name Overton Ames Lemons. Musically he had the same roots as Fats Domino, and was probably even a bit better vocally than the latter, but was not as successful with white audiences. Smiley cut his first records in 1947. He had his own biggest hit with "I Hear You Knocking" (9/55 R&B 2). Cover versions of his compositions became pop hits for others: "I Hear You Knocking" for Gale Storm and Dave Edmunds and "One Night" for Elvis Presley. Smiley died 7th October, 1966.

Robbie Robertson 1944 Canadian lead guitarist, singer and songwriter with The Band, previously Ronnie Hawkins' Hawks and Bob Dylan's accompanying band. Hits: "Up On Cripple Creek" (11/69 US 25); more successful in the UK, "The Weight" (9/68 UK 21), and "Rag Mama Rag" (4/70 UK 16). The Band split up in 1976. In 1987 an outstanding album by Robertson appeared, which yielded the hit single "Somewhere Down The Crazy River" (7/88 UK 15).

Dick Scoppettone 1945 US guitarist and singer with Harper's Bizarre.

Michael Monarch 1946 US guitarist with the group Sparrow formed in Canada in 1967. After an unsuccessful record the band moved to California, changing their name to Steppenwolf. In April 1969 Michael left the group and was replaced by Larry Byrom. In 1977 Michael turned up in the Heavy Metal band Detective.

Victor Unitt 1946 UK guitarist with Pretty Things and the Edgar Broughton Band.

Huey Lewis 1950 US singer, songwriter, harmonica player and producer. Real name Hugh Anthony Cregg. In 1967 he tramped through Europe as a street musician and then became a member of Slippery Elm, and Clover, who released their first single in November 1976. Huey was leadsinger and Nick Lowe was the producer. In 1977 Clover recorded four more singles and two albums, without success. In addition they accompanied Elvis Costello on his album MY AIM IS TRUE. In May 1979 Clover split up, and exactly a year later Huey Lewis & The News were formed. Hits: "Do You Believe In Love" (2/82 US 7), "Heart And Soul" (9/83 US 8), "I Want A New Drug" (1/84 US 6), "The Heart Of Rock 'n Roll" (4/84 US 6), "If This Is It" (7/84 US 6), "The Power Of Love" (6/85 US 1; 9/85 UK 11; 3/86 RE-UK 9), "Stuck With You" (8/86 US 1; UK 12), "Hip To Be Square" (10/86 US 3), "Jacob's Ladder" (1/87 US 1), "Doing It All For My Baby" (8/87 US 6) and "Perfect World" (7/88 US 3).

Michael Sadler 1954 Canadian leadsinger, keyboard player, bassist and songwriter. In 1976 he was a founder member of Saga, having previously played with Flood. In 1978 the first album by Saga was released, then the group became so well-known in Europe and especially in West Germany, that even Canadians thought Saga were a German group. Hit: "On The Loose" (12/82 US 26).

Deaths

Harry James 1983 US trumpeter and orchestra leader. Born 15th March, 1916.

Hits of the Day

1941	"The Band Played On" Guy Lombardo US 2 weeks	
1947	"Peg O' My Heart" Buddy Clark US 6 weeks	
1952	"Delicado" Percy Faith US 1 week	
1986	"There'll Be Sad Songs" Billy Ocean US 1 week	

6th

Birthdays

Laverne Andrews 1915 US singer, oldest of the three Andrews Sisters. Hits, see 3rd February under sister Maxine. Laverne died 8th June, 1967.

Bill Haley 1925 US singer, guitarist and songwriter. He started playing country music in the 1940s and formed the 4 Aces Of Western Swing in 1948. In the same year Bill made his first record with this band, "Too Many Parties, Too Many Pals". In 1950 he formed the Saddlemen. In 1951 Bill changed over to R&B, and in 1952 "Rock The Joint" was distinctively 'rock 'n' roll'. In 1953 he dropped the cowboy image completely and renamed his group Bill Haley & His Comets. The first record under this new name was also the first rock n' roll record in the charts, "Crazy Man Crazy" (5/53 US 12). His major hit was "Rock Around The Clock" (5/54 US 23; 1/55 UK 17; 5/55 RE-US 1; 10/55 RE-UK 1; 9/56 RE-UK 5; 12/56 RE-UK 24; 1/57 RE-UK 22; 4/68 RE-UK 20; 3/74 RE-UK 12; RE-US 39). This record has been one of the catalysts of rock 'n' roll, having sold more than 20 million copies over the years. It was recorded on 12th April, 1954, and became a hit after being used over the opening credits of the film *Blackboard Jungle*. Further hits for Bill were "Shake, Rattle & Roll" (8/54 US 7; 12/54 UK 4), "Burn That Candle" (11/55 US 9), and "See You Later Alligator" (1/56 US 6; 3/56 UK 7; 9/56 RE-UK 12). After 1958 the hits dried up. Haley died 9th February, 1981.

Della Reese 1931 US singer. Real name Delloreese Patricia Early. At first she sang gospel with Mahalia Jackson between 1945 and 1949, then she became a member of the Clara Ward Singers with Erskine Hawkins. In 1957 she became a solo artist. Hit: "Don't You Know" (9/59 US 2). In the USA she is also considered to be an outstanding actress who presents her own TV shows.

Gene Chandler 1937 US singer and songwriter. Real name Eugene Dixon. In 1955 he formed his own group, the Gaytones. In 1957 he became a member of the Dukays, then spent three years with the US Army in Germany, and finally returned to the Dukays. He had two smaller hits with this band, before landing his first hit, however the band were uncredited, "Duke Of Earl" (1/62 US 1). Further hits, "Groovy Situation" (7/70 US 12), and "Get Down" (2/79 UK 11).

Jet Harris 1939 UK bassist and songwriter in the first successful lineup of the Shadows. In 1962 he formed a partnership with Shadows-colleague Tony Meehan after a brief solo career. Greatest solo hit, "Man With The Golden Arm" (8/62 UK 12). Hits with Meehan, "Diamonds" (1/63 UK 1), "Scarlett O'Hara" (4/63 UK 2) and "Applejack" (9/63 UK 4). Comeback attempts regularly failed because of so-called "mental problems". In 1975 Jet said in an interview, "Two bottles of vodka a day, that's about my level."

Jan Bradley 1944 US singer. In 1962 Jan made his first record. Hit: "Mama Didn't Lie" (1/63 US 14).

Rik Elswit 1945 US guitarist. In 1971 he joined the group Dr. Hook formed in 1968.

Graham Oliver 1952 UK guitarist with Saxon formed in 1977.

David Smith 1952 UK singer with Real Thing.

John Keeble 1959 UK drummer with Spandau Ballet.

Deaths

Louis Armstrong 1971 US jazz trumpeter. He died in New York of a heart condition. Born 4th July, 1900.

Van McCoy 1979 US multi-instrumentalist. Cause of death: heart attack. Born 6th January, 1944.

Hits of the Day

1963	"Easier Said Than Done" Essex	US 2 weeks
1974	"Rock The Boat" Hues Corporation	US 1 week
1985	"Sussudio" Phil Collins	US 1 week

Miscellany

1964 The première of the first Beatles film, *A Hard Day's Night*, took place in the presence of Princess Margaret and Lord Snowdon.

7th

Birthdays

Anton Karas 1906 Austrian zither player and composer. He was 43 years old when he wrote the music for the film *The Third Man*. It became a worldwide hit and million seller, "The Third Man Theme" (2/50 US 1). In 1966 Karas opened a bar in Vienna called The Third Man. In the evenings he played the title song live, the lights were turned down and the waiters stopped serving the guests, to the annoyance of the latter. Karas made a mint with just this one hit. He died 10th January, 1985.

Lloyd 'Tiny' Grimes 1916 US guitarist, and singer who was considered to be the co-developer of 'Bop'. He was a member of Cats & The Fiddle, and the Art Tatum Trio before forming his own trio in the late 1940s, and then his own band, The Rocking Highlanders. Grimes who used to play a guitar with only four strings, was among the first to electrically amplify his guitar. He was in the US R&B charts once, with "Midnight Special" (11/48 R&B 12). He died of meningitis 4th March, 1989.

Elton Britt 1917 US country singer and yodeller. Real name James Britt Baker. In the 1930s he made his first records and cut the most popular country song to date with the number "There's A Star-Spangled Banner Waving Somewhere" (9/42 US 7). Elton also appeared in many films and TV shows. He died 23rd June, 1972.

Charlie Louvin 1927 US country singer and songwriter. Real name Charlie Elzer Loudermilk. In 1943 he worked together with his brother Ira as Foggy Mountain Boys in their own radio show. In 1947 they appeared together for the first time as Louvin Brothers, and in 1949 they made their first records. They split up in 1963. Charlie appeared in the films, *Music City USA* and *Golden Guitar*. The biggest hit as Louvin Brothers were, "I Don't Believe You've Met My Baby" (1/56 C&W 1) and for Charlie as a soloist, "I Don't Love You Anymore" (6/64 C&W 4). Their style of singing was copied by other duos like the Everly Brothers.

Mary Ford 1928 US singer. Real name Colleen Summer. She was successful with her husband, married from 1949 to 1963, as Les Paul & Mary Ford. For hits, see 9th June. Mary died 30th September, 1977.

Joe Zawinul 1932 Austrian composer and jazz rock multi-instrumentalist. Real first names Josef Erich. His career started as a pianist and bass clarinetist in jazz with Hans Koller, Fatty George and Friedrich Gulda from the early 1950s. In 1959 Maynard Ferguson employed him for his group. Between 1961 and 1970 he played in the Cannonball Adderly Quintet. At the end of 1971 Joe formed Weather Report who were successful worldwide until 1985. In 1987 he formed his new group, Weather Update.

Ringo Starr 1940 UK drummer, singer, songwriter and film actor. Real name Richard Starkey. He played with the Eddie Clayton Skiffle Group and with Rory Storm & The Hurricanes before becoming a member of the Beatles in 18th August, 1962 until they split up. Then he started a solo career. Hits: "It Don't Come Easy" (4/71 UK & US 4), "Back Off Boogaloo" (4/72 UK 2; US 9), "Photograph" (10/73 UK 8; US 1), "You're Sixteen" (12/73 US 1; 2/74 UK 4), "Oh My My" (3/74 US 5), "Only You" (11/74 US 6; UK 28) and "No No Song" (2/75 US 3). Ringo was once asked why he had so many rings on his fingers. His answer was, " 'cause I can't get them all in my nose." A funny guy.

Warren Entner 1944 US guitarist with the Grass Roots.

Jim Rodford 1945 UK bass player with Argent, Phoenix and from 1978 with the Kinks.

Rob Townsend 1947 UK drummer with Family. After that as a studio musician with Medicine Head, Kevin Ayers, Axis Point and others. From 1982 he was a member of the Blues Band and also of the Dave Kelly Band.

Larry Reinhardt 1948 US guitarist. In 1970 he joined Iron Butterfly formed in 1966.

David Hodo 1950 US singer with Village People.

Clive Jackson 1962 UK singer and guitarist, called 'The Doctor' of Doctor & The Medics. Hit: "Spirit In The Sky" (5/86 UK 1).

Deaths

George Morgan 1975 US country musician. Born 28th June, 1924.

Hits of the Day

1960	"Good Timin' " Jimmy Jones UK 3 weeks
1962	"The Stripper" David Rose US 1 week
1966	"Sunny Afternoon" Kinks UK 2 weeks
1973	"Will It Go Round In Circles" Billy Preston US 2 weeks
1984	"When Doves Cry" Prince US 5 weeks

8th

Birthdays

Louis Jordan 1908 US singer, clarinetist, saxophonist and songwriter. For many he is considered to be the father of modern R&B. He started as a professional musician in 1929 with Louis Armstrong, then played with various orchestras like Chick Webb. In 1938 Louis formed his first band, Elks Rendezvous, which evolved into Tympany Five in 1939. From 1942 he appeared in several films. Hits:

"G. I. Jive" (5/44 US 1), "Is You Is Or Is You Ain't (Ma' Baby)" (7/44 US 2), "Caldonia Boogie" (6/45 US 6), "Buzz Me" (1/46 US 9), "Stone Cold Dead In The Market (He Had It Coming)" (7/46 US 7) with Ella Fitzgerald, "Choo Choo Ch'Boogie" (8/46 US 7), "Ain't Nobody Here But Us Chickens" (1/47 US 6), "Open The Door, Richard" (3/47 US 6), "Baby, It's Cold Outside" (6/49 US 9) again with Ella, and "Saturday Night Fish Fry" (10/49 US 21 and still a million seller!). He made records right up until 1973. Louis died 4th February, 1975.

Billy Eckstein 1914 US singer and leader of his own orchestra. He started his career with Earl Hines, with whom he sang from 1939 to 1943, having the hit "Stormy Monday Blues" (4/43 US 23). Then Billy formed his own jazz band which included such crack musicians as Charlie Parker, Dizzy Gillespie, Art Blakey, Miles Davis and singer Sarah Vaughan. He was successful as a soloist from 1945 to 1956. His nickname was Mr. B., his real name William Clarence Eckstein. Hits: "A Cottage For Sale" (10/45 US 8), "Prisoner Of Love" (4/46 US 10), "My Foolish Heart" (3/50 US 6) and "I Apologize" (3/51 US 6), all titles mentioned were million sellers.

Jerry Vale 1932 US singer. Real name Genaro Louis Vitaliano. He was successful in the USA from 1953 to 1966. Biggest hit: "You Don't Know Me" (7/56 US 14).

Steve Lawrence 1935 US singer and actor. Real name Steven Leibowitz. In 1952 he made his first records. He married singer Eydie Gorme in 1957, with whom he also sang on records together as a duo. Solo hits: "Party Doll" (2/57 US 5), "Footsteps" (3/60 US 7; UK 4) and "Go Away Little Girl" (11/62 US 1).

Jai Johanny Johanson 1944 US drummer with the Allman Brothers Band, which had two drummers. In between, he played as a session musician for Charlie Daniels, Marshall Tucker Band and Sea Level. Real name John Lee Johnson.

Ricky Wolff 1945 UK guitarist with the Flowerpot Men and White Plains.

Willie Wilson 1947 UK drummer with Syd Barrett, Quiver, Cochise, Sutherland Brothers, David Gilmour, Roy Harper and Pretty Things.

Andy Fletcher 1961 UK synthesizer player with Depeche Mode.

Hits of the Day

1950 "Mona Lisa" Nat 'King' Cole US 8 weeks
1957 "(Let Me Be Your) Teddy Bear" Elvis Presley US 7 weeks

1965 "I'm Alive" Hollies UK 2 weeks
1972 "Lean On Me" Bill Withers US 3 weeks
1972 "Puppy Love" Donny Osmond UK 5 weeks
1989 "Good Thing" Fine Young Cannibals US 1 week

9th

Birthdays

Joe Liggins 1916 US singer, pianist, songwriter and bandleader. Early on, he was trying to obtain a big-band sound with a small combo. He had his first hit with "The Honeydripper" (8/45 R&B 1; 10/45 US 13). The record became a million seller. Further hits were "Got A Right To Cry" (2/46 US 12) and "Pink Champagne" (6/50 US 30); both were million sellers in 1950. Joe was active in the music business up to his death on 1st August, 1987.

Ed Ames 1927 US singer and actor. He started a quintet, the Ames Brothers, during his adolescence in Boston with his brothers Gene, Joe, and Vic (alias Ulrick). In the late 1940s he obtained a recording contract. Hits, see under oldest brother Joe, 3rd May. In 1959 the group split up, Ed attended acting school and began his career as a TV actor, playing Indian Mingo for 4 years in the series *Daniel Boone*. In addition, he started a successful solo career in 1965. Hit: "My Cup Runneth Over" (1/67 US 8). From the early 1970s he was no longer in the charts.

Lee Hazlewood 1929 US singer, songwriter and producer. He wrote a number of instrumental hits for his protègé Duane Eddy. In the 1960s Lee sang. Hits, with Nancy Sinatra, "Jackson" (6/67 US 14), "Lady Bird" (10/67 US 20) and "Did You Ever" (8/71 UK 2).

Donald McPherson 1941 US leadsinger with Main Ingredient. He died 4th July, 1971 and was replaced by Cuba Gooding.

Bon Scott 1946 Australian singer and songwriter of Scottish origin. In 1966 he started in the group Valentines, in the middle of 1970 he formed Fraternity. At the end of 1974 he joined AC/DC as leadsinger replacing Dave Evans (the group had been formed in Sydney in 1973). The group had their biggest hit with "Touch Too Much" (2/80 UK 29). Bon died 19th February, 1980 and was replaced by Brian Johnson.

Debbie Sledge 1954 US singer and oldest of the sibling group Sister Sledge, who cut their first records in 1971. Hits: "He's The Greatest Dancer" (2/79 US 9; UK 6), "We Are Family" (4/79 US 2; UK 8; 11/84 RE-UK 33), "Lost In Music" (8/79 UK 17; 9/84 RE-UK 4) and "Frankie" (6/85 UK 1).

Marc Almond 1959 UK singer, and songwriter. Complete first names Peter Marc. In 1979 he formed the duo Soft Cell with Dave Ball. Biggest hits: "Tainted Love" (8/81 UK 1; 1/82 US 8 – the records remained in the charts for a total of 43 weeks in the USA!), "Say Hello, Wave Goodbye" (2/82 UK 3), "Torch" (5/82 UK 2) and "What" (8/82 UK 3). In early 1984 the duo split up, Marc carried on as a soloist and had his first hit with Bronski Beat, "I Feel Love (Medley)" (4/85 UK 3). First Top Thirty hit as a solo artist was "Stories Of Johnny" (8/85 UK 23) while his biggest hit was "Something's Gotten Hold Of My Heart" (1/89 UK 1), featuring Gene Pitney.

Hits of the Day

1955	"Rock Around The Clock" Bill Haley US 8 weeks
1955	"Learning The Blues" Frank Sinatra US 2 weeks
1964	"House Of The Rising Sun" Animals UK 1 week
1966	"Paperback Writer" Beatles US 1 week (2nd time)
1977	"Undercover Angel" Alan O'Day US 1 week
1983	"Every Breath You Take" Police US 8 weeks
1988	"The Flame" Cheap Trick US 2 weeks
1988	"Nothing's Gonna Change My Love For You" Glenn Medeiros UK 4 weeks

---

10th

Birthdays

Sandy Stewart 1937 US singer, real name Sandra Ester Galitz. She was working in Eddie Fisher's and Perry Como's TV shows when she was a teenager. Her only hit was "My Coloring Book" (12/62 US 20).

Ian Whitcomb 1941 UK singer, songwriter and book author. As an artist he had the hit, "You Turn Me On (Turn On Song)" (5/65 US 8). As an author he wrote an interesting book on the development of pop music from rag to pop, called *After The Ball*.

Jerry Miller 1943 US guitarist and founder member of Moby Grape in 1966.

Beaky 1944 UK guitarist and drummer with the group Dave Dee, Dozy, Beaky, Mick, and Tich. Real name John Dymond.

Arlo Guthrie 1947 US singer, guitarist and songwriter. Son of the legendary Woody Guthrie. He created interest with his album ALICE'S RESTAURANT in November 1967, just a month after his father's death. It was a 19-minute talking blues and, perhaps, a little self-indulgent. However in 1969 it formed the basis of a film. Hit for Arlo, "The City Of New Orleans" (7/72 US 18), written by Steve Goodman.

Ronnie James Dio 1948 US singer and songwriter with Elf, Ritchie Blackmore's Rainbow and Black Sabbath. Ronnie also made solo records. Hit: "Rock 'n' Roll Children" (8/85 UK 26).

Dave Smalley 1949 US guitarist with the Raspberries from their inception in 1970 until 1973. After that with Dynamite.

Rik Emmett 1953 Canadian guitarist, singer, and songwriter with Triumph formed in 1975. Rik had played with Act III before that. Hits: "Hold On" (6/79 US 38) and "Somebody's Out There" (8/86 US 27).

Neil Tennant 1954 UK singer and songwriter with the Pet Shop Boys. Before forming this duo with Chris Lowe in 1984, he wrote for the teenager's 'bible' *Smash Hits*. The first version of "West End Girls" (11/85 UK 1; 3/86 US 1) recorded in 1984, was a flop; but the re-mixed version was successful a year later. Further hits: "It's A Sin" (6/87 UK 1; 9/87 US 9), then with Dusty Springfield "What Have I Done To Deserve This" (8/87 UK 2; 12/87 US 2), "Always On My Mind" (12/87 UK 1; 3/88 US 4), "Heart" (4/88 UK 1), "Domino Dancing" (9/88 UK 7; US 18) and "It's Alright" (7/89 UK 5). With the help of the Pet Shop Boys, both Dusty Springfield and Liza Minnelli revived their careers, at least in Europe.

Derry Grehan 1957 Canadian guitarist and songwriter for Honeymoon Suite.

Deaths

Jelly Roll Morton 1941 US R&B pianist. Born 20th September, 1885.

Arthur Fiedler 1979 US violinist and leader of the Boston Pops Orchestra. Born 17th December, 1894.

John Hammond 1987 US jazz musician and A&R man. Born on 15th December, 1910.

Hits of the Day

1940 "Make-Believe Island" Mitchell Ayres US 2 weeks
1961 "Tossin' And Turnin'" Bobby Lewis US 7 weeks
1965 "Satisfaction" Rolling Stones US 4 weeks
1976 "Afternoon Delight" Starland Vocal Band US 2 weeks

11th

Birthdays

Bill Snyder 1916 US pianist, composer and bandleader, who with his orchestra had million seller "Bewitched" (4/50 US 3) from the Broadway musical, Pal Joey.

Thurston Harris 1931 US singer and saxophonist. In 1953 he made his first records as a member of the Lamplighters. As a soloist he had his biggest hit with "Little Bitty Pretty One" (10/57 US 6). Harris died 14th April, 1990 of a heart attack.

Tab Hunter 1931 US film actor and singer. Real name Arthur Gelien. He made his first films in 1948. In 1957, by now an established film star, he made records as well. Hits: "Young Love" (1/57 US & UK 1) and "Ninety-Nine Ways" (3/57 US 11; UK 5). In 1971 Hunter said, "That star business is over. I was just lucky over the last few years. Now I am just one of many actors looking for a job. And acting is still what I do best."

Terry Garthwaite 1938 US guitarist, singer and songwriter with Joy Of Cooking, one of the first rockbands to be led by two women, Terry and Tony Brown. The group was formed in 1967 and kept going till 1973, after which Terry carried on as a soloist. In 1977 she formed Joy, a new version of the old band, which however did not last much longer than one album. After that, Terry worked again as a soloist.

Commander Cody 1944 US singer and pianist with Commander Cody And His Lost Planet Airmen, formed in 1968. Real name Gordon Frayne. The band played a mixture of boogie-woogie, western swing, country and rockabilly, which wasn't particularly commercial. Another birthdate quoted is 19th July.

Bonnie Pointer 1951 US singer and co-founder of the Pointer Sisters in 1969. Hits and history of the group can be found under sister Anita, 23rd January. Bonnie left the family group in 1978 and tried as a soloist. Her biggest hit was "Heaven Must Have Sent You" (6/79 US 11).

Peter Brown 1953 US singer, keyboard player, songwriter and sound engineer. Hits: "Do Ya Wanna Get Funky With Me" (9/77 US 18), and, together with Betty Wright "Dance With Me" (3/78 US 8).

Richie Sambora 1960 US lead guitarist with the group Bon Jovi formed in March 1983.

Mel Appleby 1966 UK singer with sister Kim as the duo Mel & Kim. Complete name Melanie Appleby. Before their singing careers took off, they were two of the best fashion models in London. The production team of Stock/Aitken/Waterman wrote many of their hits: "Showing Out" (9/86 UK 3), "Respectable" (3/87 UK 1), "F.L.M." (7/87 UK 7) and "That's The Way it Is" (2/88 UK 10). Mel died of cancer on 18th January, 1990 aged only 24.

Deaths

George Gershwin 1937 US composer. Died during an operation on a brain tumour in Hollywood. Born 26th September, 1898.

Hits of the Day

1960 "Alley-Oop" Hollywood Argyles US 1 week
1970 "Mama Told Me Not To Come" Three Dog Night US 2 weeks
1981 "Ghost Town" Specials UK 3 weeks
1987 "Alone" Heart US 3 weeks

12th

Birthdays

Oscar Hammerstein 1895 US lyririst. After Oscar had tried in vain to write plays, he started writing lyrics for Broadway shows in the 1920s. After some difficulties to begin with, he was successful with *Showboat* (1928) and *Carmen Jones* (1943). When librettist Lorenz Hart, who had worked closely with Richard Rodgers, died, Oscar and

Richard started to collaborate. This resulted in such classics as *Oklahoma!* (1943), *Carousel* (1945), *South Pacific* (1949), *The King And I* (1951) and *The Sound Of Music* (1959). Many of these musicals were made into successful films. Hammerstein produced many of these own shows, as well as many others too, like. *Annie Get Your Gun*. Oscar received the Pulitzer Prize in 1944 for *Oklahoma!* He died 23rd August, 1960.

Van Cliburn 1934 US pianist. Complete name Harvey Lavan Cliburn. His recording of the Piano Concerto No. 1 (1958) by Tchaikovsky was the first classical album to be a million seller in the USA.

Bill Cosby 1937 US film actor, comedian, singer and songwriter. Greatest pop-hit, "Little Ole Man (Uptight – Everything's Alright)" (9/67 US 4). His first seven albums, released from 1964 onwards, were all million sellers. He co-starred with Robert Culp in the TV series *I Spy*, and *The Cosby Show* has been a hit for NBC for years with some estimates making it the most successful TV Series currently running.

Swamp Dogg 1942 US singer and producer. Real name Jerry Williams Jr. He made his first records as Little Jerry in 1954. Hit: "Baby You're My Everything" (1/66 R&B 32). From the beginning of the early 1970s he appeared as Swamp Dog. Hit: "Mama's Baby – Daddy's Maybe" (4/70 R&B 33).

Christine McVie 1943 UK singer, pianist and songwriter. When her surname was still Perfect, she sang with the blues group Chicken Shack, with whom she made a number of good albums; she was voted best blues singer in the UK. Hit, with Chicken Shack, "I'd Rather Go Blind" (5/69 UK 14). The other influential blues group in the UK in the late 1960s was Fleetwood Mac. At a recording session Christine met bass player John McVie, whom she married a little later. In August 1970, after Peter Green had left Fleetwood Mac, Christine joined. After a few years of little success, they recorded album RUMOURS in 1975 which sold over 15 million copies worldwide. Hits: "Go Your Own Way" (1/77 US 10; UK 38), "Dreams" (4/77 US 1; 7/77 UK 24), "Don't Stop" (4/77 UK 32; 7/77 US 3), "You Make Loving Fun" (10/77 US 9), "Tusk" (10/79 US 8; UK 6), "Sara" (12/79 US 7; UK 37), "Hold Me" (6/82 US 4), "Oh Diane" (12/82 UK 9), "Big Love" (3/87 US 5; UK 9), "Little Lies" (8/87 US 4; UK 5) and "Everywhere" (11/87 US 14; 4/88 UK 4). In 1984 Christine released a solo album, which included the hits, "Gotta Hold On Me" (1/84 US 10) and "Love Will Show Us How" (4/84 US 30).

Jeff Christie 1946 UK multi-musician and singer with the band Christie. In 1968 he composed "Yellow River" (5/70 UK 1; 7/70 US 23), which he offered to the Tremelo-

es: they thanked him but declined. So he formed his own band and recorded the title himself. The follow-up hit was "San Bernadino" (10/70 UK 7).

Walter Egan 1948 US singer and songwriter. Hit, and million seller: "Magnet And Steel" (5/78 US 8). This record was recorded and produced with the help of Fleetwood Mac musicians.

John Wetton 1949 UK bass player, singer, and songwriter with Mogul Thrash, Family, King Crimson, Uriah Heep, Roxy Music and, from 1981, leadsinger of Asia. Hits: "Heat Of The Moment" (4/82 US 4) and "Don't Cry" (7/83 US 10; UK 33). From 1987 he played with Phil Manzanera as Wetton/Manzanera.

Eric Carr 1950 US drummer, from 1981 with Kiss, replacing Peter Criss. He died on November 24th, 1991.

Liz Mitchell 1952 Jamaican singer. In 1969 she had a part in the Berlin performances of *Hair*, and in the early 1970s she became a member of the Les Humphries Singers, where she met Malcolm Magaron. As a result, they formed Malcolm Locks. Her friend Marcia Barrett, who lived in Hamburg, suggested that they all join a new group Boney M which had just been formed by Frank Farian. Frank Farian once said that all the members of the group were replaceable except for Liz Mitchell. Their biggest hits were "Daddy Cool" (12/76 UK 6), "Sunny" (3/77 UK 3), "Ma Baker" (5/77 UK 2), "Belfast" (10/77 UK 8), "Rivers Of Babylon/Brown Girl In The Ring" (4/78 UK 1; 6/78 US 30), "Rasputin" (9/78 UK 2), "Mary's Boy Child/Oh My Lord" (12/78 UK), "Hooray! Hooray! It's A Holi-Holiday" (4/79 UK 3), and "El Lute" (8/79 UK 12).

Deaths

Minnie Riperton 1979 US singer and songwriter. She died of cancer. Born 8th November, 1948.

Chris Wood 1983 UK singer and multi-instrumentalist. Died after a long illness of liver disease. Born 24th June, 1944.

Hits of the Day

1952	"Auf Wiederseh'n Sweetheart" Vera Lynn US 9 weeks
1957	"All Shook Up" Elvis Presley UK 7 weeks
1962	"I Can't Stop Loving You" Ray Charles UK 2 weeks
1969	"In The Year 2525" Zager & Evans US 6 weeks
1975	"Tears On My Pillow" Johnny Nash UK 1 week

1980 "Xanadu" Olivia Newton-John UK 2 weeks	

1980 "Xanadu" Olivia Newton-John UK 2 weeks
1986 "Papa Don't Preach" Madonna UK 3 weeks
1986 "Holding Back The Years" Simply Red US 1 week

Jay Uzzell 1942 US singer and leader of the Corsairs, an R&B vocal-quartet which consisted of the three brothers Jay, James, & Moses Uzzell and their cousin George Wooten. Jay's nickname was Bird. They made their first records in 1961. Greatest hit: "Smoky Places" (12/61 US 12).

13th

Birthdays

Ernest Gold 1921 US composer, born in Vienna and emigrated to the USA in 1939. From the 1940s to the 1960s he composed and arranged countless film scores. His biggest success was the music for the film *Exodus*, which became a million seller in the version by piano-duo Ferrante & Teicher in 1960. He also wrote music for *On The Beach*, and for *It's A Mad Mad Mad Mad World*. Ernest is the father of songwriter and singer Andrew Gold.

Stephen Jo Bladd 1942 US drummer with the J. Geils Band.

Jim McGuinn 1942 US guitarist, singer, keyboard player, songwriter and co-founder of the Byrds. In 1964 they started as the Jet Set, then called themselves Beefeaters, but then decided on Byrds, spelled incorrectly on purpose, like the Beatles so to speak. McGuinn had worked previously with the Limelighters, the Chad Mitchell Trio, and as a session musician with Bobby Darin and Judy Collins. In January 1965, the Byrds met Bob Dylan who had a contract with the same record company. He gave them "Mr. Tambourine Man" (5/65 US & UK 1): Of the Byrds only Jim McGuinn played an instrument on the record, for the rest, session musicians played and the other Byrds sang. Further hits: "All I Really Want To Do" (7/65 US 40; UK 4) and "Turn! Turn! Turn!" (10/65 US 1; UK 26). In 1967, under the influence of a East-Asian subudcult, Jim changed his first name to Roger. In 1969 finally, he was the last one left of the original lineup. He carried on working as Byrds with a changing lineup until 1973. After that he made solo records and became a member of Bob Dylan's Rolling Thunder Revue. In 1977 Roger formed Thunderbyrd. Shortly afterwards he joined up with former band members Gene Clark and Chris Hillman, and recorded as McGuinn, Clark, Hillman. Hit: "Don't You Write Her Off" (3/79 US 33). After 1980 he carried on as a soloist.

Hits of the Day

1957 "Banana Boat Song" Harry Belafonte
1959 "Lonely Boy" Paul Anka US 4 weeks
1974 "Rock Your Baby" George McCrae US 2 weeks
1981 "Bette Davis Eyes" Kim Carnes
1985 "A View To Kill" Duran Duran US 2 weeks

Miscellany

1973 At the John Wayne Theatre in Bueno Park, California, Phil Everly furiously threw his guitar to the ground and left the stage during the concert. His brother Don, the other half of the Everly Brothers told the audience, "The Everly Brothers have already been dead for 10 years."

1985 Live-Aid took place simultaneously in the UK and the USA. It became the musical event of the year and earned the organiser Bob Geldof a nomination for the Nobel Peace Prize.

14th

Birthdays

Woody Guthrie 1912 US father of folk music. Real first names Woodrow Wilson. He was already writing songs at the time of the Great Depression, calling Americans to solidarity, which was the inspiration for the song "This Land Is Your Land". In 1939 he became friends with Pete Seeger with whom he formed the Almanac Singers in 1941, which then became the Weavers. Woody's style of singing was later adopted by Bob Dylan and many other folk singers. In 1954 Guthrie had to go into a New York hospital because of an incurable nerve disease inherited from his mother. He died there 3rd October, 1967. Many of his compositions have became standards over the years. His son Arlo performs some of his songs and has even emulated his style, but he has never come close to the genius of his father. A true genius.

Del Reeves 1933 US country singer, guitarist, song-writer and host of his own TV show. He is called the 'Dean Martin of Country Music'. His career started in 1961. Greatest hit, "Girl On The Billboard" (3/65 C&W 1).

Bob Scholl 1938 US singer and leader of the Mellow-Kings a white singing group who had their greatest hit with the number "Tonite, Tonite" (8/57 US 77; 1/61 RE-US 95). Bob died 27th August, 1975.

Vince Taylor 1939 UK singer, songwriter and guitarist who tried to be the answer to Elvis in the late 1950s. When he was unable to obtain any success in his home-country he tried his luck in France, where he landed a hit in 1961 with the self-penned "Brand New Cadillac".

Chris Cross 1954 UK bass player with Ultravox. Real surname Allen.

Deaths

Clarence White 1973 US guitarist and singer in one of the many lineups of Byrds. He was run over by a hit-and-run driver. Born 7th June, 1944.

Hits of the Day

1962 "Roses Are Red" Bobby Vinton US 4 weeks
1979 "Bad Girls" Donna Summer US 5 weeks

15th

Birthdays

Cowboy Copas 1913 US country singer and guitarist. Real first names Lloyd Estel. He is a specialist in songs in 3/4 time and was among the first to record the song "Tennessee Waltz" (5/48 C&W 3). He had his biggest pop-hit with "Don't Leave My Poor Heart Breaking" (12/51 US 15); his biggest country hits were "Signed, Sealed & Delivered" (1/48 C&W 2; 9/61 RE-C&W 10) and "Alabam" (7/60 C&W 1). He was killed with Patsy Cline and Hawkshaw Hawkins in a plane crash on 5th March, 1963.

Tommy Dee 1940 US country D.J., who wrote a song about the airplane crash which killed Buddy Holly, Big Bopper and Ritchie Valens. Carol Kay sang and while Tommy narrated: "Three Stars" (3/59 US 11).

Johnny Sea 1940 US country singer and guitarist. Real surname Seay. Between 1959 and 1968 he was in the country charts. He reached his highest position in the pop charts with "Day For Decision" (6/66 US 35), a patriotic answer to the record "Eve Of Destruction" by Barry McGuire.

Millie Jackson 1944 US singer and songwriter. In the early 1960s she worked as a model in New York, then became a full-time singer in 1964, cutting her first records in 1970. She also formed the trio Facts Of Life. Millie's solo hits: "Ask Me What You Want" (3/72 US 27) and "Hurts So Good" (9/73 US 24).

Peter Lewis 1945 US guitarist with Peter & The Wolves and Moby Grape.

Linda Ronstadt 1946 US singer. She started during her schooldays with her sister and a brother, as the folk trio The 3 Ronstadts. In 1964 she formed the group Stone Poneys. Hit: "Different Drum" (11/67 US 13). In 1968 Linda started her solo career. Her backing group in 1971 consisted of Glenn Frey, Don Henley, Randy Meisner and Bernie Leadon, who were to become the Eagles a little later. Greatest hits for Linda: "You're No Good" (12/74 US 1), "When Will I Be Loved" (4/75 US 2), "Blue Bayou" (9/77 US 3; 1/78 UK 35) with James Ingram, "Somewhere Out There" (12/86 US 2; 7/87 UK 8) from the film *An American Tail*, and with Aaron Neville, "Don't Know Much" (9/89 US 2; 11/89 UK 2). Most of her hits were produced by Peter Asher, formerly of Peter & Gordon.

Ian Campbell 1948 UK guitarist and flautist of Middle Of The Road.

Artimus Pyle 1948 US drummer with Lynyrd Skynyrd, Atlanta Rhythm Section and APB.

Trevor Horn 1949 UK singer, guitarist, songwriter and producer. After playing in Tina Charles', Trevor formed the duo Buggles with Geoff Downes in 1979. They had a hit with their very first record, "Video Killed The Radio Star" (9/79 UK 1; 11/79 US 40). Both Buggles' members became members of Yes in 1980, Trevor as a singer to replace Jon Anderson and Geoff on keyboards for Rick Wakeman. But after one album and a US tour the band split up again. Horn became an influential producer, working with ABC, Dollar, Frankie Goes To Hollywood and the German band Propaganda, among others. Among his greatest successes was "Do They Know It's Christmas" by Band Aid, which is the biggest selling record of all time in Britain. Musicians who have worked with him have described him as 'difficult', which may be putting it mildly.

Geoffrey Richardson 1950 UK violinist, guitarist, and flautist with Caravan, Rupert Hine, Murray Head and Penguin Cafe Orchestra.

David Pack 1952 US lead guitarist, pianist and singer with Ambrosia. He also worked with Alan Parsons, and as a solo artist.

Alicia Bridges 1953 US singer and songwriter. Hit: "I Love The Nightlife (Disco 'Round)" (7/78 US 5; 11/78 UK 32).

Ian Curtis 1956 UK singer, songwriter and guitarist. Founder of Joy Division. Committed suicide May 18, 1980.

Deaths

Bill Justis 1982 US saxophonist. Born 14th October, 1926.

Bobby Day 1990 US singer and songwriter. Born July 1st, 1932.

Hits of the Day

1955	"Dreamboat" Alma Cogan UK 2 weeks	
1974	"Sugar Baby Love" Rubettes	
1989	"If You Don't Know Me By Now" Simply Red US 1 week	

16th

Birthdays

Mindy Carson 1927 US singer and radio/TV presenter. After she had won the radio's young people's contest 'Stairway To The Stars', Mindy started out in the Paul Whiteman band, becoming the singer in Harry Cool's band in the same year. Hit with Harry, "Rumours Are Flying" (10/46 US 12). After that, she sang solo. Greatest hits: "Candy And Cake" (3/50 US 12), "My Foolish Heart" (4/50 US 6) and "Wake The Town And Tell The People" (8/55 US 13). In 1958 she appeared in the Broadway show *The Body Beautiful*: in the 1960s she withdrew from show business.

William Bell 1939 US singer and songwriter. Real surname Yarborough. In 1953 he started with Rufus Thomas' band, and then became a founder member of the Del Rios, and later sang with the Phineas Newborn orchestra. From 1962 to the middle of 1965 he was in the US Army and afterwards continued his solo career which he had begun in 1961. Hits, with Judy Clay, "Private Number" (11/68 UK 8), and as a soloist had the million seller "Tryin' To Love Two" (2/77 US 10). William set up the Peachtree and Wilbe record companies; his own records appeared with the latter from the mid-1980s.

Anthony Jackson 1940 UK bassist and lead singer with the Searchers, formed in 1960, until August 1964. He is the lead singer on all the group's great hits: "Sweets For My Sweet" (6/63 UK 1), "Sugar And Spice" (10/63 UK 2), "Needles And Pins" (1/64 UK 1; 3/64 US 13) and "Don't Throw Your Love Away" (4/64 UK 1; US 16). He was replaced by newcomer Frank Allen (formerly of Cliff Bennett & The Rebel Rousers) on bass, and Mike Pender took over as leadsinger. Jackson formed Tony Jackson & The Vibrations, who released three singles, their only success being "Bye Bye Baby" (10/64 UK 38). From the middle of 1965 he worked as a solo artist, but no hits materialised. He is still touring.

Desmond Dekker 1941 Jamaican singer and songwriter, real surname Dacres. Apart from Jimmy Cliff, he was one of the first successful reggae musicians. Hits, "007 (Shanty Town)" (7/67 UK 14), "Israelites" (3/69 UK 1; 5/69 US 9; 5/75 RE- UK 10), "It Mek" (6/69 UK 17) and "You Can Get It If You Really Want" (8/70 UK 2).

John Arthy 1942 UK tuba player, bassist and leader of the Pasadena Roof Orchestra.

Thomas Boggs 1947 US drummer with the Box Tops.

Ray Major 1949 UK guitarist and singer. In 1975 he replaced Ariel Bender in Mott The Hoople, after that British Lions.

Stewart Copeland 1952 US drummer and songwriter. In the mid-1970s he played on two albums by Curved Air, then with Eberhard Schoener, and in early 1977 he was a co-founder of Police. In addition, Stewart put a 10 inch album on the market as Clark Kent in June 1978, which was a complete flop. He also released solo records under his own name and, from 1989, played with Animal Logic.

Deaths

Harry Chapin 1981 US singer and songwriter. Died in a traffic accident, when a truck drove into the back of his blue 1975 VW Golf on Long Island. Chapin suffered a heart attack. Born 7th December, 1942.

Wayne King 1985 US bandleader with the nickname 'The Waltz King'. Born 18th June, 1906.

Hits of the Day

1964	"It's All Over Now" Rolling Stones UK 1 week
1966	"Hanky Panky" Tommy James & The Shondells US 2 weeks
1977	"Da Doo Ron Ron" Shaun Cassidy US 1 week

17th

Birthdays

Red Sovine 1918 US country singer, guitarist and songwriter. Real first names Woodrow Wilson. He was called the 'King Of Truck Driving songs'. From 1947 he played with his own band, the Echo Valley Boys. From the mid-1950s he was successful as a solo artist. First No. 1 hit in the country charts, "Giddyup Go" (11/65). Then he got into the pop charts with the million seller "Teddy Bear" (7/76 US 40; 6/81 UK 4). He died 4th April, 1980 after a traffic accident.

Spencer Davis 1941 UK guitarist and founder of the Spencer Davis Group, formed in 1963 with Stevie Winwood as leadsinger (Hits under 12th May). Spencer taught German at Birmingham University at the time. When Stevie Winwood left the band in 1967 to form Traffic, the group went into a decline.

Gale Garnett 1942 New Zealand folk singer. In 1951 she came to the USA and later appeared as an actress in several TV series. Hit: "We'll Sing In The Sunshine" (8/64 US 4).

Zoot Money 1942 UK keyboard player and singer. Real first names George Bruno. He played with Blues Incoporated briefly, in 1963/4 he formed the Big Roll Band. In 1968 he joined Eric Burdon & The Animals and then started a solo career. As a session musician, he has worked with artists like Peter Green and Family. From 1972 he played with Ellis, and from 1974 as a session musician again, with Scaffold, Eddie Harris, Alexis Korner, Kevin Coyne, Eric Burdon, Lonnie Donegan and Georgie Fame. He resumed his solo career with the album MR MONEY (1980). When the Animals re-formed in 1983, Zoot was enlisted.

Mick Tucker 1948 UK drummer with Sweet.

Geezer Butler 1949 UK bass player with Black Sabbath. Real first name Terry.

Eric Campbell 1950 UK bassist and pianist with Middle Of The Road.

Phoebe Snow 1952 US singer, guitarist, and songwriter. Real surname Laub. Her career began in the early 1970s in Greenwich Village. Hits: "Poetry Man" (1/75 US 5) and, with Paul Simon, "Gone At Last" (8/75 US 23). In 1981, she took a sabbatical from the music business returning in 1989 with the outstanding SOMETHING REAL.

Mandy Smith 1970 UK singer. Real first names Amanda Luise. During her teens, Mandy had a relationship with oldest Rolling Stone Bill Wyman, which earned her headlines, and then a record contract. Hits: "I Just Can't Wait" (3/87), and "Boys And Girls" (5/88). In the middle of 1989 she married Bill Wyman and together they opened a restaurant in London called 'Sticky Fingers'.

Deaths

Billie Holiday 1959 US blues singer. She died after taking a heroin overdose. Born 7th April, 1915.

John Coltrane 1967 US jazz saxophonist. Died as the result of a serious liver disease. Born 23rd September, 1926.

Roosevelt Sykes 1983 US blues pianist, singer, and songwriter. Born 31st January, 1906.

Hits of the Day

1976	"The Roussos Phenomenon" Demis Roussos UK 1 week
1982	"Fame" Irene Cara UK 2 weeks

Miscellany

1891 Haile Selassie I., Emperor of Ethiopia was born. For many reggae musicians and followers (Rastafarians), he was the one who was to lead them back into the Promised Land. He died 27th August, 1975.

1899 James Cagney was born in New York. He started as a variety singer and tap dancer; in 1931 he became an actor. Trade mark: aggression and immorality – the personification of the small-time gangster. And if that wasn't in demand, he played the irrepressible Irishman. He died 30th March, 1986.

1939 Cab Calloway recorded the title "Jumpin' Jive" which is considered to be the first million selling R&B number.

1968 In London, the animated movie *Yellow Submarine* had its premiere, for which the Beatles had written four new songs.

18th

Birthdays

Lou Busch 1910 US pianist and songwriter. From the late 1940s he worked as an arranger for Kay Starr and Dean Martin. Under the psuedonym Joe 'Fingers' Carr he released about 15 solo piano albums, and from one of these "Sam's Song" (6/50 US 7), and "Portuguese Washerwoman" (5/56 US 19). Lou died 19th September, 1979.

Screamin' Jay Hawkins 1929 US singer and songwriter. Real first name Jalacy. After a career as an amateur boxer he made records in the mid-1950s. Best-known record, "I Put A Spell On You" (1956).

'Papa' Dee Allen 1931 US percussion player and songwriter with War. Real first names Thomas Sylvester. He was co-writer of "World Is A Ghetto", "Low Rider", "Summer", "The 'Cisco Kid" and "Why Can't We Be Friends". He died 30th August, 1988 of a stroke.

Don Allen 1938 US drummer with the String-A-Longs.

Brian Auger 1939 UK keyboard player and songwriter with Steampacket, Trinity, Oblivion Express, on solo albums and as a studio musician.

Dion 1939 US singer and songwriter. Real name Dion Di Mucci. In 1957 he formed Dion & The Timberlanes, and a year later Dion & The Belmonts. Hits: "A Teenager In Love" (4/59 US 5; 6/59 UK 26) and "Where Or When" (12/59 US 3). After that he had hits as a solo artist, "Runaround Sue" (9/61 US 1; 11/61 UK 11), "The Wanderer" (12/61 US 2; 2/62 UK 10; 5/76 RE-UK 16), "Lovers Who Wander" (4/62 US 3), "Ruby Baby" (1/63 US 2) and "Abraham, Martin & John" (10/68 US 4). After trying to get back into business with the Belmonts in 1967 and 1972, Dion sang Christian songs for several years. In 1989 he returned to the rock business with the album YO FRANKIE, produced by Dave Edmunds and Bryan Adams.

Frank Farian 1941 German singer, songwriter and producer. Real name Franz Reuther. In the early 1960s he started out in the Saarbrucken area, forming his own group. They released their first records in 1963/4. In 1968 the band, broke up and he got a recording contract as a solo artist, calling himself Frank Reuther; after a few flops, he called himself Frank Farian. He came to prominence as a producer with the group Boney M. He wrote and produced a string of hits for them: "Daddy Cool" (12/76 UK 6), "Ma Baker" (5/77 UK 2), "Rivers Of Babylon" (4/78 UK 1; 6/78 US 30) and "Mary's Boy Child – Oh My Lord" (12/78 UK 1). In 1981 he seemed to lose interest in Boney M, but returned in 1988 as producer and songwriter for Milli Vanilli.

Lonnie Mack 1941 US guitarist and singer, real surname McIntosh. Biggest hit: "Memphis" (6/63 US 5), an instrumental version of the Chuck Berry song.

Martha Reeves 1941 US singer. She started her career as a singer with Del-Phis. In 1962 she formed her own band, which she called Martha & The Vandellas. Hits: "Heatwave" (8/63 US 4), "Quicksand" (11/63 US 8), "Dancing In The Street" (8/64 US 2; 10/64 UK 28; 1/69 RE-UK 4), "Nowhere To Run" (2/65 US 8; 4/65 UK 26), "I'm Ready For Love" (10/66 US 9; 12/66 UK 29) and "Jimmy Mack" (2/67 US 10; UK 21; 8/70 RE-UK 21). In November 1967 she changed the group's name to Martha Reeves & The Vandellas and had a hit, "Honey Chile" (11/67 US 11; 1/68 UK 30). After 1972 Martha made solo records.

Robin McDonald 1943 UK guitarist and bassist with the Dakotas, the backing band of Billy J. Kramer. From June 1968 to March 1969 he played with Cliff Bennett, and after that with Engelbert Humperdink's backing group.

Danny McCulloch 1945 UK bass player. From the end of 1962 he played with the group, The Savages, which featured Lord Sutch as vocalist. From 1966 he played with the Animals before becoming a solo artist in 1968, and then played with Reg King in 1971.

Tim Lynch 1946 US guitarist with Flamin' Groovies.

Phil Harris 1948 UK lead guitarist with Ace from their inception in December 1972 until March 1976.

Dave Vasco 1948 UK lead guitarist with Clancy.

Wally Bryson 1949 US guitarist with the Raspberries, Tattoo, and Photomaker.

Glenn Hughes 1950 US singer with Village People. He was the 'man in leather'.

Cesar Zuiderwyk 1950 Dutch drummer with Golden Earring.

Ricky Skaggs 1954 US country singer and multi-instrumentalist. After being promoted produced for years as a popstar, in the early 1980s he became really successful in the country charts. His first hit was "Crying My Heart Out Over You" (1/82 C&W 1).

Terry Chambers 1955 UK drummer with XTC.

Johnny B. Frank 1957 US bass player with Kingdom Come.

Audrey Landers 1958 US singer and actress. She was best-known for the role of Afton Cooper *Dallas* in the TV series which she played from 1981 to 1984. She was successful in Germany with the records "Manuel Goodbye" (4/83), and "Little River" (10/83). Audrey was an impressive dancer in *Chorus Line* (1985).

Nigel Twist 1958 UK drummer with Alarm.

Deaths

Robert Fuller 1966 US lead singer and guitarist with Bobby Fuller Four. The circumstances surrounding his death remained unexplained. The police assumed suicide, friends spoke of murder. Born 22nd October, 1943.

Nico 1988 US singer, songwriter and keyboards. Born 16th October, 1938.

Hits of the Day

1942	"Jingle, Jangle, Jingle" Kay Kyser	US 8 weeks
1960	"I'm Sorry" Brenda Lee	US 3 weeks
1963	"Confessin'" Frank Ifield	UK 2 weeks
1964	"Rag Doll" Four Seasons	US 2 weeks
1983	"Baby Jane" Rod Stewart	

19th

Birthdays

Sue Thompson 1926 US singer. Real name Eva Sue McKee. Hits: "Sad Movies (Make Me Cry)" (9/61 US 5), "Norman" (12/61 US 3), "James (Hold The Ladder Steady)" (9/62 US 17) and "Paper Tiger" (1/65 US 23; UK 30).

George Hamilton IV 1937 US pop/country folksinger, guitarist, songwriter and TV presenter. From the mid-1950s he was successful in the pop charts. Hits: "A Rose And A Baby Ruth" (11/56 US 6), "Why Don't They Understand" (12/57 US 10; 3/58 UK 22) and "Abilene" (6/63 US 15; C&W 1). From the early 1960s until 1978 he was regularly in the country charts.

Vikki Carr 1938 US singer, real name Florencia Bisenta de Casillas Martinez Cordona. In the early 1960s she regularly appeared in Ray Anthony's TV show. Her greatest hit was "It Must Be Him" (6/67 UK 2; 9/67 US 3).

Allan Gorrie 1946 UK bassist and singer with the Average White Band. As a session musician he played with Chaka Khan, B.A. Robertson, and Talk Talk.

Bernie Leadon 1947 US guitarist, singer and songwriter. His career began in 1958 with Scottsville Squirrell Barkers, and was a member of Hearts & Flowers from 1964 to 1968, with Dillard & Clark from August 1968 to May 1969, played with Linda Ronstadt's accompanying group the Corvettes for 5 months, and became a member of the Flying Burrito Brothers in September 1969. In April 1971 he again played with Linda Ronstadt for four months, and in August 1971 became a co-founder of the Eagles. Bernie stayed until September 1975 and was replaced by Joe Walsh. He played with the Bernie Leadon/Michael Georgiades Band, and worked as a session musician with David Bromberg, Andy Fairweather-Low, Chris Hillman, Helen Reddy, Chi Coltrane, Rita Coolidge and Stephen Stills.

Brian May 1947 UK guitarist, songwriter and occasionally also a singer with Queen. As a teenager he was with the group The Others, who released a single in Great Britain and the USA. In 1967 he formed Smile who also released a single. In 1970 Brian was a founder member of Queen.

Keith Godchaux 1948 US pianist. He played in Dave Mason's backing band. In 1971, he and his wife Donna joined the Grateful Dead. In April 1979 both were asked to leave on account of 'musical differences'. Further plans did not materialize as Keith had a car accident two days after his 32nd birthday, and died on 23rd July, 1979.

Allen Collins 1952 US lead guitarist with Lynyrd Skynyrd, who survived the air crash in 1977 in which singer Ronnie van Zant, Stevie Gaines, and the latter's sister Carrie lost their lives. In 1982 Allen formed the Rossington-Collins Band with former Lynyrd Skynyrd colleagues Gary Rossington, Bill Powell, and Leon Wilkeson. When this group split up in 1982, he carried on with the Allen Collins Band. After a car crash in 1986 he was paralyzed from the waist down. Allen died 23rd January, 1990 of pneumonia.

Silver Pozzoli 1953 Italian singer. He is supposed to have started out as a backing singer for David Crosby, Steve Winwood and Stevie Wonder. In 1983 he became leadsinger of the group Club House. Hit: "Do It Again/Billie Jean" (7/83 UK 11). In 1985 he became a solo artist. First hit, "Around My Dream" (5/85).

Deaths

Lefty Frizzell 1975 US country artist. Born 31st March, 1928.

Hits of the Day

1967 "All You Need Is Love" Beatles UK 3 weeks
1975 "Give A Little Love" Bay City Rollers UK 3 weeks
1975 "Listen To What The Man Said" Wings US 1 week
1980 "It's Still Rock 'n' Roll To Me" Billy Joel US 2 weeks
1986 "Invisible Touch" Genesis US 1 week

20th

Birthdays

Sleepy La Beef 1935 US rockabilly singer. Real first names Thomas Paulsley.

Jo Ann Campbell 1938 US singer. Greatest hit, "(I'm Not The Girl On) Wolverton Mountain" (8/62 US 38). She turned up for the last time as Jo Ann & Troy, with husband Troy Seals, in the lower echelons of the charts.

T. G. Sheppard 1944 US singer, real name Bill Browder. He tried as a pop star in the early 60s under the name Brian Stacey. No success. After that he worked as a record promoter for several years, and then finally turned to country music in 1974. He had his first country No. 1 in the same year with "Devil In The Bottle" (11/74 C&W 1). Biggest pop hit: "I Loved 'Em Every One" (3/81 US 37). 'T. G.' was an abbreviation for 'The Good'. Throughout the 1980s he was in the country charts regularly, hitting the No. 1 position 14 times.

Kim Carnes 1945 US singer, pianist and songwriter. She was a member of the New Christy Minstrels in the late 1960s with husband Dave Ellingson and Kenny Rogers. In 1971 Kim and Dave left the group and recorded "Nobody Knows" for the film *Vanishing Point*. In 1974 Kim's first solo album appeared. Before her solo career picked up momentum, she sang many different jingles for commercials. She has been in the charts since 1978. Hits: "Don't Fall In Love With A Dreamer" (3/80 US 4), with Kenny Rogers, and "Bette Davis Eyes" (3/81 US 1; 5/81 UK 10).

John Lodge 1945 UK bassist. His career started with El Riot & The Rebels, formed the Carpetbaggers, was then with John Bull Breed, and then the Falcons, before joining the Moody Blues in September 1966 to replace Clint Warwick. Two members of this band, Ray Thomas and Mike Pinder, had already played together with John in El Riot & The Rebels. Beside his membership of the Moody Blues he made solo records or with band colleague Justin Hayward.

John Almond 1946 UK keyboards and woodwind. In the late 1960s he played with John Mayall, then he released an album made in Hollywood in 1969. After that he formed Johnny Almond & The Music Machine, and finally, with guitarist Jon Mark, the Mark Almond Band, who played a rather mellow form of jazz-rock.

Carlos Santana 1947 Born in Mexico, he formed his own band, Santana, in San Francisco in 1966. Carlos is a very stylish guitarist, who has cut a string of highly individual albums. He is also a songwriter and occasionally a singer. He has played with John McLaughlin and Stanley Clarke, when he wasn't touring with his own band. Hits, for Santana: "Evil Ways" (1/70 US 9), "Black Magic Woman" (11/70 US 4), "Oye Como Va" (2/71 US 13), "Everybody's Everything" (10/71 US 12), "Samba Pa Ti" (9/74 UK 27), "She's Not There" (10/77 UK 11; US 27), "Winning" (4/81 US 17) and "Hold On" (8/82 US 15).

Tony Thorpe 1947 UK guitarist, singer and pianist with the Rubettes.

Paul Cook 1956 UK drummer with the Sex Pistols and after their split-up with the Professionals.

Michael McNeil 1958 UK pianist with Simple Minds.

Dig Wayne 1962 US singer with the British band Jo Boxers, who were successful from 1983. Hits: "Boxer Beat" (2/83 UK 3) and "Just Got Lucky" (5/83 UK 7).

Deaths

Roy Hamilton 1969 US singer. Died of a stroke. Born on 16th April, 1929.

Hits of the Day

1940	"Fools Rush In (Where Angels Fear To Tread)" Glenn Miller US 1 week
1956	"Why Do Fools Fall In Love" Frankie Lymon & The Teenagers UK 3 weeks
1961	"Temptation" Everly Brothers UK 2 weeks
1963	"Surf City" Jan & Dean US 2 weeks
1968	"Grazing In The Grass" Hugh Masekela US 2 weeks
1968	"Jumpin' Jack Flash" Rolling Stones
1987	"It's A Sin" Pet Shop Boys

Miscellany

1940 The US specialist magazine *Billboard* published the first weekly pop chart, 'Bestsellers in Stores'. It included 10 positions. The first number one was "I'll Never Smile Again" by Tommy Dorsey and his orchestra. The featured vocalist was Frank Sinatra. In addition to this pop chart in the USA, there were also following charts, 'Music Box Machine', 'Billboard Regional Favourites', and 'Radio Airplay Charts'. It is still customary for the US charts to appear for the following weekend, that is why the results of the first charts does not appear until our Hits of the Day on 27th July.

21st

Birthdays

Kay Starr 1922 US singer, real name Katherine Starks. She has been a successful solo artist in the USA since 1948. She started as a hillbilly singer, then sang with the bands of Glenn Miller, Bob Crosby and Charlie Barnett. Hits: "Hoop-Dee-Doo" (5/50 US 2), "Bonaparte's Retreat" (5/50 US 4), "I'll Never Be Free" (8/50 US 3), with Tennessee Ernie Ford, "Wheel Of Fortune" (2/52 US 1), "Comes A-Long A-Love" (9/52 US 9; 12/52 UK 1), "Side By Side" (1/53 US 3; 4/53 UK 7), "Changing Partners" (12/53 US 7; 3/54 UK 4), "Rock And Roll Waltz" (12/55 US 1; 2/56 UK 1) and "My Heart Reminds Me" (9/57 US 9).

Kim Fowley 1942 US songwriter, producer, manager, keyboard player and singer, who was born in Manila. Son of actor Douglas Fowley, who played the 'Doc' in the TV series *Wyatt Earp*. Kim began his career as a street singer, shoeshiner, dancer, and fortune-teller, and then played with the Jayhawks and the Sleepwalkers in 1957. From then on, he became a talent scout. In 1959 he produced Paul Revere & The Raiders, then the Murmaids, Hollywood Argyles, B. Bumble & The Stingers, and the Rivingtons, all had hits under his direction, sometimes with his compositions. In the mid-1960s he went to the UK and produced Slade, Family, Dave Mason and Jim Capaldi. From 1967 he also made solo albums on a regular basis.

Barry Whitham 1946 UK drummer with Herman's Hermits.

Cat Stevens 1947 UK singer, guitarist and songwriter, real name Stephen Demetri Georgiou. He had his first hits with "Matthew And Son" (1/67 UK 2) and "I'm Gonna Get Me A Gun" (3/67 UK 6). He also wrote for other artists like "Here Comes My Baby", for the Tremeloes and "First Cut Is The Deepest" for P. P. Arnold. At the end of 1967 his career seemed over. Doctors diagnosed T.B.. In 1970 he returned fit and well with "My Lady D'Arbanville" (6/70 UK 8), "Peace Train" (9/71 US 7), "Morning Has Broken" (1/72 UK 9; 3/72 US 6), "Oh Very Young" (3/74 US 10), and "Another Saturday Night" (8/74 US 6; UK 19). Until 1977 further, very good records appeared, then he withdrew from the business completely. In February 1979 he became a Muslim, calling himself Yusuf Islam.

Larry Tolbert 1950 US drummer with Raydio, and as a session musician.

Lee Aaron 1962 Canadian singer and songwriter.

Deaths

Champion Jack Dupree 1992 US blues pianist in Europe

Hits of the Day

1958	"Yakety Yak" Coasters US 1 week
1958	"Hard Headed Woman" Elvis Presley US 2 weeks
1966	"Get Away" Georgie Fame UK 1 week
1973	"Bad, Bad Leroy Brown" Jim Croce US 2 weeks
1973	"Welcome Home" Peters & Lee UK 1 week

22nd

Birthdays

Margaret Whiting 1924 US singer who started her solo career in 1946. In the early 1940s she sang with Freddie Slack's orchestra, having the hit "That Old Black Magic" (2/43 US 10), with Billy Butterfield "Moonlight In Vermont" (2/45 US 15 and a million seller!), with Paul Weston "It Might As Well Be Spring" (10/45 US 6). Hits, as a solo artist: "Guilty" (12/46 US 4), "Now Is The Hour (Maori Farewell Song)" (2/48 US 2), "A Tree In The Meadow" (7/48 US 1), "Far Away Places" (12/48 US 2), together with Johnny Mercer "Baby, It's Cold Outside" (5/49 US 3), and together with Jimmy Wakely "Slippin' Around" (9/49 US 1). She stayed in the record business until 1967.

Chuck Jackson 1937 US singer. In 1957 he left college and became a member of the gospel group Raspberry Singers. Between 1957 and 1959 he was with the Dell-Vikings. He made his first solo record in 1960. Biggest hit: "Any Day Now (My Wild Beautiful Bird)" (4/62 US 23).

George Clinton 1940 US singer and songwriter. In the 1950s George formed his first group, the Parliaments. Hit: "(I Wanna) Testify" (7/67 US 20). Out of this groups like Parliament – whose hits included the million sellers "Tear The Roof Off The Sucker (Give Up The Funk)" (5/76 US 15), and "Flashlight" (2/78 US 16) – and Funkadelic – hit and million seller "One Nation Under A Groove (Part 1)" (9/78 US 28) – were born. Clinton was the leader of both bands. But he also collaborated with other groups like Bootsy's Rubber Band, Brides Of Funkenstein, Parlet, Horny Horns, P. Funk All Stars among others. From 1982 George was a solo artist. Greatest success "Atomic Dog" (1/83 R&B 1). His nickname is 'Mr. Funkadelic'.

Thomas Wayne 1940 US singer, surname Perkins. His brother Luther played with Johnny Cash in the 50s. Thomas had one hit with "Tragedy" (1/59 US 5). He died 15th August, 1971.

Estelle Bennett 1944 US singer. In 1958 she formed the Darling Sisters with her sister Veronica and her cousin Nedra Talley Ross. In 1962 they sang on some Phil Spector productions and were renamed the Ronettes. They split up in 1966. For hits, see 10th August under Veronica.

Richard Davies 1944 UK pianist, singer, and songwriter for Supertramp. He started in the late 1960s with the band Joint. In 1969 he formed Supertramp. The group was supposed to have been called Daddy, but then the inspiration for the group's name came from the book, 'The Autobiography Of A Supertramp' by W. H. Davies, which was published in 1910. Hits: "Dreamer" (2/75 UK 13; 9/80 US 15), "The Logical Song" (3/79 UK 7), "Breakfast In America" (6/79 UK 9), "Take The Long Way Home" (10/79 US 10) and "It's Raining Again" (10/82 US 11; UK 26).

Bobby Sherman 1945 US actor and singer, star of many TV shows like *Shindig* between 1964 and 1966, *Here Come The Brides* between 1968 and 1970 and *Getting Together* in 1971/2. In the late 1960s he cut a few records which became hits: "Little Woman" (8/69 US 3), "La La La (If I Had You)" (11/69 US 9), "Easy Come, Easy Go" (2/70 US 9), and "Julie, Do Ya Love Me" (8/70 US 5), all million sellers.

Don Henley 1947 US drummer, singer, and songwriter for the Eagles. He started in the summer of 1963 with the group Four Speeds, then joined Felicity, who changed their name to Shiloh in 1969, and cut a record produced by Kenny Rogers in 1970, which, according to Don, was dreadful. In April 1971 Don became a member of Linda Ronstadt's backing band, which was to become the Eagles in 1971. By contrast with groups like the Byrds and the Flying Burrito Brothers, whose out put was based on country music, the Eagles country-ish harmonies were based upon a solid rock foundation. Hits: "Witchy Woman" (9/72 US 9), "Best Of My Love" (11/74 US 1), "One Of These Nights" (5/75 US 1; 8/75 UK 23), "Lyin' Eyes" (9/75 US 2; 11/75 UK 23), "Take It To The Limit" (12/75 US 4; 3/76 UK 12), "New Kid In Town" (12/76 US 1; UK 20), "Hotel California" (2/77 US 1; 4/77 UK 8), "Heartache Tonight" (10/79 US 1; UK 40), "The Long Run" (12/79 US 8), and "I Can't Tell You Way" (2/80 US 8). In 1981 the group announced they splitting up to follow solo projects. Hits, for Don: "Leather And Lace" (10/81 US 6) with Stevie Nicks, "Dirty Laundry" (10/82 US 3), "The Boys Of Summer" (11/84 US 5; 2/85 UK 12), "All She Wants To Do Is Dance" (2/85 US 9) and "The End Of The Innocence" (6/89 US 8).

Al DiMeola 1954 US guitarist and composer. He came to prominence in 1974 as a member of Chick Corea's Return To Forever. From 1975 he made solo records.

Hits of the Day

1965	"Mr. Tambourine Man" Byrds UK 2 weeks
1989	"Toy Soldier" Martika US 2 weeks
1989	"You'll Never Stop Me Loving You" Sonia UK 2 weeks

23rd

Birthdays

Cleveland Duncan 1935 US leadsinger, with the group Penguins, formed in 1954. Their biggest hit was "Earth Angel (Will You Be Mine)" (12/54 US 8, R&B 1), which is said to be the most successful R&B record of all time.

Madeline Bell 1942 US singer who obtained a recording contract in the UK in 1964. After her biggest hit, "I'm Gonna Make You Love Me" (2/68 US 26), she formed Blue Mink in 1969 with Roger Cook. Hits: "Melting Pot" (11/69 UK 3), "Good Morning Freedom" (3/70 UK 10), "Banner Man" (5/71 UK 3) and "Randy" (6/73 UK 9). Throughout her years with Blue Mink she continued her solo career, but none of her records left a trace in the charts.

Tony Joe White 1943 US singer, guitarist and songwriter. Hits: "Polk Salad Annie" (7/69 US 8) and "Groupie Girl" (6/70 UK 22). He wrote the hit "Rainy Night In Georgia" for Brook Benton calling himself a 'bayou rock singer'. His hits were produced by Billy Swan. His work with Tina Turner on her album FOREIGN AFFAIR released in 1989 was most impressive. Wrote "Games People Play".

Dino Danelli 1945 US drummer with the Young Rascals. In 1973/74 he played with Bulldog, in 1977 with Pepper, in 1978/79 with Photomaker, and from 1982 with Little Seven.

Andy Mackay 1946 UK saxophonist and songwriter. He played oboe with the London Symphony Orchestra, before joining Roxy Music in 1971. He also made several solo albums and is one of the most sought-after session musicians in the UK, having played with Rock Follies, Mickey Jupp, Godley & Creme, Paul McCartney and the Pet Shop Boys.

David Essex 1947 UK singer, songwriter and actor. Real name David Cook. He started in 1964 as the drummer with the group Everons. In 1965 he made his first solo record – it flopped – as did the next seven singles (all recorded from 1965 to 1970). David then starred in the musical *Godspell* playing the part of Jesus, from October, 1971. In 1972 he starred in the film *That'll Be The Day* with Ringo Starr. The film was very successful. In September 1973 David was signed by CBS; this really got his recording career going properly. He was produced by Jeff Wayne. Hits: "Rock On" (8/73 UK 3; 11/73 US 5), "Gonna Make You A Star" (10/74 UK 1), "Hold Me Close" (9/75 UK 1), "Oh What A Circus" (8/78 UK 3) and "A Winter's Tale" (12/82 UK 2). In the meantime, he continued to develope as an actor. In 1974 he co-starred with Adam Faith and Larry Hagman in *Stardust*, the sequel to *That'll Be The Day*; in 1978 he played the part of Che Guevara in the London West End musical *Evita*; and played the part of Fletcher Christian in 1983 in a musical version of *Mutiny On The Bounty*.

Blair Thornton 1950 Canadian guitarist with Bachman-Turner Overdrive from 1974 to 1979. He replaced Tim Bachman.

Dennis Greaves 1957 UK singer, guitarist, and songwriter who formed the group Nine Below Zero in the late 1970s: in their early days they usually played cover versions of R&B numbers. After a recording number of unsuccessful singles, Dennis dissolved the band and formed the quintet Truth in the summer of 1982. Hit: "Confusion (Hits Us Every Time)" (1/83 UK 22). In 1986 Dennis left with fellow founder member Mick Lister and carried on as a duo.

Martin Lee Gore 1961 UK guitarist, synthesizer player and songwriter for Depeche Mode. Hits, see 9th May, under David Gahan. In 1989 his first solo album, COUNTERFEIT, appeared.

Tim Kellett 1964 UK trumpeter and keyboard player with Simply Red since October, 1985.

Deaths

Keith Godchaux 1979 US pianist with Grateful Dead. He died as the result of a car accident. Born 19th July, 1948.

Kay Kyser 1985 US trumpeter and orchestra leader. Born 18th June, 1906.

Hits of the Day

1964	"A Hard Day's Night" Beatles UK 3 weeks
1969	"Honky Tonk Woman" Rolling Stones UK 5 weeks
1977	"I Feel Love" Donna Summer UK 4 weeks
1977	"Looks Like We Made It" Barry Manilow US 1 week
1983	"Wherever I Lay My Hat" Paul Young UK 3 weeks
1988	"Hold On To The Night" Richard Marx US 1 week

24th

Birthdays

Robert Farnon 1917 Canadian songwriter and orchestra leader, who is considered to be the most influential arranger of 'light music'. He started as a composer with Canadian Broadcasting Corporation, played with Percy Faith, finally had his own show with CBC, and worked for commercial radio stations. In the Second World War he came to Britain with the Canadian Army Music Corps. After 1945 he stayed in Britain and wrote the music for more than 30 films, among them *Expresso Bongo* (1959), starring Cliff Richard.

Barbara Jean Love 1941 US singer with Friends Of Distinction.

Heinz 1942 UK bassist and singer, born in Hagen, Germany; surname Burt. He started with the Tornados in 1960, who were Billy Fury's backing group to begin with, but who then had an instrumental hit with the record "Telstar" (8/62 UK 1; 11/62 US 1), produced by Joe Meek. Looking back, the British group Tornados were the first to reach the No. 1 position in the American charts. Heinz, the first male peroxide blonde of the British pop scene, was the group's sex symbol. In the middle of 1963 he left to start a solo career. Hit: "Just Like Eddie" (8/63 UK 5), a tribute to Eddie Cochran. In the late 1960s Eddie withdrew after participating in several pop films. In 1976 he turned up as an actor on television.

Alan Whitehead 1946 UK drummer with Marmalade.

Mike Karn 1958 UK saxophonist with Japan. Real name Anthony Michaelides.

Deaths

Peter Sellers 1980 UK singer and actor. Died after a heart attack. Born 8th September, 1925.

Hits of the Day

1943	"You'll Never Know" Dick Haymes US 7 weeks
1943	"Let's Get Lost" Vaughn Monroe US 7 weeks
1954	"Three Coins In The Fountain" Four Aces US 1 week
1968	"I Pretend" Des O'Connor UK 1 week
1971	"Indian Reservation" Raiders US 1 week
1971	"Get It On" T. Rex UK 4 weeks

1976	"Don't Go Breaking My Heart" Kiki Dee & Elton John UK 6 weeks
1976	"Kiss And Say Goodbye" Manhattans US 2 weeks
1982	"Eye Of The Tiger" Survivor US 6 weeks

Miscellany

1978 The film *Sgt. Pepper's Lonely Hearts Club Band* produced by Robert Stigwood has its premiere in New York. Although such artists as Peter Frampton (as Billy Shears), and the Bee Gees (as the Henderson Brothers) took part, and such crack musicians as Aerosmith, Alice Cooper and Earth Wind & Fire were involved with the soundtrack, the film and the accompanying record were a flop with the critics, and what was more important, with the public. A sound reflection the market reacted rightly and would not accept 'carbon copies'.

25th

Birthdays

Don Ellis 1934 US jazz trumpeter, composer and bandleader. Real first names Donald Johnson. He was very influential in the 1960s and 1970s. Don died 17th December, 1978.

Manuel Charlton 1941 UK guitarist with Nazareth.

Bruce Woodley 1942 Australian guitarist with the Seekers.

Jim McCarty 1943 UK drummer with the Yardbirds, after which he formed a duo with Keith Relf and then played with Renaissance and Box Of Frogs.

Tom Dawes 1944 US bassist with Cyrkle.

Steve Goodman 1948 US singer, guitarist and songwriter who was discovered by Kris Kristofferson. He wrote the hit "The City Of New Orleans" for Arlo Guthrie. His best-known composition was "Banana Republics". Steve died 20th September, 1984.

Mark Clarke 1950 UK bassist with Colosseum (1970/71), Uriah Heep (1971/72), Tempest (1972/73) and Rainbow (1977). In between he was a session musician with Ken Hensley, Natural Gas, Richard T. Bear, Billy Squire, Michael Bolton, Ian Hunter, Mountain and Henry Gross.

Verdine White 1951 US bass player and percussionist with Earth, Wind & Fire. He was also a session musician on records by Ramsey Lewis, Deodato, Emotions, Star Guard, Valerie Carter and Harvey Mason.

Gary Shaughnessy 1953 UK lead guitarist with Sweet Sensation.

Deaths

Big Mama Thornton 1984 US R&B singer. She died after a heart attack. Born 11th December, 1926.

Hits of the Day

1942	"Don't Sit Under The Apple Tree (With Anyone Else But Me)" Glenn Miller US 2 weeks
1970	"Close To You" Carpenters US 4 weeks
1987	"Who's That Girl" Madonna UK 1 week

Miscellany

1965 Bob Dylan had just returned from a tour of the UK. At the Newport Folk Festival he was announced by Peter Yarrow of Peter, Paul & Mary, and surprised everyone. He played with members of the Paul Butterfield Blues Band: the first song was "Maggie's Farm", featuring Bob on electric guitar. The audience were astonished. He wasn't even dressed like a folksinger any more. Bob wore a black leather jacket, a frilled shirt, black jeans, and – the symbol of Swinging London of those days, boots with high heels. The audience were not impressed, and someone shouted, "Go back to the Ed Sullivan Show!" Dylan later said of that evening, "I didn't have tears in my eyes – I was just surprised and probably a bit drunk."

26th

Birthdays

Erskine Hawkins 1914 US trumpeter, bandleader and songwriter. Between 1936 and 1948 he was in the charts with his own orchestra. Hits: "Tuxedo Junction" (12/39 US 7, Glenn Miller had a No. 1 with this title, but Erskine was the composer) and "Tippin' In" (4/45 US 9).

Al Banks 1937 US leadsinger with the Turbans. Hit: "When You Dance" (11/55 US 33). In 1961 the group split up.

Bobby Hebb 1941 US singer, songwriter and multi- instrumentalist. Hit: "Sunny" (6/66 US 2; 9/66 UK 12).

Neil Landon 1941 UK singer with Ivy League, Flowerpot Men, Fat Mattress and Main Horse Airline.

Brenton Wood 1941 US singer, songwriter and pianist. Real name Alfred Smith. In 1958 he first recorded with Little Freddy & The Rockets. Brenton had his greatest hit as a soloist with "Gimme Little Sign" (8/67 US 9; 12/67 UK 8).

Dobie Gray 1942 US singer, songwriter, and actor. Real name Leonard Victor Ainsworth. He had his first hit with "The In Crowd" (1/65 US 13; UK 25). After several unsuccessful years he joined the group Pollution in 1971, and then surprised everyone with a solo hit, "Drift Away" (2/73 US 5). As an actor he was on Broadway, and in the L. A. production of *Hair*.

Mick Jagger 1943 UK singer, songwriter, harmonica player and film actor. Complete first names Michael Philip. After singing with the group Little Boy Blue & The Blue Boys in London in 1960, which also included his friend, Keith Richard, (both were from Dartford in Kent), he joined Alexis Korner's Blues Incorporated. On 12th July, 1962 the Rolling Stones made their debut. In the band were Mick, Keith, Brian Jones, Dick Taylor and Tony Chapman. In December 1962 William Perks alias Bill Wyman replaced Dick, and in January 1963 Charlie Watts came in for Tony. This was the lineup which was to be so successful from 1964, and is still going strong. When Brian Jones left the group, he was replaced by Mick Taylor in June 1969, and he in turn was replaced by Ron Wood. Over the years, the Rolling Stones have had eight No. 15 in the UK and another eight in the USA: "(I Can't Get No) Satisfaction" (8/65 UK & US 1), and "Get Off Of My Cloud" (10/65 UK & US 1), "Ruby Tuesday" (1/67 UK 3; US 1; the B-side of this title in the USA was "Let's Spend The Night Together"), "Honky Tonk Woman" (7/69 UK & US 1), "Angie" (9/73 UK 5; US 1), and "Miss You" (5/78 US 1; UK 3). Mick had a solo hit in 1985 with "Just Another Night" (2/85 US 12; UK 32). Further hits, without the Rolling Stones, were "State Of Shock" (6/84 US 3; UK 14) with the Jacksons, and "Dancing In The Street" (8/85 US 7; UK 1) a duet with David Bowie. He appeared as an actor in *Ned Kelly* and in *Performance* (both 1970).

Roger Taylor 1949 UK drummer and songwriter with Queen. Complete surname Meddows-Taylor. In 1967 he formed the band Smile with Brian May. At the end of 1970 they both became founder members of Queen. In addition, he made solo albums, and in 1987 was founder and guitarist of the group Cross.

Duncan Mackay 1950 UK pianist with Baker Gurvitz Army, John Hiseman, Cockney Rebel, and 10 CC. He is also on records by Alan Parsons and Kate Bush, and as a soloist.

Danny Stagg 1960 US guitarist and bass player with Kingdom Come.

Miranda Joyce 1962 UK saxophonist, songwriter, and singer with the Belle Stars formed in 1980. Hits, "Iko Iko" (6/82 UK 35; it was featured in the film *Rain Man* with Dustin Hoffman and Tom Cruise, and therefore, appeared in the charts again: 3/89 US 14), and "Sign Of The Times" (1/83 UK 3).

Hits of the Day

1952	"Half As Much" Rosemary Clooney US 3 weeks
1962	"I Remember You" Frank Ifield UK 7 weeks
1975	"The Hustle" Van McCoy US 1 week
1980	"Use It Up And Wear It Out" Odyssey UK 2 weeks
1986	"Sledgehammer" Peter Gabriel US 1 week

27th

Birthdays

Juan Llossas 1900 'Tango King', Died 21st May, 1957.

Homer 1918 US country guitarist. Real name Henry D. Haynes. He formed the duo Homer & Jethro together with Kenneth C. Burns from 1932. The pair presented witty parodies of great pop hits. They even got into the charts themselves with "The Battle Of Kookamonga" (9/59 US 14), a parody on "The Battle Of New Orleans". Homer died 7th August, 1971.

Harvey Fuqua 1929 US leadsinger with the Moonglows, who were one of the classic R&B groups of the 1950s. The group started as Crazy Sounds, but were re-christened Moonglows by the popular disc jockey Alan Freed. But they also made records as Moonlighters. Hits: "Sincerely" (3/55 US 20) and "See Saw" (9/56 US 25). In 1958 Fuqua left the group, recruited new musicians, including Marvin Gaye, and made records as Harvey & The Moonglows. Hit: "Ten Commandments Of Love" (9/58 US 22). In the early 1960s Fuqua set up his own record label and produced the group Spinners, which he had

formed in 1961. In 1972 Fuqua reformed the Moonglows and re-released "Sincerely" 72 (8/72 R&B 43).

Nick Reynolds 1933 US singer and guitarist with the Kingston Trio. The group split up in 1968.

Bobbie Gentry 1944 US singer, guitarist, pianist, bassist, banjo player and songwriter. Born Roberta Streeter. She surprised the pop-world with her own composition "Ode To Billie Jo" (8/67 US 1; UK 13). Other hits: "I'll Never Fall In Love Again" (8/69 UK 1) and, with Glenn Campbell, "All I Have To Do Is Dream" (12/69 UK 3; 2/70 US 27). She has been married to singer Jim Stafford since 1978.

Maureen McGovern 1949 US singer. Hits: "The Morning After" (6/73 US 1 from the film *Poseidon Adventure*), "The Continental" (6/76 UK 16) and "Different Worlds" (7/79 US 18; theme of the TV series *Angie*).

Michael Vaughn 1950 UK lead guitarist and singer with Paper Lace.

Suzi Carr 1953 US singer with Will To Power.

Mark Stanway 1957 UK keyboard player with Magnum.

Hits of the Day

1940	"I'll Never Smile Again" Tommy Dorsey US 12 weeks
1974	"Annie's Song" John Denver US 2 weeks
1974	"Rock Your Baby" George McCrae UK 3 weeks
1985	"There Must Be An Angel" Eurythmics UK 1 week
1985	"Everytime You Go Away" Paul Young US 1 week

28th

Birthdays

Rudy Vallee 1901 US singer, bandleader, saxophonist, clarinetist, songwriter and actor. Real first names Herbert Pryor. From 1929 to 1946 he had a number of hits in the USA as Rudy Vallee & His Connecticut Yankees. He hit No. 1 five times: "Honey" (3/29), "Stein Song (University Of Maine)" (3/30), "Brother, Can You Spare A Dime?"

(11/32), "Vieni, Vieni" (10/37) and "As Time Goes By" (3/43). He died 3rd July, 1986.

Frankie Yankovic 1915 US accordion player, songwriter and record company owner. He made his first records in 1932 with the Slowene Folk Orchestra on his own label Yankee Label. He called himself and his band Frankie Yankovic & His Yanks. Hits: "Just Because" (5/48 US 9), and the million seller "Blue Skirt Waltz" (3/49 US 12). Frankie is a member of the International Polka Hall Of Fame and, in 1986, received the first ever Grammy awarded for the best polka recording.

George Cummings 1938 US guitarist with Dr. Hook.

Michael Bloomfield 1943 US guitarist and songwriter with Bob Dylan, John Hammond, Al Kooper, Moby Grape, the Paul Butterfield Blues Band, Electric Flag, as a trio with John Paul Hammond and Dr. John, KGB, Blues Blood, James Cotton Blues Band, and with several solo albums. Michael died 15th February, 1981.

Rick Wright 1945 UK pianist and singer with the group Pink Floyd formed in 1965, and on solo records. In between, he also played with Zee.

Jonathan Edwards 1946 US singer and songwriter. In 1965 he formed the bluegrass band Sugar Creek. Hit and million seller as a solo artist, "Sunshine" (11/71 US 4). After that he became a producer.

Peter Doyle 1949 Australian singer with the New Seekers from 1970 to 1973. He was replaced by Peter Oliver.

Simon Kirke 1949 UK drummer with Maniacs, Heatwave, Black Cat Bones, and finally with Free. After the band split up, Simon and Paul Rodgers formed Bad Company in 1973. As a session musician he has worked with Frankie Miller, Jim Diamond, Jim Capaldi, Jon Lord and among others.

Steven Peregrine Took 1949 UK percussionist and background singer with Tyrannosaurus Rex, formed as a duo in 1967 by Marc Bolan. In 1969 he left Marc and was replaced by Mickey Finn. Steven formed the group Pink Fairies. He died 27th October, 1980.

Gregg Guiffria 1951 US pianist with Angel.

Rachel Sweet 1962 US singer and songwriter. Hits: "B-A-B-Y" (12/78 UK 35) and, with Rex Smith, a star of several Broadway musicals, "Everlasting Love" (6/81 US 32; 8/81 UK 35).

Hits Of The Day

1945 "On The Atchinson, Topeka, And The Santa Fe" Johnny Mercer US 8 weeks

1951	"Come On-A My House" Rosemary Clooney US 8 weeks
1956	"I Want You, I Need You, I Love You" Elvis Presley US 1 week
1956	"I Almost Lost My Mind" Pat Boone US 4 weeks
1958	"Patricia" Perez Prado US 1 week
1960	"Please Don't Tease" Cliff Richard UK 1 week
1966	"Out Of Time" Chris Farlowe UK 1 week
1973	"I'm The Leader Of The Gang" Gary Glitter UK 4 weeks
1979	"I Don't Like Mondays" Boomtown Rats UK 4 weeks

29th

Birthdays

Mikis Theodorakis 1925 Greek composer. His greatest claim was his score for the film *Zorba The Greek* (1964).

Randy Sparks 1933 US head and founder of the New Christy Minstrels, formed in 1961 and who soon became one of the leading folk groups of the 1960s. Members of the band included Barry McGuire and Kenny Rogers, who later had successful solo careers. The group's biggest hit was "Green, Green" (6/63 US 14), written by Sparks and McGuire.

Geddy Lee 1953 Canadian singer, bassist and songwriter with the trio Rush. They were in the American charts from 1977 with hits like "Spirit Of Radio" (3/80 UK 13) and "New World Man" (9/82 US 21). In addition, Geddy made the record "Take Off" (1/82 US 16) together with Canadian comic duo, Bob & Doug McKenzie.

John Sykes 1959 UK guitarist, singer and songwriter. He played with Tygers Of Pan Tang (1981) and with Thin Lizzy (from December 1981). In November 1983 he joined Whitesnake and, with David Coverdale, became the main composer.

Deaths

Sir John Barbirolli 1970 British conductor. Born 2nd December, 1899.

Cass Elliott 1974 US singer with Mamas & Papas. She died after a heart attack brought on by choking on a sandwich. Where exactly, is unclear, some say in a London hotel, others say in the London apartment of Harry Nilsson. Born 19th September, 1943.

Pete Drake 1988 US steel guitarist. Born 8th October, 1932.

Hits of the Day

1955 "Rose Marie" Slim Whitman UK 11 weeks
1967 "Light My Fire" Doors US 3 weeks
1972 "Alone Again (Naturally)" Gilbert O'Sullivan US 4 weeks

Miscellany

1965 In London the second Beatles film *Help* has its world premiere.

30th

Birthdays

Chris McGuire 1929 US singer, and the oldest of the McGuire Sisters, who were very popular in the USA between 1954 and 1962. Hits: "Goodnight, Sweetheart, Goodnight" (6/54 US 7), "Sincerely" (1/55 US 1; 7/55 UK 14), "Something's Gotta Give" (6/55 US 5) and "Sugartime" (12/57 US 1).

Ed Byrnes 1933 US actor, and speaker on records. Real name Edward Breitenberger. He played the part of Gerald Lloyd Kookson III, called Kookie in the TV series *77 Sunset Strip* (1958–1963). Kookie was always combing his pompadour hairdo, which was the theme for the record "Kookie, Kookie (Lend Me Your Comb)" (4/59 US 4; UK 27). Connie Stevens took the lead vocal. After no more parts were offered him in the USA, either on TV or in films, he acted in several spaghetti westerns in Europe from 1967. In the 1970s he returned to the USA and appeared in endless episodes of numerous action-series.

Buddy Guy 1936 US blues guitarist and singer. Real first name George. He started playing professionally in 1953.

Paul Anka 1941 Canadian singer and songwriter. While spending his summer vacation, July to September with his uncle in Los Angeles in 1956, he made his first tentative steps into show business. His father, who owned a restaurant in Ottawa, financed the production of one record, "I Confess". Although the R&B group Cadettes, who had just had the hit "Stranded In The Jungle", were singing in the background, the record was a flop. In October, 1956, back at school in Canada, Paul started working on the song "Diana". The inspiration for the song was the Anka family's babysitter Diana Ayoub, who was 18 at the time, and therefore, beyond Paul's reach as he was just 15. In April 1957 he won a trip to New York. While there, he knocked at all the relevant doors of record companies. Don Costa of ABC Records was enthusiastic about the boy, and signed him up. A year later, thanks to "Diana" (7/57 US 1; 9/57 UK 1), Paul was a millionnaire. Among his other many hits were "I Love You Baby" (11/57 UK 3), "You Are My Destiny" (1/58 US 7; UK 6), "(All Of A Sudden) My Heart Sings" (12/58 US 15; UK 10), "Lonely Boy" (6/59 US 1; UK 3), "Put Your Head On My Shoulder" (8/59 US 2; 10/59 UK 7), "Puppy Love" (2/60 US 2; UK 33) and "You're Having My Baby" (7/74 US 1; 9/74 UK 6). He sang the latter with Odia Coates, although she was not credited. Paul Anka was also a prolific composer of material for other artists: "It Doesn't Matter Anymore" became the only number 1 hit for Buddy Holly in the UK; "She's A Lady" in 1971 was a million seller for Tom Jones; and in 1969 Paul wrote the English lyrics for the French song "My Way" which became a world hit for Frank Sinatra. Paul appeared in various Hollywood films between 1958 and 1962. He composed the theme song for the war film *The Longest Day* (1962), as well as acting in it. Even in the late 1980s, he was still in the record business, produced by Jack White (!).

David Sanborn 1945 US saxophonist. He played with Paul Butterfield Blues Band, B. B. King, Henry Gross, Bruce Springsteen, Cat Stevens, Ian Hunter, and many others. Made very good solo albums.

Jeffrey Hammond-Hammond 1946 UK bassist with Jethro Tull from 1971 to 1975.

Joyce Jones 1949 US singer. She sang with the female soul trio Debronettes, who were renamed First Choice in 1973. Hits: "Armed And Extremely Dangerous" (3/73 US 28; 5/73 UK 16) and "Smarty Pants" (8/73 UK 9).

Hugh Nicholson 1949 UK guitarist. His career began with Marmalade in 1971 and, from 1974, he played with Blue.

Frank Stallone 1950 US singer, and brother of Rambo and Rocky. Hit: "Far From Over" (7/83 US 10), from the film *Staying Alive*.

Kate Bush 1958 UK singer and songwriter. In 1974 Dave Gilmour of Pink Floyd heard Kate singing her own songs, paid for her to make demo recordings in a studio, and helped her get a contract with EMI. They decided to wait a little with Kate as a singer, encourage her to carry on writing songs, to train her voice, and take dancing and acting lessons. Which she did. In addition she was gathering live-experience in London pubs with her K. T. Bush Band. In January 1978 her first record was released, "Wuthering Heights" (2/78 UK 1). Further hits included "The Man With The Child In His Eyes" (6/78 UK 6), "Babooshka" (7/80 UK 5), and "Running Up That Hill" (8/85 UK 3; US 30). Then she had a hit with Peter Gabriel, "Don't Give Up" (11/86 UK 9).

Hits of the Day

1949 "Some Enchanted Evening" Perry Como US 5 weeks
1966 "Wild Thing" Troggs US 2 weeks
1977 "I Just Want To Be Your Everything" Andy Gibb US 3 weeks
1988 "Roll With It" Steve Winwood US 4 weeks

31st

Birthdays

Roy Milton 1907 US R&B singer, drummer and bandleader. Strongly influenced by gospel music, Roy joined various groups during the late 1920s. He had his first band Roy Milton & His Solid Senders in the 1930s. In the mid-1940s he released his first records on his own label. His first chart entry was the million seller "R. M. Blues" (8/46 US 20). From then until 1953 Roy had almost 20 Top Ten hits in the US R&B charts. Roy stayed in the music busines until the 1980s, and died after a stroke in September 1983.

Morey Carr 1932 US singer with the Playmates.

Bonnie Brown 1937 US singer. She was successful from 1955 with her sister Maxine and brother Jim Edward. First they appeared as Jim Edward, Maxine & Bonnie Brown, then from 1959 as The Browns. They had their biggest hits during that time with "The Three Bells" (7/59 US 1; 9/59 UK 6) and "The Old Lamplighter" (3/60 US 5). In 1967 the trio split up, Jim Edward and Maxine carried on working as solo artists.

Daniel Boone 1942 UK singer and songwriter. Real name Peter Lee Sterling. In 1958 he formed the band Beachcombers, went to London as a session musician in 1959, and wrote songs for Tom Jones and Kathy Kirby. Hits, for Daniel: "Daddy Don't You Walk So Fast" (8/71 UK 17) and "Beautiful Sunday" (4/72 UK 21; 6/72 US 15).

Lobo 1943 US singer, guitarist and songwriter. Real name Kent Lavoie. He played with several groups including Rumours, Sugar Beat, Me & The Other Guys, and 1961 Legends, which included, among others, Jim Stafford and Gram Parsons, and then became a solo artist in the early 1970s. Hits: "Me And You And A Dog Named Boo" (4/71 US 5; 6/71 UK 4), "I'd Love You To Want Me" (9/72 US 2; 6/74 UK 5) and "Don't Expect Me To Be Your Friend" (12/72 US 8). He had pop hits until the end of the 1970s, and then appeared more frequently in the country charts. He also formed the country group Wolfpack with Narvell Feltz and Kenny Earle.

Gary Lewis 1946 US drummer, singer and leader of the band Gary Lewis & The Playboys, formed in 1964. Real surname, like his father's, the film actor Jerry Lewis, Levitch (see under 16th March). Hits, by the band: "This Diamond Ring" (1/65 US 1), "Count Me In" (4/65 US 2), "Save Your Heart For Me" (7/65 US 2), "Everybody Loves A Clown" (9/65 US 4), "She's Just My Style" (12/65 US 3), "Sure Gonna Miss Her" (3/66 US 9) and "Green Grass" (5/66 US 8). At the beginning of 1967 Gary was conscripted into the Army, and after 1968 the band split up.

Bob Welch 1946 US singer, guitarist, and songwriter. He started with Head West, became a member of Fleetwood Mac in 1971, stayed till 1974, formed Paris, and then carried on as a solo artist. Hit: "Sentimental Lady" (10/77 US 8); among the backing singers were Christine McVie and Lindsey Buckingham of Fleetwood Mac.

Karl Green 1947 UK bass player with Herman's Hermits.

Carlo Karges 1951 German guitarist and songwriter with Nena.

Hugh MacDowell 1953 UK cellist with ELO from 1971, and occasionally with Wizzard.

Daniel Ash 1957 UK guitarist and singer with the formation Bauhaus formed in 1978, and after they had split up in July 1983, with Tones On Tail, and Love & Rockets.

Norman Cook 1963 UK bass player and singer with the Housemartins. After the band was dissolved in 1988 – according to their own statement, they had originally planned to stay together for three years, – Norman released his first solo record in 1989, "Won't Talk About It" (7/89 UK 29).

Deaths

Jim Reeves 1964 US country-pop singer. Killed when his private plane crashed. Born 20th August, 1924.

Hits of the Day

1959	"Living Doll" Cliff Richard UK 6 weeks	
1968	"Mony Mony" Tommy James & Shondells UK 2 weeks	
1971	"You've Got A Friend" James Taylor US 1 week	

August

1st

Birthdays

Morris Stoloff 1898 US orchestra leader, composer, and violinist, who was already playing with the Los Angeles Philharmonic Orchestra when he was a child. In 1928, when the film industry discovered sound and required the music necessary for it, Morris became concert leader for the film company Paramount, and in 1936 became musical director for Columbia Pictures, and became a freelance musical director in 1940. Morris was awarded three Oscars for his scores of the films *Cover Girl* (1944), *The Jolson Story* (1946), and *Song Without End* (1960). His greatest hit in the pop charts was Moonglow And Theme From 'Picnic' (4/56 US 1; 6/56 UK 7). Morris died 16th April, 1980.

Lionel Bart 1930 UK songwriter, real surname Begleiter. In 1956 he formed the Cavemen with Tommy Steele. After Tommy had become a star, Lionel turned more to songwriting. He wrote "Living Doll" for Cliff Richard and "Do You Mind" for Anthony Newley. In the early 1960s he got more involved with musicals and film scores, writing the script, music and lyrics for *Oliver!* (1968).

Jerry Garcia 1942 US guitarist, singer, songwriter and producer. Real first names Jerome John. In 1964 he was co-founder of Mother McCree's Uptown Jug Champions, who underwent several name changes during the next few months. In 1965 they became the Warlocks, then by the end of the year they were Grateful Dead, a name Garcia just happened upon in the Oxford Dictionary. In 1966 the first albums by Grateful Dead were released. As a producer, Jerry worked with Jefferson Airplane in 1966; and in 1970, he produced New Riders Of The Purple Sage, and played on their records too. In 1971 he made his first solo album. In 1986, when Grateful Dead were on tour, with Bob Dylan and Tom Petty & The Heartbreakers, Garcia suffered from fatigue; the doctors diagnosed diabetes. In 1987, after a seven-year hiatus, IN THE DARK appeared, featuring "Touch Of Grey" (7/87 US 9), which became the group's first Top Ten hit.

Geoff Britton 1943 UK drummer with Gun, East Of Eden, Wild Angels, Wings, Rough Diamond, Manfred Mann's Earthband, Raphael Ravenscroft and Key.

Boz Burrell 1946 UK bass player and singer with King Crimson, Centipede, and from 1974 with Bad Company. Real first name Raymond.

Rick Coonce 1947 US drummer with the Grass Roots.

Tommy Bolin 1951 US guitarist. Died December 4th, 1976.

Robert Cray 1953 US blues guitarist, singer, songwriter and, in 1973, formed his own band. For a long time he was known more in blues circles, but had his first great success with the album FALSE ACCUSATIONS in 1985. Hit: "Smoking Gun" (2/87 US 22) from the album Strong Persuader, which is one of the best-selling blues albums in US of all time – it reached No. 13.

Joe Elliot 1959 UK singer and songwriter with the band Def Leppard formed in 1977. Hits: "Photograph" (3/83 US 12), "Rock Of Ages" (6/83 US 16), "Animal" (8/87 UK 6; 10/87 US 19), "Hysteria" (11/87 UK 26; 1/88 US 10), "Love Bites" (7/88 UK 11; US 1) and "Pour Some Sugar On Me" (2/89 UK 15; US 12).

Deaths

Joe Liggins 1987 US singer and bandleader. Born 9th July, 1916.

Hits of the Day	
1963	"(You're The) Devil In Disguise" Elvis Presley UK 1 week
1964	"A Hard Day's Night" Beatles US 2 weeks
1970	"The Wonder Of You" Elvis Presley UK 6 weeks
1981	"Green Door" Shakin' Stevens UK 4 weeks
1981	"Jessie's Girl" Rick Springfield US 2 weeks

1987	"La Bamba" Los Lobos UK 2 weeks
1987	"Shakedown" Bob Seger US 1 week

Miscellany

1971 In New York Madison Square Garden, an audience of 40,000 watched two charity benefit concerts organized by George Harrison in aid of the suffering population of East Pakistan, The Concert For Bangladesh. The artists gave their services for free – and it was quite a starstudded lineup: George Harrison, Ravi Shankar, Ringo Starr, Leon Russell, Bob Dylan, Badfinger, Eric Clapton, Billy Preston, Klaus Voormann, and many more. The concerts were recorded, and the earnings were to be made available to Bangladesh. Net income was estimated at $243,418 and $10 million were expected from the sales of the triple album. Difficulties experienced by artists involved with different record companies hindered the speedy transfer of the monies. Finally George Harrison transferred $2 million dollars of his own money, and it took until 1981 for a further cheque in the amount of 8.8 million dollars to reach UNICEF. Harrison meant well, but it goes to show that in the case of rock concerts for charitable concerns, more business sense was needed than was displayed by Harrison and his organisation.

2nd

Birthdays

Hank Cochran 1935 US singer and songwriter, real name Garland Perry. He worked with the young Eddie Cochran as Cochran Brothers (although the two weren't related) and made rockabilly records. After splitting up as a duo, Hank went to Nashville in 1959, and worked as a songwriter. He wrote "I Fall To Pieces", "Funny Way Of Laughin' " and "Make The World Go Away". Hank had a few smaller hits in the country charts, the biggest being "Sally Was A Good Old Girl" (9/62 C&W 20).

Garth Hudson 1937 US pianist with Band. Sought-after session musician.

Edward Patten 1939 US singer with Gladys Knight & The Pips.

Dave Govan 1940 US singer with the Jayhawks, who later became the Vibrations, and who also made records as the Marathons.

Doris Kenner 1941 US singer with the R&B girls' group Shirelles, who had formed as Poquellos during the members' schooldays. The first records were made in 1958. Doris, whose real surname was Coley, left the group in 1968, but came back in 1975. Hits by the Shirelles, see 10th June under Shirley Alston.

Andy Fairweather-Low 1950 UK singer, guitarist, and songwriter with Amen Corner, formed in 1966. Hits: "Bend Me, Shape Me" (1/68 UK 3), "High In The Sky" (7/68 UK 6), "(If Paradise Is) Half As Nice" (1/69 UK 1; 2/76 RE-UK 34) and "Hello Suzie" (6/69 UK 4). In the early 1970s Andy formed Fair Weather. Hit: "Natural Sinner" (7/70 UK 6). From 1974 he made solo records. Hits: "Reggae Tune" (9/74 UK 10), and "Wide Eyed And Legless" (12/75 UK 6). In addition to further solo releases, Andy guested as a session musician on records by the Who, Ian Drury, Georgie Fame, Willie & The Poor Boys in 1985 and Helen Watson in 1989. Andy duetted with Helen on "Hanging Out The Washing (In A Small Backyard)", on which he showed his qualities as a singer.

Andrew Gold 1951 US singer, multi-instrumentalist and songwriter. Son of composer Ernest Gold and singer Marni Nixon. He formed groups like Doberman, Herd, and Wails with Peter Bernstein, son of Elmer in the mid-1960s. In 1969, again with Peter, Carla Bonoff and others he formed Bryndle. The group got a recording contract, worked on an album for six months, which was not released in the end. In 1971 Bryndle split up, and Andrew, still with Peter Bernstein, formed the Rangers. In 1974 he toured with Linda Ronstadt for nine months, and played on her album HEART LIKE A WHEEL, being featured on the single "You're No Good" as lead guitarist, pianist, drummer and percussionist. In 1975 his own first album was released, and he continued to play as a session musician on countless records by colleagues, like Art Garfunkel: he plays guitar, piano and drums on "I Only Have Eyes For You". From 1977 he was successful as a solo artist with hits like "Lonely Boy" (3/77 US 7; UK 11), "Thank You For Being A Friend" (2/78 US 25; 10/78 UK 42) and "Never Let Her Slip Away" (3/78 UK 5). In 1985 he formed Wax with Graham Gouldman. Hit: "Building A Bridge To Your Heart" (8/87 UK 12).

Steve Hillage 1951 UK guitarist, synthesizer player, singer, songwriter and producer. He played with Spyrogyra, Caravan, Khan, Ottawa Company, Kevin Ayers, Decadence, Gong, and from 1976 as a soloist. In 1985 he produced the first album by Cock Robin.

Clive Wright 1953 US guitarist with Cock Robin. The band was produced by Steve Hillage, who played guitar on the hit "When Your Heart Is Weak" (5/85 US 35).

Apollonia 1961 US singer and songwriter, real name Patty Kotero. She was the leader of the group Apollonia 6, which was comprised of Prince's acolytes. She co-starred with him in the film *Purple Rain* (1983). The two other members of the group, Brenda Bennett and Susan Moonsie, had previously been with Vanity 6. The biggest hit by the trio was "Sex Shooter" (9/84 R&B 14).

Pete de Freitas 1961 UK drummer and songwriter with Echo & The Bunnymen. In September 1979 Pete joined the band formed in 1977. He died in a traffic accident on 15th June, 1989.

Deaths

Enrico Caruso 1921 Italian tenor. Born 27th June, 1873.

Brian Cole 1972 US bass player with Association. Died of a heroin overdose. Born 1944.

Hits of the Day

1941	"Intermezzo (Souvenir de Vienne)" Guy Lombardo US 1 week
1975	"One Of These Nights" Eagles US 1 week
1980	"Magic" Olivia Newton-John US 4 weeks
1986	"The Lady In Red" Chris de Burgh UK 3 weeks
1986	"Glory Of Love" Peter Cetera US 2 weeks

3rd

Birthdays

Beverly Lee 1941 US singer with the Shirelles.

Sean Tyla 1947 UK guitarist and songwriter with Man, Ducks Deluxe, and from 1977 as leader of his own group the Tyla Gang. From 1980, a solo artist.

B. B. Dickerson 1949 US bass player with War.

John Graham 1951 US guitarist and percussionist who joined Earth, Wind & Fire in June 1973.

Ian Bairnson 1953 UK guitarist, bassist, singer, percussionist and songwriter. In 1974 he joined Pilot as the fourth member. He also worked with Alan Parsons Project, as a solo artist, Panarama and Keats. As a session musician Ian guested on records by Bucks Fizz, Esther Ofarim and Eberhard Schoener, which illustrates his versatility.

Ian Crichton 1956 Canadian guitarist and songwriter for Saga.

James Hetfield 1963 US singer, guitarist and songwriter with Metallica. The band released its first album in 1983. They had their first hit singles with "Harvester Of Sorrow" (9/88 UK 20) and "One" (2/89 US 35; 4/89 UK 13).

Hits of the Day

1946	"To Each His Own" Freddy Martin US 2 weeks
1946	"I Surrender" Perry Como US 1 week
1961	"Well I Ask You" Eden Kane UK 1 week
1963	"So Much In Love" Tymes US 1 week
1968	"Hello, I Love You" Doors US 2 weeks
1985	"Into The Groove" Madonna UK 4 weeks
1985	"Shout" Tears For Fears US 3 weeks

Miscellany

1963 Saturday evening. Tonight's programme at the Cavern Club in Liverpool is: Escorts, Roadrunners, Johnny Ringo & The Colts, Merseybeats and the Beatles. It is the 294th and last appearance of the Beatles at this club where their career began. They made their first appearance here on 21st March, 1961. That evening they alternated with the Bluegenes, who later became the Swinging Blue Jeans. In less than two and a half years so much had changed for the Beatles. The singles "Love Me Do", "Please Please Me" and "From Me To You" had already been released. On the 12th August, 1963 "She Loves You" would appear, entering the UK charts at No. 1: 500,000 copies of this single had already been ordered. When they made their last appearance at the Cavern Club, their future was already secured.

4th

Birthdays

Big Dee Irwin 1939 US singer, real name Ervin Difossco. During his military service with the Air Force, stationed in Greenland, he formed the Pastels in 1954. After leaving the Air Force, the group carried on professionally and scored with "Been So Long" (3/58 US 24). In 1959 the band split up, and Irwin carried on as a soloist, but he only had one hit "Swinging On A Star" (5/63 US 38; 11/63 UK

7) a duet with Little Eva. Later he produced the group Tribe, and in 1976 made records under the name Difossco.

Frankie Ford 1939 US singer, real name Frank Guzzo. While still at school, he formed his own band Syncopaters. In 1958 he cut his first solo records. Biggest hit: "Sea Cruise" (2/59 US 14), accompanied and written by Huey 'Piano' Smith. Apart from all the many New Orleans artists with the record company Ace, Frankie Ford appeared somewhat exotic, firstly because he was white, secondly because he seemed like a synthesis of Elvis Presley and Ricky Nelson.

Timi Yuro 1940 US singer, complete name Rosemarie Timothy Aurro Yuro. She started singing in 1952 at her parents' Italian restaurant. In 1959 she got her first recording contract. She had her first and biggest hit with "Hurt" (7/61 US 4), an English language version of the Fausto Leali hit "A Chi". In 1980 she lost her voice and had to undergo several operations.

David Carr 1943 UK keyboard player with the Fortunes.

Paul Martin Layton 1947 UK bassist and singer with the New Seekers. Before that Paul was a celebrated child star.

Klaus Schulze 1947 German pianist and songwriter, who is called the "German electronic genius". He played with Tangerine Dream, Ash Ra Tempel, and from 1971 as a much sought-after session musician.

Roy Flowers 1951 UK drummer with Sweet Sensation.

Paul Reynolds 1962 UK lead guitarist, singer and songwriter with A Flock Of Seagulls.

Hits of the Day

1956	"My Prayer" Platters US 5 weeks
1958	"Poor Little Fool" Ricky Nelson US 2 weeks
1960	"Shakin' All Over" Johnny Kidd & The Pirates UK 1 week
1966	"With A Girl Like You" Troggs UK 2 weeks
1973	"Morning After" Maureen McGovern US 2 weeks
1990	"Itsy Bitsy Teeny Weeny" Bombalurina UK 3 weeks

Miscellany

1980 John Lennon had not made a record for six years. Even the press were reticent about John and Yoko. They had made headlines once more on 2nd July, 1980. A Holstein cow which the couple had owned was sold to Steve Potter for a record price of 265,000 dollars. (Nobody ever checked on Mr. Potter's mental state, however, he did purchase the cow for an amusement park, the New York State Fairgrounds in Syracuse, N.Y.) Then John and Yoko went to the Hit Factory in Manhattan in order to begin work on the album DOUBLE FANTASY at the recording studio. The record company which was to release the album had not yet been decided. Not until 22nd September, 1980 did David Geffen announce that the record would be released on his new independent label, Geffen. This took place 17th November, 1980.

5th

Birthdays

Bobby Braddock 1940 US country songwriter, singer and pianist. In 1965/66 he played with Marty Robbins' band and then became a solo artist. He wrote the hit "D.I.V.O.R.C.E." for Tammy Wynette, and for George Jones "He Stopped Loving Her Today", "Her Name Is . . .", and many others.

Damita Jo 1940 US singer, surname DuBlanc. Supposedly she was already singing with Steve Gibson & The Red Caps in 1951, and not only that, she is supposed to have married him. From 1958 Damita sang as a solo artist. Hits: "I'll Save The Last Dance For You" (10/60 US 22), (an answer to the Drifters song "Save The Last Dance For Me"), and "I'll Be There" (7/61 US 12).

Airto Moreira 1941 Brazilian percussionist, drummer, pianist, singer, and songwriter. He is married to his permanent musical partner Flora Purim.

Sammi Smith 1943 US country singer, who appeared in public at the tender age of 12. In 1967 she went to Nashville. Since then she has been in the country charts regularly. First successes were in 1968 and her biggest hit was the million seller, "Help Me Make It Through The Night" (1/71 US 8).

Rick Derringer 1947 US singer, guitarist, and songwriter, real name Richard Zehringer. In 1963 he formed Rick & The Raiders. This group became the Rick Z. Combo, and in 1965 the McCoys. The title "My Girl Sloopy" by the Vibrations, appeared in March 1964, and "Hang On Sloopy" (8/65 US 1; UK 5) became the first million seller for the McCoys. A further hit was "Fever"

(11/65 US 7; UK 44). In 1969 the McCoys became the backing group for Johnny Winter, and they also did some work with brother Edgar. From 1974 Rick made solo records too. Hit: "Rock n' Roll, Hoochie Koo" (1/74 US 23). As a session musician he worked with Steely Dan, Dan Hartman, Todd Rundgren, Bette Midler, Donald Fagen, Meatloaf, Bonnie Tyler and many others.

Gregory Leskiw 1947 Canadian guitarist and singer with Wild Rice, Guess Who (from July 1970 to April 1972) and Mood Jgajga.

Chris Jagger 1949 UK singer, brother of Mick Jagger. He made a few records in a style similar to his brother.

Samantha Sang 1953 Australian singer whose real name is Cheryl Gray and who began her career at a Melbourne radio station. In the late 1960s she was a top star in her home country. In the early 1970s she came to the UK, where she met the Bee Gees. Robert Stigwood, the manager of the group advised her to change her name to Samantha Sang. With the help of the Bee Gees – Barry and Robin wrote the song, and Barry sang with her – she had a hit with "Emotion" (11/77 US 3; 2/78 UK 11).

Pete Burns 1959 UK singer and songwriter for Dead Or Alive. Real first names, Peter Jozzepi. Pete Burns made his recording debut in the late 1970s with the group Nightmares In Wax. He left this group in order to form Dead Or Alive in 1980. After three singles released on indie-labels, they secured a contract with a large record company in 1982. They had their first hit with "That's The Way (I Like It)" (3/84 UK 22) produced by German Zeus B. Held a cover version of the hit by K. C. & The Sunshine Band. Real success eluded them until Dead Or Alive changed their producers to Stock/Aitken/Waterman. Hits: "You Spin Me Round (Like A Record)" (12/84 UK 1; 6/85 US 11), "Lover Come Back To Me" (4/85 UK 11) and "Brand New Lover" (9/86 UK 31; 11/86 US 15).

Richard Huxley 1942 UK guitarist with the Dave Clark Five.

Deaths

Marilyn Monroe 1962 US actress and singer. Probably died of an overdose of sleeping tablets; it was never really explained. Born 1st June, 1926.

Hits of the Day

1944	"Swinging On A Star" Bing Crosby	US 9 weeks
1944	"G. I. Jive" Louis Jordan	US 2 weeks

1965	"Help!" Beatles	UK 3 weeks
1978	"Miss You" Rolling Stones	US 1 week
1989	"Batdance (From 'Batman')" Prince	US 1 week
1989	"Swing The Mood" Jive Bunny & The Mastermixers	UK 5 weeks

Miscellany

1957 From September 1952, the programme 'Bandstand' broadcast in Philadelphia by WFIL-TV channel 6 had become more and more popular with teenagers. From this time on, the programme was networked every weekday at 15:00 hours throughout the entire USA and was now called 'American Bandstand'. In the first programme, among others, Billy Williams appeared with "I'm Gonna Sit Right Down And Write Myself A Letter", and the Chordettes with "Just Between You And Me". The following day, the main attraction was Dale Hawkins with "Suzie Q.", and the day after upcoming star Paul Anka sang "Diana". Over the course of the years, every important star, with the exception of Elvis Presley, were to appear on this programme. It made the presenter of the programme, Dick Clarke, a star and millionnaire.

6th

Birthdays

Robert Mitchum 1917 US film actor, who is among the great Hollywood stars. As a singer he was at least once in the country charts, "Little Ole Wine Drinkin' Me" (5/67 C&W 9).

Baden Powell 1936 Brazilian jazz guitarist.

Mike Sarne 1939 UK singer, film actor and director. Real name Michael Scheur. He started his acting career in 1957; in 1962, more for a joke, he recorded the title "Come Outside" (5/62 UK 1), with actress Wendy Richard. The next record was also a duet – this time with Billie Davis, "Will I What?" (8/62 UK 18). After 1963 he was back in the film business. In 1970, after two films which he had written and directed, were ripped apart by the critics to such an extent, that he disappeared from the scene for good.

Allan Holdsworth 1948 UK guitarist and violinist. He played with, Nucleus, Tempest, Bill Bruford, Soft Machine, Jean-Luc Ponty, among others and as a solo artist.

Carol Pope 1949 Canadian singer and songwriter who was born in Manchester and emigrated with her parents when she was five. She started as the member of a band called O, which became the Bullwhip Brothers, X-Rated Bullwhip Brothers, and finally in the mid-1970s Rough Trade.

Pat McDonald 1952 US singer and songwriter who was in the duo Timbuk 3 with his wife Barbara Kooyman. Pat started with the rock group Essentials which split up in 1984. After that Barbara and he travelled about as streetsingers with a taped bass and drums accompaniment. They themselves played guitar and harmonica. In 1986 their first album appeared. Hit: "The Future's So Bright I Gotta Wear Shades" (10/86 US 19; 1/87 UK 21).

Randy DeBarge 1958 US singer and bass player with the sibling group DeBarge.

Jamie Kensit 1963 UK guitarist and keyboard player with Eighth Wonder. His birthdate is sometimes given as 5th August.

Mike Elliott 1939 UK saxophonist with the Foundations.

Deaths

Bix Beiderbecke 1931 US jazz trumpeter of German origin. He died of pneumonia. Born 10th March, 1903.

Hits of the Day

1988 "The Only Way Is Up" Yazz & Plastic Population UK 5 weeks

---

Miscellany

1954 This day marks the beginning of an incredible story. The small record company Sun Records in Memphis released the first single record by their new artist Elvis Presley. The record number was SUN 209. On the A-side was "That's Alright Mama", and on the B-side "Blue Moon Of Kentucky". The record was not placed in any of the charts, neither in the Hot 100 nor in the R&B charts, nor in the country charts. His first record in the charts was, SUN No. 217 "Baby Let's Play House/I'm Left, You're Right, She's Gone" (7/55 C&W 5). His first No. 1 in the charts is SUN 223: "I Forgot To Remember To Forget" (9/55 C&W 1). He appeared for the first time at No. 1 in the R&B charts with "Heartbreak Hotel" (3/56 R&B 3; US

1), at which time he was under contract with the electronics giant RCA.

7th

Birthdays

Freddie Slack 1910 US Boogie-Woogie-pianist, bandleader, and composer who played with Ben Pollack (1935/36), with Jimmy Dorsey (1936–39), and with Bill Bradley. With Bradley he was on the hit "Beat Me, Daddy, Eight To The Bar" (8/40 US 2). From 1942 to 1946 he was credited with his own orchestra and had 10 hits in the USA. Singers were usually Ella Mae Morse or Margaret Whiting. Hits: "Cow Cow Boogie" (7/42 US 9), and "The House Of Blue Lights" (5/46 US 8). Freddie died 10th August, 1965.

Felice Bryant 1925 US songwriter. Together she formed one of the most successful songwriting teams of the 1950s and 1960s with husband Boudleaux.

Stan Freberg 1926 US radio disc jockey, already before the Second World War, he was providing voice-overs for animated cartoon characters, and from 1951 a recording artist. His great strength were satires on endless TV series. Hits included "St. George & The Dragonet" (10/53 US 1) and "Sh-Boom" (10/54 US 14; UK 15).

Roland Kirk 1936 US jazz multi-instrumentalist and composer. He died 5th December, 1977.

Charles Pope 1936 US singer with the Tams.

Ron Holden 1939 US singer with one hit, "Love You So" (4/60 US 7).

B. J. Thomas 1942 US singer. B. J. is for Billy Joe. He started with the group Triumphs while still at school. Hit: "I'm So Lonesome I Could Cry" (2/66 US 8). After that as a solo artist with "Hooked On Feeling" (11/68 US 5), "Raindrops Keep Fallin' On My Head" (11/69 US 1; 2/70 UK 38), "I Just Can't Help Believing" (6/70 US 9) and "(Hey Won't You Play) Another Somebody Done Somebody Wrong Song" (2/75 US 1). In the mean time B. J. was more at home in country and gospel territory, reaching the top of the country charts in the 1980s with "Whatever Happened To Old Fashioned Love" (2/83 C&W 1), and "New Looks From An Old Lover" (7/83 C&W 1).

Another remarkable number was "Rock & Roll Shoes" (8/84 C&W 14), a duet with Ray Charles.

Bruce Dickinson 1958 UK singer and songwriter. He started with the group Samson, and joined Iron Maiden in 1981 to replace Paul Di'anno. Hits: "Run To The Hills" (2/82 UK 7; 12/85 RE-UK 26), "Two Minutes To Midnight" (8/84 UK 11), "Can I Play With Madness" (3/88 UK 3), "The Evil That Men Do" (8/88 UK 5) and "The Clairvoyant" (11/88 UK 6).

Tim Renwick 1949 UK guitarist and songwriter. He played with the Albion Country Band and was a co-founder of Quiver, who called themselves Sutherland Brothers & Quiver, after they had been joined by the Sutherland Brothers in 1973. Tim is also a highly sought-after session musician, playing with Al Stewart, Dana Gillespie, Gary Brooker, Elton John, Clif Richard and Andy Gibb.

Andy Fraser 1952 UK bassist, keyboard player, singer and songwriter. After playing with John Mayall for two months, he was fired. He became a founder member of Free in May 1968. In May 1971 the group split up. Andy formed the group Toby and was back at a reunion of Free in January 1972. In July 1972 he left Free again and formed Sharks with Chris Spedding. In 1975 he recorded as the Andy Fraser Band and played on albums by Eno and Robert Palmer.

Deaths

Babe Norvel Hardy 1957 US film comedian. Born 15th January, 1892.

Homer 1971 US country guitarist. Born 27th July, 1918.

Eddie Calvert 1978 UK trumpeter. Born 15th March, 1922.

Esther Phillips 1984 US singer. Born 23rd December, 1935.

Hits of the Day

1954	"Sh-Boom" Crew-Cuts US 9 weeks
1965	"I'm Henry VIII, I Am" Herman's Hermits US 1 week
1971	"How Can You Mend A Broken Heart" Bee Gees US 4 weeks
1976	"Don't Go Breaking My Heart" Elton John & Kiki Dee US 4 weeks
1982	"Come On Eileen" Dexy's Midnight Runners UK 4 weeks

8th

Birthdays

Victor Young 1900 US orchestra leader and composer. He started as a concert violinist, then became a bandleader and directed the radio shows of Al Jolson and others. He wrote the music for many films. He had his first million seller with Judy Garland, "Over The Rainbow" (9/39 US 5). Further million sellers were, "Too-Ra-Loo-Ra-Loo-Ral" (10/44 US 4), and "Galway Bay" (1/49 US 3) with Bing Crosby. His biggest hits, with the orchestra, were, "She's A Latin From Manhattan" (6/35 US 1), "The High And The Mighty" (8/54 US 6) and "Around The World In 80 Days" (5/57 US 13). Victor died 11th November, 1956.

Jimmy Witherspoon 1923 US blues singer, bassist and songwriter. He made his first records in 1945 and had his greatest hit with "Ain't Nobody's Business, Parts 1 & 2" (3/49 R&B 1). He worked with Count Basie, Gerry Mulligan, Woody herman, Earl Hines, Mel Lewis, Eric Clapton, and also as a solo artist.

Webb Pierce 1926 US country singer, who is one of the more flamboyant characters around – he owns the luxury villa with a guitar-shaped swimming pool, which tourists still like to come and visit in Nashville. Webb was successful from 1952. His first 31 records reached the Top Ten positions in the Country & Western charts. Both Faron Young and Floyd Cramer played in his backing band at the beginning of their careers. Biggest hits: "More And More" (11/54 US 22), a million seller and "I Ain't Never" (8/59 US 24). His success lasted well into the 1980s. He died on February 24th 1991.

Mel Tillis 1932 US country singer and songwriter. He had his first success as a singer in 1958, and during the course of the years reached the No. 1 position in the country charts 6 times: "I Ain't Never" (8/72), "Good Woman Blues" (10/76), "Hard Healer" (1/77), "I Believe In You" (5/78), "Coca Cola Cowboy" (6/79), and "Southern Rains" (12/80). Mel also sang duets with Webb Pierce, Glen Campbell and Nancy Sinatra. As a songwriter he supplied hits like "Detroit City", and "Ruby, Don't Take Your Love To Town" for other artists. Mel is considered to be the most famous stutterer in country music, his stuttering has in fact become his trade mark. When he sings, it all flows. Mel also appeared in several films.

Joe Tex 1933 US singer and songwriter. Real name Joseph Arrington. He won one of the youth contests at the famous Apollo Theatre in Harlem in 1954. In 1955 he released his first records, but was not successful until 1964. Hits: "Hold What You've Got" (12/64 US 5), "Skinny Legs And All" (10/67 US 10), "I Gotcha" (1/72 US 2), and "Ain't Gonna Bump No More (With No Big Fat Woman)" (4/77 US 12; UK 2). He recorded as Soul Clan with Solomon Burke, Arthur Conley, Don Covay and Ben E. King. Only hit: "Soul Meeting" (7/68 R&B 34). Joe also wrote hits for other artists, like James Brown and Jerry Butler. He has always been a model for Mick Jagger's performances on stage. In 1972 Joe converted to the Muslim faith and – henceforth called himself Joseph Hazziez. He died 13th August, 1982.

Don Jacobucci 1938 US singer with the Regents, who called themselves Runarounds after 1962.

Philip Balsley 1939 US singer with the Kingsmen formed in 1955, and who were successful as the Statler Brothers from the mid-1960s.

Jay David 1942 US drummer with Dr. Hook.

Michael Johnson 1944 US singer and guitarist. In 1966 he studied classical guitar in Spain. He toured with the Chad Mitchell Trio together with John Denver in 1967/68. From 1978 he worked as a solo artist. Hits: "Bluer Than Blue" (4/78 US 12) and "This Night Won't Last Forever" (8/79 US 19). From the mid-1980s Michael turned up in the country charts. Hits: "Give Me Wings" (9/86 C&W 1) and "The Moon Is Still Over Her Shoulder" (1/87 C&W 1).

David Grant 1956 UK singer and songwriter with the duo Linx, whose biggest hit was "Intuition" (3/81 UK 7). In 1982 the duo split up and David Grant carried on as a soloist. Hits: "Watching You, Watching Me" (7/83 UK 10) and "Could It Be I'm Falling In Love" (3/85 UK 5) a duet with Jaki Graham.

Ali Score 1956 UK drummer and songwriter with A Flock Of Seagulls.

Chris Foreman 1958 UK guitarist and songwriter. Nickname Chrissie-Boy. He was a founder member of Madness in 1976.

Deaths

Russ Morgan 1969 US pianist and orchestra leader. Born 29th April, 1904.

Cannonball Adderley 1975 US jazz musician. He died of a stroke. Born 15th September, 1928.

Hits of the Day

1952	"Vaya Con Dios (May God Be With You)" Les Paul & Mary Ford US 11 weeks
1960	"Itsy Bitsy Teenie Weenie Yellow Polka Dot Bikini" Brian Hyland US 1 week
1963	"Sweets For My Sweet" Searchers UK 2 weeks
1987	"I Still Haven't Found What I'm Looking For" U2 US 2 weeks

---

9th

Birthdays

Billy Henderson 1939 US singer with the Spinners.

Peter Leslie Gavin 1946 UK drummer with Shades, Bluesology, Jody Grind, Heads, Hands & Feet, Vinegar Joe, and others.

Marinus Gerritsen 1946 Dutch bass player, keyboard player, and songwriter with Golden Earring.

John 'Pazz' Parry 1946 UK singer with the Bonzo Dogs, Pasadena Roof Orchestra, and as a solo artist.

Barbara Mason 1947 US singer and songwriter. Her first hit was also her biggest, "Yes, I'm Ready" (5/65 US 5). She stayed in the record business until the mid-1980s.

Benjamin Orr 1955 US singer and bassist with Cars.

Kurtis Blow 1959 US singer, rapper, disc jockey and songwriter. Real name Kurt Walker. In 1976 he started as a rapping DJ in clubs in Harlem. At the same time he began his association with Grandmaster Flash. In November 1979 Kurtis got a recording contract and was among the first rappers to receive a 12" gold disc: the record was "The Breaks (Part 1)" (9/80 US 87). Other hits included "Christmas Rappin' " (12/79 UK 30) and "If I Ruled The World" (1/86 UK 24).

Whitney Houston 1963 US singer, with strong musical family background: her mother, is Emily 'Cissy' Drinkard Houston, leadsinger with Sweet Inspirations, who had recorded as a group and were also, perhaps, the best backing vocalists in the business: they backed Elvis Presley on several records. Cissy Houston also made solo records. Another member of the family is Dionne Warwick, she is Whitney's cousin. In 1985 the first solo album by

Whitney appeared, which became an instant hit. Hits: "Saving All My Love For You" (8/85 US 1; 11/85 UK 1), "How Will I Know" (12/85 US 1; UK 5), "Greatest Love Of All" (3/86 US 1; UK 8), "I Wanna Dance With Somebody (Who Loves Me)" (5/87 US & UK 1), "Didn't We Almost Have It All" (8/87 US 1; UK 14), "So Emotional" (10/87 US 1; UK 5), "Where Do Broken Hearts Go" (2/88 US 1; UK 14), "Love Will Save The Day" (5/88 UK 10; 7/88 US 9) and "One Moment In Time" (9/88 US 5; UK 1).

Hits of the Day

1947 "Smoke! Smoke! Smoke! (That Cigarette)" Tex Williams US 6 weeks

1947 "Peg O' My Heart" Three Suns US 4 weeks

1967 "San Francisco" Scott McKenzie UK 4 weeks

1975 "Barbados" Typically Tropical UK 1 week

1975 "Jive Talkin' " Bee Gees US 2 weeks

1980 "The Winner Takes It All" Abba UK 2 weeks

10th

Birthdays

Jimmy Dean 1928 US country singer, pianist, guitarist and songwriter. Real name, Seth Ward. He began his career in 1948 with the Tennessee Haymakers, and formed his own group Texas Wild Cats in 1952. From 1953 he was successful as a solo artist. Hits: "Big Bad John" (10/61 US 1; UK 2), "P. T. 109" (3/62 US 8; this song was about action by John F. Kennedy on a torpedo boat called P. T. 109, which was sunk in 1943; as we know, he survived.), and "I.O.U." (5/76 US 35). The last record did not climb all that far up the charts, but it was a million seller and a tribute to his mother by Jimmy Dean.

Eddie Fisher 1928 US singer and actor. At age 18 he sang with Buddy Morrow's band. In 1949 he became known in the USA for his appearances on Eddie Cantor's radio show. A year later he was a star. He had his most successful period in the first half of the 1950s: the biggest hits – most were million sellers – were "Any Time" (12/51 US 2), "Tell Me Why" (1/52 US 4), "Wish You Were Here" (7/52 US 1; 11/53 UK 8), "Lady Of Spain/Outside Of Heaven" (9/52 US 6; 1/53 UK 1), "I'm Walking Behind You" (5/53 US & UK 1), "Oh Mein Papa!" (12/53 US 1; UK 9), "I Need You Now" (9/54 US 1; 11/54 UK 13) and

"Cindy, Oh Cindy" (10/56 US 10; UK 5). After that Eddie became better known for his wives. On 26th September, 1955 he married singer Debbie Reynolds, whom he left three years later for Liz Taylor. Then she left him, in order to marry Richard Burton. Eddie then consoled himself with Connie Stevens. Whoever wishes to know more about the subject, should read his biography, 'Eddie – My Life, My Loves', published in 1981. As an actor he appeared in *All About Eve* (1950) and *Butterfield 8* (1960), among others. He had his own regular television shows between 1953 and 1959.

Sal Cuomo 1939 US singer with the Regents, who called themselves Runarounds from 1962.

Bobby Hatfield 1940 US singer with the blue-eyed soul duo Righteous Brothers which were formed in 1962. Hits: "You've Lost That Loving Feeling" (12/64 US & UK 1; 2/69 RE-UK 10; 11/77 RE-UK 42), "Unchained Melody" (7/65 US 4; UK 14), "(You're My) Soul And Inspiration" (3/66 US 1; UK 15) and "Rock And Roll Heaven" (5/74 US 3). Bobby also made solo records, unsuccessfully.

Les Humphries 1940 UK pianist and songwriter. He started with the group Wonderland and, from 1969, was the leader of the Les Humphries Singers. Hits: "We Are Goin' Down Jordan" (9/71), "Mexico" (9/72), "Mama Loo" (3/73), and "Kansas City" (1/74).

Veronica Bennett 1945 US singer and leader of the Ronettes, who started as the Darling Sisters in New York in 1958. From 1962 they worked as backing singers on Phil Spector productions. Consequently the Ronettes were formed. Hits: "Be My Baby" (8/63 US 2; 10/63 UK 4) and "Baby, I Love You" (12/63 US 24; UK 11). Phil Spector produced the group, which split up in 1966, and married Veronica in 1968, who now called herself Ronnie. In 1974 they were divorced. Veronica also made records as Ronnie Spector, without success.

Lary Larden 1945 US leadsinger, together with brother Dennis, and guitarist with Every Mother's Son. Greatest hit: "Come On Down To My Boat" (5/67 US 6).

Mick Clarke 1946 UK bass player with the Rubettes.

Ian Anderson 1947 UK singer, flautist and songwriter. He formed the Blades in 1963, named after James Bond's favourite club. This group developed into the John Evans Band in 1965, which then became Jethro Tull in 1968. Hits: "Living In The Past" (5/69 UK 3; 11/72 US 11), "Sweet Dream" (11/69 UK 7), "The Witch Promise" (1/70 UK 4) and "Bungle In The Jungle" (11/74 US 12).

Patti Austin 1948 US singer, who got a recording contract from her godfather Quincy Jones in 1981. As a child she was promoted by Dinah Washington and Sammy Davis Jr. At age 19 she regularly sang commercial jingles. She was on many records by Michael Jackson, Billy Joel, Paul Simon, and many other CTI and CBS artists' records. She is also on the album THE DUDE by Quincy Jones which was released in April 1981. In 1982 she released her first solo album. Hit: the million seller "Baby Come To Me" (4/82 US 1; 2/83 UK 11), in a duet with James Ingram. In 1988 she took part in the film *Tucker*.

Andy Cresswell-Davis 1949 UK singer, keyboard player, and songwriter with the group, Korgis, formed in 1979. Before that he had worked with Blue Crew, Strange Fruit, Kynd and Stackridge. After Korgis split up in 1980, he played for Tears For Fears. In 1984 Korgis reformed.

Lorraine Samantha Jean Pearson 1967 UK singer with 5 Star.

Deaths

Freddie Slack 1965 US boogie-woogie-pianist, composer and bandleader. Born 7th August, 1910.

Hits of the Day

1956	"Whatever Will Be Will Be" Doris Day UK 6 weeks	
1959	"A big Hunk O' Love" Elvis Presley US 2 weeks	
1961	"You Don't Know" Helen Shapiro UK 3 weeks	
1963	"Fingertips, Part 2" Stevie Wonder US 3 weeks	
1974	"Feel Like Makin' Love" Roberta Flack US 1 week	

11th

Birthdays

June Hutton 1921 US singer, who sang with different groups from the early 1940s, like the Pied Pipers from 1944 to 1950. She was also with Frank Sinatra when he recorded his first big hits with Axel Stordahl. June married Axel. She was successful as a soloist in the early 1950s. Hit: "Say You're Mine Again" (5/53 US 21). June died 2nd May, 1973.

Michael Hugg 1942 UK drummer and songwriter with Manfred Mann in the early days, when the band was still commercially successful. In the 1970s Hugg was a soloist. In addition, he played with McGuinness Flint (1972), and in 1984 with Lords Of The New Church.

Guy Villari 1942 US leadsinger with the group Desires formed in 1958. In the same year they made a demo tape of "Barbara Ann" which had been written for a sister of one of the group's members. A little later they called themselves Regents, and in the early 1960s the band split up. When the title finally reached the charts as "Barbara-Ann" (5/61 US 13) the group no longer existed. But after that success, the group reformed again, called themselves Runarounds and recorded the title "Runaround" (7/61 US 28). After that they disappeared into obscurity.

Michael James Kale 1943 Canadian bass player with Guess Who.

Peter 'Max' Donath 1944 Drummer with the Lords.

Jeff Hanna 1947 US guitarist with the Nitty Gritty Dirt Band.

Bill Hurd 1948 UK keyboard player and singer with the Rubettes. In 1979 he joined Suzi Quatro's backing band.

Eric Carmen 1949 US singer, bassist, guitarist and songwriter with the band Raspberries, formed in 1970. Hits: "Go All The Way" (7/72 US 5), "I Wanna Be With You" (11/72 US 16) and "Overnight Sensation" (9/74 US 18). The group split up in 1975. Eric carried on as a solo artist. Hit: "All By Myself" (12/75 US 2; 4/76 UK 12), based on the second movement of the Rachmaninoff second piano concerto.

Erik Braunn 1950 US lead guitarist and songwriter with Iron Butterfly. As a 17-year old he played on the celebrated "In-A-Gadda-Da-Vida". He left the band in September 1969, formed Flintwhistle, and then re-formed Iron Butterfly in February 1975. They released two albums, which Erik wrote almost entirely alone and was leadsinger. After that, the band split up again.

Bryan Bassett 1954 US lead guitarist with the group Wild Cherry.

Joe Jackson 1954 UK singer, songwriter and pianist. In 1974 he joined the British pub band Edward Bear, joined Arms And Legs in 1976, with whom he released three unsuccessful singles which he had written. In 1977 he left the group and became house pianist at the Playboy Club in Portsmouth. In 1978 he tried to interest London record companies in demos of his own songs. Finally, he received a contract with A&M Records. In October 1978 his first record was released: "Is She Really Going Out With Him" (6/79 US 21; 8/79 UK 13). Further hits: "It's Different For Girls" (1/80 UK 5), "Steppin' Out" (8/82 US 6; 1/83 UK

6) and "You Can't Get What You Want (Till You Know What You Want)" (4/84 US 15).

Richie Ramone 1957 US drummer who joined the Ramones in 1983. Real surname Beau.

Alan Frew 1959 Canadian singer and songwriter with the group Glass Tiger, formed in 1982. Alan emigrated from Scotland to Canada at the age of 16. In 1986 the debut album by Glass Tiger appeared. Hits: "Don't Forget Me (When I'm Gone)" (7/86 US 2; 10/86 UK 29) and "Someday" (11/86 US 7).

Paul Gendler 1960 UK guitarist with Modern Romance.

Hammish Seeloghan 1964 UK singer with the Pasadenas.

Charlie Sexton 1968 US singer, guitarist, pianist, and songwriter, who made his first album in 1985. When he was 13, he was playing with the Joe Ely Band and was working with Bob Dylan, Don Henley, Keith Richards and Ron Wood. First solo hit, "Beat's So Lonely" (12/85 US 17).

Deaths

Percy Mayfield 1984 US singer, pianist and songwriter. Died after a heart attack. Born 12th August, 1920.

Hits of the Day

1960	"Please Don't Tease" Cliff Richard UK 2 weeks (2nd time)
1962	"Breaking Up Is Hard To Do" Neil Sedaka US 2 weeks
1984	"Ghostbusters" Ray Parker Jr. US 3 weeks

12th

Birthdays

Percy Mayfield 1920 US singer, pianist and songwriter. In the late 1940s Percy moved from Texas to the West Coast, and worked with Amos Milburn, Cecil Gant and Jesse Belvin for the Specialty label before forming his own band in 1950. Percy became one of the first great R&B stars, and continued his career into the 80s. His first million seller was "Please Send Me Someone To Love" (10/50

R&B 1; US 26). Percy also wrote songs like "Hit The Road Jack" for Ray Charles. He died 11th August, 1984.

Joe Jones 1926 US singer and pianist. He worked with B. B. King in the early 1950s as pianist and butler. In 1954 he made his first records. He had his biggest hit with "You Talk Too Much" (9/60 US 3). He worked as a producer with the Dixie Cups and Alvin Robinson.

Porter Wagoner 1927 US country singer and songwriter. He was successful from the mid-50s. Biggest hit in the country charts: "Misery Loves Company" (1/62 C&W 1), written by Jerry Reed. It was Porter who championed Dolly Parton by inviting her to appear on his regular TV show from 1967. It had started in 1960. The two duetted on "Please Don't Stop Loving Me" (8/74 C&W 1).

Buck Owens 1929 US country singer, guitarist, saxophonist, trumpeter and songwriter. Real first names Alvis Edgar. From the early 1950s he played with his own band Schoolhouse Playboys, and then as a session guitarist for stars like Wanda Jackson, Faron Young and Sonny James. Then he became lead guitarist in Tommy Collins' band. From 1975 he worked as a solo artist. Between 1963 and 1972 he reached the No. 1 position in the country charts 20 times. His first hit was "Act Naturally" (4/63), re-recorded in 1965 by the Beatles and sung by Ringo Starr. Buck's biggest pop hit was "I've Got A Tiger By The Tail" (2/65 US 25). During the course of his career, he sang duets with several artists like Emmylou Harris and Dwight Yoakam; with the latter, Buck had the hit, "Streets Of Bakersfield" (7/88 C&W 1).

Rod Bernard 1940 US singer with one hit, "This Should Go On Forever" (3/59 US 20).

Albie Donnelly 1947 UK saxophonist, flautist and singer with Supercharge. As a session musician he played with Graham Parker and the Boomtown Rats.

Ozzie Yue 1947 UK guitarist and singer with Supercharge.

Ron Mael 1948 US pianist, and songwriter, real name Ronald Day. In the late 1960s he formed the band Halfnelson with his brother Russell. After two unsuccessful albums, the brothers went to the UK in 1972 to form the group Sparks there. Hits: "This Town Ain't Big Enough For the Both Of Us" (5/74 UK 2), "Amateur Hour" (7/74 UK 7), and "Beat The Clock" (7/79 UK 10).

Mark Knopfler 1949 UK guitarist, singer and songwriter. In July 1977, he, a part time teacher, his brother David, a social worker, sociologist John Illsley and session drummer Pick Withers scratched together 120 pounds, to record a demo tape in London with five songs on it, and called themselves Dire Straits, in order to clarify their financial situation. One tape with these songs reached BBC disc jockey Charlie Gillet, who played it in his weekly programme 'Honky Tonk'. An employee of a record company heard it and was so impressed that he signed the group. In January 1978, even before the first record had been released, Dire Straits played 16 gigs, supporting Talking Heads on their UK tour. In February they recorded their first album for only 12,500 produced by Muff Winwood. In May 1978 "Sultans Of Swing" (2/79 US 4; UK 8) appeared, which was one of the five numbers on the demo tape. Further hits: "Romeo And Juliet" (1/81 UK 8), "Private Investigations" (9/82 UK 2), "Money For Nothing" (7/85 UK 4; US 1), "So Far Away" (4/85 UK 20; 3/86 US 19) and "Walk Of Life" (11/85 US 7; 1/86 UK 2). Mark also writes and plays for others like Bob Dylan and Tina Turner. In late 1989 he formed Notting Hillbillies, which was a more low key operation than Dire Straits, although Dire Straits continued, releasing an album in late 1991.

Kid Creole 1950 US singer, songwriter and producer. Real name Thomas August Darnell Browder, also known as Argyle Knepf. In the mid-1950s he formed Dr. Buzzard's Original Savannah Band in New York, which played so-called mulatto-music; they had a hit with "Whispering/Cherchez La Femme/Se Si Bon" (11/76 US 27). In 1979 he formed Kid Creole & The Coconuts, with whom he had the hits "I'm A Wonderful Thing Baby" (5/82 UK 4), "Stool Pidgeon" (7/82 UK 7) and "Annie I'm Not Your Daddy" (10/82 UK 2). Kid also made solo records.

Pat Metheny 1954 US jazz guitarist and songwriter. He wrote the score for the film *The Falcon & The Snowman* with David Bowie; the title of which was "This Is Not America" (2/85 US 32; UK 14).

Jurgen Dehmel 1958 German bass player and songwriter with the group Nena.

Roy Hay 1961 UK guitarist and keyboard player with Culture Club.

Tanita Tikaram 1969 UK singer, guitarist, and songwriter, who was born in Munster, Germany. In 1988 she released her first album, and was one of the great surprises of the year. Hits: "Good Tradition" (7/88 UK 10), and "Twist In My Sobriety" (10/88 UK 22).

Deaths

Kyu Sakamoto 1985 Japanese singer, who was the very first Japanese to reach the very top of the American charts, "Sukiyaki" (5/63 US 1; UK 6). The song was really called "Ue O Muite Aruko", which means 'I look straight ahead when I leave.' Kyu was one of over 520 victims who died in a Japanese jumbo-jet crash – only four people survived.

Hits of the Day

1967 "A Whiter Shade Of Pale" Procol Harum
1972 "School's Out" Alice Cooper UK 3 weeks
1978 "Three Times A Lady" Commodores US 2 weeks
1989 "Right Here Waiting" Richard Marx US 3 weeks

Miscellany

1967 This was the first appearance of Fleetwood Mac at the National Jazz & Blues Festival. After that, because they were so impressive, they received a recording contract.

13th

Birthdays

George Shearing 1919 UK pianist and songwriter who was blind from birth. At age 18 he made his first records. In the UK between 1939 and 1946 he was voted best swing pianist several times. In 1946 he went to the USA, in 1948 he played with the Oscar Pettiford Trio, and just a little later was leading a quartet with Buddy Franco, before forming his own quintet in 1949. Hit: "September In The Rain" (5/49 US 25). Shearing's best-known composition was "Lullaby Of Birdland" (1952) supposedly written in 10 minutes.

Jimmy McCracklin 1921 US blues singer, pianist, and harmonica player. In the mid-1940s he was a professional boxer, in 1945 he made his first records. In 1949 he formed his own band with the Blues Blasters. His biggest hit was "The Walk" (2/58 US 7).

Tony Bennett 1926 US singer, real name Anthony Dominick Benedetto. His singing career started while he was at High School, and then while in the US Army, he sang with various bands. Bob Hope gave him his first opportunity to appear in front of a large audience in 1950. In the same year he received a recording contract with CBS. Percy Faith and his orchestra were also under contract to this company, and would back Tony on all his records over the next few years. Hits: "Because Of You" (6/51 US 1), "Cold, Cold Heart" (7/51 US 1), "Rags To Riches" (9/53 US 1), "Stranger In Paradise" (11/53 US 2; 4/55 UK 1), and "In The Middle Of An Island" (8/57 US 9). Tony has recorded throughout the 1980s.

Dave 'Baby' Cortez 1938 US organist, singer and songwriter. Complete name David Cortez Clowney. He sang with the group Pearls, was a session keyboard player in the late 1950s, and then had his biggest hit with "The Happy Organ" (3/59 US 1), which was followed by "Rinky Dink" (7/62 US 10).

Joe Scott Hill 1939 US guitarist and singer with Priscilla Coolidge and Jesse Ed Davis, after that he joined Canned Heat and the Flying Burrito Brothers.

Sean James Stokes 1940 UK singer and bass player with the Bachelors.

Craig Douglas 1941 UK singer, real name Terry Perkins. He specialised in singing cover versions of US hits. This brought him seven Top Ten hits from 1959 to 1962; the biggest being "Only Sixteen" (8/59 UK 1), originally recorded by Sam Cooke.

Cliff Fish 1949 UK bassist and singer with Paper Lace.

Dan Fogelberg 1951 US singer, guitarist, pianist and songwriter. He made his first album in 1971, and was a guest musician on records by Jackson Browne, Van Morrison and Randy Newman. Solo hits: "Longer" (12/79 US 2), "Same Old Lang Syne" (12/80 US 9), "Hard To Say" (8/81 US 7), "Leader Of The Band" (11/81 US 9) and "The Language Of Love" (2/84 US 13).

Feargal Sharkey 1958 UK singer, who was leadsinger of the Undertones in 1978. Hits: "Teenage Kicks" (10/78 UK 31), "Jimmy Jimmy" (4/79 UK 16) and "My Perfect Cousin" (4/80 UK 9). In June 1983 the band split up, Sharkey formed Assembly with Vince Clark. Hit: "Never, Never" (11/83 UK 4). From the end of 1984 he was a solo artist. Hits: "A Good Heart" (10/85 UK 1), and "You Little Thief" (1/86 UK 5).

Deaths

King Curtis 1971 US saxophonist. He was stabbed to death during a punch-up in front of his apartment. It was Friday, 13th. He was born 7th February, 1934.

Bill Chase 1974 US trumpeter, composer, and bandleader. He played drums first, then trumpet. He played with Maynard Ferguson, then Stan Kenton, Woody Herman, before forming his own jazz-rock group Chase in

1971. The Chase album was voted the pop album of the year by the specialist magazine "Downbeat". Bill died, hardly 40 years old, in an air crash.

Joe Tex 1982 US singer and songwriter. Died of a heart attack. Born 8th August, 1933.

Hits of the Day

1964 "Do Wah Diddy Diddy" Manfred Mann UK 2 weeks

1966 "Summer In The City" Lovin' Spoonful US 3 weeks

1983 "Give It Up" K. C. & The Sunshine Band UK 3 weeks

14th

Birthdays

Buddy Greco 1926 US composer, arranger, jazz-pianist, and singer, real first name Armando. In 1948 he had a million seller with "Ooh Look-A There, Ain't She Pretty" (12/47 US 15). Shortly after that, he became the singer with the Benny Goodman band, in which he was also a pianist. Hit: "It Isn't Fair" (4/50 US 13). In 1960 he appeared in the charts with his own orchestra and the million seller "The Lady Is A Tramp" (7/60 UK 26).

Dash Crofts 1940 US singer, drummer, multi-instrumentalist and keyboard player. He started with the group Champs (having teamed up with Jim Seals), who had already had their hit "Tequila" (3/58 US 1; UK 5). As members of Champs, Jim and Dash also played on "Too Much Tequila" (1/60 US 30). In the mid-1960s they formed the Dawnbreakers, and finally in 1970 appeared as the duo Seals & Crofts. Hits: "Summer Breeze" (9/72 US 6), "Diamond Girl" (5/73 US 6) and "Get Closer" (4/76 US 6).

David Crosby 1941 US singer, guitarist, and songwriter. Real surname van Cortland. After playing with Les Baxter's Balladeers, he became a founder member of Jet Set in August 1964, who then changed their name to Beefeaters. Three members of this band, Jim McGuinn, Gene Clark and David were joined in October 1964 by Michael Clarke and Chris Hillman, which became the original lineup of the Byrds. In October 1967 David publicly questioned the circumstances surrounding the assassination of

John F. Kennedy. The Byrds threw him out. He produced Joni Mitchell and played sporadically with Buffalo Springfield. When they split up, he formed the trio Crosby, Stills & Nash with Stephen Stills and Graham Nash. Hits: "Marrakesh Express" (7/69 US 28; UK 17), "Just A Song Before I Go" (5/77 US 7) and "Wasted On The Way" (6/82 US 9). In June 1969 the trio was expanded to a quartet with the addition of Neil Young, who remained for three albums. Hit: "Woodstock" (3/70 US 11). David made albums with Graham Nash and worked as a soloist. In 1988 the quartet reformed for the album AMERICAN DREAM.

Gil Bridges 1942 US saxophonist with Rare Earth. Also worked as a flautist, percussionist and singer.

Tim Bogert 1944 US bass player with Vanilla Fudge, Cactus, Beck, Bogert & Appice, Boxer, Rod Stewart, and finally in 1981 with a solo album.

Larry Graham 1946 US bassist and singer with Sly & The Family Stone, and from 1973 with his own band, Graham Central Station. Hit: "Your Love" (8/75 US 39). In the 1980s he was a solo artist. Hit: "One In A Million You" (6/80 US 9).

George Newsome 1947 UK drummer with the British group Climax Blues Band formed in 1968.

Sharon Bryant 1956 US singer and songwriter with the band Atlantic Starr formed in 1976, which consisted of eight men and one woman. Biggest hit was "Secret Lovers" (12/85 US 3; 3/86 UK 10). In 1985 Sharon left the group and was replaced by Barbara Weathers. Sharon built up a studio with her husband, formed a production company and released her first solo album in 1989. Hit: "Let Go" (8/89 US 34).

Deaths

Bertolt Brecht 1956 German author, lyricist, director, theatre critic, playwright, pacifist and Marxist. Born 10th February, 1989.

Big Bill Broonzy 1958 US blues artist. Died of lung cancer. Born 26th June, 1893.

Johnny Burnette 1964 US singer and songwriter. Died in a fishing accident. Born 25th March, 1934.

Joe Venuti 1978 US jazz violinist. Died of cancer. Born 1st September, 1904.

Roy Buchanan 1988 US rock and blues guitarist. He hanged himself in a prison cell in Fairfax, after being arrested for drunkenness. Born 23rd September, 1939.

Hits of the Day

1948 "You Call Everybody Darlin'" Al Trace US 6 weeks

1948 "Love Somebody" Doris Day & Buddy Clark US 5 weeks

1953 "Moulin Rouge" Mantovani UK 1 week

1966 "I Got You Babe" Sonny & Cher US 3 weeks

1968 "Fire" Crazy World Of Arthur Brown UK 1 week

15th

Birthdays

Hugo Winterhalter 1909 US orchestra leader who worked for record company RCA from 1950 to 1963, and backed Eddie Fisher, Perry Como, Kay Starr, the Fontane Sisters, Eddy Arnold and the Ames Brothers on their bigger hits. He himself had some 30 hits in the USA with his orchestra between 1949 and 1956, nine of them reached the Top Ten. The biggest hit was "Canadian Sunset" (7/56 US 2), with a piano solo by Eddie Heywood. Hugo died 17th September, 1973.

Buster Brown 1911 US singer, harmonica player and songwriter. He made his first records in the 40s and then wrote the hit "Fannie Mae" (12/59 R&B 1; 2/60 US 38). He died 31st January, 1976.

Oscar Peterson 1925 Canadian composer, pianist, and bandleader. His popularity as a jazz musician can be compared to that of Louis Armstrong. He worked as a solo artist, in a trio and with the best jazz musicians in the business.

Jackie Brenston 1930 US singer, songwriter, and saxophonist. He played with the Ike Turner band, the Kings Of Rhythm. In 1951 he recorded "Rocket 88" (5/51 R&B 1), produced by the legendary Sam Phillips, who leased it to the Chess label; it was credited to Jackie Brenston & His Delta Cats. Although it was his only hit many consider it to be the first real R 'n R song. Jackie died 15th December, 1979.

Floyd Ashton 1933 US singer with the Tams.

Bobby Helms 1933 US country singer, guitarist, and songwriter. He had his first crossover success with the number "Fraulein" (3/57 C&W 1; 7/57 US 36). Further pop hits were "My Special Angel" (10/57 US 7; UK 22) and "Jingle Bell Rock" (12/57 US 6).

Bill Pinkney 1933 US singer with the Drifters.

'Stix' Hooper 1938 US drummer and songwriter. Real first name Nesbert. In the 1950s he formed the Modern Jazz Sextet, which became the Nite Hawks, the Jazz Crusaders, and from 1972 the Crusaders. Stix also released solo records besides his work with the group.

Pete York 1942 UK drummer and songwriter with the Spencer Davis Group, Hardin & York, and as a session musician.

Jimmy Webb 1946 US songwriter and singer. He wrote hits for Glen Campbell, Fifth Dimension and Richard Harris.

Kate Taylor 1949 US singer and younger sister of James Taylor.

Thomas Aldridge 1950 US drummer with Black Oak Arkansas, Pat Travers and Ozzy Osbourne.

Bobby Caldwell 1951 US singer, guitarist, saxophonist, bassist, pianist and songwriter, who formed his first group, Rooftops, during his teens and played at 'high school hops'. He started writing music for commercials early on, and was then responsible for more than 100 soundtracks for Walt Disney's 'New Mickey Mouse Club' TV show. In the early 1970s he made his first records, on which he usually played all the instruments himself. Hit: "What You Won't Do For Love" (12/78 US 9). His compositions have since been recorded by Roberta Flack, Dionne Warwick, Toni Tennille, Natalie Cole and Peabo Bryson.

MCA 1967 US singer with the Beastie Boys. Real name Adam Yauch. Hits, see under 31st October, King Ad-Rock.

Deaths

Thomas Wayne 1971 US singer. Died in a car crash. Born 22nd July, 1940.

Norman Petty 1984 US songwriter. Born 25th May, 1927.

Hits of the Day

1953	"No Other Love" Perry Como US 4 weeks
1960	"It's Now Or Never" Elvis Presley US 5 weeks
1964	"Everybody Loves Somebody" Dean Martin US 1 week
1981	"Endless Love" Diana Ross & Lionel Richie US 9 weeks
1987	"I Just Can't Stop Loving You" Michael Jackson UK 2 weeks

Miscellany

1969 The three-day festival at Woodstock began. Motto: 'Peace & Music'. About 400,000 spectators came. Among others, the following appeared, Crosby, Stills, Nash & Young, Jimi Hendrix, CCR, Canned Heat, Janis Joplin, Richie Havens, Who, Joan Baez, Santana, Joe Cocker and Iron Butterfly.

16th

Birthdays

Al Hibbler 1915 US singer for eight years with Duke Ellington's band, and finally as a solo artist from 1951. Hits: "Unchained Melody" (4/55 US 3; UK 2) and "He" (10/55 US 4). Al has been blind since birth which however was not noticeable at his appearances with Ellington's orchestra. Duke always walked shoulder to shoulder to the microphone with Al. Al stayed there and after the performance Ellington would come over and escort him off stage again.

Ernie Freeman 1922 US pianist, composer and orchestra leader. He was musical director on records by artists like Frank Sinatra, Dean Martin, Sammy Davis Jr. and Connie Francis. Between 1957 and 1962 he cut instrumentals, including the hit "Raunchy" (11/57 US 4). He recorded as Sir Chauncey and is the pianist on records by B. Bumble & The Stingers. Hit: "Nut Rocker" (3/62 US 23; 4/62 UK 1; 1/72 RE-UK 19). Ernie died on 16th May, 1981.

Fess Parker 1925 US actor and singer. He played the main part in the film *Davy Crockett* (1955), in the series of the same name (1954/55) and in the TV series, *Daniel Boone* (1964-70). Hits: "Ballad Of Davy Crockett" (3/55 US 5) and "Wringle Wrangle" (1/57 US 12).

Bill Evans 1929 US jazz pianist and composer. He played with the Miles Davis sextet and was one of the most innovative pianists of the Post-Bop epoch. Bill died 15th September, 1980.

Eydie Gorme 1931 US singer who cut her first records in 1956. In 1957 she married Steve Lawrence, whom she partnered sang in duets. Hits, as a solo artist: "Love Me Forever" (12/57 US 24; UK 21), "Yes, My Darling Daughter" (5/62 UK 10) and "Blame It On The Bossa Nova" (1/63 UK 32; US 7). Hit for Steve and Edie: "I Want To Stay Here" (7/63 US 28; UK 3).

Ketty Lester 1934 US TV actress and singer. Real name Revoyda Frierson. In 1962 she had four hits entries in the charts, the biggest was "Love Letters" (2/62 US 5; 4/62 UK 4). Both Dick Haymes (1945) and Alison Moyet (1987) scored with the same title.

Barbara George 1942 US singer and songwriter who had her biggest hit with "I Know (You Don't Love Me No More)" (11/61 US 3).

Kevin Ayers 1944 UK bassist and songwriter with the band Soft Machine, which he formed co-founded in 1965. He remained until 1968, formed the Whole World until 1970 and then Soporifics in 1974. After that, he launched a solo career and did session work for musician Alan Parsons, among others.

Gordon Fleet 1945 UK drummer with the Australian group Easybeats formed in 1964. Before that he played with the Mojos, managed by Brian Epstein.

Gary Loizzo 1945 US singer and guitarist with Gary & The Nite Lights, which he formed in Chicago in 1966. In the same year and after an unsuccessful single, they changed their name to American Breed. Hit, and million seller: "Bend Me, Shape Me" (12/67 US 5; 2/68 UK 24).

Barry Hay 1948 Dutch singer, flautist, and songwriter with Golden Earring, formed in 1961. Their most successful international hits were "Radar Love" (12/73 UK 7; 5/74 US 13) and "Twilight Zone" (11/82 US 10).

James Taylor 1953 US singer, who, in February 1978, joined the group Kool & The Gang formed in 1964. In order to distinguish himself from the folk-rock artist of the same name, James used the initials J.T. after his first name. Hits: "Lady's Night" (10/79 US 8; UK 9), "Too Hot" (1/80 US 5; UK 23), "Celebration" (10/80 US 1; UK 7), "Get Down On It" (12/81 UK 3; 2/82 US 10), "Joanna" (11/83 US 2; 2/84 UK 2) and "Cherish" (5/85 UK 4; 7/85 US 2). In February 1988 he left the group and started a solo career.

Madonna 1958 US singer and songwriter. Real name Louise Ciccone. In her home town of Bay City, Michigan she took lessons in ballet, jazz, and modern dance. In the late 1970s she went to New York and appeared there for two years with the dance company of Pearl Lange & Alvin Ailey. After that, she went to Paris, took singing lessons and appeared for a while with the troupe of disco artist Patrick Hernandez. Frustrated by all this she returned to New York in the 1980s, and learned to play guitar, keyboards and drums. Then she recorded her first self-penned songs, which were immediate disco hits, and finally in 1983 they became pop hits: "Holiday" (10/83 US 16; 1/84 UK 6; 8/85 RE-UK 2), "Borderline" (3/84 US 10; 1/86 UK 2), "Lucky Star" (3/84 UK 14; 8/84 US 4), "Like A Virgin" (11/84 US 1; UK 3), "Material Girl" (2/85 US 2; UK 3), "Crazy For You" (3/85 US 1; 6/85 UK 2), "Angel" (4/85 US 5; 9/85 UK 5), "Into The Groove" (7/85 UK 1), "Dress You Up" (8/85 US 5; 12/85 UK 5), "Gambler" (10/85 UK 4), "Live To Tell" (4/86 US 1; UK 2), "Papa Don't Preach" (6/86 US & UK 1), "True Blue" (10/86 US 3; UK 1), "Open Your Heart" (12/86 US 1; UK 4), "La Isla Bonita" (3/87 US 4; UK 1), "Who's That Girl" (7/87 US & UK 1), "Causing A Commotion" (9/87 US 2; UK 4), "Like A Prayer" (3/89 US & UK 1). She also appeared as an actress and acquitted herself very well to the immense chagrin of her critics.

Deaths

Robert Johnson 1938 US blues singer, guitarist, and songwriter. It was reported that he had been poisoned by a rival or jealous husband. Born 8th May, 1911.

Elvis Presley 1977 US rock 'n' roll star. He would have had a performance the next day. Ginger Alden found him in his bathroom in Graceland – dead. The cause of death was heart failure. Later it became known that high consumption of drugs had contributed to his death. Born 8th January, 1935. The 'King' is dead.

Hits of the Day

1975 "Can't Give You Anything (But My Love)" Stylistics UK 3 weeks
1986 "Papa Don't Preach" Madonna US 2 weeks

17th

Birthdays

Larry Clinton 1909 US trumpeter, songwriter and bandleader. From 1937 to 1941, and again from 1948 to 1950 he had his own orchestra. Hits: "Cry, Baby Cry" (3/38 US 1), "My Reverie" (8/38 US 1), "Heart And Soul" (10/38 US 1) and "Deep Purple" (2/39 US 1). When he was not conducting his own band, he played with Tommy or Jimmy Dorsey. Larry died 2nd May, 1985.

Georgia Gibbs 1920 US singer. She appeared under her real name Freda Gibson (or Gibbons) in the 'Lucky Strike Radio Show' in 1937/38, and sang in the early 1940s, now as Georgia Gibbs, with Hudson DeLange, Frankie Trumbauer, Artie Shaw, and in the 'Gary Moore – Jimmy Durante Show' (as 'Her Nibbs, Miss Gibbs'). From 1950 she was successful as a solo artist. Hits: "Kiss Of Fire" (4/52 US 1), "Tweedle Dee" (1/55 US 2; 4/55 UK 20), "Dance With Me Henry (Wallflower)" (3/55 US 1) and "The Hula Hoop Song" (10/58 US 32).

Wayne Raney 1921 US singer and harmonica player, who appeared first with the Raney Family Gospel Singers, then with the Delmore Brothers and finally as a solo artist. Hit: "Why Don't You Howl Off And Love Me" (7/49 C&W 1; 10/49 US 22).

Sam Butera 1927 US R&B saxophonist and singer. The grandson of Italian immigrants to the USA, born in New Orleans, he made records with his own band in the early 1950s.

Mark Dinning 1933 US singer, brother of the three Dinning Sisters. He made his first records in 1957, and his main claim to fame was "Teen Angel" (12/59 US 1; 3/60 UK 37), written by his sister Jeannie. He died 22nd March, 1986.

Luther Allison 1939 US blues singer and guitarist. He formed the group Rolling Stones with his brother Gran in 1954, which was renamed the Four Jivers later on. He also worked as a solo artist.

Ed Sanders 1939 US singer and guitarist with the group Fugs formed in 1956, as a solo artist, and with Vanity.

Gary Talley 1947 US lead guitarist with the Box Tops.

Sib Hashian 1949 US drummer with Boston from 1975 to 1980.

Steve Price 1951 US drummer with Pablo Cruise and as a session musician for Grace Slick, Rick James, Alex Call and Mary Jane Girls.

Kevin Rowland 1953 UK singer, guitarist, and songwriter. He began his career with the group Lucy & The Lovers in 1977. Next he played on the record "Johnny Won't Get To Heaven" by the Kill Joys. In July 1978, he formed Dexy's Midnight Runners. Hits: "Geno" (3/80 UK 1), "There, There, My Dear" (7/80 UK 7), "Come On Eileen" (7/82 UK 1; 1/83 US 1) and "Jackie Wilson Said (I'm In Heaven When You Smile)" (10/82 UK 5). In the autumn of 1983 things became quiet for the band. In 1985 an album appeared – Rowland insisted that no single be extracted from it. In autumn 1986 the single "Because Of You" (11/86 UK 13) is credited to Dexy's Midnight Runners, but in actual fact it was really a solo record by Kevin. After that there was lengthy pause, then in mid-1988 he appeared with new records as Kevin Rowland Of Dexy's Midnight Runners.

Colin Moulding 1955 UK bassist and songwriter with the new wave band XTC formed in 1976.

Belinda Carlisle 1958 US singer and songwriter. She began with the L.A. punk band Germs, and was a co-founder of Go-Gos in 1978. Hits: "We Got The Beat" (1/82 US 2) and "Vacation" (7/82 US 8). From 1985 she carried on her career as a solo artist. Hits: "Mad About You" (5/86 US 3), "Heaven Is A Place On Earth" (9/87 US 1; 12/87 UK 1), "I Get Weak" (1/88 US 2; UK 10), "Circle In The Sand" (4/88 US 7; UK 4) and "Leave A Light On" (9/89 US 11; UK 4).

Maria McKee 1964 US singer, songwriter and guitarist. At age 16 she appeared in L.A. clubs with her half brother Brian MacLean, who had played with Love previously. After that she formed Lone Justice, which accompanied U2 and Alarm on their US tour. In 1985 her first album appeared. Maria wrote "A Good Heart" for Feargal Sharkey, which reached No. 1 in the British charts.

Deaths

Paul Williams 1973 US singer with the Temptations. He was found dead in his car, shot in the head. Born 2nd July, 1939.

Hits of the Day

1968 "People Got To Be Free" Rascals US 5 weeks
1974 "The Night Chicago Died" Paper Lace US 1 week
1974 "When Will I See You Again" Three Degrees UK 2 weeks

18th

Birthdays

Cisco Houston 1918 US folk singer, guitarist, and songwriter. Real first names Gilbert Vandine. He was friends with artists like Woody Guthrie and worked with Pete Seeger and the Almanac Singers. He himself was successful with "Rose, Rose I Love You" (6/51 US 21). During the 1950s he appeared in folk clubs and universities with Sonny Terry and Brownie McGhee. Cisco was one of those who made folk music appealing to young people in the late 1950s/early 1960s. Bob Dylan, for example, was one of his admirers. Cisco died on 19th April, 1961.

Johnny Preston 1939 US singer. Complete name John Preston Courville. Johnny was discovered by the disc jockey and songwriter J. P. 'Big Bopper' Richardson, who wrote his first hit, "Running Bear" (10/59 US 1; 2/60 UK 1). Possibly because of Big Bopper's death (in the air crash that killed Buddy Holly and Richie Valens as well), this composition was pushed even more by the US radio stations. Two further hits followed, "Cradle Of Love" (3/60 US 7; UK 2) and "Feel So Fine" (6/60 US 14; 8/60 UK 18). After that Johnny Preston slipped into obscurity.

Carl Wayne 1944 UK singer and founder of Carl Wayne & The Vikings in 1964. The group included drummer Bev Bevan and made three unsuccessful singles, before becoming the first lineup of Move in February 1966. This lineup included Roy Wood, who began to guide the musical direction of the band. In late 1969 Carl left the band and was replaced by Jeff Lynne. Carl started a fresh career in TV.

Sarah Dash 1945 US singer with Patti LaBelle & The Blue Belles, later abbreviated to La Belle. In addition, she sang on records by the Marshall Tucker Band, Alice Cooper, David Johansen and former colleague Nona Hendryx. Sarah released a solo album in 1980.

Barbara Harris 1945 US singer with the New York soul trio Toys. In 1965 they appeared on the TV show 'Shindig', after that, they had hits with the million seller "A Lover's Concerto" (9/65 US 2; 11/65 UK 5) and "Attack" (12/65 US 18; UK 36). After that, they could be seen again in the film *The Girl In Daddy's Bikini*. She had no more hits after 1966.

Vince Melouney 1945 Australian guitarist in the early lineup of the Bee Gees. In February 1967, when the three Bee Gees had been contracted to Robert Stigwood, who at that time was still the partner of Brian Epstein, two extra Australians were hired. One was Vince and the other Colin Peterson. When arguments over their musical direction flared up between the three brothers in March 1969 the group effectively broke up for a while. Melouney and Peterson were not re-engaged.

Dennis Elliott 1950 UK drummer with Foreigner and as a session musician with Ian Hunter, among others.

19th

Birthdays

Harry Mills 1913 US singer with the Mills Brothers. He died 28th June, 1982.

Ginger Baker 1939 UK drummer and songwriter. Real first name Peter. He started as a drummer with Acker Bilk and Terry Lightfoot. After that he met bassist Jack Bruce who was in the Bert Courtley band, played with Blues Incorporated, and then in 1963 again with Jack Bruce in the Graham Bond Organisation. Other bands he belonged to, included Cream, Blind Faith, Ginger Baker's Airforce and Baker-Gurvitz Army. He is very sought-after as a session musician and his excursion into Afro-rock was intriguing.

Jonathan 1940 UK singer and songwriter. Real name Roger James Cook. Together He was successful with Roger Greenaway as David & Jonathan. Hits: "Michelle" (1/66 UK 11; US 18) and "Lovers Of The World Unite" (7/66 UK 7). Both had previously sung with the group Kestrels, and had written the hit "You've Got Your Troubles" for the Fortunes. Freddie & The Dreamers and Petula Clark also had hits with songs by Greenaway/Cook. In the middle 1968 they ceased as David & Jonathan but carried on working as a songwriting team. Andy Williams, White Plains and Blue Mink (Roger Cook sang with Madeline Bell for them), had Top Ten hits by 'Cookaway Music'. In 1976 Jonathan went to Nashville and wrote country hits for artists like Don Williams and Crystal Gayle.

Johnny Nash 1940 US singer, guitarist, songwriter and actor, who was thought by many to be Jamaican. He grew up in Houston, Texas. Barely 13 years old, he was already singing regularly in radio shows and on television. His recording career began in 1957, having a hit with "A Very Special Love" (12/57 US 23). He was modestly successful with "The Teen Commandments" (12/58 US 29) in conjunction with Paul Anka and George Hamilton IV. He carried on making unsuccessful records for the next few years and writing songs which were hits for others like "What Kind Of Love Is This" for Joey Dee (1962). In 1965 he set up his own record company JoDa. In 1968, having moved to Jamaica, he had hits with "Hold Me Tight" (8/68 UK 5; 9/68 US 5), "You Got Soul" (1/69 UK 6), "Cupid" (4/69 UK 6; 11/69 US 39), "Stir It Up" (4/72 UK 13; 2/73 US 12), "I Can See Clearly Now" (6/72 UK 5; 9/72 US 1) and "Tears On My Pillow" (6/75 UK 1).

Don Fardon 1943 UK singer, real name Donald Maughn. He started with the band Sorrows, which lasted until 1967. Hit: "Take A Heart" (9/65 UK 21). After that, he continued as a solo artist, and was successful with "(The Lament Of The Cherokee) Indian Reservation" (8/68 US 20; 10/70 UK 3).

Billy J. Kramer 1943 UK singer with Billy J. Kramer & The Dakotas, formed in 1963. Real name William Howard Ashton. Before that he played with the Liverpool band The Coasters, and was discovered there by Brian Epstein. It was Epstein who brought him together with the Manchester band Dakotas. George Martin was the producer of the new group. Hits: "Do You Want To Know A Secret" (5/63 UK 3), "Bad To Me" (8/63 UK 1; 5/64 US 9) and "Little Children" (2/64 UK 1; 4/64 US 7). Billy later tried as a soloist, unsuccessfully.

Ian Gillan 1945 UK singer and songwriter. In May 1965 he joined the group Episode Six formed in 1963. The group made a number of singles together with him, which were successful especially in Lebanon. The group played in Beirut for two months, at which time all three singles were in the Lebanese Top Ten. Ian Gillan said, "The charts were compiled by a few record shops. All in all they didn't really sell many records, but for us it was a first taste of stardom." With a few changes, but always with Roger Glover and Ian, the group lasted until June 1969. Then both of them joined Deep Purple, forming most successful lineup of this band. At this time, Ian Gillan had already made himself a name in the musical *Jesus Christ Superstar*, where he sang the lead part. Hits for Deep Purple: "Black Night" (8/70 UK 2), "Strange Kind Of Woman" (2/71 UK 8), "Fireball" (11/71 UK 15) and "Smoke On The Water" (5/73 US 4; 4/77 UK 21). In June 1973 Ian left Deep Purple, and formed the Ian Gillan band in 1975, which was then called Gillan from August 1978. Hits: "Trouble" (10/80 UK 14) and "New Orleans" (3/81 UK 17). Albums by this group were extremely successful in the 1980s. In 1983 Ian sang briefly with Black Sabbath, and in 1984 the most successful lineup of Deep Purple reformed again.

Elliot Lurie 1948 US lead guitarist and singer for the group Looking Glass formed in 1969. Their greatest hit and million seller was "Brandy (You're A Fine Girl)" (6/72 US 1). In 1973 the band split up, and Elliot tried as a solo artist.

John Deacon 1951 UK bassist and songwriter for Queen. As did the other members of the group, John also had a side-project which was called Immortals.

Joey Tempest 1963 Swedish singer and songwriter with Europe. Hits: "The Final Countdown" (11/86 UK 1; 1/87 US 8), "Rock The Night" (1/87 UK 12; 5/87 US 30), "Carrie" (4/87 UK 22; 8/87 US 3) and "Superstitious" (8/88 UK 34; US 31).

Deaths

Blind Willie McTell 1959 US blues singer, guitarist, and songwriter. Born 5th May, 1901.

Dorsey Burnette 1979 US rockabilly singer and songwriter. He died of a heart attack. Born 28th December, 1932.

Hits of the Day

1950 "Good Night Irene" Weavers with Gordon Jenkins US 13 weeks

1957 "Tammy" Debbie Reynolds US 5 weeks

1967 "All You Need Is Love" Beatles US 1 week

1978 "Three Times A Lady" Commodores UK 5 weeks

20th

Birthdays

Jack Teagarden 1905 US jazz musician, innovative traditional jazz trombonist and singer. Real first names Weldon John. His career began with Ben Pollack in 1928. He stayed with Pollack until 1933, then played with Red Nichols, Benny Goodman, and Paul Whiteman, and in between with his own orchestra. Hits: "Someone Stole

Gabriel's Horn" (9/33 US 7) and "The Sheik Of Araby" (6/39 US 14). From 1947 to 1951 he played with the Louis Armstrong All Stars. Jack died 15th January, 1964.

Jim Reeves 1924 US country singer and songwriter. Real first names, James Travis. It is possible he may have become a great baseball player but for an ankle injury, which put a stop to a promising career. When you hear Jim Reeves' pleasant voice, it does not seem surprising that he became a disc jockey next. He worked in Shreveport, Louisiana, the home of the 'Louisiana Hayride'. In 1950 he cut his first recordings, and in 1953 he had his first million seller with the Top Country Hit of the Year, "Mexican Joe" (4/53 US 23). After this record he become one of the few artists in the USA who were successful simultaneously both in the country and pop charts. His greatest hits were "Four Walls" (4/57 US 11), "He'll Have To Go" (12/59 US 2; 4/60 UK 12), "I Love You Because" (2/64 UK 5), "I Won't Forget You" (6/64 UK 3; 11/64 C&W 3) and "Distant Drums" (4/66 C&W 1; 8/66 UK 1). While the latter was in the charts, he died when his private plane crashed on 31st July, 1964. His records were re-released at regular intervals in the UK and the USA. Even in the 1980s his singles were still turning up in the country charts. It seems typically American that the last Top Ten entry in the C&W chart was "Have You Ever Been Lonely (Have You Ever Been Blue)" (11/81 C&W 5), a duet with Patsy Cline. Like Jim, Patsy died in an air crash (1963).

John Lantree 1940 UK bassist with the Honeycombs.

Isaac Hayes 1942 US singer, pianist, songwriter and producer. He started as a session musician with Otis Redding, and other artists on the Stax label. He wrote a number of well-known soul hits, like "Soul Man" and "Hold On! I'm A Comin' " with songwriter David Porter. In the late 1960s Isaac released his first solo records. His biggest hit was "The Theme From Shaft" (10/71 US 1; 12/71 UK 4), from the film *Shaft*, for which he received an Oscar. He also had further success as a composer of film music: *Tough Guys* and *Truck Turner*.

Jim Pankow 1947 US trombonist and songwriter with Chicago since their formation in 1966. Jim wrote "Make Me Smile" (4/70 US 9), "Just You And Me" (9/73 US 4) and "Old Days" (4/75 US 5). As well as this, he worked as a session musician with Leon Russell, the Bee Gees, Knack, Joe Vitale, Toto, Don Felder, Rufus and David Foster.

Robert Plant 1948 UK singer and songwriter. After the Yardbirds split up in July 1968, Jimmy Page and bassist Chris Dreja decided to continue as the New Yardbirds. The group was booked for a ten-day tour through Scandinavia. When Page wanted to take on new musicians in the group, Chris Dreja left to become a photographer. Former session musician and arranger John Paul Jones joined them as bassist. Terry Reid and B. J. Wilson of Procol Harum declined the offer of becoming members. However, Reid suggested 19-year old singer Robert Plant. Jimmy Page and the band manager Peter Grant saw Robert Plant at an appearance with the band Hobbstweedle in Birmingham. Plant had already made his recording debut in 1966 as a member of the group Listen. In 1967 he released two solo singles which were both unsuccessful. In the same year he became a member of Band Of Joy (this band never released any records at the time, but in 1978 Polydor issued archive material). Page made Robert an offer, he accepted and suggested John Bonham as the drummer for the New Yardbirds. After the group had cut their first album in two weeks, they started to tour. Back in the UK Jimmy Page heard a quote by Keith Moon which he liked, " . . . going down like a lead Zeppelin": Keith's description of performances that were absolutely dreadful from start to finish. Page left the 'a' out of lead, and created Led Zeppelin. Hits: "Whole Lotta Love" (11/69 US 4), "Immigrant Song" (11/70 US 16), "Black Dog" (12/71 US 15), and "The Ocean" (6/73). The group always sold more albums than singles. As a result, the album track "Stairway To Heaven" was probably their best known; it was never released as a single because of its length. After John Bonham's death on 25th September, 1980, the other members of the group declared that after the 'loss of our dear friend', they no longer wished to continue as a group. From April 1981 Plant sang every so often with his band Honeydrippers, and released his first solo album BIG LOG (7/83 UK 11; 9/83 US 20) in July 1982. The Honeydrippers scored with "Sea Of Love" (10/84 US 3). Since then, rumours have flourished of an impending reformation of Led Zeppelin with Bonham's son replacing his father. Plant, meanwhile, continues to release solo albums intermittently.

Phil Lynott 1951 UK singer, bassist and songwriter. Son of Brazilian-Irish parents. He started with Black Eagles, Skid Row, Sugar Shack and Orphanage. In 1970 he formed Thin Lizzy. Hits: "Whisky In A Jar" (1/73 UK 6), "The Boys Are Back In Town" (5/76 UK 8; US 12), "Waitin' For An Alibi" (3/79 UK 9) and "Killer On The Loose" (9/80 UK 10). In between he made solo records and guested on records by Gary Moore, Jeff Wayne (WAR OF THE WORLDS) and others. Hits, with Gary: "Parisienne Walkways" (4/79 UK 8) and "Out In The Fields" (5/85 UK 5). Lynott died after being in a coma for a week on 4th January, 1986.

Doug Fieger 1952 US singer, guitarist, and songwriter. In the early 1970s he began as a bassist with the group Sky.

In the mid-1970s he worked as a session musician, and was briefly with the German group Triumvirat. Knack formed in May 1978. Hits: "My Sharona" (6/79 US 1; UK 6) and "Good Girls Don't" (9/79 US 12). In 1982 the band split up, Fieger formed Doug Fieger's Taking Chances. He was with Was (Not Was) as a guest singer in 1983, and was on the album, BORN TO LAUGH AT TORNADOES by the Tornados.

Gary Lalonde 1955 Canadian bassist with Honeymoon Suite.

Mike McKenzie 1955 UK guitarist with Child.

Richard Zatorski 1957 Australian keyboard player and songwriter with Real Life.

Deaths

Thad Jones 1986 US trumpeter and composer. He died of cancer. Born 28th March, 1923.

Hits of the Day

1977 "Angelo" Brotherhood Of Man UK 1 week
1977 "Best Of My Love" Emotions US 4 weeks

21st

Birthdays

Count Basie 1904 US jazz pianist, composer, band leader and arranger. He played with almost everyone in pop and jazz and was considered by many to be second only to Duke Ellington. After William Basie (his real name) had accompanied variety artists in their performances, he first played with Walter Page's Blue Devils and then with Bennie Moten's band from 1929 to 1935. After the latter's death, Basie took over the helm retaining the best musicians; within a few years it was one of the best-known bands on the jazz scene. Because of his exceptional soloists, especially tenor saxophonist Lester Young, singer Jimmy Rushing, and the simple but swinging piano style of the Count himself, he was able to build up a consistent reputation. For more than four decades the name Basie

was synonymous with excellence. His biggest commercial success was the novelty number "Open The Door, Richard" (2/47 US 1). The Count died 26th April, 1984.

Christiane Legrand 1930 French singer who sang with the Blue Stars from 1955 to 1957, with Double Six Of Paris from 1958 to 1960, and after that as a soloist with the Swingle Singers. In 1964 her brother Michel wrote the music for the film *The Umbrellas Of Cherbourg*. Christiane's voice was featured on the soundtrack. She had a hit in France in the same year with "Les Parapluies De Cherbourg".

Kenny Rogers 1938 US singer who was successful in the pop and country charts. Real first names Kenneth Donald. After playing in the High School band Scholars from 1958, he started as a bassist and singer in the Bobby Doyle Trio, one of the most popular, jazzy sounding groups from Houston. After that he sang briefly with Kirby Stone Four, and from 1966 was one of the New Christy Minstrels. In 1967 Kenny formed the First Edition, which after their first two hits were renamed Kenny Rogers & The First Edition. Hits: "Just Dropped In (To See What Condition My Condition Was In)" (2/68 US 5), "Ruby, Don't Take Your Love To Town" (6/69 US 6; 10/69 UK 2) and "Something's Burning" (2/70 UK 8; US 11). From the mid-1970s Kenny has released solo records: "Lucille" (3/77 US 5; UK 1), "She Believes In Me" (4/79 US 5), "Coward Of The Country" (11/79 US 3; 1/80 UK 1), "Lady" (10/80 US 1; UK 12), and "I Don't Need You" (6/81 US 3). Additionally, he sang duets with a variety of partners: "Islands In The Stream" (8/83 US 1; 10/83 UK 7), with Dolly Parton; "We've Got Tonight" (1/83 US 6; UK 28) with Sheena Easton; "Don't Fall In Love With A Dreamer" (3/80 US 4), with Kim Carnes and "What About Me?" (9/84 US 15), with Kim Carnes and James Ingram. And if that was not enough, Kenny hosted the TV variety show '*Rollin'*' in 1972, and acted in the films *The Gambler*, *Coward Of The County* and *Six Pack*.

James Burton 1939 US guitarist. At age 16 he played the guitar solo on "Suzie Q" by Dale Hawkins, then on many early hits by Ricky Nelson, and from 1969 to 1977 he worked as a session musician on records by Elvis Presley. In 1971 he made the unsuccessful solo album THE GUITAR SOUND OF JAMES BURTON. James is still a sought-after session musician.

Harold Reid 1939 US singer with the Statler Brothers.

Tom Coster 1941 US pianist and songwriter for Santana. He joined them as a replacement for Gregg Rolie. After that he carried on as a session musician and solo artist.

Jackie DeShannon 1944 US songwriter and singer, real name Sharon Myers. She made her first records in

1959 as Sherry Lee Myers. In 1960 she went to Los Angeles and started working as a songwriter: to date, she has written over 600 compositions, among them hits for the Byrds, Brenda Lee, Rick Nelson, Bobby Vee, Searchers and Helen Shapiro. She became known to the US public when she supported the Beatles on a 26 concert-tour in 1964. Jackie has appeared in several films also. She had one of her biggest hits as co-writer of the song "Bette Davis Eyes" for Kim Carnes. Jackie had hits with "What The World Needs Now Is Love" (5/65 US 7) and "Put A Little Love In Your Heart" (6/69 US 4).

Glenn Hughes 1952 UK bassist and singer who played with Trapeze from 1968 to 1973. After that he was a member of Deep Purple from June 1973 to March 1976. After Trapeze reformed for six months in 1977 Glenn embarked on a solo career.

Joe Strummer 1952 UK singer, guitarist and songwriter with the band Clash formed in 1976. He was born as John Mellors in Ankara, Turkey. He started with the R&B group 101ers. Clash were one of the first successful punk bands in the UK. Hits: "London Calling" (12/79 UK 11; 5/88 RE-UK 46), "Bankrobber" (8/80 UK 12) and "Rock The Casbah" (1/82 UK 30; 10/82 US 8). After several of the original members of Clash left, Strummer disbanded the group in the Spring of 1986. In 1991, he joined the Pogues for a world tour.

Kim Sledge 1957 US singer with the sibling group Sister Sledge.

Peter Slaghuis 1963 Dutch hairdresser, disc jockey, scratcher, songwriter and sound engineer. Peter called his first project Video Kids, with whom he had the hit "Woodpeckers From Space" (2/85). In 1988 he formed the group Hithouse. Hit: "Jack To The Sound Of The Underground" (11/88 UK 14). Peter remixed "I Can't Wait" (3/86 US 3; 5/86 UK 2) for Nu Shooz, turning it into a hit.

Deaths

Joe Dassin 1980 French pop singer. Born 5th November, 1938.

Hits of the Day

1943	"In The Blue Of The Evening" Tommy Dorsey US 3 weeks
1953	"I Believe" Frankie Laine UK 3 weeks (3rd time)
1968	"Mony Mony" Tommy James & The Shondells UK 1 week (2nd time)
1971	"I'm Still Waiting" Diana Ross UK 3 weeks

22nd

Birthdays

John Lee Hooker 1917 US blues singer, guitarist and songwriter. He worked with Robert Nighthawk from 1931 to 1933, after that with various gospel groups, like the Fairfield Four in 1938. In 1943 John went to Detroit, cutting his first records in 1948: "Boogie Chillun" (1/49 R&B 1) and "I'm In The Mood" (10/51 R&B 1; US 30). Both records were million sellers in 1948, as well as "Dimples" in 1963, although the latter was never in the charts. In 1980 John Lee took a part in the film *Blues Brothers*. In late 1989 he released the excellent album THE HEALER, which included such well-known musicians as Carlos Santana, Bonnie Raitt, Robert Cray, Los Lobos, Canned Heat, and George Thorogood. The follow-up, MR LUCKY, in 1991, featured a similar stellar line up of backing musicians.

Sonny Thompson 1923 US pianist, songwriter and bandleader. Real first name Alfonso. He cut his first records in 1946 and was a session musician for artists on the King, Federal and DeLuxe labels throughout the early 1950s. He was successful himself with "Long Gone" (5/48 R&B 1; 7/48 US 29), which was a million seller in 1948.

Bob Flanigan 1926 US leadsinger with the Four Freshmen, who were formed in 1948 as the Toppers. In 1950 they went professional, after being discovered by Stan Kenton, who helped them get a recording contract. In 1951 they appeared in the film *Rich, Young And Pretty*. Hits: "Mood Indigo" (11/54 US 24) and "Graduation Day" (5/56 US 17).

Dale Hawkins 1938 US rockabilly singer, guitarist, songwriter and bandleader. Real first names Delmar Allen. In 1956 he made his first records and had his biggest hit with the original version of "Suzie Q" (6/57 US 27).

Fred Milano 1939 US singer with the Belmonts.

Ron Dante 1945 US singer who had a number of million sellers, but never in his own name. He always worked with session musicians who only ever met for the relevant recordings. First with the Detergents, "Leader Of The Laundromat" (12/64 US 19), a parody on the hit by the Shangrilas "Leader Of The Pack". Then Ron was the principal vocalist for the Archies. Hits: "Sugar Sugar" (7/69 US 1; 10/69 UK 1) and "Jingle Jangle" (11/69 US 10). He was also the vocalist for the Cuff Links. Hits: "Tracy" (9/69 US 9; 11/69 UK 4) and "When Julie Comes Around" (3/70 UK 10). Attempts to launch a solo career failed. From 1975 he produced Barry Manilow.

Donna Godchaux 1947 US singer from 1974 with the Grateful Dead and New Riders Of The Purple Sage.

Sam Neely 1948 US singer and songwriter. Hit: "Loving You Just Crossed My Mind" (9/72 US 29).

Frank Marino 1954 US guitarist, singer and songwriter, who formed the group Mahogany Rush in Montreal in 1970. In the late 1970s they became a heavy-metal band under the name Frank Marino & Mahogany Rush. The group did not have a hit.

Ian Mitchell 1958 UK bassist with Bay City Rollers, Rosetta Stone, and finally with his own band, in which he was leadsinger, guitarist, keyboard player and songwriter.

Roland Orzabal 1961 UK guitarist, keyboard player, singer and songwriter with Tears For Fears. Complete name, Roland Orzabal de la Quintana. He played in a schoolband with Curt Smith when he was 13, and in Graduate in 1980, forming Tears For Fears in 1981. Hits: "Mad World" (10/82 UK 3), "Change" (2/83 UK 4), "Pale Shelter" (4/83 UK 5), "Shout" (12/84 UK 4; 6/85 US 1), "Everybody Wants To Rule The World" (3/85 UK 2; US 1; 5/86 RE-UK 5), "Head Over Heels" (6/85 UK 12; 9/85 US 3) and "Sowing The Seeds Of Love" (9/89 UK 5; US 2).

Debbie Peterson 1961 US drummer and songwriter with the Bangles.

James DeBarge 1963 US singer and keyboard player with the sibling group DeBarge. He joined the existing group in 1982.

Hits of the Day

1958	"When" Kalin Twins UK 5 weeks
1963	"Bad To Me" Billy J. Kramer UK 3 weeks
1964	"Where Did Our Love Go?" Supremes US 2 weeks
1970	"Make It With You" Bread US 1 week
1987	"Who's That Girl" Madonna US 1 week

23rd

Birthdays

Gene Kelly 1912 US dancer and singer. Beside Fred Astaire he is considered to be the greatest singing dancer of film history. His career started in 1938 on Broadway in *Leave It To Me*. Especially remarkable were his performances in *An American In Paris* (1951), and *Singin' In The Rain"* (1952). However, unlike Astaire, Gene only had two US

hits, and those were duets with Judy Garland. The better of the two was "For Me And My Gal" (1/42 US 3), the title song of his first film.

Bob Crosby 1913 US singer, bandleader and songwriter. From 1935 to 1942 he was singing periodically with the Dorsey Brothers band: he was featured on "Lullaby Of Broadway" (4/35 US 1). After this success, he formed his own band, which specialised in dixieland jazz. They had their first hit with "In A Little Gypsy Tea Room" (6/35 US 1), not sung by Bob, but by Frank Tennille, father of Toni. Further hits were "Whispers In The Dark" (8/37 US 1), "Day In, Day Out" (9/39 US 1), "Over The Rainbow" (9/39 US 2), "With The Wind And The Rain In Your Hair" (3/40 US 2) and "Down Argentine Way" (11/40 US 2). Bob Crosby & His Orchestra had hits until 1951, and was considered to be one of the top dance bands of the era. Bob's orchestra also backed his older brother Bing on a few hits like "You Must Have Been A Beautiful Baby" (12/38 US 1).

Tex Williams 1917 US country singer, guitarist and songwriter. Real first name Sol. In 1930 Tex worked for a radio station in Illinois, in the mid-1930s he and his band, the Reno Racketeers, moved to California and appeared in many western films. Then he became the singer in the Spade Cooley band and in 1946 he formed his own group, Western Caravan. From then until 1974 he was regularly in the country charts. In the 1960s he had his own TV series. His biggest crossover hit was "Smoke! Smoke! Smoke! (That Cigarette)" (7/47 US 1). Tex died on 11th October, 1985.

David 1942 UK singer and songwriter, real name Roger Greenaway. Until 1976 his career progressed parallel to that of his colleague Jonathan (see 19th August). After the latter moved to the USA, David carried on as a songwriter and producer in the UK. He revived the flagging career of the Drifters in the 1970s.

Anthony Micale 1942 US leadsinger with the Reflections. Hit: "(Just Like) Romeo & Juliet" (4/64 US 6).

Keith Moon 1947 UK drummer with the Who. In 1975 he released his only solo album, TWO SIDES OF THE MOON. He died 7th September, 1978, and was replaced by Kenny Jones of the Faces.

Rick Springfield 1949 Australian singer, guitarist and songwriter. He started with the group Zoot, and when nothing came of that, he went to the USA in 1972 to start a solo career. His first hit was "Speak To The Sky" (8/72 US 14). When his career stagnated, he became an actor, and played a lead part in the US TV series *General Hospital*, which exposed him to the general public. He re-launched his solo career, and things went better this time round.

Hits: "Jessie's Girl" (3/81 US 1; 3/84 UK 43), "Don't Talk To Strangers" (3/82 US 2) and "Love Somebody" (3/84 US 5).

Marion Valentino 1955 UK singer and guitarist with Doll. Hit: "Desire Me" (1/79 UK 28).

Bobby Gubby 1961 UK singer with Bucks Fizz, and who released the title song of the BBC TV series *Big Deal* (12/84 UK 65; 10/85 RE-UK 46) written by him in December 1984, under the name Bobby G.

Deaths

Rudolph Valentino 1926 Hollywood's silent movie star. Born 6th May, 1895.

Oscar Hammerstein 1960 US songwriter. Together with Richard Rogers he formed one of the most successful musical writer teams in the USA. Born 12th July, 1895.

David Rose 1990 US composer, bandleader & arranger. Born 15th June, 1910.

Hits of the Day

1969 "Honky Tonk Woman" Rolling Stones US 4 weeks
1975 "Fallin' In Love" Hamilton, Joe Frank & Reynolds US 1 week
1980 "Ashes To Ashes" David Bowie UK 2 weeks
1986 "I Want To Wake Up With You" Boris Gardiner UK 3 weeks

24th

Birthdays

Arthur Crudup 1905 US blues singer, guitarist, and songwriter. He also appeared under the names Percy Lee and Elmer James. In the 1940s he sang with the gospel group Harmonizing Four, and made his first records in 1941, and toured with Elmore James and Sonny Boy Williamson. He retired from the music business completely between 1953 and 1959. In the meantime, Elvis Presley had sited him as his biggest influence; and in 1959, Arthur started to record again. In 1970 he toured England, and in 1974 with Bonnie Raitt. Arthur had his first hit with "Rock Me, Mama" (5/45 R&B 3). He became known especially

for "That's All Right", which was later one of Elvis Presley's first hits. Elvis also covered "My Baby Left Me", another Arthur 'Big Boy' Crudup composition. Elvis thanked Crudup nicely in 1956, but never sent any money. Shortly before Crudup's death, Elvis' publishers were going to pay him 60,000 dollars, but they changed their minds, because a law suit would have been cheaper. So Crudup died in complete poverty on 23rd March, 1974.

Wynonie Harris 1915 US R&B singer, drummer, and songwriter, who was one of the pioneers of the R&B era. He sang and played drums in his own group in the 1930s. In 1944 he cut his first records with Lucky Millinder's band. Finally, Johnny Otis got him into R&B. He played in Lionel Hampton's and Big Joe Turner's bands. Wynonie had fifteen hits in the R&B charts between 1946 and 1952; the two biggest were "Good Rockin' Tonight" (5/48 R&B 1) and "All She Wants To Do Is Rock" (8/49 R&B 1). He recorded into the 1960s, but died on 14th June, 1969, while working as a waiter in a bar.

Louis Teicher 1924 US pianist. From 1947 he played with Arthur Ferrante as the duo Ferrante & Teicher. Hits: "Theme From The Apartment" (7/60 US 10), "Exodus" (11/60 US 2; 3/61 UK 6), "Tonight" (10/61 US 8) and "Midnight Cowboy" (11/69 US 10).

William Winfield 1929 US leadsinger with the Harptones, who were formed as an R&B group in Harlem in 1953, and were first called Harps.

David Freiberg 1938 US bassist with Quicksilver Messenger Service and Jefferson Starship.

Mason Williams 1938 US guitarist and songwriter. His best-known number is "Classical Gas" (6/68 US 2; 8/68 UK 9), which is a practise piece for many other guitarists. If they can play it, they must be pretty good. As a songwriter Mason wrote "Cindarella Rockefella" for Esther & Abi Ofarim and several successful TV and film themes.

Ernie Wright 1939 US singer with Little Anthony & The Imperials.

Carl Mann 1942 US singer, pianist and songwriter. He formed his first band at the age of 12, and made his first records in 1957. Carl always tried a little of everything, first a bit of country music, then a bit of rock 'n roll and blues. In 1959 he signed a recording contract with the Sun label. His very first record was quite successful "Mona Lisa" (6/59 US 25). But Carl had obviously overdone things, remembering that he was only 17 at the time. He had to take a break for a long while. When he returned it was too late. He played with Carl Perkins' band from 1962 to 1964. From 1967 to 1974 he retired completely from the music business and then turned up again for a while in

1976 with "Twilight Time" (5/76 C&W 100). Whether "Mona Lisa", "Pretend" or "Twilight Time", he always sang cover versions of old songs.

John Cipollina 1943 US guitarist and songwriter with Quicksilver Messenger Service from 1965 to 1970. After that he played with his own band Copperhead, Man and the Dinosaurs. He died 29th May, 1989.

James Brady 1944 US singer with the L.A. trio Sandpipers. They had their biggest hits with "Guantanamera" (7/66 US 9; 9/66 UK 7) and "Come Saturday Morning" (12/69 US 17).

Jim Capaldi 1944 UK drummer, singer and songwriter. He started the Hellions when he was 17 with Luther Grosvenor and Dave Mason, who then changed their name to Deep Feeling. In April 1967 Traffic was formed, Jim stayed with the group until they broke up in December 1974. From 1972, he had been cutting solo albums. Hits: "Love Hurts" (10/75 UK 4) and "That's Love" (4/83 US 28).

Malcolm Duncan 1945 UK saxophonist with Average White Band and as a session musician.

Ken Hensley 1945 UK pianist, singer, and songwriter. In 1965 he was one of the founder members of the group Gods. The band kept going until February 1969, then Ken became a member of the Cliff Bennett Band for four months, played with Toe Fat for six months, and finally, in December 1969, he became a founder member of Uriah Heep. Ken also made solo albums and played with Blackfoot.

Jean-Michel Jarre 1948 French pianist. International hit: "Oxygene IV" (8/77 UK 4).

Mike Derosier 1951 Canadian drummer with Heart.

Jeffrey Daniel 1955 US singer with the trio Shalamar formed in November 1978. He stayed until January 1984, went to England, and became a TV presenter of the British spin- off of the US series *Soul Train*.

Mark Bedford 1961 UK bassist with Madness.

Deaths

Louis Prima 1978 US singer and trumpeter. Born 7th December, 1912.

Hits of the Day

1940 "Where Was I?" Charlie Barnet US 2 weeks
1959 "Three Bells" Browns US 4 weeks
1974 "(You're) Having My Baby" Paul Anka & Odia Coates US 3 weeks

---

1985 "Power Of Love" Huey Lewis & The News US 2 weeks

25th

Birthdays

Leonard Bernstein 1918 US composer, pianist and conductor. From 1945 he wrote music for Broadway shows, like *Peter Pan* (1950) and *Candide* (1956). In 1957 he wrote the music for *West Side Story*; the lyrics were written by Stephen Sondheim, based on Shakespeare's Romeo And Juliet. He was principal conductor of the New York Philharmonic Orchestra from 1959 to 1969. Bernstein also wrote symphonies, ballets, musicals and film scores. He died on 14th October, 1990.

Wayne Shorter 1933 US saxophonist, composer, and bandleader. He played with Miles Davis, Art Blakey and Weather Report.

Walter Williams 1942 US singer with the O'Jays.

Gene Simmons 1949 US bass player, singer and songwriter with the hard-rock band Kiss formed in 1972. In January 1974 they signed a recording contract. Hits: "Rock And Roll All Night (Live Version)" (11/75 US 12), "Beth" (9/76 US 7), "I Was Made For Loving You" (5/79 US 11) and "Crazy Crazy Nights" (10/87 UK 4). Until 1983 the group were heavily disguised by make-up. On 18th September, 1983 they made an exclusive MTV appearance without the trademark make-up, whether the impact was frightening or not has not been recorded. Gene, real surname Klein, also made solo records.

Rob Halford 1951 UK singer with Judas Priest who were formed in 1969 and released records from 1974. Hits: "Take On The World" (1/79 UK 14), "Living After Midnight" (3/80 UK 12) and "Breaking The Law" (6/80 UK 12).

James Warren 1951 UK singer, guitarist, bassist and songwriter for the group Korgis who were formed in 1979. In 1968 James started his career with Dawn, then joined Stackridge, whose musical influences ranged between the Beatles and the Wurzels. Hits, for Korgis: "If I Had You" (6/79 UK 13) and "Everybody's Got To Learn Sometime" (5/80 UK 5; 10/80 US 18). In the early 1980s the band split up. James concentrated more on songwriting and on session work. In 1984 the Korgis re-formed.

Elvis Costello 1954 UK singer, guitarist, and song-writer, son of bandleader Ross McManus, so his real name is Declan Patrick McManus. Early on Elvis began writing his own songs. At age 16 he left school, and became a computer operator in a Liverpool factory. On the side he appeared as D. P. Costello in folk clubs (Costello was his mother's maiden name). In 1976 he formed the country rock group Flip City, who made a demo tape, and sent it to the record company Stiff which had just been set up. They signed him up, and a little later his first records were released. Hits: "Oliver's Army" (2/79 UK 2), "I Can't Stand Up For Falling Down" (2/80 UK 4), "A Good Year For Roses" (10/81 UK 6), and "Veronica" (3/89 UK 31; US 19).

Damian McKee 1958 UK singer and guitarist with Rosetta Stone. The band was intended as a successor to the Bay City Rollers, but only German teenies seemed to fall for it. Hit: "(If Paradise) Is Half As Nice" (3/78).

Nigel Durham 1965 UK drummer with Saxon.

Deaths

Stan Kenton 1979 US bandleader. Born 19th February, 1912.

Hits of the Day

1958	"Little Star" Elegants US 1 week
1958	"Bird Dog" Everly Brothers US 1 week
1960	"Apache" Shadows UK 5 weeks
1962	"The Locomotion" Little Eva US 1 week
1973	"Brother Louie" Stories US 2 weeks
1973	"Young Love" Donny Osmond UK 4 weeks
1979	"We Don't Talk Anymore" Cliff Richard UK 4 weeks
1979	"My Sharona" Knack US 6 weeks

26th

Birthdays

Jimmy Rushing 1903 US blues singer who sang with many of the great bands of the era. Real first names James Andrew. He was one Count Basie's most successful singers between 1936 and 1948, having hits with "Stop Beatin' Round The Mulberry Bush" (10/38 US 6), "Jimmy's Blues" (10/45 US 10) and "Blue Skies" (9/46 US 8), which was featured in the film of the same name. In addition, Jimmy also recorded with Benny Goodman, scoring with "This Year's Kisses" (1/37 US 1), Earl Hines, Dave Brubeck, Bob Crosby, and Benny Moten. He also cut a number of good blues records. Jimmy died 8th June, 1972.

Chris Curtis 1941 UK drummer and songwriter with the Searchers. Real name Christopher Crummey.

Vic Dana 1942 US singer who had 15 hits from 1961 to 1970. His biggest hit was "Red Roses For A Blue Lady" (2/65 US 10).

Valerie Simpson 1946 US singer and songwriter, usually with husband Nickolas Ashford (see 4th May).

Robert Cowsill 1950 US guitarist and singer with the Cowsills.

Billy Rush 1952 US guitarist with Asbury Jukes who played with Southside Johnny.

John O'Neill 1957 UK guitarist and songwriter with the Undertones.

Hits of the Day

1965	"I Got You Babe" Sonny & Cher UK 2 weeks
1967	"Ode To Billie Joe" Bobbie Gentry US 4 weeks
1972	"Brandy (You're A Fine Girl)" Looking Glass US 1 week
1978	"Grease" Frankie Valli US 2 weeks

27th

Birthdays

Lester Young 1909 US jazz tenor saxophonist and composer. He played with Count Basie from 1936 to 1940, also Benny Goodman, Coleman Hawkins and Teddy Wilson. He became popular through his record with Billie Holiday. Lester died 15th March, 1959.

Carter Glen Stanley 1925 US country guitarist and singer. Together with his younger brother Ralph Edmond, he formed the Clinch Mountain Boys in 1946. Later they appeared as the Stanley Brothers. Hit: "How Far To Little Rock" (3/60 C&W 17). Carter died 1st December, 1966.

Alice Coltrane 1937 US jazz keyboard player, harpist and composer. Her maiden name was McLeod. In 1966 she married John Coltrane, having become a member of his quartet the same year.

Tommy Sands 1937 US singer and film actor. He was married to Nancy Sinatra from 1960 to 1965. He had eleven US hits from 1957 to 1960, including "Teen-Age Crush" (2/57 US 2), "Goin' Steady/Ring My Phone" (5/57 US 16), and "The Old Oaken Booket" (8/60 UK 25). As an actor Tommy appeared in *The Longest Day* in 1962 and appeared in countless episodes of the TV series *Hawaii 5-0* in the early 1970s.

Phil Shulman 1937 UK singer, trumpeter and flautist. He formed the nucleus of Simon Dupree & The Big Sound with his brothers Ray and Derek. Their biggest hit was "Kites" (11/67 UK 9). From 1969 they changed their name to Gentle Giant.

Daryl Dragon 1942 US pianist and songwriter, son of the well-known US orchestra leader Carmen Dragon. Daryl first worked for the Beach Boys, and it was Mike Love who gave him the nickname 'Captain', then later he worked together with his wife Toni Tennille as Captain & Tennille. Most of their hits were written by Toni (see 8th May).

Malcolm Allured 1945 UK drummer with Showaddywaddy.

Jeff Cook 1949 US guitarist, violinist and singer for Alabama.

Willie DeVille 1950 US singer, guitarist, and songwriter. Real name William Borsay. In the mid-1970s he formed the group Mink DeVille, which called itself a punk band, but was more an R&B group. In 1977 the debut album by the group appeared, which included their first hit "Spanish Stroll" (8/77 UK 20). Willie cut some good albums and has a rather gorgeous diamond in one of his teeth.

Laurie Wisefield 1952 UK guitarist and songwriter with Home, and from 1974 as a replacement for Ted Turner with Wishbone Ash.

Alex Lifeson 1953 Canadian guitarist, singer, and songwriter with the rock trio Rush who released their first album in 1973. Hits: "Spirit Of Radio" (3/80 UK 13), "Tom Sawyer" (10/81 UK 25) and "New World Man" (9/82 US 21).

Glenn Matlock 1956 UK bassist. He played with the Sex Pistols until he was thrown out in 1977, and replaced by Sid Vicious. After that Glenn formed the Rich Kids, and in the early 1980s formed the Spectors.

Deaths

Brian Epstein 1967 UK manager of the Beatles and other UK artists. He was found dead at home, and there was talk of suicide. Born 19th September, 1934.

Bob Scholl 1975 US singer with the Mello-Kings. Died after a boating accident. Born 14th July, 1938.

Stevie Ray Vaughan 1990 US guitarist, singer and composer. Born October, 1954. Killed in an aircrash.

Hits of the Day

1964 "Have I The Right" Honeycombs UK 2 weeks
1977 "Float On" Floaters UK 1 week
1988 "Monkey" George Michael US 2 weeks

28th

Birthdays

Billy Grammer 1925 US country singer and guitarist. He made his first records in 1949. He was one of the first great session guitarists in Nashville and played on many of the biggest hits of other artists. As a soloist, he had his biggest hit with "Gotta Travel On" (11/58 US 4).

John Perkins 1931 Canadian singer with the Crew-Cuts formed in 1952, who had started as the the Cana-daires and changed their name to Crew-Cuts in spring 1954. In the same year they began to cover songs by black R&B groups. Hits: "Crazy 'Bout Ya Baby" (5/54 US 8), "Sh-Boom" (7/54 US 1; 10/54 UK 12), "Ko Ko Mo (I Love You So)" (1/55 US 6), "Earth Angel" (2/55 US 3; 4/55 UK 4) and "Gum Drop" (8/55 US 10). In the latter half of the 1950s as R' n' R groups demonstrated that white audiences would accept the original versions, the Crew-Cuts disappeared from the scene again, and in 1963 they split up.

Clem Cattini 1938 UK drummer with the Tornados, and then later on as a session musician with Joe Cocker, Lou Reed, the Bee Gees, Justin Hayward, Mike Batt, and many others.

Ann Honey Lantree 1943 UK drummer with the Honeycombs.

David Soul 1943 US actor and singer. Real last name Solberg. He played the part of Ken Hutchinson in the TV series *Starsky & Hutch* from 1975 to 1979. But his first larger role in a TV series was as Joshua Bolt in *Here Come The Brides* from 1968 to 1970. In the mid-1960s David had worked as a folksinger. After his success as Hutch, the opinion seemed to be that he would do well as a recording artist. At least in 1977 things worked out. Hits: "Don't Give Up On Us" (12/76 UK & US 1), "Going In With My Eyes Open" (3/77 UK 2), "Silver Lady" (8/77 UK 1), and "Let's Have A Quiet Night In" (12/77 UK 8).

Ken Andrews 1946 UK pianist, drummer, and vibraphonist with Middle Of The Road.

Daniel Seraphine 1948 US drummer and songwriter with Chicago.

Hugh Cornwell 1949 UK guitarist, singer, and songwriter with the Stranglers formed in 1975. They came to attention as one of the most successful 'Punk' bands although they seemed to have their orgins with the Doors; subsequently, they have managed to evolve their own highly individual style. Biggest hits: "Golden Brown" (1/82 UK 2), "Strange Little Girl" (7/82 UK 7), and "All Day And All Of The Night" (1/88 UK 7). Hugh also made solo records, made a record in 1979 with Robert Williams, and wrote some music for the anti-nuclear war film *When The Wind Blows*.

Wayne Osmond 1951 US guitarist and saxophonist with the Osmonds.

Kim 1961 UK singer with the duo Mel & Kim, with her sister. Surname Appleby. For hits, see 11th July, under Mel.

Hits of the Day

1948	"Twelfth Street Rag" Pee Wee Hunt	US 8 weeks
1961	"Wooden Heart" Joe Dowell	US 1 week
1968	"Do It Again" Beach Boys	UK 1 week

29th

Birthdays

Charlie Parker 1920 US jazz saxophonist, composer and bandleader, nickname "Bird". In the 1940s and 1950s he was one of the most influential performers of the be-bop era. He died 12th March, 1955.

Dinah Washington 1924 US blues singer. Real name Ruth Lee Jones. Her work with Lionel Hampton from 1943 to 1946 made her popular as a jazz singer too. Hits: "What A Diff'rence A Day Makes" (5/59 US 8), "Baby (You've Got What It Takes)" (1/60 US 5), with Brook Benton and "A Rockin' Good Way (To Mess Around And Fall In Love)" (5/60 US 7). Dinah was married seven times. She died 14th December, 1963.

Dick Halligan 1943 US pianist, trombone player, and flautist with Blood, Sweat And Tears.

Chris Copping 1945 UK bass player and pianist with Procol Harum from 1970.

Tony Eyers 1947 UK producer and songwriter who accidentally became a member of a group in 1975. Session musicians had recorded one of his compositions which turned into a hit; therefore it was necessary to find musicians to promote it. The resulting groups were called Airbus and 5000 Volts, both featured Tony. Hits: "I'm On Fire" (9/75 UK 4; US 26), and "Dr. Kiss Kiss" (7/76 UK 8).

Dave Jenkins 1947 US guitarist, bass player, and leadsinger of Pablo Cruise. Before that he was with Stoneground. Pablo Cruise had two major hits with "Whatcha Gonna Do?" (4/77 US 6), and "Love Will Find A Way" (6/78 US 6), but after 1982 there were no more hits.

Michael Jackson 1958 US singer, songwriter and dancer. During his childhood, he became a star as the leadsinger of the Jackson 5, and then from 1976 as the Jacksons. Hits: "I Want You Back" (11/69 US 1; 1/70 UK 2), "ABC" (3/70 US 1; 5/70 UK 8), "The Love You Save" (5/70 US 1; 8/70 UK 7), "I'll Be There" (9/70 US 1; 11/70 UK 4), "Mama's Pearl" (1/71 US 2; 4/71 UK 25), "Never Can Say Goodbye" (4/71 US 2; 7/71 UK 33), "Dancing Machine" (3/74 US 2), "Enjoy Yourself" (11/76 US 6), "Show You The Way To Go" (4/77 US 28; 6/77 UK 1), "Shake Your Body (Down To The Ground)" (2/79 US 7; UK 4), and "State Of Shock" (6/84 US 3; UK 14), with Mick Jagger. In addition to his career with his brothers, Michael showed his credentials as a solo artist with hits like "Got To Be There" (10/71 US 4; 2/72 UK 5), "Rockin' Robin" (3/72 US 2; 5/72 UK 3), "Ben" (8/72 US 1; 11/72 UK 7), "Don't Stop Till You Get Enough" (7/79 US 1; 9/79 UK 3), "Rock With You" (11/79 US 1; 2/80 UK 7), "One Day In Our Life" (5/81 UK 1), "Billie Jean" (1/83 US & UK 1), and "Beat It" (2/83 US 1; 4/83 UK 3); the last two were extracted from the album THRILLER which had sales of over 45 million copies and is the best-selling album of all time. After that he went on with "I Just Can't Stop Loving You" (8/87 US & UK 1), "Bad" (9/87 US 1; UK 3), "The Way You Make Me Feel" (11/87 US 1; UK 3), "Man In The Mirror" (2/88 US 1; UK 21), and "Dirty Diana" (5/88 US 1; 7/88 UK 4). Michael also recorded with other artists like Paul McCartney: "The Girl Is Mine" (11/82 US 2; UK 8) and "Say Say Say" (10/83 US 1; UK 2). He published his autobiography 'Moonwalk', in 1988.

Rick Downey 1953 US drummer and singer who joined Blue Oyster Cult in 1981.

Pebbles 1964 US singer and songwriter, real name Perri McKissack. Before starting her solo career she worked with Con Funk Shun and Sister Sledge. In 1988 her first solo album appeared. Hits: "Girl Friends" (1/88 US 5; 3/88 UK 8), and "Mercedes Boy" (5/88 US 2).

Deaths

Jimmy Reed 1976 US blues singer. Born 6th September, 1925.

Hits of the Day

1942	"We Wouldn't Love You" Kay Kyser US 2 weeks
1970	"War" Edwin Starr US 3 weeks
1981	"Japanese Boy" Aneka UK 1 week
1987	"Never Gonna Give You Up" Rick Astley UK 5 weeks
1987	"La Bamba" Los Lobos US 3 weeks

30th

Birthdays

Kitty Wells 1919 US country singer, 'The Queen Of Country Music'. Born Muriel Ellen Deason in Nashville. Her singing career started on a local station at age 16. In 1938 she married Johnny Wright who was also a country singer. He gave her the stage name Kitty Wells. In 1949 she made her first records and in 1952 had her first No. 1 in the US country charts with "It Wasn't God Who Made Honky Tonk Angels" (8/52 US 27). Until the early 1970s she was regularly in the country charts. In 1976 she entered the 'Country Music Hall Of Fame'. The son of Johnny Wright and Kitty Wells, Bobby Wright, started recording when he was 11, and has been in the country charts also since 1967.

John Phillips 1935 US guitarist, singer, and songwriter. He formed the Smoothies and then the folk-trio Journeymen with Scott McKenzie; the latter released three albums with Capitol after 1961. In 1964 Phillips formed New Journeymen together with Denny Doherty, Michelle Gilliam, and Cass Elliott. In late 1965 they signed a recording contract and renamed themselves Mamas & Papas. Barry McGuire had, in the meantime, recorded the John Phillips composition "California Dreaming", and released it in October 1965. The Mamas & Papas now recorded their own version of the title with the same playback, and it became a million seller in March 1966. For hits, see 6th April, under Michelle Gilliam Phillips, who had married John in 1962. In July 1968, the Mamas & Papas and the Phillips couple split up. In May 1970 the first album by John Phillips appeared which featured his only solo hit "Mississippi" (5/70 US 32). In late 1971 the group joined up again, but after one album they split up again. In July 1980 Phillips was arrested on a charge of cocaine possession. In April 1981 he was sentenced to five years, but after 30 days the sentence was commuted to 250 hours of community work. He undertook a lecture tour of the United States, preaching against drugs. In March 1982 John and Denny Doherty went on a reunion tour. The parts of the two female singers (Michelle had since married Dennis Hopper, and Mama Cass had died in London at the age of 32) were taken by John's daughter McKenzie and Spanky McFarlane who was previously with Spanky & Our Gang. This line-up did not release any new material, but the tour of the USA was very successful. To date, the most recent successful song was "Kokomo", written by John Phillips and Scott McKenzie for the Beach Boys in 1988. John had once composed the international hit "San Francisco" for Scott.

John McNally 1941 UK guitarist and singer with the Searchers.

Chuck Colbert 1944 US bass player with American Breed.

Micky Moody 1950 UK guitarist and singer with Zoot Money, Juicy Lucy, Snafu and Whitesnake.

Dana 1951 Irish singer, real name Rosemarie Brown, who while still a schoolgirl, won the Eurovision song contest for Ireland in Amsterdam on 21st March 1970, with "All Kinds Of Everything" (4/70 UK 1). Hits: "Please Tell Him That I Said Hello" (1/75 UK 8) and "It's Gonna Be A Cold Cold Christmas" (12/75 UK 4). Dana still makes records occasionally but mainly works in pantomime.

Kenny Andrews 1952 US singer who joined the group Darts in 1978/79 as a replacement for Den Hegarty. Hit: "Duke Of Earl" (7/79 UK 6).

Ronald Beitle 1954 US drummer with Wild Cherry.

Deaths

Thomas Sylvester 'Papa Dee' Allen 1988 US singer and songwriter with War. Born 18th July, 1931.

31st

Birthdays

Arthur Godfrey 1903 US singer, who was successful from 1947 to 1952. Hits: "Too Fat Polka" (11/47 US 2), "Slap 'Er Down Again, Paw" (2/48 US 7), and "Dance Me Loose" (12/51 US 6). Arthur is one of the best-known personalities in the history of US television and radio. From 1949 to 1959 his TV show was a must as a launch-pad for upcoming artists. Artists like the Everly Brothers, Pat Boone, and the McGuire Sisters became known through him. His reputation was sealed in 1953, when he fired Julius LaRosa during a live programme. Arthur Godfrey died 16th March, 1983.

Jerry Allison 1939 US drummer, singer and songwriter for the Crickets, with and without Buddy Holly.

Van Morrison 1945 UK singer and songwriter, real first names George Ivan. At age 15 he started with the band Monarchs as a saxophonist. In 1964 he formed Them. Hits: "Baby Please Don't Go" (1/65 UK 10), "Here Comes The Night" (3/65 UK 2; 5/65 US 24), and "It's All Over Now Baby Blue" (2/74). Morrison left Them in 1966, and started making records mainly in the USA. Hits: "Brown-Eyed Girl" (7/67 US 10), "Domino" (11/70 US 9) and "Whenever God Shines His Light" (12/89 UK 20), in a duet with fellow christian Cliff Richard. Van can always reckon on a strong loyal stock of fans.

Peter Gage 1947 UK guitarist with Gene Washington, Dada, Vinegar Joe, Elkie Brooks, and as a session musician.

Rudolf Schenker 1948 German guitarist and song-writer for the Scorpions

Rick Roberts 1949 US singer, guitarist, and songwriter who joined the Flying Burrito Brothers in 1971, released solo records in 1972 and 1973 respectively, and formed the country band Firefall in 1974. The band had eleven us hits between 1976 and 1983. Their biggest hit was "You Are The Woman" (8/76 US 9).

Gina Schock 1957 US drummer from 1979 with the band Go-Gos formed in 1978.

Glenn Tilbrook 1957 UK guitarist, singer and song-writer with the band U.K. Squeeze formed in 1974, and who later dropped the 'U.K.'

Tony De Franco 1959 US leadsinger with the family group De Franco Family. Their biggest hit was the million seller "Heartbeat – It's A Lovebeat" (9/73 US 3).

Debbie Gibson 1970 US singer and songwriter, real first name Deborah Ann. She set up a small studio at home when she was 13, where she recorded her own composi-tions. She earned her first wages singing in commercials. Her first real success came with the album OUT OF THE BLUE in 1987. Her first self-written (!) hit was "Only In My Dreams" (5/87 US 4; 9/87 UK 54; 3/88 RE-UK 11). Further hits: "Shake You Love" (10/87 US 4; 1/88 UK 7), "Out Of The Blue" (1/88 US 3; 5/88 UK 19), "Foolish Beat" (4/88 US 1; 7/88 UK 9), "Lost In Your Eyes" (1/89 US 1; UK 34) and "Electric Youth" (4/89 US 11; UK 14).

Micellany

1928 The premiere performance of the *Threepenny Opera* in the Berliner Theater am Schiffbauerdamm. The audi-ence were outraged and fascinated, shocked and over-whelmed. What Weill/Brecht had put on stage was the Berlin which so many preferred to ignore, the Berlin of beggars, prostitutes, tramps, the poor, and destitute.

September

1st

Birthdays

Joe Venuti 1904 US violinist who ranked alongside Stephane Grappelli in the post-War era as one of the key jazz violinists. Joe always kept his birthdate a secret during his lifetime. Dates between 3rd December, 1894 and 1st September, 1904 can be found in the relevant literature. Let us take the youngest version. He died 14th August, 1978.

Boxcar Willie 1931 US country singer, real name Cecil Travis Martin. He made his debut singing on radio when he was 10, later worked as a disc jockey and, in 1975, returned to live performance. In the 1980s he had a few smaller hits in the country charts, the most successful one being "Bad News" (3/82 C&W 36).

Conway Twitty 1933 US singer and songwriter. Real name Harold Lloyd Jenkins. Conway made his first records for Sun Records in the late 1950s. In 1958 he had a monster hit with "It's Only Make Believe" (9/58 US & UK 1). This was followed by "Mona Lisa" (7/59 US 29; UK 5), and "Lonely Boy Blue" (12/59 US 6). After 1962 success waned in the pop charts. But after 1966 Conway was regularly in the country charts and is the fifth most successful country artist of all time. He had a minor crossover hit with more with "You've Never Been This Far Before" (7/73 C&W 1; US 22). Twitty is so well-known in the States, that he has built his own complex for his fans called Twitty City, in Hendersonville, Tennessee.

Diane Ray 1941 US singer with only one hit, "Please Don't Talk To The Lifeguard" (8/63 US 31).

Archie Bell 1944 US singer and songwriter. While still at school, he formed his own band Archie Bell & The Drells who made their first records in 1967. They had their biggest hit with million seller "Tighten Up" (3/68 US 1). When the record was in the charts, Archie was just doing his military service. They had a follow-up hit with "I Can't Stop Dancing" (7/68 US 9) and, after that they failed to crack the top twenty.

Barry Gibb 1946 UK singer and songwriter for the Bee Gees; oldest of the three brothers, who appeared in public in the 1950s as the Blue Cats. Then the family emigrated to Australia, the Gibbs moved back to Britain in 1967, by which time the Bee Gees were already stars in Australia. Hits: "Massachusetts" (9/67 UK 1; 11/67 US 11), "World" (11/67 UK 9), "Words" (1/68 UK 8; US 15), "I've Gotta Get A Message To You" (8/68 UK 1; US 8), "Lonely Days" (12/70 US 3; UK 33) and "How Can You Mend A Broken Heart" (6/71 US 1). From 1972 to 1975 it looked as though the Bee Gees' career were over. The brothers saw less and less of one another and moved to the USA. But then came "Jive Talkin' " (5/75 US 1; UK 5), "You Should Be Dancing" (7/76 US 1; UK 5), "Love So Right" (9/76 US 3), "How Deep Is Your Love" (9/77 US 1; UK 3), "Stayin' Alive" (12/77 US 1; 2/78 UK 4), "Night Fever" (2/78 US 1; 4/78 UK 1), "Too Much Heaven" (11/78 US 1; UK 3), "Tragedy" (2/79 US & UK 1), "Love You Inside Out" (4/79 US 1; UK 13), and "You Win Again" (9/87 UK 1). Barry's solo activities were not particularly successful, but he collaborated with Samantha Sang on "Emotion" (11/77 US 3; 2/78 UK 11) and with Barbra Streisand on "Guilty" (11/80 US 3; UK 34) and "What Kind Of Fool" (1/81 US 10).

Greg Errico 1949 US drummer with Sly & The Family Stone, Santana, and as a studio musician with Lee Oskar, Bill Wyman and David Soul.

Russ Field 1949 UK guitarist with Showaddywaddy.

Steve Goetzman 1950 US drummer with Exile.

Peter Hewson 1950 UK singer, songwriter and founder of Chicory Tip, who were successful with an English version of a German song written by Michael Holm, called "Son Of My Father" (1/72 UK 1).

Bruce Foxton 1955 UK bass player with Jam, who released a solo record in 1984.

Gloria Estefan 1957 US singer and songwriter, born in Havana. In 1973 the Miami Latin Boys were formed in Miami. They played mainly in restaurants, at weddings and parties. In 1974 Gloria was present at one of their gigs, and the leader of the band, Emilio Estefan offered her a job as a singer with the band. From 1975 she became a permanent member and the group now called themselves Miami Sound Machine. In 1978 Emilio and Gloria got married. In 1979 they released their first self-financed album in Spanish. They became stars in Central and South America. From September 1984 they recorded in English too, which broadened their appeal. From August 1987 their records were credited to Gloria Estefan & The Miami Sound Machine, and from 1989 to Gloria Estefan only. Hits: "Dr. Beat" (8/84 UK 6), "Conga" (10/85 US 10), "Bad Boy" (3/86 US 8; 5/86 UK 16), "Words Get In The Way" (6/86 US 5), "Rhythm Is Gonna Get You" (5/87 US 5; 12/88 UK 16), "Can't Stay Away From You" (11/87 US 6; 2/89 UK 7), "Anything For You" (3/88 US 1; 7/88 UK 10), "1-2-3" (6/88 US 3; 10/88 UK 9), "Don't Wanna Lose You) (7/89 US 1; UK 6) and "Here We Are" (12/89 US 6).

Hits of the Day

1962 "Sheila" Tommy Roe US 2 weeks
1984 "What's Love Got To Do With It" Tina Turner US 3 weeks
1990 "The Joker" The Steve Miller Band UK 2 weeks

2nd

Birthdays

Russ Conway 1927 UK pianist and composer, real name Trevor H. Stanford. In 1955, having been in the navy for a long time, he became a club pianist. After that he accompanied Lita Rosa, Gracie Fields, among others, and then signed a solo contract with EMI. Russ had about twenty hits from 1957 to 1963, the most successful being "Side Saddle" (2/59 UK 1) and "Roulette" (5/59 UK 1).

Horace Silver 1928 US jazz pianist, composer and bandleader.

Robert Lee Dickey 1939 US singer. He formed the duo James & Bobby Purify in the late 1950s with his cousin, James Purify. Hit, "I'm Your Puppet" (10/66 US 6; 4/76 UK 12). In the late 1960s the partnership broke up and James continued as a solo artist, until Ben Moore came along and called himself Bobby Purify.

Rosalind Ashford 1943 US singer with the Vandellas, who accompanied Martha Reeves on records and at concerts.

Joe Simon 1943 US singer and songwriter he made his first records with the Golden Tones in 1960. From 1965 he was successful as a soloist. His biggest hits were "The Chokin' Kind" (3/69 US 13), "Drowning In The Sea Of Love" (11/71 US 11), and "Power Of Love" (7/72 US 11), all million sellers. In addition, Joe was successful with "Get Down, Get Down (Get On The Floor)" (4/75 US 8). His best known title in Europe was "Step By Step" (2/73 US 37; 6/73 UK 14). Joe was successful in the R&B charts right into the 1980s.

Jack White 1944 German songwriter, producer, and singer. Real name Horst Nussbaum. He went to Holland where he made his first records which were unsuccessful. Having discovered a talent for songwriting and producing, he took care of various German and European artists, after which he moved to the States, and successfully produced Laura Branigan, Audrey Landers, David Hasselhoff and Engelbert, among others.

Richard Coughlan 1947 UK drummer and songwriter with Caravan.

Mik Kaminski 1951 UK violinist, cellist, and songwriter. He joined the Electric Light Orchestra in September 1973. He had the hit "Clog Dance" (2/79 UK 17), under the pseudonym Violinski.

Steve Porcaro 1957 US pianist, singer and songwriter. In 1978 he was one of the founder members of Toto. As are all the members of the band, Steve is a sought-after studio musician.

Fritz McIntyre 1958 UK keyboard player with Simply Red.

Hits of the Day

1972 "Alone Again (Naturally)" Gilbert O'Sullivan US 2 weeks
1972 "You Wear It Well" Rod Stewart UK 1 week
1989 "Cold Hearted" Paula Abdul US 1 week

3rd

Birthdays

Memphis Slim 1915 US blues singer, pianist, and songwriter. Real name Peter Chatman. As his chosen name indicates, he originated from Memphis, went to Chicago in 1937, and played there with Bill Broonzy. In 1940 he made his first records. Among his biggest hits were "Messin' Around" (5/48 R&B 1), "Blue And Lonesome" (7/49 R&B 2) and "The Come Back" (11/53 R&B 3). In 1961 he moved to Paris, where he died on 24th February, 1988.

Hank Thompson 1925 US country singer, guitarist, and songwriter. His real first names are Henry William. He was one of the leading western-swing-band leaders of the 1950s. His own first band was called His Brazos Valley Boys, and he made his first records in 1946. He had his first hit with "Humpty Dumpty Heart" (1/48 C&W 2). Further hits included "The Wild Side Of Life" (3/52 C&W 1; 6/52 US 27) – this record was at No. 1 for 15 weeks and became a million seller – "Rub-A-Dub-Dub" (5/53 C&W 1), "Wake Up Irene" (12/53 C&W 1) – an answer to the song "Goodnight Irene" – and "Squaws Along The Yukon" (8/58 C&W 2). He continued to chart until 1983.

Tompall Glaser 1933 US country singer, oldest of the Glaser Brothers, who signed a recording contract with Marty Robbins' label in 1957. They had to wait until 1966 before the hits started coming. In 1973, they split up and re-formed for two years in 1980. Their biggest hits were "Rings" (8/71 C&W 7) and "Lovin' Her Was Easier (Than Anything I'll Ever Do Again)" (5/81 C&W 2). In addition, all three Glaser brothers embarked on solo careers with varying degrees of success.

Freddie King 1934 US blues singer, guitarist and songwriter. Real surname, Christian. He formed his own band in Chicago in the 1950s, called the Every Hour Blues Boys. In 1956 he made his first solo records Hit: "Hide Away" (4/61 US 29). He died 28th December, 1976.

Al Jardine 1942 US singer and guitarist. He was in the original lineup of Kenny & The Cadets (Kenny was Brian Wilson), which became Carl & The Passions, the Pendeltons, and finally the Beach Boys in 1961. However, Al left the band in February 1962, in order to continue his studies, and was replaced by guitarist David Marks. He played on some of the early records by the Beach Boys. But when things really got going, it was Brian Wilson who wanted the old lineup of the band back together again. Al came back in January 1963. David formed the group Dave Marks & The Marksmen.

Gary Walker 1944 US singer and drummer, real surname Leeds. Gary was already playing drums in his early teens, and was a co-founder of the Standells in 1963, but left them after two singles. Then he became a member of Johnny Rivers' band, and after that with P. J. Proby. In August 1964 he formed the Walker Brothers with John Maus and Scott Engel. For hits by the band, see under Scott Engel (9th January). In May 1967 the trio announced they were splitting up. Gary formed the group Rain, who disappeared into obscurity. In August 1975 the Walker Brothers reformed in the original lineup, but split up again in July, 1978. Gary's solo career was moderately successful.

George Biondo 1945 US bass player. He replaced Nick St. Nicholas in Steppenwolf in June 1970.

Eric Bell 1947 UK guitarist with the group Thin Lizzy formed in 1969. He left the band in January 1974 and played with the Noel Redding Band in 1975/76.

Don Brewer 1948 US drummer, singer and songwriter with Terry Knight & The Pack, and was a founder member of Grand Funk Railroad in 1968.

Leroy Smith 1952 UK pianist with Sweet Sensation.

Deaths

Al Wilson 1970 US singer, guitarist, and harmonica player, as well as songwriter for Canned Heat. He was found in the garden of fellow band member Bob 'The Bear' Hite. Al Wilson who suffered from deep depression, died of an overdose of tranquillizers. Born 4th July, 1943.

Hits of the Day

1949 "You're Breaking My Heart" Vic Damone US 4 weeks

1955 "Yellow Rose Of Texas" Mitch Miller US 6 weeks

1966 "Sunshine Superman" Donovan US 1 week

1977 "Way Down" Elvis Presley UK 5 weeks

1983 "Sweet Dreams" Eurythmics US 1 week

1983 "Red Red Wine" UB 40 UK 3 weeks

4th

Birthdays

Meade Lux Lewis 1905 US 'barrel house' piano player and composer. In 1929 he recorded "Honky Tonk Train Blues" which became successful in 1976 for Keith Emerson. Lewis was considered to be one of the best boogie-pianists. He died in a car accident on 7th June, 1964.

Merald Knight 1942 US singer and percussionist with Gladys Knight & The Pips.

Gary Duncan 1946 US singer, guitarist, synthesizer player and songwriter with Quicksilver Messenger Service, formed in 1965. After 1972 nothing much was heard of the band until there was a brief reunion in 1975, and in 1986 the album PEACE BY PIECE appeared. Gary was still leadsinger.

Greg Elmore 1946 US drummer in the first successful lineup of Quicksilver Messenger Service.

Ronald LaPread 1946 US bass player and songwriter with the Commodores.

Martin Chambers 1951 UK drummer with the Pretenders, and as a session musician.

Deaths

Dottie West 1991 US country singer and songwriter. Born 11th October, 1932.

Hits of the Day

1943	"It Can't Be Wrong" Dick Haymes	US 1 week
1961	"Michael" Highwaymen	US 2 weeks
1965	"Help!" Beatles	US 3 weeks
1968	"I've Got To Get A Message To You" Bee Gees UK 1 week	
1971	"Uncle Albert/Admiral Halsey" Paul McCartney US 1 week	
1976	"Dancing Queen" Abba	UK 6 weeks
1976	"You Should Be Dancing" Bee Gees	US 1 week
1982	"Eye Of The Tiger" Survivor	UK 4 weeks
1982	"Abracadabra" Steve Miller Band	US 1 week

Miscellany

1962 For the first time John, Paul, George and Ringo were recording together. They were in Studio 2 at EMI's, St. John's Wood Studio. All that day they rehearsed six numbers. Two of them, "Love Me Do" and "P.S. I Love You", were recorded that evening. George Martin was not satisfied with "Love Me Do" until they had done 17 takes; it was finally released as the Beatles first single on October 5th, and reached No. 17 in the English charts. How the story went on, see 11th September.

5th

Birthdays

Sunnyland Slim 1907 US blues singer, pianist, and songwriter. Real name Albert Luandrew. He cut his first records in 1946 and played, with Muddy Waters and Tampa Red among others.

Walt Ford 1931 US singer with the Rays.

John Stewart 1939 US singer, guitarist and songwriter. He started with the Cumberland Three, in 1961 he replaced Dave Guard in the Kingston Trio and remained until 1967. After that, he made solo records, first with an acoustic guitar, then with an electric guitar and rock accompaniment. Hit: "Gold" (5/79 US 5). His best-known composition is "Daydream Believer", which became a hit for the Monkees.

Al Stewart 1945 UK singer, songwriter and guitarist who has been making records since the late 1960s. Hits: "Year Of The Cat" (12/76 US 8; UK 31), and "Time Passages" (10/78 US 7), produced by Alan Parsons.

Dean Ford 1946 UK singer, guitarist, and harmonica player. Real name Thomas McAleese. He formed Dean Ford & The Gaylords in 1961, who became Marmalade in 1966. Hits: "Ob-La-Di, Ob-La-Da" (12/68 UK 1), "Reflections Of My Life" (12/69 UK 3; 3/70 US 10), and "Rainbow" (7/70 UK 3). In 1975 Dean left the group, emigrated to the USA and made his first solo album, which was produced by Alan Parsons.

Freddie Mercury 1946 UK singer, and songwriter, born Frederick Bulsara on Zanzibar. He started with Wreckage, and then launched a solo career with a new re-recording of the Beach Boy hit "I Can Hear Music", under the pseudonym Larry Lurex. In 1971 Queen were formed. Hits: "Killer Queen" (10/74 UK 2; 2/75 US 12), "Bohemian Rhapsody" (11/75 UK 1; 1/76 US 9), "Somebody To Love" (11/76 UK 2; US 13), "We Are The Champions/We Will Rock You" (10/77 UK 2; US 4), "Crazy Little Thing Called Love" (10/79 UK 2; 12/79 US 1), "Another One Bites The Dust" (8/80 US 1; UK 7), "Radio Ga-Ga" (2/84 UK 2; US 16), "I Want To Break Free" (4/84 UK 3), "A Kind Of Magic" (3/86 UK 3), "I Want It All" (5/89 UK 3) and "Break Through" (7/89 UK 7). The group had one hit with David Bowie, "Under Pressure (11/81 UK 1; US 29). Freddie made solo records too. The most successful were "Love Kills" (9/84 UK 10), "I Was Born To Love You" (4/85 UK 11) and "The Great Pretender" (3/87 UK 4). He had a hit "Barcelona" (11/87 UK 8), with Montserrat Caballe. He died of Aids on November 24th, 1991.

Buddy Miles 1946 US drummer and songwriter with Electric Flag, Buddy Miles Express, Jimi Hendrix, Carlos Santana and Nils Lofgren.

Loudon Wainwright III 1946 US satirical songwriter, singer and guitarist. Hit: "Dead Skunk" (1/73 US 16).

Dave 'Clem' Clempson 1949 UK guitarist and songwriter with Michael Chapman, Bakerloo, Colosseum, Humble Pie, Rough Diamond, Cozy Powell, Jack Bruce and Rod Argent.

Paulie Carmen 1953 US singer with Champaign which was named after her hometown, not the drink. The group consisted of musicians who worked in a studio in Champaign. After finishing session work for other artists, they would sing the odd song or two together. These beginnings resulted in a band being formed who had a hit with "How 'Bout Us" (2/81 US 12; 5/81 UK 5). Further hits followed until 1984, then the group slipped back into oblivion.

Sal Solo 1958 UK singer, guitarist, keyboard player, and songwriter for Classics Nouveaux. Hit: "Is It A Dream" (3/82 UK 11). In late 1984 Sal commenced a solo career and scored with "San Damiano (Heart And Soul)" (12/84 UK 15).

Dweezil Zappa 1969 US singer, guitarist, songwriter, and son of Frank Zappa. He released his first solo album, HAVIN' A BAD DAY, when he was 17, then he was on the album HEARTBEAT by Don Johnson, with the Fat Boys, and with Maria Vidal. In 1988 Dweezil's next album appeared, MY GUITAR WANTS TO KILL YOUR MAMA.

Deaths

Josh White 1969 US folk blues musician. Born 11th February, 1915.

6th

Birthdays

Jimmy Reed 1925 US singer, guitarist, harmonica player and songwriter. Real first names James Mathis. Blues musician Eddie Taylor taught Jimmy guitar when he was just seven years old. In 1953 Jimmy made his first records, and was successful predominantly in the R&B charts from 1955. His two biggest hits were "Honest I Do" (9/57 US 32) and "Baby What Do You Want Me To Do" (2/60 US 37). Elvis covered some of Jimmy's compositions like "Big Boss Man" and "Ain't That Loving You Baby"; furthermore "Bright Lights, Big City" has been covered by a wide variety of artist. He died 29th August, 1976.

Dave Bargeron 1942 US trumpeter with Blood, Sweat & Tears, and from 1970 for Jerry Hyman. Dave also recorded with Donald Fagen, Joe Cocker, Michael Franks and Paul Simon.

Mickey Waller 1944 UK drummer with the Jeff Beck Group, Steampacket, De Luxe Blues Band, and as a session musician for Rod Stewart, Long John Baldry and Andy Bown.

Roger Waters 1944 UK singer, bassist and songwriter with Pink Floyd, formed in 1965. In the early days Syd Barrett determined the musical direction of the band, but when he left Pink Floyd in 1968, Roger changed took over most of the writing chores. Throughout the 1970s and up to 1984, Pink Floyd albums were guaranteed massive worldwide sales. In May 1984 the first solo album by Roger appeared, THE PROS AND CONS OF HITCH HIKING. After that the band appeared to split up. When Roger's colleagues, David Gilmour, Nick Mason, and Rick Wright started to record again in 1987 under the name of Pink Floyd, Roger tried to get a court order to stop them continuing using the name. He lost the case. Further solo activities by Roger were no longer successful, possibly because Pink Floyd fans reacted against his action. Hits for Pink Floyd: "Arnold Layne" (3/67 UK 20), "See Emily Play" (6/67 UK 6), "Money" (5/73 US 13), "Another Brick

In The Wall" (12/79 UK & US 1), and "Not Now John" (5/83 UK 30). Of their many successful albums, DARK SIDE OF THE MOON ought to be mentioned, as this record remained on the US charts for over 560 weeks, and sold 10 million copies alone in the USA.

Sylvester 1947 US singer and songwriter. Surname James. He worked with the group Crockettes in San Francisco. From 1978 he was successful as a solo artist with the rising disco wave: "Dance (Disco Heat)" (8/78 US 19; 11/78 UK 29) and "You Make Me Feel (Mighty Real)" (8/78 UK 8; 1/79 US 36). Sylvester died 16th December, 1988.

James Litherland 1949 UK guitarist with Bandit, Colosseum and Dick Heckstall-Smith.

Stella Barker 1954 UK singer with the Belle Stars.

Louis Molino 1954 US drummer with Cock Robin.

Banner Thomas 1954 US bass player with Molly Hatchet.

Buster Bloodvessel 1958 UK leadsinger with the ska-revival-band Bad Manners, formed in 1980. Real name Douglas Trendle. The group arrived just in time for the two-tone-'Ska revival' movement. Hits: "Special Brew" (9/80 UK 3), "Can Can" (6/81 UK 3), "Walking In the Sunshine" (9/81 UK 10) and "My Girl Lollipop (My Boy Lollipop)" (7/82 UK 9).

Pal Gamst Waaktaar 1961 Norwegian guitarist with A-Ha.

Deaths

Ernest Tubb 1984 US country singer, born 9th February, 1914.

Tom Fogerty 1990 US singer and guitarist. Born November 9th, 1941.

Hits of the Day

1952	"I Wish You Were Here" Eddie Fisher US 1 week	
1967	"The Last Waltz" Engelbert Humperdinck UK 5 weeks	
1975	"Sailing" Rod Stewart UK 4 weeks	
1975	"Rhinestone Cowboy" Glen Campbell US 2 weeks	
1980	"Upside Down" Diana Ross US 4 weeks	
1980	"Start" Jam UK 1 week	
1986	"Venus" Bananarama US 1 week	

7th

Birthdays

Al Caiola 1920 US guitarist, and orchestra leader. Real firstnames Alexander Emil. He worked with Hugo Winterhalter and Percy Faith, for whom he played guitar on "Delicado" (4/52 US 1). Then he joined the film company United Artists, and was responsible for the music "The Magnificent Seven" (12/60 US 35; 7/61 UK 34) for the film of the same name. Another hit for Al was the music for the TV series *Bonanza* (4/61 US 19).

Arthur Ferrante 1921 US pianist, who was successful with Louis Teicher (see 24th August).

Sonny Rollins 1929 US jazz saxophonist and composer. Real first names Theodore Walter. Beside John Coltrane, he is considered to be one of the most important saxophonists to emerge since WWII.

Johnny Duncan 1931 US singer, who was successful with skiffle music in the UK. His greatest hit was "Last Train To San Fernando" (7/57 UK 2).

Little Milton 1934 US singer, and guitarist, real name James Campbell. He played with Eddie Cussick's band, then was a session guitarist for Trumpet Records, had his own band in 1951, and finally played with Ike Turner. The latter introduced him to Sun Records in July 1953. Milton's first record appeared in December of the same year, and was called "Beggin' My Baby". But he never had a hit until 1962, when he began to make found regular in roads into the R&B charts upto 1983. His biggest hit was "We're Gonna Make It" (3/65 US 25; R&B 1).

Buddy Holly 1936 US singer, guitarist, and songwriter. Real names Charles Hardin Holley. Within two years he became one of the first superstars of R n' R. Buddy released records under his own name and with his backing group, the Crickets. Hits under the group name: "That'll Be The Day" (8/57 US & UK 1; 1/58 RE-UK 29), "Oh, Boy!" (11/57 US 10; UK 3), and "Maybe, Baby" (3/58 US 17; UK 4). Hits, as Buddy Holly: "Peggy Sue" (11/57 US 3; UK 6; 4/68 RE-UK 32), "Rave On" (5/58 US 37; UK 5), "It Doesn't Matter Anymore" (2/59 UK 1; US 13), "Brown Eyed Handsome Man" (6/63 UK 3), "Bo Diddley" (6/63 UK 4) and "Wishing" (9/63 UK 10). Holly crashed in a private plane on 3rd February, 1959 with Ritchie Valens and Big Bopper, all occupants died.

Ronnie Dove 1940 US singer who had eleven hits in the US Top Forty between 1964 and 1966, including "Right

Or Wrong" (10/64 US 14) and "One Kiss For Old Times Sake" (3/65 US 14).

Alfa Anderson 1946 US singer with the band Chic formed in 1976.

Gloria Gaynor 1949 US singer, who sang with the Soul Satisfiers in the early 1970s. After that she had a successful solo career with "Never Can Say Goodbye" (11/74 US 9; UK 2) and "I Will Survive" (12/78 US 1; 2/79 UK 1).

Chrissie Hynde 1951 US born singer, guitarist and songwriter. She formed the Pretenders in London in 1978, before that, she had been a music journalist with the 'New Musical Express'. Hits: "Brass In Pocket" (11/79 UK 1; 2/80 US 14), "Talk Of The Town" (4/80 UK 8), "I Go To Sleep" (11/81 UK 7) and "Back On The Chain Gang" (10/82 UK 17; 12/82 US 5). In 1982 bassist Pete Farndon left the band and died 14th April, 1983, guitarist James Honeyman-Scott had died 16th June, 1982. Chrissie had a baby by Ray Davies in February 1983, and married Simple Minds singer Jim Kerr on 5th May, 1984, and had a baby by him also. The Pretenders' time seemed to be over. Then a record was released by UB 40 with guest singer Chrissie Hynde, "I Got You Babe" (7/85 US 28; UK 1). In 1986, Chrissie appeared again with new musicians: Robbie McIntosh and Blair Cunningham of Haircut 100, T. M. Stevens and Bernie Worrell of Talking Heads, again as the Pretenders. Hits: "Don't Get Me Wrong" (10/86 US 14; UK 10), and "Hymn To Her" (12/86 UK 8).

Dave King 1953 US bass player with the German group Snowball, Embryo, Niagara, and with Eberhard Schoener, Peter Maffay, Udo Lindenberg, Donna Summer, Herbert Gronemeyer, Amanda Lear, Boney M and Caro.

Margot Chapman 1957 US singer and keyboard player for the Starland Vocal Band.

Robin Beck 1961 US singer and songwriter. Her year of birth is more likely to be 1956, because when she appeared in the charts with "First Time" (10/88 UK 1), and reached the No. 1 slot – according to her own statement – she was already over 30. The song was originally a commercial jingle for Coca Cola, which was then re-arranged as a pop song. In her home country Robin had worked as a background singer for many years. According to press releases from her record company, she has sung with Chaka Khan, David Bowie, Irene Cara, and Michael McDonald. Subsequently she had hits in Germany.

Jermaine Stewart 1962 US singer and songwriter of the disco genre. As a teenager he appeared as a dancer in the well-known American TV musical programme 'Soul Train'. Then he worked as a backing singer for Shalamar, Gladys Knight, Millie Jackson and Culture Club. From 1984 he was in the charts regularly. Hits: "We Don't Have To Take Our Clothes Off" (5/86 US 5; 8/86 UK 2), "Say It Again" (1/88 UK 7; 3/88 US 6), "Get Lucky" (4/88 UK 13) and "Don't Talk Dirty To Me" (10/88).

Calvin Williams 1966 US singer with B.V.S.M.P.

Deaths

Keith Moon 1978 UK drummer with the Who. The cause of death was an overdose of heminervin, a tranquillizer prescribed by his doctor. Born 23rd August, 1946.

Hits of the Day

1940	"The Breeze And I" Jimmy Dorsey US 1 week
1985	"Dancing In The Street" David Bowie & Mick Jagger UK 4 weeks
1985	"St. Elmo's Fire" John Parr US 2 weeks

8th

Birthdays

Jimmie Rodgers 1897 US singer, guitarist, and songwriter. Real first names James Charles, his nickname was 'The Singing Brakeman'. He is considered to be the 'Father of Country Music', as he was the first country singer to sell records in appreciable quantities. He was also one of the first to draw upon and be influenced by the blues of the Deep-South and the rural hill-billy music of the Appalachians. On 4th August, 1927 he recorded "The Soldier's Sweetheart" (12/27 US 9), which became a million seller, as did "Blue Yodel" (3/28 US 2). Within a short period of time Jimmie had composed over 100 songs, which became a model for generations of country musicians. He made his last record on 24th May, 1933. Two days later, he died of TB.

Milton Brown 1903 US country singer and bandleader. He is considered to be the founder of western-swing with Bob Wills. They both played with the Light Crust Doughboys before Milton formed his own band, Milton Brown & His Musical Brownies. He died 13th April, 1936.

Peter Sellers 1925 UK actor and one of the most charismatic figures personalities of British show business. Real first name Richard Henry. He was one of the best and most versatile actors in Britain, making films from 1951 to 1979. Among his most idiosyncratic are *Dr. Strangelove, Or How I Learned To Love The Bomb* (1964), *What's New Pussycat* (1965), *Casino Royale* (1967), and the *Pink Panther* series of films, in which he played the part of Inspector Clouseau. As a member of the Goons, he had the hits with "I'm Walking Backwards For Christmas/Bluebottle Blues" (6/56 UK 4), and "Ying Tong Song/Bloodnok's Rock 'n' Roll" (9/56 UK 3; 7/73 RE-UK 9). He was in the charts as a solo artist with "Any Old Iron" (8/57 UK 17), and "A Hard Day's Night" (12/65 UK 14). Together with colleague. He recorded two duets with Sophia Loren, "Goodness Gracious Me" (11/60 UK 4) and "Bangers And Mash" (1/61 UK 22). Sellers died 24th July, 1980.

Harland Howard 1927 US country songwriter and singer. From 1960 he was one of the most important songwriters in Nashville, writing "Heartaches By The Number" and "I Fall To Pieces". His efforts As a singer, he was less successful. His only hit was "Sunday Morning Christian" (4/71 C&W 38).

Patsy Cline 1932 US country singer. Real first names Virginia Peterson Hensley. She sang in clubs in her home town Winchester, Virginia, and appeared publicly in Nashville in 1948. But she did not become known until she appeared on *Arthur Godfrey's Talent Scouts* TV show in January, 1957. Shortly afterwards, she had her first hits with, "Walkin' After Midnight" (3/57 US 12), "I Fall To Pieces" (5/61 US 12) and "Crazy" (10/61 US 9). Patsy died in a plane crash on 5th March, 1963, in which Cowboy Copas and Hawkshaw Hawkins, two other country stars, also died. In 1985 a film about her life was made called *Sweet Dreams*.

Billy Parsons 1934 US country singer, songwriter and guitarist. He appeared in the pop charts with "The All American Boy" (12/58 US 2; 4/59 UK 22), which he wrote himself. Billy was credited in error on the record by the record company. The real artist, was Bobby Bare, who at the time when the record became a hit, was completing his military service. So Billy went on tour and moved his lips to Bobby's record. Parsons had no hits of his own.

John Sylvia 1935 US singer with the Tune Weavers.

Dante Drowty 1941 US singer and leader of Dante & The Evergreens. The band was formed while he was still at High School, and made a few trial recordings, which were heard by Lou Adler and Herb Alpert. The pair thought they were good and became their manager and producer. Hit, "Alley-Oop" (5/60 US 15).

Sal Valentino 1942 US singer with the Beau Brummels. Real name Salvatore Williard Spanpinato. The group was formed in 1964. Hit: "Just A Little" (4/65 US 8). The band split up in 1968, and re-formed again with the original lineup in 1974. As success did not materialise, they packed it in again. Also lead the band Stoneground.

Peter Bellamy 1944 UK singer and arranger. Founder member of the traditional folk group, Young Tradition, who did much to increase awareness in the heritage of the English folk song. He died in Keighley, Yorkshire, on September 24th, 1991.

Kelly Groucutt 1945 UK bassist, guitarist, and singer with ELO until 1985, and as a solo artist.

Ron 'Pig-Pen' McKernan 1945 US singer, pianist and harmonica player for Grateful Dead, which he co-founded in 1965. Ron died 8th March, 1973.

Dean Daughtry 1946 US keyboard player and songwriter. He played with the Candy Men and was then a founder member of Atlanta Rhythm Section in 1970.

Michael Lardie 1958 US keyboard player, guitarist and songwriter with Great White.

David Lewis 1958 US guitarist, singer, and songwriter with the band Atlantic Starr, formed in 1976.

David Steele 1960 UK bassist and songwriter, who was a founder member of Beat in 1978. After the ska revival was over in the UK after 1983, he formed the Fine Young Cannibals with band colleague Andy Cox.

Hits of the Day

1951 "Because Of You" Tony Bennett US 10 weeks
1973 "Let's Get It On" Marvin Gaye US 1 week
1984 "I Just Called To Say I Love You" Stevie Wonder UK 6 weeks

---

9th

Birthdays

Russell Hardy 1941 UK pianist. He formed the band Kilburr & the High Roads with Ian Drury in 1970.

Otis Redding 1941 US soul singer, pianist, songwriter and producer, whose great idol was Sam Cooke, although he first copied Little Richard, which is evident on "Shout Bamalama" in 1960. At the time, Otis was still working with Johnny Jenkins & The Pinetoppers. From 1963 he exemplified all that was best in Southern soul music. After a few hits in 1965, he was on the way to becoming a superstar, when he crashed in a small private plane on 10th December, 1967. He did not live to see the success of "(Sittin' On) The Dock Of The Bay" (1/68 US 1; UK 3), which he had recorded three days before his death. Many consider him to be one of the best soul singers of all time along with James Brown.

Inez Foxx 1942 US singer, who made her first records as Inez Johnston in 1960. She had a hit with "Mockingbird" (6/63 US 7; 2/69 UK 34), with her brother, as Charlie & Inez Foxx. It was written by Charlie. She continued to work with her brother until 1969, then carried on as a solo artist.

Dee Dee Sharp 1945 US singer. Real name Dione LaRue. She started as a backing singer, working with Chubby Checker, among others. In 1962 she started a solo career, scoring with "Mashed Potato Time" (3/62 US 2) and "Ride!" (10/62 US 5). In 1967 she married successful songwriter and producer Kenny Gamble.

Doug Ingle 1946 US singer, keyboard player and songwriter for Iron Butterfly, which Doug formed in 1966, and which is considered to be one of the first heavy-metal rockbands. The band's best-known song "In-A-Gadda-Da-Vida" (8/68 US 30) was written by Doug; the album of the same name is one of the best-selling rock albums of all time. The band split up in 1972, but reformed in 1975 without Doug.

Trevor Leslie Oakes 1946 UK guitarist with Showaddywaddy.

Billy Preston 1946 US singer, pianist, and songwriter. When he was 10 he was allowed to accompany Mahalia Jackson on the organ on a TV show. She was so taken with him that she took him on tour. In 1958 he played the part of young blues composer W. C. Handy in a film, while Nat 'King' Cole played the part of the adult W. C. Handy. After that, Preston toured Europe with Little Richard and Sam Cooke, and recorded for Sam Cooke's record company SAR. During one of Little Richard's concerts at the Starclub in Hamburg, Billy met the Beatles, whom he played with on "Get Back" some years later. In fact the number of musicians he has played with is astonishing: the Beatles, the Rolling Stones, Ray Charles, Sly & The Family Stone, Little Richard, Sam Cooke and George Harrison. In 1969, his solo career picked up momentum with hits like "That's The Way God Planned It" (7/69 UK 11), "Outa-Space" (4/72 US 2), "Will It Go Round In Circles" (3/73 US 1), "Space Race" (9/73 US 4), "Nothing From Nothing" (7/74 US 1) and "With You I'm Born Again"

(12/79 UK 2; 3/80 US 4) with Syreeta. As a songwriter he wrote "You Are So Beautiful" for Joe Cocker.

Freddy Weller 1947 US singer, guitarist, and songwriter who played with Billy Joe Royal in the mid-60s. In September 1967 he joined Paul Revere & The Raiders. Freddy was the lead vocalist on "Indian Reservation (The Lament Of The Cherokee Reservation Indian)" (4/71 US 1) the only million seller by this lineup. While he was still with the Raiders, he started a solo career in 1969, and was a bassist and guitarist with Joe South. He had over 30 hits in the country charts between 1969 and 1980; the biggest being a cover version of the Joe South-hit "Games People Play" (4/69 C&W 2). As a songwriter he wrote "Dizzy" and "Jam Up Jelly Tight" with Tommy Roe.

Larry Stabbins 1949 UK saxophonist, flautist, and songwriter with Working Week.

David A Stewart 1952 UK guitarist, pianist, and songwriter. In 1977 he formed the group Tourists with Annie Lennox, and from 1981 the pair joined up in Eurythmics (for hits, see 25th December).

Peter Noone 1963 UK bassist with Cross.

Deaths

Norrie Paramour 1979 UK orchestra leader, songwriter and arranger, born in 1914. Norrie was A&R Manager for EMI Columbia from 1950 to 1968. It was he, who directed the careers of Cliff Richard, Frank Ifield, the Shadows, and Helen Shapiro. During the 1960s he had his own instrumental hits with "Theme From 'A Summer Place'" (3/60 UK 36) and "Theme From 'Z Cars'" (3/62 UK 33). Norrie wrote several pieces of film music and was the leader of the BBC Midland Radio Orchestra from 1972.

Hits of the Day

1957	"Diana" Paul Anka US 1 week
1965	"(I Can't Get No) Satisfaction" Rolling Stones UK 2 weeks
1972	"Mama Weer All Crazee Now" Slade UK 3 weeks
1978	"Boogie Oogie Oogie" A Taste Of Honey US 3 weeks
1989	"Hangin' Tough" New Kids On The Block US 1 week
1989	"Ride On Time" Black Box UK 6 weeks

10th

Birthdays

Francis Craig 1900 US pianist and composer, who led his own bands from the 20s. It was he, who helped singers like Kitty Kallen and Dinah Shore in their early days. He had his greatest successes with million seller "Near You" (8/47 US 1) and "Beg Your Pardon" (1/48 US 3). He died 19th November, 1966.

Yma Sumac 1922 Peruvian singer, who claims her real name is Zoila Imperatriz Charrari Sumac del Castillo. Others say her name is simply Amy Camus. She is of Indian-Spanish descent, and has been making concert tours all around the world since 1941. She created a sensation with her 4-octave vocal range. Her nickname is 'Nightingale of the Andes'. In 1947 she appeared for the first time at Carnegie Hall in the USA. In 1950 she had a hit with "Anthem of the Sun God" and No. 1 US album VOICE OF THE XTABAY. Later, she appeared in low budget films, withdrew from the business completely in 1962, and then returned in 1987 for a three-week guest performance in New York.

Roy Brown 1925 US blues singer, pianist, and songwriter. He had already formed a gospel group called Rookie Four in 1937. In 1942 he became a professional boxer in Los Angeles. In 1945, he resumed his singing career and was considered to be one of the founders of New Orleans Rhythm & Blues. At this time, he made his first records. He wrote the well-known number "Good Rockin' Tonight" (6/48 R&B 13), but his biggest hits were "'Long About Midnight" (10/48 R&B 1), "Hard Luck Blues" (6/50 R&B 1), and "Let The Four Winds Blow" (5/57 R&B 5; 7/57 US 29). He died 25th May, 1981.

Danny Hutton 1942 US singer and songwriter, born in Ireland and grew up in the USA. He started as a free-lance producer in the mid-1960s, as a session singer and solo artist. His biggest hit was "Roses And Rainbows" (10/65 US 73). After auditioning unsuccessfully for a place with the group Monkees, he formed Three Dog Night in 1968. The band had 21 Top-100 hits from 1969 to 1975, among them seven million sellers: "One" (5/69 US 5), "Mama Told Me Not To Come" (5/70 US 1; 8/70 UK 3), "Joy To The World" (3/71 US 1), "An Old Fashioned Love Song" (11/71 US 4), "Black And White" (8/72 US 1), "Shambala" (5/73 US 3) and "The Show Must Go On" (3/74 US 4). The group split up in 1976, and Hutton managed US punk bands. In June 1981 the three original members of Three Dog Night reformed, but failed to make any impression on the charts.

Jose Feliciano 1945 US singer, guitarist and songwriter; born blind in Puerto Rico. At age 5, he moved to New York with his parents. As a child, he became an accomplished guitarist and made his first stage appearances when he was nine in Spanish Harlem, New York. In the early 1960s he became known in folk music circles in Greenwich Village, and made his first records in 1963, which were destined for the US-Latin market. He had a broke through into the pop charts in 1968 with "Light My Fire" (7/68 US 3; 9/68 UK 6).

Barriemore Barlow 1949 UK drummer with Jethro Tull. He replaced original drummer Clive Bunker in May 1971. Barriemore also worked as a session musician for Brian Protheroe, Maddy Prior, Kerry Livgren, Robert Plant, and John Miles. After Ian Anderson, leader of Jethro Tull, had worked with drummer Mark Craney on his solo album in June, 1980, he stopped working with Barlow.

Vic Collins 1950 UK guitarist with the Kursaal Flyers. In 1985 he turned up with Long Ryders.

Joe Perry 1950 US guitarist and songwriter with Aerosmith, formed by him in 1970. In 1979 he left the group because he never really got on with singer Steven Tyler who wrote most of the songs for the group. He formed Joe Perry Project, and in April 1984 Aerosmith reformed with the original members.

Don Powell 1950 UK drummer with Slade.

Johnnie Fingers 1956 Irish keyboard player and singer with Boomtown Rats who lasted from 1975 to 1986.

Pat Mastelotto 1955 US drummer with Mr. Mister, and as a session musician with Cock Robin, Pointer Sisters, Jack Wagner, Patti LaBelle and Vanity.

Carol Decker 1957 UK singer and songwriter. In 1982 she met Ronnie Rogers in the group Lazers. In 1986, the two of them formed a songwriting team, which resulted in the group T'Pau being formed. Hits: "Heart And Soul" (5/87 US 4; 8/87 UK 4), "China In Your Hand" (10/87 UK 1), "Valentine" (1/88 UK 9) and "I Will Be With You" (6/88 UK 14).

Siobhan Fahey 1960 Irish singer and songwriter. She formed the UK trio Bananarama in 1981 with two girl-friends with whom she shared a flat. For hits, see under colleague Karen Woodward on 2nd April. In August 1987, Siobhan married Dave A. Stewart, half of Eurythmics. A little later, she left the group and was replaced by Jacqui Sullivan. In autumn 1988, she formed Shakespear's Sister with US singer, guitarist, and songwriter, Marcella Detroit. Hits: "You're History" (7/89 UK 7) and "Stay" (2/92 UK 1).

Hits of the Day

1949	"Someday" Vaughn Monroe US 2 weeks
1954	"Little Things Mean A Lot" Kitty Kallen UK 1 week
1964	"You Really Got Me" Kinks UK 2 weeks
1966	"You Can't Hurry Love" Supremes US 2 weeks
1983	"Maniac" Michael Sembello US 2 weeks
1988	"Sweet Child O'Mine" Guns 'N' Roses US 2 weeks
1988	"A Groovy Kind Of Love" Phil Collins UK 2 weeks

Miscellany

1973 Mick Jagger and Keith Richards had chosen the title 'Starfucker' for their new album. Ahmet Ertegun and record company Atlantic were determined not to release the record with that name, but Mick Jagger was just as stubborn, and not willing to make any concessions. After the album had waited months for its release, the title was changed to STAR STAR, but the lyrics were left as they were. Inspite of this, the BBC put the record on their play list on 10th September, 1973. In defence of the original title, Mick Jagger said, "If girls can do it, then I don't see why I can't write about it – it is exactly what I see." During a concert tour of the USA in 1975, while the number was being played, a huge 5 meter long phallic balloon was released from the stage. In San Antonio, Texas, the group was threatened with arrest if they tried to release a balloon there. They refrained.

11th

Birthdays

Jimmie Davis 1902 US singer, songwriter, and twice (1944 – 48, and 1960 – 64), Governor of Louisiana. Country music was an important part of his life, but after his time at university he was a full time professor of history. During his college days he started with Tiger Four, and made his first records in 1929. Hits: "Nobody's Darling But Mine" (12/37 US 19), "Meet Me Tonight In Dreamlight" (12/38 US 13) and "There's A New Moon Over My Shoulder" (2/45 C&W 1). In the 1940s he had a hit as a songwriter. Gene Autry recorded his title "You Are My Sunshine". Later, Jimmie got more involved with gospel music. In 1972 he became a member of the Country Music Hall Of Fame.

Ben Hewitt 1935 US singer and songwriter who sang like Elvis Presley, only – he wasn't Elvis Presley.

Charles Patrick 1938 US leadsinger with the Doo-Wop group Monotones. Hit: "Book Of Love" (3/58 US 5).

Bernie Dwyer 1940 UK drummer with Freddie & The Dreamers.

Leo Kottke 1945 US guitarist, singer and songwriter. From 1971 he made successful albums, including DREAMS AND ALL THAT STUFF (11/74 US 45).

Bob Catley 1947 UK leadsinger with Magnum, who released their debut album in 1976. Hit: "Start Talking Love" (5/88 UK 22).

John Martyn 1948 UK guitarist, singer and songwriter. In 1986 he celebrated his 20th anniversary in the business. Highly thought of, he never did manage a hit but his best known song remains "May You Never". Either solo, or with changing musicians, he performs music which was a hybrid of folk, blues, jazz and pop.

Dennis Tufano 1948 US guitarist and singer with the Buckinghams, formed in 1966. Well-known producer James William Guercio tried out the Chicago sound with them, which was then perfected by the group Chicago in 1969. The Buckinghams' career was prematurely halted when they were arrested on drugs charges in 1968. Hits: "Kind Of A Drag" (12/66 US 1), "Don't You Care" (3/67 US 6), and "Mercy, Mercy, Mercy" (6/67 US 5).

Tommy Shaw 1953 US guitarist, singer, and songwriter with Styx from 1975. From 1984 he made solo records as well. Hit: "Girls With Guns" (9/84 US 33).

Jon Moss 1957 UK drummer with Culture Club.

Mick Talbot 1958 UK pianist and songwriter. He started with Merton Parkas and Dexy's Midnight Runners, before forming the duo Style Council in 1982 with Paul Weller, formerly of the Jam.

Deaths

Lorne Greene 1987 Canadian actor and narrator. He died of heart failure. Born 12th February, 1915.

Peter Tosh 1987 Jamaican singer and songwriter, who was shot dead in his home by burglars. Born 9th October, 1944.

Hits of the Day

1943 "Sunday, Monday Or Always" Bing Crosby US 7 weeks

1943 "All Or Nothing At All" Frank Sinatra US 2 weeks

1953 "Look At That Girl" Guy Mitchell UK 6 weeks

1959 "Only 16" Craig Douglas UK 4 weeks

1968 "Hey Jude" Beatles UK 2 weeks

1971 "Go Away Little Girl" Donny Osmond US 3 weeks

1976 "Shake Your Booty" K.C. & The Sunshine Band US 1 week

1982 "Hard To Say I'm Sorry" Chicago US 2 weeks

Miscellany

1962 The Fab Four are back in the studio again, in order to work on their first single record. George Martin brought drummer Andy White into the studio, who was to play instead of Ringo Starr. Ringo was banished to playing tambourine in the background. Even the number "P.S. I Love You" was re-recorded, with Ringo playing maracas. The version of "Love Me Do" produced that day, was the one included on their first album PLEASE PLEASE ME, which was released on 22nd March, 1963.

12th

Birthdays

Maurice Chevalier 1888 French chansonnier and film actor. He celebrated his first successes in Paris revue-theatres, and in 1909 he partnered Mistinguette. After the First World War, he appeared in London, and from 1921 again in Paris and also in Argentina. In 1927 he appeared in films, like *The Love Parade* (1930), and *Gigi* (1957). He died on 1st January, 1972.

Eddy Howard 1914 US singer, songwriter, and orchestra leader. He sang in various bands, before becoming the singer with Dick Jurgens from 1934 to 1940 and had a hit with "In An Old Dutch Garden (By An Old Dutch Mill)" (12/39 US 3). After that, he formed his own band, which continued to be successful until 1955. Hits, and million sellers: "To Each His Own" (6/46 US 1) and "Sin" (9/51 US 1). Eddy died 23rd May, 1963.

Ella Mae Morse 1924 US jazz singer. In 1939 she sang with Jimmy Dorsey, and after that, with Freddie Slack, with whom she had her first hits, "Cow Cow Boogie" (7/42 US 9), and "The House Of Blue Lights" (5/46 US 8).

George Jones 1931 US country singer. He is the second most successful country artist of all time. He first recorded in 1953, and had the first of 140 hits in 1955, which continued until 1980. By contrast with many of his colleagues, he failed to crossover into the pop charts. However, he often hit No. 1 in the C&W charts. Among his most successful recordings were "White Lightening" (3/59 C&W 1), "Tender Years" (6/61 C&W 1) and "A Good Year For The Roses" (11/70 C&W 2). He also sang duets with Ray Charles, Brenda Lee, Gene Pitney, and Tammy Wynette, to whom he was married from 1969 to 1975. As a rockabilly singer, George made records in the names of Thumper Jones, and Hank Smith. As with most of country artists, he had a nickname, 'Rolls Royce of Country Singers'.

Gus Backus 1937 US singer. Real first names Donald Edgar. In 1955 he was a co-founder of the Dell-Vikings, who were all members of the US Air Force stationed in Pittsburgh. Hits: "Come Go With Me" (2/57 US 4), and "Whispering Bells" (7/57 US 9). In mid-1957 the nucleus of the group split up with, some continuing as Dell-Vikings, the others, including Gus, recorded for Mercury as Del-Vikings. Hit: "Cool Shake" (7/57 US 12). In the late 1950s Gus was transferred to West Germany where he stayed after completing his military service. [He had a successful career there as a pop singer throughout the 60s.] Then in the 1970s he seemed to have disappeared from the face of the earth. It turned out he was working as a foreman in the oilfields in New Mexico. He tried a comeback in Germany in the late 1980s, when it failed, he went back to the USA.

Tony Bellamy 1940 US guitarist with Redbone.

Maria Muldaur 1943 US singer, maiden name Maria Gracia Rosa Domenica d'Amato. Together. She was a member of Jim Kweskin's Jug Band with husband Geoff. Maria started with the Even Dozen Jug Band, which included John Sebastian, Stefan Grossman and Steve Katz. From 1972, when she divorced her husband, she made solo records. Hits: "Midnight At The Oasis" (2/74 US 6; 6/74 UK 21), and "I'm A Woman" (12/74 US 12).

Barry White 1944 US singer, songwriter and producer. Even though he may not look like it, for many he was the sex symbol of the 1970s. At age 16 he played with the L.A. R & B band Upfronts; at age 18 he wrote and arranged "The Harlem Shuffle" for Bob & Earl (1964), which was later covered by the Rolling Stones (1986). In 1973 he made his first record. Hits, and million sellers: "I'm Gonna Love You Just A Little More, Baby" (4/73 US

3; 6/73 UK 23), "Never, Never Gonna Give Ya Up" (10/73 US 7; 1/74 UK 14), "Can't Get Enough Of Your Love, Babe" (8/74 US 1; UK 8), "You're The First, The Last, My Everything" (11/74 US 2; UK 1), "It's Ecstasy When You Lay Down Next To Me" (8/77 US 4). His background singers were successful as Love Unlimited, he himself led the Love Unlimited Orchestra. Hit, and million seller: "Love's Theme" (12/73 US 1; 2/74 UK 10). After hearing very little of him in the 1980s, Barry staged a comeback in 1989, but throughout he has been a big draw on the cabaret circuit.

Colin Young 1944 UK singer, born in Barbados. In 1968 he replaced Clem Curtis in the Foundations, formed in 1967, and was leadsinger on the hits, "Build Me Up, Buttercup" (11/68 UK 2; 1/69 US 3) and "In the Bad Old Days" (3/69 UK 8).

Will Birch 1948 UK drummer and songwriter with the Kursaal Flyers and with Records.

Gerry Beckley 1952 US guitarist, singer, pianist, drummer, and songwriter with America. As a session musician Gerry also worked on records by Paul Williams, Mike Hugg, Dan Fogelberg and David Cassidy.

Neil Peart 1952 Canadian drummer and songwriter with Rush.

Barry Andrews 1956 UK keyboard player, with King Crimson, and from 1977 with XTC. He also recorded with Iggy Pop, Robert Fripp and Shriekback.

Brian Robertson 1956 UK guitarist with Thin Lizzy, Motorhead, Wild Horses and Frankie Miller Band.

Hits of the Day

1963 "She Loves You" Beatles UK 4 weeks
1970 "Tears Of A Clown" Smokey Robinson & The Miracles UK 1 week

---

13th

Birthdays

Bill Monroe 1911 US country singer and songwriter. He was considered to be the 'Father of Blue Grass Music'. He recorded from 1936 as Monroe Brothers with brother Charlie and started a solo career in the 1940s, backed by his own band. His most successful record was "Kentucky Waltz" (3/46 C&W 3). Bill also wrote the number "Blue Moon Of Kentucky", which the young Elvis Presley recorded.

Dick Haymes 1916 Singer, songwriter and film actor, born in Buenos Aires, and grew up in Europe. In 1936 he went to the USA, wrote songs, sang on the radio, and played small parts in films. Then he tried to sell his own compositions to Harry James, who engaged him in 1939 as a replacement for Frank Sinatra. Hits: "A Sinner Kissed An Angel" (12/41 US 15), and "I'll Get By (As Long As I Have You)" (4/44 US 1); the latter did not get into the pop charts until 1944, although it was recorded in April, 1941. Dick also sang "Idaho" (8/42 US 4) with Benny Goodman and recorded with Tommy Dorsey. From 1943 he was successful as a solo artist: "It Can't Be Wrong" (6/43 US 1), "You'll Never Know" (7/43 US 1), and the million seller "Little White Lies" (4/48 US 2). Dick also duetted with Helen Forrest on ten hits. The two biggest were "Long Ago (And Far Away)" (4/44 US 2) and "I'll Buy That Dream" (9/45 US 2). From 1938 to 1953 he was in more than ten films. As he obviously never became a US citizen, and used this as a reason to avoid conscription into the army in the Second World War, he had difficulties entering the USA again after a sojourn abroad with his fourth wife Rita Hayworth. He was not deported, but his career suffered greatly. In 1960 and in 1971 Dick was bankrupt. From the mid-1960s he lived in Ireland, and only appeared occasionally in American nightclubs and on TV programmes. He died 30th March, 1980.

Mel Torme 1925 US singer, and songwriter, who also worked as a producer, pianist, drummer, and actor. Real name Melvin Howard. At the age of four, he sang on radio with the Coon-Sanders band. At age 9 he acted in TV soap operas. In 1942 he played drums in a band led by Chico Marx. In 1944 he formed his own band, the Meltones, and sang with Artie Shaw in 1945/46. Hit: "I Got The Sun In The Morning" (7/46 US 17). Then he started a solo career. Hits: "Careless Hands" (3/49 US 1), "Again" (4/49 US 3), "Mountain Greenery" (4/56 UK 15; 7/56 RE-UK 4) and "Comin' Home Baby" (12/62 US 36; UK 13). Among his most successful compositions was the "Christmas Song", which was a hit for Nat King Cole in 1946 and is re-issued annually. Mel also appeared in several films and presented TV musical spectaculars.

James Johnson 1939 US singer with the Jayhawks. Hit: "Stranded In The Jungle" (6/56 US 18). They renamed themselves Vibrations in 1960. Hits: "The Watusi" (2/61 US 25) and "My Girl Sloopy" (3/64 US 26). In between they made a record "Peanut Butter" (4/61 US 20) as Marathons.

Dave Quincy 1939 UK keyboard player and saxophonist with the Jet Blacks, Manfred Mann's Chapter 3, If, Q, and as a session musician with P. J. Proby, J. J. Jackson and Paul Jones. In 1973 he formed Zzebra, who were successful initially but failed to consolidate.

David Clayton-Thomas 1941 UK singer and songwriter. Real name David Thomsett. In the second half of the 1960s, he was successful on the Canadian Circuit. In 1969 he replaced Al Kooper in Blood, Sweat & Tears, formed in 1968. Hits: "You've Made Me So Very Happy" (3/69 US 2; UK 35), "Spinning Wheel" (5/69 US 2) and "When I Die" (10/69 US 2). In 1972, David started a solo career, but in 1974 he returned to the group. After 1976, Blood, Sweat & Tears reformed periodically with changing lineups although Bobby Colomby and David Clayton-Thomas remained through every permutation, which was necessary as Bobby was the owner of the group name.

Peter Cetera 1944 US singer, bassist, and songwriter with the band Chicago Transit Authority formed in 1966, and who called themselves plain Chicago in July 1969 after a quarrel with the Chicago public transport system of the same name. Before that, various members had already played with Missing Links and with Big Thing. Chicago were one of the first successful jazz-rock bands. From the beginning of the 1970s, having undergone a change of musical-direction, the band became more and more successful. Hits: "25 or 6 To 4" (7/70 UK 7; US 4), "Saturday In The Park" (8/72 US 3), "Just You 'n' Me" (9/73 US 4), "If You Leave Me Now" (8/76 US 1; 10/76 UK 1), "Hard To Say I'm Sorry" (6/82 US 1; 8/82 UK 4), "Hard Habit To Break" (8/84 US 3; 11/84 UK 8) and "You're The Inspiration" (11/84 US 3; 1/85 UK 14). In 1981 Peter released his first solo record and in 1985 he finally split from Chicago, being replaced by Jason Scheff, son of Jerry Scheff, bassist for Elvis Presley of many years standing. Solo hits for Peter: "Glory Of Love" (6/86 US 1; 8/86 UK 3), and in a duet with Amy Grant, "The Next Time I Fall" (9/86 US 1), and "One Good Woman" (7/88 US 4).

Randy Jones 1952 US singer with Village People.

Den Hegarty 1954 UK singer and founder of the Darts in 1976. Before that, as had several other members of this group, he had sung with Rocky Sharpe & The Replays. Just like that band, the Darts reworked old doo-wop hits of the 1950s; both Showaddywaddy and Sha-Na-Na followed a similar path. Hits: "Come Back My Love" (1/78 UK 2), "Boy From New York" (5/78 UK 2) and "It's Raining" (8/78 UK 2). After this success, Den left the group and was replaced by American Kenny Andrews.

Joni Sledge 1956 US singer with Sister Sledge.

Zak Starkey 1965 UK drummer, and son of Ringo Starr.

Hits of the Day

1952	"You Belong To Me" Jo Stafford US 12 weeks
1962	"She's Not You" Elvis Presley UK 3 weeks
1980	"Feels Like I'm In Love" Kelly Marie UK 2 weeks
1986	"Don't Leave Me This Way" Communards UK 4 weeks
1986	"Take My Breath Away" Berlin US 1 week

14th

Birthdays

Pete Agnew 1946 UK bass player and songwriter with the Shadettes, from which Nazareth was formed in 1968.

Steve Gaines 1949 US guitarist who replaced Ed King in Lynyrd Skynyrd from 1975. He died in an airplane crash on 20th October, 1977.

Paul Kossoff 1950 UK guitarist and songwriter, son of British actor David Kossoff. He played with Black Cat Bones, and from 1968 with Free, after 1971 as a soloist, and with the band, Back Street Crawler. Paul died on 19th March, 1976.

Barry Cowsill 1955 US singer and bassist with the Cowsills.

Morton Harket 1959 Norwegian singer and songwriter with A-Ha. Hits: "Take On Me" (7/85 US 1; 9/85 UK 2), "The Sun Always Shines On TV" (11/85 US 20; 1/86 UK 1), "Train Of Thought" (4/86 UK 8), "Hunting High And Low" (6/86 UK 5), "I've Been Losing You" (10/86 UK 8), "Cry Wolf" (12/86 UK 5), "The Living Daylights" (7/87 UK 5), "Stay On These Roads" (3/88 UK 5), "Touchy!" (8/88 UK 11) and "You Are The One (Remix)" (12/88 UK 13).

Deaths

Furry Lewis 1981 US blues musician. Born 6th March, 1893.

Billy Vaughn US band leader and composer, born on April 12th, 1919.

Hits of the Day

1940 "Sierra Sue" Bing Crosby US 4 weeks
1946 "Five Minutes More" Fran Sinatra US 4 weeks
1974 "I Shot The Sheriff" Eric Clapton US 1 week

15th

Birthdays

Roy Acuff 1903 US country singer, fiddler and song-writer. Roy played in a Madison Show in 1932/33, after which he formed his own band, the Tennessee Cracker Jets. From 1935 he had a new group called Crazy Tennesseans, made his first records in 1936, and recorded his two biggest hits with "Great Speckle Bird" (9/38 US 13), and the million seller "Wabash Cannonball" (12/38 US 12). In 1937 he appeared in the Grand Ole Opry, and then played with a new band, the Smoky Mountain Boys. In 1942 he set up a music publishing company together with Fred Rose, which has become one of the largest publishing companies over the years. The pair also set up the Hickory record label in the late 1950s. Roy was the first artist to be accepted into The Hall Of Fame in his lifetime, that was in 1962. His nickname is the 'King Of Country Music'. Roy who was successful with "The Prodigal Son" (2/44 US 19) in the 1940s occasionally sang in the ensuing years and released records on his Hickory label right into the 1970s.

Snooky Pryor 1921 US blues harmonica player, singer, and drummer. Real first names, James Edward. He has been making records since the late 1940s.

Cannonball Adderley 1928 US alto and soprano sax-ophonist, composer and bandleader. Real first names Julian Edwin. He is considered to be one of the most eminent alto saxophonists of modern jazz. He became known to a larger public with his quintet, which included pianist Joe Zawinul. Hit: "Mercy, Mercy, Mercy" (1/67 US 11). He died 8th August, 1975.

Jimmy Gilmer 1940 US singer, who replaced Chuck Tharp in the Fireballs in 1960. It was Norman Petty who introduced Jimmy to the group. They called themselves Jimmy Gilmer & The Fireballs for quite a number of years. Hit: "Sugar Shack" (9/63 US 1). Norman Petty also took on the management of the band and as he also looked after Buddy Holly when Holly died many of his compositions

were reworked by Petty with the help of Jimmy Gilmer & The Fireballs. In late 1967 they recorded as the Fireballs again. Hit: "Bottle Of Wine" (12/67 US 9).

Les Braid 1941 UK bass player with Swinging Blue Jeans.

Lee Dorman 1942 US bass player, singer, pianist, and songwriter, with Iron Butterfly and Captain Beyond.

Frederick Eugene Byrd 1971 UK singer with B.V.S.M.P.

Deaths

Bill Evans 1980 US jazz musician. He died of the results of a perforated stomach ulcer. Born 16th August, 1929.

Hits of the Day

1945 "Till The End Of Time" Perry Como US 10 weeks
1962 "Sherry" Four Seasons US 5 weeks
1962 "She's Not You" Elvis Presley UK 2 weeks
1966 "All Or Nothing" Small Faces UK 1 week
1973 "Delta Dawn" Helen Reddy US 1 week
1990 "Show Me Heaven" Maria McKee UK 4 weeks

16th

Birthdays

Joe Reisman 1924 US saxophonist, orchestra leader, composer and arranger for film industry, Broadway and television. In the 1950s he produced many of RCA's record releases. He himself played in the bands of Bob Crosby and Louis Prima, and also made records as a soloist. He had his greatest success with "Armen's Theme" (12/56 US 46).

Charlie Byrd 1925 US jazz guitarist and composer, who introduced Stan Getz to the 'bossa nova' and recorded with him on a few occasions. On the one hand Charlie himself cut over 40 albums, which can be termed mellow at best, while, on the other hand, he is considered to be an outstanding jazz guitarist.

B. B. King 1925 US singer, guitarist, and songwriter; real first name Riley probably *the* blues man. In the late

1940s he had his own radio shows as a disc jockey in the name of Riley King 'Blues Boy Of Beale Street'. This 'Blues Boy' became the abbreviation B. B.. In 1938 he formed the Elkhorn Singers gospel quartet; he played with Bobby Bland and Johnny Ace as the Beale Streeters in 1947. From 1949 he regularly made recordings. From 1951 right into the 1980s he had over 70 hits in the R&B charts, including "Three O'Clock Blues" (12/51 R&B 1), "You Know I Love You" (9/52 R&B 1), "Please Love Me" (6/53 R&B 1), and "You Upset Me Baby" (11/54 R&B 1). From 1957 he began to have some hits in the pop charts with "The Thrill Is Gone" (12/69 US 15), and "I Like To Live The Love" (12/73 US 28). B. B. has received awards as best jazz singer and/or best guitarist of the year, becoming a role model for many successive generations of musicians.

Little Willie Littlefield 1931 US pianist, singer, guitarist and songwriter. He made his first records in 1946. He composed "Kansas City", which he had already recorded as "K. C. Lovin'" in 1952. His most successful recordings were "It's Midnight" (8/49 R&B 3) and "Farewell" (11/49 R&B 5).

Richard Blandon 1934 US leadsinger of the Dubs, an R & B quintet. Hit: "Could This Be Magic" (11/57 US 23).

Joe Butler 1943 US drummer with Lovin' Spoonful.

Bernie Calvert 1944 UK bass player, replaced Eric Haydock in the Hollies from 1966. Before that he played with Dolphin.

Betty Kelley 1944 US singer with Martha Reeves & The Vandellas.

Sonny Lemaire 1947 US bass player and songwriter with Exile.

Kenny Jones 1948 UK drummer with the Small Faces, Faces, Rod Stewart and the Who. As a session musician he played with everyone from Mike Batt to Jerry Lee Lewis.

David Bellamy 1950 US singer, guitarist, keyboard player, and songwriter with the Bellamy Brothers, who made their professional debut in 1958. David worked with the Accidents, and wrote the title "Spiders And Snakes" for Jim Stafford. From 1968 to 1971 he was with the band Jericho, which included his brother Howard. From 1976 they were successful as the Bellamy Brothers. Hits, see under his brother Howard, 2nd February.

Charles Fearing 1956 US guitarist with Raydio and a sought-after session musician.

Richard Marx 1963 US singer, pianist, guitarist and songwriter. At the age of five Richard sang commercial jingles, in common with his mother, which were written by his father. His career began as a songwriter and backing singer for Bob Seger and Kenny Rogers. It was Lionel Richie who recognized Richard's talent, and advised him to start a solo career. In 1987 his debut album appeared, which established his credentials. Hits: "Don't Mean Nothing" (6/87 US 3), "Should've Known Better" (9/87 US 3), "Endless Summer Nights" (1/88 US 2), "Hold On To The Nights" (5/88 US 1), "Satisfied" (5/89 US 1), "Right Here Waiting" (7/89 US 1; 9/89 UK 2) and "Angelia" (10/89 US 4).

Deaths

Marc Bolan 1977 UK singer, guitarist and songwriter. Died after a car accident. Born 30th September, 1947.

Hits of the Day

1972 "Black And White" Three Dog Night US 1 week
1989 "Don't Wanna Lose You" Gloria Estefan US 1 week

17th

Birthdays

Hank Williams 1923 US country singer, guitarist and songwriter. Real first names Hiram King. He appeared in radio shows in Montgomery as 'The Singing Kid' when he was quite young. While still a teenager he formed his group The Drifting Cowboys. His first records were cut in 1946. He appeared in the pop charts for the first time with "Move It On Over" (8/47 C&W 4). This song contained some of the ingredients of rock 'n' roll was about. Further hits: "Love Sick Blues" (3/49 C&W 1 for 16 weeks!; 5/49 US 21), "Cold Cold Heart" (3/51 C&W 1; US 27), "Hey, Good Lookin'" (7/51 C&W 1; 9/51 US 29), "Jambalaya (On The Bayou)" (8/52 C&W 1; US 20), "Kaw-Liga" (2/53 C&W 1; US 23) and "Your Cheatin' Heart" (2/53 C&W 1; US 25). Most of these numbers were million sellers. His nickname was 'Shakespeare Of Country Music' and it is certainly true that he was the leading songwriter of country music. Even the song titles indicated that his range of emotions was liable to erratic changes. Problems with his wife Audrey, a strong inferiority complex, and alcoholism contributed towards his being banished from the Grand Ole Opry in August 1952. Shortly before his death, he married the exceptionally pretty Billie Jean Jones Eshlimar, but that did not help him; ill and psychologically burnt-out, he died on 1st January 1953 of a heart attack on the back seat of his Cadillac on the way to a show in Canton, Ohio. His death was attributed to his excessive drinking, as he was only 29 years old. In 1961 he was entered in the Country Music Hall Of Fame and in 1987, in the Rock 'n' Roll Hall Of Fame. He influenced the style of country music in his time and strongly influenced pop music. George Hamilton played the part of Hank Williams in the film biography *Your Cheatin' Heart* made in 1964.

Bill Black 1926 US bassist and songwriter who played on most of the records made by Elvis Presley before being conscripted into the army. From 1959 with his own combo he had hits with "White Silver Sands" (3/60 US 9) and "Don't Be Cruel" (9/60 US 11; 11/60 UK 32). Bill cropped up in the US pop charts until January 1965. He died 21st October, 1965.

Sil Austin 1929 US saxophonist and songwriter. Complete first name Sylvester. He played with the Tiny Bradshaw Band, before forming his own group. Hit: "Slow Walk" (11/56 US 17).

Phil Cracolici 1937 US leadsinger with the Mystics, a quintet from Brooklyn, New York. Hit: "Hushabye" (5/59 US 20).

Lamonte McLemore 1940 US singer with the Hi-Fi's which became the Versatiles, and finally Fifth Dimension.

Fee Waybill 1950 US singer and songwriter with the Tubes. The group formed at the end of the 1960s. Fee only became a member because he was the only one who had a car large enough to accomodate all their instruments. It was not until later that it turned out he could sing well. Over the course of the years, the band's appearances became progressively more theatrical. From 1976 they began to chart and their biggest hit was "She's A Beauty" (4/83 US 10).

Deaths

Jimmy Yancey 1951 US blues and boogie pianist. Died of diabetes. Born 20th February, 1898.

Hugo Winterhalter 1973 US orchestra leader. Died of cancer. Born 15th August, 1909.

Hits of the Day

1954 "Three Coins In A Fountain" Frank Sinatra UK 3 weeks

1955 "Ain't That A Shame" Pat Boone US 2 weeks
1977 "I Just Want To Be Your Everything" Andy Gibb US 1 week (2nd time)

18th

Birthdays

Jimmie Rogers 1933 US singer, guitarist, pianist and songwriter, not to be confused with country star (8th September). While he was still with the Air Force, he formed his first band. In 1959 he had his own NBC TV series in the USA. Hits: "Honeycomb" (8/57 US 1; 11/57 UK 30), "Kisses Sweeter Than Wine" (11/57 US 3; UK 7), "Secretly" (5/58 US 3) and "English Country Garden" (6/62 UK 5). On 1st December, 1967, he was found in his car with a fractured skull; he had to recuperate for a whole year. He returned to the stage on 28th January, 1969.

Frankie Avalon 1939 US singer. Real name Francis Avallone. He began to play in bands when he was only 14. In the mid-1950s he played with Paul Whiteman on radio and TV appearances. In 1957 he was a singer and trumpeter with Rocco & His Saints. In the same year he played in the film *Discjockey Jamboree*. First solo hit: "Dede Dinah" (1/58 US 7). Frankie was one of the typical high school rockers of the late 1950s. His biggest hits were "Venus" (2/59 US 1; 4/59 UK 16) and "Why" (11/59 US 1; 1/60 UK 20). He also appeared in films in the 1960s. However, after 1962 he disappeared from the pop charts. In 1976 he recorded a disco version of his hit "Venus", but it only managed to reach No. 46. In 1987 he appeared in the film *Back To The Beach* with Annette Funicello with whom he had already made 'surfing' films in the early 1960s. He also sang a version of "California Sun" in this film.

Alan King 1946 UK guitarist with the group Ace, and as a session musician.

Kerry Livgren 1949 US guitarist, pianist, and songwriter for Kansas, formed in 1970. The group was previously called White Clover.

Dee Dee Ramone 1952 US bass player and in 1974 cofounder of the Ramones. Real name Douglas Colvin.

Martin Beedle 1961 UK drummer with Cutting Crew.

Joanne Catherall 1962 UK singer with Human League.

Ian Spice 1966 UK drummer with Breathe.

Ricky Bell 1967 US singer with the children's group New Edition formed in 1982.

Deaths

Jimi Hendrix 1970 US guitarist, singer, and songwriter. He choked to death on his own vomit, after drinking alcohol with sleeping tablets. Born 27th November, 1942.

Rob Tyner 1991 US drummer with MC5. Born December 12th 1944.

Hits of the Day

1961 "Take Good Care Of My Baby" Bobby Vee US 3 weeks

1971 "Hey Girl, Don't Bother Me" Tams UK 3 weeks

1976 "Play That Funky Music" Wild Cherry US 3 weeks

19th

Birthdays

Billy Ward 1921 US pianist and leader of Billy Ward & His Dominoes. Billy had formed the Ques in 1950, who received a record contract and changed their name to Dominoes in the same year, after winning a youth contest at the Apollo and appearing on Arthur Godfrey's *Talent Scout Show*. Clyde McPhatter was lead singer until 1953. When he left the group, Jackie Wilson became leadsinger until 1957. Hits: the million seller "Sixty Minute Man" (5/51 R&B 1; 8/51 US 17), "Have Mercy Baby" (5/52 R&B 1), "Stardust" (6/57 US 12; 9/57 UK 13) and "Deep Purple" (9/57 US 20; 11/57 UK 30). The group split up in the early 1960s.

Nini Rosso 1926 Italian trumpeter and songwriter. Real first name Celeste. Hits: "Il Silenzio" (8/65 UK 8), and "Montanara" (12/66).

Nick Massi 1927 US bass player, from 1960 to 1965 with the Four Seasons. Real name Nicholas Macioci.

Brook Benton 1931 US singer and songwriter. Real name Benjamin Franklin Peay. He started in the early 1940s with Camden Jubilee Singers, went to New York in 1948, and joined Bill Langford's Langfordaires. In 1951 he sang with the Jerusalem Stars, and made his first solo record in 1953. He was successful from 1958, and his biggest hits were "It's Just A Matter Of Time" (1/59 US 3), "The Boll Weevil Song (5/61 US 2; 7/61 UK 30), "Hotel Happiness" (11/62 US 3) and "Rainy Night In Georgia" (1/70 US 4). In addition, he recorded duets with Dinah Washington, "Baby (You've Got What It Takes)" (1/60 US 5) and "A Rockin' Good Way (To Mess Around And Fall In Love)" (5/60 US 7). Brook died 9th April, 1988.

Brian Epstein 1934 UK manager. The most important day of his life was probably 28th October, 1961: a customer walked into the record shop NEMS in Liverpool, and asked for the record "My Bonnie" by the Beatles: The manager of the shop was called Brian Epstein. While searching for the record, Brian found the Beatles in the Cavern Club. He became their manager in December 1961. Later he signed up other artists like Gerry & The Pacemakers, Billy J. Kramer, Cilla Black, Tommy Quickly, the US band Cyrkle, and US singer Eric Anderson. On 27th August, 1967, while the Beatles were meditating in Wales with the Maharishi Mahesh Yogi, Epstein died of an overdose of sleeping tablets.

Bill Medley 1940 US singer and songwriter. After playing previously with the Paramours, he formed the duo Righteous Brothers with Bobby Hatfield in 1962, and started making records in 1963. For hits, see 10th August, under Bobby. In November 1967 Bill left the duo, in order to carry on as a solo artist, club owner, and country artist, where he had had a hit with "I Still Do" (4/84 C&W 17). In 1987 he duetted with Jennifer Warnes on "(I've Had) The Time Of My Life" (9/87 US 1; UK 6) and returned to the charts again with the help of the film *Dirty Dancing*.

Paul Williams 1940 US songwriter, singer and actor. He appeared in *Planet Of the Apes*, and *Smokey & The Bandit*. As a songwriter he was responsible for "We've Only Just Begun", and "Rainy Days And Mondays" by the Carpenters, "Just An Old Fashioned Love Song" by Three Dog Night, and "Evergreen (Love Theme from A Star Is Born)" by Barbra Sreisand, for which he received an Oscar in 1976. As a film composer he wrote the music for the Muppet Movie.

Cass Elliott 1943 US singer. Real name Ellen Naomi Cohen. She started with Cas Elliott & The Big Three, who changed their name to Mugwumps. In 1965 she became a member of Mamas & Papas, for hits, see 6th April. From mid-1968 she sang as a solo artist. Hits: "Dream A Little

Dream Of Me" (7/68 US 12; UK 11) and "It's Getting Better" (6/69 US 30; 8/69 UK 8). She died 29th July, 1974.

David Bromberg 1945 US guitarist. He played on records by Bob Dylan, Jonathan Edwards, Gordon Lightfoot, Rick Derringer, Sha-Na-Na and Ringo Starr. He was never particularly successful as a solo artist.

Freda Payne 1945 US jazz and soul singer. Together with sister Scherrie who joined the Supremes when Diana Ross left, she studied singing in their hometown Detroit. In the 1960s she sang with Pearl Bailey, Quincey Jones and Duke Ellington. In 1965 she made her first solo record, and was successful from the early 1970s. Hits: "Band Of Gold" (4/70 US 3; 9/70 UK 1) and "Bring The Boys Home" (6/71 US 12). Both records were million sellers. In the early 1980s she was a presenter on the talk show *For You, Black Woman*.

John Coghlan 1946 UK drummer. His career started with the Cadets in 1962, and then he joined the Spectres in September 1962, which became Traffic Jam in May 1967, and finally Status Quo in August 1967. In 1982 John left the group, in order to form his own group, Diesel. He was replaced by Pete Kircher.

Lol Creme 1947 UK guitarist, singer, songwriter, and video maker. Real first name Lawrence. In 1963, during the first British beat boom, he was a member of the Manchester band Sabres. After the initial euphoria had died away, Lol studied graphic design and art. There he met Kevin Godley. During the next few years, Lol concentrated on his course, and worked for the British publishers Pan Books. In September 1969, he made a record with his colleague Kevin as Frabjoy & Runcible, on which Graham Gouldman and Eric Stewart played as studio musicians. In August 1970, the four above named musicians made several records as Hotlegs, played together with Neil Sedaka on his comeback albums SOLITAIRE and THE TRA-LA-LA DAYS ARE OVER in 1971, and made demo tapes in 1972 which they sold to Jonathan King. He advised them to use the name 10 CC. The quartet stayed together until 1976, then Godley & Creme left and carried on as a duo with further success. They also formed a film production company, Media Lab, which has gone from strength to strength.

Twiggy 1949 UK actress, model, singer and icon of the 1960s. Hit: "Here I Go Again" (8/76 UK 17).

Nile Rodgers 1952 US guitarist, songwriter and producer. After they had already played together from 1970 in various New York clubs, Nile and Bernard Edwards formed a rock trio in 1972 called Big Apple Band. During the course of the next three years, they played a lot in clubs, and accompanied the group New York City and Carol Douglas. Slowly but surely they changed from rock to the newly-developing disco sound. In 1977, they changed their name to Chic having recruited singer Norma Jean Wright. Hits: "Dance, Dance, Dance (Yowsah Yowsah Yowsah)" (10/77 US & UK 6), "Everybody Dance" (4/78 US 38; UK 9), "Le Freak" (10/78 US 1; UK 7), "I Want Your Love" (2/79 US 7; UK 4), and "Good Times" (6/79 US 1; UK 5). As a producer, Nile worked successfully for Sister Sledge, Sheila B. Devotion, Diana Ross, Debbie Harry, David Bowie, Thompson Twins, and the first successful album by Madonna, LIKE A VIRGIN. In 1983 Nile recorded his own solo album, ADVENTURES IN THE LAND OF THE GOOD GROOVE. He played in the Honeydrippers with Robert Plant, Jimmy Page, and Jeff Beck. In 1987 he formed the trio Outloud, without Bernard.

Rex Smith 1955 US actor, Broadway musical star and singer. His biggest hit was the million seller "You Take My Breath Away" (4/79 US 10). He had a further success with "Everlasting Love" (6/81 US 32; 8/81 UK 35) with Rachel Sweet.

Rusty Egan 1957 UK songwriter and drummer with Rich Kids, Visage and Phil Lynott.

Lita Ford 1958 UK leadsinger, singer, and songwriter with the Runaways formed in Los Angeles in 1976. In April 1979 the group split up, and the individual members tried their luck as soloists with varying degrees of success. In April 1984 a solo album by Lita was released. From 1988 she was successful with "Kiss Me Deadly" (3/88 US 12) and "Close My Eyes Forever (Remix)" (3/89 US 8), a duet with Ozzy Osbourne.

Deaths

Red Foley 1958 US country star. Born 17th June, 1910.

Gram Parsons 1973 US guitarist. Born 5th November, 1946.

Hits of the Day

1960	"The Twist" Chubby Checker US 1 week
1970	"Ain't No Mountain High Enough" Diana Ross US 3 weeks
1970	"Band Of Gold" Freda Payne UK 6 weeks
1981	"Prince Charming" Adam & The Ants UK 4 weeks
1987	"I Just Can't Stop Loving You" Michael Jackson US 1 week

20th

Birthdays

Jelly Roll Morton 1890 US blues pianist, singer, composer, and bandleader. Real name Ferdinand Joseph Lemott. His year of birth is also listed as 1885. Jelly Roll liked to make himself appear older, in order to substantiate his claim to have invented jazz in 1902. In keeping with this story is the fact that he was considered to be one of the most charismatic personalities of the blues and jazz fraternity. His most successful record was "The Black Bottom Stomp" (1/27 US 13). He died 10th July, 1941.

Gogi Grant 1924 US singer. Real name Audrey Brown. Hits: "Suddenly There's A Valley" (10/55 US 9) and "There's A Wayward Wind" (4/56 US 1; 6/56 UK 9). She dubbed the vocal for Ann Blyth in the film *The Helen Morgan Story*, (1957).

Richard Stephens 1940 US guitarist with the String-A-Longs.

Mick Rogers 1946 UK singer and guitarist with Manfred Mann's Earthband formed in 1971. He sang the hit "Joybringer" (9/73 UK 9). In 1975 he was replaced by Chris Thompson. Mick played with Aviator, and from 1983 with the Dave Kelly Band.

Joe Leeway 1949 UK synthesizer player and singer, with the Thompson Twins, who aren't twins at all, but a trio. For hits, see under Tom Bailey on 18th January. Joe left the group in 1989.

Chuck & John Panozzo 1949 US bassist and US drummer with Styx.

Alannah Currie 1957 UK singer, saxophonist and percussionist, and songwriter with the Thompson Twins.

David Hemmingway 1960 UK drummer with the Housemartins from 1987.

Deaths

Jim Croce 1973 US singer, songwriter, and guitarist. Crashed in a small private plane. Born 10th January, 1943.

Ben Webster 1973 US jazz tenor saxophonist. Born 27th February, 1909.

Steve Goodman 1984 US songwriter and singer. Died of leukemia. Born 25th July, 1948.

Hits of the Day

1969	"Sugar, Sugar" Archies US	4 weeks
1969	"Bad Moon Rising" CCR UK	3 weeks
1975	"Fame" David Bowie US	1 week
1986	"Stuck With You" Huey Lewis & The News US	3 weeks

21st

Birthdays

Jimmy Young 1923 UK singer, who began his professional singing career in 1949. In 1951 he made his first records. Hits: "Eternally" (8/53 UK 8), "Unchained Melody" (5/55 UK 1), "The Man From Laramy" (9/55 UK 1), "Chain Gang" (3/56 UK 9) and "More" (9/56 UK 4). From 1964, his recording career was over, but in 1967 he made a name for himself as a radio presenter.

Ward Lamar Swingle 1927 US singer, pianist, and saxophonist. In 1951 he went to Paris, and studied the piano with Walter Gieseking. In 1956 he moved to Paris for good. He formed the Blue Stars there, then Double Six Of Paris. In 1963 he formed the Swingle Singers, who specialized in singing classical works without lyrics. At least the record, "Bach's Greatest Hits" reached No. 15 in the US pop charts in the autumn of 1963. Baroque music, Mozart and madrigals were his field of activity from then on.

Leonard Cohen 1934 Canadian singer and songwriter. Leonard started with the country group Buckskin Boys in 1954, after which he made a name for himself as a poet and storyteller. During this period, several of his songs were recorded by Judy Collins and Tim Hardin. His appearance on stage at the Big Sur Festival 1967 made him known as a singer, his first album appeared in 1968, which included his composition "Suzanne". He had his greatest hit with "Lover Lover Lover" (12/74). Jennifer Warnes released an album in 1987 called FAMOUS BLUE RAINCOAT, a collection of Cohen songs, among them "First We Take Manhattan".

22nd

Dickey Lee 1941 US pop and country singer and songwriter. Real name Dick Lipscomb. He made his first records in 1957 for Sun Records. Hit: "Patches" (8/62 US 6). By the mid-1960s his pop hits had dried up. He turned to country music and was successful with "Rocky" (8/75 C&W 1); and he continued to appear in the C&W charts right into the 1980s.

Kevin Murphy 1943 US pianist with American Breed in the end phase. From them Ask Rufus developed, followed by Rufus.

Don Felder 1947 US guitarist and songwriter. In January 1974 he joined the Eagles formed in 1971, as their fifth man. Don had been previously with Flow, and had worked as a session musician and engineer on records by David Blue and Crosby & Nash. When Don joined together with the Eagles for the album ONE OF THESE NIGHTS, the group was transformed into one of the most influential of the 1970s. Felder is co-writer of the band's biggest hit, "Hotel California". In 1981 Don, like all the other members of the group, started a solo career.

Phil 'Animal' Taylor 1954 UK drummer with Motorhead from 1975 to 1983.

Henry Priestman 1955 UK keyboard player and guitarist with the Christians.

Deaths

Jaco Pastorius 1987 US bass player. Mortally wounded during a fight with a club manager. Born 1st December, 1951.

Hits of the Day

1946	"To Each His Own" Ink Spots US 1 week
1956	"Lay Down Your Arms" Anne Shelton UK 4 weeks
1959	"Sleep Walk" Santo & Johnny US 2 weeks
1961	"Reach For The Stars/Climb Ev'ry Mountain" Shirley Bassey UK 1 week
1963	"Blue Velvet" Bobby Vinton US 3 weeks
1968	"Harper Valley PTA" Jeannie C. Riley US 1 week
1974	"Kung Fu Fighting" Carl Douglas UK 3 weeks
1974	"Can't Get Enough Of Your Love" Barry White US 1 week
1985	"Money For Nothing" Dire Straits US 2 weeks

Birthdays

Leroy Holmes 1913 US orchestra leader, real first name Alvin. Working for record company MGM, he was responsible for recordings by Tommy Edwards and Connie Francis. Leroy won four Oscars including one for among others his biggest hit, "The High And The Mighty" (7/54 US 9).

Joni James 1930 US singer, real name Joan Carmella Babbo. She started as a dancer at the age of 12. During her time at high school, she worked as a model, and in the late 1940s toured as a dancer throughout Canada. Finally she made her first records in 1952. Hits, and million sellers: "Why Don't You Believe Me" (10/52 US 1; 3/53 UK 11), "Have You Heard" (1/53 US 4), and "Your Cheatin' Heart" (2/53 US 7). Further hits were "How Important Can it Be?" (2/55 US 2) and "You Are My Love" (10/55 US 6). Joni remained successful until the early 1960s.

Mike Patto 1942 UK singer and songwriter. Real name Mike McCarthy. He started with Mike Patto & The Breakaways in the early 1960s, sang with Bow Street Runners, Chicago Line Blues Band, and formed Timebox in 1966. Hit: "Beggin' " (7/68 UK 38). Timebox became Patto until 1973. This was followed by a short guest appearance with Spooky Tooth, and then in 1975, by his own band Boxer. On 4th March, 1979, Mike died after a long illness of cancer of the larynx.

David Coverdale 1951 UK singer and songwriter he joined Deep Purple in September 1973 as a replacement for Ian Gillan. Before that he was a sales assistant in a fashion boutique. David made his debut on the album BURN. The band were already arguing among themselves and split up in March 1976. David made a solo album entitled WHITESNAKE, which was released in May 1977. From January 1978 he called his own band Whitesnake after the album. Hits: "Fool For Your Loving" (4/80 UK 13; 10/89 US 37), "Here I Go Again" (11/82 UK 34; 6/87 US 1; 10/87 RE-UK 9) and "Is This Love" (6/87 UK 9; 10/87 US 2).

Debby Boone 1956 US singer, daughter of Pat Boone. Real first names Deborah Ann. In 1977 she had the hit of the year in the USA, "You Light Up My Life" (9/77 US 1), from the film of the same name. The record was at No. 1 for 10 weeks.

Joan Jett 1960 US guitarist, singer and songwriter for the 'all-female-hard-rock-band' Runaways formed in

1976, who recorded a few singles and albums, and split up in 1979. Joan went to London and made a few records there with former Sex Pistols members Paul Cook and Steve Jones. In July 1980 she was taken to hospital with a heart valve infection and pneumonia. When she was well again, she formed Joan Jett & The Blackhearts. Hits: "I Love Rock 'n' Roll" (2/82 US 1; 4/82 UK 4), "Crimson And Clover" (5/82 US 7), "I Hate Myself For Loving You" (6/88 US 8) and "Little Liar" (10/88 US 19). In 1987 she played the part of the leader of a rock 'n' roll band called Barbusters in the film *Light Of The Day*.

Deaths

Irving Berlin 1989 US composer. Died in his sleep at the age of 101. Born 11th May, 1888.

Hits of the Day

1966 "Distant Drums" Jim Reeves UK 5 weeks
1973 "Let's Get It On" Marvin Gaye US 1 week
1973 "Angel Fingers" Wizzard UK 1 week
1979 "Cars" Gary Numan UK 1 week
1984 "Missing You" John Waite US 1 week

23rd

Birthdays

John A. Lomax 1875 US folk musician, who set up the folk music archives in 1928, which accumulated 26,000 entries over the course of the years. He died 26th January, 1948.

John Coltrane 1926 US jazz saxophonist and composer. First his style was pure bop, but gradually he developed his own highly personal form of improvisation which led the way to free jazz. He died 17th July, 1967.

Ray Charles 1930 US singer, pianist, and songwriter. Surname Robinson. At the age of 5 he went partially blind, and at age 7 went completely blind. In 1947 he formed the Maxim Trio that played music in the style of the Nat King Cole Trio. Hit: "Confession Blues" (4/49 R&B 2). From the early 1950s he was successful as a soloist. He had his first hit in his own name with "Baby Let Me Hold Your Hand"

(2/51 R&B 5). While his influence has been far-reaching, he is the third most successful R&B artist after James Brown and Aretha Franklin. In the mid-1950s he became an R&B star with "I've Got A Woman" (1/55 R&B 1), "A Fool For You" (7/55 R&B 1) and "Drown In My Own Tears" (2/56 R&B 1). From 1957 he hit the pop charts with "What'd I Say" (7/59 US 6), "Georgia On My Mind" (9/60 US 1; 12/60 UK 24), "Hit The Road Jack" (9/61 US 1; UK 6), "I Can't Stop Loving You" (5/62 US & UK 1), "You Don't Know Me" (7/62 US 2; 9/62 UK 9), "Take These Chains From My Heart" (4/63 US 8; UK 5), "Busted" (9/63 US 4; UK 21) and "Crying Time" (12/65 US 6) among others. Whether it is country, R&B jazz or pop, Ray Charles is at home in any of these fields.

Les McCann 1935 US jazz pianist and singer. While his solo career flourished, he also worked with Eddie Harris, Roberta Flack, Jimmy Witherspoon, and Doldinger's Passport.

Ben E. King 1938 US singer and songwriter. Real name Benjamin Earl Nelson (sometimes the surname is given as Soloman). He started with the Four B's, was with the Moonglows briefly, and from 1956 with the Five Crowns. He became successful when the Five Crowns became the newly formed Drifters, and he became leadsinger. With him they had hits like "There Goes My Baby" (6/59 US 2) and "Save The Last Dance For Me" (9/60 US 1; UK 2). From May 1960 he started a solo career: "Spanish Harlem" (12/60 US 10), "Stand By Me" (5/61 US 4; UK 27; 10/86 RE-US 9) and "Supernatural Thing" (2/75 US 5).

Roy Buchanan 1939 US guitarist, singer and songwriter. In the 1950s, he was playing in Dale Hawkins' band. In the early 1960s he made a few solo singles and started as a session musician with Freddie Cannon and for Leiber/Stoller. In the early 1970s he was introduced as the 'best unknown guitarist in the world' on a US TV special. In 1972 the readers of 'Guitar Player' voted him the best new guitarist. In the same year a solo album by Roy appeared. Following that, he released a number of good blues-rock albums. But he hadn't the stuff of which superstars are made! When the Rolling Stones asked him to replace Brian Jones, he thanked them but declined, as it would be too much razzmatazz for his liking. He hanged himself in a 'drying out' cell on 14th August, 1988.

Tim Rose 1940 US singer and songwriter with Big Three, and as a soloist. Good albums but no hits.

Jeremy Steig 1942 US jazz flautist with a number of solo records, but who also played rock with Johnny Winter, among others.

Steve Boone 1943 US bassist with Lovin' Spoonful.

Julio Iglesias 1943 Spanish singer, who has sung on over 60 albums in five different languages, and sold more than 100 million records. That got him into the Guinness Book Of Records. Sometimes he is referred to as the Spanish Frank Sinatra. Among his biggest international hits are "Begin The Beguine" (10/81 UK 1), "Quiereme Mucho (Yours)" (3/82 UK 3), "To All The Girls I've Loved Before" (3/84 US 5; UK 17), with Willie Nelson, and "My Love" (8/88 UK 5).

Wallace & Walter Scott 1943 US leadsingers of the Whispers, formed in 1964. In 1964, they made their first records and began to be successful in 1969. Hits: "And The Beat Goes On" (2/80 US 19; UK 2), "It's A Love Thing" (2/81 US 28; UK 9) and "Rock Steady" (5/87 UK 38; US 7).

Paul Peterson 1945 US singer and actor. He was a Mouseketeer when he was a teenager. From 1958 to 1966 he played the part of Jeff Stone in the Donna Reed Show. In 1962 it was thought he could become a singer too, and he managed hit "My Dad" (11/62 US 6). The record was voted the worst record of the year 1962. After the Donna Reed Show had finished, the same happened to Paul's career. In the late 60s he made headlines mainly with his drug habits and fast cars. In the 70s he published a series of novels with a James Bond-like hero called Eric Safeman. In 1977 he published a book called, 'Walt, Mickey & Me'.

Duster Bennett 1946 UK blues singer, guitarist, harmonica player, and songwriter. He made a few very good albums, and died much too early on 25th March, 1976.

Jerry Corbetta 1947 US singer, pianist, and songwriter for Sugarloaf. Hits: "Green Eyed Lady" (8/70 US 3) and "Don't Call Us, We'll Call You" (12/74 US 9).

Neal Smith 1947 US drummer with Alice Cooper, Billion Dollar Babies, Plasmatics, and Buck Dharma.

Bruce Springsteen 1949 US singer, guitarist and songwriter. At age 14 he played in the band Castiles, which made records that were never released. He formed the group Child, which became Steel Mill, Dr. Zoom & The Sonic Boom, and finally, the Bruce Springsteen Band. In 1972 he secured a contract which guaranteed him 10 albums; the first GREETINGS FROM ASBURY PARK appeared in January, 1973. Immediately he was hailed as the 'new Bob Dylan', and other groups like Manfred Mann and the Hollies started to cover his compositions. By the beginning of the 1980s finally, Bruce had broken through into mainstream. Hits: "Hungry Heart" (11/80 US 5), "Dancing In The Dark" (5/84 US 2; UK 28; 1/85 RE-UK 4), "I'm On Fire" (2/85 US 6; UK 5), "Glory Days" (6/85 US 5; 8/85 UK 17), "I'm Going Down" (9/85 US 9), "My

Hometown" (12/85 US 6), "Brilliant Disguise" (10/87 US 5; UK 20), and "Tunnel Of Love" (12/87 US 9).

Deaths

Robbie McIntosh 1974 UK drummer with the Average White Band. He died of a drug overdose when he was age of 24.

Hits of the Day

1957	"That'll Be The Day" Crickets US 1 week
1957	"Honeycomb" Jimmie Rogers US 4 weeks
1965	"Make It Easy On Yourself" Walker Brothers UK 1 week
1967	"The Letter" Box Tops US 4 weeks
1972	"Baby Don't Get Hooked On Me" Mac Davis US 3 weeks
1978	"Dreadlock Holiday" 10 CC UK 1 week
1989	"Girl I'm Gonna Miss You" Milli Vanilli US 2 weeks

24th

Birthdays

Anthony Newley 1931 UK actor, composer, singer and film director. His acting career started as an apprentice before graduating to films in 1947: one of his most memorable performances was the Artful Dodger in *Oliver Twist*. After many other films, he played the part of and R 'n' R singer in *Idle On Parade* (1959), and wrote the theme song. Over the next three years he had a number hits: "I've Waited So Long" (5/59 UK 3), "Why" (1/60 UK 1), "Do You Mind" (3/60 UK 1), and "Strawberry Fair" (11/60 UK 3). His mannerisms and phrasing were later copied by the young David Bowie. Anthony continued to be successful as a songwriter, penning "Goldfinger" for the James Bond film of the same name.

Barbara Allbut 1940 US singer with the trio Angels, who began as starlets in the late 1950s. In 1960 they made their first records. Hits, "'Til" (10/61 US 14) and "My Boyfriend's Back" (8/63 US 1). After 1964 the hits ceased.

Phillis Allbut 1942 US singer, exactly two years to the day younger than her sister Barbara. She too was with the Angels.

Gerry Marsden 1942 UK singer, guitarist and songwriter with Gerry & The Pacemakers. He played with various Liverpool skiffle bands, and formed his own band in 1958, called the Mars Bars, and then finally formed the Pacemakers with his brother Freddie. In 1962 Brian Epstein put them under contract which at that time was a sure-fire recipe for success. Hits: "How Do You Do It?" (3/63 UK 1; 7/64 US 9), "I Like It" (5/63 UK 1; 9/64 US 17), "You'll Never Walk Alone" (10/63 UK 1), "I'm The One" (1/64 UK 2), "Don't Let The Sun Catch You Crying" (4/64 UK 6; US 4), and "Ferry Cross The Mersey" (12/64 UK 8; 2/65 US 6), the titlesong of the first film made with the whole group. In 1965 the Mersey sound lost much of its impact and Gerry disappeared into the relative obscurity of the cabaret circuit. In 1968 the group split up, and he started a solo career. After two unsuccessful singles, he was invited to appear as the male lead in the extremely successful West End musical *Charlie Girl*. At the time Joe Brown had been playing the part. Gerry played this role for five years, then became a presenter of a childrens' programme on ITV. He was often called on by English TV companies as an expert witness of the Merseybeat era. This led to him re-forming the Pacemakers in 1975 and going on tour, which was very lucrative, especially in the US. In 1979, after working as a solo artist for a while, he started off on another tour with the Pacemakers, a 'Sound Of The 60s Tour'. Over the course of the years "You'll Never Walk Alone" had become the anthem of Liverpool F.C. and indeed of the entire English football scene. In May 1985, 35 people died and many more were injured in a fire during a football match at the Bradford City ground in Yorkshire. The 'Bradford Disaster Fund' was set up to benefit victims and dependents: a group, calling themselves The Crowd, recorded "You'll Never Walk Alone" (6/85 UK 1) again, and donated all the royalties to the fund. Among those featured were Paul McCartney, Graham Gouldman, John Entwhistle, Kiki Dee, Tony Christie, and Gerry Marsden. Another further benefit record "Ferry Cross The Mersey" (5/89 UK 1) was released to help the victims of yet another football stadium disaster this time in the spring of 1989 – in Sheffield. Once again Gerry was one of the guiding lights and singers.

Linda McCartney 1942 US pianist, singer, songwriter and photographer. She married Beatle Paul McCartney on 12th March, 1969, she was the daughter of George Eastman, a lawyer. She played keyboards with Paul McCartney's group Wings. She also made solo records like "Seaside Woman" (6/77 US 59) as Suzy & The Red Stripes.

Kjell Asperud 1946 Norwegian singer, percussionist, and songwriter for Titanic. Hit, "Sultana" (9/71 UK 5).

Jerry Donahue 1946 UK guitarist, and singer with Fotheringhay, Heads, Hands & Feet, Sandy Denny, Fairport Convention, Joan Armatrading, Gerry Rafferty, Ralph McTell, and others.

M. C. Miker 'G' 1967 Rapper, who had his biggest hit with "Holiday Rap" (8/86 UK 6).

Deaths

Peter Bellamy 1991 UK folk singer and arranger. Born September 8th, 1944.

Hits of the Day

1964	"I'm Into Something Good" Herman's Hermits UK 2 weeks
1966	"Cherish" Association US 3 weeks
1977	"Best Of My Love" Emotions US 1 week (2nd time)
1983	"Tell Her About It" Billy Joel US 1 week
1983	"Karma Chameleon" Culture Club UK 6 weeks
1988	"Don't Worry Be Happy" Bobby McFerrin US 2 weeks
1988	"He Ain't Heavy, He's My Brother" Hollies UK 2 weeks

25th

Birthdays

John Locke 1943 US keyboard player and songwriter with Spirit, formed in 1967. After that he played with Simon Stoke's Black Whip Band, Nazareth and Randy California. In 1989 John appeared at the several re-unions of Spirit.

Onnie McIntyre 1943 UK guitarist, singer, and songwriter with the Average White Band formed in Scotland in 1972. Before that, he was with the group Dream Police.

Michael Douglas 1944 UK pianist with OMD in 1981.

Burleigh Drummond 1951 US percussionist, and singer with Ambrosia, who were successful from 1975 to 1982. Hits: "How Much I Feel" (9/78 US 3) and "Biggest Part Of Me" (4/80 US 3). He also played on the album TALES OF MYSTERY AND IMAGINATION by Alan Parsons.

John Fiddler 1947 UK singer, songwriter, and multi-instrumentalist with Medicine Head. Hits: "One And One Is One" (5/73 UK 3), and "Rising Sun" (8/73 UK 11). Later, John played with the British Lions, which comprised former members of Love Affair and Mott. In 1986 he made an unsuccessful comeback with Medicine Head. Finally he was with Box Of Frogs.

Deaths

John Bonham 1980 UK drummer with Led Zeppelin. He died of suffocation after choking on vomit in his sleep. Born 31st May, 1948.

Jimmy Wakely 1982 US country singer. Born 16th February, 1914.

Miles Davis 1991 US trumpeter, composer and arranger. Born May 25th, 1926.

Hits of the Day

1954 "Hey There" Rosemary Clooney US 6 weeks
1965 "Eve Of Destruction" Barry McGuire US 1 week
1968 "Those Were The Days" Mary Hopkin UK 6 weeks
1982 "Abracadabra" Steve Miller Band US 1 week (2nd time)

26th

Birthdays

George Gershwin 1898 US composer, songwriter, and pianist. Real name Jacob Gershvin. He had already written a hit "Swanee" in 1919. Al Jolson sang the song in the show 'Sinbad', and sold more than 2 million copies of the record. Hits for George: "Rhapsody In Blue" (10/24 US 3), which he recorded with Paul Whiteman's concert orchestra; he played piano himself on "Rhapsody In Blue" (9/27 US 7); and "An American In Paris" (6/29 US 7). He also wrote the opera *Porgy And Bess* (1935). He died 11th July, 1937.

Ted Weems 1901 US orchestra leader, trombonist and songwriter. Real name Wilfred Theodore Weymes. In 1922 he formed his first band, which was successful until 1948.

Hits: "Somebody Stole My Gal" (2/24 US 1), "Piccolo Pete" (9/29 US 2), "The Man From The South" (1/30 US 1), "Heartaches" (3/47 US 1) recorded in 1933, "I Wonder Who's Kissing Her Now" (10/47 US 3) recorded in 1939 with singer Perry Como, – his biggest hit, and "Mickey" (11/47 US 10). Ted died 6th May, 1963.

Marty Robbins 1925 US country singer, guitarist, and songwriter, who had his own radio show together with K-Bar Cowboys in the late 1940s. Real name Martin David Robinson. He had his own television show from 1951, which was called "Western Caravan". Marty also appeared in several films, had his own record label Robbins from 1958, and was an enthusiastic stock car racer. From 1952 he made solo records, was immediately successful in the C&W charts and was the ninth most successful country artist. After giving his ballads a slight Mexican flavour in the mid-1950s, he became successful in the pop charts. Hits: "I'll Go On Alone" (12/52 C&W 1), "A White Sport Coat (And A Pink Carnation)" (4/57 US 2), "El Paso" (11/59 US 1; 1/60 UK 19), "Don't Worry" (1/61 US 3) and "Devil Woman" (7/62 US 16; 9/62 UK 5). Robbins died 8th December, 1982.

Julie London 1926 US singer and actress. Real surname Peck. As a teenager she sang in West Coast bands. Her looks secured her a film contract in 1944. In 1955 she released her first album, JULIE IS HER NAME, on which she sang romantic love songs accompanied only by bass and guitar. This album included her biggest and only hit: "Cry Me A River" (11/55 US 9; 4/57 UK 22).

George Chambers 1931 US bassist and singer, who was already appearing in the 1950s with his brothers, Willie, Lester and Joe, as a gospel quartet. From the early 1960s they called themselves Chambers Brothers. Hit: "Time Has Come Today" (8/68 US 11).

Dick Heckstall-Smith 1934 UK saxophonist who played with Alexis Korner, Graham Bond, John Mayall and Colosseum. Dick also released records as a solo artist but became seriously ill in 1991 and ceased working.

Joe Bauer 1941 US drummer with Youngbloods.

Bryan Ferry 1945 UK singer, keyboard player, and songwriter for the band Roxy Music formed in 1971, and from 1973 as a soloist. Hits, with the band: "Virginia Plain" (8/72 UK 4), "Love Is The Drug" (10/75 UK 2; 12/75 US 30), "Dance Away" (4/79 UK 2), "Angel Eyes" (8/79 UK 4), "Over You" (5/80 UK 5), "Oh Yeah (On The Radio)" (8/80 UK 5), and "Jealous Guy" (2/81 UK 1), and as a soloist: "A Hard Rain's Gonna Fall" (9/73 UK 10), "Let's Stick Together" (6/76 UK 4; 10/88 RE-UK 12), "Extended Play" (8/76 UK 7), "This Is Tomorrow" (2/77 UK 9) and "Slave To Love" (5/85 UK 10).

Lynn Anderson 1947 US country singer. After she had been voted 'California Horseshoe Queen' in 1966, her success as a country singer commenced. From 1968 she appeared regularly in the *Lawrence Welk Show*. She has had over 60 hits in the country charts since 1966. She reached No. 1 five times, with her first No. 1 being her biggest pop hit and million seller, "Rose Garden" (11/70 US 3; 2/71 UK 3). Lynn is the daughter of Liz Anderson, who was successful as a songwriter and also appeared in the C&W charts a few months before Lynn Anderson became successful.

Olivia Newton-John 1948 Australian singer, born in Great Britain, and who emigrated with her parents at the age of 5. In 1964 she won a youth competition and the prize was a trip to London. She cut a single record there in May 1966, which was a flop. In September of the same year, she met Bruce Welch of the Shadows, who invited her to play *Cinderella* with Cliff Richard and the Shadows at the London Palladium. Instead, she flew home for Christmas. A little later, she returned and moved in with Bruce Welch in London. In 1970 she became a member of the group Tomorrow, which released two unsuccessful singles and split up again. Finally it was Cliff Richard who helped her on her way to stardom. In January, 1971, a single was released: the B-side was "Don't Move Away", a duet with Cliff. After that, she toured Europe with him. In April 1971 she had her own first hit with "If Not For You" (3/71 UK 7; 5/71 US 25). Among her other hits were million sellers like "Let Me Be There" (11/73 US 6), "If You Love Me (Let Me Know)" (4/74 US 5), "I Honestly Love You" (8/74 US 1; 11/74 UK 22), "Have You Never Been Mellow" (1/75 US 1), "Please Mr. Please" (6/75 US 3), "Hopelessly Devoted To You" (7/78 US 3; 11/78 UK 2), "A Little More Love" (11/78 US 3; UK 4), "Magic" (5/80 US 1; 8/80 UK 32), and "Physical" (10/81 US 1; UK 7). Among her other hits were "Xanadu" (6/80 UK 1; 8/80 US 8), with ELO; "You're The One I Want" (4/78 US & UK 1) and "Summer Nights" (8/78 US 5; UK 1) with John Travolta, her co-star in the movie *Grease*; and in addition, there were hits with Andy Gibb, Cliff Richard, and David Foster.

Stuart Tosh 1951 UK drummer with Pilot, Alan Parsons Project, and from 1977 with 10 CC. In addition, he has recorded with Roger Daltrey, Graham Gouldman and Eric Stewart.

Craig Chaquico 1954 US guitarist and songwriter with Jefferson Starship and their successor, Starship.

Tracey Thorne 1962 UK singer and songwriter. Tracey started with the Marine Girls, with whom she released two albums. In 1982 she made a solo album. In 1984 she formed the duo Everything But The Girl with Ben Watt. Greatest hit, "I Don't Want To Talk About It" (7/88 UK 3).

Deaths

Bessie Smith 1937 US blues singer. She died after a car accident. Born 15th April, 1894.

Hits of the Day

1942	"He Wears A Pair Of Silver Wings" Kay Kyser US 4 weeks
1953	"You You You" Ames Brothers US 8 weeks
1958	"Carolina Moon/Stupid Cupid" Connie Francis UK 6 weeks
1960	"My Heart Has A Mind Of Its Own" Connie Francis US 2 weeks
1964	"Oh, Pretty Woman" Roy Orbison US 3 weeks
1987	"Didn't We Almost Have It All" Whitney Houston US 2 weeks

27th

Birthdays

Don Nix 1941 US singer, saxophonist, guitarist, songwriter and producer. He formed the Instrumentals with schoolfriends Duck Dunn and Steve Cropper in the late 1950s. With these same musicians and a few more, who all worked as a session musicians in Memphis, the Mar-Keys came into being in 1959. Hit: "Last Night" (7/61 US 3). Cropper and Dunn became members of Booker T. & The MGs. Don became a producer and partner of Leon Russell. Over the years he has produced artists like Lonnie Mack, John Mayall, Jeff Beck, Delaney & Bonnie, and the British band Skin Alley. He himself released albums from time to time, which were good but too eclectic. As a songwriter he was responsible for the classic "Goin' Down", among others.

Alvin Stardust 1942 UK singer. Real name, Bernard William Jewry. In many ways his career was similar to that of Gary Glitter; Stardust, too, had changed his name and went through several ups and downs. In the early 1960s he recorded as Shane Fenton & The Fentones. Major hits: "I'm A Moody Guy" (10/61 UK 22) and "Cindy's Birthday" (7/62 UK 19). The drummer of the Fentones was Bobby Elliott who was to become a member of the Hollies later on. Among the many artists who were suddenly made unfashionable by the Beatles, was Shane Fenton. In 1965 he became a manager and worked with artists like the Hollies and Lulu. From 1973 he changed his name to

Alvin Stardust. Hits: "My Coo-Ca-Choo" (11/73 UK 2), "Jealous Mind" (2/74 UK 1), "Pretend" (9/81 UK 4), "I Feel Like Buddy Holly" (5/84 UK 7) and "I Won't Run Away" (10/87 UK 7).

Randy Bachman 1943 Canadian guitarist, singer and songwriter who started with Allan & The Silvertones in the early 1960s. This band became the Reflections, then Chad Allen & The Expressions and, finally, Guess Who in 1963. Hits: "These Eyes" (4/69 US 6), "Laughing" (7/69 US 10) and "American Woman/No Sugar Tonight" (3/70 US 1; 5/70 UK 19). In July 1970 Randy left the band to form Brave Belt with his old pal Chad Allen. In 1972 he formed Bachman-Turner Overdrive with his brothers Tim and Robby, and C. F. Turner. Hits: "You Ain't Seen Nothing Yet" (9/74 US 1; 11/74 UK 2) and "Roll On Down The Highway" (1/75 US 14; UK 22). In April 1977 Randy left, as they abbreviated their name to BTO, and started a solo career. When that didn't work, he joined the group Iron Horse in May 1979. After two unsuccessful albums, the band split up in the middle of 1980. In September 1984 Randy reformed BTO with his brother Tim and C. F. Turner. They didn't have any hits, but the trio toured successfully in North America.

Barbara Dickson 1947 UK singer and songwriter. She started as a folksinger and sang in a trio with Rab Noakes and Archie Fisher, who each made their first solo albums in the early 1970s – Barbara's being FROM THE BEGGER'S MANTLE. In the show *John, Paul, George, Ringo & Bert* she accompanied herself on the piano, which had its premiere in Liverpool, and then in London: the critics all agreed that she was one of the highlights. From 1976, now under contract with RSO, she was successful as a solo artist with "Answer Me" (1/76 UK 9) and "January, February" (3/80 UK 11). She also had a hit with "I Know Him So Well" (1/85 UK 1) from the musical *Chess*, duetting with Elaine Paige.

Meatloaf 1947 US singer, real name Marvin Lee Aday. He has been in the record business since the 1970s. He played the part of Eddie in the film *The Rocky Horror Picture Show*. Hits: "Two Out Of Three Ain't Bad" (3/78 US 11; 8/78 UK 32), "You Took The Words Right Out Of My Mouth" (5/78 UK 33; 1/79 US 39) and "Dead Ringer For Love" (11/81 UK 5), a duet with Cher.

Greg Ham 1953 Australian saxophonist, keyboard player and flautist with Men At Work, formed in 1979.

Robbie Shakespeare 1953 Jamaican bassist and songwriter. Extremely successful with Sly Dunbar as studio musician. The two released records as the duo Sly & Robbie. Hit: "Boops (Here To Go)" (3/87 UK 12).

Shaun Cassidy 1958 US singer and actor, half-brother of David Cassidy and son of thespian couple Jack Cassidy and Shirley Jones. Like David, Shaun also became known through a TV series which was aimed mainly at a young audience. He played the part of Joe Hardy in *The Hardy Boys* between 1977 and 1979. During this period he also had his biggest hits as a singer: "That's Rock 'n' Roll" (7/77 US 3), "Da Do Ron Ron" (5/77 US 1) and "Hey Deanie" (11/77 US 7). After that, he appeared in *Breaking Away* for two years; when that finished in 1981, he was too old, at 23, for the youth market. In 1987 he played a part in the US soap opera *General Hospital*, and tried a comeback as a singer in 1989.

Deaths

Rory Storm 1972 UK singer with his own band Hurricanes, whose claim to fame was in having had Ringo Starr as a drummer. Storm committed suicide. Real name Alan Caldwell.

Charlie Monroe 1975 US country musician. He died of cancer. Born 4th July, 1903.

Gracie Fields 1979 UK singer. Born 9th January, 1898.

Jimmy McCulloch 1979 UK guitarist. Born 4th June, 1952.

Hits of the Day

1941	"Blue Champagne" Jimmy Dorsey US 1 week
1952	"I Went To Your Wedding" Patti Page US 10 weeks
1975	"I'm Sorry" John Denver US 1 week
1980	"Don't Stand So Close To Me" Police UK 4 weeks

28th

Birthdays

Naphtali Kupferberg 1928 US singer with the Underground band Fugs and as a solo artist.

Brigitte Bardot 1934 French actress, sex symbol of the 1950s and 1960s. As a singer she was successful in France with the Serge Gainsbourg composition "Harley Davidson" (1967), and "Bonnie & Clyde" (1968), a duet with Serge.

Koko Taylor 1935 US blues singer. Real name Cora Walton. She made her first records with J. B. Lenoir in

1963. She had her biggest hit with "Wang Bang Doodle" (4/66 R&B 4). In 1987 she recorded with Blues Machine.

Nick St. Nicholas 1943 Born Klaus Kassbaum in Hamburg, Germany. He joined the Canadian group Steppenwolf as bassist, after the group had passed its peak.

Helen Shapiro 1946 UK singer and actress. While still at school she was called a 'foghorn' because of her masculine voice. She was still at school when she had her first hit with "Don't Treat Me Like A Child" (3/61 UK 3), however her dress-sense belied her tender years. Further hits: "You Don't Know" (6/61 UK 1), "Walking Back To Happiness" (9/61 UK 1), "Tell Me What He Said" (2/62 UK 2), and "Little Miss Lonely" (7/62 UK 8). After 1964 she disappeared from the charts. As an actress she appeared in *It's Trad, Dad!* and *Play It Cool* (both in 1962). Later she appeared as Nancy in a revival of Lionel Bart's musical *Oliver!*, and became more of a jazz singer. In 1987 she recorded some of Johnny Mercer's songs.

Peter Hope-Evans 1947 UK singer and harmonica player in a duo with John Fiddler as Medicine Head. For hits, see 25th September. Peter also played with Family, Roger Chapman, Pete Townshend, Linda Lewis and Johnny G.

Finbar Furey 1948 Irish folk musician, who formed a duo with brother Eddie, but it was augmented by other family members from time to time.

Jimmy Bo Horne 1949 US disco singer. Hit: "Dance Across The Floor" (4/78 US 38), which was written and produced by Harry 'K.C.' Casey, was his only hit.

Paul Burgess 1950 UK drummer, with 10 CC, Eric Stewart, Graham Gouldman, Gilbert O'Sullivan, Corey Hart, Camel and Colour Field.

Andy Ward 1952 UK drummer with Camel, John's Children, Brew and Philip Goodhand-Tait's Band.

Jim Diamond 1953 UK singer and songwriter who became a clubsinger at 16, and toured especially the German Air Bases with the band Gully Foyle in the early 1970s. In 1975 he formed Bandit, who released their first album in 1977. As punk was in vogue, Bandit were out of kilter and they split up. Jim worked with Alexis Korner and then, in the late 1970s, formed a band in L.A. with Carmine Appice and Earl Slick. Before they even recorded, the band split up because of financial difficulties. Jim returned to Great Britain, produced Zoot Money and joined up with Tony Hymas, former pianist with Jeff Beck and Jack Bruce, to form Ph. D. They had a hit with "I Won't Let You Down" (4/82 UK 3); just as he was about to be successful, he contracted hepatitis and couldn't promote the album "Is

It Safe?". In 1984 Jim started a solo career and had hits with "I Should Have Known Better" (11/84 UK 1), and "Hi Ho Silver" (2/86 UK 5).

Annabel Lamb 1955 UK singer, pianist and songwriter. Hit: "Riders On The Storm" (8/83 UK 27).

Jennifer Rush 1960 US singer and songwriter who started her career under her real name, Heidi Stern. From 1983 she sang as Jennifer Rush. Hits: "Ring Of Ice" (12/85 UK 14), "The Power Of Love" (7/85 UK 1), "Destiny" (9/85), "I Come Undone" (2/87) and "Flames Of Paradise" (5/87 US 36), a duet with Elton John.

Hits of the Day

1961 "Johnny Remember Me" John Leyton UK 1 week (2nd time)
1968 "Hey Jude" Beatles US 9 weeks
1974 "Rock Me Gently" Andy Kim US 1 week

29th

Birthdays

Gene Autry 1907 US country singer, songwriter and actor. Before becoming a saxophonist with the Fields Brothers Madison Show, he worked as a cowboy and telegraph operator for the Frisco Railroad. Finally he decided to play guitar, because he could accompany himself singing better than with a saxophone. In 1929/30 Gene sang on a radio station in Tulsa, and shortly afterwards, he made his first records. In 1934 he appeared in his first film, *Old Santa Fe*. More than 90 films were to follow. From 1940 he broadcasted on the radio programme 'Melody Ranch'. After his military service, between September 1945 and 1956, he continued broadcasting on with radio and owned several record companies and the California Angels Baseball-Team. In 1969 he was entered in the Country Music Hall Of Fame. Gene had his first million seller in 1935 with "That Silver-Haired Daddy Of Mine" (8/35 US 7), recorded in 1931 with Jimmy Long. He wrote his own second million seller, "Here Comes Santa Claus (Down Santa Claus Lane)" (12/47 US 9; 12/48 RE-US 8; 1/50 RE-US 24). His biggest hit was "Rudolph, The Red-Nosed Reindeer" (12/49 US 1; 12/50 RE-US 3; 12/51 RE-US 16; 12/52 RE-US 12; 12/53 RE-US 26), which was followed by another seasonal million seller, "Frosty The Snowman" (12/50 US 7; 12/52 RE-US 23).

Jerry Lee Lewis 1935 US singer, pianist and song-writer, who was discovered by and signed to the small Sun record company. In 1956 Jerry's father sold 33 dozen eggs, to make the journey from Ferriday, Louisiana to Memphis. They were determined to audition for Sam Phillips of Sun Records. When they got there, he had just left for Nashville: Jerry demonstrated what a stubborn kind of fellow he could be: when they wouldn't let him in, he said that he would sit on the doorstep until they let him to cut his demo tape. Finally someone let him in, the recordings were made, and they told him to come back in a month. When Jerry came back a month later, Sam Phillips was there, and re-corded "Whole Lotta Shakin' Goin' On" (6/57 US 3; 9/57 UK 8). Shortly after the record had been released, it was banned by most radio stations, because the lyrics were too vulgar. This did not prevent it from becoming a hit. His stubbornness and a touch of vulgarity has seemed to course through his career. His personal life has always attracted criticism: he married when he was sixteen, married again when he was seventeen and then married his thirteen-year-old cousin in December 1957. The latter caused a tour of the UK to be cancelled. He was not divorced from this cousin until February 1970. She filed the divorce because she said that in thirteen years of marriage to Jerry Lee Lewis, she had spent only three whole nights alone with him. Further hits: "Great Balls Of Fire" (11/57 US 2; UK 1), "Breathless" (3/58 US 7; UK 8) and "What'd I Say" (4/61 US 30; UK 10). In the mid-1960s, Jerry's career as a rock artist went into a decline. However, he continued to be successful in the country charts with most of his R 'n' R titles. 'The Killer' had over 60 hits to 1986, six of them at No. 1.

Jean-Luc Ponty 1942 French violinist, pianist, and composer who played with a symphony orchestra before turning to jazz in the late 1950s. He played with Frank Zappa, George Duke, John McLaughlin, and as a solo artist.

Tommy Boyce 1944 US songwriter and singer, who worked in a duo with Bobby Hart. They wrote a number of hits for others and even had a hit themselves once with "I Wonder What She's Doing Tonight" (12/67 US 8). In 1975 Tommy and Bobby toured with two Ex-Monkees, Davy Jones and Mickey Dolenz.

Timmy Donald 1946 UK drummer with White Trash, Quiver, Cody, and Blue.

Nick Taylor 1946 US guitarist and singer with Bloodrock.

Mark Farner 1948 US singer and songwriter with Grand Funk Railroad, formed in 1968. Mark was first with Terry Knight & The Pack with another band member, drummer Don Brewer. Terry became the manager and producer of Grand Funk until he was thrown out in March 1972. Then success came. Hits: "We're An American

Band" (7/73 US 1), "The Loco-Motion" (3/74 US 1), "Some Kind Of Wonderful" (12/74 US 3) and "Bad Time" (4/75 US 4). In 1976 the band split up, and was re-formed in 1981 with Mark, but they could no longer reach the charts. In 1977 Mark released a solo album.

Mike Pinera 1948 US guitarist with Blues Image, and from 1970 with Iron Butterfly replacing Erik Braun, then with Cactus, Ramatam, Thee Image, Alice Cooper, and as a solo artist.

Mari Wilson 1957 UK singer, who fulfilled a wish for herself with "Just What I Always Wanted" (9/82 UK 8).

Matt and Luke Goss 1968 UK twins, singers, and drummer and songwriter respectively of the group Bros. In 1984 they started as Gloss. In addition to the twins, there was bassist Craig Logan. The trio signed a recording contract in April 1987, and released their first single "I Owe You Nothing" (6/88 UK 1) in August of the same year, but it did not become a hit until it was re-issued after the success of "When Will I Be Famous" (1/88 UK 2), and "Drop The Boy" (3/88 UK 2). After that, they became pinups of the youth market with hits like "Cat Among The Pigeons" (12/88 UK 2), "Too Much" (7/89 UK 2), "Chocolate Box" (10/89 UK 9) and "Sister" (12/89 UK 10).

Hits of the Day

1958	"It's All In The Game" Tommy Edwards US 6 weeks
1960	"Tell Laura I Love Her" Ricky Valance UK 3 weeks
1973	"We're An American Band" Grand Funk Railroad US 1 week
1973	"Eye Level" Simon Park Orchestra UK 4 weeks
1979	"Message In A Bottle" Police UK 3 weeks
1984	"Let's Go Crazy" Prince US 2 weeks

30th

Birthdays

Jill Corey 1935 US singer. Real name Norma Jean Speranza. Her biggest of five hits was "Love Me To Pieces" (8/57 US 11), the theme tune of the CBS TV show *Studio 1 Summer Theater*.

Z. Z. Hill 1935 US blues singer and songwriter. Real first name Arzel. In 1963 he cut his first records and recorded for his brother's label, Hill, in 1970. He had 16 hits in the R&B charts between 1964 and 1984, which included "Don't Make Me Pay For His Mistakes" (2/71 R&B 17) and "Love Is So Good When You're Stealing It" (6/77 R&B 15). Hill died 27th April, 1984.

Johnny Mathis 1935 US singer. He started his education as an opera singer in San Francisco when he was 13. In 1956 he went to New York and has sold almost as many albums as Elvis Presley and Frank Sinatra. Hits singles: "It's Not For me To Say" (4/57 US 5), "Chances Are" (9/57 US 1), "A Certain Smile" (6/58 US 14; 9/58 UK 4), "Gina" (9/62 US 6), "When A Child Is Born" (11/76 UK 1), and "Too Much, Too Little, Too Late" (3/78 UK 3; US 1), with Deniece Williams. He also recorded duets with Gladys Knight and Dionne Warwick.

Gus Dudgeon 1942 UK producer, who produced artists like Elton John, Kiki Dee, the Strawbs, John Kongos, Magna Carta, Audience, Tea & Symphony, Chris Rea, Elkie Brooks, and Joan Armatrading; sometimes he was featured as a percussionist or backing singer on their records.

Frankie Lymon 1942 US singer and songwriter. The group Premiers, formed in 1955 became Frankie Lymon & The Teenagers shortly after. Frankie was just 13 years old at the time. Hits: "Why Do Fools Fall In Love" (2/56 US 6; 6/56 UK 1), "I Want You To Be My Girl" (4/56 US 13), I'm Not A Juvenile Delinquent" (3/57 UK 12) and "Baby Baby" (4/57 UK 4). In 1957 he left the group and tried, unsuccessfully, as a solo artist. Drug problems cost him his life. He died 28th February, 1968.

Dewey Martin 1942 US singer, drummer and songwriter. First he was a folk singer, then with Dillards, and finally as a drummer with Buffalo Springfield. After the band split up, he formed Dewey Martin's Medicine Ball. It was unsuccessful.

Marilyn McCoo 1943 US singer with Fifth Dimension, formed in 1966. Hits: "Up Up And Away" (6/67 US 7), "Stoned Soul Picnic" (6/68 US 3), "Aquarius/Let The Sunshine In" (3/69 US 1; UK 11), "Wedding Bell Blues" (9/69 US 1; 1/70 UK 16), "One Less Bell To Answer" (10/70 US 2), and "(Last Night) I Didn't Get Top Sleep At All" (4/72 US 8), (apart from "Up Up And Away", all were million sellers). Marilyn married Billy Davis Jr. another member of fifth Dimension in 1969. They left the group in 1976 and carried on as a duo. Hit, and million seller: "You Don't Have To be A Star (To Be In My Show)" (9/76 US 1; 3/77 UK 7). From the beginning of the 1980s the two recorded as solo artists. Marilyn became the hostess of the TV show *Solid Gold*.

Mike Harrison 1945 UK singer, pianist, and songwriter. He started with the V.I.Ps which became Art, and finally formed Spooky Tooth in 1967, with whom he stayed until February 1974. After that, he started a solo career and became a member of Chris Stainton's band.

Sylvia Peterson 1946 US singer with the Chiffons.

Marc Bolan 1947 UK singer, songwriter and guitarist. Real name Marc Feld. In November 1965 he changed his stage name from Toby Tyler to Marc Bolan, and released "The Wizard". In 1966 further singles appeared which also flopped. In May 1967 he became a member of John's Children, in September of the same year he formed the acoustic duo Tyrannosaurus Rex, later abbreviated to T. Rex. Hits: "Debora" (5/68 UK 34; 4/72 RE-UK 7), "Ride A White Swan" (10/70 UK 2), "Hot Love" (2/71 UK 1) "Get It On" (7/71 UK 1; 1/72 US 10), "Jeepster" (11/71 UK 2), "Telegram Sam" (1/72 UK 1), "Metal Guru" (5/72 UK 1), "Children Of The Revolution" (9/72 UK 2), "Solid Gold Easy Action" (12/72 UK 2), "20th Century Boy" (3/73 UK 3), and "The Groover" (6/73 UK 4). After that his career waned, just as Marc was going to launch a comeback his girlfriend Gloria Jones crashed her small black Mini-Cooper into a tree, and Marc died 16th September, 1977. Like many other deceased rock stars, Marc Bolan's music enjoyed a considerable revival some ten years after his death.

Deborah Allen 1953 US singer and songwriter. Born Deborah Lynn Thurmond. After writing hits for Sheena Easton, Tanya Tucker, and others, she tried for herself. Her first hit was "Baby I Lied" (10/83 US 26).

Basia 1956 Polish singer, surname Trzetrzelewska. Her musical career began when she was sixteen. While she was touring the USA, she decided to stay there, and then she went to live in Britain. She became a singer with Matt Bianco. Hits: "Get Out Of Your Lazy Bed" (2/84 UK 15) and "Yeh Yeh" (10/85 UK 7). In 1986 she decided to carry on working under her first name only.

Dave Betts 1957 Canadian drummer with Honeymoon Suite.

Hits of the Day

1965 "Tears" Ken Dodd UK 5 weeks
1972 "How Can I Be Sure" David Cassidy UK 2 weeks
1978 "Summer Nights" John Travolta & Olivia Newton-John UK 7 weeks
1978 "Kiss You All Over" Exile US 4 weeks

Deaths

Mary Ford 1977 US singer who was successful with her husband of the time as Les Paul & Mary Ford. She died of diabetes. Born 7th July, 1928.

Miscellany

1955 After only 3 films he became the idol of the young – James Dean. He died in a car crash. Born 8th February, 1931.

October

1st

Birthdays

Richard Harris 1930 Irish actor and singer. He studied music and drama in London. In 1956 he appeared on stage for the first time, and in 1958 he appeared in his first film. Among his most successful films were *The Guns Of Navarone* (1961), *Mutiny On The Bounty*, with Marlon Brando (1962), *The Bible* in which he played Cain (1966), *Camelot* – as King Arthur (1967) and *The Wildgeese*, with Richard Burton (1978). As a singer he had only one success with "McArthur Park" (5/68 US 2; 7/72 RE-UK 38).

Geoff Stephens 1934 UK singer and songwriter. He started his career as a sketch writer for the BBC. After that, he wrote hits for the Applejacks, ("Tell Me When"), and for Dave Berry ("The Crying Game"). He discovered and produced Donovan, and finally turned a collection of studio musicians into the New Vaudeville Band, who made records in the style of the 30s. Hits: "Winchester Cathedral" (9/66 UK 4; US 1), "Peek-A-Boo" (1/67 UK 7) and "Finchley Central" (5/67 UK 11).

Julie Andrews 1935 UK singer and actress. Real name Julia Elizabeth Wells. She first appeared onstage in the London show *Starlight Roof* in 1947. In the late 1940s/early 1950s she broadcasted on a regular radio programme called 'Educating Archie'. Her very English accent made her ideal for casting in musicals with British parts. She played the part of Polly Brown in the New York production of *The Boy Friend*. In 1956, again in New York, she was Eliza in the stage production of *My Fair Lady*. When *My Fair Lady* was filmed in 1964, everyone thought Julie would get the leading part, but it went to Audrey Hepburn instead, whose singing parts were taken by Marni Nixon. In the same year, Julie took the lead part in Walt Disney's production of *Mary Poppins*, and received an Oscar as Best Actress. Later she also received an Emmy award. In the 1970s she appeared in Las Vegas. In 1981, under the influence of her second husband Blake Edwards who strove to change her image, she appeared in the nude in the film *S.O.B.* In the same year she starred in *Victor Victoria*. In 1963 she made an album of country songs LOVE ME TENDER, the title track was a duet with Johnny Cash.

Jerry Martini 1943 US saxophonist with Sly & The Family Stone. As a session musician he worked with Mike Bloomfield, Rubicon, David Werner and Two Tons.

Scott McKenzie 1944 US singer and songwriter. In the early 60s he started with the group Smoothies, which was led by John Phillips, later of the Mamas & Papas. The group developed into the Journeymen, who split up after three albums. After John had established himself as a songwriter, Scott recorded the John's composition "San Francisco (Be Sure To Wear Some Flowers In Your Hair)" (5/67 US 4; 7/67 UK 1), which became an international hit. He had a further hit with "Like An Old Time Movie" (10/67 US 24; UK 50), then he disappeared until 1988 when he co-wrote "Kokomo" for the Beach Boys with John Phillips.

Barbara Parritt 1944 US singer with the Toys.

Donny Hathaway 1945 US singer, keyboard player, songwriter and producer. He worked with the Impressions, Carla Thomas, Jerry Butler, the Staple Singers and Roberta Flack, with whom he once went to art school, and later sang several duets: "Where Is The Love" (6/72 US 5; 8/72 UK 29), "The Closer I Get To You" (2/78 US 2; 5/79 UK 42) and "Back Together Again" (5/80 UK 3). He died after jumping out of a fifteenth floor window of the New York Essex House Hotel, on 13th January, 1979. His daughter, Lalah Hathaway is currently one of the brightest prospects.

Rob Davies 1947 UK guitarist with Mud.

Martin Turner 1947 UK bassist and songwriter for Wishbone Ash.

Cub Koda 1948 US guitarist, leadsinger and song-writer. Real first names Michael John. In 1969 he formed the trio The Station, which later became Brownsville Station. Hit, and only million seller: "Smokin' In The Boys Room" (10/73 US 3; 4/74 UK 27). In the middle of 1979 the band split up, Koda carried on as a solo artist and did session work on an album by Blackfoot.

Mariska Veres 1948 Dutch singer with Shocking Blue. Hit: "Venus" (12/69 US 1; UK 8).

Howard Hewett 1955 US singer with the group Shalamar formed in 1977. When the band was formed, it consisted of various sessions singers, who sang a medley of Motown hits under the title 'Uptown Festival' (3/77 US 25; 5/77 UK 30) for producers David Griffey and Simon Soussan. An album of the same name reached No. 8 in the US album charts. In 1978 the two producers set up the record label Solar (Sound Of Los Angeles Records), and formed Shalamar. From the TV programme 'Soul Train' two dancers, Jody Watley and Jeffrey Daniels were recruited and Gerald Brown was engaged as leadsinger. After the first album had been recorded, Gerald was replaced by Howard Hewett in January 1979. Hits: the million seller, "The Second Time Around" (12/79 US 8), "I Can Make You Feel So Good" (3/82 UK 7), "A Night To Remember" (6/82 UK 5), "There It Is" (9/82 UK 5), "Dead Giveaway" (6/83 US 22; UK 8), and "Dancing In The Sheets" (3/84 US 17). In 1984 Watley and Daniels were replaced by Delisa Davis and Micki Free.

Andy Walton 1957 UK drummer with Kenny.

Martin Cooper 1958 UK saxophonist with OMD.

Deaths

Al Jackson 1975 US drummer with Booker T. & The MGs. He was shot to death by burglars in his house in Memphis. Born 27th November, 1935.

Freddy Martin 1983 US saxophonist and bandleader. Born 9th December, 1906.

Hits of the Day

1977 "Star Wars Title Theme" Meco US 2 weeks
1983 "Total Eclipse Of The Heart" Bonnie Tyler US 4 weeks

2nd

Birthdays

Jimmy Torres 1939 US lead guitarist with the String-A-Longs. Hit: "Wheels" (1/61 US 3; UK 8).

Lolly Vegas 1939 US guitarist, singer and songwriter for Redbone, the first American Indian group to be successful in the States; they were formed in 1968. Hits: "Witch Queen Of New Orleans" (9/71 UK 2; 11/71 US 21) and the million seller, "Come And Get Your Love" (1/74 US 5). Pat Vegas, Lolly's brother also played in the band. The pair wrote hits for P. J. Proby Bobbie Gentry, Aretha Franklin and the Righteous Brothers.

Ronald Meagher 1941 US guitarist with Beau Brummels.

Don McLean 1945 US singer and songwriter. In 1971 he turned up out of nowhere with "American Pie" (11/71 US 1; 1/72 UK 2). It tells the story of US pop music in 8 and 1/2 minutes, and Don arrived at the conclusion that after Buddy Holly's death nothing noteworthy was written again. Further hits: "Vincent" (3/72 US 12; 5/72 UK 1), which was about painter Vincent Van Gogh and "Crying" (5/80 UK 1; 1/81 US 5). The song "Killing Me Softly With His Song", a hit for Roberta Flack in spring 1973, is about Don McLean. In the meantime Don has turned more to country music.

Richard Hell 1949 US bassist, singer, and songwriter with the Neonboys formed in 1971. The nucleus of this group became Television in 1973. In 1975 Richard left and formed the Heartbreakers in London. In 1976 he left this group too, and formed the Voidoids. Richard released two solo albums, appeared in the film *Smithereens* in 1982, withdrew from the music business and worked as a journalist. His real last name is Meyers.

Michael Rutherford 1950 UK bassist, songwriter and singer with the band Genesis formed in 1966. Before that he played with the Anons. In 1979 and 1982 Mike released solo records in addition to his work with the group. From 1985, beside his work with Genesis, he started the band Mike & The Mechanics with Paul Carrack as leadsinger. Hits: "Silent Running" (11/85 US 6; 2/86 UK 21), "All I Need Is A Miracle" (3/86 US 5), and "Living Years" (1/89 US 1; UK 2).

Sting 1951 UK bassist, singer, songwriter and pianist with Police. Real name Gordon Sumner. His nickname Sting came from his liking for black and yellow striped pullovers and dates back to his career in the early 1970s.

In 1974 he became a member of Last Exit, which released an unsuccessful single "Whispering Voices" in 1975. Sting was bassist and leadsinger. In 1977 Police were formed and paid to have their first single "Fall Out" produced and released in February of the same year. It cost them £150. At the same time the group were backing US singer Cherry Vanilla on her UK tour. In October 1977 Police went to Munich to help Eberhard Schoener record his album VIDEO FLASHBACK. In January 1978 they started recording their own first album. In February 1978 the group appeared on a TV commercial for Wrigley's Chewing Gum, and had to dye their hair blond. As the new-wave/punk movement was at its height, US audiences thought that all groups had to have peroxide-blond hair and so Police fitted the bill. In April 1978 "Roxanne" (2/79 US 32; 4/79 UK 12) was released; initially, it failed and only became a hit later on. As the group had committed to work with Eberhard Schoener and his Laser Theatre in West Germany, they could not promote "Roxanne" properly. In addition, Sting had been offered the part of Ace in the film *Quadrophenia*. In 1979 Police started a run of hits: "Can't Stand Losing You" (7/79 UK 2), "Message In A Bottle" (9/79 UK 1), "Walking On The Moon" (12/79 UK 1), "Don't Stand So Close To Me" (9/80 UK 1; 2/81 US 10), "De Do Do Do, De Da Da Da" (10/80 US 10; 12/80 UK 5), "Every Little Thing She Does Is Magic" (9/81 UK 1; US 3), "Every Breath You Take" (5/83 UK & US 1), "King Of Pain" (8/83 US 3; 1/84 UK 17), and "Wrapped Around Your Finger" (7/83 UK 7; 1/84 US 8). While working with Police, Sting made solo records. Hits: "Spread A Little Happiness" (8/82 UK 16), "If You Love Somebody Set Them Free" (6/85 US 3; UK 26), "Fortress Around Your Heart" (8/85 US 8), "Russians" (12/85 UK 12; US 16), and "We'll Be Together" (10/87 US 7). Besides all this, Sting carried on with his film career. In 1979 he played the part of Eddie Cochran in *Radio Out*, in 1984 he played Feyd Rautha in *Dune*, in 1985 co-starred with Meryl Streep in *Plenty*, and in 1987 with Kathleen Turner in *Julia & Julia*. One of his most striking performances was his contribution to the Dire Straits Song "Money For Nothing" (7/85 US 1; UK 4). As if he hadn't enough to do already, he also organized concerts in aid of Amnesty International and the Brazilian rain forests.

Ish Ledesma 1952 Cuban leadsinger and guitarist with the band Foxy formed in 1975, four of the five members had fled from Cuba to Florida in 1959. Hits: "Get Off" (7/78 US 9) and "Hot Number" (3/79 US 21).

Philip Oakey 1955 UK singer and songwriter for Human League, which was formed from the group Future in autumn of 1977. Hits: "Love Action" (8/81 UK 3), "Don't You Want Me" (12/81 UK 1; 2/82 US 1), "Mirror Man" (11/82 UK 2; 10/83 US 30), "(Keep Feeling) Fascination" (4/83 UK 2; US 8), and "Human" (8/86 UK 8; US 1). Oakey had a hit with Georgio Moroder on "Together In Electric Dreams" (9/84 UK 3).

Robbie Nevil 1961 US singer, songwriter and guitarist. He wrote songs for the Pointer Sisters and Vanity, among others, before releasing his first solo album in 1986. Hits: "C'est La Vie" (9/86 US 2; 12/86 UK 3), "Dominoes" (2/87 US 14; 5/87 UK 26) and "Wot's It To Ya" (6/87 US 10).

Tiffany 1971 US singer, complete name Tiffany Renee Darwish. In 1987 she turned up in the series La la la Lolitas, and as a child made 'Music For Children'. Hits: "I Think We're Alone Now" (8/87 US 1; 12/87 UK 1), "Could've Been" (11/87 US 1; 3/88 UK 4), "I Saw Him Standing There" (2/88 US 7; 5/88 UK 8), "All This Time" (11/88 US 6) and "Radio Romance" (11/88 UK 13; 2/89 US 35).

Deaths

Rock Hudson 1985 US film actor. Died of AIDS. Born 17th November, 1925.

Hits of the Day

1965	"Hang On Sloopy" McCoys US 1 week
1971	"Maggie May/Reason To Believe" Rod Stewart US 5 weeks
1982	"Pass The Dutchie" Musical Youth UK 3 weeks
1982	"Jack & Diane" John Cougar (Mellencamp) US 4 weeks

3rd

Birthdays

Albert Collins 1932 Texas born US blues guitarist, singer and songwriter. Dubbed 'King of the Telecaster' he made his first records in 1955.

James Darren 1936 US singer and actor. Real name James Ercolani. He first came to attention in 1956 as an actor in US 'teen' films. From 1959 he was also successful as a singer in this market. Hits: "Goodbye Cruel World" (10/61 US 3; UK 28) and "Her Royal Majesty" (2/62 US 6;

UK 36). After 1963 it all seemed to be over. James somehow managed to keep his teen appeal. Then he played in TV series like *Time Tunnel*, and finally he had another minor hit with "You Take My Heart Away" (3/77 US 52), from the film *Rocky*. His birthdate is also sometimes quoted as 8th June, 1936.

Eddie Cochran 1938 US singer, songwriter, and guitarist. Real first names Edward Ray. Together with Hank Cochran, who was not related to him as his real name was Garland Perry, he formed the duo Cochran Brothers in 1954, who made country and rockabilly records. In 1956 Eddie's first solo record "Skinny Jim/Half Loved" appeared, which however, left no trace in the charts. Their first hit was "Sittin' In The Balcony" (3/57 US 18) written by John D. Loudermilk. The real Eddie, who was just as rebellious as James Dean, wrote songs like "Summertime Blues" (8/58 US 8: 11/58 UK 18; 4/68 RE-UK 34), and "C'mon Everybody" (11/58 US 35; 3/59 UK 6). After his fans in the USA had deserted him, he concentrated more on Britain, where he had his last big hit, "Three Steps To Heaven" (5/60 UK 1). Eddie died after a car accident on 17th April, 1960. Just like Buddy Holly, Eddie too has exerted a major influence on the R 'n' R market.

Alan O'Day 1940 US singer, pianist, and songwriter with compositions like "Angie Baby" for Helen Reddy and "Rock 'n' Roll Heaven" for the Righteous Brothers were by him. Hit: "Undercover Angel" (4/77 US 1).

Chubby Checker 1941 US singer, real name Ernest Evans. After earning his living plucking chickens, he launched his singing career as he could do good imitations of Fats Domino: indeed his name was derived from Domino: – Chubby after Fats, Checker after Domino. On his first hit, "The Class" (5/59 US 38), he imitated the voices of Fats, the Coasters, Elvis, and the Chipmunks. And then his career seemed to be over again. Then however, he recorded a cover version of a Hank Ballard song and since then, he is widely regarded as having discovered "The Twist". "The Twist" (8/60 US 1; 11/61 RE-US 1; 1/62 UK 14) and "White Christmas" are the only records to have reached No. 1 again in the USA after an absence of over a year. Further hits: "Pony Time" (1/61 US 1; 3/61 UK 27), "Let's Twist Again" (6/61 US 8; 8/61 UK 37; 12/61 RE-UK 2), "Let's Twist Again/The Twist" (11/75 UK 5), "The Fly" (9/61 US 7), "Slow Twistin'" (3/62 US 3; UK 23), and "Limbo Rock" (9/62 US 2; 11/62 UK 32). He made records right into the 80s, but they were not particularly successful.

Lindsey Buckingham 1947 US singer, guitarist, and songwriter. First he worked in a duo with Stevie Nicks, then both joined Fleetwood Mac in 1974. From the beginning of the 1980s he released solo records as well. Hits: "Trouble" (10/81 US 9; 1/82 UK 31), and "Go Insane" (7/84 US 23). In June 1988 Lindsey announced that he was leaving Fleetwood Mac for good. He was replaced by Billy Burnette and Rick Vito.

Stevie Ray Vaughan 1954 US guitarist, singer and songwriter. One of the most impressive blues guitarists of his generation, his career was abruptly ended, when he was killed in an aircrash on August 27th, 1990.

Jack Wagner 1959 US actor who played the part of Frisco Jones in the TV series *General Hospital*, and singer. Hit: "All I Need" (10/84 US 2).

Tommy Lee 1962 US drummer, singer and songwriter with the heavy metal band Mötley Crüe.

Deaths

Woody Guthrie 1967 US folk musician and probably one of the greatest in that field. He died of an inherited nerve disease, Huntington's chorea. Born 14th July, 1912.

Hits of the Day

1987 "Pump Up The Volume" M.A.R.R.S. UK 2 week

4th

Birthdays

Leroy Van Dyke 1929 US singer and songwriter. Leroy worked as a newspaper reporter, was in the US army in the early 1950s and worked as a auctioneer after that. It was a song about precisely that subject which earned him his first hit, "Auctioneer" (11/56 US 19). Four years later he had another hit with "Walk On By" (10/61 US 5; 1/62 UK 5). After that, he could be found mainly in the country charts until 1977.

Lloyd Green 1937 US steel guitarist and dobro player who was one of the top session men in Nashville, and produced several solo records. He played with Billy Crash Craddock, Don Williams, and Crystal Gayle.

Marlena Davies 1944 US singer with the Orlons.

Nona Hendryx 1944 US singer, who started with the Blue Belles in 1961. They became Patti LaBelle & The Blue Belles, and then just LaBelle. The trio split up in 1977. After that, Nona released solo records.

Jim Fielder 1947 US bassist with Mothers Of Invention, Tim Buckley, Buffalo Springfield, Chris Hillman, Gene Clark, Neil Sedaka, and Blood, Sweat & Tears.

Barbara Kooyman 1957 US singer and songwriter who started as Barbara K & The Cat's Away, then joined the Essentials, and there met Pat McDonald with whom she formed the duo Timbuk 3. The hits are under 6th August, Pat McDonald.

Deaths

Janis Joplin 1970 US blues and rock singer. She was found dead in her motel room. Cause of death: heroin overdose. Born 19th January, 1943.

Hits of the Day

1941	"Piano Concerto In B-Flat" Freddy Martin US 8 weeks
1962	"Telstar" Tornados UK 5 weeks
1975	"Hold Me Close" David Essex UK 3 weeks
1975	"Fame" David Bowie US 1 week (2nd time)
1980	"Another One Bites The Dust" Queen US 3 weeks

5th

Birthdays

George Jones Jr. 1936 US leadsinger with the Edsels, whose song "Rama Lama Ding Dong" recorded in 1958 became a hit later on, (5/61 US 21), and even later still a rock classic.

Abi Ofarim 1937 Israeli, real name Abraham Reichstadt. He formed the successful duo Esther & Abi Ofarim with his wife, Esther. They had international hits between 1963 and 1968. Biggest hit: "Cinderella Rockefella" (2/68 UK 1). After the divorce from his wife, his solo projects remained unsuccessful.

Johnny Duncan 1938 US country singer. After working as a disc jockey for years, he thought that he could sing too. From 1967 he was successful in the country charts, and to date has had over 40 hits. The main ones are "Thinkin' Of A Rendezvous" (10/76 C&W 1), "I Couldn't Have Been Any Better" (2/77 C&W 1), and "She Can Put Her Shoes Under My Bed (Anytime)" (3/78 C&W 1).

Carlos Mastrangelo 1938 US singer with the Belmonts. He was replaced by Frank Lyndon in May 1962.

Richard Street 1942 US singer who joined the Temptations in 1971 as a replacement for Paul Williams. He sang on "Papa Was A Rollin' Stone" (10/72 US 11; 12/72 UK 14) and "Masterpiece" (2/73 US 7). The Temptations are the fourth most successful soul artists after James Brown, Aretha Franklin, and Ray Charles; therefore, they are the most successful soul group of all time.

Steve Miller 1943 US singer, guitarist and songwriter. As a teenager he played with his brother Jimmy and Boz Scaggs in the Marksmen. After leaving school, he played in various bands with Scaggs, then he went to Chicago to play blues. He formed the Miller Goldberg Blues Band and with Barry Goldberg released one single. In 1966 he formed the Steve Miller Blues Band, which later became Steve Miller Band, and finally was abbreviated to his name only. Hits: "The Joker" (10/73 US 1), "Rock'n Me" (8/76 US 1; 10/76 UK 11), "Fly Like An Eagle" (12/76 US 2), "Jet Airliner" (4/77 US 8) and "Abracadabra" (5/82 US 1; UK 2).

Brian Connolly 1945 UK leadsinger and songwriter with the group Sweet, who were very successful between 1971 and 1978. Hits: "Co-Co" (6/71 UK 2), "Little Willy" (6/72 UK 4; 1/73 US 3), "Wig-Wam Bam" (9/72 UK 4), "Blockbuster" (1/73 UK 1), "Hell Raiser" (5/73 UK 2), "Ballroom Blitz" (9/73 UK 2; 6/75 US 5), "Teenage Rampage" (1/74 UK 2), "The Sixteens" (7/74 UK 9), "Fox On the Run" (3/75 UK 2; 11/75 US 5) and "Love Is Like Oxygen" (1/78 UK 9; US 8). In May 1979 Brian left Sweet for a solo career, he was unsuccessful. After that, he formed New Sweet, who were also unsuccessful.

Brian Johnson 1947 UK singer and songwriter, first with Geordie, whose biggest hit was "All Because Of You" (3/73 UK 6), and from 3rd April, 1980 with AC/DC as a replacement for the late Bon Scott.

B. W. Stephenson 1949 US singer, songwriter and guitarist, died on April 28th 1988.

Eddie Clarke 1950 UK guitarist and songwriter with Motorhead; who left in 1982.

Harold Faltermeyer 1952 German songwriter, producer and pianist from Munich, who became a successful composer of film and TV scores in the USA. Hit: "Axel F" (3/85 US 3; 6/85 UK 2), from the film *Beverly Hills Cop*. Before going to the USA, he could be heard in Germany on records by Konstantin Wecker, Amanda Lear, Giorgio Moroder, Donna Summer, Laura Branigan and GLS United.

Russell Mael 1953 US singer and songwriter, real name Dwight Russell Day. He and his brother Ron were the nucleus of Sparks, who were internationally successful. They started out there as children, modelling teenager fashions, and attended lectures on film directing. In 1970 they formed the band Halfnelson together with two other musicians. In 1971 Todd Rundgren produced a record, which was not successful. Then they changed their name to Sparks and released two further records which also disappeared in oblivion. In 1973 the Maels left the other musicians, went to London and tried as Sparks there. In England their crazy melodies with their peculiar lyrics and eccentric allusions quickly became popular. Hits: "This Town Ain't Big Enough For The Both Of Us" (5/74 UK 2) and "Amateur Hour" (7/74 UK 7). When success faded, they went to Munich to work with Giorgio Moroder, who produced "Beat The Clock" (7/79 UK 10).

Bob Geldof 1954 Irish singer, songwriter and leader of Boomtown Rats, who were formed in 1975 and had more than 10 Top 30 hits in the UK from 1977 to 1984. The biggest were "Like Clockwork" (6/78 UK 6), "Rat Trap" (10/78 UK 1), "I Don't Like Mondays" (7/79 UK 1), "Someone's Looking At You" (1/80 UK 4) and "Banana Republic" (11/80 UK 3). In August 1982, Bob played the lead part in the film *The Wall*, which was based on the album by Pink Floyd which was released in 1979. In November 1984 the Boomtown Rats finally split up. Bob wrote and organized the Band Aid Project with Midge Ure, "Do They Know It's Christmas?" (12/84 UK 1; US 13; 12/85 RE-UK 3), and became the organiser of the Live Aid Concert on 13th July, 1985 for Aid to Ethiopia. "Do They Know It's Christmas" became the best selling single in the U.K. Bob was knighted by the Queen for his services, and he was talked about as a candidate for the Nobel Peace Prize. Bob made solo records from 1986. Hit: "This Is The World Calling" (11/86 UK 25). He married English TV presenter Paula Yates and in 1987 appeared in milk commercials on British TV.

Lee Thompson 1961 UK saxophonist, singer and songwriter with Madness.

Miscellany

1962 The first record by the Beatles, "Love Me Do" was released. George Martin had produced two versions, one on 4th September, 1962 with Ringo Starr on drums, and another on 11th September, 1962 with session drummer Andy White on the drums. Ringo played tambourine. The version without Ringo playing drums appeared.

6th

Birthdays

Robin Shaw 1945 UK bassist with White Plains and Flowerpot Men.

Millie 1947 Singer, born on Jamaica as Millicent Smith, but because of her size she always maintained her surname was Small. She was one of the first artists from the West Indies to have a hit in the UK. This song had a touch of reggae, blue beat and ska, which earned her the nickname 'The Blue Beat Girl', "My Boy Lollipop" (3/64 UK 2; 5/64 US 2). Playing harmonica on the record was Rod Stewart.

Thomas McClary 1949 US lead guitarist and songwriter with the Commodores and as a solo artist.

Kevin Cronin 1951 US singer, pianist, and songwriter who, in 1971, joined the group REO Speedwagon, formed in 1967, and replaced Terry Luttrell. The group were named after a fire engine from the year 1911. Kevin in turn was replaced by Mike Murphy in 1973, as Kevin wanted to start a solo career. After nothing came of it, he went back to the group in 1975, replacing Murphy. In 1977 they started having hits. Hits: "Keep On Loving You" (11/80 US 1; 4/81 UK 7), "Take It On The Run" (3/81 US 5; 5/81 UK 19), "Keep The Fire Burnin'" (6/82 US 7) and "Can't Fight This Feeling" (1/85 US 1; 3/85 UK 16).

Gavin Sutherland 1951 UK bassist, guitarist, singer and songwriter. He joined the band Quiver (formed 1970) in 1972 with his brother Ian, who were then called Quiverlands, and then Sutherland Brothers & Quiver. Hit: "Arms Of Mary" (4/76 UK 5). As a songwriter Gavin had written the hit "Sailing" which was a monster hit for Rod Stewart.

Richard Jobson 1960 UK singer and songwriter for Skin Alley and for the punkband Skids, who made records between 1977 and 1981. Hit: "Into The Valley" (2/79 UK 10). He was the only one who remained through the years, all other members changed. In 1984 he turned up with the group Armoury Show. In 1989 he made solo records. In addition, he has worked as a TV presenter.

Danny Simcic 1962 Australian drummer with Real Life.

Deaths

Johnny O'Keefe 1978 Australian R 'n' R singer. Born 19th January, 1935.

Nelson Riddle 1985 US orchestra leader. Born 1st June, 1921.

Hits of the Day

1973 "Half Breed" Cher US 2 weeks
1979 "Sad Eyes" Robert John US 1 week
1990 "A Little Time" Beautiful South UK 1 week

7th

Birthdays

Uncle Dave Macon 1870 US country singer. Real first names David Harrison. He was the first great solo star at Nashville's Grand Ole Opry. He died 22nd March, 1952. In 1966 he was entered in the Country Music Hall Of Fame.

Vaughn Monroe 1911 US singer, bandleader and trumpeter. Hits: "There I Go" (10/40 US 1), "My Devotion" (8/42 US 1, "When The Lights Go On Again (All Over The World)" (10/42 US), "Let's Get Lost!" (5/43 US 1), "There! I've Said It Again" (3/45 US 1), "Let It Snow! Let It Snow! Let It Snow!" (12/45 US 1), "Ballerina" (11/47 US 1), "Riders In The Sky (A Cowboy Legend)" (4/49 US

1) and "Someday" (8/49 US 1). Vaughn was successful until 1954, appeared in many films and was often on radio. He died 21st May, 1973.

Al Martino 1927 US singer, and in his youth a friend of Mario Lanza. Real name Alfred Cini. His very first hit was also a million seller, "Here In My Heart" (5/52 US 1; 11/52 UK 1). Hits: "Now" (1/53 UK 3), "Wanted" (6/54 UK 4; 10/54 RE-UK 17), "I Love You Because" (4/63 US 3), "I Love You More And More Every Day" (2/64 US 9), "Spanish Eyes" (12/65 US 15; 7/73 UK 5) and "To The Door Of The Sun (Alle Porte Del Sole)" (12/74 US 17). As an actor he played a part which might have better suited Frank Sinatra, namely the part of Johnny Fontane in *The Godfather* (1972).

Colin Cooper 1939 UK singer, saxophonist and songwriter with Climax Blues Band.

Martin Murray 1941 UK guitarist with the Honeycombs.

Tony Sylvester 1941 US singer with Main Ingredient, born in Panama, real first names Enrique Antonio. He left the band in 1973 and became a producer for Ben E. King, Linda Lewis and Sister Sledge.

Dino Valente 1943 US singer, guitarist and songwriter from 1970 with the band Quicksilver Messenger Service formed in 1965. Real name Chester Powers. He started as a folksinger with solo albums. He wrote the million seller "Get Together" (1969).

Kevin Godley 1945 UK drummer, songwriter, singer, and keyboard player. He started with the Sabres, Mockingbirds, Hotlegs, 10 CC and finally went on with the duo Godley & Creme. Hits: "Under Your Thumb" (9/81 UK 3), "Wedding Bells" (11/81 UK 7), "Cry" (3/85 UK 19; 7/85 US 16) and "A Little Piece Of Heaven" (4/88).

Robert Webber 1945 US lead guitarist and singer with Sugarloaf.

David Hope 1949 US bassist with Kansas.

David Taylor 1950 UK bassist with Edison Lighthouse.

John Cougar Mellencamp 1951 US singer, songwriter and producer who formed his first band at age 14, released his first solo record in 1976, and rose to be a star in the early 1980s. Hits: "Hurts So Good" (5/82 US 2), "Jack & Diane" (8/82 US 1; 10/82 UK 25), "Lonely One Night" (8/85 US 6), "Small Town" (10/85 US 6), "Rock In The USA" (1/86 US 2), "Paper In Fire" (8/87 US 9) and "Cherry Bomb" (10/87 US 8).

Cathy Carsons 1953 US singer with Hot.

Tico Torres 1953 US drummer with Bon Jovi. Real first name Hector.

Sam Brown 1964 British singer and songwriter. Her father Joe Brown was a successful artist in the 1950s/60s in the UK, and her mother was one of the Vernon Girls. She was a backing singer for the Small Faces early on, also for Adam & The Ants, and Spandau Ballet. Her own first solo album was released in 1988. Hit: "Stop!" (2/89 UK 4).

Deaths

Mario Lanza 1959 US singer. Died in a clinic in Rome. Born 31st January, 1921.

Johnny Kidd 1966 UK singer and songwriter with his own band. Died after a car accident. Born 23rd December, 1939.

Smiley Lewis 1966 US R 'n' R artist. Died of stomach cancer. Born 5th July, 1920.

Hits of the Day

1944 "You Always Hurt The One You Love" Mills Brothers US 5 weeks
1989 "Miss You Much" Janet Jackson US 4 weeks

8th

Birthdays

Pete Drake 1932 US steel guitarist, who was one of the leading session musicians in Nashville. He played on hundreds of hits; among them were records by Elvis Presley, Jim Reeves, Joan Baez and Bob Dylan. In the 1950s he formed his own band, called Sons Of The South. After making a name for himself in Nashville, he made solo records. As Pete Drake & His Talking Steel Guitar he had the hit, "Forever" (3/64 US 25). In 1977, because he disliked the way the big record companies treated their country artists, he set up his own record label. On 29th July, 1988 he died where he had played most of his life, in Nashville.

Doc Green 1934 US singer with the Drifters from 1959 to 1966. Died 10th March, 1989 of cancer.

George Bellamy 1940 UK guitarist with the Tornados.

Dave Arbus 1941 UK violinist, founder and leader of East Of Eden. He is the only musician to stay with the group over the years. The band had their only hit with a title which was unusual for the charts, "Jig-A-Jig" (4/71 UK 7). Dave was also be featured heard on "Baba O'Riley" by the Who.

Buzz Clifford 1942 US singer, real first name Reese Francis. Only hit: "Baby Sittin' Boogie" (1/61 US 6; 3/61 UK 17). It is possible that it was the cute babies' voices which assured the success of the record; they were the children, a boy and a girl, of the producer. After that, Buzz changed to country music, however, he had no success in the respective charts.

Susan Raye 1944 US country singer and TV/film actress. From 1968 she appeared regularly with Buck Owens. As a solo artist, she was successful from 1970 mainly in the country charts. Her biggest hits were "L.A. International Airport" (2/71 C&W 9; 4/71 US 54), "Pitty, Pitty, Patter" (7/71 C&W 6), and "(I've Got A) Happy Heart" (11/71 C&W 3). She had hits in the country charts right into the early half of the 1980s.

Butch Rillera 1945 US drummer with Redbone.

Ray Royer 1945 UK guitarist and in 1966 founder member of Procul Harum. In 1967 he was replaced by Robin Trower.

Tony Wilson 1947 UK bassist and songwriter with Hot Chocolate, formed in 1970. He had already written songs with Errol Brown for other artists like "Bet Your Life I Do" for Herman's Hermits. Their composition "Brother Louie" became a million seller in the United States for the group Stories. For hits by Hot Chocolate, see 12th November under Errol Brown.

Johnny Ramone 1948 US guitarist with the Ramones. Real name John Cummings.

Hamish Stuart 1949 UK singer, guitarist, songwriter and bassist. In 1972 he replaced Michael Rosen in the Average White Band which had been formed the year before. Before that, Hamish had played with Forever More. From the end of 1974 the AWB were successful first of all in the USA. Hit: "Pick Up The Pieces" (12/74 US 1; 2/75 UK 6), "Cut The Cake" (4/75 US 10; UK 31), and "Let's Go Round Again" (4/80 UK 12). After 1982 the group split up. Hamish was also a session musician and worked with Chaka Khan, David Sanborn, Melissa Manchester, Michael Franks, Kenny Loggins and Leo Sayer. In the late 1980s he also played with Paul McCartney on his album "Flowers In The Dirt", and then accompanied him on his world tour in 1989.

Robert 'Kool' Bell 1950 US bassist and founder of Kool & The Gang. In 1964 they started out as jazz group, The Jazziacs. In 1967, as The Soul Music Revue, they accompanied soul artists who appeared in their home town Jersey City. In 1968 they turned increasingly to rhythm & blues, first as The New Dimensions, then as the New Flames, and finally as Kool & The Flames. In order, however, to avoid being confused with James Brown's Famous Flames, they changed their name to Kool & The Gang in the same year. In 1969 they secured their first recording contract; since then they have become permanent fixtures on the rhythm & blues and soul scenes. The principal hits until 1978 (before that the group had no permanent leadsinger until 1978 when James 'J. T.' Taylor joined them, for hits with him see 16th August under Taylor) were "Jungle Boogie" (12/73 US 4) and "Hollywood Swinging" (4/74 US 6), both million sellers.

Hits of the Day

1954	"Hold My Hand" Don Cornell UK 4 weeks
1955	"Love Is A Many Splendoured Thing" Four Aces US 6 weeks
1964	"Oh, Pretty Woman" Roy Orbison UK 2 weeks
1977	"Silver Lady" David Soul UK 3 weeks
1988	"Love Bites" Def Leppard US 1 week
1988	"Desire" U2 UK 1 week

9th

Birthdays

Pat Burke 1937 Jamaican saxophonist and flautist with the British group Foundations.

John Lennon 1940 UK singer, guitarist and songwriter with the Beatles and from 1969 as a solo artist. His major hits without the Beatles were "Give Peace A Chance" (7/69 UK 2; US 14), "Instant Karma (We All Shine On)" (2/70 UK 5; US 3), "Power To The People" (3/71 UK 7; US 11), "Imagine" (10/71 US 3; 11/75 UK 6; 12/80 RE-UK 1), "Happy X-mas (War Is Over)" (12/72 UK 4; 12/80 RE-UK 2), "Whatever Gets You Through The Night" (9/74 US 1; UK 36), "Number Nine Dream" (12/74 US 9; 2/75 UK 23), "(Just Like) Starting Over" (11/80 US & UK 1), "Woman"

(1/81 US 2; UK 1), "Watching The Wheels" (3/81 US 10; UK 30) and "Nobody Told Me" (1/84 US 5; UK 6). He was shot dead on 8th December, 1980.

John Entwhistle 1944 UK bassist and songwriter with the Who. In addition he made solo records and played with the group Ox.

Peter Tosh 1944 Jamaican guitarist, singer, and songwriter. Real name Winston Hubert MacIntosh. He started in the Wailers in 1963 with Bob Marley. The first single "Simmer Down" was one of the big hits of the year in Jamaica. In the 1970s Peter started a solo career. In spite of support from Mick Jagger, the longed-for success did not materialise. Hit: "(You Gotta Walk) Don't Look Back" (10/78 UK 43). He died 11th September, 1987.

Jackson Browne 1948 US singer, guitarist, pianist and songwriter, born in Heidelberg. He started as a guitarist with the Nitty Gritty Dirt Band, was with Tim Buckley and Nico 1967/68, and from 1969 was successful as a songwriter for Tom Rush, Byrds, Bonnie Raitt and Linda Ronstadt. In 1972 he had his first hit "Doctor My Eyes" (3/72 US 8) as a solo artist. He was co-writer of "Take It Easy", the first hit by the Eagles. Further hits for Jackson: "Running On Empty" (2/78 US 11), "Somebody's Baby" (7/82 US 7) and "Lawyers In Love" (7/83 US 13).

Michael Lee Smith 1951 US leadsinger of the group Starz. Hit: "Cherry Baby" (3/77 US 33).

Shona Laing 1955 New Zealand singer, keyboard player and songwriter. She has been making records since 1972. In 1975 she went to Britain and wrote songs there for Johnny Logan and Kelly Marie. In 1979 she became a member of Manfred Mann's Earthband. From the beginning of the 1980s she worked as a solo artist, recording songs like "Not A Kennedy" (1985).

Deaths

Jacques Brel 1978 Belgian chanson singer. Died of cancer. Born 8th April, 1929.

Hits of the Day

1948	"A Tree In The Meadow" Margaret Whiting US 5 weeks
1959	"Here Comes The Summer" Jerry Keller UK 1 week
1961	"Hit The Road, Jack" Ray Charles US 2 weeks
1965	"Yesterday" Beatles US 4 weeks

1971	"Maggie May" Rod Stewart UK 5 weeks
1976	"5th Of Beethoven" Walter Murphy US 1 week

10th

Birthdays

Ivory Joe Hunter 1914 US R & B singer, pianist, and songwriter. In 1933 he cut his first records and in 1944, he set up his own record companies. In 1945 he had his first hit with "Blues At Sunrise" (12/45 R&B 3), and his first No. 1 with "Pretty Mama Blues" (6/48 R&B 1) on his Pacific label. His song "I Almost Lost My Mind" (1/50 R&B 1) was a hit in the US in 1956 for Pat Boone. Boone's version brought Hunter to a wider white audience, which enabled him to have hit with "Since I Met You Baby" (11/56 US 12). In the late 1960s he changed to country music. He died on 8th November, 1974.

Thelonius Monk 1917 US pianist, composer and bandleader. He played with Charlie Parker, Dizzy Gillespie, Miles Davis, Sonny Rollins, and made solo records. Monk died 17th February, 1982.

Denis D'Ell 1943 UK pianist, guitarist, harmonica player, and singer with the Honeycombs. Real surname Dalziel. The band was formed in 1963 as the Sherabos. They changed their name to Honeycombs in honour of their female drummer Honey Lantree. Howard and Blaikley discovered the group in a London pub and wrote several hits for the group, including "Have I The Right" (7/64 UK 1; 9/64 US 5) and "That's The Way" (8/65 UK 12). In the 1970s Denis tried as a solo artist.

Alan Cartwright 1945 UK bassist with Procul Harum from 1972 to 1977.

Jerry LaCroix 1945 US singer, saxophonist, and harmonica player with Edgar Winter's White Trash, Blood, Sweat & Tears and Rare Earth. Jerry also made solo albums.

John Prine 1946 US folk singer songwriter whose best known songs "Paradise" and "Sam Stone".

Midge Ure 1953 UK singer, guitarist, keyboard player, and songwriter. In 1972 he started with the group Salvation, who changed their name to Slik in 1974. Hit: "Forever And Ever" (1/76 UK 1). In 1977 the band split up, Midge became co-founder of Rich Kids, and replaced Brian Robertson briefly in Thin Lizzy in 1979. In April 1979 he joined Ultravox. Hits: "Vienna" (1/81 UK 2), "All Stood Still" (6/81 UK 8), and "Hymn" (11/82 UK 11). In June 1982 Midge released a solo record "No Regrets" (6/82 UK 9), produced by Steve Harley, and also worked with Visage, but still remained a member of Ultravox. Further hit, "Dancing With Tears In My Eyes" (5/84 UK 3) followed. In November 1984 he collaborated with Bob Geldof (see 5th October) on the Band Aid project. In September 1985 Midge released a solo album, and shortly afterwards he went on tour. Hit: "If I Was" (9/85 UK 1).

David Lee Roth 1955 US singer and songwriter. He was a member of Red Ball Jets, which became Mammoth with the Van Halen brothers. After becoming the loudest group west of the Mississippi, they called themselves Van Halen in 1975. In 1978 they had their first hit and million seller, "Jump" (1/84 US 1; UK 7). After his first solo hit "California Girls" (1/85 US 3), David announced in June 1985 that he was leaving Van Halen. In February 1986, the record company Warner Brothers tried to persuade brothers Eddie and Alex that they could no longer use the name Van Halen without David. They ignored this and engaged Sammy Hagar as a replacement for David. Further solo hits for David: "Just A Gigolo/I Ain't Got Nobody" (3/85 US 12) and "Just Like Paradise" (1/88 US 6; 3/88 UK 27).

Tanya Tucker 1958 US country singer, who had her first hits in the country charts when she was 13. Since then she has had ten No. 1s; her biggest crossover hit was "Lizzy And The Rain Man" (4/75 C&W 1; US 37).

Al Connelly 1960 Canadian guitarist with Glass Tiger.

Martin Kemp 1961 UK bassist with Spandau Ballet.

Michael Bivins 1968 US singer with New Edition.

Deaths

Eddie Cantor 1964 US singer and actor, born 31st January, 1892.

Hits of the Day

1953	"St. George And The Dragonet" Stan Freberg US 4 weeks
1960	"Mr. Custer" Larry Verne US 1 week
1963	"Do You Love Me" Brian Poole & The Tremeloes UK 3 weeks
1970	"Cracklin' Rose" Neil Diamond US 1 week
1987	"Here I Go Again" Whitesnake US 1 week

11th

Birthdays

Art Blakey 1919 US jazz drummer and bandleader. His group, Jazz Messengers, provided a starting point for many young musicians. He died on October 16th, 1990.

Ennio Morricone 1928 Italian composer who worked, from the early 1960s, the film industry. His music for so-called spaghetti westerns, like *A Fistful Of Dollars* (1964), *The Good, The Bad, & The Ugly* (1966), and *Once Upon A Time In The West* (1968) made him world famous. He also released some of his compositions under the pseudonym Leo Nichols.

Dottie West 1932 US country singer and songwriter. Real name Dorothy Marie Marsh. She got her nickname, 'The Country Sunshine', from a commercial jingle which she wrote for Coca-Cola. In the mid-1950s she worked for a TV station in Cleveland, and was at the Grand Ole Opry from 1964. She was in the country charts from 1963 until the mid-1980s. Her biggest crossover hit was "What Are We Doin' In Love" (3/81 US 14), Kenny Rogers provided backing vocals. She died on September 4th, 1991.

Daryl Hall 1948 US singer, pianist, and songwriter. Real surname Hohl. He was successful from 1976 as Hall & Oates with John Oates. Both grew up in Philadelphia, and sang there as teenagers in doowop groups. In 1967 Hall made his first record with Kenny Gamble & The Romeos, then formed the Temptones, played with Gulliver in 1969 and, from 1972 teamed up with John Oates. Hits: "Sara Smile" (4/76 US 4), "She's Gone" (8/76 US 7; a RE entry from the year 1974), "Rich Girl" (2/77 US 1), "Kiss On My List" (11/80 UK 33; 2/81 US 1), "Private Eyes" (9/81 US 1; 4/82 UK 32), "I Can't Go For That (No Can Do)" (11/81 US 1; 1/82 UK 8), "Maneater" (10/82 UK 6; US 1), "Family Man" (4/83 UK 15; US 6), "Say It Isn't So" (10/83 US 2), "Out Of Touch" (10/84 US 1), and "Method Of Modern Love" (12/84 US 5; 2/85 UK 21). In 1986 Daryl had a successful solo hit with "Dreamtime" (8/86 US 5; UK 28).

Andrew Woolfolk 1950 US saxophonist and flautist with Earth, Wind & Fire, and as a session musician.

Deaths

Edith Piaf 1963 French chansonnière; born 19th December, 1915.

Tex Williams 1985 US country artist, who died of lung cancer, born 23rd August, 1917.

Hits of the Day

1967	"Masachusetts" Bee Gees UK 4 weeks
1969	"Je T'Aime Moi Non Plus" Jane Birkin & Serge Gainsbourg UK 1 week
1975	"Bad Blood" Neil Sedaka US 3 weeks
1986	"When I Think Of You" Janet Jackson US 2 weeks
1986	"True Blue" Madonna UK 1 week

12th

Birthdays

Sam Moore 1935 US soul singer who had several hits with his partner David Prater as Sam & Dave: "Soul Man" (9/67 US 2; 11/67 UK 24), and "I Thank You" (1/68 US 9; UK 34). He started with a gospel group called Melionaires. In 1961 Sam and Dave met, and started recording together in 1962. Success arrived in 1966 after being produced by Isaac Hayes and David Porter.

Melvin Franklin 1942 US singer with the Temptations. Real name David English. He has been with the group since they were formed in 1962. The Temptations had their origins in the 1950s in various groups like Questions, Elegants, Distants and Primes. Melvin was a member of a new group, Elgins, which was a hybrid of all the others: later they were renamed the Temptations.

James Dewar 1946 UK bassist with Stone The Crows and from 1973 with Robin Trower's band.

Rick Parfitt 1948 UK guitarist, singer, and songwriter. Real name Richard Harrison. He played with the Highlights from August 1964 to March 1967. When the Spectres changed to Traffic Jam, and then finally called themselves Status Quo, Rick joined the group. Musically the group has combined hard-rock with boogie. Hits: "Pictures Of Matchstick Men" (1/68 UK 7; 5/68 US 12), "Caroline" (9/73 UK 5), "Down, Down" (12/74 UK 1), "Rockin' All Over The World" (10/77 UK 3), "Whatever You Want" (9/79 UK 4), "What You're Proposing" (10/80 UK 2), and "Marguerita Time" (12/83 UK 3). In 1985 the band gave "farewell" concerts, but then released "In The Army Now"

(10/86 UK 2) and "Burning Bridges (On And Off And On Again)" (12/88 UK 5).

David Vanian 1956 UK singer. In May 1976 he joined Damned. Before that he had been a grave digger. In November 1976 the debut single "New Rose" was released, which did not reach the charts. In February 1978 the band split up. David played with the Doctors Of Madness, but in September 1978 three members of Damned joined up again as Les Punks, then as Doomed, and finally as Damned again. Hits: "Love Song" (5/79 UK 20), "Grimly Fiendish" (3/85 UK 21) and "Eloise" (2/86 UK 3).

Deaths

Gene Vincent 1971 US R 'n' R singer and songwriter. He survived the car crash which killed Eddie Cochran in the UK, although he was badly injured. Whether this contributed to his death 11 years later is a matter of speculation. He died of internal haemorrhaging, when he had just decided to try a comeback. Chances seemed good, especially as the British still liked Gene a lot. Born 11th February, 1935.

Ricky Wilson 1985 US singer and guitarist, born on March 19, 1953.

Hits of the Day

1961	"Michael" Highwaymen UK 1 week
1963	"Sugar Shack" Jimmy Gilmer & The Fireballs US 5 weeks
1974	"Annie's Song" John Denver UK 1 week
1985	"The Power Of Love" Jennifer Rush UK 5 weeks
1985	"Oh Sheila" Ready For The World US 1 week

13th

Birthdays

Anita Kerr 1927 US singer, pianist, songwriter and producer. She was born Anita Jean Grob. In 1949 she formed the Anita Kerr Singers, and from 1951 she made records. She made an important contribution to the Nashville sound, working with Jim Reeves, the Browns and Red Foley. In the early 1960s Anita was one of the first women to produce country records. She never turned up in the charts with her Singers, but as Anita & Th'So-And-Sos she had a minor hit with "Joey Baby" (2/62 US 91).

Nana Mouskouri 1936 Greek singer, who was successful from 1961. One of her many hits was "White Rose of Athens" (8/61).

Chris Farlowe 1940 UK singer, guitarist, and songwriter, real name John Henry Deighton. He was just 13 years old when he formed his first band, John Henry Skiffle Group. In 1957 he won the All-England Skiffle Championship with his group. In 1959, now more interested in R&B and R'n'R, he formed the Thunderbirds. In 1962 they released their first record, which was a flop. After further unsuccessful singles, Chris released a single in August 1965 in the name of Little Joe Cook. Many who heard this record, were of the opinion that it must be by a black American blues singer. In October Chris received a record contract with Immediate Records, but "The Fool" produced by Eric Burdon was a flop again. In February 1966 Mick Jagger produced "Think" (2/66) for Chris Farlowe, which was a Jagger/Richard composition. Another of their compositions, "Out Of Time" (6/66 UK 1), was a direct hit. In May 1968 the Thunderbirds split up. Chris withdrew from the music business and looked after his small London antique shop, which specialized in Second World War memorabilia. In September 1970 he returned with the band Hill, and then became a member of Colosseum. In November 1971 he became the singer in Atomic Rooster. After that, he only performed sporadically.

Art Garfunkel 1941 US singer. Art began his career with Paul Simon in 1957 as the duo Tom & Jerry. Tom Graph was Art Garfunkel, Jerry Landis was Paul Simon. After a brief spell, they became Simon & Garfunkel. For their hits and history, see under Paul, 5th November. Art has worked as a solo artist since the 1970s. Hits: "All I Know" (9/73 US 9), "I Only Have Eyes For You" (8/75 US 18; UK 1), "What A Wonderful World" (1/78 US 17), with James Taylor and Paul Simon, and "Bright Eyes" (3/79 UK 1).

Robert Lamm 1944 US pianist, singer and songwriter with Chicago since they were formed in 1967. Hits by the band up to 1985 can be found under 13th September, Peter Cetera. The hits without Peter, "Will You Still Love Me" (11/86 US 3), "I Don't Wanna Live Without Your Love" (6/88 US 3), "Look Away" (9/88 US 1) and "What Kind Of Man Would I Be" (12/89 US 5).

Sammy Hagar 1947 US singer, guitarist and songwriter. He started in 1973 as leadsinger of Montrose and made solo records from 1975. Hits: "Your Love Is Driving Me Crazy" (12/82 US 13), and "I Can't Drive 55" (9/84 US 6). After David Lee Roth left Van Halen, Sammy became the leadsinger at the beginning of 1986. Hits: "Why Can't This Be Love" (3/86 US 3; UK 8) and "When It's Love" (7/88 US 5; UK 28).

Peter David Spencer 1948 UK drummer with Smokie.

Craig McGregor 1949 UK bassist from 1975 with band Foghat formed in 1971.

John Edward Coley 1951 US singer and songwriter. He formed the duo England Dan & John Ford Coley with Danny Seals, brother of Jim Seals of Seals & Crofts. Hits: "I'd Really Love To See You Tonight" (6/76 US 2; 9/76 UK 26), "Nights Are Forever Without You" (10/76 US 10), "We'll Never Have To Say Goodbye Again" (2/78 US 9) and "Love Is The Answer" (3/79 US 10).

Marie Osmond 1959 US singer of the Osmond clan. Hits: "Paper Roses" (9/73 US 5; 11/73 UK 2) as a solo artist and, with brother Donny, "I'm Leaving It (All) Up To You" (7/74 US 4; UK 2) and "Morning Side Of The Mountain" (11/74 US 8; UK 5). When the Osmonds ceased to be popular in the late 1970s, they looked for new areas to conquer and found country music. In the mid-1980s Marie became very successful with "Meet Me In Montana" (7/85 C&W 1) with Dan Seals, "There's No Stoppin' Your Heart" (11/85 C&W 1), and "You're Still New To Me" (8/86 C&W 1) with Paul Davis.

Joey Belladonna 1960 US singer, and songwriter with Anthrax. First Hits: "I Am The Law" (2/87 UK 32) and "I'm The Man" (12/87 UK 20).

Hits of the Day

1979 "Don't Stop 'Til You Get Enough" Michael Jackson US 1 week
1984 "I Just Called To Say I Love You" Stevie Wonder US 3 weeks

---

14th

Birthdays

Jimmy Liggins 1922 US singer and guitarist, who was trained by the famous Archie Moore to be a professional boxer. Then he became a driver for his brother Joe's band, taught himself to play guitar, and made his first records in 1947. His biggest hit was "Drunk" (10/53 R&B 4). From 1958 to 1978 he was the owner of his own record company and ran a music school.

Bill Justis 1926 US saxophonist and songwriter, who worked for the record company Sun from 1957. He did arrangements for Jerry Lee Lewis, Johnny Cash and Charlie Rich. He himself had a hit in his own right with "Raunchy" (11/57 US 2; 1/58 UK 11). In the 1960s he formed his own record company Play Me, worked for RCA, Monument, and ABC, where he produced Fats Domino in 1963. He died 15th July, 1982.

Kenny Roberts 1927 US country singer and yodeller. He had his biggest hit with the million seller, "I Never See Maggie Alone" (9/49 US 9).

Robert Parker 1930 US saxophonist, singer, and bandleader. In the 1950s and 1960s he was one of the leading session musicians in New Orleans, playing with Professor Longhair, Joe Tex and Ernie K-Doe. As a solo artist, he had a hit with "Barefootin'" (4/66 US 7; UK 24).

Cliff Richard 1940 UK singer, real name Harry Webb. Since 1958, either with or without the Shadows, he has been one of the most popular British recording artists. His first hit was "Move It" (9/58 UK 2). Hits: "Living Doll" (7/59 UK 1; 11/59 US 30), "Travellin' Light" (10/59 UK 1), "Please Don't Tease" (6/60 UK 1), "I Love You" (12/60 UK 1), "The Young Ones" (1/62 UK 1), "The Next Time/Batchelor Boy" (12/62 UK 1), "Summer Holiday" (2/63 UK 1), "Rote Lippen Soll Man Kussen" (10/63 G 1), "The Minute You're Gone" (3/65 UK 1), "Congratulations" (3/68 UK 1), "Devil Woman" (5/76 UK 9; 7/76 US 6), "We Don't Talk Anymore" (7/79 UK 1; 9/79 US 7), and "Dreamin'" (8/80 UK 8; US 10). He also recorded with Olivia Newton-John, Sarah Brightman, Sheila Walsh, Phil Everly, and Elton John. A new version of "Living Doll" (3/86 UK 1), with the group The Young Ones, was a further hit for Cliff. In 1988 he had the Christmas No. 1 in the UK with "Mistletoe And Wine" (12/88 UK 1). In mid-1989 his 100th single was released amid much promotional fuss, "The Best Of Me" (6/89 UK 2). He shows no sign of retiring in the near future.

Marcia Barrett 1945 Member of Boney M.

Colin Hodgkinson 1945 UK bassist and singer with Alexis Korner, Brian Auger, Back Door, Cozy Powell, Schon & Hammer, Whitesnake and Mick Jagger.

Justin Hayward 1946 UK singer, pianist, guitarist, and songwriter. He released solo singles with various record companies and was a member of the Wild Three. In 1967 he joined the Moody Blues, formed in 1964 and replaced Denny Laine. Hits: "Nights In White Satin" (12/67 UK 19; 8/72 US 2; 12/72 RE-UK 9; 11/79 RE-UK 14), "Question" (2/70 UK 2; 5/70 US 21), "Your Wildest Dreams" (4/86 US 9), and "I Know You're Out There Somewhere" (6/88

US 30). Justin also made records as a soloist and with fellow band member John Lodge. Solo-hit "Forever Autumn" (7/78 UK 5) and, with Lodge, "Blue Guitar" (10/75 UK 8).

Dan McCafferty 1946 UK singer and songwriter with Nazareth, formed in 1969. They got their name from "The Weight" by Band. Nazareth tried to find a middle path between hard-rock and pop. First hits: "Broken Down Angel" (5/73 UK 9) and "Bad Bad Boy" (7/73 UK 10). While doing this, they had hits with "This Flight Tonight" (10/73 UK 11), a Joni Mitchell composition and "Love Hurts" (11/75 US 8), which was popularised by the Everly Brothers. Dan also made solo records.

Ivory Tilmon 1948 US singer with the Detroit Emeralds.

Chris Amoo 1952 UK leadsinger and songwriter for Real Thing. Hits: "You To Me Are Everything" (6/76 UK 1; 3/86 RE-UK 5), "Can't Get By Without You" (9/76 UK 2; 5/86 RE-UK 6), and "Can You Feel The Force" (2/79 UK 5; 8/86 RE-UK 24). The RE-UK versions are so-called "Decade Remixes."

Thomas Dolby 1958 UK singer, guitarist, pianist, and songwriter. Real name Thomas Morgan Robertson. From 1977 to 1979 he played keyboards with groups like Members, Passions and Fall. In 1979 he played with Camera Club for a few months, and accompanied Lene Lovich on a US tour. In 1981 he released his first single on his own Independent Label, Armageddon. Although the record did not sell well, the group Foreigner became interested in him, and asked him to work with them on their album '4'. After that, he played for Def Leppard. In July 1981 he set up another label and sold a worldwide license for it to EMI. In 1982 his first album appeared which was especially successful in the USA. On it was his first hit, "Windpower" (8/82 UK 31). Further hits included "She Blinded Me With Science" (2/83 US 5) and "Hyperactive!" (1/84 UK 17).

Karyn White 1965 US singer. In 1984 she was leadsinger with Legacy, who had their greatest success with "Don't Waste The Night" (3/85 R&B 44). In addition she worked as a session singer in Los Angeles. She had her first hit with "Facts Of Love" (12/86 US 27) with jazz keyboardist Jeff Lorber. After that, she provided backing vocals for Ray Parker Jr., the Commodores and Richard Marx, before receiving a solo contract in 1987. She was successful as a soloist from 1988. Hits: "The Way You Love Me" (10/88 US 7), "Superwoman" (1/89 US 8; 6/89 UK 11), and "Secret Rendezvous" (5/89 US 6; 9/89 UK 22).

Deaths

Bing Crosby 1977 US singer. He died of a heart attack on the golf course. Born 2nd May, 1904.

Leonard Bernstein 1990 US composer, conductor and arranger. Born August 25th, 1918.

Hits of the Day

1944 "A Hot Time In The Town Of Berlin" Bing Crosby & Andrews Sisters US 6 weeks

1944 "I'll Walk Alone" Dinah Shore US 4 weeks

1955 "Man From Laramie" Jimmy Young US 4 weeks

1957 "Wake Up Little Susie" Everly Brothers US 4 weeks

1972 "Ben" Michael Jackson US 1 week

1972 "Mouldy Old Dough" Lieutenant Pigeon UK 4 weeks

15th

Birthdays

David Carroll 1913 US orchestra conductor and arranger. Real name Nock Schrier. He worked with the Crew Cuts, Diamonds, Gaylords, Vic Damone, Rusty Draper, and Georgia Gibbs. His hits: "Melody Of Love" (1/55 US 8) and "It's Almost Tomorrow" (11/55 US 20).

Nellie Lutcher 1915 US singer, pianist, and songwriter. She was already playing piano in the same band as her father played bass when she was a teenager. After that, she played with the big band Southern Rhythm Boys. In 1935 she moved to the west coast, and appeared there in various clubs for 10 years. In 1947 she had her first big hits with "Hurry On Down" (9/47 US 20) and "He's A Real Gone Guy" (11/47 US 15). In the late 1950s her career waned.

Mickey Baker 1925 US guitarist, songwriter and singer. Real name McHouston Baker. He was a sought-after session guitarist by record companies like King, Savoy, Aladdin, Atlantic and many others. He formed the duo Mickey & Silvia with Silvia Robinson. The pair were in the charts between 1957 and 1961. Their biggest hit was "Love Is Strange" (1/57 US 11) and, in 1965, it was a hit for the Everly Brothers also.

Barry McGuire 1935 US singer and songwriter. Barry was a member of the group New Christy Minstrels, formed in 1961, for whom he and Randy Sparks, founder of the group, wrote their biggest hit, "Green, Green" (6/63 US 14). Barry had his biggest hit as a solo artist with "Eve Of Destruction" (8/65 US 1; UK 3).

Chris Andrews 1938 UK singer and songwriter. He started with the band Chris Ravel & The Ravers in the late 1950s and had his first success as a songwriter with "The First Time" and "We Are In Love" for Adam Faith, and "Girl Don't Come" and "Long Live Love" for Sandie Shaw. From the mid-1960s he also recorded his own compositions. Hits: "Yesterday Man" (10/65 UK 3), "To Whom It Concerns" (12/65 UK 13) and "Pretty Belinda" (6/69). Chris tried to make a comeback several times, hitherto without success.

Marv Johnson 1938 US singer, pianist and songwriter. He had his first recording contract as a solo artist in 1958 with Kudo. In January 1959 Marv recorded the first single for Berry Gordy's Tamla Motown label, "Come To Me" (3/59 US 30), although it was licensed to United Artists. The first records on Motown didn't materialize until November 1961. Further hits by Marv: "You Got What It Takes" (11/59 US 10; 2/60 UK 5), "I Love The Way You Love Me" (3/60 US 9; 5/60 UK 35), and "I'll Pick A Rose For My Rose" (1/69 UK 10). To this day, he is still active and records occasionally for the Motor City label.

Fela Anikulapo Kuti 1938 Nigerian singer, saxophonist, trumpeter, pianist, composer, and bandleader. Kuti is a musician who was also politically active inspite of persecution and intimidation; he has tried to become President of Nigeria. He released more than 50 albums with political content. He became known in Europe mainly through his work with Ginger Baker.

Don Stevenson 1942 US drummer with the rockband Moby Grape formed in 1966.

Richard Carpenter 1946 US pianist, singer, and songwriter. He formed a jazz trio in the mid-1960s with sister Karen and bassist Wes Jacobs. After two singles they won a so-called 'Battle Of The Bands' contest in the Hollywood Bowl, and thereupon received a record contract with RCA as the Richard Carpenter Trio. Four tracks were recorded, which however, were never released. In 1968 Jacobs left the trio to study music. The two siblings formed Spectrum which appeared mainly in Disneyland, the 'Troubador' and Whiskey-A-Go-Go. Besides this, Karen and Richard recorded several demos at session bassist Joe Osborn's house, which Joe sent to Herb Alpert, head of A&M Records. He was enthusiastic and, in April 1969, they were signed up as the Carpenters. They were very successful between 1969 and 1983. For hits, see 2nd March under Karen. After Karen died 4th February, 1983, Richard made a solo album in mid-1985, called TIME; he sang most of the vocals, while both Dusty Springfield and Dionne Warwick contributed. The record did not appear until October 1987 and was a flop.

Chris de Burgh 1948 UK singer, guitarist, and songwriter, born in Argentina, real name Christopher Davidson. In September 1974 he received a recording contract with A&M Records, and two months later he played support for label colleagues Supertramp on their 'Crime Of The Century' tour. In February 1975 his debut album appeared, entitled FAR BEYOND THESE CASTLE WALLS, from which the first single "Hold On" was taken. The critics nearly somersaulted with enthusiasm, but record buyers did not. His second single "Flying" was high in the Brazilian charts for several months, the Britons did not seem to care. During the course of the next few years several more good albums appeared, none of which got into the charts. All this changed finally with "Lady In Red" (7/86 UK 1; 2/87 US 3). Chris had a further hit with "Missing You" (10/88 UK 3).

Frank DiMino 1951 US singer and songwriter with the heavy-metal band Angel formed in 1975. The group started amid a plethora of publicity but their only hit was "Ain't Gonna Eat Out My Heart Anymore" (4/78 US 44).

Tito Jackson 1953 US guitarist with the sibling group Jackson 5. Real first names Toriano Adaryll.

Deaths

Cole Porter 1964 US songwriter, born 9th June, 1891.

Bobby Lester 1980 US singer with the Moonglows. Born on 13th January, 1930.

Jud Strunk 1981 US singer. He died in an air crash. Born 11th June, 1936.

Hits of the Day

1966	"Reach Out, I'll Be There" 4 Tops US 2 weeks
1977	"You Light Up My Life" Debby Boone US 10 weeks
1988	"Red Red Wine" UB 40 US 1 week
1988	"One Moment In Time" Whitney Houston UK 2 weeks

16th

Birthdays

Big Joe Williams 1903 US blues singer, guitarist, harmonica and accordion player and songwriter, who is supposed to have made his first records in 1918.

Max Bygraves 1922 UK singer and entertainer. Real first name Walter. He received the nickname 'Max' for imitating famous British comedian Max Miller in his early days. After the war, Bygraves played in night clubs, music halls, and recorded a medley of Al Jolson songs. In 1949 he played a small part in a film. In the early 1950s he could be seen quite often at the London Palladium, and did one season with Judy Garland. In the first year of the British pop chart, Bygraves was in it: "Cowpuncher's Cantata" (11/52 UK 11; 1/53 RE-UK 6), "Heart Of My Heart" (5/54 UK 7), "Gilly Gilly Ossenfeffer Katezenellenbogen By The Sea" (9/54 UK 7), "Meet Me On The Corner" (11/55 UK 2), "You Need Hands/Tulips From Amsterdam" (5/58 UK 3), "Jingle Bell Rock" (12/59 UK 7), and "Fings Ain't Wot They Used To Be" (3/60 UK 5). After disappearing almost completely from the charts in the 1960s, he had another hit with "Deck Of Cards" (10/73 UK 13).

Bert Kaempfert 1923 German multi-instrumentalist, orchestra leader, producer and composer. He recorded with Tony Sheridan and the Beatles in 1961. Hits with his orchestra: "Wunderland Bei Nacht" (11/60 US 1), and "Red Roses For A Blue Lady" (1/65 US 11). He wrote the music for the Frank Sinatra hits, "Strangers In The Night", and for the Al Martino hit, "Spanish Eyes" which Bert had called "Moon Over Naples". Kaempfert died 21st June, 1980.

Emile Ford 1937 UK singer with Emile Ford & The Checkmates. He was born Emile Sweetman in Nassau, Bahamas, and came to Britain with his parents when he was a child. Emile is considered to be the first black man to live in Britain and land a great hit there, although both W´nifred Atwell and Shirley Bassey managed it before him. A few other interesting points: his title was the longest question ever posed in a No. 1 position in a pop chart: "What Do You Want To Make Those Eyes At Me For" (11/59 UK 1). At the same time Adam Faith shared the No. 1 position with him for a week with "What Do You Want", which was the first time that 2 records shared the top position. Further hits for Emile were "On A Slow Boat To China" (2/60 UK 3), and "Counting Teardrops" (12/60 UK 4).

Nico 1938 US singer, songwriter and keyboards. Vocalist with Velvet Underground for their first album, having been one of Andy Warhol's acolytes. Later, she cut a number of highly eclectic solo albums. She died on July 18th, 1988.

Dave Lovelady 1942 UK drummer with Fourmost.

Fred Turner 1943 Canadian bassist, singer, and songwriter with Brave Belt, which became Bachman-Turner Overdrive in 1972. After they split up, Fred played with Bryan Adams and with Union in the early 1980s.

Bob 'Ace' Weir 1947 US guitarist and singer with Grateful Dead. Real name Robert Hall. From 1972 he was a soloist with King Fish, Bob Weir Band, and Bobby & The Midnites.

Tony Carey 1953 US singer, guitarist, keyboard player and songwriter. His career began with the US group Blessings and in September 1975 became a member of Ritchie Blackmore's Rainbow. In May 1977 he left the band, went on a two-week session job to Frankfurt in 1978, got stuck in Germany and worked as a solo artist; while there he was the instigator of the Planet P Project and he also worked with Peter Maffay. Hits as a solo artist: "A Fine Fine Day" (3/84 US 22), "The First Day Of Summer" (6/84 US 33), and "A Room With A View". In the meantime he has specialized in writing incidental music for a German TV crime series.

Danny McIntosh Jr. 1954 UK guitarist with Hazard and Bandit. Danny also played with Alexis Korner, Dollar, Quick, Chi Coltrane, and Annabella.

Gary Kemp 1959 UK guitarist and songwriter. His group Makers formed in 1976, became Spandau Ballet in 1979. Hits: "To Cut A Long Story Short" (11/80 UK 5), "Chant No. 1 (I Don't Need This Pressure On)" (7/81 UK 3), "Lifeline" (10/82 UK 7), "True" (4/83 UK 1; 8/83 US 4), "Gold" (8/83 UK 2; 11/83 US 29), "Only When You Leave" (6/84 UK 3; US 34), "I'll Fly For You" (8/84 UK 9) and "Through The Barricades" (11/86 UK 6).

Deaths

Gene Krupa 1973 US jazz drummer. Born 15th January, 1909.

Art Blakey US jazz drummer and bandleader. Born 11th October, 1919.

Hits of the Day

1959 "Mack The Knife" Bobby Darin UK 2 weeks
1976 "Mississippi" Pussycat UK 4 weeks
1976 "Disco Duck" Rick Dees & His Cast Of Idiots US 1 week

17th

Birthdays

Cozy Cole 1909 US drummer. Real first names William Randolph. In 1928 he became a professional drummer and formed his own band. In 1930 he made his first records with Jelly Roll Morton. In the 1930s he played with Benny Carter, Cab Calloway, and Benny Goodman, and between 1949 and 1953 with Louis Armstrong. In 1954 he formed a school for percussionists with Gene Krupa. In the 1950s he had the pop hits, "Topsy Part II" (8/58 US 3; 12/58 UK 29), "Topsy Part I" (9/58 US 27), and "Turvy Part II" (12/58 US 36). Cozy was seen as a musician in the films *Make Mine Music* (1944) and the *Glenn Miller Story* (1954). He died 29th January, 1981.

Alan Howard 1941 UK bassist with the Tremeloes until 1966.

Gary Puckett 1942 US singer and guitarist with the Outcasts, who were formed in 1967 and changed their name to Gary Puckett & The Union Gap. Hits, and million sellers: "Woman Woman" (11/67 US 4), "Young Girl" (3/68 US 2; UK 1; 6/74 RE-UK 6), "Lady Willpower" (6/68 US 2; 8/68 UK 5), and "Over You" (9/68 US 7). In 1971 the band split up. Gary's solo activities were a failure.

James Seals 1941 US guitarist, saxophonist, violinist and singer. He formed the duo Seals & Crofts. Seals started as a member of the Champs and played on their hit "Tequila" (2/58 US 1; 4/58 UK 5); later on, Dash Crofts joined this band too. The pair stayed with the Champs until the mid-1960s, and then formed the Dawnbreakers. In the early 1970s they became a duo. Hits: "Summer Breeze" (9/72 US 6), "Diamond Girl" (5/73 US 6) and "Get Closer" (4/76 US 6).

Ziggy Marley 1968 Jamaican reggae singer and songwriter, who tried to follow in his father Bob's footsteps. Real first name David. He had his first hit with "Tomorrow People" (5/88 US 39; UK 22) as Ziggy Marley & The Melody Makers.

Deaths

Billy Williams 1972 US singer, born 28th December, 1916.

Tennessee Ernie Ford 1991 US singer, born 13th February, 1919.

Alberta Hunter 1984 US blues singer, born 1st April, 1895.

Hits of the Day

1960 "Save The Last Dance For Me" Drifters US 1 week

1964 "Do Wah Diddy Diddy" Manfred Mann US 2 weeks

1970 "I'll Be There" Jackson 5 US 5 weeks

1981 "It's My Party" Dave Stewart & Barbara Gaskin UK 4 weeks

1981 "Arthur's Theme" Christopher Cross US 3 weeks

1987 "You Win Again" Bee Gees UK 4 weeks

1987 "Lost In Emotion" Lisa Lisa & Cult Jam US 1 week

18th

Birthdays

Lotte Lenya 1898 Austrian actress and singer. She was considered to be an outstanding interpreter of the works of Brecht/Weill, and she was first married to Kurt Weill. She emigrated in 1933 and died in New York 27th November, 1981.

Melina Mercouri 1925 Greek actress, singer, and politician. Real name Maria Amalia Mersuris. Among her best known films are *Never On Sunday* (1959), *Phaedra* (1961), *Tokapi* (1964), and *A Dream Of Passion* (1978). She is married to film director Jules Dassin. As a singer she was known especially for her strident political views. Her most successful record was "Ta Pedia Tou Pirea", known to us as "Never On A Sunday", from the film of the same name. From 1967 to 1974 Melina lived in exile due to her resistance against fascism. In 1974 she returned and ran for a seat in Parliament. In 1977 she succeeded, and has been Greek Minister for Culture since 1981.

Chuck Berry 1926 US rock musician and songwriter. The list of titles written by him reads like a history of R 'n' R. Many of his songs were covered by other artists, like the Beatles and Rolling Stones. 1955 was a lucky year for Berry. Muddy Waters advised him to go to Leonard Chess, the owner of Chess Records. Berry's first title was to be called "Ida May" but Chess altered the title to "Maybellene" (8/55 US 5), and sent the record to Alan Freed, *the* R 'n' R D.J. of the period, and after being designated co-writer he played the record until it became a hit. Further hits: "Roll Over Beethoven" (6/56 US 29), "School Days" (4/57 US 3; 7/57 UK 24), "Rock & Roll Music" (11/57 US 8), "Sweet Little Sixteen" (2/58 US 2; 4/58 UK 16), "Johnny B. Goode" (4/58 US 2), "Let It Rock/Memphis Tennessee" (10/63 UK 6), "No Particular Place To Go" (5/64 US 10; UK 3). He had his biggest hit was a 'novelty' song, which had nothing to do with R 'n' R: "My Ding-A-Ling" (8/72 US 1; 10/72 UK 1). In 1987 Chuck Berry published his autobiography, and he has threatened to write another book.

Cynthia Weil 1937 US songwriter. She wrote many of the most memorable hits of the 1960s with her husband Barry Mann.

Russ Giguere 1943 US guitarist and singer with Association.

Laura Nyro 1947 US songwriter, singer, and pianist. Real surname Nigro. She made an abortive attempt as an artist in the mid-1960s. But her compositions were much sought-after: "And When I Die" for Blood, Sweat & Tears, as well as hits for 5th Dimension and Three Dog Night, Barbra Streisand, Aretha Franklin, Frank Sinatra, and Linda Ronstadt. However, she did record a string of fine albums.

Joe Egan 1949 UK keyboard player, singer and songwriter. He started with Big Three, formed Stealers Wheel with Gerry Rafferty in 1972, and then tried as a solo artist, without success. Joe was also on records by Andy Fairweather and Rab Noakes.

Dick Crippen 1956 UK bassist with Tenpole Tudor.

Denise Dufort 1957 UK drummer with Girlschool.

Deaths

Orville 'Hoppy' Jones 1944 US singer with the Ink Spots. Born 17th February, 1905.

Hits of the Day

1969 "I Can't Get Next To You" Temptations US 2 weeks
1969 "I'll Never Fall In Love Again" Bobbie Gentry UK 1 week
1986 "Every Loser Wins" Nick Berry UK 3 weeks

19th

Birthdays

George Cates 1911 US composer, arranger, producer, and orchestra leader, who worked with Bing Crosby, Teresa Brewer, the Andrews Sisters, and others. He was the musical leader for 25 years in the Lawrence Welk TV-Show. He had his biggest hit with "Moonglow And Theme From 'Picnic" (4/56 US 4).

Dave Guard 1934 US singer, guitarist, and banjo player with the Kingston Trio formed in 1957. Dave left the group in 1961, tried as a solo artist and then with the Whisky Hill Singers. He died on March 22nd, 1991.

Larry Chance 1940 US singer and leader of the Earls, a white doo-wop-quartet from the Bronx. Real name Larry Figueiredo. Hit: "Remember Then" (12/62 US 24).

Keith McCormack 1940 US guitarist and singer with the String-A-Longs.

George McCrae 1944 US singer, he played around with various bands for years until he had a lucky break, "Rock Your Baby" (6/74 US & UK 1). Two further hits followed, "I Can't Leave You Alone" (10/74 UK 9), and "It's Been So Long" (7/75 UK 4), then his success waned. He also released records with his wife Gwen and became her manager. He died of cancer on 24th January, 1986.

Divine 1945 US singer and actor. After appearing in the films *Pink Flamingo* and *Polyester*, he was seen as a glittering extrovert and absolute cult figure. From 1983 the opulent transvestite who resembled a blown-up Dolly Parton, was successful with titles like "Shoot Your Shot" (1/83), "You Think You're A Man" (7/84 UK 16), and "Walk Like A Man" (4/85 UK 23). He died in 1988 of heart disease.

Keith Reid 1945 UK lyricist responsible for the hits by Procul Harum.

Jeannie C. Riley 1945 US country singer, real name Jeanne Carolyn Stephenson. In the mid-1960s she went to Nashville, sang on demo tapes, and worked as a secretary. She had her first and biggest hit with the Tom T. Hall song, "Harper Valley P.T.A." (8/68 US 1; 10/68 UK 12). She still appeared in the country charts until 1976.

Wilbert Hart 1947 US singer. He formed the nucleus of the Delfonics with his brother William, which started in 1965 as the Four Gents. They made their first records in 1967. Their major hits were "La-La Means I Love You" (2/68 US 4; 7/71 UK 19), and "Didn't I (Blow Your Mind

This Time)" (1/70 US 10; 4/71 UK 22), produced by Thom Bell and they paved the way for the 'Philly sound' of 1970s.

Peter Solley 1948 UK keyboard player with Chris Farlowe, Los Bravos, Arthur Brown, Terry Reid, Paladin and Snafu among others.

Daniel Woodgate 1960 UK drummer with Madness from 1978.

Sinitta 1966 US singer who was successful in the UK with the help of production team Stock/Aitken/Waterman. Hits: "So Macho/Cruisin' " (3/86 UK 47; 6/86 RE-UK 2), "Toy Boy" (7/87 UK 4), "Cross My Broken Heart" (2/88 UK 6) and "Right Back Where We Started From" (6/89 UK 4).

Hits of the Day

1940	"Only Forever" Bing Crosby US 9 weeks
1946	"Rumours Are Flying" Frankie Carle US 9 weeks
1956	"A Woman In Love" Frankie Laine UK 4 weeks
1961	"Walkin' Back To Happiness" Helen Shapiro UK 3 weeks
1974	"Nothing From Nothing" Billy Preston US 1 week
1974	"Sad Sweet Dreamer" Sweet Sensation UK 1 week
1985	"Take On Me" A-Ha US 1 week

20th

Birthdays

Stuart Hamblen 1908 US singer, actor and songwriter. From 1925 he worked for radio. In the early 30s he went to Hollywood, played in many westerns, and then with his own band on radio. He had his biggest hit with the self-penned "This Ole House" (8/54 C&W 2; 11/54 US 26) which was later covered by others. Stuart died on 8th March, 1989.

Wanda Jackson 1937 US singer, guitarist, pianist, and songwriter, who was successful with a particularly raunchy blend of rockabilly and country. Already at age 13 she had a daily programme with a local radio station in her home town. In 1954 she made her first records with Hank Thompson, and in the same year she made "You Can't Have My Love" (7/54 C&W 8) with Billy Gray. After a tour with Elvis Presley, she wanted to be a rock singer. Hits: "Let's Have A Party" (8/60 US 37; UK 32), and "In The Middle Of Heartache" (10/61 US 27). From 1961 until 1974 Wanda was regularly in the country charts.

Ray Jones 1939 UK bassist with the Dakotas.

Jay Siegal 1939 US singer with the Tokens.

Ric Lee 1945 UK drummer with Ten Years After.

Larry Gonsky 1949 US keyboard player with Looking Glass.

Roy Gordon Zabludowsky 1950 South African guitarist with the group Proudfoot.

Alan Greenwood 1951 US pianist with the band Foreigner formed in 1976. He also made records with Ian Lloyd, Spys and Joe Lynn Turner.

Tom Petty 1953 US singer, guitarist, and songwriter. He started with Mudcrutch in the late 1960s and formed Tom Petty & The Heartbreakers in 1975. Hits: "Don't Do Me Like That" (11/79 US 10), "Don't Come Around Here No More" (3/85 US 13), "Jammin' Me" (4/87 US 18), "I Won't Back Down" (4/89 US 12; UK 28), and "Free Fallin' " (11/89 US 7). He and the band accompanied Stevie Nicks on "Stop Draggin' My Heart Around" (7/81 US 3). In 1988 Tom became one of the Travelling Wilburys.

Mark King 1958 UK bassist, singer, and songwriter with the band Level 42 formed in 1980. Before that, Mark had played as a drummer and been involved with Project M in 1979. Hits: "The Sun Goes Down (Living It Up)" (7/83 UK 10), "Something About You" (9/85 UK 6; 2/86 US 7), "Lessons In Love" (4/86 UK 3; 4/87 US 12), "Running In The Family" (2/87 UK 6), "To Be With You Again" (4/87 UK 10), and "It's Over" (9/87 UK 10).

Johnny Dee 1961 Canadian singer, guitarist, and songwriter with Honeymoon Suite, who were successful from 1984. Hit: "Feel It Again" (3/86 US 34).

Tad Winklarz 1965 Pianist and saxophonist with the Canadian group Chalk Circle.

Deaths

Ronnie van Zant, Steve Gaines & Cassie Gaines 1977 US members of Lynyrd Skynyrd, who were on a US tour when they died in an air crash. The new album by the band had just been released, a macabre touch being that the album cover showed them standing in a sheet of flame.

Merle Travis 1983 US country singer, guitarist, and songwriter. Born 29th November, 1917.

Jo Ann Kelly 1990 UK blues singer and guitarist and sister of Blues Band member Dave Kelly. Born 5th January 1944.

Hits of the Day

1960 "Only The Lonely" Roy Orbison UK 2 weeks
1962 "Monster Mash" Bobby 'Boris' Pickett US 2 weeks
1973 "Angie" Rolling Stones US 1 week
1979 "Video Killed The Radio Star" Buggles UK 1 week
1979 "Rise" Herb Alpert US 2 weeks
1984 "Freedom" Wham! UK 3 weeks

21st

Birthdays

Owen Bradley 1915 US pianist and band leader. He had a hit with "Blues Stay Away From Me" (12/49 US 11), which was credited to Own Bradley & His Quintet. He and his musicians recorded with the Four Aces, Georgia Gibbs, and the Mills Brothers.

Dizzy Gillespie 1917 US jazz trumpeter, songwriter, singer and bandleader. Real first names John Birks. He played with Teddy Hill (1937), Cab Calloway (1939/40), Ella Fitzgerald (1941), Lucky Millinder (1942), Earl Hines (1943) and Billy Eckstine (1944), before developing Bebop with Charlie Parker in 1945. One of his best known compositions was "Salt Peanuts" (11/45 US 22).

Doctor Ross 1925 US blues one-man band. Real first name Isaiah. His "Cat Squirrel" became an early vehicle for Cream's rock improvisations.

Norman Wright 1937 US singer with the Dell-Vikings.

Jimmy Beaumont 1940 US singer with the Skyliners. Hits: "Since I Don't Have You" (2/59 US 12) and "Pennies From Heaven" (5/60 US 24).

Manfred Mann 1940 South African pianist and songwriter. Real name Michael Lubowitz. In 1962 he formed the jazz oriented Mann-Hugg Blues Brothers with Mike Hugg. From May 1963 they played pop and rock music as Manfred Mann. Hits: "Do Wah Diddy Diddy" (7/64 UK 1; 9/64 US 1), "Sha La La" (10/64 UK 3; US 12), and "Pretty Flamingo" (4/66 UK 1; 6/66 US 29). In the middle of 1966 the band changed their leadsinger from Paul Jones to Mike D'Abo, and their record company. Biggest hit: "Mighty Quinn (Quinn The Eskimo)" (1/68 UK 1; 3/68 US 10). In June 1969 the band split up. The group Emanon was formed, which, when read backwards is 'no name': it did not last long. In November 1969, still as the duo Mann and Hugg, they formed Manfred Mann Chapter 3. They played more jazz oriented music which was not very commercial. From March 1972 they were finally successful as Manfred Mann's Earthband. Hits: "Blinded By The Light" (8/76 UK 6; 11/76 US 1), and "Davy's On The Road Again" (5/78 UK 6).

Steve Cropper 1941 US guitarist with Booker T. & The MGs. He is a sought-after session musician and was also successful as a producer.

Elvin Bishop 1942 US guitarist and songwriter. In 1965 he was a co-founder of the Paul Butterfield Blues Band. In 1968 he started a solo career and scored with "Fooled Around And Fell In Love" (3/76 US 3; 5/76 UK 34); the vocalist was Mickey Thomas, later with Jefferson Starship.

Ron Elliott 1943 US singer, guitarist and songwriter with the Beau Brummels formed in 1964. Hits: "Love Love" (1/65 US 15) and "Just A Little" (4/65 US 8). The band split up in July 1967. Ron made a 'progressive' rock album together with Sal Valentino. In December 1968 these two split up worked as solo artists played in groups like Pan and Stoneground, and then joined up again in 1974. The resulting album was unsuccessful and, in mid-1975 the band split up again.

Kathy Young 1945 US singer. She had a hit with "A Thousand Stars" (10/60 US 3) with the group Innocents.

Lee Loughnane 1946 US trumpeter with Chicago.

Tetsu Yamauchi 1947 Japanese bass player with Free and the Faces. Sought-after session musician.

John Bundrick 1948 US keyboard player, singer, songwriter, and producer. He was a sought-after studio musician in Houston/Texas, then went to the UK, became a member of Free, Back Street Crawler, and made solo records. His nickname is Rabbit.

Charlotte Caffey 1953 US guitarist with the Go-Gos.

Phillip Chen 1954 UK bassist with Keef Hartley Band, Jeff Beck, Rod Stewart, and Butts Band.

Eric Faulkner 1954 UK guitarist with the Bay City Rollers.

Julian Cope 1957 UK singer, bassist, guitarist, and songwriter. He played with Crucial Three, Nova Mob and A Shallow Madness, before forming the new-wave group Teardrop Explodes in 1978. Hit: "Reward" (1/81 UK 6). The band split up at the end of 1982, and Julian began a solo career. Hit: "World Shut Your Mouth" (9/86 UK 19).

Steve Lukather 1957 US lead guitarist with Toto. Steve is a sought-after session musician, who has worked with Boz Scaggs, Elton John, Olivia Newton-John, Neil Diamond and Joe Cocker, among others.

Deaths

Bill Back 1965 US bass player. He died of a brain tumour. Born 17th September, 1926.

Hits of the Day

1957 "Chances Are" Johnny Mathis US 1 week
1957 "Jailhouse Rock" Elvis Presley US 7 weeks
1967 "To Sir, With Love" Lulu US 5 weeks
1972 "My Ding-A-Ling" Chuck Berry US 2 weeks
1989 "That's What I Like" Jive Bunny & The Mastermixers UK 3 weeks

---

22nd

Birthdays

Annette Funicello 1942 US singer, and actress. In 1955 she became a member of the Walt Disney Organisation Mousketeer, a kind of Mickey Mouse Fan Club. The record label Disneyland produced the first single by Annette, "Tall Paul" (1/59 US 7). Further hits: "O Dio Mio" (2/60 US 10), and "Pineapple Princess" (8/60 US 11). After 1961 she was too old to carry on running around with Mickey Mouse ears. She disappeared from the charts, but turned up beside Frankie Avalon in a number of 'Beach Movies'. In 1976 she had a regular TV show called 'Easy Does It'. In 1987 she returned in the film *Back To The Beach*, with Frankie Avalon. A slight case of *deja vu*.

Robert Fuller 1943 US singer and leader of the Bobby Fuller Four. Hits: "I Fought The Law" (1/66 US 9; 4/66 UK 33) and "Love's Made A Fool Of You" (4/66 US 26). On 18th July, 1966, Robert was found suffocated in his car in front of his house in Hollywood. Whether it was suicide, or as some said murder, was never established. His brother Randy wanted to carry on with the band, but they were unsuccessful.

Leslie West 1945 US guitarist, singer, and songwriter. Real surname Weinstein. He started as a member of the Vagrants and formed the group Mountain with bassist Felix Pappalardi in 1969. Hit: "Mississippi Queen" (4/70 US 21). Mountain considered themselves the successors of the recently disbanded group Cream. Mountain lasted until 1972, then Leslie left and formed West, Bruce & Laing with Jack Bruce and Corky Laing. They split up two years later, after several records. Then followed solo albums by Leslie and several reunions of Mountain.

Eddie Brigati 1946 US singer and songwriter, who started his career with Joey Dee & The Starliters. When he left in 1964 with some of the other Starliters, they formed a new band Young Rascals: Brigati and Felix Cavaliere (see 29th November) wrote and sang most of the hits. From 1969 they called themselves just Rascals. In 1971 the group split up, and Brigati turned up on records by Jackie Lomax, Danny O'Keefe, Roy Buchanan and the Average White Band.

Deaths

Tommy Edwards 1969 US singer, born 17th February, 1922. Some sources give the date of death as 23rd October.

Hits of the Day

1964 "(There's) Always Something There To remind Me" Sandie Shaw UK 3 weeks
1988 "Groovy Kind Of Love" Phil Collins US 2 weeks

23rd

Birthdays

Charles Foxx 1939 US songwriter, singer, and manager for his sister Inez, with whom he sometimes sang on her records.

Ellie Greenwich 1940 US songwriter, who wrote many of the great hits of the 1960s with her husband Jeff Barry. Apart from Gerry Goffin and Carole King, Greenwich/Barry were one of the most sought after songwriting teams of the 1960s pop, composing "Da Doo Ron Ron", "Be My Baby", "Then He Kissed Me", "Chapel Of Love", "River Deep Mountain High", "Hanky Panky", "Do Wah Diddy Diddy", and "Leader Of the Pack", among others. They also appeared as artists. Ellie first tried as Ellie Gay, then as Ellie G & The Jets and with Jeff she formed the duo Raindrops. By multitracking their voices, they were able to sound like a group. Their greatest success was "The Kind Of Boy You Can't Forget" (8/63 US 17). That was it, so back to songwriting! In 1965 she and her husband were divorced, but they carried on working together. It was they who helped the young Neil Diamond get his break in 1966 by producing his first nine hits. In the 1970s Ellie worked as a session singer, and was on records by Blondie, Dusty Springfield, and Cyndi Lauper. In addition, she occasionally released albums, on which she sang her own songs: ELLIE GREEN COMPOSES, PRODUCES, AND SINGS (1967), and LET IT BE WRITTEN, LET IT BE SUNG (1974). In the 1980s she carried on working as a songwriter, collaborating with other partners like Ellen Foley.

Greg Ridley 1947 UK bassist with Art, Spooky Tooth, and Humble Pie, after that more as a session musician.

Richie Bull 1948 UK bassist and banjo player with Kursaal Flyers.

Wurzel 1949 UK guitarist from August 1983 with Motorhead. Real name Michael Burston.

Dwight Yoakam 1956 US country singer and songwriter, who reminded one a little of Elvis Presley in his early days. In 1985 he made his first record, and has been in the country charts since 1986. His first big hits were "Streets Of Bakersfield" (7/88 C&W 1) with Buck Owens, and "I Sang Dixie" (11/88 C&W 1).

Deaths

Al Jolson 1950 US singer and actor. Born on 26th March, 1886.

Michael Holliday 1963 UK singer. He shot himself. Born 24th November, 1928.

Leonard Lee 1976 US singer and songwriter. Died after a heart attack. Born 29th June, 1935.

Hits of the Day

1953 "Hey Joe" Frankie Laine UK 2 weeks
1961 "Runaround Sue" Dion US 2 weeks
1976 "If You Leave Me Now" Chicago US 2 weeks
1982 "Do You Really Want To Hurt Me" Culture Club UK 3 weeks

24th

Birthdays

Sonny Terry 1911 US blues harmonica player, singer, and songwriter. Real name Saunders Terrell. He was playing harmonica already at age 8. In 1922 he went blind in his left eye and in 1927, in his right eye. In 1939 he met Brownie McGhee and they played together for until his death. Sonny died 11th March, 1986.

Steve Conway 1920 UK singer. Real name Walter James Groom. He was among the best known British singers between the Second World War and the beginning of rock 'n' roll. However, as there was no British hit parade, it is difficult to gauge Steve's popularity. He died 19th April, 1952.

Willie Mabon 1925 US blues singer, pianist, harmonica player and songwriter. In 1947 he formed the Blues Rockers, and made his first recordings as Big Willie. He had hits in his real name: "I Don't Know" (12/52 R&B 1) and "I'm Mad" (4/53 R&B 1). Willie died 19th April, 1985.

Bill Wyman 1926 UK bassist with the Rolling Stones, who was successful also as a soloist. Hit: "(Si Si) Je Suis Un Rock Star" (7/81 UK 14). In early biographies of the Rolling Stones his birthyear was given as 1941. Later it was corrected to 1936 and even later still the London correspondent of the German 'Stern' magazine had a look at Bill's birth certificate (Reg. No. 850 6 A) at a London Registry Office, which showed that he was born in 1926. This corresponds to an entry permit by Danish customs which also has the year 1926, and gives as a source for that year Wyman's passport No. 69269. Bill is considered to be the archivist of the Rolling Stones, who makes absolutely sure that anything that can be collected about the band, is kept.

Gilbert Becaud 1927 French singer and songwriter. Real name Francois Silly, nickname Monsieur 100,000 Volts. In 1952 Edith Piaf discovered him, he had his first hit with "Les Croix" in 1953. During the course of his long career he appeared in the USA and in the USSR. In addition to his many hits in France, he has been successful in other European countries too. Hit: "A Little Love And Understanding" (3/75 UK 10). Many of his songs were translated into English and became hits for other artists.

Big Bopper 1930 US songwriter and singer. Real name Jilles Perry (J. P. or Jape) Richardson. He started as a D.J.

25th

and became known across the USA when he broadcasted continuously for 122 hours on his radio station. He wrote songs like "Running Bear" for Johnny Preston. He had just had a hit of his own with "Chantilly Lace" (8/58 US 6; 12/58 UK 12), when he died in a plane crash on 3rd February, 1959. Ritchie Valens and Buddy Holly died in the same crash.

Santo Farina 1937 US steel guitarist who entered the charts together with his brother as Santo & Johnny. Their claim to fame was the instrumental "Sleep Walk" (7/59 US 1; 10/59 UK 22).

Ted Tempelman 1944 US leadsinger, trumpeter and drummer for the group Harper's Bazaar formed in 1963, whose biggest hit was "59th Street Bridge Song (Feelin' Groovy)" (2/67 US 13; UK 34). In 1970 the group split up. Ted became the successful producer of Captain Beefheart, Little Feat, Van Morrison, Doobie Brothers and Van Halen.

Edgar Broughton 1946 UK singer, guitarist and songwriter. In the late 1960s he formed the underground group Edgar Broughton Band. Hits: "Out Demons Out" (4/70 UK 39) and "Apache Dropout" (2/71 UK 35). But their secret hit was and still is "Hotel Room".

Jerry Edmonton 1946 Canadian drummer with Steppenwolf.

Rob van Leeuwen 1946 Dutch guitarist with Shocking Blue.

Paul & Barry Ryan 1948 UK songwriter (Paul) & singer (Barry). Real surname Sapherson. Their mother was successful as Marion Ryan with "Love Me Forever" (1/58 UK 5). In the mid-1960s the twins began to produce records. Hit: "Don't Bring Me Your Heartaches" (11/65 UK 13). In mid-1967 Paul only wanted to write songs, so Barry carried on as a soloist and had the hit "Eloise" (10/68 UK 2). After that they slipped into obscurity and Barry's attempted comeback in 1989 failed.

Dale Griffin 1950 UK drummer with Mott The Hoople and British Lions.

Alan Jackman 1958 UK drummer with Outfield.

Hits of the Day

1942 "(I've Got A Gal In) Kalamazoo" Glenn Miller US 8 weeks
1960 "I Want To Be Wanted" Brenda Lee US 1 week
1987 "Bad" Michael Jackson US 2 weeks

Birthdays

Eddie Lang 1902 US guitarist. He is one of the best early jazz legends. Real name Salvatore Massaro. The violinist Joe Venuti was one of his schoolfriends. Just as he did, Eddie began with the violin. From 1925 he made records as a solo artist, formed a duo with Joe Venuti, played with Paul Whiteman and Red Nichols, and backed Bing Crosby. As Ed Lang he led his own orchestra. He died 26th March, 1933.

Jeanne Black 1937 US singer, who had her only pop hit with the answer to Jim Reeves hit "He'll Have To Go", which was "He'll Have To Stay" (5/60 US 4; UK 41).

Helen Reddy 1942 Australian singer who was born into a show business family. She was onstage for the first time when she was 4. In the early 1960s she had her own TV show. In 1966 she went to New York and followed her fortune in the USA. Biggest hits, and million sellers: "I Am Woman" (6/72 US 1), "Delta Dawn" (6/73 US 1), "Leave Me Alone (Ruby Red Dress)" (11/73 US 3) and "Angie Baby" (10/74 US 1; 1/75 UK 5).

Jon Anderson 1944 UK leadsinger and songwriter with the group Yes formed in 1968. Before that, he had sung in various bands for 12 years, these included the Warriors, which his brother Tony led, and who released their debut single in 1964, and two further singles in 1967. In its early days, Yes did not pay much attention to singles, it was more important to produce good albums (the same was true for Led Zeppelin). Still, they had "Roundabout" (2/72 US 13) and "Wonderous Stories" (9/77 UK 7). In actual fact, several good albums did appear up to 1980. Then Anderson left, in order to make solo records. He had several hits with Vangelis, as Jon & Vangelis (see under 29th March), then Yes carried on from 1983, more commercially than ever before. Hit: "Owner Of A Lonely Heart" (11/83 US 1; UK 28).

Kathy 'Taffy' Danoff 1944 US singer with the Starland Vocal Band.

John Hall 1947 UK drummer with the Equals.

Glen Tipton 1948 UK guitarist with Judas Priest.

Chris Norman 1950 UK singer with the group Smokie, who were successful between 1975 and 1981. Hits: "If You Think You Know How To Love Me" (7/75 UK 3), "Living Next Door To Alice" (12/76 UK 5; US 25), "Lay Back In The Arms Of Someone" (3/77 UK 12), "It's Your Life"

(7/77 UK 5), "Oh Carol" (5/78 UK 5), and "Mexican Girl" (9/78 UK 19). He was successful with Suzi Quatro on "Stumblin' In" (11/78 UK 41; 1/79 US 4). After 1981 the band split up. Chris tried as a soloist and was able to rely on his loyal German fans.

Nick Thorp 1964 UK bassist with the band Curiosity Killed The Cat formed in 1983.

Matthias Jabs 1956 Guitarist with the Scorpions.

John Leven 1963 Norwegian bassist with Europe.

Hits of the Day

1941 "(Lights Out) 'Til Reveille" Kay Kyser US 2 weeks

1969 "Sugar Sugar" Archies UK 8 weeks

1975 "I Only Have Eyes For You" Art Garfunkel UK 2 weeks

1980 "Woman In Love" Barbra Streisand US & UK 3 weeks

1986 "True Colors" Cyndi Lauper US 2 weeks

26th

Birthdays

Mahalia Jackson 1911 US gospel singer, who according to her own statement, sang only to the glory of God. She also said, "They always asked me to sing blues. Everyone who has a voice like mine can sing blues, but I never sang it because I had been brought up to believe it was wrong. Down in the south, jazz has never been accepted as really good music. I sing what I have sung all my life in church, and I believe in it." She had her greatest hit and million seller with "Move On Up A Little Higher" (1/48 US 21). Mahalia died on 27th January, 1972.

Michael Piano 1944 US singer with the trio Sandpipers.

Keith Strickland 1953 US drummer with the B 52s formed in 1976.

Daniel John Ohm 1963 US singer, who made his first records in 1988.

Deaths

Alma Cogan 1966 UK singer. She died of cancer. Born 18th May, 1932.

Hits of the Day

1974 "Then Came You" Dionne Warwicke & Spinners US 1 week

1974 "Everything I Own" Ken Boothe UK 3 weeks

1985 "Saving All My Love For You" Whitney Houston US 1 week

27th

Birthdays

Kai Warner 1926 Orchestra leader and brother of James Last. Real name Werner Last. He died 9th July, 1982.

Floyd Cramer 1933 US pianist and songwriter, who became a sought-after session musician in the mid-1950s. He played on most of the early records by Elvis Presley, Jim Reeves and the Browns. In the late 1950s he wrote a few songs himself: "Last Date" (10/60 US 2), "On The Rebound" (3/61 US 4; UK 1), and "San Antonio Rose" (6/61 US 6; UK 36).

Philip Catherine 1942 Guitarist born in London of an English mother and Belgian father. He is one of the best jazz-rock guitarists. Philip became a professional musician when he was 17. In the early 1970s he played with Jean-Luc Ponty, Pork Pie, Charlie Mariano, Larry Coryell, Chet Baker and Toots Thielemans.

Hazell Dean 1956 UK singer and songwriter. Real name Hazell Dean Poole. Hits: "Searchin' " (4/84 UK 6), "Whatever I Do (Wherever I Go)" (7/84 UK 4), "Who's Leaving Who" (3/88 UK 4) and "Maybe (We Should Call It A Day)" (6/88 UK 15).

Simon Le Bon 1958 UK singer, guitarist, and songwriter for Duran Duran, who were formed in 1978 and whom Simon joined in April 1980. With that came hits like "Hungry Like A Wolf" (5/82 UK 5; 12/82 US 3), "Save A Prayer" (8/82 UK 2; 2/85 US 16), "Is There Something I Should Know?" (3/83 UK 1; 5/83 US 4), "Union Of The Snake" (9/83 UK 3; 11/83 US 3), "New Moon On Monday" (1/84 US 10; UK 9), "The Reflex" (4/84 UK & US 1), "The Wild Boys" (11/84 UK & US 2), "A View To Kill" (5/85 US 1; UK 2), "Notorious" (11/86 UK 7; US 2), "I Don't Want Your Love" (10/88 UK 14; US 4), and "All She Wants Is" (12/88 US 22; UK 9). In between Simon worked on a project called Arcadia who scored with "Election Day" (10/85 UK 7; US 6).

Eddie Hind 1961 UK singer and songwriter with the German/English duo Picnic At The Whitehouse. In 1985 Muff Winwood, brother of Steve, signed them to CBS and commented that they would make headlines.

Deaths

Xavier Cugat US Band leader. Born 1st January 1900.

Alma Gluck 1938 US singer, born 11th May, 1884.

Oliver Nelson 1975 US saxophonist, pianist, composer, and leader of his own band. He died of a heart attack. Born 4th June, 1932.

Steven Peregrine Took 1980 UK percussionist and singer. Born 28th July, 1949.

Hits of the Day

1966 "Reach Out I'll Be There" Four Tops UK 2 weeks
1973 "Midnight Train To Georgia" Gladys Knight & The Pips US 2 weeks
1973 "Daydreamer" David Cassidy UK 3 weeks
1979 "One Day A Time" Lena Martell UK 3 weeks
1990 "Undrained Melody" Righteous Brothers UK 4 weeks

28th

Birthdays

Cleo Laine 1927 UK singer and actress. Real name Clementina Dinah Campbell. In 1940 she appeared in the film *Thief Of Baghdad*. In 1951 she became a professional singer and worked with John Dankworth's band from 1952. In 1958 she married John, but left the band and only worked with them sporadically. Her biggest solo hit was "You'll Answer To Me" (9/61 UK 5).

Charlie Daniels 1936 US country guitarist, singer, violinist, and songwriter. In the late 1950s he formed his own first band, the Jaguars; they stayed together until 1967. Elvis recorded Charlie's composition "It Hurts Me" in 1963. Charlie became a session musician in Nashville and played with Bob Dylan, Ringo Starr, Leonard Cohen, Pete Seeger, Marty Robbins and countless other country stars.

In addition he produced four albums by the Youngbloods. In 1971 he finally started his own group, the Charlie Daniels Band. Hits: "Uneasy Rider" (6/73 US 9) and "The Devil Went Down To Georgia" (6/79 US 3; 9/79 UK 14).

Graham Bond 1937 UK R&B multi-instrumentalist and songwriter. His career began on alto saxophone in the Don Rendell quintet. In 1962 he replaced Cyril Davis in Alexis Korner's Blues Incorporated. After that, mainly playing Hammond organ, he formed a trio with Jack Bruce and Ginger Baker, which later was expanded to a quartet with John McLaughlin. They called themselves Graham Bond Organisation. When Bruce and Baker left, in order to form Cream with Eric Clapton, Jon Hiseman joined the band. In 1968 Graham dissolved the group, went to the USA, and made solo records there. He played once again with Ginger Baker with Air Force, and turned up in other short-lived projects. In 1973 drugs and personal problems led to a nervous breakdown. He commited suicide on 8th May, 1974 when he jumped under a train on the London underground system.

Curtis Lee 1941 US singer and songwriter with one hit, "Pretty Little Angel Eyes" (7/61 US 7), produced by Phil Spector.

Hank B. Marvin 1941 UK guitarist and songwriter. Real name Brian Rankin. In 1957 he formed the skiffle group Rail Roaders with Bruce Welch in his home town Newcastle. In May 1958 they went to London and formed the Five Chesternuts. They released one unsuccessful single. Then they were engaged as backing musicians for Cliff Richard, who was to tour Britain as a supporting group for the Kalin Twins in October 1958. From this developed Cliff Richard & The Drifters, who became the Shadows in July 1959, because there was already an American group called Drifters. Hits: "Apache" (7/60 UK 1), "Man Of Mystery/The Stranger" (11/60 UK 5), "Frightened City" (5/61 UK 3), "Kon-Tiki" (9/61 UK 1), "Wonderful Land" (3/62 UK 1), "Guitar Tango" (8/62 UK 4), "Dance On" (12/62 UK 1), "Foot Tapper" (3/63 UK 1), "Atlantis" (6/63 UK 2), "The Rise And Fall Of Flingel Bunt" (5/64 UK 5), and "Don't Cry For Me Argentina" (12/78 UK 5). In January 1968 Hank released his first solo single, "London's Not So Far". The record was not a success, but Cliff Richard recorded it later. Later Cliff and Hank duetted on "Throw Down A Line" (9/69 UK 7) and "Joy Of Living" (2/70 UK 25). In the early 1970s the Shadows played with changeable and partly unrecognizable line-ups, the exceptions being Hank Marvin and Bruce Welch who carried on the group name. In 1986, as in 1959, Hank played guitar on the new recording of "Living Doll" (3/86 UK 1) with Cliff and The Young Ones. In October 1988, when Hank was living in Australia, he came to London especially to play at the Dockland Open Air Concert with Jean-Michel Jarre. It cost Jarre £20,000.

Wayne Fontana 1945 UK singer and songwriter with Wayne Fontana & The Mindbenders. Real name Glynn Ellis. First he started the skiffle group Velfins in Manchester, then the Jets. In 1963 he made a demo for the record company Fontana, hence his stage name; his backing group included Eric Stewart, who finally became the Mindbenders. Hits: "Um Um Um Um Um Um" (10/64 UK 5) and "Game Of Love" (2/65 UK 2; US 1). Then Wayne wanted to launch a solo career in 1966. Hit: "Pamela Pamela" (12/66 UK 11). The Mindbenders were successful without Wayne, as Eric Stewart had taken over as leadsinger, "A Groovy Kind Of Love" (1/66 UK 2; 4/66 US 2).

Telma Hopkins 1948 US singer with Dawn.

Ricky Lee Reynolds 1948 US guitarist and singer with Black Oak Arkansas.

Stephen Morris 1957 UK drummer with New Order.

Deaths

Earl Bostic 1965 US saxophonist. Died of a heart attack. Born 25th April, 1920.

Hits of the Day

1950 "All My Love" Patti Page US 5 weeks
1978 "Hot Child In The City" Nick Gilder US 1 week

29th

Birthdays

Fanny Brice 1891 US singer, actress, and dancer. Real name Fannie Borach. From 1910 to 1923 she could be seen and heard in nearly all of the Ziegfeld Follies shows. In 1928 she played in some film musicals: *Nightclub*, and *My Man* (both 1928). Fanny was known as 'Baby Snooks' on 1940s radio. She had 5 hits as a singer in the 1920s, the biggest was "My Man" (2/22 US 1). Fanny's life was the inspiration for the Broadway musical *Funny Girl*, which was filmed in 1968 with Barbra Streisand as lead. In 1975 the sequel *Funny Lady* was released. Fanny died 29th May, 1951.

Ray Steinberg 1942 US singer with the Reflections, whose greatest hit was "(Just Like) Romeo & Juliet" (4/64 US 6).

Denny Laine 1944 UK guitarist, singer and songwriter. Real name Brian Arthur Hines. In the early 1960s he formed the band Denny & The Diplomats and was a founder member of Moody Blues in 1964. Hit: "Go Now" (12/64 UK 1; 2/65 US 10). In August 1966 he left the band and was replaced by Justin Hayward. Denny became a member of the Electric String Band, and received a solo contract which resulted in no hits. After that, he joined Balls, Ginger Baker's Airforce and finally Paul McCartney's Wings in 1971. In 1982 he left McCartney and carried on his solo career.

Peter Green 1946 UK guitarist, singer and songwriter. Real surname Greenbaum. He started out with the groups Looners and Shotgun Express, before replacing Eric Clapton in July 1966 in John Mayall's Bluesbreakers. Beside Mayall and Green, the other musicians in the band were Mick Fleetwood and John McVie. In July 1967 the Bluesbreakers, without John Mayall, recorded an album for Mike Vernon, owner of the Blue Horizon label, backing US blues musician Eddie Boyd. Mike Vernon was so taken with their playing, that he offered them their own recording contract. They became known as Peter Green's Fleetwood Mac, and a little later Peter Green was dropped from the group name. In addition, they played on various 'Blue Horizon' records by Otis Spann and Duster Bennett. It was Green who initially gave the group its musical identity by writing hits like "Black Magic Woman" (4/68 UK 37) (later a hit for Santana), "Albatross" (12/68 UK 1; 5/73 RE-UK 2), "Man Of The World" (4/69 UK 2), "Oh, Well" (10/69 UK 2), and "The Green Manalishi (With The Two Pronged Crown)" (5/70 UK 10). A further hit was the Little Willie John number, "Need Your Love So Bad" (7/68 UK 31; 7/69 RE-UK 32). On 11th April, 1970, when the band were just touring Europe and were playing in Munich, Peter announced that he was leaving the band. He left in May. His reason was that he hated all the razzmatazz, the behaviour and posturing of the record industry and everything to do with it. After that, he is supposed to have worked as a gravedigger and hospital porter. When a cheque for 30,000 pounds was given to him in January, 1977, he threatened the bearer with an air rifle; he was promptly committed to a mental hospital for a spell. He tried a comeback in July 1979, with the album IN THE SKIES; other solo albums appeared, which were all good, but not for the charts. Now lives as a recluse.

David Paton 1951 UK leadsinger, bassist and songwriter with the band Pilot, formed in 1974. Hits: "Magic" (11/74 UK 11; 4/75 US 5) and "January" (1/75 UK 1). Later he was one of a number of musicians who worked on various projects with Alan Parsons; he was also a member of Camel and Keats. As a session musician David was also on records by Kate Bush, Chris de Burgh, Chris Rea, Jimmy Page and Elton John.

Arnell Carmichael 1952 US keyboard player and singer with Raydio, lead by Ray Parker whom he continued to record with. As a session musician he worked with La Toyah Jackson, Maxine Nightingale, Leo Sayer, Billy Preston and Diana Ross.

Stephen Luscombe 1954 UK synthesiser player, singer and songwriter with Blancmange who were successful from 1982. Hits: "Living On The Ceiling" (10/82 UK 7), "Blind Vision" (5/83 UK 10), and "Don't Tell Me" (4/84 UK 8).

Randy Jackson 1961 US singer with the sibling group Jackson 5.

Deaths

Duane Allman 1971 US guitarist and leader of the Allman Brothers band. He was killed in a motor bike accident. Born 20th November, 1946.

Woody Herman 1987 US jazz musician and orchestra leader. Died of heart failure and pneumonia. Born 16th May, 1913.

Hits of the Day

1955 "Autumn Leaves" Roger Williams US 4 weeks
1966 "96 Tears" ? & The Mysterians US 1 week
1977 "Yes Sir, I Can Boogie" Baccara UK 1 week
1983 "Islands In The Stream" Kenny Rogers & Dolly Parton US 2 weeks
1988 "Orinoco Flow" Enya UK 3 weeks

30th

Birthdays

Eddie Holland 1939 US songwriter who started his career as a singer. He formed a songwriting team with his brother Brian and Lamont Dozier, which quickly became one of Tamla-Motown's prize assets. The three of them wrote hits for the Supremes, Four Tops, and Marvin Gaye. As did many famous songwriters, he also tried to be a singer. He only scored with "Jamie" (1/62 US 30).

Grace Slick 1939 US singer, and songwriter. She was born Grace Wing, became a model, and married Jerry Slick, with whom she formed the band Great Society in 1965. In 1966 she joined the group Jefferson Airplane, also formed in 1965, as a replacement for singer Signe Anderson. Hits: "Somebody To Love" (4/67 US 5) and "White Rabbit" (6/67 US 8). The band carried on until 1974. Some of the previous members including Grace, carried on with solo projects, when they reformed as Jefferson Starship. In 1978, when the band blamed Grace because a disappointed audience had set fire to the stage on the Lorelei on 17th June, 1978, she left the group, but came back in March 1981. Hits by Jefferson Starship: "Miracles" (8/75 US 3), and "Count On Me" (3/78 US 8). In 1985 the group name was changed again to just Starship. Grace was still with them. Hits: "We Built This City" (9/85 US 1; 11/85 UK 12), "Sara" (12/85 US 1) and "Nothing's Gonna Stop Us Now" (1/87 US 1; 3/87 UK 1). In November 1988 Grace, Paul Kantner, Jorma Kaukonen, Marty Balin, and Jack Casady five of the original members of Jefferson Airplane – re-grouped to work on a new project. When the result was released in August 1989, under their old name, the group Starship continued to release records as well.

Otis Williams 1941 US singer, real surname Miles. In the 1950s he sang with groups like Distants and Primes. In 1960 they called themselves Elgins, and shortly after that, they became the Temptations. For hits until 1971, see Eddie Kendricks under 17th December, after that, see Richard Street under 5th October.

Chris Slade 1946 UK drummer. He started with Tom Paxton in 1971, and was with Manfred Mann's Earthband from 1972 to 1978. After that, he played with Frankie Miller, Uriah Heep, Gary Numan, Denny Laine, and from 1985 with Firm.

Timothy B. Schmit 1947 US bassist and singer. He started in 1962 with the folk trio Tim, Tom & Ron. In 1963 he was with the Surfband Contenders, then with the New Breed, who called themselves Glad from 1968. In February 1970 he joined Poco and then joined the Eagles in September 1977. After the Eagles had split up, he played as a session musician with Elton John, Bob Seger, America, Joe Walsh, Crosby, Stills & Nash, and many others. In 1984 he issued a solo album.

Geoff Beauchamp 1962 UK lead guitarist with Eighth Wonder.

Deaths

Georges Brassens 1981 French chansonnier. Born 22nd October, 1921.

Hits of the Day

1943 "Pistol Packin' Mama" Al Dexter US 8 weeks
1959 "Travellin' Light" Cliff Richard UK 5 weeks
1982 "Who Can It Be Now" Men At Work US 1 week

Miscellany

1938 Orson Welles broadcast his famous radio play *War Of The Worlds* based on the novel by H. G. Wells. Although it had been announced as a radio play several times, panic errupted among the population, because many believed in a real invasion from Mars. Even during the programme, it was pointed out several times that it was only a radio play; many did not hear this, because they had already taken to their heels.

31st

Birthdays

Ray Smith 1934 US singer, guitarist and pianist. Hit: "Rockin' Little Angel" (1/60 US 22). He died 29th November, 1979.

Tom Paxton 1937 US guitarist, folk singer, and songwriter. In the early 1960s he went to Greenwich Village and met Bob Dylan, Phil Ochs, Peter, Paul & Mary, and Pete Seeger. It was especially Pete who helped Tom get going. In 1965 the album RAMBLIN' BOY appeared – Tom's nickname – which included "The Last Thing On My Mind" and the title track. His compositions were recorded by John Denver, the Kingston Trio, and many others.

Kinky Friedman 1944 US country-rock songwriter and singer, whose nickname was 'Frank Zappa of Country Music'. Real first name Richard. In 1966 he cut his first records with his own band, which he called King Arthur & The Carrots. After that, he went to Borneo with the Peace Corps; on his return to Los Angeles in 1971, he formed the Texas Jew Boys. In 1973 Kinky released his first solo album SOLD AMERICAN which included "Let Saigons Be Bygones" and "We Reserve The Right To Refuse Service To You". Perhaps his most famous composition was called "They Ain't Making Jews Like Jesus Any-

more". This type of black humour and a concentration of 'four letter words' prevented Kinky and his band from appearing in the Grand Ole Opry.

Russ Ballard 1947 UK guitarist, songwriter, singer, and producer. He started with the Roulettes, who were Adam Faith's backing band. Then he joined Unit Four Plus Two, who were already passed their peak; then, he was a founder member of Argent. Hit: "Hold Your Head Up" (3/72 UK 5; 6/72 US 5). From the mid-1970s Russ worked as a solo artist; despite never having a hit himself, he wrote many of hits for others. As a session musician he was on records by Roger Daltrey and America.

Moon Martin 1950 US singer, songwriter and guitarist. Real first name John. He started with the band Southwind, which released three albums between 1969 and 1972. He wrote for Mink de Ville and many others. In 1978 he formed his own band. Hit: "Rolene" (8/79 US 30).

Bernard Edwards 1952 US bassist, songwriter and producer. He started with Nile Rodgers in the group Chic.

Tony Brock 1953 UK drummer with the Babys and as a session musician for Rod Stewart, Eddie Money, Randy Vanwarmer and Jimmy Barnes.

Johnny Clegg 1953 UK singer, guitarist and songwriter. At the age of six he moved to Zimbabwe with his parents, and grew up there and in South Africa. When he was 14 he learned the language and music of the Zulus, in spite of apartheid laws. This landed Johnny in prison for the first time at age 15, because he had worked with black musicians in their township. In 1976 he formed an unsegregated band Juluka, which became Johnny Clegg & Savuka in 1986. The best known number of both groups was "Scatterlings of Africa".

Tony Bowers 1956 UK bassist with Alberto Y Los Trios Paranoias, Moth Men and, from 1984, Simply Red.

Larry Mullen 1961 UK drummer with U 2.

Johnny Marr 1963 UK guitarist and songwriter with the Smiths formed in 1982. In mid-1987 the group split up because Marr went to the USA to work with Talking Heads. In 1991, he formed Electronic.

Annabella Lwin 1965 UK singer with Bow Wow Wow. Real name Myant Mayant Aye. She was born in Rangoon, Burma. The first single by the group Bow Wow Wow, who were managed by Malcolm McLaren, was "C'30, C'60, C'90, Go!" (7/80 UK 30), it was released on cassette only, as was the second single by the group. McLaren was of the opinion that in future, most kids would be taping records from their radio in order to be able to walk around with their Walkmans and listen to music anywhere. Hits:

"Go Wild In The Country" (1/82 UK 7), and "I Want Candy" (6/82 UK 9). In 1984 Annabella left the group and carried on as a solo artist making records in her own first name. The group changed their names to Chiefs Of Relief and produced quite acceptable pop music.

King Ad-Rock 1966 US singer and songwriter with the Beastie Boys formed in 1981. Real name Adam Horovitz. The group developed from a hardcore rock into a white rap band. Hits: "(You Gotta) Fight For Your Right (To Party!)" (12/86 US 7; 2/87 UK 11), "No Sleep Till Brooklyn" (5/87 UK 14), and "She's On It" (7/87 UK 10).

Alistair McErlaine 1968 UK guitarist and songwriter with the Scottish group Texas formed in 1987.

Hits of the Day

1942 "White Christmas" Big Crosby US 11 weeks
1960 "Save The last Dance For Me" Drifters US 2 weeks (2nd time)
1963 "You'll Never Walk Alone" Grery & The Pacemakers UK 4 weeks
1964 "Baby Love" Supremes US 4 weeks
1970 "Woodstock" Matthews Southern Comfort UK 3 weeks

Miscellany

1942 "White Christmas" by Bing Crosby reached No 1 for the first time in the USA. During the course of the next few years, the record was to appear in the charts a few more times: 12/43 US 6; 12/44 US 5; 12/45 US 1, 12/46 US 1, 12/47 US 3, 12/48 US 6, 12/49 US 5, 12/50 US 13, 12/51 US 13, 12/53 US 21, 12/54 US 21, 12/55 US 7, 12/56 US 65, 12/57 US 34, 12/58 US 66, 12/59 US 59, 12/60 US 26, 12/61 US 12, 12/62 US 38. Bing was successful in the UK after the title had begun to fade in the USA: 12/77 UK 5, 12/85 UK 69.

November

1st

Birthdays

Bill Anderson 1937 US singer and songwriter. In 1957 he was a disc jockey and wrote about sporting events. From 1958 till the end of the 1980s he had a number of hits in the C&W charts. His biggest crossover hit was "Still" (4/63 US 8). Bill could be seen in various films as an actor and presented the TV game show 'Fandango'. His nickname is 'Whispering Bill'.

Mike Bernie 1944 UK tenor saxophonist with Wizzard.

Ric Grech 1946 UK bassist, violinist and singer. He started with Family, and bacame a member of the super group Blind Faith along with Steve Winwood, Ginger Baker, and Eric Clapton. Then he played with Ginger Baker's Airforce, KGB, and Traffic. As a session musician he was on records by the Bee Gees, Muddy Waters and Rod Stewart and he also made solo albums. Ric died 17th March, 1990.

Robert Yeazel 1946 US guitarist and singer with Beast and Sugarloaf.

Dan Peek 1950 US guitarist, singer, and songwriter with America.

Ronald Bell 1951 US saxophonist and songwriter for Kool & The Gang.

Chris Morris 1954 UK guitarist with Paper Lace.

Lyle Lovett 1957 US singer and songwriter. Lyle worked as a journalist, and studied German. In the 1970s he started to write songs and from 1979 he appeared in public. In 1986 he was signed by MCA, who sold him and his group as a western swing band. He had his first hit with the self-penned "Cowboy Man" (11/86 C&W 10). His songs, which are anything but fussy lyrically, demonstrate strong powers of observation.

Eddie MacDonald 1959 UK bassist with the group Alarm formed in 1981.

Mags Furuholmen 1962 Norwegian keyboard player and songwriter with A-Ha.

Rick Allen 1963 UK drummer with Def Leppard.

Hits of the Day

1957	"That'll Be The Day" Crickets UK 3 weeks
1969	"Suspicious Minds" Elvis Presley US 1 week
1975	"Island Girl" Elton John US 3 weeks

2nd

Birthdays

Earl Carroll 1937 US leadsinger with Cadillacs, who originated as the Carnations formed in 1953. Earl's nickname was Speedy. The greatest hit for the group was a derivation of this nickname to "Speedoo" (12/55 US 17). The Cadillacs are considered to be the first R&B vocal group who did their own choreography for stage performances. They had a further hit with "Peek-A-Boo" (12/58 US 28). In 1961 Earl became a member of the Coasters, who were passed their peak.

David 'Jay' Black 1938 US leadsinger, with Jay & The Americans. In 1962 he joined that band and replaced John 'Jay' Traynor. The band had already had a hit with "She Cried" (3/62 US 5) with Traynor; now, became even more successful with "Come A Little Bit Closer" (9/64 US 3), "Cara Mia" (6/65 US 4), and "This Magic Moment" (12/68 US 6). In 1970 the group split up, and Black carried on as a solo artist.

Bruce Welch 1941 UK guitarist, singer, and songwriter. He formed the nucleus of the Shadows with Hark.

B. Marvin. The two of them had already played skiffle music in their younger days. In 1958 they formed the Drifters, Cliff Richard's backing band. After the original US Drifters heard about this, they had to change their name to Shadows. Bruce wrote songs for Cliff over the years and worked with him.

Keith Emerson 1944 UK pianist and songwriter. He started backing P. P. Arnold, before which he had played with the unknown group Gary Farr & The T-Bones. In September 1967 the group Nice was formed. Hit: "America" (7/68 UK 21). During those days Keith was celebrated as the 'Jimi Hendrix' of the keyboards, his stage performance included using a knife on the keyboard. When success eluded them, Nice split up, and in June 1970, Emerson formed Emerson, Lake & Palmer, which lasted until December 1978. Hits: "From The Beginning" (10/72 US 39) and "Fanfare For The Common Man" (6/77 UK 2). In between, he cut solo records, like "Honky Tonk Train Blues" (4/76 UK 21). In the early 1980s Keith composed soundtracks for films and TV programmes. In 1985 Keith and Greg Lake agreed to make records together again. However, Carl Palmer did not want to join in, and was replaced by Cozy Powell. In mid-1986 Powell left and Carl Palmer rejoined in 1987, but after several unsuccessful rehearsals the project was dropped. In February 1988 Keith, Carl Palmer, and Robert Berry formed the group 3, which released an unsuccessful album.

John David Souther 1945 US guitarist, singer and songwriter. He started with Glenn Frey in Longbranch Pennywhistle, then played with Glenn as a duo, and then when Glenn joined the Eagles, John went solo. J. D. wrote, among other things, hits for the Eagles, Bonnie Raitt and Linda Ronstadt. As a session musician he has worked with the cream of West Coast musicians. He co-founded the Souther, Hillman, Furay Band, who had a hit with "Fallin' In Love" (8/74 US 27). As a soloist J. D. was successful from the late 1970s. HIt: "You're Only Lonely" (9/79 US 7). He had a further hit as a duo with James Taylor, "Her Town Too" (3/81 US 11).

Les 'Chip' Hawkes 1946 UK bassist with the Tremeloes, father of Chesney Hawkes.

Dave Pegg 1947 UK bassist with Steeleye Span, Fairport Convention and Jethro Tull. In addition, as a session musician he is on many albums by British folk-oriented musicians.

Deaths

Mississippi John Hurt 1966 US blues musician. He died after a heart attack. Born 3rd July, 1893.

Hits of the Day

1974 "You Haven't Done Nothing" Stevie Wonder US 1 week
1985 "Part Time Lover" Stevie Wonder US 1 week

3rd

Birthdays

Brian Poole 1941 UK singer and guitarist with Brian Poole & The Tremeloes, formed in 1959. At the time Brian was still wearing glasses like Buddy Holly and trying to copy his idol. When the music scene in Britain changed with the advent of the Beatles in 1963, Brian Poole & The Tremeloes tried to avoid comparison with Buddy Holly & The Crickets: Poole exchanged his glasses for contact lenses. Hits: "Twist & Shout" (7/63 UK 4), "Do You Love Me" (9/63 UK 1), "Candy Man" (1/64 UK 6), and "Someone Someone" (5/64 UK 2). In January 1966 Brian left the band for a solo career. His ploy failed and The Tremeloes enjoyed success internationally without Brian. He still performs, with his band Electrix.

Bert Jansch 1943 UK guitarist, singer and songwriter. For many years he was considered to be the best folk-guitarist in the UK, and was an inspiration to Donovan. In 1962 he formed the group Pentangle, who played together until 1972. After that, Bert made records as a solo artist and session musician.

Nick Simper 1946 UK bassist, singer, and songwriter. In 1964 he started his professional career with Buddy Britten & The Regents, in 1966 he played with Johnny Kidd & The Pirates. After Johnny's death, Nick carried on with the rest of the Pirates until May 1967, and after that played both in Screaming Lord Sutch's band and in Billie Davis' band until October 1967. He was with the Flowerpot Men until February 1968 and after that, became a member of Roundabout, which just a month later, in March 1968, became Deep Purple. In July 1969 he left the band, and was replaced by Roger Glover, who joined along with new singer Ian Gillan, both previously of Episode Six. Nick played with Marsha Hunt's band, and again with Lord Sutch, before forming Warhorse in August 1970. The band stayed together until May 1974. After that, he worked as a session musician for four years, and then formed a new band, Fandango, in April 1978.

Lulu 1948 UK singer, real name Marie McDonald McLaughlin Lawrie. When she was just 15 years old, she led the group Glen Eagles, who changed their name to Luvvers and became one of the first successful groups of the beat-era. They had their first hit with a new version of the Isley Brothers' song "Shout" (5/64 UK 7); it was another hit for Lulu 22 years later, as "Shout – Brand New 1986 Recording" (7/86 UK 8). In between she had several hits: "Leave A Little Love" (6/65 UK 8), "The Boat That I Row" (4/67 UK 6), "To Sir With Love" (9/67 US 1), "Me The Peaceful Heart" (11/68 UK 9), "I'm A Tiger" (11/68 UK 9), "Boom-Bang-A-Bang" (3/69 UK 2), and "The Man Who Sold The World" (1/74 UK 3). In between (from 1969 to 1973) she was married to Maurice Gibb of the Bee Gees.

Adam Ant 1954 UK singer and songwriter with the band Adam & The Ants formed in 1977. Real name Stuart Leslie Goddard. Before that he had played with Bazooka Joe and B-sides. In January 1979 Adam & The Ants released their first single, which flopped. A year later, the Ants left Adam. Parts of the group became Bow Wow Wow. In February 1980 Adam formed a new group with the old name. Hits: "Dog Eat Dog" (10/80 UK 4), "Antmusic" (12/80 UK 2), "Kings Of The Wild Frontier" (2/81 UK 2), "Stand And Deliver" (5/81 UK 1), "Prince Charming" (9/81 UK 1), and "Ant Rap" (12/81 UK 3). He had his first solo hit as Adam Ant with "Goody Two Shoes" (5/82 UK 1; 11/82 US 12). He had further hits with "Friend Or Foe" (9/82 UK 9) and "Puss 'N' Boots" (10/83 UK 5). In the mid-1980s things became quiet for Adam, and by the end of the 80s he was preparing a comeback.

Marilyn 1962 UK singer who was one of Boy George's side kicks. Real name Peter Robinson. Hit: "Calling Your Name" (11/83 UK 4).

Ian McNabb 1962 UK singer, guitarist, keyboard player, and songwriter for the trio Icicle Works formed in 1980. Hits: "Love Is A Wonderful Color" (1/84 UK 15) and "Whisper To A Scream (Birds Fly)" (4/84 US 37).

Deaths

Mort Shuman 1991 US singer and songwriter. Born 12th November 1936.

Hits of the Day

1951	"Cold Cold Heart" Tony Bennett US 6 weeks
1956	"Green Door" Jim Lowe US 3 weeks
1956	"Love Me Tender" Elvis Presley US 5 weeks
1960	"It's Now Or Never" Elvis Presley UK 8 weeks
1962	"He's A Rebel" Crystals US 2 weeks

1979	"Pop Muzik" M US 1 week
1984	"Caribbean Queen" Billy Ocean US 2 weeks

4th

Birthdays

Dickie Valentine 1929 UK singer and film actor. From 1949 Dickie sang with Ted Heath's band, and from 1953 he had a successful solo career and developed into a teenage-idol. Greatest hits: "Finger Of Suspicion" (12/54 UK 1), "Mister Sandman" (12/54 UK 5), "I Wonder" (6/55 UK 4) and "Christmas Alphabet" (11/55 UK 1). He died on 6th May, 1971.

James Honeyman Scott 1957 UK bassist and songwriter with the Pretenders formed in 1978. He died 16th June, 1982.

Mark Jefferis 1960 UK singer with T.X.T.

Lena Zavaroni 1963 UK child star. Hit: "Ma, He's Making Eyes At Me" (2/74 UK 10).

Hits of the Day

1965	"Get Off Of My Cloud" Rolling Stones UK 3 weeks
1972	"I Can See Clearly Now" Johnny Nash US 4 weeks
1978	"You Needed Me" Anne Murray US 1 week
1989	"Listen To Your Heart" Roxette US 1 week

5th

Birthdays

Roy Rogers 1911 US actor, and country singer. Real name Leonard Franklin Slye. In 1930 he moved from his hometown Cincinnatti to California, and joined various groups, like the Hollywood Hillbillies, Rocky Mountaineers and the Texas Outlaws. Then he formed his own group, the International Cowboys. In 1934 he formed the

Pioneer Trio with Bob Nolan and Tim Spencer, which later became the Sons Of The Pioneers. Roy called himself Dick Weston in those days, and he appeared in the film *Rhythm On The Range* under this name in 1936. In 1937 he started a solo career. He had his first hit with "Hi-Yo, Silver" (7/38 US 13). In 1938 he was the lead actor in the film *Under Western Stars*. During the course of his career, Roy made 91 films and more than 100 half-hourly western shows. In most films, his horse Trigger was his co-star; when the horse died, it was stuffed and displayed in the Roy Rogers Museum. In contrast to his competitors, Gene Autrey and Tex Ritter, Roy's records were only by-products. He attained his real popularity as a film actor, and must have earned his millions; his fortune is estimated at 100 million dollars.

Ike Turner 1931 US pianist, guitarist, singer, songwriter, talent scout and producer. He started his career at the age of 11, when he accompanied blues musicians like Sonny Boy Williamson and Robert Nighthawk on the piano. In 1951 his band Kings Of Rhythm recorded "Rocket '88" at the Sun Studios in Memphis featuring leadsinger and saxophonist, Jackie Brenston; the single was credited to Brenston and is considered to be one of the first rock 'n' roll singles. Turner became one of the top session guitarists and in the 1950s he produced Junior Parker, Howlin' Wolf, B. B. King, Roscoe Gordon and Johnny Ace. In 1956 when the Kings Of Rhythm were playing in St. Louis, he discovered Annie Mae Bullock among the audience, married her in 1958, and appeared with her as Ike & Tina Turner. Hits, see under 26th November. In July 1976 he was divorced from Tina Turner. All further projects by Ike were not especially successful. In July 1988 he was sentenced to a year in prison for possession of and trafficking in drugs.

Paul Simon 1942 US singer, songwriter and guitarist. He wrote his first songs in 1955 with his schoolfriend Art Garfunkel. Paul had played with the band White Rabbit previously. In 1957 Paul and Art recorded "Hey Schoolgirl" (12/57 US 49) as Tom & Jerry, Jerry Landis being Paul Simon. Further records followed, which however, were not successful. In 1958 Paul released the solo record "True Or False" as True Taylor. In 1959, when they finally left high school, Tom & Jerry split up, and lost track of each other. Paul studied English, recorded demo tapes for other singers on the side, and released further singles as Jerry Landis. Between 1960 and 1963, still studying, he made records as Tico, Tico & The Triumphs and carried on as Landis. In 1963, Paul was influenced by the rising folk-boom in the USA, and tried his luck in New York's Greenwich Village. In 1964 he joined up with Art Garfunkel again, and in October of that year they released the album,

WEDNESDAY MORNING, 3 A.M., which was unsuccessful. In January 1965 the pair split up again. Paul went to the UK and played in folk clubs there. CBS released the single "The Sounds Of Silence" (11/65 US 1) from the above album without telling Paul or Art. The original version was remixed: drums, percussion and a light electric guitar were added. It became a hit. In November 1965 Paul, who was still in England, heard of the record's success, and went back to the USA. During the following four years Simon & Garfunkel became superstars. Hits: "Homeward Bound" (2/66 US 5; UK 9), "I Am A Rock" (5/66 US 3; UK 17), "Mrs. Robinson" (4/68 US 1; 7/68 UK 4), "The Boxer" (4/69 US 7; UK 6), "Bridge Over Troubled Water" (2/70 US & UK 1), "Cecilia" (4/70 US 4) and "El Condor Pasa" (9/70 US 18). In early 1970 it became clear that the pair would split up. Now and again they would come reform for special occasions like a Grammy event in March 1971 or an NBC Saturday Night Live Show in October 1975. In 1971 Paul's first solo album appeared, which sparked off another phase in his career and included "Mother And Child Reunion" (2/72 US 4; UK 5). Further hits: "Kodachrome" (5/73 US 2), "Loves Me Like A Rock" (8/73 US 2; UK 39), "50 Ways To Leave Your Lover" (12/75 US 1; UK 23), "Slip Slidin' Away" (10/77 US 5; 12/77 UK 36), "Late In the Evening" (8/80 US 6), and "You Can Call Me Al" (8/86 US 44; UK 4; 3/87 RE-US 23). Most remarkable was Paul's album GRACELAND which was released in 1987 and was the record of the year.

Gram Parsons 1946 US guitarist, banjo player, singer, and songwriter. Real name Cecil Ingram Connor. The story of Gram and his family reads like a tragedy. Gram is from Florida where his grandfather owned a plantation, which produced a third of the entire Florida lemon harvest; he bequeathed Gram an annual income of 30,000 dollars for the rest of his life. Gram seemed to have inherited his musical ability from his father, whose main interests were music, alcohol and hunting. Gram's father had always wanted to be a musician, but in his youth musicians had such a bad name, that he became a flight engineer instead. Gram remembers his father having all kinds of musical instruments around the home. Gram's father shot himself Christmas 1959. Gram's mother married again in 1961, a gigolo from New Orleans known all about town. The day before Gram left high school, his mother died of acute alcoholism. The family nanny became Gram's stepmother; she was only four years older than Gram himself. She tried, to the best of her ability, to save the family fortune. His stepfather drank himself to death. Gram's musical career began quite early. His first band together with schoolfriends was called Pacers, later changed to Legends. They played light, melodic rock 'n' roll titles, especially at dances. In the early 1960s Gram turned to folk music. He played with Jim Stafford, who became successful as a soloartist in 1973/74, and with Kent Lavoie, who later became the soloartist Lobo, in a trio that were very similar to the Kingston Trio. From September 1961 to June 1965 Gram played with the Shilos, who played a mixture of traditional and modern music. In October 1965 Gram joined the Int. Submarine Band, which played country rock. In March 1968 Gram left the group and joined the Byrds; it was his influence and background that guided them towards country music. The country album SWEETHEART OF THE RODEOS influenced musicians, like Elvis Costello, Emmylou Harris, and Tom Petty, but did not sell well. In December 1968 Gram and Byrds colleague Chris Hillman joined the Flying Burrito Brothers. In February 1973 finally Gram Parsons formed his own group Gram Parsons & The Fallen Angels, who played country music., but Gram drank too much, took too many drugs and seemed to suffer from serious mental problems. In 1973 he entered a pact with his friend and manager Phil Kaufman: if one of them should die, the other would burn his body in the desert. Two months later, on 19th September, 1973, Gram was found dead in a motel. The cause of death was alcohol and morphine. He was to be buried in New Orleans, but the coffin waiting for transport at Los Angeles Airport, was stolen by Phil Kaufman and a friend. They drove it to a place near the Joshua Tree National Monument and burned the body. Phil had kept his promise – and had to pay a 300 dollar fine.

Peter Noone 1947 UK singer. In 1961 Peter had a part in the British TV soap opera *Coronation Street*. After that he received an offer to play a part in a film beside Judy Garland. His parents were against this, so he never became the film star Peter Noone. In 1963 he became a member of the group The Heartbeats in his hometown Manchester, Peter used Kovac as his surname. In the same year, the band was renamed Herman & His Hermits, and then abbreviated to Herman's Hermits, with Peter as leadsinger. In 1964 British producer Mickie Most attended a concert by the group, and discovered an astonishing likeness between Peter and the young John F. Kennedy. In addition, he thought that Peter was an excellent singer for the group because he was good-looking. The man was right. Hits: "I'm Into Something Good" (8/64 UK 1; 10/64 US 13), "Can't You Hear My Heartbeat" (1/65 US 2), "Silhouettes" (2/65 UK 3; 4/65 US 5), "Wonderful World" (4/65 UK 7; US 4), "Mrs. Brown You've Got A Lovely Daughter" (4/65 US 1), "I'm Henry VIII, I Am" (7/65 US 1), "A Must To Avoid" (12/65 UK 6; US 8), "Listen People" (2/66 US 3), "Leaning On The Lamp Post" (4/66 US 9), "Dandy" (10/66 US 5), "No Milk Today" (10/66 UK 7; 2/67 US 35), "There's A Kind Of Hush" (2/67 UK 7; US

4), "Sunshine Girl" (7/68 UK 8), "Something's Happened" (12/68 UK 6), "My Sentimental Friend" (4/69 UK 2), and "Years May Come, Years May Go" (2/70 UK 7). In 1970 the group split up, Peter tried as a soloist, only hit, "Oh You Pretty Thing" (5/71 UK 12), written by David Bowie, who also played piano on the record. After that, Peter Noone continued to make solo records and reformed the group at irregular intervals to tour on the 'oldies circuit'. In 1980, by which time Noone was living in L.A., he formed the group the Tremblers who never managed a hit. In 1983, back in Britain, he was successful as an actor, he played a lead part in the *Pirates Of Penzance*.

Rick Cobb 1948 US drummer with Bloodrock.

Peter Hammill 1948 UK guitarist, pianist, songwriter and singer with Van Der Graaf Generator, and as a soloist.

Mike Score 1957 UK singer, keyboard player and guitarist with A Flock Of Seagulls. Hits: "I Ran" (4/82 US 9) and "Wishing (If I Had A Photograph Of You)" (11/82 UK 10; 11/83 US 26).

Rob Fisher 1959 UK keyboard player, bassist and songwriter. In 1982, after studying at the University of Bath, he formed the duo Naked Eyes with Pete Byrne. Hits: "Always Something There To Remind Me" (3/83 US 8), and "Promises, Promises" (7/83 US 11). In December 1984 the duo split up. A little later, Rob met Simon Climie when both were working with the group Scritti Politti. In mid-1986 they signed a record contract as Climie Fisher. For hits, see 7th April under Simon Climie.

Paris Grey 1965 US singer and songwriter with Inner City, who were successful from 1988 under the name 'The New Dance Sound Of Detroit'. Hits: "Big Fun" (9/88 UK 8), "Good Life" (12/88 UK 4) and "Ain't Nobody Better" (4/89 UK 10).

Bryan Adams 1959 Canadian singer, guitarist and songwriter, who has recorded since 1980. Hits: "Straight From The Heart" (3/83 US 10), "Run To You" (11/84 US 6; 1/85 UK 11), "Heaven" (4/85 US 1), "Summer Of '69" (6/85 US 5), "Heat Of The Night" (3/87 US 6), "It's Only Love" (11/85 US 15; UK 29), with Tina Turner and "Everything I Do (I Do It For You)" (10/91 US 1; UK 1)

Deaths

Johnny Horton 1960 US country singer. He died in a car accident on his way to Nashville. His widow is Billie Jean Jones, previously married to Hank Williams, who died in 1953. Born 30th April, 1927.

Barry Sadler 1989 US sergeant and singer, who was successful with his own composition "The Ballad Of The

Green Berets" (2/66 US 1; UK 24). At the age of 49 he died of heart failure in Tennessee.

Guy Lombardo 1977 Canadian pianist and orchestra leader. Born 19th June, 1902.

Hits of the Day

1954	"My Son, My Son" Vera Lynn	UK 2 weeks
1966	"Last Train To Clarksville" Monkees	US 1 week
1977	"Name Of The Game" Abba	UK 4 weeks
1983	"Uptown Girl" Billy Joel	UK 5 weeks
1988	"Kokomo" Beach Boys	US 1 week

6th

Birthdays

Ray Conniff 1916 US orchestra leader. He started as a trombonist and arranger for Bunny Berigan, Bob Crosby, Harry James, Vaughn Monroe and Artie Shaw. In the 1950s he developed their own sound with his orchestra and chorus, which was easy-listening background music. The secret of their success was a combination of instruments and voices, so interwoven that it was impossible to distinguish between instrument and human voice. Ray had million sellers with nine albums between 1957 and 1973. In addition, with his orchestra he accompanied Johnny Ray, Frankie Laine, Guy Mitchell, Marty Robbins and Johnny Mathis. His biggest hit single was "Somewhere, My Love" (6/66 US 9).

Stonewall Jackson 1932 US country singer, guitarist, and songwriter. His name is not a pseudonym, his parents named him after the confederate general Stonewall Jackson. He was in the country charts regularly between 1958 and 1973. His biggest crossover hit was "Waterloo" (5/59 US 4).

Joseph Pope 1933 US singer with the Tams.

Eugene Pitt 1937 US leadsinger with the Jive Five formed in 1959. Before that, he had played with the Genies. The Jive Five were successful between 1961 and 1965. Hit: "My True Story" (7/61 US 3).

Jim Pike 1938 US singer. He started with the Mitchell Boys Choir and Stan Kenton, before forming the Lettermen in 1960. Hits: "When I Fall In Love" (11/61 US 7) and

"Goin' Out Of My Head/Can't Take My Eyes Off You" (12/67 US 7).

P. J. Proby 1938 US singer, real name James Marcus Smith. He made his first records in 1957 in the name of Jet Powers, then with the Mello Kings and the Moondogs. In the late 1950s/early 1960s he earned his living by singing demos for Elvis Presley because his voice sounded similar, and took smaller parts in films. In 1963 he turned up in Britain as P. J. Proby. Hits: "Hold Me" (5/64 UK 3), "Somewhere" (12/64 UK 6), "Maria" (11/65 UK 8) and "Niki Hoeky" (1/67 US 23). One of his best records was the album THREE WEEK HERO, recorded in 1969 with musicians who shortly afterwards became Led Zeppelin. In 1978 he staged a comeback playing Elvis in *Elvis On Stage*. In the same year he made the album FOCUS WITH PROBY with the Dutch group Focus.

Doug Sahm 1941 US singer, songwriter and leader of the Tex-Mex rockband Sir Douglas Quintet. Hits: "She's About A Mover" (4/65 US 13; 6/65 UK 15), "Mendocino" (1/69 US 27), and "Dynamite Woman" (10/69).

Mike Clifford 1943 US singer with three hits, which included "Close To Cathy" (9/62 US 12).

George Young 1947 Australian guitarist and songwriter whose career paralleled that of Harry Vanda (see 22nd March).

Glenn Frey 1948 US guitarist, pianist, singer and songwriter. In his youth he played with Bob Seger in their hometown Detroit. He formed the duo Longbranch Pennywhistle in 1968 with John David Souther, who made two albums, and lasted three years. Then he became a founder member of the Eagles in 1971. (Hits, see 22nd July, under Don Henley). From 1982 Glenn made solo records. Hits: "The Heat Is On" (12/84 US 2; 2/85 UK 12), "Smuggler's Blues" (4/85 US 12; 7/85 UK 22), "You Belong To The City" (9/85 US 2) and "True Love" (8/88 US 13).

Frankie Miller 1949 UK singer, songwriter, and guitarist. He has played in various Scottish bands, Stoics, Jude, JB and Frankie Miller's Full House. In addition to session work with Thin Lizzy in 1974, among others Frankie chiefly pursues a solo career. Hit: "Darlin'" (10/78 UK 6).

Chris Glen 1950 UK bassist and singer with Tear Gas, the Alex Harvey Band, and the Michael Schenker Group.

Ricky Wilde 1961 UK songwriter, producer and singer, who, at the tender age of 11, tried to get into the charts with "I Am An Astronaut". This feat was accomplished by his older sister Kim Wilde later (16th November, 1960), with the help of their father Reginald Smith alias Marty

Wilde, who himself had been a pop star from 1958 to 1962 in Britain (*see* 15th April).

Deaths

Dickie Goodman 1989 US comedian and songwriter. He died of a self inflicted shotgun wound at his son Jon's house. Born 19th April, 1934.

Hits of the Day

1943	"Paper Doll" Mills Brothers US 12 weeks
1948	"Buttons And Bows" Dinah Shore US 10 weeks
1953	"Answer Me" David Whitfield UK 1 week
1954	"This Ole House" Rosemary Clooney US 3 weeks
1961	"Big Bad John" Jimmy Dean US 5 weeks
1965	"Get Off Of My Cloud" Rolling Stones US 2 weeks
1968	"With A Little help From My Friends" Joe Cocker UK 1 week
1971	"Gypsies, Tramps & Thieves" Cher US 2 weeks
1976	"Rock 'n Me" Steve Miller Band" US 1 week
1982	"Up Where We Belong" Joe Cocker & Jennifer Warnes US 3 weeks

---

7th

Birthdays

Al Hirt 1922 US trumpeter, who was successful with several jazz-oriented instrumental numbers. Nickname, 'New Orleans Trumpet King'. Before making records in his own name, he played with the Dorsey Brothers, and had his own dixieland group in the late 50s. Hits: "Java" (1/64 US 4) and "Cotton Candy" (4/64 US 15)

Mary Travers 1937 US singer with Peter, Paul & Mary. For hits, see 31st May under Peter Yarrow. In the 1970s Mary released three solo albums. Looking back today she evaluates her time with the trio as follows, 'Just how important we really were I discovered one day when I put one of our gold LPs onto the record player. It was most sobering to find that it was actually an LP by Dean Martin which had been painted gold.'

Dee Clark 1938 US singer. Real first name Delectus. He started in 1952 with the Hambone Kids, with whom he first recorded. In 1953 he joined the Golden Tones, which became the Kool Gents. A disc jockey discovered Dee at a talent contest and helped him get a recording contract. From 1957 he made solo records. Biggest hits: "Just Keep It Up" (5/59 US 18; 10/59 UK 26), and "Raindrops" (5/61 US 2). When he had no more success in the States, he suddenly turned up in Britain with another hit, "Ride The Wild Horse" (10/75 UK 16). He died on December 7th, 1990.

Johnny Rivers 1942 US singer, guitarist, producer, and songwriter. Real name John Ramistella. He made his first recordings with the Spades in Baton Rouge in 1956. In 1958 he moved from Louisiana to New York, and met Alan Freed there, who advised him to change his name and helped him to get a recording contract. In 1961 Johnny went to Los Angeles, and was the star there at "Whisky A Go Go" in 1963. His early records like "Memphis" (5/64 US 2) were cut infront of a live audience. Further hits: "Secret Agent Man" (3/66 US 3), "Poor Side Of Town" (9/66 US 1), "Baby I Need Your Lovin'" (2/67 US 3), "Rockin' Pneumonia – Boogie Woogie Flu" (10/72 US 6), and "Swayin' To The Music (Slow Dancin')" (6/77 US 10). In 1966 Johnny set up his own record company, Soul City, and signed. Fifth Dimension.

Joni Mitchell 1943 Canadian singer, guitarist, and songwriter. Maiden name Roberta Joan Anderson. She is the writer of "Woodstock" and "Both Sides Now". Hits for Joni herself were "Big Yellow Taxi" (6/70 UK 11), and "Help Me" (3/74 US 7). In addition she collaborated with James Taylor on "You've Got A Friend". The British band Nazareth had a hit with her song "This Flight Tonight". Other artists too, like Bob Dylan, Fairport Convention, Judy Collins, Tom Rush, Gordon Lightfoot, Matthews Southern Comfort, Johnny Cash and Crosby, Stills & Nash have covered her material. In 1988 she released one of her best albums with CHALK MARK IN A RAIN STORM.

Nick Gilder 1951 Canadian singer and songwriter, who was born in London and emigrated with his parents at the age of 10. In 1971 he formed Sweeney Todd with Jimmy McCulloch. From 1977 he worked as a solo artist. Hit: "Hot Child In The City" (6/78 US 1).

Kevin Scott MacMichael 1951 Canadian guitarist and songwriter with Cutting Crew.

Jellybean 1957 US disc jockey, mixmaster and producer. Real name John Benitez. He mixed the music for "Flashdance" (1982). His first production was the Madonna song "Holiday" in 1983; among his other productions were "Say Say Say" by Paul McCartney and "Love Is A Battlefield" by Pat Benatar. He had his first success as Jellybean with "Sidewalk Talk" (11/85 US 18), written by Madonna, and further ones with "Who Found Who" (7/87 US 16; 11/87 UK 10), "The Real Thing" (9/87 UK 13), "Jingo" (12/87 UK 12) and "Just A Mirage" (3/88 UK 13). What exactly Jellybean did on these records apart from sitting at the console is not clear, as the vocals were by artists such as Adele Bertai, Steven Dante and Elisa Fiorillo.

Sharleen Spiteri 1967 UK singer, guitarist, and songwriter with Texas, who released their first record in 1989. Hit: "I Don't Want A Lover" (2/89 UK 8).

Liam O'Maonlai Irish singer, keyboard player and songwriter with the Hothouse Flowers, who released their first records in 1987. They came to prominence as U2s supporting group. First Hit: "Don't Go" (5/88 UK 11).

Hits of the Day

1958 "It's All In The Game" Tommy Edward UK 3 weeks

1981 "Private Eyes" Daryl Hall & John Oates US 2 weeks

1987 "I Think We're Alone Now" Tiffany US 2 weeks

8th

Birthdays

Chris Connor 1927 US singer. In 1952/53 she sang in Stan Kenton's band. Hit: "I Miss You So" (10/56 US 34).

Patti Page 1927 US singer. Real name Clara Ann Fowler. In the late 1940s she broadcasted as Ann Fowler regularly with Al Klauser & His Oklahomans. Vocalist Patti Page sang for the Page Milk Company Show on the same radio station, when she left the station, Ann Fowler took on her job and her name. In 1947 she joined Jimmy Joy's band, and secured a recording contract and was one of the first to have her voice double-tracked. Hits: "All My Love" (8/50 US 1), "The Tennessee Waltz" (11/50 US 1), "I Went To Your Wedding" (8/52 US 1), "(How Much) Is That Doggie In The Window" (1/53 US 1; 3/53 UK 9), "Allegheny Moon" (6/56 US 2), "Old Cape Cod" (5/57 US 3) and "Hush, Hush, Sweet Charlotte (4/65 US 8). In the 1950s she sold more records than any other singer. From 1955 to 1958 she presented the *Patti Page Show* on TV, and in addition, there was the TV series *The Big Record* in 1957/8. In 1968, when the national hits stopped the C&W hits kept coming until 1982.

Ken Dodd 1929 UK singer and comedian, who made his first appearances in 1954 in variety shows. He was one of the most popular singers of romantic ballads in the UK for over 20 years. Hits: "Love Is Like A Violin" (7/60 UK 8), "Tears" (9/65 UK 1), "The River (Le Colline Sono In Fioro)" (11/65 UK 3) and "Promises" (5/66 UK 6). Ken had his last hit at the end of 1981.

Gerald Alston 1942 US singer, who replaced the late leadsinger, Georgie Smith, in the Manhattans, (formed in 1962) in 1971. Hits: "Kiss And Say Goodbye" (4/76 US 1; 6/76 UK 4), "Hurt" (10/76 UK 4) and "Shining Star" (4/80 US 5). In 1989 Gerald began a solo career..

Bonnie Bramlett 1944 US singer in a team with her husband as Delaney & Bonnie. Her maiden name was Bonnie Lynn. She was a backing vocalist for Fontella Bass, Albert King, and was the first white woman to sing in the Ikettes Ike & Tina Turner's backing vocalists. In 1968 she made her first album with Delaney whom she had married in 1967. Hit: "Never Ending Song Of Love" (5/71 US 13). In 1972 the group and marriage split up and Bonnie started a solo career. In 1980, she started to record gospel. See also 1st July.

Robert Nix 1944 US drummer with Atlanta Rhythm Section. In addition he played on records by Al Kooper, Lynyrd Skynyrd and Billy Joe Royal.

Roy Wood 1946 UK singer, songwriter, and multi-instrumentalist. He started in his hometown in 1963 with Gerry Levene & The Avengers. From 1964 to January 1966 he played with Mike Sheridan & The Nightriders and formed the group Move in February 1966. The group lasted until October 1971, and in the same month Roy formed the Electric Light Orchestra – ELO for short. In August 1972 he formed another new group, Wizzard, which became the Wizzo Band in April 1977; these lasted until March 1978. In September 1981 he started Roy Wood's Helicopters. In addition to all these projects he also made solo records. Hits: "Forever" (12/73 UK 8); with Move, "Night Of Fear" (1/67 UK 2), "Flowers In The Rain" (9/67 UK 2), "Fire Brigade" (2/68 UK 3), "Blackberry Way" (12/68 UK 1), "Brontosaurus" (4/70 UK 7), "California Man" (5/72 UK 7); with Wizzard, "Ball Park Incident" (12/72 UK 6), "See My Baby Jive" (4/73 UK 1), "Angel Fingers" (9/73 UK 1), "I Wish It Could Be Christmas Every Day" (12/73 UK 4; 12/81 RE-UK 41; 12/84 RE-UK 23), "Rock 'n' Roll Winter" (4/74 UK 6) and "Are You Ready To Rock" (12/74 UK 8).

Minnie Riperton 1948 US singer, and songwriter. She started with the Gems, who sang backing vocals on records by Johnny Nash, Etta James, Fontella Bass and Ramsey Lewis. Then Minnie sang with Rotary Connection and made solo records as Andrea Davis. When that failed, she joined the group Wonderlove in 1973, who were Stevie Wonder's resident backing vocalists. In 1974 she attempted a solo career and scored with "Lovin' You" (1/75 US 1; 4/75 UK 2). Minnie died 12th July, 1979.

Alan Berger 1949 US bassist with Southside Johnny & The Asbury Jukes.

Bonnie Raitt 1949 US singer, guitarist and songwriter. Her father John Raitt starred in the first Rodgers & Hammerstein production, *Carousel* (1945). Bonnie started to record in 1971 and acquired a reputation as a slide guitarist. In addition to her solo projects she was also featured on many records by Little Feat, Jackson Browne and James Taylor, among others. In 1990 she won three Grammys for her album NICK OF TIME, released in 1989. She received a fourth Grammy for her work with John Lee Hooker on his album THE HEALER.

Larry Burnett 1951 US guitarist, singer and songwriter with Firefall.

Ricky Lee Jones 1954 US singer, and songwriter. She made her first record in 1979 and was considered to be the discovery of the year: "Chuck E.'s In Love" (4/79 US 4; 6/79 UK 18) appealed to both critics and buyers alike. In the mid-1980s Ricky seemed to have sunk into oblivion. In the late 1980s she popped up again with the album FLYING COWBOYS, produced by Walter Becker.

Porl Thompson 1957 UK guitarist and keyboard player, who in 1984 joined the group Cure (formed in 1978).

Terry Lee Miall 1958 UK drummer with Adam & The Ants.

Alan Graham Frew 1959 UK singer, and songwriter with the Canadian group Glass Tiger. Hits: "Don't Forget Me (When I'm Gone)" (7/86 US 2; 10/86 UK 29) and "Someday" (11/86 US 7).

Leif Garrett 1961 US child film star and singer. In 1969 his acting career began, and from 1977 he was successful as a singer too with "Surfin' USA" (8/77 US 20), "Runaround Sue" (11/77 US 13) and "I Was Made For Dancin'" (11/78 US 10; 1/79 UK 4).

Deaths

Ivory Joe Hunter 1974 US R&B singer, pianist and songwriter. Died of lung cancer. Born 10th October, 1914.

Hits of the Day

1941	"You And I" Glenn Miller US 5 weeks
1962	"Love Sick Blues" Frank Ifield UK 5 weeks
1967	"Baby Now That I've Found You" Foundations UK 2 weeks
1969	"Wedding Bell Blues" 5th Dimension US 3 weeks
1975	"Space Oddity" David Bowie UK 2 weeks
1986	"Take My Breath Away" Berlin UK 4 weeks
1986	"Amanda" Boston US 2 weeks

9th

Birthdays

Roger McGough 1937 UK poet, songwriter and singer with Scaffold, Grimms and solo artist.

Tom Fogerty 1941 US guitarist with Creedence Clearwater Revival. His brother John was leader of this group. When the band split up in 1972, Tom made solo records without any special success. He died on September 6th, 1990.

Lee Anthony Graziano 1943 US drummer and trumpeter with American Breed.

James Talley 1943 US country singer.

Phil May 1944 UK singer, guitarist and songwriter with the group Pretty Things formed in 1963. Although the band made good R&B records, they never had that big commercial breakthrough. Hit: "Don't Bring Me Down" (10/64 UK 10). In 1976 Phil tried for a solo career. In 1988 a new album by the Pretty Things, OUT OF THE ISLAND, appeared. At least Phil and Dick Taylor of the original lineup were still present.

Joe Bouchard 1948 US bassist and singer with Blue Öyster Cult.

Hits of the Day

1961	"Little Sister/His Latest Flame" Elvis Presley UK 4 weeks
1974	"You Ain't Seen Nothing Yet" Bachman-Turner Overdrive US 1 week
1985	"Miami Vice Theme" Jan Hammer US 1 week

10th

Birthdays

Jane Froman 1907 US singer who sang in many Broadway musicals and radio shows in the 1930s and 1940s. In 1934 she had her first hit with "I Only Have Eyes For You" (11/34 US 20). From 1952 she had further hits with "I'll Walk Alone" (5/52 US 14) and "I Believe" (4/53 US 11). In 1943 Jane survived an airplane crash near Lisbon. In 1952 a film based on her life was made called *With A Song In My Heart*.

Billy May 1916 US orchestra leader, trumpeter and composer. His career began in 1938 in Charlie Barnet's band, in 1940 he joined Glenn Miller as lead trumpeter. Billy played the solo parts in "The Song Of The Volga Boatmen" (2/41 US 1) and "American Patrol" (7/42 US 15). After 1942 he left Miller and worked as an arranger for Woody Herman and Alvino Ray. In the early 1950s he had his own band, with whom he recorded "Charmaine" (2/52 US 17). Billy wrote arrangements for Frank Sinatra and Nat King Cole, and wrote many scores for film and TV.

Onie Wheeler 1921 US country singer and songwriter, he appeared from 1950 with his own band, Ozark Cowboys. He made his first records in 1951. Onie played together with Lester Flatt, Earl Scruggs, Pee Wee King, George Jones and Roy Acuff. He died 27th May, 1984.

Anne Shelton 1927 UK singer, who sang with Bert Ambrose's orchestra when she was only 12 on BBC radio. In 1944 she sang with Bing Crosby, and in 1950 with Percy Faith. She was the first English woman to record the title "Lili Marlene". Before there were charts in Britain, she already had a successful recording career. She had hits in the USA with "Be Mine" (1/49 US 25). In the UK she had her greatest hit with "Lay Down Your Arms" (8/56 UK 1), and her last big hit was "Sailor" (1/61 UK 10). In 1979 she sang the song "Yanks" in the film *I'll Be Seeing You*. At the Queen Mother's 80th birthday in 1980 she sang her favourite song, "You'll Never Know". Alongside Vera Lynn she is probably the best known and most successful postwar singer.

Tommy Facenda 1939 US singer. Hit: "High School USA" (10/59 US 28); there are 28 versions of this number, a different High School being named in each one.

Hubert Laws 1939 US flautist and songwriter. He played with the Jazz Crusaders from 1954, with Mongo Santamaria in 1963, with Sergio Mendez in 1965, and with Quincy Jones on various albums. Hubert made his first solo album in 1964, called THE LAWS OF JAZZ. Chick Corea, Ron Carter, and Airto Moreira all played with him. From 1969 to 1974 he played classical flute with a symphony orchestra.

Screamin' Lord Sutch 1940 UK singer. Real name David Edward Sutch. In 1958 he formed the band Savages. He copied the nickname 'Screamin' ' from US R&B artist Screamin' Jay Hawkins. Further integral parts of his stage performances were taken from old horror films, or derived from Jack The Ripper stories; sometimes he was carried on stage in a coffin, or wearing a toilet seat on his head. From December 1966 to April 1967 he played with Roman Empire, which included Ritchie Blackmore as guitarist, and Matthew Fisher as pianist. Screamin' Lord Sutch made records with musicians like Jeff Beck, Jimmy Page, Nicky Hopkins, Noel Redding and Keith Moon, which were never particularly successful. Inspite of that, he always managed to get himself talked about, even if it was as an aspiring politician. He tried several times to get into Parliament as a candidate for the Monster Raving Loony Party. He looked better than most, even if he did get far less votes.

Mel Noonan 1943 Australian singer and songwriter with New World. Hits: "Tom Tom Turnaround" (7/71 UK 6) and "Sister Jane" (5/72 UK 9).

Tim Rice 1944 UK lyricist he wrote *Jesus Christ Superstar*, *Evita* and other rock musicals with Andrew Lloyd Webber.

Greg Lake 1947 UK bassist, singer and songwriter. In January 1969 he was a founder member of King Crimson. In mid-1970 the group Emerson, Lake & Palmer were formed. The greatest hit by the group was "Fanfare For The Common Man" (6/77 UK 2), the best known title written and sung by Greg was "Lucky Man" (5/71). In late 1978 the band split up and was reformed with Cozy Powell instead of Carl Palmer in 1985 (see 2nd November, under Keith Emerson). Greg had a solo hit with "I Believe In Father Christmas" (12/75 UK 2).

Dave Loggins 1947 US singer, guitarist, and songwriter, brother of Kenny Loggins. Hit: "Please Come To Boston" (6/74 US 5) from a fine LP APPRENTICE IN A MUSICAL WORKSHOP. Dave is also on records by Bobby Bare, Jimmy Buffett, Crystal Gayle and Anne Murray.

Donna Fargo 1949 US country singer and songwriter. Real name Yvonne Vaughan. She taught at Covina High School in California, and also performed as Donna Fargo. In 1969 she made her first records, and in 1972 gave up teaching. She had the hit "The Happiest Girl In The Whole USA" (5/72 US 11). She had a further million seller with

"Funny Face" (11/72 US 5). In 1978 she was found to be suffering from multiple sclerosis. She continued to have C&W hits throughout the 1980s. Alongside that, she owns her own music publishing business.

Ronnie Hammond 1950 US singer. In 1972 he joined the group Atlanta Rhythm Section formed in 1970. Hits: "So Into You" (1/77 US 7), "Imaginary Lover" (3/78 US 7), "I'm Not Gonna Let It Bother Me Tonight" (6/78 US 14), "Do It Or Die" (5/79 US 19) and "Spooky" (8/79 US 17).

Ritchie Cole 1951 UK drummer with Stray.

Hits of the Day

1958 "It's Only Make Believe" Conway Twitty US 2 weeks

1973 "Keep On Truckin'" Eddie Kendricks US 2 weeks

1979 "Heartache Tonight" Eagles US 1 week

1984 "I Feel For You" Chaka Khan UK 2 weeks

11th

Birthdays

LaVern Baker 1929 US singer. Real name Delores Williams. When she was 17 she was singing in a Chicago nightclub as 'Little Miss Sharecropper', and recorded under this name and as Bea Baker. In 1952/53 she sang in Todd Rhodes' orchestra. After that, she toured through Europe as a solo artist, and then became one of the most influential R&B singers of the rock era from 1955. Hits: "Tweedle Dee" (1/55 US 14), "Jim Dandy" (12/56 US 17) and "I Cried A Tear" (12/58 US 6). LaVern was successful in the USA until 1966.

Narvel Felts 1938 US singer, guitarist, and songwriter. In the 1950s he tried as a rockabilly singer, when he was not particularly successful with this type of music, he went to Nashville in 1972, and tried as a country singer. His biggest hits were "Drift Away" (6/73 C&W 8), "Reconsider Me" (4/75 C&W 2) and "Lonely Teardrops" (4/76 C&W 5).

Roger Lavern Jackson 1938 UK pianist with the Tornados.

Mac Kissoon 1943 He and his sister Katie were both born in Trinidad and emigrated to Britain with their parents in the late 1950s. He formed the duo Mac & Katie Kissoon. Real surname Farthing. Hits: "Chirpy Chirpy Cheep Cheep" (7/71 US 20), "Sugar Candy Kisses" (1/75 UK 3) and "Don't Do It Baby" (5/75 UK 9).

Jesse Colin Young 1944 US singer, bassist and songwriter. Real name Perry Miller. He started as a folksinger in the early 1960s and formed the band Youngbloods in 1965. Hit: "Get Together" (9/67 US 62; 6/69 RE-US 5). The group split up in 1972 and Jesse started a solo career without success.

Pat Daugherty 1945 US bassist with Black Oak Arkansas.

Chris Dreja 1945 UK guitarist, singer, pianist, and songwriter for the Yardbirds from their founding in June 1963 until they split up in July 1968. After that, Chris became a photographer. He finally teamed up with his former colleagues to form Box Of Frogs.

Vince Martell 1945 US guitarist with Vanilla Fudge and Cactus.

Paul Cowsill 1950 US singer and keyboard player with the Cowsills.

Andy Partridge 1953 UK guitarist, singer and songwriter with XTC, formed in 1976. Hit: "Sense Working Overtime" (1/82 UK 10). Together with his fellow band members Andy also made records as Dukes Of Stratosphar, where he called himself Sir John Jones.

Ian Craig Marsh 1956 UK pianist and songwriter. He was among the founder members of Human League. His career ran a parallel course with that of Martyn Ware (see 19th May).

Mic Michaeli 1962 Norwegian keyboard player and songwriter with Europe.

Deaths

Victor Young 1956 US Orchestra leader and composer. Born on 8th August, 1900.

Berry Oakley 1972 US bass player with the Allman Brothers. Just like Duane Allman, almost exactly a year before him (29th October, 1971), he died in a motor bike accident. Born 4th April, 1948.

Dimitri Tiomkin 1979 US composer of Russian origins. Born 10th May, 1899.

Ronnie Dyson 1990 US singer. Born June 5th, 1950.

Hits of the Day

1955 "Hernando's Hideaway" Johnston Brothers UK 2 weeks
1972 "Clair" Gilbert O'Sullivan UK 2 weeks
1978 "Mac Arthur Park" Donna Summer US 3 weeks
1989 "When I See Your Smile" Bad English US 2 weeks
1989 "All Around The World" Lisa Stansfield UK 2 weeks

12th

Birthdays

Martha Tilton 1918 US singer, who became known as the singer with Benny Goodman from 1937 to 1939. She had hits with "I Let A Song Go Out Of My Heart" (5/38 US 1) and "And The Angels Sing" (4/39 US 1). Martha was successful as a solo artist also from 1944. Hit: "I'll Walk Alone" (7/44 US 4).

Jo Stafford 1920 US singer. Jo was the forces sweetheart in WW II. They gave her the nickname 'G. I. Jo'. While still at high school she studied singing and formed a trio with her two sisters Pauline and Christine. From 1940 to 1942 she sang with Tommy Dorsey, and as a member of the Pied Pipers, whom she left in 1944 for a solo career. Hits: "Candy" (2/45 US 1) together with Johnny Mercer & The Pied Pipers, "Shrimp Boats" (11/51 US 2), "You Belong To Me" (8/52 US 1; 11/52 UK 1), "Jambalaya" (8/52 US 3; 12/52 UK 11) and "Make Love To Me!" (1/54 US 1; 5/54 UK 8). Jo recorded numerous duets with musical star Gordon MacRae. Biggest hits: "My Darling, My Darling" (11/48 US 1), and the million seller "Whispering Hope" (8/49 US 4). Frankie Laine was also one of her singing partners. She was accompanied on most of her recordings by husband Paul Weston's band.

Grace Kelly 1929 US film actress who sang "True Love" (9/56 US 3; 11/56 UK 4) with Bing Crosby. The song was from her last film *High Society*. Grace had become known internationally for her co-starring role with Gary Cooper in the film *High Noon* in 1952. While she was on the Cote d'Azure in 1955 during filming of her third Hitchcock film *To Catch A Thief*, she met Monegas-

quean Prince Rainier III, whom she married 18th April, 1956. After that she was called Gracia Patricia. She died 14th September, 1982.

Bob Crewe 1931 US songwriter and producer for the Four Seasons. He wrote a number of hits for the band with keyboard player Bob Gaudio. As a producer, he wrote for Mitch Ryder, Labelle, Disco-Tex, and Frankie Valli among others. Finally Bob even managed a record company.

Charlotte Davis 1936 US singer with the Tune Weavers. Hit: "Happy, Happy Birthday, Baby" (9/57 US 5).

Mort Shuman 1936 US songwriter and singer. He wrote countless hits in the late 1950s and early 1960s with Doc Pomus: "Save The Last Dance For Me", "This Magic Moment", and "Sweets For My Sweet" for the Drifters, "Teenager In Love" for Dion & The Belmonts, "(Marie's The Name) His Latest Flame", "Surrender", "Little Sister", "A Mess Of Blues" and "Viva Las Vegas" for Elvis Presley, and "Suspicion" for Terry Stafford. As an artist (he sings in English, German and French), he had a hit with "Sorrow" (6/77). He died on 11th November, 1991.

Brian Hyland 1943 US singer. At age 12 he formed the group Delphis, and had his first great success as a soloist when he was 16 with "Itsy Bitsy Teenie Weenie Yellow Polka Dot Bikini" (7/60 US 1; UK 8). Further hits, "Ginny Come Lately" (3/62 US 21; 5/62 UK 5), "Sealed With A Kiss" (6/62 US 3; 8/62 UK 3; 6/75 RE-UK 7) and "Gypsy Woman" (9/70 US 3).

John Walker 1943 US singer with the Walker Brothers. Real last name Maus. He co-starred when he was 12 with Betty Hutton in the US TV series *Hello Mum*. After moving to the West Coast, he played the brother of Scott Engel in a TV series. Engel and Maus became bassist and lead guitarist respectively with the Dalton Brothers. When drummer Gary Leeds met up with them in 1964, they formed the trio Walker Brothers. For hits, see 9th January. In May 1967 the group split up. Maus was the first of the three to have a hit as a solo artist, "Annabella" (7/67 UK 24). In August 1975 the trio joined up again with the original crew, and in mid-1978 split up again.

Booker T. Jones 1944 US pianist and songwriter. He worked as a session musician with Steve Cropper, Al Jackson and Lewis Steinberg in 1962 for the Stax label, and as part of the group Mar-Keys. Between sessions they would play together, the results impressed label owner Jim Stewart who encouraged them to rehearse for a record. They called themselves Booker T. & The MGs. Hits: "Green Onions" (8/62 US 3; 12/79 UK 7), "Hang 'Em High" (11/68 US 9) and "Time Is Tight" (3/69 US 6; 5/69 UK 4). The acronym MG stands for Memphis Group. The group was featured backing artists like Otis Redding, Sam & Dave, Wilson Pickett, Eddie Floyd and Rufus & Carla Thomas. Booker T. built a career for himself as a producer during his years with the band, working with artists like Rita Coolidge, whose sister Priscilla he married, Earl Klugh and Bill Withers. He also started a solo career.

Neil Young 1945 Canadian singer, songwriter, and guitarist. After being a member of various high school rock bands, he formed the Mynah Birds, which included young Rick James. In 1966 he was a co-founder of Buffalo Springfield. The group split up in May 1968. Neil released his first solo album in January 1969. In June 1969 he became the fourth member of Crosby, Stills, Nash & Young. Hits: "Woodstock" (3/70 US 11), "Teach Your Children" (6/70 US 16), and "Ohio" (6/70 US 14). Beside these he released records as Neil Young & Crazy Horse; this combination has been extant off and on since January 1969 with the biggest hit being "Heart Of Gold" (2/72 US 1; UK 10). Neil Young is very much an iconoclast whose reputation out distances his overall commercial acceptance, consequently he has worked with groups like the Stray Gators, as well as Crazy Horse and Crosby, Stills & Nash. His solo career continues to exert a strong influence: as recently as 1991, the LP WELD was lauded by all who heard it.

Arthur Tavares 1946 US singer with the family group of the same name. Nickname 'Pooch'. From 1964 to 1969 the brothers appeared as Chubby & The Turnpikes.

Donald Roeser 1947 US guitarist, singer and songwriter with Blue Öyster Cult, who were formed in 1970 and became successful in 1976. Their principal hit was "Don't Fear (The Reaper)" (7/76 US 12; 5/78 UK 16).

Errol Brown 1948 UK singer and songwriter, who formed the group Hot Chocolate in 1969. Biggest hits: "Emma" (3/74 UK 3; 3/75 US 8), "You Sexy Thing" (11/75 UK 2; US 3), "So You Win Again" (6/77 UK 1; 8/77 US 31), "Every 1's A Winner" (3/78 UK 12; 12/78 US 6) and "No Doubt About It" (5/80 UK 2). In March 1984 final they had their final hit. In 1987 the Dutch DJ Ben Liebrand re-mixed "You Sexy Thing" (1/87 UK 10), adding a few instruments and the record became a hit all over again. In the same year, Errol started a solo career. He had his first hit with "Personal Touch" (7/87 UK 25).

Donald Johnson 1948 US drummer with Taste Of Honey.

Barbara Fairchild 1950 US country singer and songwriter. When she was 12, she started to appear regularly on TV. She went to Nashville when she was 18 as a songwriter and wrote hits for Loretta Lynn, Liz Anderson and Conway Twitty. In 1969 her solo career took off; her biggest hit was the "Teddy Bear Song" (2/73 US 32).

Leslie McKeown 1955 UK singer with the Bay City Rollers, one of the most successful teen bands between 1974 and 1976. Leslie joined the band in 1973 and replaced Nobby Clark. The group had been founded as Saxons in 1967. After being renamed Bay City Rollers they were sold by management as the new Beatles, which was probably staking claims a little too high. Their hits included "Bye Bye Baby" (3/75 UK 1), "Give A Little Love" (7/75 UK 1), and "Saturday Night" (10/75 US 1). In 1978 Leslie in turn was replaced by Duncan Faure, as he wished to start a solo career. Since that time he has worked the 'oldies' circuit.

Hits of the Day

1949 "Slippin' Around" Margaret Whiting & Jimmy Wakely US 3 weeks
1964 "Oh Pretty Woman" Roy Orbison UK 1 week (2nd time)
1966 "Poor Side Of Town" Johnny Rivers US 1 week
1983 "All Night Long" Lionel Richie US 4 weeks
1988 "Wild Wild West" Escape Club US 1 week

13th

Birthdays

John Paul Hammond 1942 US blues singer, guitarist, harmonica player and songwriter. In 1963 he made his first solo album. Among the musicians accompanying him were the Hawks, who shortly after became Band, Jimi Hendrix and Dr. John and Mike Bloomfield, with whom he appeared as Triumvirate. Worked as a session musician with Tina Turner on the album TINA TURNS THE COUNTRY ON in 1974. Son of John Hammond, Sr.

Timmy Thomas 1944 US singer, pianist, and songwriter. As a keyboard player he played with Donald Byrd and Cannonball Adderley, then became a session musician in Memphis. He had his first solo hit with "Why Can't We Live Together" (11/72 US 3; 2/73 UK 12). As a session musician he worked with Betty Wright, George & Gwen McCrae, Leif Garrett, Nicole and K. C. & The Sunshine Band.

Terry Reid 1949 UK singer, guitarist, and songwriter. At age 15 he was the leadsinger with Peter Jay & The Jaywalkers, after that he was a soloist and session musician, first in the UK, and then in the USA.

Wayne Parker 1960 Canadian bassist with Glass Tiger.

14th

Birthdays

John Henry Barbee 1905 US blues singer, guitarist and songwriter. Real name William George Tucker. In September 1938 he cut his first record, "Six Weeks Old Blues", which was produced in Chicago. When he returned to Luxora, Arkansas, he found another man in bed with his wife: John Henry fetched his gun and shot at the man, believing he had shot the man dead, he went into hiding. When his record started to sell well, he couldn't be found by the record company who wanted him to cut a follow-up. It wasn't until 1949 that he found out that he had only shot the man in the leg. In 1964 he returned from a tour of Europe with the American Negro Folk Blues Festival and bought his first car, with which he proceeded to run over a man a week later. He went to prison and died there on 4th November, 1964.

Walter Carlos 1939 US musician and electronics expert who was one of the first to play classical music on a Moog. His album, SWITCHED ON BACH (1968) became a million seller. He wrote most of the music for the film *Clockwork Orange*. In the 1970s he had a sex-change and altered his name to Wendy Carlos.

Freddie Garritty 1940 UK singer and songwriter. He started his career as a member of the skiffle group Red Sox. After that, he played with the John Norman Four and the Kingfishers, which became Freddie & The Dreamers in 1961. With the backash of the Beatles they became successful in 1963 with hits like "If You've Gotta Make A Fool Of Somebody" (5/63 UK 3), "I'm Telling You Now" (8/63 UK 2; 3/65 US 1), "You Were Made For Me" (11/63 UK 3) and "I Understand" (11/64 UK 5; 3/65 US 36). In October 1968 the group split up, and Freddie started the popular British children's TV programme *Little Big Time*

with Pete Birrell. In 1976 Freddie reformed Freddie & The Dreamers with new musicians and took to the burgeoning 'oldies circuit'. In 1988 he made his stage debut appearance as an actor in Shakespeare's *The Tempest*.

Marvyn Harris 1947 South African drummer with Proudfoot.

Roger Hills 1947 UK drummer. Session musician with Peter & Gordon, Paul Jones and White Plains.

James Young 1949 US guitarist, singer and songwriter for the group Styx formed in 1963.

Stephen Bishop 1951 US singer, guitarist and songwriter. In 1967 he formed the quartet Weeds. After that, he tried for seven years to obtain a solo contract. Finally he gave up and became permanently employed as a songwriter with a music publisher. It was Art Garfunkel who finally helped him get a recording contract in 1976. Hit: "On And On" (5/77 US 11). Over the next few years he recorded sporadically, but he was more successful as a songwriter: he wrote "Separate Lives" for Phil Collins and Marilyn Martin, which was featured in the film *White Nights* (1985). Phil Collins produced his album BOWLING IN PARIS (1989).

Barry Brandt 1951 US drummer with Angel.

Frankie Banali 1955 US drummer and songwriter with Quiet Riot and as a session musician.

Alec John Such 1955 US bassist with Bon Jovi.

John Andrew Banfield 1964 UK singer with the Pasadenas.

Joseph Simmons 1964 US singer and songwriter with the nickname 'Run'. He was already working as a DJ for Rap King and Kurtis Blow, in 1977. Joseph formed Run DMC with Daryl McDaniels in 1982. Hits: "Walk This Way" (7/86 US 4; 9/86 UK 8) and "It's Tricky" (5/87 UK 16).

Miscellany

1952 The British music magazine *New Musical Express* published a hitparade (chart) for the first time, and it was an American who topped the charts – see above!

15th

Birthdays

Mantovani 1905 Italian orchestra leader. First names Annunzio Paolo. In the early 1930s he formed his first orchestra in England and made his recording debut. He had his first hit with "Red Sails In The Sunset" (11/35 US 2). He became really popular in the early 1950s, when he was asked to re- arrange well known songs especially for the US market and record them with the typical Mantovani sound. The following numbers became million sellers: "Charmaine" (11/51 US 10), "The Moulin Rouge Theme (Where Is Your Heart)" (5/53 UK 1; US 13; 10/53 RE-UK 10; 12/53 RE-UK 12), and "Cara Mia" (8/54 US 10). His "Swedish Rhapsody" (10/53 UK 2; 2/54 RE-UK 12) was successful only in Britain. Mantovani died 30th March, 1980.

C. W. McCall 1928 US country singer. Real name William Fries. Fries, who worked in advertising, invented the character C. W. McCall for an advertising campaign. Then in 1973 his voice was used as the 'voice-over' for an advertising campaign. After that, he was in the C&W charts with his novelty songs up until the late 1970s. His greatest success was million seller, "Convoy" (12/75 US 1; 2/76 UK 2).

Petula Clark 1932 UK singer and actress. She started singing on the radio when she was 9, and appeared in more than 20 films between 1944 and 1951. In 1946 she made her first records but did not have her first hit until "The Little Shoemaker" (6/54 UK 7). She became internationally known with "Downtown" (11/64 UK 2; 12/64 US 1; 11/88 RE-UK 1) (remix version)". Among her other hits were "Sailor" (1/61 UK 1), "Monsieur" (9/62), "Casanova Baciami" (2/63), "My Love" (12/65 US 1; 2/66 UK 4) and "This Is My Song" (2/67 UK 1; US 3). Petula Clark was one of the most popular female singers of the 1960s.

Clyde McPhatter 1932 US singer. His career started in 1950 with the Dominoes and had a hit with the million seller "Sixty Minute Man" (8/51 US 17). In 1953 he formed the Drifters and was lead vocalist on the million seller "Honey Love" (10/54 US 21). In April 1954 he was conscripted into the army and was replaced by Dave Baughan. In 1956 Clyde started a solo career. Hits: "Treasure Of Love" (5/56 US 16; 8/56 UK 27), "A Lover's Question" (10/58 US 6) and "Lover Please" (3/62 US 7). He died 13th June, 1972.

Little Willy John 1937 US R&B singer and songwriter. Real name John Davenport. John is considered to be one of the primary movers in the development of soul music. At age 16 he cut his first records, obtaining a recording contract with King Records in 1956: he had 17 R&B hits. The most successful were "Fever" (7/56 US 24), "Talk To Me, Talk To Me" (4/58 US 20) and "Sleep" (9/60 US 13). He was considered to be one of the best blues ballad singers of the second half of the 50s, and his compositions were covered by Elvis Presley and Peggy Lee. He constantly carried a gun while at the Apollo Theatre, and he stabbed a man to death in a bar in Seattle, for which he was finally convicted to a prison sentence for manslaughter in May 1966. He died in prison on 26th May, 1968.

Anni-Frid Lyngstad 1945 Swedish singer with Abba and as a soloist as Frida. "I Know There's Something Going On" (11/82 US 13), produced by Phil Collins.

Steve Fossen 1949 US bassist with the group Army formed in 1963. This group later became White Heart and then Heart from 1974. Steve left the group in late 1981 and was replaced by Mark Andes.

Michael Cooper 1952 US singer, guitarist, and songwriter with ConFunkShun, formed in 1968. The group first called themselves Project Soul, and then from 1972 Con Funk Shun. Hit: "Ffun" (12/77 US 23).

Tony Thompson 1954 US drummer with Chic and as a session musician with Sister Sledge, Mick Jagger, Power Station, Madonna, Robert Palmer, Bernard Edwards and Nile Rodgers.

Hits of the Day

1980	"Lady" Kenny Rogers	US 6 weeks
1980	"The Tide Is High" Blondie	UK 2 weeks

16th

Birthdays

W. C. Handy 1873 US blues songwriter, publisher and cornetist. First names William Christopher. In 1895 he was bandmaster of a minstrel show. After that, he had his own band, and set up a publishing company in 1908. Among his best known compositions are "St. Louis Blues", "Beale Street Blues", "Careless Love" and "Long Gone", among others. The story of W. C. was filmed in 1957. Billy Preston

17th

Birthdays

played the young Handy, and Nat King Cole the adult Handy. He died 28th March, 1958.

Toni Brown 1938 US singer and pianist for the group Joy Of Cooking formed in 1967, which was one of the first rockbands to be lead by women. Their biggest hit was "Brownsville" (4/71 US 66). In 1973 the band split up, Toni made solo records and re-formed the group as Joy, but they were unsuccessful.

Troy Seals 1938 US guitarist, singer, songwriter and producer. In December 1964, with his wife Jo Ann Campbell, he had a minor hit with "I Found A Love, Oh What A Love" (12/64 US 67), as Jo Ann & Troy. Finally he played in a road band, backing soul musicians like James Brown, Dobie Gray, and Mentor Williams. In 1973 he made solo records, without any success.

Winfred Lovett 1943 US singer with Manhattans.

Lillian Lopez 1945 US singer with the disco trio Odyssey, who was born in the Virgin Islands. Hits: "Native New Yorker" (11/77 US 21; UK 5), "Use It Up And Wear It Out" (6/80 UK 1), "Going Back To My Roots" (5/81 UK 4), and "Inside Out" (6/82 UK 3).

Chi Coltrane 1948 US singer, pianist and songwriter. In the late 1960s she formed her own first band in Chicago. In 1972 she obtained a record contract. Her first single, "Thunder And Lightning" (9/72 US 17), was her greatest hit. Since then success has been elusive.

Pattie Santos 1949 US singer with the band It's A Beautiful Day, formed in 1967, which never got beyond cult status. The eponymous debut album (1969) included "White Bird" and became the band's best known song. They split up in 1974.

Wally Lowe 1951 UK bassist with Magnum.

Hits of the Day

1956 "Just Walkin' In the Rain" Johnny Ray UK 7 weeks

1959 "Mr. Blue" Fleetwoods US 1 week

1963 "Deep Purple" Nino Tempo & April Stevens US 1 week

1974 "Whatever Gets You Through The Night" John Lennon US 1 week

1974 "I'm Gonna Make You A Star" David Essex UK 3 weeks

1985 "A Good Heart" Feargal Sharkey UK 2 weeks

1985 "We Built This City" Starship US 2 weeks

Gordon Lightfoot 1938 Canadian singer, guitarist and songwriter. Before becoming successful as a solo artist, he worked as a pianist and arranger of advertising jingles. Next, influenced by Tom Paxton and Bob Dylan, he began to write songs, which were recorded by Ian & Sylvia and Marty Robbins. His first success as a composer was "For Lovin' Me" for Peter, Paul & Mary in January 1965. In 1966 Gordon started his own recording career. Hits: "If You Could Read My Mind" (12/70 US 5; 6/71 UK 30), "Sundown" (4/74 US 1; 8/74 UK 33) and "Wreck Of The Edmund Fitzgerald" (8/76 US 2; 1/77 UK 40). After he had become established as a composer, other artists like Bob Dylan, Johnny Cash, Glen Campbell, Jerry Lee Lewis, Barbra Streisand and Elvis Presley recorded his songs.

Gene Clark 1941 US guitarist, singer and songwriter. He started with the folk trio Surf Riders, then joined the New Christy Minstrels, and formed the trio Beefeaters with Jim McGuinn and David Crosby in August 1964, who released an unsuccessful single. These three plus Chris Hillman and Michael Clarke were the founder members of the Byrds in October 1964. In March 1966, Gene left the Byrds, because he was afraid of flying and didn't like all the touring. In October 1967 Gene played for another three weeks with the Byrds. In August 1968 he formed the group Dillard & Clark with Doug Dillard: they stayed together until December 1969. In January 1973 the original lineup of the Byrds reformed for an album. After that Gene played with Chris Hillman and Roger (formerly Jim) McGuinn occasionally. He died on May 24th, 1991.

Bob Gaudio 1942 US songwriter and keyboard player. The group Four Lovers formed in 1956 and renamed themselves Four Seasons in 1960 when Bob joined them. Before that Bob had lead Royal Teens, who had their biggest hit with "Short Shorts" (1/58 US 3). From 1962 the Four Seasons were one of the most successful US groups. For hits, see 3rd May, under Frankie Valli.

Martin Barre 1946 UK guitarist. He joined Jethro Tull in January 1969 as a replacement for Mick Abrahams.

Rod Clements 1947 UK bassist, violinist and singer with Lindisfarne, formed in 1969, and as a session musician.

Ian Sutherland 1948 UK guitarist, singer and songwriter. His career paralleled that of his brother Gavin, see 6th October.

Dean Martin Jr. 1952 US singer, and son of Dean Martin, who obtained a recording contract for his son with Frank Sinatra. A trio consisting of Dean Martin, Desi Arnaz, Jr., and Billy Hinsche called Dino, Desi & Billy was formed. Hits: "I'm A Fool" (6/65 US 17), and "Not The Lovin' Kind" (9/65 US 25). Dino died in a plane accident with the Air National Guard on 21st March, 1987.

Peter Cox 1955 UK singer, guitarist, pianist and songwriter with Go West. Hits: "We Close Our Eyes" (2/85 UK 5), "Call Me" (5/85 UK 12), and "Don't Look Down (The Sequel)" (11/85 UK 13; 8/87 US 39).

Ronald DeVoe 1967 US singer with New Edition.

Hits of the Day

1945 "Chickery Shack" Sammy Kaye US 4 weeks
1951 "Sin (It's No Sin)" Eddy Howard US 8 weeks
1958 "Tom Dooley" Kingston Trio US 1 week
1962 "Big Girls Don't Cry" Four Seasons US 5 weeks
1966 "Good Vibrations" Beach Boys UK 2 weeks
1973 "I Love You Love Me Love" Gary Glitter UK 4 weeks
1979 "When You're In Love With A Beautiful Woman" Dr. Hook UK 3 weeks
1979 "Still" Commodores US 1 week
1984 "Wake Me Up Before You Go-Go" Wham! US 3 weeks

18th

Birthdays

Johnny Mercer 1909 US singer and songwriter. He wrote his first song when he was only 15. Later he worked as a lyricist with Hoagy Carmichael, James van Heusen, Gordon Jenkins, Jerome Kern, Henry Mancini and many others. In 1933 Johnny had his first big hit with his composition "Lazybones" (7/33 US 1), played by Ted Lewis. Three years later, Benny Goodman scored with Johnny's composition "Goody Goody" (2/36 US 1). In 1937 Johnny wrote his first pieces of film music, and from 1938 made his own records. In 1942 Johnny set up a new record company with two other people, called Capitol Records, and released all his records on this label from then on. Hits: "Ac-Cent-Chu-Ate The Positive" (1/45 US 1), "Candy" (2/45 US 1), "On The Atchison, Topeka, And The

Santa Fe" (7/45 US 1), and "Personality" (1/46 US 1). During the course of his career, Johnny has written the lyrics for more than 1,000 songs, among them "That Old Black Magic", "Fools Rush In", "You Must Have Been A Beautiful Baby", "Jeepers Creepers" and "Moon River". He is considered to be one of the most influential lyricists of the twentieth century. He died 25th June, 1976.

Hank Ballard 1936 US singer and songwriter. He was discovered and helped by Johnny Otis in 1951. In 1953 he became leadsinger of the Royals replacing Lawson Smith. They recorded the hit "Get It" (8/53 R&B 6) with Hank. In 1954 they changed their name to the Midnighters and became very successful in the national and R&B charts. They were best known for their 'Annie Trilogy': "Work With Me Annie" (4/54 R&B 1; 6/54 US 22), "Annie Had A Baby" (9/54 R&B 1; US 23), and "Annie's Aunt Fanny" (12/54 R&B 10). In 1958, by which time the group called themselves Hank Ballard & The Midnighters, they recorded "Teardrops On Your Letter" (3/59 R&B 4); the B-side was "The Twist" (4/59 R&B 16; 7/60 RE-R&B 6; US 28), which became an international hit for Chubby Checker in 1960. Hank's biggest hit were "Finger Poppin' Time" (5/60 US 7) and "Let's Go, Let's Go, Let's Go" (9/60 US 6). After 1961, Hank's career in the pop charts was over. The group split up in 1965, reformed again later, but without Hank.

Don Cherry 1936 US free-jazz trumpeter, composer and multi-instrumentalist.

Con Clusky 1941 UK guitarist with the Bachelors.

Dave Irving 1946 UK drummer and singer with Supercharge.

Herman Rarebell 1949 Drummer and songwriter with the Scorpions since 1977. He also made solo records. Nickname 'Herman Ze German'.

Graham Parker 1950 UK singer, guitarist and songwriter who made his first demos with his group Rumour in 1975. Between 1976 and August 1980 he recorded with them, thereafter he released records under just his own name. Hits: "The Pink Parker" (3/77 UK 24) and "Hey Lord, Don't Ask Me Questions" (4/78 UK 32).

John Parr 1954 UK singer and songwriter. Hit: "St. Elmo's Fire (Man In Motion)" (6/85 US 1; 9/85 UK 6).

Jenny Burton 1957 US singer with C-Bank and from 1983 as a solo artist.

Kim Wilde 1960 UK singer and songwriter. Daughter of Marty Wilde. Hits: "Kids In America" (2/81 UK 2; 5/82 US 25), "Chequered Love" (5/81 UK 4), "Cambodia" (11/81 UK 12), "View From A Bridge" (4/82 UK 16), "You

Keep Me Hanging On" (10/86 UK 2; 3/87 US 1), "You Came" (7/88 UK 3), "Never Trust A Stranger" (10/88 UK 7) and "Four Letter Word" (12/88 UK 6). She had a hit duetting with Junior on, "Another Step Closer To You" (4/87 UK 6). As Mel & Kim (not to be confused with the sister duo of the same name) – in this case Mel is the comedian Mel Smith – they had a hit with "Rockin' Around The Christmas Tree" (12/87 UK 3).

Kirk Hammett 1962 US guitarist and songwriter with Metallica.

Deaths

Junior Parker 1971 US singer. He died during an eye operation. Born 3rd March, 1927.

Danny Whitten 1972 US singer, guitarist and songwriter with Crazy Horse. His composition "I Don't Wanna Talk About It" became a big hit for Rod Stewart. Danny died aged 29 of an overdose of heroin.

Lennie Tristano 1978 US jazz pianist and composer. Born 19th March, 1919.

Tom Evans 1983 UK bassist with Badfinger. He committed suicide. Born 5th June, 1947.

Hits of the Day

1950	"Harbor Lights" Sammy Kaye	US 4 weeks
1978	"Rat Trap" Boomtown Rats	UK 2 weeks

Sinatra, and "I Dream Of You" (1/45 US 4), also with Sinatra. Tommy died unexpectedly on 26th November, 1956.

Ray Collins 1937 US singer and songwriter with the Soul Giants, who were joined by Frank Zappa in 1964; they became the Muthers in 1965, then the Mothers, and finally the Mothers Of Invention. Ray stayed until the early 1970s and was replaced by singers Mark Volman and Howard Kaylan of the Turtles. In 1981, after playing with Geronimo Black and guesting on a solo album by Frank Zappa, he formed a band called Grandmothers.

Hank Medress 1938 US singer with the Tokens. Hank later became a producer, and it was he who recorded a new version of the Tokens' hit "The Lion Sleeps Tonight" with Robert John. He was also featured on records by Tony Orlando & Dawn, Pousette-Dart Band and the Weather Girls.

Charlie Coe 1944 US bassist with Paul Revere & The Raiders.

Fred Lipsius 1944 US alto-saxophonist and pianist until 1972 with the group Blood, Sweat & Tears formed in 1968.

Andrew McCulloch 1945 UK drummer with Shylimbs, King Crimson, Arthur Brown's Kingdom Come and Fields. In 1972 he was a founder member of Greenslade.

Joe Correro 1946 US drummer with Paul Revere & The Raiders. After the band split up in the early 1970s, he did session work for Hamilton, Joe Frank & Reynolds, Al Kooper, Al Jarreau, Joe Cocker, Jackie Lomax, Deodato, the Alpha Band and Tim Weissberg.

Annette Guest 1954 US singer with First Choice.

Deaths

Francis Craig 1966 US pianist, songwriter and orchestra leader. Born 10th September, 1900.

19th

Birthdays

Tommy Dorsey 1905 US trombonist, songwriter, and bandleader, who is one of the greatest trombonists in the history of jazz. He is the younger of the two Dorsey brothers, the other was Jimmy, born 29th February, 1904. From the mid 1930s both had considerable success with their own respective orchestras. During the course of his career, Tommy reached the No. 1 position in the US pop charts seventeen times between 1935 and 1953. His million sellers were "Marie" (3/37 US 1), "Boogie Woogie" (11/38 US 3; 1/43 RE-US 5), "I'll Never Smile Again" (6/40 US 1), "There Are Such Things" (11/42 US 1) with Frank

---

Hits of the Day

1954	"Hold My Hand" Don Cordell	UK 1 week (2nd time)
1964	"Baby Love" Supremes	UK 2 weeks
1966	"You Keep Me Hanging On" Supremes	US 2 weeks
1988	"Bad Medicine" Bon Jovi	US 2 weeks
1988	"First Time" Robin Beck	UK 3 weeks

20th

Birthdays

June Christy 1925 US singer, real name Shirley Luster. She started her career as Sharon Leslie in the late 1930s, but hit the bigtime when she replaced Anita O'Day in Stan Kenton's band in 1945. She had her biggest hits with this band: the two million sellers "Tampico" (7/45 US 3) and "Shoo-Fly Pie and Apple Pan Dowdy" (3/46 US 6). After the Stan Kenton band split up in the late 1950s, June worked as a solo artist; her biggest hit was "My Heart Belongs To Only You" (2/53 US 22). She died on June 21st, 1990.

Raymond Lefevre 1929 French orchestra leader who has released over 50 albums in the course of his career.

Tony Butala 1940 US singer with the Lettermen formed in 1960. They had 20 hits between 1961 and 1971; among them were "When I Fall In Love" (11/61 US 7) and "Goin' Out Of My Head/Can't Take My Eyes Off You" (12/67 US 7). From 1968, the lineup was constantly changing, but Tony made sure that the band continued. The last album to chart was in 1974.

Aubrey Lee de Cordova 1941 US bassist with the String-A-Longs.

Norman Greenbaum 1942 US singer, guitarist, and songwriter. In 1965 he formed the "psychedelic" group Dr. West's Medicine Show & Junk Band, which split up in 1967. After that, Norman embarked on a solo career, which finally bore fruit with "Spirit In the Sky" (2/70 US 3; UK 1). In 1972 his third and last album appeared, after which he withdrew from the music business and bred goats.

De Lisle McKenzie Harper 1942 UK bassist with Juicy Lucy, Johnny Nash, Freddie King, Stealers Wheel, Ginger Baker, and others.

Mike Vernon 1944 Most successful and popular UK blues record producer. Founder of Blue Horizon records.

Duane Allman 1946 US guitarist and songwriter. He formed the Kings in 1960 with brother Gregg. They played in various bands until 1965, when they formed the Allman Joys, Hourglass, and finally the Allman Brothers Band. Beside that he was an in-demand session guitarist at the Muscle Shoals and Criteria studios. The last three studio recordings by Duane can be found on the album EAT A PEACH which climbed to No. 4 in the US album charts in March 1972. Biggest hit for the Allman Brothers, without

Duane, was "Ramblin' Man" (8/73 US 2). Duane died 29th October, 1971.

Ray Stiles 1946 UK bassist and singer with Mud.

Joe Walsh 1947 US guitarist, singer and songwriter. Real name Joseph Fidler Walsh. Joe was a member of the James Gang from April 1969 to November 1971. From March 1972 to December 1973 he played with his group Barnstorm, in which Joe Vitale played drums. From January to November 1975 there was the Joe Walsh Band, and from December 1975 finally, he played with the Eagles until they split up in 1982. In between he recorded a number of solo albums. Hits, "Rocky Mountain Way" (8/73 US 23; 7/77 UK 39) and "Life's Been Good" (6/78 US 12; UK 14). In addition, as a session musician, he has guested on many records by prominent colleagues, like Steve Winwood, Ringo Starr, Diana Ross and Randy Newman, among others.

Gary Green 1950 UK guitarist with Fish-Hook and Gentle Giant.

James Brown 1957 UK drummer and singer with UB 40.

Steve Alexander 1962 UK drummer with Brother Beyond.

Mike D 1965 US singer with the Beastie Boys. Real name Michael Diamond. Hits by the group, see 31st October, under King Ad-Rock.

Hits of the Day

1965 "I Hear A Symphony" Supremes US 2 weeks
1971 "Theme From Shaft" Isaac Hayes US 2 weeks

21st

Birthdays

Coleman Hawkins 1904 US jazz tenor saxophonist. He was one of the first significant saxophonist. He played with Fletcher Henderson from 1924 to 1934, spent a considerable time in Europe, and after his return, recorded the million seller "Body And Soul" (1/40 US 13). Coleman also played with Benny Carter, Benny Goodman, and the Metronome All-Star Band. He died 19th May, 1969.

Jean Shepard 1933 US country singer and bassist. In the late 1940s she formed the female group Melody Ranch

Girls. She was regularly in the country charts between 1953 and 1978. She had her first hit – a duet with Ferlin Husky – "Dear John Letter" (9/53 US 4). The follow-up by the pair, "Forgive Me, John" (10/53 US 24), was also a national hit.

Dr. John 1940 US pianist, guitarist, drummer, singer and songwriter, who is considered to be the pioneer of "swamp-rock". Real name Malcolm John Rebennack, called 'Mac'. He started as a session musician in the 1950s in his hometown of New Orleans with Professor Longhair, Frankie Ford and Joe Tex. In the early 1960s he went to L.A. and became a session musician, mainly for Phil Spector. Beside that he played in groups like Zu Zu Band with Jesse Hill, and Morbus & The Three Ghouls. Around this time he became interested in Voodoo and magic: "Prince" Lala especially got him interested in the subject. From 1968 he recorded as a solo artist. His biggest hit was "Right Place, Wrong Time" (4/73 US 9).

Lonnie Jordan 1948 US pianist, singer and songwriter with War. Real first name Leroy. He started with the Creators in the early 1960s, which later became Night Shift. This band accompanied footballer and soul singer Deacon Jones in the late 1960s. During a performance they were spotted by British singer Eric Burdon who was hoping to start a new career in the USA and was looking for a backing group. They teamed up and the group was renamed War. In the same year they had their own first hits. Million seller hits: "Slippin' Into Darkness" (1/72 US 16), "The World Is A Ghetto" (11/72 US 7), "The Cisco Kid" (3/73 US 2), "Why Can't We Be Friends" (5/75 US 6) and "Summer" (7/76 US 7).

Alphonse Mouzon 1948 US jazz drummer, keyboard player, composer and singer. He started when he was 19 with Gil Evans, and then worked with McCoy Tyner, Larry Coryell, Joachim Kühn and Herbie Hancock.

Randy Zehringer 1949 US drummer, whose career paralleled that of his brother Rick, see 5th August.

Livingston Taylor 1950 US singer and songwriter, who, in common with siblings Alex and Kate, achieved moderate success on the back of older brother James Taylor. He had his first success in 1971, but his most significant was "I Will Be In Love With You" (10/78 US 30).

Fiachna O'Braonain 1965 UK guitarist and singer with Hothouse Flowers.

Deaths

Allan Sherman 1973 US comedian, writer and producer. Born 30th November, 1924.

22nd

Birthdays

Hoagy Carmichael 1899 US singer, pianist, bandleader, and probably one of the most productive of all American songwriters. He recorded his first song with the Hitch Happy Harmonists in 1923. In 1924 Hoagy formed his own band. Two years later he began work as a lawyer after successfully completing his studies. Frankie Trumbauer and his orchestra recorded Hoagy's composition "Riverboat Shuffle" (9/27 US 16). It was his first success, and made him forget his career as a lawyer. Hoagy formed his own band Carmichael's Collegians, and shortly afterwards it became Hoagy Carmichael & His Pals, among whom were Tommy and Jimmy Dorsey. He had his first hit with "Lazy River" (6/32 US 19). Beside Tommy and Jimmy Dorsey, Joe Venuti and Eddie Lang were also members. His biggest hit was "Huggin' And Chalkin' " (11/46 US 1). He appeared in several films between 1937 and 1955. His composition "Stardust" is apparently the most recorded love song of all time. He died 27th December, 1981.

Ron McClure 1941 US bassist ranging from jazz to rock to pop. He played with Bobby Scott, Buddy Rich, Maynard Ferguson, Herbie Mann, Wes Montgomery, and also with Tony Bennett, Dionne Warwick, the Pointer Sisters, and from 1973 to 1975 with Blood, Sweat & Tears.

Steve Caldwell 1942 US singer with the Orlons.

Jamie Troy 1942 US singer with the Classics.

Aston Barrett 1946 Jamaican bassist with the Upsetters and from 1970 with the Wailers.

Dennis Larden 1948 US guitarist and with brother Lary, first as a folk duo, then as Every Mother's Son. Their biggest hit was "Come On Down To My Boat" (5/67 US 6).

Will Danford 1949 South African bassist and singer with Proudfoot.

Little Steven 1950 US guitarist, singer and songwriter. Surname; van Zandt. He met Bruce Springsteen for the first time in late 1967, with whom he formed the group Child, which just a bit later became Steel Mill. The band split up in 1971. Van Zandt who up to this point had only played bass, became guitarist in the Bruce Springsteen Band in September 1971. During the following years, he played sometimes with Bruce Springsteen, and sometimes made records as a solo artist. Alongside that, he produced Southside Johnny & The Asbury Jukes, Gary U.S. Bonds and Jean Bouvoir.

Tina Weymouth 1950 US bassist, synthesizer player, singer and songwriter who was a founder member of the band Talking Heads, formed in 1974. In 1981 the members of the group decided to pursue their own projects for a while. Tina and her husband Chris Frantz formed Tom Tom Club. Hits: "Wordy Rapping Hood" (6/81 UK 7), and "Genius Of Love" (1/82 US 31). From the mid-1980s the two projects ran parallel.

Hits of the Day

1952 "It's In The Book" Johnny Standley US 2 weeks
1957 "Mary's Boy Child" Harry Belafonte UK 7 weeks
1967 "Let The Heartaches Begin" Long John Baldry UK 2 weeks
1975 "D.I.V.O.R.C.E." Billy Connolly UK 1 week
1975 "That's The Way" K. C. & The Sunshine Band US 1 week
1986 "Human" Human League US 1 week

23rd

Birthdays

Perez Prado 1916 Cuban pianist and songwriter who in the 1950s became "King of Mambo" with the title "El Ray Del Mambo". Hits: "Cherry Pink And Apple Blossom White" (3/55 US & UK 1) and "Patricia" (6/58 US 1; UK 8). He died on 4th December, 1983. His birthday is sometimes given as 13th November, or 11th December.

Betty Everett 1939 US singer and pianist, who cut her first records in 1958. Her first big hit was "You're No Good" (1/64 US 51), which was later covered by the Swinging Blue Jeans and Linda Ronstadt. Other hits included "The Shoop Shoop Song (It's In His Kiss)" (2/64 US 6; 10/68 UK 34) and, with Jerry Butler, "Let It Be Me" (9/64 US 5). She appeared in the R&B charts until 1978.

Anthony Bourge 1948 UK guitarist and singer with Budgie, formed in 1968; their first album appeared in September 1971.

Sandra Stevens 1949 UK singer with Brotherhood Of Man. This group was comprised session singers and musicians. First hit: "United We Stand" (2/70 UK 10; 4/70 US 13). After that, there was a pause of six years, then the group won the Eurovision song contest in 1976 with "Save Your Kisses For Me" (3/76 UK 1; 5/76 US 27). Further hits: "Oh Boy (The Mood I'm In)" (2/77 UK 8), "Angelo" (7/77 UK 1) and "Figaro" (1/78 UK 1).

Bruce Hornsby 1954 US singer, pianist and songwriter. In 1978 Bruce who had learned to play piano at high school and later studied the instrument, started an endless tour of bars and cocktail lounges through the southern states of the USA with his own band. In 1980 he and his brother moved to Los Angeles, where the pair signed a three-year contract with 20th Century Publishing Company, which was to secure them a regular income as songwriters. One year later they met Huey Lewis who was especially impressed by Bruce's piano playing. In 1983 Bruce joined. Sheena Easton's group for a long US tour. In 1985, having written songs for eight years, which nobody wanted, he formed his own band Range, and obtained a recording contract with RCA. The year after that, the first records by Bruce Hornsby & The Range appeared. Hits: "The Way It Is" (8/86 UK 15; US 1), "Mandolin Rain" (1/87 US 4) and "The Valley Road" (4/88 US 5). In the meantime, Bruce also worked with Huey Lewis, Clannad, Patti Austin, Kim Carnes and Don Henley.

Deaths

Joe Turner 1985 US R&B singer and songwriter. Born on 18th May, 1911.

Hits of the Day

1940 "Blueberry Hill" Glenn Miller US 1 week
1959 "Mack The Knife" Bobby Darin US 3 weeks (2nd time)
1963 "I'm Leaving It Up To You" Dale & Grace US 2 weeks
1974 "I Can Help" Billy Swan US 2 weeks

24th

Birthdays

Scott Joplin 1868 US pianist and composer. He was considered to be one of the greatest ragtime artists and songwriters. He wrote "The Entertainer", which became a million seller in 1974 for Marvin Hamlisch. He died 1st February, 1917.

Michael Holliday 1928 UK singer. Real name Michael Miller. He was successful from 1956 to 1960. Hits: "The Story Of My Life" (1/58 UK 1), "Stairway Of Love" (5/58 UK 3) and "Starry Eyed" (1/60 UK 1). He died 23rd October, 1963.

Pete Best 1941 UK drummer born in Madras, India. Real first names, Randolph Peter. When the Beatles formed in April 1960, he became their drummer. In the cellar of the Best family's house was the Casbah Club, which offered the young group their first opportunities for performing. In the early 1960s in Hamburg, Pete was a member of The Beatles. During the first recording sessions 18th August, 1962, Pete was fired from the group by producer George Martin, because he said Pete was not good enough. His replacement was Ringo Starr of Rory Storm. Pete formed the group Pete Best Four, which immediately received a record contract with Decca, the same company which had previously turned down the Beatles. While his group was unsuccessful, the Beatles conquered the world. Pete worked in a bread factory, tried to commit suicide and had difficulties for a long time before getting himself together again. Now he is a civil servant in Liverpool.

Gary Boyle 1941 UK guitarist, born in India. He started in the backing band of Dusty Springfield, and then played with Brian Auger for two years. As a studio musician he worked with Mike Westbrook, Mike Gibbs and Stomo Yamashta, and in late 1972 joined Isotope. From 1977 Gary released solo records.

Donald 'Duck' Dunn 1941 US bassist and songwriter with the Mar-Keys and from 1964 with Booker T. & The MGs. Donald is a sought-after session musician.

Billy Connolly 1942 UK folk singer, songwriter and comedian. He played with the Humblebums with Gerry Rafferty. From the early 1970s he became established as a comedian & solo artist. His biggest hit was a parody of the Tammy Wynette hit, "D.I.V.O.R.C.E." (11/75 UK 1). As a film actor, Billy appeared with Richard Burton in *Absolution* and Michael Caine in *Water*.

Robin Williamson 1943 UK multi-instrumentalist and singer with Incredible String Band formed in 1965, and which split up in 1974. After that he played as a session musician, with Melanie, Van Morrison and Al Stewart among others.

Lee Michaels 1945 US singer, pianist and songwriter. Lee played with the Sentinels in 1965, then with the Joel Scott Hill group; in both groups Johnny Barbata was drummer, who later joined Jefferson Airplane. In 1968 he started a solo career; his biggest hit was "Do You Know What I Mean" (7/71 US 6).

Tony Clarkin 1946 UK lead guitarist and songwriter with Magnum.

Dave Sinclair 1947 UK pianist with Wilde Flowers (1967), Caravan (1968–1971), Matching Mole (1971/72), Hatfield & The North (1972/73), and with Caravan again (1973–1976). After that he attempted a solo career. In 1981/82 he rejoined Caravan once again.

Gary Cooper 1953 US singer and songwriter in the duo Sly Fox. First hit: "Let's Go All The Way" (12/85 US 7; 6/86 UK 3).

Carmel 1958 UK female singer and songwriter with the group of the same name formed in 1982. Surname McCourt. Hits: "Bad Day" (8/83 UK 15) and "More More More" (2/84 UK 23).

Derrick Murphy 1962 Drummer with the Canadian group Chalk Circle.

Deaths

Eric Carr 1991 US drummer. Born 7th July, 1950.

Freddie Mercury 1991 UK singer and songwriter with Queen. Died of AIDS. Born September 5th 1946.

Hits of the Day

1945	"It's Been A Long Long Time" Harry James US 3 weeks	
1973	"Photograph" Ringo Starr US 1 week	
1978	"No More Tears" Barbra Sreisand & Donna Summer US 2 weeks	
1990	"Ice Ice Baby" Vanilla Ice UK 4 weeks	

25th

Birthdays

Paul Desmond 1924 US jazz alto saxophonist and songwriter. Real surname Breitenfeld. From 1951 he played with the Dave Brubeck Quartet, whose biggest hit, "Take Five" (9/61 US 25; UK 6) was written by Paul. He died 30th May, 1977.

Percy Sledge 1940 US singer, who was already singing as a teenager with the group Esquires Combo. When soul music became successful in the mid-1960s his career took off. Hits: "When A Man Loves A Woman" (4/66 US 1; UK 4; 2/87 RE-UK 2), "Warm And Tender Love" (7/66 US 17; UK 34) and "Take Time To Know Her" (3/68 US 11).

Roy Lynes 1943 UK pianist, who, in April 1965, joined the Spectres, formed in 1962. They released three unsuccessful singles, and changed their name to Traffic Jam in March 1967. In order to avoid confusion with the group Traffic formed by Steve Winwood at the same time, the band changed their name again in November 1967 to Status Quo. In July 1970 Roy left the group.

Bev Bevan 1944 UK drummer. In September 1962, He formed Denny Laine & The Diplomats with Denny Laine, and after that played with Carl Wayne & The Vikings between May 1964 and late 1965. In February 1966 Bev became a founder member of Move and was also a founder member of ELO in October 1971.

Bob Lind 1944 US singer and songwriter. Hit: "Elusive Butterfly Of Love" (1/66 US 5; 5/66 UK 5). When no more hits materialized, he withdrew from show business in the early 1970s and retired to Mexico.

Val Fuentes 1947 US drummer with It's A Beautiful Day.

Del Bromham 1951 UK guitarist, pianist and leader of the group Stray.

Steve Rothery 1959 UK guitarist with Marillion.

Stacy Lattislaw 1966 US singer who was just 12 years old when she made her first album. She was in the R&B charts from 1979, and successful in the pop charts from 1980. Hits: "Jump To The Beat" (6/80 UK 3) and "Let Me Be Your Angel" (8/80 US 21).

Deaths

Nick Drake 1974 UK singer, guitarist, and songwriter. Born 19th June, 1948. He committed suicide.

Hits of the Day

1955 "Rock Around The Clock" Bill Haley & The Comets UK 3 weeks
1965 "The Carnival Is Over" Seekers UK 3 weeks
1967 "Incense And Peppermint" Strawberry Alaram Clock US 1 week
1972 "My Ding-A-Ling" Chuck Berry UK 4 weeks
1989 "Blame It On The Rain" Milli Vanilli US 2 weeks
1989 "You Got It (The Right Stuff)" New Kids On The Block UK 3 weeks

---

26th

Birthdays

Robert Goulet 1933 US actor and singer. He played the part of Sir Lancelot on Broadway in *Camelot*. Hit: "My Love, Forgive Me (Amore, Scusami)" (10/64 US 16).

Garnet Mimms 1933 US singer, pianist and leader of Garnet Mimms & The Enchanters. Before that, he had sung in various gospel groups, and made his first record with the group Norfolk Four in 1953. After two years of military service he formed the Gainors in 1958. In 1962 he formed the Enchanters, whose biggest hit was "Cry Baby" (8/63 US 4). When the hits dried up in the USA in 1966, he turned up in Britain as Garnett Mimms & Truckin' Co. with "What It Is" (6/77 UK 44).

JimSundquistand PhilHumphrey 1937 US guitarists who both had their own groups before they joined up as the duo Fendermen in 1959. They thought of the name because both played Fender guitars. Only hit and a good example of garage rock and pre-punk music was "Mule Skinner Blues" (5/60 US 5; 9/60 UK 32).

Tina Turner 1938 US singer and actress (according to her own biography born in 1939). Real name Annie Mae Bullock. In 1965 she was discovered by Ike Turner, to whom she was married from 1958 to 1976. In 1957 she made her first records in the name of Little Ann, produced by Ike. In 1960 Ike built a show around his wife, who used to whirl around the stage even then, called the Ike & Tina Turner Revue. In the same year, their records started to sell. Hits: "A Fool In Love" (8/60 US 27), "It's Gonna Work Out Fine" (9/61 US 14), "River Deep Mountain High"

27th

Birthdays

Al Jackson 1935 US drummer and songwriter with Booker T. & The MGs. Al died 1st October, 1975.

Jimi Hendrix 1942 US guitarist, singer and songwriter. He taught himself to play guitar as a teenager and played in various high school bands. In 1959 he was conscripted into the US army and released in 1961 after an accident during parachute jumping. He started as a session musician under the pseudonym Jimmy James, playing with Sam Cooke, B. B. King, Little Richard, Jackie Wilson, Ike & Tina Turner, Wilson Pickett, King Curtis, Isley Brothers, John Paul Hammond, and Curtis Knight. In 1965 he formed his own first band, Jimmy James & The Blue Flames. In 1966 Chas Chandler of the Animals 'discovered' him, took him to London and put together the trio Jimi Hendrix Experience for him with Noel Redding on bass and Mitch Mitchell on drums. Hits: "Hey Joe" (1/67 UK 3), "Purple Haze" (3/67 UK 3), "The Wind Cries Mary" (5/67 UK 6), "All Along The Watchtower" (9/68 US 20; UK 5) and "Voodoo Chile" (11/70 UK 1). In 1969 Redding left the group and formed Fat Mattress. He was replaced by Billy Cox. A little later, in August 1969, Mitchell went too, and the band split up. Hendrix was one of the highlights of the Woodstock Festival with his own group Electric Sky Church; after that, he played with Band Of Gypsies, again with Billy Cox and drummer Buddy Miles. Jimi died 18th September, 1970.

Dozy 1944 UK bassist with Dave Dee, Dozy, Beaky, Mick & Tich. Real name Trevor Leonard Davies. Hits, see 17th December, under Dave Dee.

Eddie Rabbitt 1944 US singer, guitarist, and songwriter. Real name Edward Thomas. In 1964 he made his first records, which were unsuccessful. In 1968 he went to Nashville and became a songwriter there for the publishing company Hill & Range with a salary of 37 dollars a week. Things became better when Elvis Presley landed a million seller with Eddie's title "Kentucky Rain". His solo career picked up momentum with "Drivin' My Life Away" (6/80 US 5), "I Love A Rainy Night" (11/80 US 1), "Step By Step" (7/81 US 5) and, with Crystal Gayle, "You And I" (10/82 US 7). After 1983 Eddie was no longer in the pop charts, but regularly appeared in the country charts.

Barry Devlin 1948 Irish bassist and singer with Horslips.

(6/66 UK 3), "Proud Mary" (1/71 US 4) and "Nutbush City Limits" (9/73 UK 4; US 22). From 1974 she worked without Ike and divorced him in 1976. She seemed almost forgotten when she celebrated a shining comeback as a solo artist in 1983. Hits: "Let's Stay Together" (11/83 UK 6; 2/84 US 26), "What's Love Got To Do With It" (5/84 US 1; 7/84 UK 3), "Private Dancer" (10/84 UK 26; 1/85 US 7), "We Don't Need Another Hero" (7/85 US 2; UK 3), from the film *Mad Max Beyond Thunderdome* in which she co-starred, "Typical Male" (8/86 US 2; UK 33), "Two People" (11/86 US 30), "What You Get Is What You See" (2/87 US 13; UK 30), "The Best" (8/89 US 15; UK 5), "I Don't Wanna Lose You" (11/89 UK 8) and "Steamy Windows" (11/89 US 39).

John McVie 1945 UK bassist. He started with John Mayall's Bluesbreakers in January 1963 and stayed until mid-1967 In July 1967 John was one of the founder members of Fleetwood Mac, along with Peter Green and Mick Fleetwood, who also joined from John Mayall.

Bert Ruiter 1946 Dutch bassist and singer. When he was 19 he became a professional musician with the Jay-Jays. Then he formed a quartet called Full House and became a member of Focus in September 1971, where he replaced Cyril Havermans. In the late 1970s he turned up on records by Earth & Fire.

John Rossell 1948 UK trumpeter. In the mid-1960s he formed the Boston Showband which later became the Glitter Band.

Martin Lee 1949 UK singer with Brotherhood Of Man.

Deaths

John Rostill 1973 UK bassist with the Shadows from 1963 to 1969. He died by electrocuting himself on his bass guitar. Born 16th June, 1942.

Tommy Dorsey 1956 US trombone player, songwriter and bandleader. Born 19th November, 1905.

Hits of the Day

1949	"Mule Train" Frankie Laine US 6 weeks
1954	"This Ole House" Rosemary Clooney UK 1 week
1955	"Sixteen Tons" Tennessee Ernie Ford US 8 weeks

Kevin Kavanaugh 1951 US keyboard player and singer with Southside Johnny & The Asbury Jukes.

Charles Burchill 1959 UK guitarist and singer with Simple Minds.

Ashley Ingram 1960 UK singer and songwriter with Imagination. Hits: "Body Talk" (5/81 UK 4), "Just An Illusion" (3/82 UK 2) and "Music And Lights" (6/82 UK 5).

Deaths

Lotte Lenya 1981 Austrian actress and singer. Born 18th October, 1898.

Hits of the Day

1982 "Truly" Lionel Richie US 2 weeks

Miscellany

1896 The premier performance of 'Also Sprach Zarathustra' (Thus Spake Zoroaster) took place in Frankfurt, Germany, conducted by composer Richard Strauss. It became an 'opener' for many live shows after use in the movie *2001*.

1970 The triple album ALL THINGS MUST PASS by George Harrison was released in the USA. If one discounts his filmscore for WONDERWALL, this was his first real solo project. Phil Spector was the co-producer. Such crack musicians like Ringo Starr, Billy Preston, Gary Brooker, Eric Clapton, Gary Wright, Klaus Voorman and Dave Mason were all featured. The singles, "My Sweet Lord" and "What Is Life", were taken from the album.

28th

Birthdays

José Iturbi 1895 Spanish pianist. In 1923 he went to the USA. Jose played Chopin's "Polonaise In A-Flat" (9/45 US 20) in the film *A Song To Remember*, and it became a million seller. His other hit was "Clair De Lune" (1/46 US 21). Jose died 28th June, 1980.

Berry Gordy Jr. 1929 US songwriter and founder of the record company Tamla-Motown

Agato Barbieri 1933 Argentinian tenor saxophonist and composer. Real first name Leandro. In 1953 he played in Lalo Schifrin's band, a fellow countryman. Following that, he made records with Don Cherry, Dollar Brand, Carla Bley, Steve Lacy and Charlie Haden. He won two Grammys for the music to the film *Last Tango In Paris* (1972), in which he also appeared.

Gary Troxel 1939 US singer and songwriter with the Fleetwoods. For hits, see 29th February.

Bruce Channel 1940 US singer and songwriter. Hits: "Hey Baby" (1/62 US 1; UK 2), and "Keep On" (6/68 UK 12). Delbert McClinton played the harmonica on "Hey Baby".

Clem Curtis 1940 UK singer, born on Trinidad. In 1967 Clem was co-founder of the Foundations and their leadsinger on the hit "Baby, Now That I've Found You" (9/67 UK 1; 12/67 US 11). In 1968 he was replaced by Colin Young.

Randy Newman 1943 US singer, pianist, composer and songwriter. Randy wrote ironic songs about the 'American Way Of Life'. When he was 17 Randy had a permanent job as a songwriter. In 1967 Alan Price had a hit with Randy's composition "Simon Smith And His Amazing Dancing Bear". In 1970 his composition "Mama Told Me (Not To Come)" became a hit for Three Dog Night. Ray Charles, Ringo Starr, Peggy Lee, and Nina Simone all recorded his songs. He himself had his biggest hit with "Short People" (11/77 US 2). His albums SAIL AWAY, GOOD OLD BOYS, LITTLE CRIMINALS, and TROUBLE IN PARADISE demonstrate Randy's excellent songwriting abilities. Further more he received two Oscar nominations for his score to the film *Ragtime* (1981).

R. B. Greaves 1944 US singer and songwriter. Real first names Ronald Bertram Aloysius, nephew of Sam Cooke. He was born at the US Airforce base in Georgetown, British Guyana. He grew up in the Seminole reservation in California, Greaves is half Indian. In 1963 he went to the UK as Sonny Childe & The TNTs, but nothing much happened. Back in the USA, R.B. had his biggest hit with the million seller "Take A Letter Maria" (10/69 US 2).

Beeb Burtles 1948 Australian guitarist and songwriter for the group Zoot and in 1975 founder member of the Little River Band.

Hugh McKenna 1949 UK pianist and songwriter, who finally arrived at the Sensational Alex Harvey Band in 1972, via Bubbles, Nickelson, and Tear Gas.

David Jaymes 1954 UK guitarist, singer and songwriter, who formed Modern Romance in 1980. Hits: "Best

Years Of Our Lives" (11/82 UK 4), "High Life" (2/83 UK 8) and "Walking In The Rain" (8/83 UK 7).

John Spinks 1955 UK guitarist, singer and songwriter for Outfield. First hit: "Your Love" (2/86 US 6).

Princess 1962 UK singer. After making a punk record as a solo artist, she sang with Osibisa for two years, worked with Tai Mai and Precious Wilson, and was a successful solo artist from 1985, under the auspices of songwriting team, Stock/Aitken/Waterman. Hits: "Say I'm Your Number One" (8/85 UK 7), "After The Love Has Gone" (11/85 UK 28) and "I'll Keep On Loving You" (4/86 UK 16).

Hits of the Day

1940 "Ferryboat Serenade" Andrews Sisters US 3 weeks

1958 "Hoots Mon" Lord Rockingham's XI UK 3 weeks

1960 "Are You Lonesome Tonight" Elvis Presley US 6 weeks

1963 "She Loves You" Beatles UK 2 weeks (2nd time)

1964 "Leader Of The Pack" Shangri-Las US 1 week

1970 "I Hear You Knocking" Dave Edmunds UK 7 weeks

1987 "(I've Had) The Time Of My Life" Bill Medley & Jennifer Warnes US 1 week

---

29th

Birthdays

Billy Strayhorn 1915 US pianist and songwriter. After playing classical piano in a school orchestra in Pittsburgh, he arranged a meeting with Duke Ellington in 1938. Billy hoped to sell him a few songs. Very quickly Billy became the Duke's closest colleague – as composer, arranger, pianist, and even occasionally as his substitute. Especially, the Strayhorn composition "Take The A-Train" (7/41 US 11; 7/43 RE-US 19), which became an evergreen and the Duke Ellington signature tune. Billy died 31st May, 1967.

Merle Travis 1917 US country singer, songwriter, and guitarist. He started in the 1930s with groups like Tennessee Tomcats and Georgia Wildcats. He survived the Second World War in the Navy, then started working as a solo artist and songwriter. His song "Smoke! Smoke! Smoke! That Cigarette" became a million seller 1947 through Tex Williams who co-wrote it. "16 Tons" written by Merle alone was equally successful for Tennessee Ernie Ford in 1955. Merle himself was in the country charts between 1946 and 1966. His biggest hits in the pop charts – both were No. 1 for 14 weeks in the country charts – were "Divorce Me C.O.D." (11/46 US 25) and "So Round, So Firm, So Fully Packed" (2/47 US 21). Merle died 20th October, 1983.

John Mayall 1933 UK guitarist, singer and songwriter, whose group, Bluesbreakers, proved to be a training ground for musicians, like Eric Clapton, Peter Green, Mick Fleetwood, Mick Taylor, John McVie, Hughie Flint and Keef Hartley. In 1962 he formed his own band Blues Syndicate in his hometown Manchester. In January 1963 Alexis Korner advised Mayall to move to London. After John had worked as a barman in a pub for several months, he formed the Bluesbreakers in July 1963; among the first members was young bassist John McVie, guitarist Bernie Watson and drummer Peter Ward. In April 1964 Mayall had a record contract, and the first record released was the single "Crawling Up A Hill". From that time on he has released consistent albums, but it is not the kind of music to set the singles charts alight.

Meco 1939 US musician and producer. Surname Monardo. His speciality was making disco hits out of film music: "Star Wars Theme/Cantina Band" (8/77 US 1; 10/77 UK 7) is his most successful to date.

Chuck Mangione 1940 US jazz flugelhorn player, bandleader and songwriter. Real first names Charles Frank. He cut his first records with his older brother 'Gap' Gaspare as Jazz Brothers in 1960. They played together until 1964 and released three albums. The first solo record by Chuck appeared already in 1962. In 1965 he went to New York where he played with musicians like Woody Herman, Art Blakey, Kai Winding and Maynard Ferguson. From the early 1970s, while maintaining a high profile as a jazz musician he also had hits with "Feels So Good" (2/78 US 4) and "Give It All You Got" (1/80 US 18), which was used by the US TV station ABC, as the introductory music to the Olympic Winter Games 1980.

Dennis Doherty 1941 Canadian singer and songwriter. He started in his hometown with the Halifax Three and went to New York in 1964. There he joined up with a group of folk musicians, who had originated in bands like Big Three, Mugwumps, and Journeymen. First they were called New Journeymen, and in late 1965 they became the Mamas & Papas. From 1966 to 1968 several very successful singles and albums were released, then the group split up.

In November 1971 a reunion album appeared, which did not become a hit, and the band split up again. Dennis made two unsuccessful solo albums and became the presenter of a popular TV programme in Nova Scotia, Canada. In 1982 there was a further reunion of the Mamas & Papas, in which Cass Elliott who had died in 1974, was replaced by Elaine McFarlane, previously of Spanky & Our Gang.

Jody Miller 1941 US singer. Biggest hit, "Queen Of The House" (4/65 US 12), was a reply to Roger Miller's "King Of The Road". She appeared regularly in the country charts between 1965 and 1979.

Felix Cavaliere 1944 US singer, keyboard player, and songwriter. After playing in several bands in his home city New York, he became a member of Joey Dee & The Starliters. Together with him, Eddie Brigati and Gene Cornish played 'the Twist'. These three, plus drummer Dino Danelli formed the Young Rascals in spring 1964, who then eliminated 'Young' from their name in 1967. Hits: "Good Lovin'" (3/66 US 1), "Groovin'" (4/67 US 1; UK 8), "How Can I Be Sure" (9/67 US 4), "A Beautiful Morning" (4/68 US 3) and "People Got To Be Free" (7/68 US 1). In May 1972 the band split up, Felix made solo records and became a producer of Laura Nyro, among others. His only solo-hit was "Only A Lonely Heart Sees" (3/80 US 36).

Ronnie Montrose 1947 US guitarist, singer and songwriter. He started as a session musician and played on records by Herbie Hancock, Van Morrison, and Edgar Winter. In 1973 he refused to be lead guitarist of Mott The Hoople, and instead formed his own band Montrose with leadsinger Sammy Hagar in 1974. In 1978 Sammy left the band, which then split up. Ronnie returned to session work with the Hoodoo Rhythm Devils, Dan Hartman, Gary Wright, Earthquake, Nicolette Larson and Tony Williams among others. In 1980 Ronnie formed Gamma who cut three albums. In 1983 he was on an album by Paul Kantner.

Barry Goudreau 1951 US guitarist and songwriter. He started in 1975 with Boston, whom he left in 1980 in order to start a solo career. In 1984 he formed Orion The Hunter.

Deaths

Ray Smith 1979 US singer. He committed suicide. Born 31st October, 1934.

Hits of the Day

1941 "Chattanooga Choo-Choo" Glenn Miller US 9 weeks

1952 "Why Don't You Believe Me" Joni James US 6 weeks
1969 "Come Together/Something" Beatles US 1 week
1975 "Bohemian Rhapsody" Queen UK 9 weeks
1980 "Super Trouper" Abba UK 3 weeks
1986 "You Give Love A Bad Name" Bon Jovi US 1 week

30th

Birthdays

Brownie McGee 1915 US blues singer, guitarist and songwriter, who worked with Sonny Terry from 1939 and made records from 1940.

Allan Sherman 1924 US comedian gag writer and producer of the TV series *I've Got A Secret*. He created "Hello Muddah, Hello Faddah! (A Letter From Camp)" (8/63 US 2; UK 14) based on Ponchielli's "Dance Of The Hours". His album MY SON, THE FOLK SINGER (1962) became a million seller. He died 21st November, 1973.

Bob Moore 1932 US bassist and songwriter. In the 1950s he was a sought-after session musician, and was on records by Connie Francis, Brenda Lee, Elvis Presley and Red Foley. His band backed Roy Orbison on his early hits. Solo hit: "Mexico" (8/61 US 7).

Jimmy Bowen 1937 US bassist, singer, songwriter, producer and manager. He wrote "Party Doll" with Buddy Knox which became a million seller for Buddy in 1957. In the same year the pair wrote "I'm Stickin' With You" (2/57 US 14) for Jimmy Bowen & The Rhythm Orchids. Buddy played guitar and Jimmy sang. In 1963 Bowen went to Reprise Records and managed the recording careers of Dean Martin, Frank and Nancy Sinatra and Keely Smith. In 1969 he set up the record company Amos Records. Later he became president of MCA Records in Nashville.

Frank Ifield 1937 UK singer, who emigrated to Australia with his parents as a child. There at the age of 13, in 1950, he made his first record entitled, "Did You See My Daddy Over There". During the next few years, he became the most successful pop star in Australia. In 1959 he returned to the UK and from 1960 to the beginning of Beatlemania he was immensely popular. Hits: "I Remember You" (7/62 UK 1; 9/62 US 5), "Lovesick Blues" (10/62 UK

1), "Wayward Wind" (1/63 UK 1) and "Confessin'" (6/63 UK 1). He continued to have hits until the beginning of 1967.

Paul Stookey 1937 US singer and guitarist with Peter, Paul & Mary, formed in 1961, one of the most popular acoustic folk groups of the 1960s.

Leo Lyons 1943 UK bassist with Ten Years After.

Robert Grill 1944 US singer and bass player with Grass Roots. The songwriter P. F. Sloan and producer Steve Barri recorded "Where Were You When I Needed You" (6/66 US 28) in 1966 under the name of Grass Roots. When the record became a hit, the two decided to record with the L.A. band Thirteenth Floor, with whom Robert sang, as Grass Roots. Hits: "Let's Live For Today" (5/67 US 8), "Midnight Confessions" (8/68 US 5) and "Sooner Or Later" (6/71 US 9). In the mid-1970s the band disappeared from the scene. In 1980 a solo album by Bob Grill appeared, which he had recorded with the help of John McVie, Mick Fleetwood and Lindsey Buckingham of Fleetwood Mac. In 1981 he went on tour as Rob Grill & Grass Roots.

Roger Glover 1945 UK bassist and songwriter, who joined Deep Purple replacing Nick Simper. In 1973 he left the band, and became a producer for Judas Priest, Nazareth and Blackmore's Rainbow. In late 1978 he became a permanent member of Rainbow. When the original lineup of Deep Purple re-formed in 1984 Roger was with them.

Shuggie Otis 1953 US multi-talented musician, and son of Johnny Otis. He made a few outstanding albums in the 1970s.

John Ashton 1957 UK guitarist and songwriter with the Psychedelic Furs formed in 1977.

Richard Barbieri 1957 UK keyboard player and songwriter with Japan.

Billy Idol 1955 UK singer and songwriter. Real name William Broad. In 1977 he formed Chelsea, which became Generation X. Major hit: "King Rocker" (1/79 UK 11). He released solo records from 1982. Hits: "Eyes Without A Face" (5/84 US 4; 7/84 UK 19), "White Wedding" (7/85 UK 6), "Rebel Yell" (9/85 UK 6), "To Be A Lover" (10/86 US 6; UK 22), "Don't Need A Gun" (1/87 US 37; 3/87 UK 26), "Sweet Sixteen" (4/87 US 20; 6/87 UK 17) and "Mony Mony – Live" (8/87 US 1; 10/87 UK 7).

David McClymont 1958 UK bassist and songwriter with Orange Juice.

Stacey Q. 1958 US disco singer, whose surname is Swain. At the height of the disco wave she had her first and biggest hit with "Two Of Hearts" (7/86 US 3).

Paul Wheeler 1965 Australian drummer with Icehouse.

Hits of the Day

1940	"Trade Winds" Bing Crosby US 4 weeks
1968	"Love Child" Diana Ross & The Supremes US 2 weeks
1985	"I'm Your Man" Wham! UK 2 weeks
1985	"Separate Lives" Phil Collins & Marilyn Martin US 1 week

December

1st

Birthdays

Matt Monroe 1930 UK singer. Real name Terry Parson. While he was still carrying out his military service, he tried his luck as a singer in talent shows. Because he never got anywhere, he became a bus driver to start with. In the late 1950s he became a professional singer. George Martin recorded his parodies of Frank Sinatra songs under the name of Fred Flange: he appears on SWINGING SELLERS by Peter Sellers in 1959. Frank Sinatra who heard this record gave Matt his compliments: well done. He was successful with his own records from 1960 to 1965. Hits: "Portrait Of My Love" (12/60 UK 3), "My Kind Of Girl" (3/61 UK 5; 5/61 US 18), "Softly As I Leave You" (2/62 UK 10), "Walk Away" (9/64 UK 4; 11/64 US 23) and "Yesterday" (10/65 UK 8). Matt died 7th February, 1985.

Billy Paul 1934 US singer, real name Paul Williams. Already at the age of 11 he was singing on radio in his home town of Philadelphia. In 1952, Billy made his first records, but was not to be successful until the million seller "Me And Mrs. Jones" (11/72 US 1; 1/73 UK 12).

Lou Rawls 1935 US singer and actor. After his military period he was a member of the gospel group Pilgrim Travellers from 1956 to 1959. After that he sang backing vocals on Sam Cooke's hit, "Bring It On Home To Me" (6/62 US 10). From 1962 Lou made solo records. Hit: "You'll Never Find Another Love Like Mine" (6/76 US 2; UK 10). Especially Americans still remember his voice from advertisments for Budweiser Beer.

Sandy Nelson 1938 US drummer and songwriter. He began as a member of Kip Tyler & The Flips, in which later Beach Boy Bruce Johnston played piano. Then Sandy became a session musician and worked with Gene Vincent, the Teddy Bears, which included Phil Spector in its lineup, and Jan & Dean. Solo hits: "Teen Beat" (9/59 US 4) and

"Let There Be Drums" (10/61 US 7; 12/61 UK 3). Even before recording their second hit, Sandy lost his left foot in a motor bike accident, basically the end for a drummer. Not for Sandy.

Eric Bloom 1944 US singer, guitarist, pianist, and songwriter with Blue Oyster Cult, who issued their first album in 1972 under this name, and before that, released records as Soft White Underbelly, and Stalk-Forest Group. Hit: "(Don't Fear) The Reaper" (7/76 US 12; 5/78 UK 16).

John Densmore 1944 US drummer and songwriter with the Psychedelic Rangers. In 1965 he was a founder member of the Doors and stayed until the end of the band in 1973. After that he played with Butts Band.

Charlie Grima 1944 UK drummer with Mongrel and Wizzard.

Bette Midler 1945 US singer and actress. First successes were as Tzeitel in the musical *Fiddler On The Roof*. She won a Grammy in 1972 with the album "THE DIVINE MISS M" and became a star. Hits: "Do You Want To Dance?" (12/72 US 17), "Boogie Woogie Bugle Boy" (5/73 US 8) and "The Rose" (3/80 US 3). The last recording was a million seller and came from the film of the same name in which Bette played the part of Janis Joplin. As an actress she was also successful in *Down And Out In Beverly Hills* and *Ruthless People*. This multi-faceted talent is considered to be the only authentic cabaret artist who managed to be successful during the rock era.

Gilbert O'Sullivan 1946 Irish singer and songwriter. Real first names Raymond Edward. He started with Rick's Blues, the leader of whom was Rick Davies, who was later to form Supertramp. From the early 1970s Gilbert was successful as a solo artist. Hits: "Nothing Rhymed" (10/70 UK 8), "No Matter How I Try" (11/71 UK 5), "Alone Again (Naturally)" (3/72 UK 3; 5/72 US 1), "Ooh-Wakka-Doo-Wakka-Day" (6/72 UK 8), "Clair" (9/72 UK 1; US 2), "Get Down" (3/73 UK 1; 6/73 US 7), "Oooh Baby" (9/73 UK 18; US 25) and "Why, Oh Why, Oh Why" (11/73 UK 6).

Klaaseje Van der Wal 1949 Dutch bassist with Shocking Blue.

Jaco Pastorius 1951 US bassist with Weather Report, Joni Mitchell, Herbie Hancock, and as a solo artist. His real first names were John Francis. He died 21st September, 1987.

Steve Janson 1959 UK drummer and percussionist with Japan. Real surname Batt.

Sam Reid 1963 Canadian keyboard player and songwriter for Glass Tiger.

Deaths

Carter Stanley 1966 US country singer and guitarist. Born 27th August, 1925.

Magic Sam 1969 US blues singer and guitarist. He died after a heart attack. Born 14th February, 1937.

Lee Dorsey 1986 US singer and songwriter. Died of emphysema. Born 24th December, 1924.

Hits of the Day

1958 "To Know Him Is To Love Him" Teddy Bears US 3 weeks

1966 "Green Green Grass Of Home" Tom Jones UK 7 weeks

1973 "Top Of The World" Carpenters US 2 weeks

1984 "I Should Have Known Better" Jim Diamond UK 1 week

2nd

Birthdays

Tom McGuinness 1941 UK guitarist, singer, and songwriter with the Roosters, Casey Jones & The Engineers and most famously with Manfred Mann, from January 1964 until June 1966. After that, he formed McGuinness Flint, which lasted until February, 1972. Tom formed the duo Stonebridge McGuinness with Lou Stonebridge until 1979, and with the Blues Band from February 1979 onwards, as well as songwriting.

David Munden 1943 UK drummer with the Tremeloes.

Peter Kingsbery 1952 US bassist, singer and songwriter with the band Cock Robin formed in 1983. Hits: "When Your Heart Is Weak" (6/85 US 35) and "The Promise You Made" (6/86 UK 28).

Rick Savage 1960 UK bassist with Def Leppard.

Deaths

David Blue 1982 US singer and songwriter. He died after jogging for too long. Born 18th February, 1941.

Hits of the Day

1944 "Into Each Life Some Rain Must Fall" Ella Fitzgerald & Ink Spots US 2 weeks

1950 "The Thing" Phil Harris US 5 weeks

1957 "You Send Me" Sam Cooke US 3 weeks

1967 "Daydream Believer" Monkees US 4 weeks

1972 "Papa Was A Rolling Stone" Temptations US 1 week

1978 "Da Ya Think I'm Sexy" Rod Stewart UK 1 week

1978 "You Don't Bring Me Flowers" Barbra Streisand & Neil Diamond US 1 week

---

3rd

Birthdays

Ferlin Husky 1925 US country artist, guitarist, film actor and songwriter. After he had served in the merchant navy for five years in the 2nd World War, he started as a singer; and in the early 1950s he recorded under the pseudonyms Terry Preston and Simon Crum. As Simon Crum he had his greatest success with the novelty record "Country Music Is Here To Stay" (11/58 C&W 2). Then he became the protegee of Tennessee Ernie Ford and went to Capitol Records, who released his records from 1953, first as Ferlin Huskey, then without the 'e' in the surname. Hits: "A Dear John Letter" (9/53 US 4) with Jean Shepard, "Gone" (3/57 US 4; he had already released this title unsuccessfully as Terry Preston), and "Wings Of A Dove" (11/60 US 12). Ferlin played in the films *Mr. Rock & Roll* (1957) and *Country Music Holiday* (1958).

Andy Williams 1928 US singer, whose complete name is Howard Andrew. In his youth he appeared with his three brothers Bob, Dick and Don, as Williams Brothers Quartet, who sang along with the Bing Crosby hit, "Swinging On A Star" (5/44 US 1). In 1952 the brothers split up, Andy began a solo career. Hits: "Canadian Sunset" (8/56 US 7), "Butterfly" (2/57 US 1; 4/57 UK 1), "Are You Sincere" (2/58 US 3), "Lonely Street" (9/59 US 5), "The Village Of St. Bernadette" (12/59 US 7), "Can't Get Used To Losing You" (3/63 US & UK 2), "Almost There" (9/65 UK 2), "Can't Take My Eyes Off You" (3/68 UK 5), "Can't Help Falling In Love" (3/70 UK 3), "Home Lovin' Man" (11/70 UK 7), "(Where Do I Begin) Love Story" (2/71 US 9; UK 4) and "Solitaire" (12/73 UK 4). Andy was the host for an NBC TV programme between 1962 and 1971. His year of birth is cited from 1926 to 1936.

Ralph McTell 1944 UK folk singer, guitarist, and songwriter. Real last name May (but named for his idol Blind Willie McTell). In 1967 he wrote a song which became a hit after he had recorded it in various versions: "Streets Of London" (12/74 UK 2). Although he released many more good songs after that, he could never repeat its success. Celebrated his 25 year career in 1992.

Vic Malcolm 1946 UK guitarist with Geordie.

Ozzy Osbourne 1948 UK singer and songwriter, real first names John Michael. He started in the late 1960s with Polka Tulk, Rare Breed, and from 1968 with Earth, who changed their name to Black Sabbath in 1969 and became one of the first great heavy-metal groups. Hit: "Paranoid" (8/70 UK 4; 8/80 RE-UK 14). In late 1977 Osbourne left Black Sabbath, and was replaced by Dave Walker, but Ozzy came back again after several months. In summer 1979 he finally left the group and was replaced by Ronnie James Dio. Further successors were Ian Gillan, Glenn Hughes, and Tony Martin. In 1980 Ozzy started a solo career, backed by the group Blizzard of Oz. Hits: "Bark At The Moon" (12/83 UK 21), "So Tired" (5/84 UK 20) and "Shot In The Dark" (1/86 UK 20), he did not reach the single charts in the USA, but instead he reached platinum disc status with the albums BLIZZARD OF OZZ and DIARY OF A MADMAN in 1981, and gold with SPEAK OF THE EVIL (1982) and BARK AT THE MOON (1983). In July 1985 all the old members of Black Sabbath came together for one day, at 'Live Aid' in Philadelphia.

John Wilson 1949 UK drummer with Them (1966-68), Taste (1968-70), Cochise (1970), Stud (1971-72) and on records by Mark Ellington, Al Stewart and Ian Matthews.

Nicky Stevens 1951 UK female singer with Brotherhood Of Man.

Miscellany

1971 At the Casino in Montreux, Frank Zappa & The Mothers Of Invention were on stage when during the concert, a member of the audience fired a flare, which set fire to the roof. Nobody was hurt, but Frank Zappa lost equipment to the value of 50,000 dollars. The group Deep Purple, who happened to be in Montreux at the same time, producing their album MACHINE HEAD, used the event in one of their songs, "Smoke On The Water". In fact December 1971 seemed a bad month all round for Frank Zappa. On the 10th December, during a performance, he was knocked off stage by the jealous boyfriend of a female Frank Zappa fan, and he broke his ankle and leg. For the following nine months he was wheelchair bound.

1979 The Who played at the Riverfront Colosseum, Cincinnati. In a rush for the unnumbered seats 11 people were crushed to death.

4th

Birthdays

Eddie Heywood 1915 US pianist, songwriter and orchestra leader. He had his first million seller with "Begin The Beguine" (4/45 US 16). He wrote "Canadian Sunset" (6/56 US 2) for Hugo Winterhalter, featuring Eddie at the piano. Solo-hit: "Soft Summer Breeze" (6/56 US 11). He died after a long illness on 2nd January, 1989.

Freddy Cannon 1940 US singer, guitarist, and songwriter. Real name Frederick Anthony Picariello. As Freddy Karmon he was a member of the G-Clefs in the mid-1950s and played lead guitar on their hit, "Ka-Ding

Dong" (7/56 US 24). After that he made a demo of a song, which he had written with his mother, this finally became his first hit "Tallahassee Lassie" (5/59 US 6; 8/59 UK 17). This was followed by "Way Down Yonder In New Orleans" (11/59 US 3; 1/60 UK 3) and "Palisades Park" (5/62 US 3; UK 20). After his career was over around 1965, Freddy worked as a promotion man for the record company Buddah Records. Now and again he joined the revival shows, and in 1981 actually had a record in the charts with the Belmonts entitled "Let's Put The Fun Back In Rock 'n' Roll" (9/81 US 81).

Chris Hillman 1942 US guitarist, bassist, singer and songwriter. From 1958 to 1962 he played with he Scottsville Squirrell Barkers. Then he formed the Hillmen, who lasted until July 1964, and finally became a founder member of the Byrds in October 1964. He stayed until October 1968 and in December of the same year formed the Flying Burrito Brothers with whom he stayed until October 1971, and then joined Manassas. In 1973 he formed the Souther-Hillman-Furay Band and from the mid-70s worked as a solo artist. He also participated in various reunions of the Byrds.

Bob Mosley 1942 US bassist with Moby Grape, formed in 1966.

Dennis Wilson 1944 US drummer and songwriter. With his two brothers he formed the nucleus of the Beach Boys. Dennis, who was the only real surfer among the Beach Boys, drowned on 28th December, 1983.

Southside Johnny 1948 US singer and songwriter. Real name Johnny Lyon. With Bruce Springsteen, who always seemed to overshadow him and Steve van Zandt he was in groups like Sundance Bluesband and Dr. Zoom & The Sonic Boom in the late 1960s. After that it was Studio B and as a duo with van Zandt, Southside Johnny & The Kid. This developped into Bankstreet Bluesband. Then he joined the Blackberry Booze Band, which in turn evolved into Southside Johnny & The Asbury Jukes in 1974.

Gary Rossington 1951 US guitarist, songwriter and leader of the Rossington-Collins Band formed in 1979, which consisted of four of the five surviving members of Lynyrd Skynyrd.

Deaths

Tommy Bolin 1976 US guitarist with James Gang, Deep Purple, and as a solo artist. Cause of death was either alcohol or heroin. He was 25 years old.

Perez Prado 1983 Cuban pianist. Born 23rd November, 1918.

Hits of the Day

1954 "Mr. Sandman" Chordettes US 7 weeks
1959 "What Do You Want" Adam Faith UK 3 weeks
1965 "Turn Turn Turn" Byrds US 3 weeks
1971 "Family Affair" Sly & The Family Stone US 3 weeks
1976 "Under The Moon Of Love" Showaddywaddy UK 3 weeks
1982 "Beat Surrender" Jam UK 2 weeks

Miscellany

1956 In the Sun studios in Memphis, 706 Union Avenue, Carl Perkins was rehearsing with his usual musicians and Jerry Lee Lewis at the piano for the next possible single. During the course of rehearsals, Johnny Cash and Elvis Presley happened to drop in at the studios. A photographic session was arranged quickly for the local press, then Johnny Cash left the studio again. The other musicians were sitting around and playing about on their guitars and the piano. The tape recorder was switched on, and this is how the so-called 'million dollar session' came about, first as an illegal disc, and then officially on the market. They were not serious recordings at all, just a bit of messing about.

1980 Two months after drummer John Bonham's death Jimmy Page, Robert Plant, and John Paul Jones, announced the end of Led Zeppelin. In an explanation they said, that "after the loss of their friend, and out of respect for his family they could no longer carry on as the group Led Zeppelin."

5th

Birthdays

Sonny Boy Williamson 1899 US blues harmonica player, singer, and songwriter. Real name Aleck Ford, nickname Rice Miller. There exists a whole bunch of data on this man, his birthdate, and his name. The birthdate on his gravestone says 11th March, 1908, and in a passport which he once used to travel to Europe, the birthdate was given as 7th April, 1909. One thing is certain, he died 25th May, 1965. Sonny Boy appeared from the mid-30s at the

Grand Ole Opry. From 1941 to 1945 he played on a radio station at Helena. In 1974 he made his first records. His biggest hit was "Don't Start Me Talkin'" (10/55 R&B 3).

Don Robertson 1922 US pianist and songwriter, who had a million seller with the instrumental title "The Happy Whistler" (4/56 US 6; UK 8). Apart from that he wrote hits for other artists, like Hank Snow, Eddy Arnold, Elvis Presley, Hank Locklin, Les Paul & Mary Ford, Faron Young, Kitty Wells and Nancy Wilson.

Little Richard 1932 US singer, pianist, ans songwriter. Real name Richard Wayne Penniman. His birthdate is often given (even on record covers) as 25th December, 1935. It was his record company who had the idea of selling him as 'Santa Claus'. Winning a talent contest led to a first record with RCA-Victor in 1951. From 1953 to 1955 Richard was a member of the Tempo Toppers and a singer for the Johnny Otis Band. In 1955 he sent demo tapes to Specialty Records in L.A. On the 14th September, 1955, he went to their studios and recorded nine titles, among them his first hit, "Tutti Frutti" (1/56 US 17; 2/57 UK 29). Further hits: "Long Tall Sally" (4/56 US 6; 2/57 UK 3), "Jenny Jenny" (6/57 US 10; 9/57 UK 11), "Keep A Knockin'" (9/57 US 8; 11/57 UK 11), Good Golly, Miss Molly" (2/58 US 10; UK 8), and "Baby Face" (1/59 UK 2). In 1957, after a tour of Australia, he announced he would never sing rock 'n' roll again. In 1964 he changed his mind, and tried several comebacks, the last was "Great Gosh A'Mighty!" (3/86 US 42), from the film *Down And Out In Beverly Hills*, in which he played a part. In his heyday as a rock 'n' roller, Little Richard appeared in three early R 'n' R films, *Don't Knock The Rock*, *The Girl Can't Help It*, and *Mr Rock 'n' Roll*.

J. J. Cale 1938 US guitarist, singer, and songwriter. The initials J. J. are for Jean Jacques. In his early days he worked together with Leon Russell, Carl Radle, Phil Spector, and Delaney & Bonnie Bramlett. In 1965 he made his first album, including the original version of "After Midnight". In 1966 he formed the Leathercoated Minds, with whom he made one album. Only after Eric Clapton had been successful with his version of "After Midnight", did the name J. J. Cale get into the charts. Hit: "Crazy Mama" (1/72 US 22). J. J. still has a cult following among those who appreciate his country-blues, his laid-back style of singing and his excellent guitar playing.

Lucas Sideras 1944 Greek drummer with Aphrodite's Child.

Andy Kim 1946 Canadian singer and songwriter. Real name Andrew Joachim. During the death throes of bubble gum music in the late 1960s he co-wrote the hit, "Sugar Sugar" by the Archies. As an artist he had hits with "Baby

I Love You" (5/69 US 9) and "Rock Me Gently" (6/74 US 1; 8/74 UK 2). After that, nothing was heard of Andy for several years until he turned up with a new album in 1983, but now as Barron Longfellow.

Jim Messina 1947 US guitarist, singer and songwriter. From September 1967 to May 1968 he was bassist with Buffalo Springfield, and then formed Poco in 1968 with Richie Furay. Jim stayed until November 1970 and then formed the duo Loggins & Messina with Ken Loggins. Hit: "Your Mama Don't Dance" (11/72 US 4). In November 1976 they split up, and both attempted solo careers. When the original lineup of Poco re-formed in January 1989, Jim was featured.

Jack Russell 1960 US singer and songwriter. In 1978 he started with the group Dante Fox. In the early 1980s Great White was formed, whose debut album appeared in 1984. Hits: "Once Bitten Twice Shy" (4/89 US 5) and "The Angel Song" (9/89 US 30).

Deaths

Roland Kirk 1977 US jazz multi-instrumentalist and composer. Born 7th August, 1936.

Hits of the Day

1964	"Ringo" Lorne Greene US 1 week
1981	"Begin The Beguine" Julio Iglesias UK 1 week
1987	"Heaven Is A Place On Earth" Belinda Carlisle US 1 week

6th

Birthdays

Dave Brubeck 1920 US jazz pianist, and songwriter, first names David Warren. Dave first started to study veterinary medicine and from 1941 he was a music student at the College Of Pacific, where he led an orchestra. Following that, his studies of composition at Mills College were interrupted in 1943 because he was called up for military service. In Europe he was the leader of a military band. Back in the USA, Dave formed his first band in 1946, and in 1949 a trio evolved which was to be the nucleus of the

Dave Brubeck Quintet formed in 1951. His biggest pop hit was in 5/4 time, entitled "Take Five" (9/61 US 25; UK 6).

Steve Alaimo 1940 US singer, songwriter, and guitarist who never managed to get beyond mediocrity. Hit: "Every Day I Have To Cry" (1/63 US 46).

Jonathan King 1944 UK singer, songwriter, producer and owner of record company U.K. Records. Real first name Kenneth. While still studying English at Cambridge University, he wrote his first hit, "Everyone's Gone To The Moon" (7/65 UK 4; 9/65 US 17). During the course of the next few years he made records under several pseudonyms, Sakkarin with "Sugar Sugar" (4/71 UK 12), Shag and "Loop Di Love" (10/72 UK 4), 100 Ton & A Feather with "It Only Takes A Minute" (7/73 UK 9), Bubblerock and "(I Can't Get No) Satisfaction" (1/74 UK 9), 53rd & 3rd, Weathermen with "It's The Same Old Song" (1/71 UK 19), Sound 9418 and Father Abraphart & The Smurps. In addition to that, he writes about pop music for several music magazines, produced the first album for Genesis, whom he gave their name, and supported and discovered groups like 10 CC and Kursaal Flyers. What other names he may have used, only he himself knows. As a producer he was behind Piglets whose hit "Johnny Reggae" (11/71 UK 3) featured actress Adrienne Posta as leadsinger, she sang the number in the classic cockney dialect. Jonathan had another Top Ten hit in his own name with "Una Paloma Blanca" (9/75 UK 5). From the early 1980s he was a presenter on UK TV, although he was often working in New York for the BBC programme 'Entertainment USA'. He also had a weekly column on pop music in the British daily newspaper 'Sun'.

Kim Simmonds 1947 UK guitarist, songwriter, and founder of Savoy Brown in late 1966. Over the course of the years, the rest of the line-up changed constantly, only Kim stayed. They toured the US extensively, made a number of good albums, but had no single hits.

Miroslav Vitous 1947 Jazz-rock bassist with Weather Report, among others. He was born in Prague.

Joe Dube 1950 US drummer with Starz.

Jeff Grob 1950 US drummer with Looking Glass.

Rick Buckler 1955 UK drummer with Jam, Time UK, and Sharp.

Eddie Tenpole 1955 UK singer and songwriter with the group Tenpole Tudor formed by him in 1979. First hit: "Swords Of A Thousand Men" (4/81 UK 6).

Ben Watt 1962 UK guitarist, pianist and songwriter for Everything But The Girl. He worked with Robert Wyatt and made a solo album.

Deaths

Leadbelly (alias Huddie Ledbetter) 1949 US blues musician who influenced a whole range of folk and blues artists. Pete Seeger and Woody Guthrie were among his many admirers. Nickname, "The King Of The 12 String Guitar Players!". His exact birthdate is not known, it is thought to be 20th January, 1889.

Roy Orbison 1988 US singer, guitarist, and songwriter. While at his mother's house, in Hendersonville near Nashville, he complained about pains in his chest during the afternoon. An ambulance was called which took him to hospital, where he died after a heart attack later that day. Born 23rd April, 1936.

Hits of the Day

1952	"The Glow Worm" Mills Brothers US 3 weeks
1967	"Hello Goodbye" Beatles UK 7 weeks
1969	"Na Na Hey Hey Kiss Him Goodbye" Steam US 2 weeks
1986	"The Next Time I Fall" Peter Cetera & Amy Grant US 1 week
1986	"The Final Countdown" Europe UK 2 weeks

Miscellany

1969 The Rolling Stones wanted to end their US tour with a free concert. For this purpose, they chose the car race track at Altamont, approx. 45 minutes away from San Francisco by helicopter. This was also where the film about their performances on stage in the USA was to end. The audience were, if one might put it this way, simply unpaid extras. What seemed at first to be a 'thank you' concert by the Rolling Stones, was actually a cooly calculated business. Beside the Stones, Santana, Crosby, Stills, Nash & Young, the Flying Burrito Brothers and Jefferson Airplane appeared. During the Jefferson Airplane's set fights broke out in the audience. The Grateful Dead, who had helped organize the event, had suggested using 'Hell's Angels' as security; they – partly drunk and partly stoned – began to beat up members of the angry audience. Marty Balin of Jefferson Airplane tried to mediate in a fight between a member of the audience and a 'Hell's Angel' and was knocked unconscious while on stage. During the following performances, there were constant scuffles and fights either in front of the stage or even on stage, which was not far enough away from the audience, and too low. After everyone had played, the obligatory interval before the Stones' performance arrived. The audience became even more restless and impatient. When darkness fell, the audience had waited an hour and a half, before the Rolling Stones finally stepped on stage, the mood of the audience had reached boiling point. Mick Jagger tried to to calm down the audience and Hell's Angels, but was completely ineffective. Sometime, either between or during the numbers, "Love In Vain" and "Under My Thumb", eighteen year old Meredith Hunter drew a gun and pointed it in the direction of the stage. A Hell's Angel did what he thought he had to do, he murdered him by stabbing him repeatedly in his neck, back and forehead. Later, the Hell's Angel was cleared of murder, as he maintained Hunter was trying to kill Mick Jagger. If Woodstock was the highlight of the Love & Peace Movement, then Altamont was the end. Davis Crosby later said, about the incidents, "The Hell's Angels may have been the most obvious mistake made by the Rolling Stones, but even greater were the mistakes made by the snobbish and egotistical members of the group." In this context the following fits well:

1970 The Rolling Stones celebrated the premier performance of their film *Gimme Shelter*, which was about the tour of the previous year and included the events at Altamont.

7th

Birthdays

Edmundo Ros 1910 UK drummer, singer and bandleader, born in Venezuela. As a jazz drummer, he made his first records with Fats Waller in London in 1938. Then, in 1940, he formed his own orchestra whose influences were primarily Latin American. Hits: "Wedding Samba" (1/50 US 16), and "Melodie d'Amour" (1/58).

Louis Prima 1912 US trumpeter, singer, and songwriter. His career as a trumpeter started in his hometown of New Orleans when he was 17. In 1930 he played with Red Nichols' band in New York. In 1933 he formed his own dixieland band, played parts in several Hollywood films and in 1940 formed his own big band. He was married to singer Keely Smith, with whom he had several hits, like "That Old Black Magic" (11/58 US 18). In 1962 the couple were divorced. Solo hits for Louis, "Bell Bottom Trousers" (6/45 US 10), "Civilization" (11/47 US 8), "Buona Sera" (2/58 UK 25), and "Wonderland By Night"

(12/60 US 15). In Europe he was sometimes thought to be a rock 'n' roll artist, but he was above all an excellent jazz trumpeter. After falling into in a coma for a long time, Louis died in New Orleans on 24th August, 1978.

Bent Fabric 1924 Danish pianist and songwriter. Real name Bent Fabricius-Bjerre. When he was a teenager he formed his first jazz band and in 1950 he became head of Metronome Records in Denmark. Hit: "Alley Cat" (7/62 US 7). In Denmark he is a well-known TV personality.

Harry Chapin 1942 US singer and songwriter. His father was a jazz-drummer, and he played in a band with his brothers during his teens. Harry played guitar, banjo and trumpet. They played at the clubs in Greenwich Village and made documentary films on the side. In order to avoid being conscripted, his brothers left the country and Harry formed his own band in 1971. His first album appeared in February, 1972. Hits: "Taxi" (3/72 US 24), "W-O-L-D" (1/74 US 36; 5/74 UK 34), "Cat's In The Cradle" (10/74 US 1) and "Sequel" (11/80 US 23). In addition to his career as a recording star he was very involved with Famine Relief. He always gave a percentage of the takings from his concerts to this organisation, which sometimes amounted to 50%. While driving to a benefit concert, he was involved in a fatal accident on the Long Island Expressway on 16th July, 1981.

Johnny Mars 1942 US blues hormonica player. In 1957 he formed, Johnny Mars & The Cotton Brothers, and cut his first records in the mid-60s. Lives in the UK.

Tom Waits 1949 US singer, songwriter and film actor. His style of singing tends to take the form of monologues, while his songs are trenchant narratives chronicling seamier side of life. Without doubt, he was an antistar, although even that too can become a gimmick. A commentary on Waits, "He is to music, what Bukowski was for US literature." and "Waits is a one-man Beatnik revival." Tom started appearing in public in the late 1960s, and cut his first album in 1973.

Mike Nolan 1954 UK singer with Bucks Fizz, who were formed in 1980 to participate in the Eurovision song contest: they subsequently won in 1981 with "Making Your Mind Up" (3/81 UK 1). Over the next few years the group had a number of hits: "The Land Of Make Believe" (11/81 UK 1), "My Camera Never Lies" (3/82 UK 1), and "Now Those Days Are Gone" (6/82 UK 8). In December 1984, Mike was seriously injured in a road accident in the band's bus, and his career seemed to be over. But with "New Beginning (Mamba Seyra)" (6/86 UK 8) three years later, Bucks Fizz managed another UK Top 10 hit.

Timothy Butler 1958 UK bassist and songwriter with the Psychedelic Furs.

Nicole McCloud 1959 US singer and songwriter. Real surname McCranie. In 1985 she released her first record. Hit: "Don't You Want My Love" (4/86).

Claudia Brucken 1963 German singer and songwriter with the formation Propaganda formed in 1982. Previously, she had sung with the Dusseldorf girls quartet Topolinos. Using demo tapes, Propaganda tried to persuade a British producer to work with them. Finally, Trevor Horn, producer of Frankie Goes To Hollywood, rose to the bait. Hits: "Dr. Mabuse" (3/84 UK 27), "Eye To Eye" (6/85 UK 21), and "P:Machinery" (9/85).

Barbara Weathers 1963 US singer, who replaced Sharon Bryant in 1984 in Atlantic Starr (formed 1976). Hits, with Barbara: "Secret Lovers" (12/85 US 3; 3/86 UK 10) and "Always" (3/87 US 1; 6/87 UK 3).

Deaths

Dee Clark 1990 US singer and songwriter. Born November 7th, 1938.

Hits of the Day

1961	"Tower Of Strength" Frankie Vaughan UK 3 weeks
1963	"Dominique" Singing Nun US 4 weeks
1974	"Kung Fu Fighting" Carl Douglas US 2 weeks
1974	"You're The First, The Last, My Everything" Barry White UK 2 weeks

---

8th

Birthdays

Sammy Davis Jr. 1925 US singer, dancer, and actor, who for many, was the embodiment of the US entertainment industry with a flourishing career, on Broadway, on TV and in films. He lost his left eye in a car accident on 19th November, 1954. He formed the Will Mastin Trio in the 1940s with his father and his uncle. In 1946 he became friends with Frank Sinatra who helped him with his singing career, and later with Dean Martin, made him a member of the Sinatra clan. Hits: "Hey There" (8/54 US 16), "Something's Gotta Give/Love Me Or Leave Me" (5/55 US 9), "That Old Black Magic" (7/55 US 13; 9/55 UK 16) and "The Candy Man" (3/72 US 1). The loss of his eye and the intolerance he saw about him, made him the butt of his own biting and sometimes sarcastic sense of humour. He called himself, "the only one-eyed Jewish nigger in the world". It was he who also said, "When I first started in show business, it was said there was room for all tastes, which is why it was called variety. Nowadays there is no variety left in show business." He died after a lengthy illness on 16th May, 1990.

Jimmy Smith 1925 US jazz, funk, and soul organist and songwriter. First names, James Oscar. In 1934 he won a talent show, and in 1942 he formed a song and dance team with his father. Jimmy made his first records as a member of Don Gardner & The Sonotones in 1953. In 1956 he recorded with his own trio. Hit: "Walk On the Wild Side" (5/62 US 21). From 1966 Jimmy was also a singer.

Jerry Butler 1939 US singer and songwriter. Jerry began his career, as did many soul singers, in a gospel group. He sang with the Northern Jubilee Gospel Singers with Curtis Mayfield. After that, he developed an affinity with rhythm & blues and became a member of the Quails, and finally in 1957 joined the Roosters with Mayfield, which shortly afterwards became the Impressions. Hit: "For Your Precious Love" (6/58 US 11). From autumn 1958 Jerry started a solo career. Hits: "He Will Break Your Heart" (10/60 US 1), "Let It Be Me" (9/64 US 5) with Betty Everett, "Only The Strong Survive" (3/69 US 4) and "Ain't Understanding Mellow" (12/71 US 21) with Brenda Lee Eager.

Bobby Elliott 1942 UK drummer who in 1963 joined the Hollies (formed in 1962), where he replaced Donald Rathbone. Bobby had played with the Fentones previously.

Jim Morrison 1943 US singer and songwriter with the band Doors, formed in 1965. Hits: "Light My Fire" (6/67 US 1), "Hello I Love You" (7/68 US 1; UK 15), "Touch Me" (12/68 US 3), and "Riders On The Storm" (7/71 US 14; 9/71 UK 22; 3/76 RE-UK 33). Jim, whose performances on stage were seen as being controversial, was arrested for "lewd and lascivious behaviour" a couple of times. He left the Doors on 12th December, 1970. He died 3rd July, 1971.

Lee Pickens 1943 US guitarist with Bloodrock.

George Baker 1944 Dutch songwriter and singer with George Baker Selection. Real name Johannes Bouwens. Hits: "Little Green Bag" (3/70 US 21), "Paloma Blanca" (9/75 UK 10; 11/75 US 26) and "Morning Sky" (11/75).

Graham Knight 1946 UK bassist with Marmalade.

Gregg Allman 1947 US guitarist, keyboard player, singer, and songwriter. Real first names Gregory Lenoir. His career ran parallel to that of his brother Duane (20th November). After the latter's death, Dicky Betts became the unofficial head of the Allman Brothers Band. Gregg made more impact through his marriage to Cher in 1975, than with his music. Solo success: "Midnight Rider" (12/73 US 19).

Ray Schulman 1949 UK bassist, violinist and trumpeter with Simon Dupree & The Big Sound, which later became Gentle Giant. In 1983 he turned up on an album by Minor Detail.

Warren Cuccurullo 1956 US guitarist, singer and songwriter with Frank Zappa and a founder member of Missing Persons in 1980.

Phil Collen 1957 UK guitarist and songwriter. He started with Girl and joined the band Def Leppard, formed 1977 as a replacement for Pete Willis in 1982.

Paul Rutherford 1959 UK singer and songwriter. Paul started with the Spitfire Boys and sang their only single "Mein Kampf". He was briefly with the Opium Eaters, and then went to the USA for a while. In August 1980 the group Frankie Goes To Hollywood was formed, and Paul became the singer of the band alongside Holly Johnson. In August 1988 he signed a recording contract as a solo artist.

Deaths

John Lennon 1980 UK singer, guitarist and songwriter with the Beatles and as a soloist. In early 1975 he withdrew completely from the music business. In May 1979 he announced he would record again. On 15th November, 1980 the album DOUBLE FANTASY appeared. On 8th December, 1980 he was just returning from the record studio to his apartment at Dakota-House in New York when he was killed by seven shots fired by Mark David Chapman, whom Lennon had given an autograph only a few hours before when he left home. Born 9th October, 1940.

Marty Robbins 1982 US country and pop singer, guitarist, and songwriter. He died after a heart attack. Born 26th September, 1925.

Hits of the Day

1945	"It's Been A Long Long Time" Bing Crosby US 2 weeks
1956	"Singing The Blues" Guy Mitchell US 10 weeks
1979	"Walking On the Moon" Police UK 1 week
1979	"Babe" Styx US 2 weeks

1984	"Power Of Love" Frankie Goes To Hollywood UK 1 week
1984	"Out Of Touch" Daryl Hall & John Oates US 2 weeks
1990	"Saviours Day" Cliff Richard. UK 3 weeks

Miscellany

1961 The first record by the Beach Boys, "Surfin'" is released.

9th

Birthdays

Freddy Martin 1906 US tenor saxophonist, bandleader and songwriter who formed his own band in the early 1930s. From 1933 to 1954 he had about 85 hits in the USA and along with Guy Lombardo led one of the most successful dance bands of the era. His greatest successes were "I Saw Stars" (8/34 US 1), "Piano Concerto In B Flat" (8/41 US 1), "Rose O'Day (The Filla-Da-Gusha Song)" (1/42 US 1), "Symphony" (12/45 US 1), "To Each His Own" (8/46 US 1), "Managua, Nicaragua" (1/47 US 1) and "I've Got A Lovely Bunch Of Coconuts" (10/49 US 8). Freddy died 1st October, 1983.

Donald Byrd 1932 US jazz-rock trumpeter and composer.

Junior Wells 1934 US blues singer, harmonica player and songwriter. Real name Amos Blackmore. After playing with various groups in Chicago, he replaced Little Walter in Muddy Waters' band in 1952. After that, he played with Memphis Slim and Buddy Guy. He accompanied the Rolling Stones on a world tour with Buddy in 1972. His greatest success as a soloist was "Little By Little" (6/60 R&B 23).

David Houston 1938 US country singer, guitarist, and songwriter, who was successful from 1963 to 1981 in the C&W charts. He received his first recording contract in 1956 with Sun Records. David is a god-son of Gene Austin who helped him at the beginning of his career. David's greatest crossover hit was "Almost Persuaded" (7/66 US 24).

Sam Strain 1940 US singer with Little Anthony & The Imperials, and from 1976 with the O'Jays as a replacement for William Powell.

Rick Danko 1943 Canadian bassist, singer and songwriter with the Band, as a solo artist and as a session musician.

Kenny Vance 1943 US singer with the group Jay & The Americans formed in 1961, and from 1975 as a session singer and solo artist.

Shirley Brickley 1944 US leadsinger with the Orlons, who were formed in 1955. Hits: "The Wah Watusi" (6/62 US 2), "Don't Hang Up" (10/62 US 4; 1/63 UK 39) and "South Street" (2/63 US 3). In 1968 the group split up.

Neil Innes 1944 UK singer, guitarist, pianist and songwriter in the group Bonzo Dog Doo-Dah Band formed in 1965. Hit: "I'm The Urban Spaceman" (11/68 UK 5). Neil wrote the song and a certain Apollo C. Vermouth was credited as the producer; he was better known as Paul McCartney. The whole thing is probably a thank you for the Bonzos joining in on the *Magical Mystery Tour*. In January 1970 the band split up. Innes was briefly with McGuinness Flint and then reformed the as Bonzo Dog Band in 1972. He started a solo career in 1973, recording the album HOW SWEET TO BE AN IDIOT. After that, Neil composed and sang jungles for commercials, played parts on TV, and composed incidental music for *Monty Python's Flying Circus*. Eric Idle of Monty Python's Flying Circus and he formed the Rutles in 1977, a parody of the Beatles, and released the album and TV film ALL YOU NEED IS CASH. Neil played Ron Nasty, who was supposed to represent John Lennon. Latterly, he has worked on film scores like *Erik The Viking*.

Dennis Dunaway 1948 US bassist with Alice Cooper.

Joan Armatrading 1950 UK singer and songwriter. Joan was born in the Caribbean and came to England in 1956. She made records from 1972. Her songs were impressive especially for their outstanding lyrics. Hits: "Love And Affection" (10/76 UK 10) and "Drop The Pilot" (2/83 UK 11).

Sylvia 1956 US country singer. Complete name Sylvia Kirby Allen. In 1975 she went to Nashville and worked there as a secretary for a producer. Now and then she was used as a backing vocalist on recording sessions. In 1979 she received a record contract and has been in the C&W charts regularly ever since. Her greatest cross-over success was million seller "Nobody" (8/82 US 15).

Donny Osmond 1957 US singer and keyboard player with the family group Osmonds, which consisted of seven siblings. The older brothers had already been successful with live shows in Disneyland in 1962. In the mid-1960s Donny joined them. Hits: "One Bad Apple" (1/71 US 1), "Yo-Yo" (9/71 US 3), "Down By The Lazy River" (1/72 US 4; 3/72 UK 40), "Crazy Horses" (10/72 US 14; UK 2),

"Going Home" (6/73 US 36; UK 4), "Let Me In" (9/73 US 36; UK 2), "Love Me For A Reason" (8/74 UK 1; US 10) and "The Proud One" (5/75 UK 5; 7/75 US 22). Solo hits for Donny: "Sweet And Innocent" (3/71 US 7), "Go Away Little Girl" (8/71 US 1), "Hey Girl" (11/71 US 9), "Puppy Love" (2/72 US 3; 6/72 UK 1), "Too Young" (6/72 US 13; 9/72 UK 5), "Why" (8/72 US 13; 11/72 UK 3), "The Twelfth Of Never" (3/73 US 8; UK 1), "Young Love" (7/73 US 23; UK 1) and "When I Fall In Love" (11/73 UK 4). Hits with sister Mary: "I'm Leaving It (All) Up To You" (7/74 US 4; UK 2) and "Morning Side Of The Mountain" (11/74 US 8; UK 5). After nothing much had been heard of Donny for about ten years, he popped up again with "Soldier Of Love" (8/88 UK 29; 3/89 US 2).

Deaths

Sonny Til 1981 US leadsinger with the Orioles, formed in 1947. Real name Earlington Carl Tilghman. They are considered to be the first R&B vocal group and had eleven hits in the US R&B charts between 1948 and 1953. Pop hits: "It's Too Soon To Know" (11/48 US 13), and the million seller "Crying In The Chapel" (8/53 US 11). Sonny was 51 (56?) years old, when he died of a heart attack.

Hits of the Day

1944 "I'm Making Believe" Ella Fitzgerald & Ink Spots US 2 weeks
1972 "I Am Woman" Helen Reddy US 1 week
1978 "Mary's Boy Child" Boney M. UK 4 weeks
1978 "Le Freak" Chic US 1 week
1989 "We Didn't Start The Fire" Billy Joel US 2 weeks

10th

Birthdays

Guitar Slim 1926 US blues singer, guitarist and songwriter. Real name Eddie Jones. In 1949 he formed a trio with Huey Piano Smith and another musician. In 1951 he cut his first records as a solo artist. When he returned from the Korean War, he recorded "The Things That I Used To Do" (2/54 US 23; R&B 1 for 14 weeks and with that the greatest blues-hit of the year) among others. Ray Charles was one of the musicians, as he played the piano on this million seller. Guitar Slim died on 7th February, 1959.

Peter Sarstedt 1942 UK guitarist, singer and songwriter. He played guitar in the backing band of his older brother Richard, who was successful in the early 1960s as Eden Kane. In the late 1960s Peter started a solo career, and had hits with "Where Do You Go To My Lovely?" (2/69 UK 1) and "Frozen Orange Juice" (6/69 UK 10). Further attempts at landing hits failed. Even forming the Sarstedt Brothers with siblings Richard and Clive failed.

Chad Stuart 1943 UK singer, pianist and string instrumentalist with the duo Chad & Jeremy, see 22nd March.

Ralph Tavares 1945 US singer and oldest brother of the sibling group Tavares, who began to sing in the late 1950s. In 1963 they became professional and called themselves Chubby & The Turnpikes, in 1973 they changed their name to Tavares. Hits: "It Only Takes A Minute" (7/75 US 10), "Heaven Must Be Missing An Angel" (6/76 US 15; UK 4; 2/86 RE-UK 12), "Whodunit" (3/77 US 22; UK 5), and "More Than A Woman" (11/77 US 32; 5/78 UK 7).

Chris Kefford 1946 UK bassist with the nickname 'Ace'. In 1964 he started with Carl Wayne & The Viking, which developed into Move in February 1966. Chris stayed until April 1968 and then formed Ace Kefford Stand, which lasted until mid-1969.

Walter Orange 1946 US drummer, songwriter and singer. In the late 1960s the Jays were formed, and only Jay, who at the time was leadsinger of the group had any experience as a professional. In 1968/69 the Jays changed their name to Commodores. During the course of the years Lionel Richie developed as leadsinger and writer. After Lionel had left the group in 1982, Walter became one of the leadsingers again.

Keith Smart 1946 UK drummer with Mongrel from November 1971 until July 1972, with Wizzard from August 1972 until February 1975 and finally with the Rockin' Berries.

Jessica Cleaves 1948 US singer with Friends Of Distinction.

Brenden Harkin 1948 US guitarist with Bamboo, Free Beer, Starz, and in the 1980s with Kool & The Gang.

Johnny Rodriguez 1951 US country guitarist and singer. Real first names Juan Raul Davis. At age 7 this Chicano learned to play guitar. Later he played with high school rockbands, went to Nashville in 1971, and was with Tom T. Hall's band for two years. From 1972 he was successful as a solo artist in the country charts.

Geoff Deane 1954 UK singer and songwriter who formed the punk and reggae parodying band Leyton Buzzards in the late 1970s with David Jaymes, who later dropped the 'Leyton' and released an album as the Buzzards in 1979. As it was way behind sales expectations of the duo, they formed the more commercially oriented disco-salsa dance group Modern Romance in 1980. Hits: "Everybody Salsa" (8/81 UK 12), "Ay Ay Ay Ay Moosey" (11/81 UK 10), "Best Years Of Our Lives" (11/82 UK 4), "High Life" (2/83 UK 8) and "Walking In The Rain" (8/83 UK 7).

Paul Hardcastle 1958 UK keyboard player and songwriter. In the early 1980s he started with Direct Drive and became a member of First Light in 1982. In 1984 Paul set up his own record company, and had an international hit with "19" (5/85 UK 1; US 15) it referred to the average age of US soldiers in the Vietnam War. Further hits were "Just For Money" (11/85 UK 19), "Don't Waste My Time" (1/86 UK 8) and "The Wizard" (10/86 UK 15).

Deaths

Otis Redding 1967 US soul singer and songwriter. He had just bought himself a private aircraft in order to be more mobile during a long tour, when he crashed on the way to a concert. The other passengers in the plane were James King, Ronald Caldwell, Phalon Jones, and Carl Cunningham, all members of the Bar-Kays, who were accompanying Otis on his tour. Redding was born 9th September, 1941.

Hits of the Day

1964	"I Feel Fine" Beatles UK 5 weeks
1966	"Good Vibrations" Beach Boys US 1 week
1983	"Say Say Say" Paul McCartney & Michael Jackson US 6 weeks
1983	"Only You" Flying Pickets UK 5 weeks
1988	"Look Away" Chicago US 2 weeks
1988	"Mistletoe And Wine" Cliff Richard UK 4 weeks

11th

Birthdays

Big Mama Thornton 1926 US blues singer and songwriter, who started as a dancer and singer in a revue in the early 1940s. Real first names, Willie Mae. From the early 1950s she made records, played with Johnny Otis, Roy Milton, and Joe Liggins. She sang the original version of "Hound Dog" (3/53 R&B 1) which was a hit for Elvis

Presley three years later. She was one of Janis Joplin's idol, who covered the Thornton number "Ball And Chain". Big Mama died 25th July, 1984.

Tom Brumley 1935 US master of the steel guitar. He played with Buckaroos, Buck Owens' accompanying band, from 1963, and later became a member of Rick Nelson's Stone Canyon Band.

McCoy Tyner 1938 US jazz pianist and composer, whose career started with John Coltrane's quartet in 1960. In the meantime he has adopted an Islamic name and calls himself Sulaimon Saud.

David Gates 1940 US singer, guitarist and songwriter in the group Bread formed in 1969. The musicians in this band had previously worked as a session band and tried their luck as Pleasure Faire. Success arrived with Bread. Hits: "Make It With You" (6/70 US 1; UK 5), "If" (3/71 US 4), "Baby I'm-A Want You" (10/71 US 3; 1/72 UK 14), "Everything I Own" (1/72 US 5; 4/72 UK 32) and "The Guitar Man" (7/72 US 11; 9/72 UK 16). In 1973 the band split up, formed again briefly in 1976, and scored with "Lost Without Your Love" (11/76 US 9; UK 27); then they disappeared for good. David had modest success as a solo artist: "Goodbye Girl" (12/77 US 15) being the most significant. His composition "If" became a top hit in the UK for Telly Savalas in February 1975.

Brenda Lee 1944 US pop and country singer. Real name Brenda Mae Tarpley. When she was 12 she obtained a recording contract and was successful shortly after. Hits: "Sweet Nothin's" (12/59 US 4; 4/60 UK 4), "I'm Sorry" (5/60 US 1; UK 12), "I Want To Be Wanted" (9/60 US 1; UK 31), "Dum Dum" (6/61 US 4; UK 22), "Fool Number 1" (10/61 US 3; UK 38), "Break It To Me Gently" (1/62 US 4; UK 46), "Speak To Me Pretty" (4/62 UK 3), "All Alone Am I" (9/62 US 3; 1/63 UK 7), "Losing You" (3/63 UK 10; 4/63 US 6) and "As Usual" (12/63 US 12; UK 5). Brenda also recorded a Christmas song which was reissued annually – "Rockin' Around The Christmas Tree" (12/60 US 14; 11/62 UK 6) – and was recorded in 1958. Her nickname was 'Little Miss Dynamite'. She made country records like a cover version of Kris Kristofferson hit "Nobody Wins" (2/73 C&W 5) in the 1970s, which were successful in the country charts.

Robert Pickett 1945 US guitarist and bassist with Sugarloaf.

Spike Edney 1951 UK keyboard player with Cross.

Jermaine Jackson 1954 US bassist, singer and songwriter. He started with his brothers in the Jackson 5 formed in 1967. On 15th December, 1973 he married the daughter of Berry Gordy Jr., head of record company Tamla-Motown. When the group Jackson 5 left the company and called themselves the Jacksons, Jermaine stayed loyal to his father-in-law and his wife Hazel Joy. Jermaine was the first of the Jackson clan to attempt a solo career. Hits: "Daddy's Home" (12/72 US 9), "Let's Get Serious" (3/80 US 9; 5/80 UK 8), "Do What You Do" (10/84 US 13; 2/85 UK 6) and, with Pia Zadora, "When The Rain Begins To Fall" (10/84 UK 68; 2/85 US 54). Jermaine joined his brothers once again in 1984 for the VICTORY album and the resulting tour. This resulted in the single "Torture" (8/84 US 17; UK 26) by the Jacksons, the leadsingers were Jermaine and Michael.

Rita Ray 1954 Ghanalan singer with Rocky Sharpe and the Darts.

Nikki Sixx 1958 US bassist and songwriter with the heavy metal band Mötley Crüe formed in 1981.

Deaths

Sam Cooke 1964 US soul singer and songwriter. After a party, so the story goes, Sam mistakenly stepped into the wrong room at his motel, while not fully dressed. Thereupon the manageress of the motel, who lived in that room, felt threatened and shot him several times with fatal results. Born 22nd January, 1935.

Hits of the Day

1961	"Please Mr. Postman" Marvelettes US 1 week
1968	"Lily The Pink" Scaffold UK 3 weeks
1971	"Ernie" Benny Hill UK 4 weeks
1982	"Mickey" Tony Basil US 1 week

Miscellany

1946 Hank Williams made his first record for the small New York label Sterling.

1953 Frankie Laine was still at position No. 1 in the UK with "Answer Me". David Whitfield returned with his version of "Answer Me" back to the top position and shared it with Frankie Laine for one week.

1970 The first album of songs by John Lennon appeared since the demise of the Beatles. Before that, with Yoko Ono and The Plastic Ono Band, he had released "Two Virgins – Unfinished Music No. 1" (29th November, 1968), "Life With The Lions – Unfinished Music No. 2" (9th May, 1969), THE WEDDING ALBUM (7th November, 1969), and LIVE PEACE IN TORONTO (12th December, 1969).

In the USA alone 2.5 million copies had been ordered before its release. Compositions like "Mother" and "Working Class Hero" are classics today. The album was called JOHN LENNON/PLASTIC ONO BAND.

12th

Birthdays

Frank Sinatra 1915 US singer and film actor. Real first names Francis Albert. He is probably the greatest singer in the history of show business, ever; hardly any other artist in the world can boast that he has been on stage for more than 50 years, with success! In 1935 Frank won a talent contest as a member of the Hoboken Four, in 1937 he was a singing waiter in a restaurant in New Jersey. Well-known orchestra leader Harry James heard him and put him under contract. With that, he never looked back. Among his hits were "I'll Never Smile Again" (6/40 US 1) with the Tommy Dorsey Orchestra, "All Or Nothing At All" (6/43 US 1) with Harry James recorded in 1939, "White Christmas" (12/44 US 7; 12/45 RE-US 5; 12/46 RE-US 6), "Oh! What It Seemed To Be" (2/46 US 1), "Five Minutes More" (8/46 US 1), "Mamselle" (5/47 US 1), "Young-At-Heart" (2/54 US 2; 7/54 UK 12), "Three Coins In The Fountain" (5/54 US 7; 7/54 UK 1), "Learnin' The Blues" (5/55 US 1; 8/55 UK 2), "Love And Marriage" (11/55 US 5; 1/56 UK 3), "(Love Is) The Tender Trap" (12/55 US 7; UK 2), "All The Way" (10/57 US 2; 12/57 UK 3), "Strangers In The Night" (5/66 US & UK 1), together with his daughter Nancy "Somethin' Stupid" (3/67 US & UK 1), and "Theme From New York, New York" (5/80 US 32; 2/86 UK 4). As a film actor Frank appeared for the first time in *Las Vegas Nights* (1941). During the course of the years he appeared in about 60 films, among his most successful roles were his performances in *The House I Live In* (1946) and *From Here To Eternity* (1952), for which he received Oscars respectively. He was nominated for an Oscar for his part in the film *The Man With The Golden Arm* (1955). During the course of his career Frank had awards showered upon him, Playboy magazine voted him best singer of the year from 1958 to 1966 and 1968/69. There were Emmys and Grammys galore and, who knows what for – the medal for bravery from the State of Israel; possibly that his decision to withdraw from show business in 1971 led to it .... During the course of the 1970s Frankie announced a comeback several times – and continued to come back, as 'Ol' Blue Eyes'.

Connie Francis 1938 US singer. Real name Concetta Rosa Maria Franconera. In 1955 she made her first records, and was successful from 1957. Hits: "Who's Sorry Now" (2/58 US 4; 4/58 UK 1), "Carolina Moon/Stupid Cupid" (7/58 US 14; UK 1), "My Happiness" (12/58 US 2; 2/59 UK 4), "Lipstick On Your Collar" (5/59 US 5; 7/59 UK 3), "Everybody's Somebody's Fool" (5/60 US 1; 8/60 UK 5), "My Heart Has A Mind Of Its Own" (8/60 US 1; 11/60 UK 3) and "Don't Break The Heart That Loves You" (2/62 US 1; 4/62 UK 39). After she had been raped on 8th November 1974, Connie withdrew completely from show business, only staging a comeback in 1978.

Dionne Warwick 1940 US singer who started with the Drinkard Singers gospel group and then sang with her sister Dee Dee and her aunt Cissy Houston (mother of Whitney) as the trio Gospelaires. In the late 50s she worked as a session singer, and was discovered there by song writing team Bacharach/David, who considered Dionne's voice to be extremely suitable for their compositions. Hits: "Walk On By" (4/64 UK 9; US 6), "I Say A Little Prayer" (10/67 US 4), "(Theme From) Valley Of The Dolls" (1/68 US 2; 3/68 UK 28), "I'll Never Love This Way Again" (6/79 US 5), "Heartbreaker" (10/82 UK 2; US 10), and also together with the Spinners "Then Came You" (7/74 US 1; 10/74 UK 29), and with Elton John, Gladys Knight, and Stevie Wonder as Dionne & Friends, "That's What Friends Are For" (11/85 US 1; UK 16). In the 70s Dionne lengthened her name with an 'e' to Warwicke. The reason was that she had discovered that her first name and surname together contained 13 letters. However, after the change seemed to bring nothing but bad luck rather than fortune, she changed it back again.

Declan Clusky 1942 UK guitarist and singer with the trio Bachelors, that had been formed in Dublin in 1953, as a harmonica trio. In the 1960s they became a vocal trio and had hits from 1963 to 1968. The most successful were "Diane" (1/64 UK 1; 4/64 US 10), "I Believe" (3/64 UK 2; 6/64 US 33) and "The Sound Of Silence" (3/66 UK 3).

Mike Heron 1942 UK singer, songwriter, and multi-instrumentalist. In 1965 he formed the Incredible String Band with fellow Scot Robin Williams and made solo records from 1971.

Dicky Betts 1943 US guitarist and songwriter with the Allman Brothers. After Duane Allman's death he became the leader of the band. He wrote and sang "Ramblin' Man" (8/73 US 2), the band's biggest hit. After 1974 the group split up, Betts started a solo career and formed Great Southern. He also worked as a session musician. In 1978 Gregg Allman and Dickey Betts revived the Allman Brothers.

Mike Smith 1943 UK singer, and keyboard player with the Dave Clark Five, and later with Mike D'Abo.

Grover Washington Jr. 1943 US jazz/funk saxophonist and songwriter. At age 16 he had his own band, the Four Clefs. After that, Grover worked as a session musician and soloist. Greatest hit, sung by Bill Withers, "Just The Two Of Us" (2/81 US 2; 5/81 UK 34).

Rob Tyner 1944 US drummer with MC5. Died September 18th, 1991, in Royal Oak, Michigan.

Allan Ward 1945 UK guitarist and pianist with the Honeycombs.

Tony Williams 1945 US jazz rock drummer and songwriter with Miles Davis, Bill Evans, Stan Getz, Herbie Hancock, and with his own band Lifetime.

Clive Bunker 1946 UK drummer with McGregor's Engine in 1967 and with the newly formed band Jethro Tull from late 1968 to May 1971. After that, he formed Jude, joined Blodwyn Pig in 1974, and played with Aviator and as a session musician.

Ralph Scala 1947 US singer and songwriter with the Blues Magoos. They had their only Top Ten success with "(We Ain't Got) Nothing Yet" (12/66 US 5).

Ray Jackson 1948 UK string instrumentalist and harmonica player with Lindisfarne and as a studio musician.

Barry Blue 1950 UK songwriter and singer. Real name Barry Ian Green. He wrote hits for Gene Pitney, Cliff Richard and Tony Christie. Barry himself was successful with "(Dancing) On A Saturday Night" (7/73 UK 2) and "Do You Wanna Dance" (11/73 UK 7). He worked frequently with Lynsey de Paul.

Cy Curnin 1957 UK singer, pianist and songwriter with the band Fixx formed in 1980, which was first called Portraits. Hits: "One Thing Leads To Another" (9/83 US 4) and "Secret Separation" (5/86 US 19). As a songwriter Cy was co-writer of the Tina Turner hit "Better Be Good To Me".

Sheila E. 1959 US singer and songwriter. Real surname Escovedo. She is the daughter of percussionist Pete Escovedo who allowed his daughter to play congas when she was 5 years old. Later she sang with the Escovedo Brothers and at age 15 went on a tour of South America with her father and the group Azteca. As a studio singer she worked with Prince, George Duke, Herbie Hancock, Lionel Richie, and Marvin Gaye, before having her first own hit, "Glamourous Life" (6/84 US 7). Further hits: "The Belle Of St. Mark" (10/84 US 34; 2/85 UK 18) and "A Love Bizarre" (11/85 US 11).

Jeff Aaron Brown 1964 UK singer and dancer with the Pasadenas.

Deaths

Clifton Chenier 1987 US singer and songwriter who was considered to be the 'King of Zydeco'. Born 26th June, 1925.

Hits of the Day

1964 "Mr. Lonely" Bobby Vinton US 1 week

1963 "I Want To Hold Your Hand" Beatles UK 5 weeks

1970 "Tears Of A Clown" Smokey Robinson & The Miracles US 2 weeks

1981 "Don't You Want Me" Human League UK 5 weeks

1987 "Faith" George Michael US 4 weeks

13th

Birthdays

Ron Caines 1944 UK saxophonist, pianist and singer with East Of Eden.

Marti Webb 1944 UK singer. Hit: "Take That Look Off Your Face" (2/80 UK 3).

Tony Gomez 1948 Keyboard player with the Foundations, born in Ceylon.

Jeff 'Skunk' Baxter 1948 US guitarist, who played with the Doobie Brothers from 1974 to 1978. After that, he became a studio musician and producer. Jeff is on records by Tom Rush, Steely Dan, Joni Mitchell, Carly Simon, Little Feat and Rod Stewart.

Ted Nugent 1948 US guitarist, singer and songwriter. He was playing guitar when he was 9. In 1960 he had his first band, the Royal High Boys. From 1962 to 1964 he played with the Lourdes and then with Cobo Hall, who appeared on stage as supporting group with the Supremes and Beau Brummels. In 1965 the Amboy Dukes were formed, and from 1972 they called themselves Ted Nugent & The Amboy Dukes. From 1975 Ted played as a soloist. Hits, as Amboy Dukes: "Journey To The Center Of The Mind" (6/68 US 16), as a soloist, "Cat Scratch Fever" (8/77 US 30).

David O'List 1948 UK guitarist and songwriter. He started with the band Attack and then declined John Mayall's offer of replacing Peter Green with his Bluesbreakers. Instead, in spring 1967, he became a founder member of

Nice, whom he left in September 1968. Then he joined Roxy Music in October 1971 until February 1972, then Jet from June 1974 to July 1975 and finally as a session musician with Bryan Ferry and Tony Ashton.

Tom Verlaine 1949 US guitarist, singer and songwriter. Real name Thomas Miller. He started with the Neon Boys and formed Television in 1973. Beside such bands as Blondie, Talking Heads and Ramones, Television had their first successes in the CBGB Club in New York. Hit: "Prove It" (7/77 UK 25). In 1978 the band split up and Tom carried on as a solo artist.

Alan Love 1952 UK singer with Opal Butterfly, Referendum and Madriga, which evolved into Merlin in February 1974.

John Anderson 1954 US singer, guitarist, and songwriter. He formed his own group Living End while still a teenager. After that, he sang with his sister Donna, went to Nashville in 1962 and became permanently employed as a songwriter. In 1974 he made his first solo record. From 1977 he was regularly in the C&W charts and his biggest hit with the million seller "Swingin'" (1/83 C&W 1).

Berton Averre 1954 US guitarist and keyboard player with Knack. After the band had split up in 1983, he played on an album by the Honeys.

Austin Sorenson 1961 Norwegian singer and songwriter with Fra Lippo Lippi. Real name Per Öystein Sörensen.

Hits of the Day

1941 "I Don't Want To Set The World On Fire" Hoarce Heidt US 3 weeks

1947 "Ballerina" Vaughn Monroe US 10 weeks

1962 "Return To Sender" Elvis Presley UK 3 weeks

1986 "The Way It Is" Bruce Hornsby & The Range US 1 week

14th

Birthdays

Spike Jones 1911 US comedian who had his great fame from 1942 until 1953. Real first names Lindley Armstrong. He made fun of any music popular at the time. Thus, in amongst classical titles, suddenly shots were fired, carousing was heard, bells rang, somebody whistled loudly or there was just a lot of noise. Spike had started out as a studio drummer in Hollywood. Then in the early 1940s he formed his own band, called Spike Jones & His City Slickers. Hits: "Der Fuhrer's Face" (10/42 US 3), "Cocktails For Two" (1/45 US 4), "Chloe" (4/45 US 5), "Hawaian War Chant" (7/46 US 8), "William Tell Overture" (6/48 US 6), "All I Want For Christmas (Is My Two Front Teeth)" (11/48 US 1; 12/49 RE-US 18) and "I Saw Mommy Kissing Santa Claus" (12/52 US 7). After 1953, record buyers seemed to have had enough of his little jokes. Later, Spike played only with a dixieland band. He died 1st May, 1965.

Charlie Rich 1932 US country singer, songwriter and pianist. He started his recording career as a rockabilly artist with Sun Records. Before that, he had already played with jazz and pop bands, formed the group Velvetons and had been the host of a local TV show. At Sun Records, he backed Johnny Cash and Roy Orbison, among others. Then his own solo records started to appear. Hits: "Lonely Weekends" (3/60 US 22), "Mohair Sam" (8/65 US 21), "Behind Closed Doors" (4/73 US 15; 4/74 UK 16) and "The Most Beautiful Girl" (9/73 US 1; 2/74 UK 2). His nickname is 'Silver Fox'. In 1974 he was voted country entertainer of the year. After 1981 little was heard of him.

Frank Allen 1943 UK bassist and singer. He started in 1959 as a rhythm guitarist with Cliff Bennett & The Rebel Rousers, changed within the group to bass in autumn 1961, and in August 1964 replaced Tony Jackson in the Searchers.

Jane Birkin 1946 UK actress and singer. She became well-known in the film *Blow Up* (1966), in which she was scantily clad; it co-starred David Hemmings as a photographer. With Serge Gainsbourg, with whom she had a close friendship, she recorded the title "Je T'Aime . . . Moi Non Plus" (7/69 UK 2; 10/69 RE-UK 1; 12/74 RE-UK 31), which Serge had recorded previously already with Brigitte Bardot. However, Brigitte, after listening to the title, did not wish it to be released, so Serge had to re-record it, luckily for Jane. She had another hit in France with "Ex-Fan Des Sixties" (1978) written by Serge.

Joyce Vincent 1946 US singer with Dawn.

Patty Duke 1947 US actress and singer. Complete name Anna Maria Patricia Duke Astin. From 1955 she played in films. After receiving an Oscar for the part of the young Helen Keller in *The Miracle Worker* (1962), she became hostess of the *Patty Duke Show* on TV from 1963 to 1965. As a singer she had one notable hit, "Don't Just Stand There" (6/65 US 8).

Cliff Williams 1949 UK bassist who in June 1977 replaced Mark Evans in the band AC/DC, formed in Sydney in 1973.

Deaths

Dinah Washington 1963 US blues and jazz singer. Dinah who was suffering from the effects of serious alcohol dependency, died after taking an overdose of tranquillizers. Born 29th August, 1924.

Hits of the Day

1946 "Ole Buttermilk Sky" Kay Kyser US 2 weeks
1959 "Heartaches By The Number" Guy Mitchell US 2 weeks
1968 "I Heard It Through The Grapevine" Marvin Gaye US 7 weeks
1985 "Saving All My Love For You" Whitney Houston UK 2 weeks

15th

Birthdays

John Hammond 1910 US producer and talent scout. When he had just started out as a producer John worked with Fletcher Henderson and was responsible for the last recordings by Bessie Smith, and the first by Billie Holiday. He also looked after early recordings by Benny Goodman, who married John's sister Alice in 1942, by Count Bassie and Lester Young. After the 2nd World War, John became head of the record company Keynote, then of Majestic, and finally vice-president of Mercury Records. Then he went talent scouting for CBS and signed musicians such as Aretha Franklin, Pete Seeger, George Benson, Leonard Cohen, Bob Dylan, and Bruce Springsteen for this company. He died 10th July, 1987. Father of John Paul Hammond.

Alan Freed 1921 US disc jockey, who did a lot for R&B and for the early days of rock 'n' roll. After the payola accusation he never worked again. He died 20th January, 1965.

Rose Maddox 1926 US country singer. Born Rosea Arbana Brogdon. In the mid-1940s, she and other members of her family sang on a radio station in Modesto. She cut her first records in 1947 as Maddox Brothers and Sister Rose with her brothers Cal, Henry, Fred and Don. In 1959 the group split up and Rose started a solo career. Her biggest hit was "Sing A Little Song Of Heartache" (11/62 C&W 3). After 1964 she disappeared from the charts.

Jerry Wallace 1928 US pop/country singer, who made his first records in 1951, and had his first hit with "Little Miss One" (2/54 US 30). Further hits were, "How The Time Flies" (8/58 US 11) and "Primrose Lane" (8/59 US 8). Later he turned more to country music and had 35 hits between 1965 and 1980, his biggest being "If You Leave Me Tonight I'll Cry" (7/72 C&W 1; US 38). His nickname is "Mr. Smooth".

Jesse Belvin 1932 US singer, pianist, and songwriter, who released songs on 15 different record labels during the 1950s. By the late 1940s/early 1950s he was one of the most eminent figures in the upcoming R&B wave. His influence on pop music probably would have been even greater, had he not been killed with his wife in a car accident on 6th February, 1960. Jesse made his first recordings with the band of saxophonist Big Jay McNeely. In 1952 he recorded the title "Dream Girl" (1/53 R&B 2) with Marvin Phillips as Jesse & Marvin. Just as his career was about to take off, he was conscripted and sent to Korea. During that time he wrote "Earth Angel (Will You Be Mine)", which was recorded by the Penguins and by the Crew Cuts, and is one of the most popular R&B numbers of all time. In 1955 Jesse returned, and during the following period he made records as Gassers, Sheiks, Chargers, and Cliques. Then he recorded "Goodnight My Love" (12/56 R&B 7) under his own name. It became the signing-off melody for Alan Freed's radio show, and the piano was played by Barry White who was 11 years old at the time. In 1958 Jesse formed the group Shields, who recorded the composition "You Cheated" (8/58 US 12). He had his biggest hit with "Guess Who" (3/59 US 31) written by his wife Jo Anne.

Cindy Birdsong 1939 US singer who started her career with Patti LaBelle & The Blue Belles. When Florence Ballard left the Supremes in 1967, she was replaced by Cindy. In June 1972 Cindy left the group again, in order to look after her husband and her home.

Dave Clark 1942 UK drummer and songwriter with his band Dave Clark Five, who were formed as were so many other British beatgroups as a skiffle group. In 1962 they made their first records, which were unsuccessful. In 1963 the Mersey-boom stimulated interest in 'beatgroups' from all over the UK. Hits: "Glad All Over" (11/63 UK 1; 2/64 US 6), "Bits And Pieces" (2/64 UK 2; 4/64 US 4), "Can't You See That She's Mine" (5/64 UK 10; US 4), "Because" (8/64 US 3), "I Like It Like That" (6/65 US 7), "Catch Us If You Can" (7/65 UK 5; US 4), "Over And Over" (11/65 US 1), "You Got What It Takes" (3/67 UK 28; US 7), "Everybody Knows" (11/67 UK 2), "Red Balloon" (9/68 UK 7), "Good Old Rock 'N' Roll" (12/69 UK 7) and "Everybody Get Together" (3/70 UK 8). After that, the band split up. Dave carried on from 1971 to 1973 as Dave Clark & Friends with Mike Smith, singer of Dave Clark 5. After that he looked after his publishing interests. In 1978 he put together a retrospective of the groups career, which reached position No. 7 in the album charts. Dave owned all the publishing and performance rights to the group's career. In 1986 the musical *Time* co-written and produced by Dave had its premier in the London Dominion Theatre. The lead part was played by Cliff Richard and was later taken over by David Cassidy.

Harry Ray 1946 US singer who joined the Moments in 1970, which later in 1978 became Ray, Goodman & Brown.

Carmine Appice 1948 US drummer, singer and songwriter. In 1966 he was a co-founder of Vanilla Fudge who lasted until 1969. Carmine formed Cactus with Tim Bogert, and then with Jeff Beck, formed Beck, Bogert & Appice. Finally he worked as a session drummer and became a member of Rod Stewart's band; He often wrote material with Rod. In 1982 Vanilla Fudge re-formed again.

Don Johnson 1948 US actor and singer. Don became known through the TV series 'Miami Vice', in which he played the part of Sonny Crockett from 1984. In 1970 he had his first film role in *The Magic Garden Of Stanley Sweetheart*. In 1973 he played in *A Boy And His Dog*. After that, nothing much seemed to happen, and between 1976 and 1981 he played in five pilot films for TV series, none of which ever got off the ground. He played the main male lead in the TV film *Elvis And The Beauty Queen*, then came 'Miami Vice'. Don had his first success as a singer with "Heartbeat" (8/86 US 5). Other hits: "Till I Loved You" (10/88 US 25; UK 16) with Barbara Streisand, and "Tell It Like It Is" (7/89). Don Johnson knows how to make more money on record sales: he co-writes most of the B-sides of his hits.

Paul Simonon 1955 UK bassist, singer and songwriter with Clash, which split up in 1985.

Nick Beggs 1961 UK bassist and songwriter for Kajagoogoo. After singer Limahl had left, Nick took over singing as well. Hits: "Big Apple" (10/83 UK 8) and "The Lion's Mouth" (3/84 UK 25). When the band was no longer functioning properly, they called themselves Kaja, and then split up altogether. In 1988 Nick popped up with the group Ellis, Beggs & Howard, who had their first hit with "Big Bubbles, No Troubles" (9/88).

Deaths

Fats Waller 1943 US blues and jazz pianist. Fats was known for his excessive lifestyle and for being a worka-

holic. He died during a train journey from L.A. to New York. Born 21st May, 1904.

Glenn Miller 1944 US bandleader. While looking after US troops with the Army in Europe, he was on the way from London to Paris, when his small private plane crashed in the Channel. No traces of wreckage or evidence were ever found. Born 1st March, 1904.

Jackie Brenston 1979 US singer and songwriter. Died after a heart attack. Born 15th August, 1930.

Hits of the Day

1945	"I Can't Begin To Tell You" Bing Crosby US 6 weeks
1973	"The Most Beautiful Girl In The World" Charlie Rich US 2 weeks
1973	"Merry X-Mas Everybody" Slade UK 5 weeks
1979	"Another Brick In the Wall" Pink Floyd UK 5 weeks
1984	"Do They Know It's Christmas?" Band Aid UK 5 weeks

16th

Birthdays

Tony Hicks 1945 UK guitarist, singer and songwriter. He started with the group the Dolphins and became a founder member of the Hollies at the end of 1962.

Benny Anderson 1946 Swedish pianist, singer and songwriter. Benny first came to prominence as a member of the group Hep Stars who were very popular in Sweden in the 1960s. In 1970 Benny and Bjorn Ulvaeus joined up and with their respective wives started the group Abba. Hits, see 25th April.

Billy Gibbons 1949 US guitarist, singer and songwriter for the band ZZ Top formed in 1970. He started his career as a member of the group Moving Sidewalks, who played as supporting group in Jimi Hendrix performances. Hendrix later remembered Billy in a talk show, and said, Billy was one of the best young guitarists in the States. In 1970 the first album by ZZ Top appeared. Hits: "Tush" (7/75 US 20), "Legs" (5/84 US 8), "Gimme All Your Lovin' " (4/83 US 37; 9/83 UK 61; 10/84 RE-UK 10), "Sleeping Bag"

(10/85 US 8; UK 27), "Stages" (1/86 US 21) and "Rough Boy" (3/86 US 22; UK 23).

Deaths

Sylvester 1988 US singer. He died of AIDS. Born 6th September, 1947.

Hits of the Day

1944 "Don't Fence Me In" Bing Crosby & Andrews Sisters US 8 weeks

1950 "The Tennessee Waltz" Patti Page US 13 weeks

1955 "Christmas Alphabet" Dickie Valentine UK 3 weeks

1957 "April Love" Pat Boone US 6 weeks

1965 "Day Tripper/We Can Work It Out" Beatles UK 5 weeks

1972 "Me And Mrs. Jones" Billy Paul US 3 weeks

1978 "You Don't Bring Me Flowers" Barbra Streisand & Neil Diamond US 1 week (2nd time)

1989 "Let's Party" Jive Bunny & The Mastermixers UK 1 week

17th

Birthdays

Arthur Fiedler 1894 US violinist. He became a member of the Boston Pops Orchestra in 1915, of which he was the leader from 1930 until his death on 10th July, 1979. Greatest hit, the million seller "Jalousie" (5/38 US 13).

Karl Denver 1934 UK singer, who was successful from 1961 to 1964. Hits: "Marcheta" (6/61 UK 8), "Mexicali Rose" (10/61 UK 8), "Wimoweh" (1/62 UK 4), the English version of the South African Zulu song of the same name, and which was released in the USA as "The Lion Sleeps Tonight" by the Tokens) and "Never Goodbye" (2/62 UK 9).

Tommy Steele 1936 UK singer and songwriter, considered to be the UK's first rock 'n' roll star. Real name Thomas Hicks. In September 1956 he cut a demo for a record company, and two days later was recording his first single. Hits: "Singing The Blues" (12/56 UK 1), "Butterfingers" (5/57 UK 8), "Water, Water/Handful Of Songs" (8/57 UK 5), "Nairobi" (3/58 UK 3), "Come On Let's Go" (11/58 UK 10), "Little White Bull" (12/59 UK 6) and "What A Mouth" (6/60 UK 5). When the hits dried up in 1961, he became a successful actor on stage and in film musicals.

Art Neville 1937 US singer, pianist, and songwriter. Complete first names Arthur Lanon. Already while he was still at school, he had his own band, the Hawketts, with whom he recorded the New Orleans hit "Mardi Gras Mambo" in 1954. Later, his brothers Charles and Aaron joined the band, in 1958 Art had to join the Navy, and Aaron took over lead in the group. Back from the Navy, Art played with the Hawketts again. Despite their popularity locally, they couldn't break nationally. In the meantime, in 1962 Art formed Neville Sounds; his brothers were only temporarily involved. After Aaron had tried successfully as a solo artist in 1966, Art played with a new lineup of Neville Sounds as backing band for his brother. In 1967 Allen Toussaint engaged Art and the rhythm section as his house band, they became the Meters and played on countless hits by Lee Dorsey, Dr. John, LaBelle and Robert Palmer. In addition, they had their own instrumental hits, the greatest being "Cissy Strut" (4/69 US 23). In the meantime Aaron continued to experiment with his solo career, and brother Charles played saxophone with various jazz bands in New York. In 1975 the brothers, including youngest brother Cyril, joined up again. From 1978 they appeared together as the Neville Brothers. Aaron Neville had a hit with "Don't Know Much" in 1989, a duet with Linda Ronstadt. The Neville Brothers have become one of the most sought-after live acts on the international circuit.

Eddie Kendricks 1939 US singer. His career started with the Primes in the late 1950s, which became the Elgins and finally the Temptations in August 1961; he remained with them until June 1971. Hits: "My Girl" (1/65 US 1), "Beauty Is Only Skin Deep" (8/66 US 3; 10/66 UK 18), "I Can't Get Next To You" (8/69 US 1; 1/70 UK 13), "Ball Of Confusion" (5/70 US 3; 9/70 UK 7) and "Just My Imagination (Running Away With Me)" (2/71 US 1; 5/71 UK 8). After that, Eddie started a successful solo career, having hits with "Keep On Truckin' " (8/73 US 1; 11/73 UK 18) and "Boogie Down" (1/74 US 2; 3/74 UK 39). He rejoined the Temptations for a reunion album in 1982; in 1985, LIVE AT THE APOLLO with David Ruffin was recorded with Hall & Oates to mark the reopening of the Apollo Theatre in Harlem. In the meantime Eddie had dropped the 's' from his surname.

Paul Butterfield 1942 US harmonica player, singer, and songwriter. He played with many black blues musicians and helped to fuel a blues revival in the 1960s in the

USA. As a teenager, Paul had played live with Howlin' Wolf, Buddy Guy, Otis Rush, Little Walter and Magic Sam. In 1963 he formed the Paul Butterfield Blues Band, which included, at one time or another, musicians like Elvin Bishop, David Sanborn, Mike Bloomfield and Mark Naftalin. The group lasted until 1972, then Paul formed Butterfield's Better Days. In 1976, with ex-Band bassist Rick Danko, he formed the Danko-Butterfield Band. In 1980 he became ill with a disease of the bowels; two serious operations followed, which kept him out of the limelight until the end of 1981. He died 4th May, 1987.

Dave Dee 1943 UK singer, real name David Harman. He started as Dave Dee & The Bostons and in October 1964, changed the name to Dave Dee, Dozy, Beaky, Mick & Tich. The songwriting team, Ken Howard and Alan Blaikley, took over management of the group and produced a whole row of hits for the band: "Hold Tight" (3/66 UK 4), "Hideaway" (6/66 UK 10), "Bend It" (9/66 UK 2), "Save Me" (12/66 UK 4), "Okay!" (5/67 UK 4), "Zabadak!" (10/67 UK 3), "Legend Of Xanadu" (2/68 UK 1) and "Last Night In Soho" (7/68 UK 8). In August 1969 Dave left the band and attempted a solo career. In late 1989 Dave joined the group Marmalade and released the single "Scirocco".

Jim Bonfanti 1948 US drummer with the Raspberries.

Darryl Way 1948 UK violinist, pianist and songwriter with the band Curved Air formed in 1970. Beside that he released three solo albums as Darryl Way's Wolf. After Curved Air had split up in 1977, he worked as a session musician on records by Trace, Jethro Tull and Marianne Faithfull among others.

Paul Rodgers 1949 UK singer and songwriter. After singing with the Roadrunners and Brown Sugar, he became one of the founder members of Free in May 1968; Alexis Korner suggested the name, based on his own trio Free At Last. Hits: "All Right Now" (6/70 UK 2; 8/70 US 4; 7/73 RE-UK 15), "My Brother Jake" (5/71 UK 4) and "Wishing Well" (1/73 UK 7). These three titles were later released on the EP "Free" (2/78 UK 11). In late 1971 various tensions arose within the group and each member tried solo careers: Paul formed Peace. At the beginning of 1972 Free re-formed. In the middle of 1973 it became clear, that the band would finally split up. Paul Rodgers received an offer of joining Deep Purple as singer, which he declined. Instead, he became founder member and singer of Bad Company. Hits: "Can't Get Enough" (6/74 UK 15; 8/75 US 5) and "Feel Like Makin' Love" (7/75 US 10; UK 20). The group officially split up in mid-1983. Paul released a solo album, then joined The Firm with Jimmy Page of Led Zeppelin and Chris Slade of Manfred Mann. Hit: "Radioactive" (2/85 US 28). When Bad Company reformed later, Paul was no longer with them.

Mickey Jones 1952 US bassist, and singer with Angel, formed out of the remains of several east coast bands in 1975.

Mark Gane 1953 Canadian guitarist, keyboard player and songwriter, who became a member of Martha & The Muffins in 1975, which developed into M & M in 1984. For hits, see 18th December, under colleague Martha Johnson.

Sarah Dallin 1961 UK singer with Bananarama. For hits 2nd April under colleague Keren Jane Woodward.

Deaths

Hound Dog Taylor 1975 US blues guitarist, pianist, singer and songwriter. He died of cancer. Born 12th April, 1917.

Don Ellis 1978 US jazz trumpeter. Born 25th April, 1935.

Hit Of The Day

1966 "Winchester Cathedral" New Vaudeville Band US 2 weeks (2nd time)

18th

Birthdays

Fletcher Henderson 1898 US jazz pianist, songwriter, arranger and orchestra leader. He formed his own band in 1923, which became the first well-known jazz, big band: he had 20 US hits between 1923 and 1937. It was Fletcher who established the parameters of swing with his large band. His biggest hits were "Charleston Crazy" (4/24 US 8) and "Sugar Foot Stomp" (10/25 US 8). Fletcher played on hits by musicians like Louis Armstrong, Bessie Smith, Ethel Waters, and Benny Goodman, for whom he wrote many arrangements. He died 29th December, 1952.

Buck Ram 1908 US songwriter, producer and manager. He had his first success as co-writer of "I'll Be Home For Christmas", which became a million seller for Bing Crosby in 1943. In the early 1950s he managed the Penguins and the Platters; and wrote the latter's greatest hits. He died on January 1st, 1991.

Anita O'Day 1919 US jazz singer, who achieved fame with Gene Krupa's band in 1941. With Gene she had the hit "Just A Little South Of North Carolina" (6/41 US 4). Then she sang with the band of Stan Kenton and had her greatest success with "And Her Tears Flowed Like Wine" (9/44 US 4). Back with the Gene Krupa band Anita continued to extend her reputation before embarking on a solo career. She occasionally worked with Duke Ellington's and Benny Goodman's Bands. Alcohol and drug problems caused lenghty gaps in her career, but all in all, she remained in the music business right into the 1980s.

Sam Andrews 1941 US guitarist with the group Big Brother & The Holding Company formed in 1965.

Chas Chandler 1941 UK bassist. Real first name Bryan. In the early 1960s he played with the Alan Price combo, which became the Animals after Eric Burdon joined them in 1963. In September 1966, when it was already definite that the group would split up and they were touring the USA, Chas saw and heard a musician called Jimi Hendrix in 'Cafe Wha?' in New York. He persuaded him to go to England. Jimi went, and Chas built up a band around him and then became the manager of Jimi Hendrix Experience. On 18th September, 1970 Jimi left a message on Chas' answering machine, saying "I need help badly, man"; but it was too late to help him, he was already dead. Another successful group that Chas managed were Slade. In the 1970s Chas produced records by Eric Burdon, as well as joining the odd Animals reunion.

Keith Richards 1943 UK guitarist and songwriter with the Rolling Stones and as a solo artist.

Deke Leonard 1944 UK guitarist and songwriter. Real first name Roger. He played with several bands, until he formed Man in 1968, which lasted until 1976. In between – from 1972 to 1974 – Deke attempted a solo career. He also worked as a session musician. In 1983, on the occasion of the 25th anniversary of the London Marquee Club, Man re-formed for a live record.

Buddy Gask 1948 UK bassist and singer with Showaddywaddy.

Martha Johnson 1950 Canadian singer and songwriter who led the semi-professional band Martha & The Muffins in 1975. At this time, guitarist and keyboard player Mark Gene joined the group who decided to go into music business full-time. During the following years, they kept producing good, witty records. Their biggest hit was "Echo Beach" (3/80 UK 10). From 1984, Martha and Mark carried on as the duo M & M.

Bobby Keyes 1953 US saxophonist, who is one of the best and most well-known session musicians in the business. He has worked with the Rolling Stones, Harry Nilsson, John Lennon, Eric Clapton, Joe Cocker, and many others. Bobby also made solo records.

Greg D'Angelo 1963 US drummer with White Lion.

Hits of the Day

1959	"What Do You Want To Make Them Eyes At Me For" Emile Ford & The Checkmates UK 6 weeks
1961	"The Lion Sleeps Tonight" Tokens US 3 weeks
1982	"Save Your Love" Renee & Renato UK 3 weeks
1982	"Maneater" Daryl Hall & John Oates US 3 weeks

19th

Birthdays

Edith Piaf 1915 Singer and songwriter. Real name Edith Giovanna Gassion. It is said her father forced her to sing in the streets of Paris to earn money. She was discovered by a night club owner, and the poor street singer became the most famous chanson singer of all time, the 'sparrow of Paris' who in turn helped many talented singers and songwriters. Her song "La Vie En Rose" (1950) became a million seller, "Non Je Ne Regrette Rien" (1960) was one of her best, "Milord" (11/60 UK 24) was one of her most successful chansons. She died 11th October, 1963.

Professor Longhair 1918 US pianist, singer, drummer and songwriter. Real name Henry Roeland Byrd. He was among the best and most influential musicians from New Orleans: Fats Domino and Huey 'Piano' Smith emulated his style of playing. Dr. John called him his idol. He started as a street musician in New Orleans in the 1930s, played with the Mid-Drifs from 1947 to 1949, and then formed his own band, which he called Professor Longhair & The Four Hairs. His only hit was "Bald Head" (8/50 R&B 5). Byrd died 30th January, 1980.

Little Jimmy Dickens 1920 US country singer, who started in 1942 with Johnny Bailes & His Happy Valley Boys as 'Jimmy The Kid'. From 1949 to 1972 he was successful as a soloist. His biggest hit was "May The Bird Of Paradise Fly Up Your Nose" (10/65 C&W 1; US 15). As with all the best-known country musicians, Little Jimmy, whose real name is James Cecil, had a nickname too: Tater!

Phil Ochs 1940 US singer and songwriter. He became one of the leading protest singers in the USA in the 1960s. He committed suicide 9th April, 1976.

20th

Birthdays

Maurice White 1941 US singer, drummer and songwriter. He started as a session drummer with Chess Records in the early 1960s, working with Muddy Waters, Billy Stewart, Chuck Berry, Jackie Wilson, Etta James and the Impressions. From 1966 to 1969 he was a member of the Ramsey Lewis Trio. In 1969 he formed his own band, which were first called Salty Peppers, and then renamed Earth, Wind & Fire from 1970. Hits, and million sellers: "Shining Star" (2/75 US 1), "Sing A Song" (11/75 UK 5), "Getaway" (7/76 US 12), "Got To Get You Into My Life" (7/78 US 9; 10/79 UK 33) "September" (11/78 US 8; UK 3), "Boogie Wonderland" (5/79 US 6; UK 4) with the Emotions, "After The Love Has Gone" (7/79 US 2; UK 4) and "Let's Groove" (10/81 US & UK 3).

Alvin Lee 1944 UK guitarist, singer and songwriter of the band Ten Years After formed in 1966. He started in 1961 with the Jay Birds, who played together until November 1966, and a few days later, Ten Years After was formed, which lasted until March 1974. After that, he played as Alvin Lee & Co. until July 1976, and from February 1978 until May 1980 with Ten Years Later, from June 1980 to October 1981 as Alvin Lee Band and from November 1981 to 1982 only as Alvin Lee. Hit: "Love Like A Man" (6/70 UK 10). Alvin was always more of an album artist. The original lineup reformed in 1989.

Zal Yanovsky 1944 Canadian guitarist and songwriter. Together He was a member of the Mugwumps with John Sebastian; when they split up in 1965, the other two musicians, Cass Elliott and Denny Doherty, joined the Mamas & Papas, and Zal and John formed the band Lovin' Spoonful. Zal stayed until 1967 and then attempted a solo career.

John McEuen 1945 US guitarist, violinist and singer with the Nitty Gritty Dirt Band formed in 1966.

Limahl 1958 UK singer and songwriter, real name Christopher Hamill. His career started with the band Kajagoogoo. Hits: "Too Shy" (1/83 UK 1; 3/83 US 5) and "Oooh To Be Ah" (4/83 UK 7). After that, he started a solo career. Hits: "Only For Love" (11/83 UK 16) and "Never Ending Story" (10/84 UK 4; 3/85 US 17).

Hits of the Day

1942 "My Devotion" Vaughn Monroe US 1 week
1958 "It's Only Make Believe" Conway Twitty UK 5 weeks
1964 "Come See About Me" Supremes US 1 week
1987 "Always On My Mind" Pet Shop Boys UK 4 weeks

Paul Francis Webster 1907 US lyricist, who wrote songs like "Secret Love", "Love Is A Many Splendoured Thing", "Friendly Persuasion", "The Green Leaves Of Summer", "The Shadow Of Your Smile", "Somewhere, My Love" an "April Love". They were usually featured in films.

Larry Willis 1940 US pianist. He accompanied Hugh Masekela, Miriam Makeba, Cannonball Adderley, Stan Getz, the Four Tops, and then joined Blood, Sweat & Tears in 1972.

Bobby Colomby 1944 US drummer. He started as an accompanist with Odetta and Eric Anderson, and in 1968 was a founder member of Blood, Sweat & Tears. In 1976 he was the last musician of the original line-up to leave. Bobby became a producer.

Peter Criss 1945 US drummer and singer with the group Kiss formed in 1972. Real surname Crisscoula. In May 1980 he left the group and was replaced by Eric Carr. Peter made solo records also.

Steve Wright 1948 Australian singer with the Easybeats. As with all the other members of the band he was not born in Australia: they all emigrated from the Netherlands and the UK with their parents. After he had sung with the Langdells in the early 1960s as Chris Langdon, he became a founder member of the Easybeats in 1964 who quickly developed into the leading group in Australia. In 1966 they went to the UK, and tried to conquer the rest of the world. That worked at least with "Friday On My Mind" (11/66 UK 6; 3/67 US 16). From 1970 to 1974 Steve appeared in the Australian version of *Jesus Christ Superstar*, after which he had a solo hit in his home country with "Evie".

Anita Baker 1957 US singer, who started her career in 1976 with the group Chapter 8 formed in 1971; they split up in 1980. Anita worked in an office in Detroit and obtained a solo recording contract in 1983. Hits: "Sweet Love" (8/86 US 8; 11/86 UK 13), "Giving You The Best That I Got" (9/88 US 3) and "Just Because" (1/89 US 14).

Billy Bragg 1957 UK singer and songwriter. In 1977 he formed the punk/R&B band Riff Raff, which lasted until 1981. After working as a street musician for a while, he obtained a recording contract as a solo artist in 1983. Hits: "Between The Wars (EP)" (3/85 UK 15) and "She's Leaving Home" (5/88 UK 1). Billy created a minor stir several times for his political activities: in October 1984 he was arrested when taking part in a sit-in against apartheid policies in front of the South Africa House in London. One of the few prepared to use his pre-eminence constructively in pursuit of his beliefs.

Ray Coburn 1962 Canadian keyboard player and songwriter for Honeymoon Suite.

Deaths

Bobby Darin 1973 US singer and songwriter. On 12th December he was taken to hospital, a weakness of the heart which he had suffered from since his youth was becoming more noticeable. He was operated on 20th December, and died while still on the operating table. Born 14th May, 1936.

Hits of the Day

1941	"Elmer's Tune" Glenn Miller US 1 week
1969	"Leaving On A Jet Plane" Peter, Paul & Mary US 1 week
1969	"Two Little Boys" Rolf Harris UK 6 weeks
1975	"That's The Way" K. C. & The Sunshine Band US 1 week
1980	"Starting Over" John Lennon UK 1 week
1986	"Walk Like An Egyptian" Bangles US 4 weeks
1986	"Caravan Of Love" Housemartins UK 1 week

21st

Birthdays

Freddie Hart 1926 US country singer, guitarist and songwriter. Real name Fred Segrest. In the early 1950s he worked with Lefty Frizzell, and from 1959 he had hits as a solo artist in the C&W charts. His biggest pop hit and million seller was "Easy Loving" (8/71 US 17).

Paul 1940 US singer and songwriter, real name Ray Hildebrand. With Jill Jackson who called herself Paula, he appeared as Paul & Paula. He wrote "Hey Paula" (12/62 US 1; 2/63 UK 8), which originally was released under their real names of Ray & Jill, without success. Only when they called themselves Paul & Paula and reissued the record did it become a hit. A further hit was "Young Lovers" (3/63 US 6; UK 9); after 1963 it was all over. In 1982 the duo joined up again to cut a country record.

Frank Zappa 1940 US singer, guitarist and songwriter. He started in the late 1950s with the group Blackouts, played cocktail-music in cafés in 1960, and attempted to compose film music. In 1963 he became a member of Soots, in 1964 he played with the Soul Giants, which he called Muthers shortly after, and then Mothers of Invention. Since then, he has carved a reputation as one of rock's true eccentrics.

Carla Thomas 1942 US soul singer. Carla is the daughter of Rufus Thomas with whom she first recorded a duet in 1960. Hits, as a soloist: "Gee Whiz (Look At His Eyes)" (1/61 US 10) and "B-A-B-Y" (8/66 US 14). In a duet with Otis Redding she was successful with "Tramp" (5/67 US 26; 7/67 UK 13) and "Knock On Wood" (8/67 US 30; 10/67 UK 35).

Albert Lee 1943 UK guitarist and songwriter. Among the bands worthy of mention with whom Albert played were Neil Christian's Crusaders, Chris Farlowe & The Thunderbirds, Flintlocks, Country Fever, Joe Cocker's accompanying group, Heads, Hands & Feet, and Eric Clapton's band. Albert can also be heard as a session musician on countless records, and he also made solo records.

Gwen McCrae 1946 US singer, who was successful in the wake of husband George McCrae, by using the same writers and production team. Hit: "Rockin' Chair" (5/75 US 9).

Kevin Peek 1946 Australian guitarist, who played with Mary Hopkin, the New Seekers, Cliff Richard and Sky. He also made solo records.

Carl Wilson 1946 US guitarist, singer and songwriter. With his brothers he was already playing as Pendletones, Kenny & The Cadets and Carl & The Passions in the late 1950s. In 1961 the Beach Boys were formed, one of the very few US bands who were able to come up with something in the face of the onslaught of British beat groups in the first half of the 1960s.

Martin Belmont 1948 UK guitarist with Man, Ducks Deluxe from August 1972 to July 1975, and after that, with Graham Parker & Rumour.

Betty Wright 1953 US soul singer. She was already singing in the family's gospel choir, Echoes Of Joy, at age 3. In 1966 she made her first solo records. Major hits: "Clean Up Woman" (11/71 US 6) and "Dance With Me" (3/78 US 8) with Peter Brown.

Allan Johnson 1957 Australian bassist with Exciter and Real Life.

Tony Lewis 1957 UK bassist and singer with the trio Outfield formed in 1985. Hits: "You're Love" (2/86 US 6), "All The Love" (6/86 US 19), "Since You've Been Gone" (6/87 US 31) and "Voices Of Babylon" (3/89 US 25).

Hits of the Day

1940 "Frenesi" Artie Shaw US 13 weeks
1974 "Cat's In The Cradle" Harry Chapin US 1 week
1974 "Lonely This Christmas" Mud UK 4 weeks
1985 "Say You Say Me" Lionel Richie US 4 weeks

22nd

Birthdays

Hawkshaw Hawkins 1921 US country singer. Real first names Harold Franklin. He was successful in the C&W charts from 1948; "Slow Poke" (1/52 US 26) was his biggest hit. He was married to colleague Jean Shepard. He had just had his greatest success in the country charts with "Lonesome 7-7203" (3/63 C&W 1) when he crashed in a plane on 5th March, 1963. Two other country stars, Patsy Cline and Cowboy Copas, were killed with him.

Jorge Ben 1942 Brazilian guitarist, singer and songwriter. In his home country he was one of the most successful artists on the pop scene of the 1960s. His composition "Taj Mahal" was the basis for Rod Stewart's "Da Ya Think I'm Sexy".

Barry Jenkins 1944 UK drummer and songwriter who left the Nashville Teens and joined the Animals in 1966. When they split up in 1967, he was the only one of the old group who stayed with Eric Burdon, who then appeared as Eric Burdon & Animals, and from June 1968 as Eric Burdon & New Animals. In 1969 they all split up and Barry joined Heavy Jelly.

Rick Nielsen 1946 US singer and guitarist who formed the group Fuse in 1969, which became Sick Man Of Europe in 1971, and Cheap Trick in 1973. In 1977 the first album by this group appeared. Hits: "I Want You To Want Me" (4/79 US 7; UK 29), "The Flame" (4/88 US 1; 8/88 UK 32) and "Don't Be Cruel" (8/88 US 4).

Robin & Maurice Gibb 1949 Singers and songwriters, who with older brother Barry formed the Bee Gees. For hits and history see 1st September. Robin also made records as a soloist. Hits: "Saved By The Bell" (7/69 UK 2), and "Oh! Darling" (8/78 US 15).

Alan Williams 1950 UK guitarist, flautist and pianist with the Rubettes.

Deaths

Ma Rainey 1939 US blues singer. Born 26th April, 1886.

Hits of the Day

1958 "Chipmunks Song" David Seville US 4 weeks
1962 "Telstar" Tornados US 3 weeks
1979 "Escape (The Pinacolada Song)" Rupert Holmes US 2 weeks
1984 "Like A Virgin" Madonna US 6 weeks

23rd

Birthdays

Chet Baker 1929 US jazz trumpeter and singer. Real first name Chesney. He played in Gerry Mulligan's quartet in 1952, and after that with his own bands. He died in Amsterdam on 13th May, 1988.

Rev. James Cleveland 1932 US gospel singer and songwriter. Died February 9th 1991.

Esther Phillips 1935 US singer who played several instruments and during the course of her long career cut blues, R&B, jazz and soul records. She was born Esther Mae Jones. She was just 13 when she was discovered by Johnny Otis and signed to a recording contract. Little Esther appeared in his revue until 1954 and sang the hit "Double Crossing Blues" (2/50 R&B 1), "Mistrustin' Blues" (4/50 R&B 1) and "Cupid's Boogie" (6/50 R&B 1). In 1962 she dropped appeared the 'Little' from her name. Hits: "Release Me" (10/62 US 8) and "What A Diff'rence A Day Makes" (8/75 US 20; 10/75 UK 6). Esther died 7th August, 1984.

Johnny Kidd 1939 UK singer, guitarist and songwriter. Real name Frederick Heath. In 1959 he formed Johnny

Kidd & The Pirates, who were one of the first English hardrock groups, pre-dating the heavy metal phenomen of the 1970s and 1980's. Hits: "Shakin' All Over" (6/60 UK 1) and "I'll Never Get Over You" (7/63 UK 4). Johnny died 7th October, 1966.

Jorma Kaukonen 1940 US guitarist with Jefferson Airplane and Hot Tuna from 1972 to 1978. Jorma also made solo records.

Eugene Record 1940 US singer and songwriter with the Hi-Lites formed in 1960. In 1963 they made their first record, in 1964 they changed their name to Chi-Lites. From 1969 to 1984 they were in the US R&B charts regularly. The greatest pop hits were "Have You Seen Her" (10/71 US 3; 1/72 UK 3), "Oh Girl" (4/72 US 1; UK 14), "Homely Girl" (3/74 UK 5), "Too Good To Be Forgotten" (11/74 UK 10), "It's Time For Love" (9/75 UK 5), and "You Don't Have To Go" (7/76 UK 3). "Have You Seen Her/Oh Girl" (6/75 UK 5) were re-released in the UK as a double A-sides.

Tim Hardin 1941 US songwriter, singer and guitarist. He never had hits for himself with his outstanding compositions, but other artists like the Four Tops, Bobby Darin and Johnny Cash scored with "If I Were A Carpenter"; and Peter, Paul & Mary and Rod Stewart scored with "Reason To Believe". Tim died 29th December, 1980.

Ron Bushy 1945 US drummer with Iron Butterfly.

Luther Grosvenor 1949 UK guitarist, singer and songwriter. He started with the Hellions, then played with the V.I.P.s, Art and Spooky Tooth. He stayed with the latter from their foundation in 1967 until 1972. He also played with Stealers Wheel; in August 1973, he changed his name to Ariel Bender and joined Mott The Hoople. From mid-1975 to 1977 he played with Widow Maker. Luther also made solo records.

Dave Murray 1958 UK lead guitarist and songwriter with Iron Maiden.

Hits of the Day

1972	"Long Haired Lover From Liverpool" Little Jimmy Osmond UK 5 weeks
1978	"Le Freak" Chic US 2 weeks (2nd time)
1989	"Another Day In Paradise" Phil Collins US 4 weeks
1989	"Do They Know It's Christmas" Band Aid II UK 3 weeks

24th

Birthdays

Dave Bartholomew 1920 US songwriter, trumpeter, singer, and bandleader. Dave is considered to be the architect of the New Orleans sound of the 40s and 50s. He started as a trumpeter in Fats Pichon's band on a Mississippi steamer. In 1946 he formed his own first band in New Orleans and there discovered young pianist and singer Fats Domino, whom he produced and wrote for, contributing many of his biggest hits. He also looked after Jewel King, Roy Brown, Lloyd Price, Shirley & Lee and Smiley Lewis. Dave can be heard with his band on early records by Little Richard. Once he was even in the charts himself with "Country Boy" (2/50 R&B 14).

Lee Dorsey 1924 US singer and songwriter. He had his first career as a boxer in the name of Kid Chocolate. During a party in New Orleans, Lee met songwriter Allen Toussaint who produced his first records in 1961. Hits: "Ya Ya" (9/61 US 7), "Working In The Coalmine" (7/66 US & UK 8) and "Holy Cow" (10/66 US 23; UK 6). He died 1st December, 1986.

Ray Bryant 1931 US pianist and bandleader. After he had played in several groups, he recorded with his own trio from 1955 as Ray Bryant Combo. Hit: "The Madison, Part 1" (4/60 US 30).

Mike Curb 1944 US songwriter, producer and artist with Mike Curb Congregation. In 1964, as a student, he wrote the commercial jingle "You Meet The Nicest People On A Honda". For the group, the Hondells, who recorded the jingle, he reworked it and it became the "Little Honda" (10/64 US 9). From that time on, Curb was considered to be a 'wunderkind' in the US record business. He was a millionaire at 23, and president of MGM Records at 25, whose first job for the company was to sack 250 employees. In 1974 he became the head of Warner/Curb Records. He wrote other hits, and produced many groups whom he usually gathered up from the street, put in the studio and recorded. In this way, he discovered the Mugwumps, Electric Flag and Stone Poneys with singer Linda Ronstadt. Greatest hit for Mike Curb Congregation "Burning Bridges" (11/70 US 34).

Eddie Furey 1944 Irish folk musician, who appears with his brother as Eddie & Finbar Furey.

Lemmy 1945 UK singer, bassist, and songwriter. Real name Ian Fraser Kilmister. He started as bassist with Hawkwind and formed the group Motorhead in 1975, who are known for never playing below 126 decibels at concerts. Hits: "The Golden Years" (5/80 UK 8) and "Motorhead Live" (7/81 UK 6).

Jan Akkerman 1946 Dutch guitarist and songwriter with Johnny & The Cellar Rockers, Hunters, Brainbox, and from 1971 with the group Focus, formed in 1969. Hits: "Hocus Pocus" (1/73 UK 20; 3/73 US 9) and "Sylvia" (1/73 UK 4). He has worked as a soloist from 1976.

Paul Shuttleworth 1947 UK singer and songwriter. He started with the group Surly Bird (1969/70), was with Cow Pie (1970-72), and finally became a founder member of Kursaal Flyers (1973). They made their first records on Jonathan King's record label, but they did not sell well. Only when Mike Batt became their producer did things improve. Hit: "Little Does She Know" (11/76 UK 14).

Ian Burden 1957 UK synthesizer player with Human League.

Hits of the Day

1977 "How Deep Is Your Love" Bee Gees US 3 weeks
1988 "Every Rose Has A Thorn" Poison US 3 weeks

25th

Birthdays

Kid Ory 1889 US jazz trombonist. Real first name Edward. He played with his own orchestra from 1911. From 1912 to 1919 he led the most successful band in New Orleans, which included King Oliver, Louis Armstrong and Sidney Bechet in its lineup. He composed the well-known number "Muskrat Ramble". He died 23rd January, 1973.

Cab Calloway 1907 US singer, drummer, bandleader and songwriter. For many years Cab was considered to be the most charismatic showman in the entire music business. He became known as 'King Of Hi-De-Ho' after appearances at the Cotton Club in New York in the early 1930s. Alongside that, he led an excellent jazz band, which featured such stars as Ben Webster, Dizzy Gillespie and Cozy Cole. Hits: "Minnie The Moocher" (3/31 US 1) and "(Hep-Hep!) The Jumpin' Jive" (7/39 US 2). He appeared in the charts again and again until 1945, and in the 1950s and 1960s Cab turned up again as the singer in *Porgy & Bess* and *Hello, Dolly!*.

Tony Martin 1912 US singer, saxophonist and film actor. Real name Alvin Morris. From 1936 to 1957 he appeared in many films like Casbah (1948) as the 'romantic lover'. He appeared regularly in nightclubs from 1948 with his second wife, Cyd Charisse, who was also successful as an actress. Hits, for Tony: "It's A Blue World" (2/40 US 2), "To Each His Own" (7/46 US 4), "There's No Tomorrow" (11/49 US 2), "I Said My Pajamas (And Put On My Prayers)" (1/50 US 3), a duet with Fran Warren, "I Got Ideas" (6/51 US 3), "Stranger In Paradise" (12/53 US 10; 4/55 UK 6) and "Walk Hand In Hand" (6/56 US 10; UK 2). Tony stayed in the record business until 1957. In 1976, with his wife, he published their shared memoirs, 'The Two Of Us'.

Billy Horton 1929 US singer. He formed the Gospel Tornados with three friends in Philadelphia in 1955. Alongside that, they sang rhythm and blues as the Thunderbirds. In 1957 finally they called themselves Silhouettes. Hit: "Get A Job" (1/58 US 1).

Chris Kenner 1929 US singer and songwriter. In 1957 he made his first record. Hit: "I Like It Like That, Part 1" (5/61 US 2). He wrote, among others, "Land Of 1000 Dances" (6/63 US 77), which became an enormous soul hit for Wilson Pickett in 1966. His compositions were also recorded by Fats Domino and the Dave Clark Five. Chris died 25th January, 1976.

O'Kelly Isley 1937 US singer with the Isley Brothers. O'Kelly was the oldest of three brothers who released their first record in 1957. For hits, see 21st May, under brother Ronald. He died 31st March, 1986.

Bob James 1939 US jazz/pop keyboard player and composer. He worked as a session musician for many top stars from the late 1960s. In 1973 he became a producer and arranger for record company CTI/Kudu. In 1977 he formed his own record company Tappan Zee. Bob made a few solo albums, his most successful ones were million seller TOUCH DOWN (1978) and ONE ON ONE (1979), with Earl Klugh.

Pete Brown 1940 UK songwriter, percussionist and multi-media artist He worked with Vincent Crane, John McLaughlin, and Graham Bond, wrote most of the lyrics for Cream; in 1968 formed Battered Ornaments with guitarist Chris Spedding, and Piblokto in 1969.

Trevor Lucas 1943 Australian guitarist and singer. In the early 1960s Trevor played folk music in Australia. In 1966 he appeared at the International Folk Festival in London's Albert Hall. In 1967 he formed the folk rock group Election. In 1969 he married singer Sandy Denny, and formed the group Fotheringay with her. At the behest of

Chris Blackwell, head of Island Records, Trevor produced Traffic, Joe Cocker, T. Rex, Stephen Stills and Sandy Denny. In 1972 he became a member of Fairport Convention. After his wife had died after falling down stairs in 1978, Trevor went back to Australia, where he continued to work as a producer. He died 4th February, 1989.

John Edwards 1944 US singer with the Spinners. In 1977 he joined that group and replaced Philippe Wynne.

Henry Vestine 1944 US guitarist. In 1966 he was a founder member of Canned Heat and remained until 1969. In 1972/73 he returned and later played with Frank Zappa.

Noel Redding 1945 UK bassist, guitarist and songwriter. Real surname David. In 1968 Noel was recruited for Jimi Hendrix Experience, then played with Fat Mattress, and formed his own band in 1975. In 1990, he published his autobiography.

Jimmy Buffett 1946 US singer and songwriter. After Jimmy had worked as a freelance journalist for a while, he received a recording contract in September 1970. Exactly 324 copies of his debut album DOWN TO EARTH were sold. In 1973 he received a new recording contract and had his first hit with "Come Monday" (6/74 US 30). His greatest hit was "Margaritaville" (4/77 US 8). In the 1980s he had C&W hits.

Barbara Mandrell 1948 US country singer and multi-instrumentalist. She started in the early 1960s as a member of the family group Mandrells. In 1963 she made her first solo records. Hit: "(If Loving You Is Wrong) I Don't Want To Be Right" (3/79 US 31). From 1980 to 1982 she was the hostess of her own TV show in the USA. In 1980 and 1981 she was voted Country Entertainer of the Year.

Desireless 1952 French female singer whose "Voyage, Voyage" (10/87 UK 53; 5/88 RE-UK 5) was the surprise hit of the year 1987.

Rob Campbell 1954 UK guitarist, singer and songwriter with UB 40. Complete first name Robin. He and his brother Alistair (see 15th February under his name for their hits) are sons of Irish folk singer Ian Campbell.

Annie Lennox 1954 UK singer and songwriter. She formed Catch in 1977 with Dave Stewart and another friend; they had a small hit in the Netherlands with "Borderline". In June 1979 the group was expanded and they changed their name to Tourists. Hits: "I Only Want To Be With You" (11/79 UK 4) and "So Good To Be Back Home Again" (2/80 UK 8). In October 1980, while the band was still touring Australia, they split up. Annie and Dave carried on as Eurythmics. Hits: "Love Is A Stranger" (11/82 UK 54; 4/83 RE-UK 6; 9/83 US 23), "Sweet Dreams (Are Made Of This)" (2/83 UK 2; 4/83 US 1), "Who's That Girl"

(7/83 UK 3; 5/84 US 21), "Here Comes The Rain Again" (1/84 UK 8; US 4), "Sexcrime (1984)" (11/84 UK 4), "Would I Lie To You?" (4/85 UK 17; US 5), "There Must Be An Angel (Playing With My Heart)" (7/85 UK 1; US 22), "It's Alright (Baby's Coming Back)" (1/86 UK 12), and "Thorn In My Side" (9/86 UK 5). Annie had hits with "Sisters Are Doin' It For Themselves" (11/85 US 18; UK 9), a duet with Aretha Franklin, and "Put A Little Love In Your Heart" (11/88 US 9; UK 28), a duet with Al Green.

Shane McGowan 1957 UK singer and songwriter with the Pogues formed in 1982. In 1984 the first record by the band appeared. Hits: "Fairytale Of New York" (12/87 UK 2), with Kirsty MacColl, and "The Irish Rover" (3/87 UK 8), with the Dubliners. Sacked in 1991.

Francis Dunnery 1962 UK singer, guitarist and songwriter with It Bites. Hit: "Calling All The Heroes" (7/86 UK 6).

Deaths

Johnny Ace 1954 US singer and songwriter. Played Russian roulette – and lost. Born 9th June, 1929.

Charlie Chaplin 1977 Film actor, comedy star and songwriter. Born 16th April, 1889.

Hits of the Day

1948	"All I Want For Christmas (Is My Two Front Teeth)" Spike Jones US 3 weeks
1965	"Over And Over" Dave Clark 5 US 1 week
1971	"Brand New Key" Melanie US 3 weeks
1976	"When A Child Is Born" Johnny Mathis UK 2 weeks

26th

Birthdays

Ken Howard 1939 UK songwriter, who, with Alan Blaikley, were the most songwriting team, apart from Lennon/McCartney, in the 1960s in the UK. The pair wrote hits for Dave Dee, Dozy, Beaky, Mick & Tich, Honeycombs, Herd, Lulu and many others.

Phil Spector 1940 US songwriter, producer, and singer. He was just 17 when he formed the group Teddy

Bears with two girls of the same age. The trio recorded "To Know Him Is To Love Him" (9/58 US 1; 12/58 UK 2), which supposedly was the epitaph on Phil's father's gravestone; it was a million seller. This success earned him a job with Atlantic Records, where he wrote the hit "Spanish Harlem" with Leiber/Stoller for Ben E. King. From then on, his reputation as a writer and producer developed in leaps and bounds. Phil set up his own record company with Lester Sill in 1961 and produced the Crystals, Ronettes, and many others. Two of his best productions were "You've Lost That Lovin' Feelin'" for the Righteous Brothers and "River Deep Mountain High" for Ike & Tina Turner. He was a multi-millionaire at 21 and withdrew from the business for several years. In the early 1970s, he worked with the Beatles, individually and collectively.

Ernie & Earl Cate 1942 US singers and songwriters, who had the hit "Union Man" (2/76 US 24) as the Cate Brothers. Ernie played keyboards, and Earl played guitar. They formed a group with two other musicians which played a mixture of R&B, country and rock 'n' roll.

Paul Anthony Quinn 1951 UK lead guitarist and songwriter with Saxon formed in 1977.

Hits of the Day

1942 "Strip Polka" Kay Kyser US 2 weeks
1964 "I Feel Fine" Beatles US 3 weeks
1970 "My Sweet Lord/Isn't It A Pity" George Harrison US 4 weeks

---

27th

Birthdays

Marlene Dietrich 1901 Actress and singer, real name Maria Magdalena von Losch. She became known worldwide through the film *Der Blaue Engel* (The Blue Angel) (1930). Her biggest hit as a singer was "Too Old To Cut The Mustard" (8/52 US 12) with Rosemary Clooney. She claimed she had been photographed so often during her life that she no longer wished to be so, and became a recluse in her Paris apartment, where she died 6th May 1992.

Scotty Moore 1931 US guitarist. Real first name Winfield. Scotty played on Elvis Presley's early records. His guitar playing influenced a whole generation of rockabilly artists. In 1969 he played on an album by Mother Earth. In 1976 an album of his was released, and then he was on two albums by Billy Swan. In the meantime he has worked as a producer in Nashville.

Carl Fisher 1939 US singer. For various group names and hits, see 13th September.

Mike Pinder 1941 UK keyboard player. Mike started as a roadie with the group El Riot & The Rebels and finally became a permanent member. In May 1964 he was a founder member of the Moody Blues. He stayed until July 1978 and was replaced by Patrick Moraz. In addition, he worked as a soloist and as a studio musician with John Lennon.

Leslie Maguire 1941 UK keyboard player with Gerry & The Pacemakers.

Eddie Taylor 1941 US saxophonist who has lived in West Germany since the 70s and works there as a session musician.

Mick Jones 1944 UK guitarist, singer, and songwriter. Mick started with the instrumental group Nero & The Gladiators in the early 1960s, whose greatest hit was "Entry Of The Gladiators" (4/61 UK 37). After the band had split up, Mick played with French rock idol Johnny Hallyday for about five years. In 1971 he joined Wonderwheel and from September 1972 played with the reformed group Spooky Tooth, who had split up in late 1970. After that, he became a member of the Leslie West Band, and in February 1976 co-founder of Foreigner. After Mick had produced the album INSIDE INFORMATION by Foreigner on his own in 1988, he released his own first solo album in 1989.

Tracy Nelson 1944 US singer, pianist and songwriter. After having briefly formed two different bands and made a solo album in 1965, she formed Mother Earth in July 1966. This group was always praised a great deal, but were never commercially successful. After Tracy had sung more folk and blues to begin with, she then went more in the direction of country music in the early 1970s. From 1974 she was a solo artist, session musician and singer.

Larry Byrom 1948 US guitarist with Steppenwolf, who replaced Michael Monarch in April 1969. Larry in turn was replaced by Kent Henry in May 1971. After that, as a session musician he was on records by a variety of artists: from Mary Osmond to Joe Cocker, Dr. Hook, Roy Orbison, Joan Baez, Eddie Rabbit, to Tanya Tucker and Ronnie Milsap.

Terry Bozzio 1950 US drummer, singer, and songwriter with Missing Persons, whose trademark was Terry's sister Dale.

David Knopfler 1952 UK guitarist, singer, and songwriter, who was a founder member of Dire Straits in 1977. He is the younger brother of band leader Mark. In July 1980 he left, carried on as a solo artist, and released a number of good, but not very successful albums.

Deaths

Bob Luman 1978 US rockabilly singer. Died after having pneumonia. Born 15th April, 1938.

Hoagy Carmichael 1981 US composer. Born 22nd November, 1899.

Hits of the Day

1952 "I Saw Mommy Kissing Santa Claus" Jimmy Boyd US 2 weeks

1969 "Someday We'll Be Together" Diana Ross & The Supremes US 1 week

1975 "Let's Do It Again" Staple Singers US 1 week

1980 "There's No One Quite Like Grandma" St. Winifred's Schoolchoir UK 1 week

1986 "Reet Petite" Jackie Wilson UK 4 weeks

28th

Birthdays

Earl 'Fatha' Hines 1903 US jazz and blues pianist, singer and songwriter. Hines was one of the most influential modern jazz pianists. He started his career in the early 1920s in Louis Armstrong's band, the Hot Five. From 1928 to 1947 he led his own band, and then finally from 1948 to 1951 played again with Louis Armstrong and his All-Stars. As a solo artist, Earl had hits with "Boogie Woogie On The St. Louis Blues" (5/40 US 11) and "Stormy Monday Blues" (10/42 R&B 1; 4/43 US 23). After a hiatus, he staged a comeback in 1964 and continued to work until his death on 22nd April, 1983.

Roebuck 'Pop' Staples 1915 US guitarist and singer. In his teens he played as a blues guitarist and became a member of the Golden Trumpet Gospel Group. In the early 1950s he formed his own gospel group, the Staple Singers, in which were, in addition to his son Pervis, who left the family group in 1971, his three daughters, Cleotha, Mavis and Yvonne. In 1953 the first record was released.

During the course of the years, their style evolved away from gospel towards soul, and from 1967 they started to have hits: "I'll Take You There" (4/72 US 1; 6/72 UK 30), "If You're Ready (Come Go With Me)" (10/73 US 9; 6/74 UK 34) and "Let's Do It Again" (10/75 US 1). The group name, in the meantime, had been shortened from Staple Singers to Staples. Solo album PEACE TO THE NEIGHBORHOOD was released 1992.

Billy Williams 1916 US singer. He started as leadsinger with the Harmony Four, who had formed already in 1930 and made records as Charioteers from 1935. They became popular through regular appearances in the 'Kraft Music Hall', a sponsored radio show presented by Bing Crosby. The Charioteers had their biggest hit with "Open The Door Richard" (3/47 US 6). The group were also backing vocalists on, "Don't Forget Tonight Tomorrow" (11/45 US 9) by Frank Sinatra and "Now Is the Hour (Maori Farewell Song)" (3/48 US 6) by Buddy Clark. Billy stayed with this group until 1949. After that he worked with a quartet or as a solo artist. Hit: "I'm Gonna Sit Right Down And Write Myself A Letter" (6/57 US 3; 8/57 UK 22). In the early 1960s Billy lost his voice due to diabetes and finally withdrew to Chicago, where he worked as a social worker. He died there 17th October, 1972.

Johnny Otis 1921 US singer, drummer, vibraphonist, pianist, bandleader, songwriter, and for many the 'Father of R&B'. Real name John Veliotes, and although many believe he is black, he is of Greek descent. From 1939 on he was playing drums with various bands. In 1945 he formed his own. He discovered and produced artists like Little Esther Phillips, Charles Brown, the Robins, Big Mama Thornton, Etta James, Johnny 'Guitar' Watson, Sugarcane Harris, Little Willie John, Hank Ballard, and many others. He appeared as Kansas City Bill & Orchestra on "Hound Dog" (3/53 R&B 1), the biggest hit for Big Mama Thornton. The Johnny Otis Orchestra had hits with "Double Crossing Blues" (2/50 R&B 1), "Mistrustin' Blues" (4/50 R&B 1), and "Cupid's Boogie" (6/50 R&B 1). Hits, for Johnny Otis Show: "Ma, He's Making Eyes At Me" (11/57 UK 2), "Bye Bye Baby" (1/58 UK 20) and "Willie And The Hand Jive" (6/58 US 9).

Dorsey Burnette 1932 US rockabilly singer, bassist and songwriter. He played occasionally from 1951 with his younger brother Johnny and Paul Burlison, then in 1956/57 permanently as Johnny Burnette Trio. Very soon the brothers had made a name for themselves as songwriters, writing early hits for Ricky Nelson. Then they each launched solo careers. The biggest hit for Dorsey was "(There Was A) Tall Oak Tree" (2/60 US 23). From 1972 to 1977 he had a number of C&W hits. He died 19th

August, 1979. His son Billy has been a successful country artist since the late 1970s.

Charles Neville 1938 US saxophonist, flautist and percussionist with the Neville Brothers.

Chas 1943 UK guitarist, bassist, pianist, singer and songwriter. Complete name Charles Hodges. The story goes that Chas was playing piano in a pub, when Jerry Lee Lewis walked in the bar, in which he was to appear, and asked, "What the devil am I supposed to be doing here when you have him?" His career thus far: 1960 with the Stormers, from 1961 to 1965 with the Outlaws, after that, Cliff Bennett & the Rebel Rousers, Roy Young Band, Black Claw, and finally in 1969 founder member of Heads, Hands & Feet. In 1973 the band split up after making three good albums. Together with Dave Peacock finally, he formed the duo Chas & Dave. For hits, see 24th May, under Dave.

Edgar Winter 1946 US singer, pianist, saxophonist and songwriter. He is the younger brother of Johnny, in whose band he played in the early 1960s. Johnny was just 15, Edgar 13, when they made their first record as Johnny & The Jammers. Later they called themselves Black Plague. After that, they both tried their luck as solo artists. Edgar formed White Trash, and then the Edgar Winter Group, in which Ronnie Montrose played lead guitar, and Dan Hartman bass. Hit: "Frankenstein" (3/73 US 1; 5/73 UK 18). When the band split up in the mid-1970s, Edgar played as a solo artist, with his brother again and on records by Montrose, Meatloaf and Bette Midler.

Dick Diamonde 1947 Dutch born bassist with the Australian group Easybeats. Real name Dingeman van der Sluys.

Clive Brooks 1949 UK drummer with Groundhogs, Egg and Liar.

Alex Chilton 1950 US singer, guitarist and songwriter. In 1965 he formed the De Villes, which shortly after became the Box Tops. Hits, and million sellers: "The Letter" (8/67 US 1; UK 5) and "Cry Like A Baby" (3/68 US 2; UK 15). For many of their records, Alex was the only band member who was really involved with the productions, as all the other instruments were played by studio musicians. In 1970 the band split up, Alex formed Big Star and later made solo records. The 1987 album PLEASED TO MEET ME by the Replacements, includes the tribute "Alex Chilton".

Louis McCall 1951 US drummer with Con Funk Shun.

Richard Clayderman 1953 French pianist. Real name Phillipe Pagès. After training as a classical pianist he accompanied such French artists as Johnny Hallyday and

Michel Sardou from the end of the 60s. He married at 18 and did an apprenticeship as a banker. At 22 he got divorced and signed a recording contract as a soloist. Although his singles were not particularly successful, four of his albums alone each earned platinum discs in Germany.

Deaths

Freddie King 1976 US blues guitarist and singer. He died on stage of a heart attack. Born 3rd September, 1934.

Dennis Wilson 1983 US drummer with the Beach Boys. He drowned. Born 4th December, 1944.

Hits of the Day

1946 "The Old Lamp Lighter" Sammy Kaye US 7 weeks

1946 "(I Love You) For Sentimental Reasons" Nat 'King' Cole US 6 weeks

1959 "Why" Frankie Avalon US 1 week

1961 "Moon River" Danny Williams UK 2 weeks

1974 "Angie Baby" Helen Reddy US 1 week

1985 "Merry Xmas Everyone" Shakin' Stevens UK 2 weeks

29th

Birthdays

Virgil Johnson 1935 US singer and songwriter. He worked as an English teacher and in 1960 formed the Velvets, an R&B doowop quartet, with a few students, who caught Roy Orbison's attention. It was he who finally introduced them to his record company. Hit: "Tonight (Could Be The Night)" (5/61 US 26).

Ed Bruce 1939 US singer, songwriter and TV actor. In 1957 he made two unsuccessful records for Sun Records as a rock 'n' roller. Before that, he had already sung on records by Bill Flagg, who played rockabilly music. After his lack of success, Ed became a used car salesman and wrote songs on the side, which were recorded by Jerry Lee Lewis, Charlie Rich and Johnny Cash. In 1964 Ed went to Nashville, did TV commercials and appeared in such TV series as *Maverick*. In 1963 Tommy Roe used the number "Save Your Kisses For Me", written by Ed, as the B-side of his hit "Sheila". From 1967 Ed made his own records, his greatest success being "You're The Best Break This Old Heart Ever Had" (12/81 C&W 1). Ed is also the writer of the Waylon and Willie hit "Mamas Don't Let Your Babies Grow Up To Be Cowboys".

Ray Thomas 1941 UK flautist, saxophonist and singer with Moody Blues since their formation in 1964. Before that, like Mike Pinder, he played with El Riot & The Rebels.

Marianne Faithfull 1947 UK singer and songwriter. She was discovered by Rolling Stones' manager Andrew Loog Oldham, and Jagger/Richards wrote her first hit, "As Tears Go By" (8/64 UK 9; 11/64 US 22). This was followed by "Come And Stay With Me" (2/65 UK 4; US 26), "This Little Bird" (5/65 UK 6; US 32) and "Summer Nights" (7/65 UK 10; 9/65 US 24). After 1967 her career seemed to be over, but Marianne made headlines as Mick Jagger's girlfriend. In the late 1970s she was back again, better than ever, "The Ballad Of Lucy Jordan" (11/79 UK 48) and "Broken English" (6/80).

Cozy Powell 1947 UK drummer and songwriter. He played with the Jeff Beck Group from April 1971 to June 1972, and formed Beast in November of the same year, which became Bedlam in May 1973, and which lasted until April 1974. In addition, Cozy made solo records. Hits: "Dance With The Devil" (12/73 UK 3) and "Na Na Na" (8/74 UK 10). In May 1974 he started Cozy Powell's Hammer until April 1975, then played with Strange Brew for two months and drummed with Rainbow from September 1975. After Ritchie Blackmore had joined up again with old colleagues of Deep Purple, Cozy became a member of Emerson, Lake & Palmer for one album.

Robert Parissi 1950 US singer, guitarist and leader of Wild Cherry, formed in 1976. Hit: "Play That Funky Music" (6/76 US 1; 10/76 UK 7).

Yvonne Elliman 1951 US singer, born on Hawaii. She had her first success on stage and in films as Mary Magdalen in *Jesus Christ Superstar*. Her first hit "I Don't Know How To Love Him" (4/71 US 28) was extracted from this rock opera. After singing in Eric Clapton's band from 1974 to 1977, who at the time were signed to the RSO label, she was given the opportunity to record for RSO. This company also had the Bee Gees under contract, who wrote her hit "Love Me" (10/76 US 14; UK 6). For the film *Saturday Night Fever* Yvonne recorded the title "If I Can't Have You" (1/78 US 1; 5/78 UK 4). If she isn't making solo records, she has cropped up on endless records as a session singer.

Roger Voudouris 1954 US singer, guitarist and songwriter. Even during his high school days, he had his own band, which he called the Roger Voudouris Loud As Hell Rockers. Later, a little more sober, the band toured as opening act for John Mayall, Stephen Stills, the Doobie Brothers, and others. In 1979 Roger had the solo hit "Get Used To It" (3/79 US 21), it remained his only hit.

Deaths

Fletcher Henderson 1952 US jazz pianist and orchestra leader. After a stroke which he suffered at Christmas 1950, causing him to retire. Born 18th December, 1898.

Paul Whiteman 1967 US orchestra leader. Born 28th March, 1890.

Tim Hardin 1980 US songwriter, singer, and guitarist. Died of an overdose of heroin. Born 23rd December, 1941.

Hits of the Day

1945	"White Christmas" Bing Crosby US 2 weeks
1951	"Cry" Johnnie Ray US 11 weeks
1960	"I Love You" Cliff Richard UK 2 weeks
1973	"Time In A Bottle" Jim Croce US 2 weeks

30th

Birthdays

Bo Diddley 1928 US guitarist, singer, and songwriter who could also play several other instruments. Real name Elias (or Ellis) Bates McDaniel. He was one of the early legends of rock 'n' roll whose compositions were covered by many British R&B bands like the Rolling Stones. He had his first hit with the double A-sided single "Bo Diddley/I'm A Man" (5/55 R&B 1), and his greatest with "Say Man" (9/59 US 20; R&B 3).

Skeeter Davis 1931 US country singer. Real name Mary Frances Penick. Her career, however, began in the pop charts; she had her first hit with Betty Jack Davis as the Davis Sisters with "I Forgot More Than You'll Ever Know" (10/53 US 18). Shortly after this hit, Betty died in a car accident. Skeeter carried on as a soloist. From 1958 until 1976 she was regularly in the country charts. Hits: "The End Of The World" (1/63 US 2) and "I Can't Stand Mad At You" (9/63 US 7).

John Hartford 1937 US string instrumentalist and songwriter. He worked as a session musician in Nashville. He never had a hit himself, but wrote "Gentle On My Mind" (5/67 C&W 60), which became an international for Glen Campbell and Dean Martin.

Del Shannon 1939 US singer and songwriter. Real name Charles Westover. During his military service with the US Army Del had his own radio show called 'Get Up And Go' on American Forces Network in Germany. Back in the USA he worked in a carpet shop in the daytime, and sang in nightclubs at night. He was discovered there and given a recording contract. Hits: "Runaway" (3/61 US & UK 1), "Hats Off To Larry" (6/61 US 5; 9/61 UK 6), "Hey Little Girl" (11/61 US 38; 3/62 UK 2), "Swiss Maid" (11/62 UK 2), "Little Town Flirt" (12/62 US 12; UK 4), and "Keep Searchin' (We'll Follow The Sun)" (11/64 US 9; 1/65 UK 3). After the hits dried up he carried on working as a songwriter, composing "I Go To Pieces" for Peter & Gordon among others, as a producer, and also as an artist. In the UK, he still had many fans and his occasional concerts were always well attended; both Tom Petty and Jeff Lynne were great fans. Tom produced Del's last hit "Sea Of Love" (12/81 US 33) and it was supposed that after Roy Orbison's death, Del might take his place with the Travelling Wilburys. It never came to that, because Del died 8th February, 1990.

Kenny Pentifallo 1940 US drummer with Southside Johnny & The Asbury Jukes.

Michael Nesmith 1943 US guitarist, singer and songwriter. His career began as Michael Blessing, under which he cut his first records. Alongside that, he wrote songs for other artists, including the Stone Poneys' hit "Different Drum". Like Davy Jones, Michael had answered an ad in the paper in 1965, which was looking for 'four crazy characters'. Stephen Stills was rejected (because of his bad teeth), Danny Hutton also, (who went on to form Three Dog Night), and Charles Manson (quite rightly!). Thus were created the Monkees. In March 1970 Michael formed his own group whom he called Michael Nesmith & The First National Band. Hits: "Joanne" (8/70 US 21), and "Rio" (3/77 UK 28). Michael did not participate in later reunions of the Monkees.

Davy Jones 1945 US singer, also with the Monkees. For hits, see 8th March, under Mickey Dolenz.

Patti Smith 1946 US singer and songwriter, who was referred to as a 'new-wave singer/poet'. Bob Dylan is supposed to have influenced her lyrics and Elvis Presley her style of performance, she said at the time. Her boyfriend at the time, Allen Lanier of Blue Oyster Cult introduced her to rock music. Patti wrote some lyrics for the band. In 1974 her first single appeared, "Piss Factory", which was about every day life in industrial society. Patti had her biggest hit with "Because The Night" (4/78 US 13; UK 5) written by her and Bruce Springsteen. In the early 1980s she married ex-MC5 guitarist Fred 'Sonic' Smith and withdrew from the music business until 1988.

Jeff Lynne 1947 UK singer, guitarist, and songwriter. In February 1966, Roy Wood, who until that time had been with Mike Sheridan & The Nightriders, formed his own band Move. Shortly after, Mike left his own band, Jeff Lynne joined and they renamed themselves Idle Race on May 1966. During the course of the next four years, the band released some outstanding albums, which however, did not sell very well. In February 1969 Roy Wood asked Jeff Lynne to join his band Move, but he declined. When Roy renewed the offer in early 1970, Jeff agreed. In October 1971 he and Roy formed a new band, Electric Light Orchestra. Hits: "Livin' Thing" (10/76 US 13; UK 4), "Telephone Line" (5/77 UK 8; US 7), "Don't Bring Me Down" (8/79 US 4; UK 3) and "Hold On Tight" (7/81 US 10; UK 4). Together with Olivia Newton-John they were successful with "Xanadu" (6/80 UK 1; 8/80 US 8). When Roy Wood started his new project Wizzard in August 1972, Jeff took over the helm of ELO. In October 1988 Roy Orbison, Tom Petty, George Harrison, Bob Dylan and Jeff joined together as the Travelling Wilburys, which was intended to be fun more or less. After Roy Orbison's death, the album by the Travelling Wilburys became immensely successful.

Geoff Peacey 1949 UK keyboard player and guitarist with Boston Show Band and Lake. He also played on records by Rudolf Rock & Schocker, Elephant, and others.

Dave Stewart 1950 UK pianist and songwriter. He started with the group Hatfield And The North, formed in 1972 who had no success. In the early 1980s he became a solo artist. Hits: "What Becomes Of The Brokenhearted?" (3/81 UK 13) with guest singer Colin Blunstone, and "It's My Party" (9/81 UK 1), a duet with Barbara Gaskin.

Tracey Ullman 1959 UK singer and actress. She appeared in London in the stage show *Elvis* with Shakin' Stevens. In the early 1980s she was the main actress, in the BBC TV series *Three Of A Kind*. She got a recording contract, after meeting the wife of Stiff records boss at the hairdressers. Hits: "Breakaway" (3/83 UK 4), "They Don't Know" (9/83 UK 2; 3/84 US 8) and "Move Over Darling" (12/83 UK 8). Later she went to the USA and had her own TV show which clearly demonstrated Tracey's talent for comedy.

Deaths

Richard Rodgers 1979 US composer. Born 28th June, 1902.

31st

Birthdays

Rex Allen 1920 US country singer, guitarist, and actor in western films. From 1944 he made a name for himself with his own radio shows. In 1949 he could be heard on a network programme all over the States. Rex made his first film in 1950, called *The Arizona Cowboy*; in which he repeated the same formula for the next 31 films made between 1950 and 1957. Horse Koko was a frequent partner in the films. Rex was the narrator of more than 80 Walt Disney films. As a singer he turned up in 1949 in the country charts. Hits: "Crying In The Chapel" (8/53 US 8) and "Don't Go Near The Indians" (9/62 US 17).

Odetta 1930 US folk blues singer, guitarist, songwriter and actress. Her complete name is Odetta Holmes Felious Gorden. She was already earning her living as a singer in 1952 and among her early admirers were Pete Seeger and Harry Belafonte. In 1956 Odetta released her first album. Many more records followed until 1974. In between, she appeared in operas and films. In 1986, after twelve years, she made a new album called MOVIN' IT ON, recorded live.

John Brian Alford 1939 UK singer, who appeared as Allisons with Bob Day. Hit: "Are You Sure" (2/61 UK 2).

Andy Summers 1942 UK guitarist and songwriter. In the early 1960s he played with Zoot Money in the Don Robb Band, became a member of Alexis Korner's Blues Incorporated, and then was a founder member in February 1964 of Zoot Money's Big Roll Band. He stayed there until July 1967 and in the same month became co-founder of Dantalian's Chariot, with whom he played until April 1968. After that he went to Soft Machine for three months and was a member of Eric Burdon & The Animals from July 1968 to December 1968. In all those years his artist's name was Andy Somers; then he left the music business and stayed in California. In January 1975 he turned up with the Kevin Coyne band, then for three months with Strontium 90 and finally from July 1977 he replaced Henry Padovani in Police. Just like his Police colleague Sting, Andy too played on several albums by Eberhard Schoener, which were released between 1977 and 1979. In the meantime Andy recorded solo albums and with Robert Fripp.

John Denver 1943 US singer, guitarist and songwriter. Real name John Henry Deutschendorf. He started as a member of the Chad Mitchell Trio in 1965, replacing Chad Mitchell. His composition "Leaving On A Jet Plane" became a hit for Peter, Paul & Mary in 1969, and it established his reputation. His solo career took off with a string of hits: "Take Me Home, Country Roads" (4/71 US 2), "Sunshine On My Shoulders" (1/74 US 1), "Annie's Song" (6/74 US 1; 8/74 UK 1), "Back Home Again" (9/74 US 5), "Thank God I'm A Country Boy" (3/75 US 1), and "I'm Sorry/Calypso" (8/75 US 1): all were million sellers. In the 1980s he recorded duets with artists like Placido Domingo, Sylvie Vartan and Emmylou Harris.

Peter Quaife 1943 UK bassist with the Kinks since 1962 when they were still called Ravens. He left the group on 6th April, 1969, and was replaced by John Dalton.

Burton Cummings 1947 Canadian singer, keyboard player and songwriter. In the spring of 1966 he replaced Chad Allen in the group Guess Who, formed in 1963. Hits: "These Eyes" (4/69 US 6), "Laughing" (7/69 US 10), "No Time" (12/69 US 5), "American Woman/No Sugar Tonight" (3/70 US 1; 5/70 UK 19), "Share The Land" (10/70 US 10) and "Clap For The Wolfman" (7/74 US 6). In 1975 Burton broke up the group and started a solo career. Hit: "Stand Tall" (10/76 US 10). In April 1985 Burton stole back into the limelight, cutting the benefit record "Tears Are Not Enough" with other Canadian musicians. The project was to be similar to USA for Africa and "We Are The World", but it became an international flop, although musicians like Neil Young, Bryan Adams, Joni Mitchell, Anne Murray and Gordon Lightfoot worked with Burton.

Donna Summer 1948 US singer and songwriter who was dubbed 'The Queen Of Disco'. Real name LaDonna Adrain Gaines. In 1967 she went to Europe and played in the musical *Hair* in Munich, then *Porgy & Bess* at the Volksoper in Vienna, and in *Showboat*. Giorgio Moroder and Pete Belotte discovered her when she was a backing vocalist and they produced her first solo records. Hits: "Love To Love You Baby" (12/75 US 2; UK 4), "I Feel Love" (7/77 UK 1; US 6), "Love's Unkind" (12/77 UK 3), "Last Dance" (5/78 US 3), "MacArthur Park" (9/78 US 1; UK 5),

"Heaven Knows" (1/79 US 4; UK 34), "Hot Stuff" (3/79 UK 11; US 1), "Bad Girls" (5/79 US 1; 7/79 UK 14), "Dim All The Lights" (8/79 US 2; UK 29), "No More Tears (Enough Is Enough)" (10/79 US 1; UK 3) a duet with Barbra Streisand, "On The Radio" (1/80 US 5; UK 32), "The Wanderer" (9/80 US 3), "She Works Hard For The Money" (5/83 US 3; UK 25), "This Time I Know It's For Real" (2/89 UK 3; 4/89 US 7), and "I Don't Wanna Get Hurt" (5/89 UK 7).

Willy Ray Ingram 1950 US saxophonist with the German group Spider Murphy Gang.

Tom Hamilton 1951 US bassist with Aerosmith, formed in 1970.

Deaths

Bert Berns 1967 US songwriter, producer and talent scout. Real surname Russell. He wrote "Twist And Shout", "Hang On Sloopy", "Piece Of My Heart", "I'm Gonna Run Away From You" and "Brown Eyed Girl". In 1964 he went to the UK and discovered and produced Zulu and Them. In 1965 he set up his own record company Bang Records, for which he brought Van Morrison to the USA and discovered the McCoys and Neil Diamond. Bert died after a heart attack aged only 38 years old.

Rick Nelson 1985 US singer, TV star and actor. He crashed in a private plane. Born 8th May, 1940.

Hit Of The Day

1966 "I'm A Believer" Monkees US 7 weeks

Index of Names

Index of Names

Banks, Ron 10 May *133*
Banks, Tony 27 Mar *84*
Barbata, John 1 Apr *91*
Barbee, John Henry 14 Nov *315*
Barber, Chris 17 Apr *108*
Barbieri, Agato 28 Nov *326*
Barbieri, Richard 30 Nov *329*
Barbirolli, Sir John 29 Jul *208*
Barclay, Nicole 21 Apr *111*
Bardens, Peter 19 Jun *173*
Bardot, Brigitte 28 Sep *268*
Bare, Bobby 7 Apr *98*
Baretto, Ray 29 Apr *119*
Bargeron, Dave 6 Sep *246*
Barker, Michael 12 Jan *12*
Barker, Stella 6 Sep *247*
Barlow, Barriemore 10 Sep *251*
Barre, Martin 17 Nov *317*
Barrère, Paul 3 Jul *186*
Barrett, Aston 22 Nov *321*
Barrett, Marcia 14 Oct *285*
Barrett, Syd 6 Jan *6*
Barron, Blue 22 Mar *78*
Barry, Jeff 3 Apr *93*
Barry, Len 12 Jun *166*
Bart, Lionel 1 Aug *212*
Bartholomew, Dave 24 Dec *353*
Bartley, Jock 16 May *139*
Bartram, Dave 23 Mar *79*
Basia 30 Sep *271*
Basie, Count 21 Aug *232*
  26 Apr *117*
Bass, Colin 4 May *126*
Bass, Fontella 3 Jul *186*
Bassett, Bryan 11 Aug *221*
Bassey, Shirley 8 Jan *8*
Bathelt, Hans 2 Jul *185*
Bators, Stiv 4 Jun *159*
Batt, Mike 6 Feb *35*
Battin, Skip 2 Feb *31*
Bauer, Joe 26 Sep *266*
Baxter, Jeff 'Skunk' 13 Dec *343*
Baxter, Les 14 Mar *71*
Bayer-Sager, Carol 8 Mar *64*
Beaky 10 Jul *192*
Beard, Frank 11 Jun *165*
Beauchamp, Geoff 30 Oct *299*
Beaumont, Jimmy 21 Oct *292*
Becaud, Gilbert 24 Oct *294*
Bechet, Sidney 14 May *136 - 137*
Beck, Jeff 24 Jun *178*
Beck, Robin 7 Sep *248*
Beck, Shorty 6 Jun *160*
Beckenstein, Jay 14 May *137*
Becker, Walter 20 Feb *48*
Beckley, Gerry 12 Sep *254*
Bedford, Mark 24 Aug *236*
Beedle, Martin 18 Sep *258*
Beef, Sleepy La 20 Jul *201*
Beefheart, Captain 15 Jan *14*
Beggs, Nick 15 Dec *346*
Beiderbecke, Bix 10 Mar *67*
  6 Aug *217*
Beitle, Ronald 30 Aug *240*

Belafonte, Harry 1 Mar *58*
Bell, Andy 25 Apr *116*
Bell, Archie 1 Sep *242*
Bell, Eric 3 Sep *244*
Bell, Madeline 23 Jul *204*
Bell, Maggie 12 Jan *11*
Bell, Ricky 18 Sep *259*
Bell, Robert 'Kool' 8 Oct *281*
Bell, Ronald 1 Nov *302*
Bell, William 16 Jul *197*
Belladonna, Joey 13 Oct *285*
Bellamy, David 16 Sep *257*
Bellamy, George 8 Oct *280*
Bellamy, Howard 2 Feb *31*
Bellamy, Peter 24 Sep *265*
  8 Sep *249*
Bellamy, Tony 12 Sep *253*
Belmont, Martin 21 Dec *351*
Belushi, John 24 Jan *22*
  5 Mar *62*
Belvin, Jesse 15 Dec *345*
  6 Feb *35*
Ben, Jorge 22 Dec *352*
Benatar, Pat 10 Jan *10*
Bennett, Brian 9 Feb *38*
Bennett, Cliff 4 Jun *158*
Bennett, Duster 23 Sep *264*
  25 Mar *82*
Bennett, Estelle 22 Jul *203*
Bennett, Pat 7 Apr *98*
Bennett, Tony 13 Aug *223*
Bennett, Veronica 10 Aug *220*
Bennie, Daniel 13 Mar *70*
Benno, Marc 1 Jul *184*
Benson, George 22 Mar *78*
Benson, Ray 16 Mar *73*
Benton, Brook 19 Sep *259*
  9 Apr *101*
Berger, Alan 8 Nov *310*
Berlin, Irving 11 May *134*
  22 Sep *263*
Bernard, Rod 12 Aug *222*
Bernie, Mike 1 Nov *302*
Berns, Bert 31 Dec *362*
Bernstein, Leonard 14 Oct *286*
  25 Aug *236*
Berry, Chuck 18 Oct *289*
Berry, Dave 6 Feb *35*
Berry, Jan 3 Apr *93*
Best, Pete 24 Nov *323*
Betts, Dave 30 Sep *271*
Betts, Dicky 12 Dec *342*
Bevan, Bev 25 Nov *324*
Bilk, Mr Acker 28 Jan *25*
Biondo, George 3 Sep *244*
Birch, Will 12 Sep *254*
Birdsong, Cindy 15 Dec *345*
Birkin, Jane 14 Dec *344*
Birrell, Pete 9 May *131*
Bishop, Elvin 21 Oct *292*
Bishop, Stephen 14 Nov *315*
Bivins, Edward 15 Jan *14*
Bivins, Michael 10 Oct *282*
Black, Bill 17 Sep *258*

Black, Cilla 27 May *150*
Black, David 'Jay' 2 Nov *302*
Black, Jeanne 25 Oct *295*
Blackmore, Ritchie 14 Apr *105*
Blackwell, Otis 16 Feb *45*
Blackwell, Robert 23 May *146*
Bladd, Stephen Jo 13 Jul *195*
Blades, Jack 24 Apr *114*
Blaikley, Alan 23 Mar *79*
Blake, Norman 10 Mar *67*
Blakely, Alan 1 Apr *91*
Blakey, Art 11 Oct *283*
  16 Oct *288*
Blakey, Michael 12 Jan *12*
Bland, Billy 5 Apr *96*
Bland, Bobby 27 Jan *25*
Blandon, Richard 16 Sep *257*
Blank, Boris 15 Jan *14*
Bley, Carla 11 May *134*
Bleyer, Archie 12 Jun *165*
  20 Mar *77*
Bloodvessel, Buster 6 Sep *247*
Bloom, Bobby 28 Feb *56*
Bloom, Eric 1 Dec *330*
Bloomfield, Michael 28 Jul *208*
  15 Feb *44*
Blow, Kurtis 9 Aug *219*
Blue, Barry 12 Dec *343*
Blue, David 18 Feb *47*
  2 Dec *331*
Bogert, Tim 14 Aug *225*
Boggs, Thomas 16 Jul *197*
Bogle, Bob 16 Jan *14*
Bohannon, Hamilton 7 Mar *64*
Bolan, Marc 16 Sep *257*
  30 Sep *271*
Bolder, Trevor 9 Jun *163*
Bolin, Tommy 1 Aug *212*
  4 Dec *333*
Bolton, Michael 26 Feb *54*
Bon, Simon Le 27 Oct *296*
Bond, Graham 28 Oct *297*
  8 May *130*
Bond, Johnny 1 Jun *155*
  12 Jun *166*
Bond, Ronnie 4 May *126*
Bonds, Gary U. S. 6 Jun *160*
Bonfanti, Jim 17 Dec *348*
Bonham, John 25 Sep *266*
  31 May *154*
Bono 10 May *133*
Bono, Sonny 16 Feb *44*
Boone, Daniel 31 Jul *210*
Boone, Debby 22 Sep *262*
Boone, Pat 1 Jun *155*
Boone, Steve 23 Sep *263*
Booth, Simon 12 Mar *69*
Bopper, Big 24 Oct *294*
  3 Feb *33*
Bostic, Earl 25 Apr *115*
  28 Oct *298*
Botkin, Perry Jr. 16 Apr *107*
Bouchard, Joe 9 Nov *310*
Bourge, Anthony 23 Nov *322*

Index of Names

Durham, Nigel 25 Aug 237
Dusty, Slim 13 Jun 166
Dwyer, Bernie 11 Sep 252
Dyke, Leroy Van 4 Oct 276
Dyke, Roy 13 Feb 42
Dylan, Bob 24 May 147
Dyson, Ronnie 11 Nov 312
    5 Jun 159
Eaglin, Snooks 21 Jan 19
Earl, Colin 6 May 127
Earl, Roger 16 May 139
Easton, Sheena 27 Apr 118
Eastwood, Clint 31 May 154
Eckstein, Billy 8 Jul 191
Eddy, Duane 26 Apr 116
Edelhagen, Kurt 8 Feb 37
Edge, Graeme 30 Mar 87
Edmonton, Jerry 24 Oct 295
Edmunds, Dave 15 Apr 106
Edney, Spike 11 Dec 341
Edwards, Bernard 31 Oct 300
Edwards, John 25 Dec 355
    9 May 131
Edwards, Jonathan 28 Jul 208
Edwards, Nokie 9 May 130
Edwards, Stuart 9 Jun 163
Edwards, Tom 27 Mar 84
Edwards, Tommy 17 Feb 45
    22 Oct 293
Eede, Nick van 14 Jun 168
Egan, Joe 18 Oct 290
Egan, Rusty 19 Sep 260
Egan, Walter 12 Jul 194
Ehart, Philip 4 Feb 33
Elliman, Yvonne 29 Dec 359
Ellington, Duke 24 May 147
    29 Apr 119
Elliot, Joe 1 Aug 212
Elliott, Bobby 8 Dec 337
Elliott, Cass 19 Sep 259
    29 Jul 208
Elliott, Dennis 18 Aug 229
Elliott, Mike 6 Aug 217
Elliott, Ron 21 Oct 292
Ellis, Barbara 20 Feb 48
Ellis, Don 17 Dec 348
    25 Jul 205
Ellis, Ralph 8 Mar 64
Ellis, Simon 18 May 141
Ellis, Steve 7 Apr 99
Elmes, Vic 10 May 133
Elmore, Greg 4 Sep 245
Elswit, Rik 6 Jul 189
Emerson, Keith 2 Nov 303
Emmett, Rik 10 Jul 192
Endsley, Melvin 30 Jan 28
Engel, Scott 9 Jan 9
Engemann, Bob 19 Feb 47
Ennis, Ray 26 May 149
Eno, Brian 15 May 138
Entner, Warren 7 Jul 190
Entwhistle, John 9 Oct 281
Enya, 17 May 140
Epstein, Brian 19 Sep 259
    27 Aug 238

Eric, Wreckless 18 May 141
Errico, Greg 1 Sep 242
Essex, David 23 Jul 204
Estefan, Gloria 1 Sep 243
Estes, Sleepy John 25 Jan 23
    5 Jun 159
Eva, Little 29 Jun 182
Evan, John 28 Mar 85
Evans, Bill 15 Sep 256
    16 Aug 226
Evans, Mal 5 Jan 5
Evans, Mark 2 Mar 60
Evans, Paul 5 Mar 62
Evans, Rick 20 Jan 18
Evans, Rod 19 Jan 17
Evans, Tom 18 Nov 319
    5 Jun 159
Everett, Betty 23 Nov 322
Everly, Don 1 Feb 30
Everly, Phil 19 Jan 17
Eyers, Tony 29 Aug 239
Fabares, Shelley 19 Jan 17
Fabian, 6 Feb 35
Fabric, Bent 7 Dec 336
Facenda, Tommy 10 Nov 311
Fadden, Jimmy 9 Mar 66
Fagen, Donald 10 Jan 9
Fahey, John 28 Feb 56
Fahey, Siobhan 10 Sep 251
Fairchild, Barbara 12 Nov 314
Fairley, Patrick 14 Apr 105
Fairweather-Low, Andy 2 Aug 213
Faith, Adam 23 Jun 177
Faith, Percy 7 Apr 98
    9 Feb 39
Faithfull, Marianne 29 Dec 359
Falco 19 Feb 47
Falconer, Earl 23 Jan 21
Faltermeyer, Harold 5 Oct 278
Fambrough, Henry 10 May 132
Fame, Georgie 26 Jun 180
Fardon, Don 19 Aug 230
Fargo, Donna 10 Nov 311
Farian, Frank 18 Jul 199
Farina, Johnny 30 Apr 120
Farina, Mimi 1 May 122
Farina, Richard 30 Apr 121
Farina, Santo 24 Oct 295
Farley, Colin 24 Feb 52
Farlowe, Chris 13 Oct 284
Farndon, Pete 12 Jun 166
    14 Apr 105
Farner, Mark 29 Sep 270
Farnham, John 1 Jul 184
Farnon, Robert 24 Jul 205
Farris, Steve 1 May 123
Faulkner, Eric 21 Oct 292
Faulkner, Vic 27 Feb 55
Fearing, Charles 16 Sep 257
Felder, Don 21 Sep 262
Feliciano, Jose 10 Sep 251
Felix, Julie 14 Jun 167
Felts, Narvel 11 Nov 312
Fender, Freddy 4 Jun 158

Fenn, Rick 23 May 146
Ferguson, Doug 4 Apr 95
Ferguson, Jay 10 May 133
Ferguson, Johnny 22 Mar 78
Ferguson, Larry 14 Apr 105
Ferguson, Maynard 4 May 125
Ferrante, Arthur 7 Sep 247
Ferrone, Steven 25 Apr 116
Ferry, Bryan 26 Sep 266
Fiddler, John 25 Sep 266
Fiedler, Arthur 10 Jul 192
    17 Dec 347
Fieger, Doug 20 Aug 231
Field, Russ 1 Sep 242
Fielder, Jim 4 Oct 277
Fields, Gracie 27 Sep 268
Finch, Richard 25 Jan 23
Fingers, Johnnie 10 Sep 251
Finn, Mickey 3 Jun 157
Finn, Neil 27 May 151
Finn, Tim 25 Jun 179
Fish 25 Apr 116
Fish, Cliff 13 Aug 224
Fisher, Carl 27 Dec 356
Fisher, Eddie 10 Aug 220
Fisher, Jerry 1 Mar 58
Fisher, Matthew 7 Mar 64
Fisher, Morgan 1 Jan 1
Fisher, Rob 5 Nov 306
Fisher, Roger 14 Feb 43
Fitzgerald, Ella 25 Apr 115
Flack, Roberta 10 Feb 39
Flanigan, Bob 22 Aug 233
Flash, Grandmaster 1 Jan 1
Flatt, Lester 11 May 134
    28 Jun 181
Fleet, Gordon 16 Aug 227
Fleetwood, Mick 24 Jun 177
Fleming, Rochelle 11 Feb 40
Fletcher, Andy 8 Jul 191
Flint, Bernie 26 May 149
Flint, Hughie 15 Mar 72
Flowers, Roy 4 Aug 215
Floyd, Eddie 25 Jun 179
Floyd, King 13 Feb 42
Fogelberg, Dan 13 Aug 224
Fogerty, John 28 May 152
Fogerty, Tom 6 Sep 247
    9 Nov 310
Foley, Red 17 Jun 171
    19 Sep 260
Fontana, Wayne 28 Oct 298
Ford, Billy 9 Mar 65
Ford, Dean 5 Sep 245
Ford, Emile 16 Oct 288
Ford, Frankie 4 Aug 215
Ford, John 1 Jul 184
Ford, Lita 19 Sep 260
Ford, Mary 30 Sep 272
    7 Jul 190
Ford, Tennessee Ernie 13 Feb 42
    17 Oct 289
Ford, Walt 5 Sep 245
Foreman, Chris 8 Aug 219

Index of Names

Index of Names

Index of Names

Index of Names

Index of Names

Index of Names

Index of Names

Index of Names

Index of Groups

Index of Groups

Index of Groups

Index of Groups

Index of Groups